THE GOSPEL RESTORED

A Discourse

Walter Scott

ii

The Gospel Restored: A Discourse

Published by:
Gospel Armory Publishing
Bowling Green, Kentucky
www.GospelArmory.com

Printed in the United States of America

ISBN: 978-1-942036-19-7

TABLE OF CONTENTS

PUBLISHER'S NOTE

There have been some minor changes made to this material – primarily some changes in punctuation and updating the chapters in Bible citations from roman numerals to regular numbers. A detailed table of contents has been added for easier reference. However, an effort was made to keep the substance of the material the same.

—The Publisher

PREFACE

The professors of our holy religion having unhappily strayed from the scriptures and true Christianity, there seemed to be no remedy in any thing but a return to original ground. This suggested itself to many, in different places, almost simultaneously, about the beginning of the present century, and numerous churches were formed about that time, both in Europe and America, resembling, more or less, the churches planted by the Apostles, or the church of Jerusalem instituted by the Lord Jesus himself.

These churches, with few exceptions, adopted the holy scriptures as their exclusive guide in religion, and rejected the dangerous creeds and confessions of Christendom, which have operated so fatally on the unity of the church. This formed the first positive step towards that return to original ground, for which the present century is distinguished.

In 1823 a plea for a particular ecclesiastical order was put forth publicly, by Brother Alexander Campbell. This for distinction's sake was called the ancient order. Others had, before this time, taken the scriptures alone; but this master-stroke gave a fresh impulse to religious inquiry, and, by a single expression, "Ancient Order," limited that inquiry to a very important branch of our religion as a first step.

Presiding, at that time, over a church which had already attained the ancient order, or at least as much of it as seems even now to be attained, the gospel, or rather a uniform authoritative plan of preaching it, became more the object of my attention, as may be seen from a few essays published in the C. Baptist, cut short, however, by the then limited knowledge of the extraordinary topic which had been selected; in 1827 the True Gospel was restored. For distinction's sake it was styled the Ancient Gospel.

The present century, then, is characterized by these three successive steps, which the lovers of our Lord Jesus have been enabled to make, in their return to the original institution. First the Bible was adopted as sole authority in our assemblies, to the exclusion of all other books. Next the Apostolic order was proposed. Finally the True Gospel was restored.

The above very general notice of the progress and order of the present reformation, is deemed sufficient to make the reader feel whither it is we desire to bring him by this discourse, namely, to the gospel; and not to a plea for any particular order, or to any discussion of the previous question concerning the supreme and exclusive authority of the holy scriptures.

A volume of unbroken discourse of the true gospel is still a desideratum. Since 1827, it has floated through our periodicals in essays and fragments of essays very unlike the living orations in which it was then set forth to the public for acceptance. Those are scattered over a wide field, and necessarily apart from each other; so that when a disciple would invite a friend, or fellow professor, or relative, to a perusal of what has been learned and written of the gospel since that time, he must needs invite him to the review of numerous volumes, a task by no means acceptable to readers in general.

In the tenth number of the Millenial Harbinger, for 1831, the restoration of the true gospel is referred to, in the following manner: "Brother Walter Scott, who, in the fall of 1827, arranged the several items of faith, repentance, baptism, remission of sins, the Holy Spirit, and eternal life, restored them in this order to the church, under the title of ancient gospel, and preached it successfully to the world—has written a discourse," &c. In the Evangelist for 1832 the following paragraph, of the connection between the above elements and sin which they are intended to destroy, occurs. "In regard to sinners and sin, six things are to be considered—the love of it, the practice of it, the state of it, the guilt of it, the power of it, and the punishment of it. The first three relate to the sinner; the last three to sin. Now faith, repentance, and baptism, refer to the first three, the love, and practice, and state of sin; while remission, the Holy Spirit, and the resurrection relate to the last three, the guilt, and power, and punishment of sin. In other words, brethren, to make us see the beauty and perfection of the gospel theory as devised by God; faith is to destroy the love of sin, repentance to destroy the practice of it, baptism the state of it, remission the guilt of it, the Spirit the power of it, and the resurrection to destroy the punishment of sin; so that the last enemy, death, will be destroyed."

On the original arrangement of the elements of the gospel then and on the analysis of sin contained in the preceding paragraph, the present volume is built. It comprehends a connected discourse of the true gospel of Christ, and has been written by request of some of the most intelligent among our brethren. The task might have fallen upon some one more able to perform it; but as none has yet appeared to occupy this ground, we have yielded to the wishes of those who were perhaps better judges in the case than ourselves, and have done the best we could.— May the reader derive as much profit from reading it as the author has been gladdened while writing it.

A discourse on the elements of any science, admits of but little elegance, except so much as attaches to correctness of description and accuracy of definition. The reader, therefore, must not hope to meet with much of it in these elementary orations, which are of the didactic and demonstrative kind chiefly. With this monition to the reader, we commend the book to the protection of God, and to the patronage of the public and the brethren.

WALTER SCOTT

A DISCOURSE OF THE TRUE GOSPEL

SECTION FIRST–INTRODUCTORY

CHAPTER I

The Fall of Our First Parents and Their Expulsion from Paradise Considered

The fall of man, and his recovery by Jesus Christ our Lord form a great drama, of which God is the author. The chief personage is the Messiah, and his mighty and subtle antagonist is an archangel in arms. The parties are demons and angels, the theatre is the universe, the stage the world, and its government the subject in debate. The plot lies in bringing good out of evil; happiness out of misery, almighty power from feminine weakness, light out of darkness, glory from the grave. The catastrophe consists of the seizure and perdition of the traitor angel with all his powers, and of the final triumph of the son of man with all his saints.

On this system of things, characterized by such splendid points and splendid personages, enriched by such an endless variety of under-plot and interlude, and played off on a stage boundless as the great globe itself, observations and reflections uninteresting would supercede apology, for they would admit of none. If, therefore, the present discourse has faults, and who can doubt it, they are to be attributed to the writer and not to his subject.—He confesses it, they are to be attributed to the writer.

CHAPTER II

Of the Three States of Man

The Scriptures describe man as having existed in three states, a natural, a preternatural state, and a state of respite. The first is described as good, the second as evil, and the third as partaking of both good and evil. The good is that in which man existed before the fall; the evil, that into which he was plunged by the fall; and the state of respite is that in which he now exists.

The first was a natural state, because it was that in which be was created; and we style it the good, because it is so denominated in the scriptures,—thus, And God saw every thing that he had made, and behold it was very good.

The preternatural state is so named, because it lay beyond man's natural condition, and because in it every thing, guilt, condemnation, shame, fear, death, was wholly ulterior to his nature. We designate it the evil state, because all its points are evil and only evil.

The state of respite is so named, because in it man is vouchsafed a respite for life, the present life. It is of a mixed nature partaking of both good and evil; it is inferior to the first or natural state, and superior to the second or preternatural state; it possesses neither the goods of the former, nor the evils of the latter: it is a condition in which man may either improve, or abuse, the life which has been lent him by his good, and wise, and all-benevolent Creator. Revealed religion is the means by which he may improve life, and become what God would have him to be; and to contemn or reject this, is to insult God and abuse the life which he has lent us.

The first and the last of these states are of God, and on that account they may be styled divine. In the former man was admitted to personal and sensible intercourse with his Creator; in the latter this is denied him; in this, faith is substituted for knowledge; and in it, of man, when he has reached his highest attainment, it can only be said, he walks "as if seeing him that is invisible." The second state originated with Satan, and may, therefore, well be styled the state of evil.

But let us inquire more particularly into the history of man in these three states. We shall begin with the first or natural, in which every thing was pronounced, by the Creator, to be very good.

CHAPTER III

Of the First State in General

The great points, or prominent features in this original constitution of things, are our first parents themselves, their peculiar privileges, their innocence, their capacity for knowledge, duty, and happiness, their trial, and temptation, their fall, and expulsion, and the time they continued in Paradise. Though their temptation, fall, and expulsion may be deemed by the reader to belong more properly to the state of evil inasmuch as they were of Satan rather than of God. But the state of the case is this, they were tempted by Satan, they fell of themselves, and were expelled by God. The good and evil states seem here to run into each other; for the temptation, which was an evil, occurred in the good state, while the expulsion, which was a real good, took place in the evil state, the fall being the point at which both states in reality touched one another.

CHAPTER IV

Of the Superiority of the Religious Principle of the First State

Man's mental acquisitions by his own experience is called knowledge, his acquisitions by the experience of others is styled faith, the total of his acquisitions, therefore, consists of knowledge and faith. What man knew of the existence of the Deity in his natural state, was knowledge; in the present state of respite, it is faith.

Faith may be increased indefinitely without being exalted to knowledge. A man may vouch to me the existence of an object, and his testimony may be confirmed by that of two, or two thousand more; and this, again, by that of an indefinite number of other witnesses; still my belief, however strengthened, is not exalted to knowledge; I am still compelled in the case to trust to the experience of others; and till I have a sensible experience of my own, of the existence of the object in question, my acquisition is not knowledge but faith. This continuous and indefinite approach of faith to knowledge, appears a little paradoxical; but it is certainly no less obvious than that in Mathematics one line may be made to approach another forever without the possibility of touching it. And this is absolutely true. It is so with knowledge and faith, which, however near they approach each other, are, notwithstanding, never the same.

In this point of view the revealed religion of the present state is inferior to the order of things in man's primitive condition, in which he was, on account of his innocence, admitted to sensible communion with the Deity. But this defectiveness in the principle of our religion, is to be done away at the return of the Messiah, when the pure in heart shall be permitted again to see God, and man once more be honoured with face to face intercourse with his Creator.

It was, therefore, a distinguished and exalted privilege of the natural state of man, that in it he was admitted to sensible communion with his Maker. The divine existence was, therefore, not a matter of faith to him, as it is to men now.—He enjoyed a sensible proof of this, the grand fundamental of all religion. We possess this only as faith. When, therefore, man fell from his natural condition, knowledge yielded to faith, and a state of things, in which man knew there was a God, was bartered away for that out of which he could be delivered only by the principle of believing that there is a God. Instead of enjoying his own experience on this point, he has now to trust to the experience of others, that is, he has to depend on particular revelations granted through the ministrations of particular men, as Adam, Enoch, Noah, Abraham, Moses, David, Isaiah, Daniel, Malachi, John the Baptist, and Our Lord and Saviour, who declares, that he had seen the Father.[1] Meanwhile, faith is the only remaining organ of communion with God, found in the constitution of man; and hence the propriety of that saying of the Apostle. "Without faith it is impossible to please God;" because besides this, there is in us no other foundation for either knowledge or duty in relation to the Deity.

It is worthy of observation, that, in harmony with the preceding remarks, the scriptures never speak of Adam's faith. Samuel, and David, and Sampson, and Gideon, and Jeptha, and Moses, and Joseph, and Jacob, and Isaac, and Abraham, and Noah, and Enoch, and even Abel, Adam's son, are all celebrated in scripture for their faith, and for their noble deeds of righteousness rendered to God on this principle; but here the chain ends, or rather begins; and Adam who enjoyed knowledge of the divine existence, is, in regard to faith, passed over in profound silence.

CHAPTER V

Of the Nature of Man in General

Rational and animal life, like organic and animal life, are blended in man with such admirable felicity as perhaps to baffle the nicest sagacity to declare with indubitable certainty, where the one begins and the other ends. Not that they are inseparable, or absolutely incapable of a distinct existence, for in the vegetable world, we see organic life apart from animal life; in the purely animal tribes organic and animal life exists distinct from rational life; and in heavenly intelligences reason, doubtless exists apart from both the former modes of being. In man the whole three modes of existence, organic, animal, and rational unite and run into each other with such surprising subtilty as frequently to confound our reason.

It may be observed of them in general, that organic life is beheld in its most distinct form in the growth and development of the vegetable kingdom.

Animal life is distinguished for sensation, and it discerns tastes, smells, sounds, colors, motions, actions, heights, distances, expressions, and so forth; but here somewhere it ends and reason begins.

Rational life is characterized by its powers to perceive order, contrivance, design, cause and effect, the fitness, relations and uses of

---

[1] John 6:46

things in the natural and moral worlds. While animal life is perfected in sensation, rational life enables us to perceive that all things throughout nature, are distributed according to certain vital, mechanical, and mathematical laws of proportion, fitness, correspondence, contrast, contrariety and so forth.

It will be perceived, therefore, that, if man were purely animal, he would have no moral conception of power, wisdom, order, and goodness; but only ideas of relation and design purely instinctive. The forms, colours, and attitudes of vegetables would be seen by him as they are, without ever suggesting to him a single idea of the vital and mechanical forces which combine for their development; he would drink of the stream and recline upon its banks without at all inquiring into the operation of those powers, which make the one run and the other stand still. Light and shade would he seen by him without reference to that system of optics by which they are separated and distributed through the universe: and like other animals he would grow, decline, and die, alike ignorant of nature and him who made it.

But though man is animal in sensation, and rational in thought, in his existence he is purely animal: and as that is the point in which we desire to look at him for the present, we shall submit the following short chapter on animal life as contra-distinguished from life eternal.

CHAPTER VI

Of Human Life in Particular

There are two kinds of life spoken of in the holy scriptures, eternal life and animal life. The former is essential and independent; the latter is, secondary and dependant on something without itself. All animals are possessed of this last species of life; and depend for their subsistence on the things of external nature, as air, and food. Eternal life is an essential attribute of God, and of his Son, and of the Holy Spirit. The holy angels also are gifted with the element of immortality in this manner, as is Satan too, who has been created with the same attribute and like good angels is of a never-dying nature. It is not so with man; who is both animal and mortal in his constitution. This, however, is as fortunate for him as it is admirably declarative of the wisdom of his Creator; for had Adam been constituted independent of external nature, and endowed with life in himself he would then, like the holy angels, have been immortal and could not have died. When he sinned, therefore, he would have been in a condition like that of Satan himself. But Satan is in a state of condemnation, and as he cannot die, has to be seized by a stratagem and punished for ever, a fact which gives origin to the scripture phrase, "eternal fire,"—the punishment prepared for never-dying beings, the devil and his angels, and not originally for man; who is a creature of time and capable of death. The fire, however, in which Satan and his angels will be punished for ever, will also form the punishment of wicked men. "Depart from me you cursed into everlasting fire prepared for the devil and his angels." This is called "the second death;" over those, who share in the first resurrection, and are gifted with the attribute of innate life or immortality, this dire ruin, the scriptures assure us, shall exert no influence. "Blessed and holy is he, who has part in the first resurrection, for over such the second death has no power."

The state only, and not the life of Adam then, was different in kind from our own: his life was animal, weak, and corruptible; ours is the same. We depend on external nature; so did he; he was susceptible of fatigue, and required sleep; we also require sleep, and are susceptible of fatigue; his life was conditional, and lent him for a time; our life also is a loan, and will be required of us, as his was required of him.

CHAPTER VII

Of Man in Regard to Knowledge and Duty

We now exist at an immense distance from the times of the primitive pair, and enjoy the exalted privilege of beholding human nature wonderfully developed, and of ascertaining what it is through the medium of its own doings, now spread forth before us in various tissues of natural, moral, and religious action, transpiring through a lapse of ages extending from Paradise to the present time.

It is an interesting truth in the inductive history of man, that he has been essentially the same in all ages. For instance, he has, every where, in all ages, and under all circumstances, been endowed with a capacity for knowledge, and a sense of duty. His physical and moral powers, for the perfection of these endowments, have ever been the same also.

Man's desire of knowledge is wonderful, he has ever made his sense, and consciousness, and reason, either in the form of experience or observation, in all places pay tribute to this master passion. In the gratification of it, he has left nothing untouched. His appetite for knowledge has prompted and spurred him on to investigate every thing. Conscious of the imperfection of his senses, he has whetted his genius to supply, by its inventions, their deficiency, and by his ingenuity has enlarged the sphere of their operation to the utmost limits of the system he inhabits. By means of instruments, of his own construction and invention, he descends into the microscopic world and examines the anatomy, actions, and instincts of beings so small, that millions of them can swim about in a drop of water with as much freedom as a whale in the ocean. And by means of the telescopic apparatus he bounds into the other extreme of nature, and beholds vast worlds, suns, and planets and globes, hundreds of times larger than our own; but which must have continued forever unknown to his most active sense unless his inventions had aided him in their discovery.

He is a being of lofty ambition; he has invented science and reduced it to system; he has organized states and adorned them with the arts of peace or strengthened them with the munitions of war. He has by his divine art subdued the elements, and made the most subtle agents of nature bow to his designs. Having discovered the relation which the products of the soil bear to his life and happiness, he has in all ages availed himself of this discovery and so vexed and teased with spade and plough the earth, that her lawns and valleys, her plains and undulating hills have ever flourished with the blessings and ornaments of life. The ocean, the most wonderful of the creatures of God, he has subdued to subserve his lofty enterprise; he goes down to the sea in ships, and traces in the mighty waters the footsteps of the Eternal. He circumnavigates the globe, and by the exuberance and riches of foreign climes supplies the poverty and deficiencies of his own. He grasps the wind in his fist, and tames the tempestuous blast. Around the world he rides upon the storm: he flies upon the wings of the wind, and by his art draws down the lightning out of the clouds; he weighs the planets in a balance, and lays the measuring line around the sun himself; he understands tides, and calculates equinoxes, recessions, and eclipses for thousands of years to come.

But the wonder of all this is increased when his achievements are contemplated relatively to the small number of his mental powers; for notwithstanding his endless variety in art; his valour in war, and sublimity in science, notwithstanding the magnitude and boldness of his designs, all his powers and productions are resolvable ultimately into but two classes of positive ideas, namely, ideas of what is, and ideas of what ought to be; in other words, ideas of knowledge, and duty.

Is man then, with all his ambition and claims to distinction, a creature of merely two thoughts, of two positive classes of ideas? It is even so; with all his struggles of body and agonies of soul, his pretensions to mind, and talent, and genius, he possesses no more; and his other positive powers of speech and action are involved in this necessity; nor can all the men of an age, or of all ages, either in the things of science, society, or religion, by any power either of thought or word or deed, transcend this necessity. For what are the writings of Homer, and Virgil, and Xenophon, and Cicero, and Tacitus, and Demosthenes, what are the works of the ancient moralists, philosophers, and rhetoricians, and of the moderns, Bacon, Newton, Locke, Des Cartes and all the British and Continental sages, statesmen, and orators, but their ideas of what is, and what ought to be—their ideas of knowledge and duty.

In this respect man differs supremely from his Maker, who, besides knowing what is and what ought to be, knows also what is not and what ought not to be, and speaks of things before they come into existence as "though they were." All things exist in the divine mind originally and without a type, and not as they do in ours, reflected from nature and acquired by the actual exercise of our senses. This power of knowing things that are not, is an admirable endowment, and is not possessed but by the uncreated nature. The universe, with all its sentiments of power, wisdom, and goodness, is not a copy of any thing but the idea of itself in the mind of its great architect. All that has been and all that is to be, the resurrection, our glorification, and eternal life, are known and seen by him as though they had already occurred. In a word "He knows the end from the beginning;" and is not like men, all whose knowledge can be traced ultimately to the exercise of their senses.

CHAPTER VIII

Of Man's Capacity for Happiness

In conformity with his animal and rational nature man is gifted with a capacity for pain and pleasure, and happiness and misery; when things affect him by their properties, or relations, they produce what is called pleasure, or pain of body; when they affect him only by their ideas, they cause happiness, or misery of mind; and when they operate upon him by the double influence of their properties and the ideas of their properties, that is, when they affect us both physically and mentally they produce happiness or misery, and pain or pleasure according to their nature, and the relations which they bear to these feelings and sensations. The words pain and pleasure, therefore, are here made to have a physical signification and to relate to the body; while happiness and misery have a mental meaning and are applied to the mind.

The author of our being has instituted the following connections among these things. With the knowledge and use of a thing he has united pleasure, or pleasurable sensations of body; with the abuse of it pain, or painful sensations. Analogous to this are the things of our mental or moral nature in which the chain is as follows, Knowledge, duty, and happiness; and knowledge, disobedience, and misery.

In these connections the divine benevolence is very obvious; for the chain might not have been so extended by one link at least. We might have known, for instance, the articles proper to be selected for food and have attended to them with faultless scrupulosity, and all the purposes, which they are designed to fill, might have been attained by the very same processes by which they now obtain, irrespective of the capacity, which we possess, of enjoying pleasure in the use of them; but the Creator, in addition to our capacity to use a thing, has graciously superadded the power of deriving a real pleasure from the use of it; for we not only eat, but by the sense of tasting, we eat with real pleasure. The abuse of things is just as certainly attended by pain, and the reasoning on the side of the divine benevolence, is here the same.

In mental or moral matters the reasoning is the same also.—We might have known duty, and attended to it without any of that enjoyment which now attaches to the performance of it; but here again we are met by the divine benevolence, and feel that, in every act of duty, we are made to taste a real happiness; hence that saying of our Lord and Saviour to his disciples, "Seeing you know these things, happy are you if you do them." Disobedience is just as certainly followed by misery of mind.

When we look at man in his natural state we are compelled to regard him as being perfectly happy; violence and deceit had not entered his borders; pain of body and misery of mind were consequently far away, and equally unknown to him in that happy condition. He was full of knowledge; his duty was all before him; he attended to it, and was completely blest. Sin, guilt, misery, and pain were wholly preternatural and lay beyond his state of unstained obedience; nor could he purchase the fatal knowledge of those things but by a price almost too terrible to name,—disobedience.

Such, indeed, seems to have been the perfection of our First Parents in regard to happiness, that they do not appear to have even once thought of their own native defencelessness; nor does it seem to have occurred to them once, that they were naked, till the misery resulting from their shame for the past and fear of the future, flashed upon their minds the whole state of the case, and caused them with intolerable mortification, to feel that now they were wholly unprepared to meet their Creator as when in a state of conscious innocence. In brief, they felt they were naked; they felt they were in their persons defenceless, ignorant of death, afraid to meet it, and incapable of either resisting, or escaping it. "And they heard the voice of the Lord God walking in the garden in the cool of the day; and Adam and his wife hid themselves from the presence of the Lord God among the trees of the garden. And the Lord God called unto Adam, and said to him, Where art thou? And he said, I heard thy voice in the garden and was afraid, because I was naked; and I hid myself."

Innocence, then, is a glorious feast; it is the feast of the soul; while misery, like an evil angel, is the inseparable companion of disobedience; misery, indeed, follows sin as the shadow follows the form of the hated

Hyena, when it roams in quest of prey at the sultry hours of noon amid the wretched cottages of the sun burnt Hagarenes; but righteousness is like the resurrection morn; it is full of hope; it is full of heaven. Happiness, mental moral happiness, therefore, is to be referred for its origin to obedience to God; while obedience itself is to be referred to law, law to authority, and authority to right, and right to his property in us by creation, by preservation, by purchase, by inheritance; for we belong to God and to the Son of God by all these obligations; and to acknowledge God and his Son is eternal life.

The fact that our minds are operated on chiefly by ideas of things, should teach us on all occasions to seek correct knowledge; and never to clothe things with fancied properties, and excellencies which they do not possess, if so our happiness will be ill-founded and false. On the other hand we are equally liable to err by clothing matters and things with imaginary evil, and so render ourselves miserable by the creative energies of our own doubtful fancy.

Knowledge, and happiness, with the authority granted to him, were doubtless the grand points in man, which constituted him an illustrious image of the Deity. "Let us make man in our own image, and after our likeness let him have dominion over" &c.

CHAPTER IX

Concerning our First Parents in Paradise

With the above observations on our general nature, let us look at our first parents as they existed in Paradise before the Fall. Like us they were endowed with the love of knowledge, and a sense of duty; and we shall see that they must have inhabited that blissful abode for a hundred years at least, sinless and wholly unconscious of the happiness which introduces to each other's acquaintance the sexes, enjoying undisturbed felicity with God and one another, tracing in heaven above and on the earth beneath all sensible indications of the divine power, wisdom, and goodness. Surely nothing can excel in innocence and happiness the ideas suggested to us of this youthful pair in Paradise; for they must, as they arose under the moulding fingers of their great Creator, have been of surpassing loveliness.

> Two of far nobler shape, erect and tall.
> God-like erect, with native honor clad,
> In naked majesty, seem'd lords of all.
> For contemplation he and valour form'd.
> For softness she and sweet attractive grace,
> He for God only, she for God in him.
> His fair large front and eye sublime declared

Absolute rule, and hyacinthian locks
Round from his parted forelock manly locks
Clustering, but not beneath his shoulders broad,
She as a vail down to the slender waist
Her unadorned golden irises wore
Disheveled, but in wanton ringlets waived
As the vine curls her tendrils.—
Grace was in all her steps, heaven in her eye,
In every gesture dignity and love.
————————————————The loveliest pair
That ever since in love's embraces met.

Language and the knowledge of things, to a certain extent, were probably conferred on Adam by inspiration. Dr. Johnson thought it absolutely impossible for man to invent speech or even to discover that he was possessed of that power. But having attained these things by a gift from God, we may well suppose, that much of his time was spent in the company of the unrivaled beauty to whom God had espoused him, in the pursuit of knowledge, exercising their new-born senses on the qualities of things, and employing their reason in separating and distinguishing the various objects by which, in that happy state, they were surrounded; and as both were necessarily under the same state of pupilage, their bliss, in cultivating the understanding and affections of each other, must have been complete. The origin of this *chef d'oeuvre* of nature, Eve, the side of Adam from which she was taken—taught her that she was the keeper of his heart; while he could look upon her only as a second self—his lovelier and better part, or to give it in his own words when he first beheld her, This is now bone of my bone and flesh of my flesh.—That our First Parents, during the long period of a hundred years, with all the facilities which they possessed for learning, in their intercourse with angels and with God himself, did not attain to very high degrees of knowledge, it would be difficult for us to imagine; on the contrary we are compelled to believe, that in that time they must have acquired prodigious stores of information on all terrestrial things. They watched no doubt earliest morn and dewy eve, and the changes of the slightly varied year as it passed over the gorgeous paradisiacal seat in which it had pleased their Creator to place them. They eyed with pleasing wonder the effects, in that happy abode, of the budding spring, and saw with delight when Taurus through the regions of Eden

In rosy hillocks rolled the summer day.

Then came golden autumn not unadmired and the crisped winter, scarcely felt in those temperate realms. No doubt the motions of the heavenly bodies, and of the earth, and all the phenomena of which they are the sources, were the objects of their constant investigation, as well as the sources of unfading delight.

While thus quaffing unmeasured draughts of pleasure in the society of each other, and drinking down fresh knowledge everyday from the pure and inexhaustible fountains by which they were everywhere surrounded in the new-born world, what remained but that they should next learn their duty to each other and to their God. This, indeed, as we have seen, was all of which their nature was capable; for beyond knowledge and duty their inexperienced thought was unqualified to extend.

CHAPTER X

Of the Trial of Adam in Knowledge

In respect to knowledge and duty, therefore, it pleased Almighty God to put their attainments to the test. But as knowledge must precede duty the intellectual trial very properly preceded the moral one. "And the Almighty caused all the beasts of the field and all the fowls of the air" to come to Paradise and pass in review before Adam their lord. His knowledge of them must have been as accurate as it was extensive; for it is added, that "Whatever Adam called every living thing that was the name thereof; and he gave names to all cattle and to the fowls of the air and to every beast of the field; but for Adam there was not found an help meet for him." It is the will of God that all his rational creatures should both feel and acknowledge their dependence on him; and, therefore, the animals seem to have been brought before Adam that he might be made to feel that among them all "There was not a help meet for him." In this view of the matter Milton represents Adam as supplicating the Deity for a wife; but of this the holy scriptures are absolutely silent. From seeing the animals in pairs, Adam might be led to reason from their case to his own; but from the nature of the human mind which, in regard to the objects of its knowledge, limits itself, as we have seen, to the things that are, without ability to conceive of those things that are not, it was impossible for him to conceive of any thing beyond that which had come under the review of his senses. Moreover no being but God could have conceived originally the idea of so beautiful, lovely, and unrivaled a creature as is woman. It was enough that, in comparing the condition of the lower animals with his own, he saw himself to be solitary, felt that he was alone. In this manner he was prepared to set a proper estimate upon his beautiful partner the moment she was presented to him by God; and her pearless perfections enabled him also to see at a glance the infinite superiority of the divine mind above the human—to see what an inestimable endowment it is to be able to know things that are not, and to speak of them, and even form them as though they had already been in actual existence. Thus, Adam having gained, either by inspiration, or by actual experience, all necessary knowledge of things natural, the Creator bestowed on him a partner or second self, by whom and with whom he could enter upon the consideration of things moral, the relations and obligations by which human beings are connected with one another. We shall see that our first parents, in a state of complete adolescence, must have spent the first century of their existence in Paradise. It is possible also, that their Creator saw good to allow them to spend the greater portion of that hundred years in acquiring a knowledge of nature and of their moral relations to each other, before he put their sense of duty to that religious test which eventuated in their fall. In the intellectual trial Adam was alone, and he acquitted himself well, and gave full proof of his competence to instruct his future partner, and of God's divine and provident benevolence, that as he had made man, so he had at once endowed him with the knowledge necessary for life, and had not left him to perish in the midst of abundance from ignorance of the uses of things.

CHAPTER XI

Of the Trial of Our First Parents in Duty

We now come to a part of our subject which relates to the moral trial of our first Parents, or to that part of God's economy which put to the test the sense of obligation and duty which our First Parents owed to their munificent and all-wise Creator.—Let us in a few words look at knowledge and duty as they now commend themselves to mankind generally. It is a curious fact that in almost all our colleges, universities, academies, and common schools, and even churches, the course of education is formed with a reference rather to the former than to the latter and inculcates knowledge rather than duty; there is no comparison between the intellects and morals of the scholars, in knowledge they are giants; in practical goodness they are dwarfs; they know every thing, and do nothing. Intellect among them, like the starry chestnut, mounts to the clouds; morality, practical morality, stunted and flowerless creeps along the ground.

Again, it is in religion as it is in society; for as we are accustomed to act and think in one department of life, so we are inclined to act and think in every other department. A man shall believe with his whole soul, that the author of Christianity is a heaven-sent messenger, feel perfectly convinced of the truth of the gospel, and even of his own duty to obey it, yet he does not, he will not obey it. Nevertheless he will greedily swallow down any amount of knowledge you choose to impart to him on these topics, and sit and listen, and reason and receive, and be still the same. He will believe, but he will not obey. He will receive knowledge and admire it, but repudiate duty and even abhor it. Yet duty is a pervading topic; everywhere there is duty to our parents, duty to our children, duty to husbands, duty to wives, duty to servants, duties to masters, duties to slaves, duties to relations immediate and remote, to friends, fellow citizens, and to our fellow-men. Yet, the thing does not commend itself to the hearts of men, and win their kindliest regard as does knowledge. How many attend our public assemblies to hear and learn! How few return from them determined to obey!

Now if this is man in his most experienced condition, if this is man in these latter ages on whom the ends of the world have come, if this is man with the teachings of practical life and all the observation and experience of nearly six thousand years, what was to be expected of him in his infantile state, a child in experience, tenderly educated in a Paradise of pleasure, and the darling of a kind God and all good angels? It was with him as it is with ourselves; he yielded to his love of knowledge, and offered, at the shrine of fancied wisdom, the sacrifice of duty which he owed to God.

It may be made a question, why we are fonder of knowledge than obedience; for knowledge abstract from purposes of utility, is an empty thing. The reason seems to be this, that man in pursuing knowledge feels more sovereignty and less dependence directly, than when acting in obedience to the calls of duty. Men desire to be gods, to be the sovereign arbiters of their own conduct, or to do as they choose;—they dread responsibility, because it implies dependence, and dependence weakness, and weakness misery "doing or suffering." But this is inadmissible in the economy of God's government; for as we are dependant on God for all that we are, and all that we know, so he wills that we shall be responsible to him for all that we do. He is the fountain of all authority even as he is the source of all power and goodness and wisdom; he gave us life and sustains us in it; and wills that we should account to him for the gracious loan of such an incomparable blessing.

But it does not follow that because God is good man will be grateful. He may be exceedingly bountiful, we may be exceedingly unthankful; he may be great and we may not acknowledge his greatness; he may be very good, we very ungrateful. It is proper, therefore, with such ambitious feelings for independence as we possess, that we should be tried, that it should be proved of what metal we are, and whether we be as good as we would affect to be great, whether we will prove as grateful to God as we are ready to partake of his bounties, whether we are as willing he should reign over our life as we are willing to enjoy that life at his hand.

It was proper, therefore, that Adam should be morally tried as well as intellectually; it was proper to ascertain whether he could be grateful when God was good; whether he chose to obey that authority whose divine power had given him all things richly to enjoy; whether he chose to be ruled by God as he chose to live by him; for man's obligation to God and dependence on him is the cause of all duty.

If God had created man as he is, and had left him to pursue knowledge and the devices of his own heart, without inculcating dependence and a sense of moral obligation, then we might have judged that man was never made by God at all, but was the offspring of chance, or fate, or a diabolical power; and if the Scriptures had not inculcated these things on man, and shown that, from the beginning, God had held man responsible for his actions, we might have doubted their divinity, in as much as they would have been so defective, that men understanding the whole of human nature would have been unable to believe them.

But now the scriptures speak in perfect harmony with the most correct views which we have yet been able to obtain of human nature, and of the obligations we owe to him on whom we are altogether dependant for life and all the things which we enjoy; for they show that, as we are formed creatures of knowledge and duty, so God would deal with us according to this our proper nature, and be served and reverenced by us in subjecting both our love of knowledge and sense of duty to his authority.—To do this is righteousness; not to do this is sin.

In this view of things then it pleased the Almighty God to put the virtue, gratitude, or sense of duty of our first parents to the test, in the following manner.

"And the Lord God commanded the man, saying, of every tree of the Garden thou mayest freely eat; but of the tree of the knowledge of good and evil, thou shalt not eat; for in the day thou eatest thereof thou shall surely die."

CHAPTER XII

Of Law in General, and of the Law in Paradise in Particular

Law means rule, and is intended to give direction to action, The force of law depends on the existence of previous authority in him who makes it, and on the condition and capability and reason of obedience of those for whom it is designed. If law comes to us unsupported unrecommended by these things, it is then either of no authority, or it is tyranny. If there is no authority in the law maker, there can and will be no authority in the law made. But supposing the authority to be perfect (though there can exist no authority for tyranny anywhere) but the law incongruous with the condition, capability, and reason of obedience in those for whom it was made, it would not be law but tyranny; it would be oppression and not safety, and would produce confusion and not good order. But where the right to make law exists and the rule adapts itself to the condition, capability, and reason of obedience of those for whom it is designed, personal safety and the security of property will be the result and the law will be admitted.

In the case before us no one will doubt God's right to make law; nor, indeed, will any person presume deny the obligation of Adam to obey it, for certainly all possible reason of obedience rested on him why he should honor the Ruler.

Moreover the law was in harmony, perfect harmony with his capabilities and opened for him a sphere of action commensurate with his active powers, so that his gratitude to God could play with a healthy freedom and in so doing would afford proof to himself, to angels, and to God, that it was alive, had a name, and a local habitation in his breast. His circumstances also were favorable to the keeping of the law. First, because the fruit of every other tree in the garden was given him on which to subsist, Second, because gratitude prompted him rather to obedience than to disobedience. Third, the tree of life was of free access to him; so that, if his ambition should aspire to any thing beyond his natural and present happy condition, he "could eat and live forever." And it stood full before him to guard his virtue and stimulate his perseverance.

CHAPTER XIII

Of Trial and of Temptation

It may not be improper in this place to make the necessary distinction which exists between a trial and a temptation. In a trial there is an injunction and inducement to abstain from evil, or practice some good, as the case may be: in a temptation there is an injunction and inducement either to practice evil or to abstain from some good, as the case may be. For instance Adam was tried, the Saviour was tempted; or our first parents were tried by God and tempted by the Devil, and so of other cases:—Trial is of God and is natural and necessary to the perfection of both our intellectual and moral nature; temptation is diabolical, degrading, insulting, and has Satan for its author. It was highly gracious in God to test the virtue of our first parents; but most diabolical in Satan to tempt our blessed Saviour with the government of the world, in order to cause him to do evil—to fall down and worship him instead of the Divine Father. We are to count it all for joy when we fall into divers trials, knowing that the trial of our faith worketh patience; the testing of our principles is the exaltation of our graces and virtues, and is of God; but as he cannot be tempted to evil, so neither does he tempt any man to evil: "but every man is tempted when he is drawn away of his own lust and enticed; and lust when it has conceived bringeth forth sin, and sin when it is perfected bringeth forth death."

Both the intellectual and moral trial of our first parents must have greatly enlarged their happiness, which is the end and perfection of both knowledge and duty; and no doubt it was to increase the amount of their joys that their blessed Creator tried both their knowledge and their sense of duty. What indeed could fill our father Adam with more constant heart-felt satisfaction than to know, when his Creator put his understanding to the test, he had so acquitted himself as to secure his entire approbation? Adam had attained to a knowledge of some leading feature in the nature of each of the animals, as the test imports, and naming them according to this master passion, instinct, or external conformation, his judgment was admitted as correct, and his naming of them authority for the style by which they were to be known and spoken of in future times. *And whatever Adam called every living creature that was the name thereof.* It was an act of unmixed goodness then in the Divine Creator thus to put our father's knowledge to the test; for it had a direct tendency to increase his happiness by assuring him of his own attainments in knowledge, of the approbation of his Maker, and of his own authority over all inferior natures in the world of which he was the lord. On this occasion and subsequently Adam must have felt not merely like a man, but like a man clothed with authority and full of wisdom.

But was the trial of his moral nature, his goodness, less intended to increase his happiness than the trial of his intellectual nature or wisdom? Most assuredly no. Surely it was to amplify the joys of our first parents that God subjected to the test of obedience their grateful reverence for his authority. It can very easily be proved that Adam's happiness never could have been complete unless he had been put on trial. This may appear at first thought, somewhat paradoxical; but it is no less true on that account. In the first place, Adam, agreeably to his nature, must in the contemplation of all that God had done for him and given to him, in creating him, exalting him to the lordship of the world, and in bestowing upon him his last best gift, his lovely partner Eve, have felt gratitude, an excess, if I may so speak, of gratitude to God, his benefactor and Creator. But it would have been painful rather than pleasant, to have confined this gratitude to his bosom alone. When this virtue, so natural to man, is conceived in the heart, it necessarily seeks to discover itself by the overt powers of speech and action, and will not contentedly lie concealed in the breast of its possessor; it will issue in words or works. By putting Adam on trial, therefore, he created for him a sphere in which his gratitude could play with a freedom commensurate with his natural constitution as a being of moral action as well as of words and thoughts. If gratitude be good in feeling, it is still better for its owner when it is allowed to discover itself in words, and best of all when it is found in action.—The happiness of its possessor is then complete; for he has then given to his benefactor the most unequivocal testimony of moral reciprocity of which his nature is capable; for action good or evil is principle perfected, and as Milton says,

————————————————a grateful mind
By owing owes not, but still pays, at once
Indebted and discharged; what burden then?

Let the reader follow us in patience while with an humble reliance on the scriptures.

"We may assert Eternal Providence,
And justify the ways of God to man."

Thus the moral, like the intellectual trial of our first parents was not only in accordance with their nature as beings of knowledge and duty, but in perfect harmony with that happiness which it is the highest ambition of our nature to possess; and it was, as we have seen, most certainly intended by God to enlarge the sphere of their blessedness and increase its amount, that this probationary scheme was introduced.

To God, then, the maker of Heaven and Earth, to God the only wise, and the only good, the greatest and the best, be everlasting honor and praise. Amen.

CHAPTER XIV

Of the Tree of Life and of the Tree of the Knowledge of Good and Evil

In the fertile district of Eden and around the sources of the four celebrated rivers of Pison, Gihon, Heddekel, and Euphrates, God planted the garden which by way of eminence we call Paradise.

Now if He has distinguished for beauty many parts and portions of the habitable globe at large, if he has struck forth everywhere in all the earth such glorious landscape, so much of the beautiful, and picturesque, we may well suppose that the garden of the world planted by His own hand, was an abode of the highest beauty and adorned with every sentiment of order, grandeur, variety, and sublimity, "For out of the ground made the Lord God to grow every tree that is pleasant to the sight, and good for food; the tree of life also in the midst of the garden and the tree of the knowledge of good and evil; and the Lord God took the man, and put him into the garden to dress and keep it. And the Lord God commanded the man, saying, Of every tree of the garden thou mayest freely eat; but of the tree of the knowledge of good and evil thou mayest not eat: for in the day thou eatest thereof thou shalt surely die."

Paradise, under the name of "The garden of God" is, several times in the scriptures made an object of comparison, and fertile and beautiful districts of country are likened to the garden of God. Where Eden was situate avails not to inquire. In it God was pleased to plant the garden in which he placed the original ancestors of mankind; and in the midst of the garden two trees, the tree of life and the tree of the knowledge of good and evil, forming as it were a central crown to the wide-spreading landscape of the Paradise of God.

Of the one it was permitted man freely to eat. Of the other he was not to eat. It was to stand forever in his presence the untouched unstained symbol of his own obedience and gratitude to God. To him the one was an ordinance of life, the other of death, and both stood before him in the midst of his home inviting him to good and dissuading him from evil, like law and gospel before his innumerable descendants of latter times.

Had he partaken of the tree of life before the fall, and he was at perfect liberty by the word of the Lord God to do so, the other tree and the commandment respecting it would, doubtless, have been withdrawn, for he could not have died; the case of Satan, moreover, sufficiently demonstrates how unsafe it is to put immortal beings under law. So when he eat of the forbidden tree he was separated from both, lest he should "Eat of the tree of life also and live for ever." This would have been equally dangerous in his sinful state, as Satan's case again proves.

But the two trees being contiguous to each other in the centre of the landscape, and apart from all the rest; our first parents, by their reverence for the divine commandment and the delight they took in obeying the Lord God their Creator, practised so admirable a self denial, that they seem, from the narrative, never once during their long stay in Paradise to have approached either of them till the fatal day of the fall, a circumstance to be regarded by all their descendants as proof positive of the exceeding gravity and chasteness of their original virtue and of their admirable piety towards their Creator whom they loved, and honored, and adored.

Our First Parents, then, were tried of God, tempted by Satan, and sinned themselves. Their trial was natural, necessary, and exalting; their temptation degrading, dangerous, diabolical; and their fall fatal, guilty, deadly. The fall is the point at which the two states of good, and evil meet and touch one another. The trial and the interdict was of God, the temptation was of Satan; and the dire calamity was their own act, their own voluntary act, all things considered.

CHAPTER XV

Of the Time Our First Parents Continued in Paradise

If we contemplate mankind as they existed in the earliest ages, we discover by scripture that they were distinguished for very long life.

Noah was nine hundred and fifty years old when he died. His father was upwards of seven hundred, and his grandfather Methuselah almost a thousand. Enoch was translated at the age of three hundred and sixty-five, Jared was only seven years younger than Methuselah, and the father of all, Adam, expired only at the advanced age of nine hundred and thirty years!

Human life may be divided into five different periods, infancy, adolescence, puberty, manhood, and old age. Infancy extends from birth to the second dentition, adolescence from the second dentition to puberty, puberty to the period of marriage, and manhood from marriage to old age. Since the flood men have run through the whole of these five periods in at most eighty years; but the antediluvians, generally, did not pass through them but in eight or nine hundred years; consequently each of those divisions of human life, was much more extended in them than in us. We reach the second dentition or receive our second set of teeth about the age of seven years, and at that time pass from childhood to the period of adolescence or boyhood.—Thus we fulfil the first period of our life in the lapse of seven short years; but this could not have been their case. Their childhood must have been extended proportionately with the whole of their existence. We exhaust the period of adolescence or boyhood at about fifteen, and at that age attain to puberty.—But this they could not have done. Adolescence or boyhood was surprisingly extended in them; they do not seem to have reached maturity before one hundred years; consequently the age, at which they were blessed with children, was not until that number of years had passed over them, Lamech was one hundred and eighty-two years old before Noah was born. Methuselah was one hundred and eighty-seven at the birth of Lamech. When Enoch was born his father Jared was one hundred and sixty-two, Jared's father again was one hundred and eighty-five; and Adam was one hundred and thirty at the birth of his third son, Seth. Thus we see that as human life extended itself, not to tens but to hundreds, the different periods into which it is divisible were proportionately extended, and that the antediluvians generally, who lived for eight or nine hundred years, did not attain the age of puberty till they were a hundred at least.

In this respect our first parents resembled their immediate descendants. Adam was blessed with his third son, Seth, only when he had attained his hundred and thirtieth year; and his first son, Cain, was not born to him till after his expulsion from Paradise. Therefore, being expelled just before he reached puberty and having three sons, Cain, Abel, and Seth immediately after his expulsion and before he attained one hundred and thirty, it follows evidently that he could not have lived less than one hundred or more than one hundred and thirty years in Paradise; he must consequently have been created in a state of entire adolescence; and thus, by a wise providence, he felt himself, at his creation, equally removed from the feebleness of childhood and the disquietude of that age which lies immediately beyond adolescence.

To this view of the matter one objection only, of any moment, can be opposed; and that is apparent rather than real; that the divine Father gave commandment to the original ancestors of mankind, while in the garden, to fill the earth with their own species. To this we answer, that the Creator, being supremely peculiar in his attributes, speaks of those things that are not as though they truly existed. He did not, therefore, speak but with a reference to the mature nature of those whom, at the moment, he was graciously pleased to address; and gave them commandment in relation to a period of their existence, which was immediately to follow the happy state of adolescence in which he had created them. This is a mode of speech by no means unusual in the holy scriptures. At the flood, the Lord said to Noah, his proclaimer of righteousness, "The end of all flesh is come before me." But the deluge did not occur till one hundred and twenty years after this had been uttered. To Abraham He said, "A father of many nations have I constituted thee." Yet Abraham was then without a child. In this, as in many other instances, and particularly in the words relating to the increase of our species, the Great God speaks of those things that are not as though they were.

Milton, on the contrary, supposes our "beloved first parents to have been created in perfect manhood and, in a splendid poetical fiction, describes their nuptials as occurring at the moment of their first introduction to each other.

> ————————————————To the nuptial bower
> I led her blushing like the morn; all Heaven
> And happy constellations, on that hour,
> Shed their selectest influence; the earth
> Gave signs of granulation, and each hill.
> Joyous the birds, fresh gales and gentle airs
> Whispered it to the woods, and from their wings
> Flung rose, flung odors from the spicy shrub,
> Disparting, till the amorous bird of night
> Sung spousal, and bid haste the Evening Star
> On his hill top to light the bridal lamp.

This ravishing gloss of our great Bard is encumbered with insuperable difficulty, inasmuch as it is incongruous with some of the most obvious points of that extremely general narrative in which the holy scriptures comprise the history of our First Parents. While the fact, that in Paradise they flourished in the innocence of unconscious adolescence and did not while there taste of the happiness of marriage, derives indubitable support from the letter of the sacred oracle, which to poets, as well as to all others, is the only safe guide when discoursing of things religious. It was not till after the fall and their expulsion from Paradise that Cain, their eldest, was born.

THE EVIL STATE CONSIDERED

CHAPTER XVI

Of the Evil State in General

The great and dreadful things of this State are all of an evil nature, and were ulterior to man's original condition. Sin, guilt, cowardice, shame, condemnation, death constitute its leading features. These evils were not man's by birthright, they are not his by right of inheritance; but were unlawfully purchased by him at the promptings of that ferocious spirit, who dared to purchase a knowledge of them with the loss of heaven.

We have, heretofore, been looking at man in his native abode, clothed with innocence and full of happiness, basking is the sunshine of divine favor and swaying his unstained sceptre over a peaceful world. The scene is now to be changed from good to evil, from happiness to misery, from pleasure to pain; temptation is to take the place of trial, and sin of righteousness, guilt is to be substituted for innocence, and cowardice and shame for the courage and serenity of conscious worth. Satan now usurps the place of God, or rather opposes him; and ruin and dismay trample upon order and primitive security, till death enters and by a destruction unavoidable and irresistible reigns triumphant over a fallen world.

CHAPTER XVII

Of the Temptation by Satan

As the successful trial of Adam's understanding, in the naming of the animals, had a direct tendency to inspire him with a consciousness of his own intelligence, and thereby to increase his self-satisfaction and by consequence his happiness, so it very necessarily prepared him for that higher trial to which his virtue was put in the commandment respecting the forbidden fruit.—Naturally considered Adam's understanding in the one case was as severely tried as in the other case was his gratitude and loyalty to God. And it may safely be affirmed that all of us would rather venture on the one trial than the other. All of us would, doubtless, esteem it much less difficult to abstain from the fruit of a certain tree than to come off with honor in a case like that of Adam's, in which he was to seize upon some action, instinct, or external appearance in the forms of all the animals as a reason for the name to be imposed upon them for all future time.

Indeed, it must have appeared a training of a very gentle and gracious character for the Lord God to demand of him as a test of his reverence only a simple abstinence from the fruit of one tree: and the matter was rendered still more amiable by what was said of the other vegetable products of that happy home of man, that he was at liberty freely to eat of them all; and this goodness was still further heightened by its including the tree of life itself, which seems to have been planted by the side of the interdicted tree in order to show to man, that his benevolent and holy Creator would rather that he should partake of absolute immortality by the one than sin and death by touching the other. The trial was wholly of a negative character, and enjoined nothing to be done, but only something to be left undone; and in this Adam had no habit to contend with and conquer; for he had never partaken of this tree as food. Indeed, he was, in this view of the matter, by no means free to fall; the balance of motive was all on the side of perseverance.

The fact is, that Adam very probably never would have sinned, but on account of his affection for his unsuspecting partner, who, not having so great an experience in trial, and never having like him tasted the happiness resulting from conscious superior wisdom, became more a proper object of fiendish duplicity, and, therefore, she actually fell before the temptation.

Still the mother of mankind was tried, and in trial gave proof of an innate virtue not inferior to that possessed by her husband. And had trial, which was of God, been the only test to which her fidelity was put, she would, doubtless, have triumphed and continued in innocence forever. But to trial by God succeeded temptation by Satan, and though she had sustained the one, she could not resist the other. Though she had lived and rejoiced under the trial or fatherly prohibition which said "Thou shalt not eat thereof lest thou die:" she could not withstand the deceitful suggestion, "You shall be as gods, knowing good and evil."

How singularly adapted to human nature on its weakest side is the temptation of the Fiend! "You shall be as gods knowing good and evil." To this day do men sacrifice duty to knowledge: superior wisdom is the ambition of all. Strange as it may seem scarcely the man exists, who would not rather that you would blame his heart than his head, who would not be called knave rather than fool, who would not rather be thought ungrateful than incapable. And yet *Si ingratum dixeris, omnia dixeris*—If you call a man ungrateful you call him every thing that is bad.

The temptation, therefore, is founded on a consummate knowledge of human nature, and is directed to that popular and specious weakness in man, by which, to this day he is ever prepared to apologise for neglect of duty, his admiration of a diviner wisdom. The profound knowledge of human nature which directed this temptation and the bold but succinct subtilty with which it is addressed to the object of it could be possessed, at this early date of human history, only by a being of the very highest order of intelligence; and the language used concerning Satan, under the symbolical name of the "Serpent" implies both his superior knowledge, and subtilty.

Now the serpent was more subtle than any beast of the field which the Lord God had made. And he said unto the woman, Yea, hath God said, Ye shall not eat of every tree of the garden? And the woman said unto the serpent, We may eat of the fruit of the trees of the garden; but of the fruit of the tree which is in the midst of the garden, God hath said, Ye shall not eat of it, neither shall ye touch it, lest ye die. And the Serpent said unto the woman, Ye shall not surely die; for God doth know that in the day ye eat thereof, your eyes shall be opened, and ye shall be as gods, knowing good and evil.

Your eyes shall be opened.—Man is, as has been observed, endowed with a capacity for knowledge and duty, and is susceptible of the two sentiments of misery and happiness. As knowledge and obedience are ever followed by happiness, so knowledge and disobedience are the certain sources of misery. The devil knew this by experience; he had purchased this knowledge at the expense of heaven itself. There was a time when his experience, his natural and happy experience, reached only to knowledge, duty, and enjoyment; but he had fatally become wiser; his eyes had been opened; and he now felt what it was to know evil by being undutiful, and to taste of misery by sacrificing his happiness to his ambition. And thus were our First Parents also to taste of misery, the consciousness of having done evil by yielding to his suggestions.

"And when the woman saw, that the tree was good for food, and that it was pleasant to the eyes, and a tree to be desired to make one wise, she took of the fruit thereof, and did eat, and gave also to her husband with her, and he did eat And the eyes of them both were opened, and they knew they were naked."

Alas! that a knowledge of misery should be purchased at so fatal a price. How deplorable to behold two beings hitherto innocent, pious, and happy, thus pushed all naked and unprepared into a state in which they must inevitably live in misery, or but for the mercy of God die in despair! How dreadful to know evil by loosing our righteousness, and misery by casting away our happiness.

But let the reader please take notice to what is meant by a state of misery. It is a state in which, from a sense of sin and a fear of punishment, the mind is disturbed in such a way as to be afraid of God and ashamed of itself and consequently unhappy, a state of feeling wholly unknown to beings innocent of the violation of law.

The reason why we would have the reader to attend to this account of the state of misery is, because it is a principle business of the gospel, of which we shall immediately speak, to excise or cut out of the conscience this intolerable burden—the sense of guilt, and to replant in the human heart, as in its native seat, the joys of innocence, the joys of the spirit of God.

CHAPTER XVIII

Of the Fall of Our First Parents

It has been noted in the preceding pages that there is a difference between trial and temptation; there is a difference also between both of these and sin; temptation and sin are not an identity; for one may be tempted without sinning, as was the case with our Saviour; and a being may sin without being tempted, as was the case with Satan when he seduced man.

Sometimes, however, sin and that which tempts to the commission of it are so closely connected that they are distinguished with difficulty, as in the case of Joseph; and some sins never would be committed perhaps, but for the supposed goods with which they are associated, as in the case of Judas.

But when a man does commit sin it is because he believes it to be best, all things considered. This is the case with all who sin; for it is a voluntary evil, sin of ignorance excepted; no man needs to sin unless he chooses; the love of sin, therefore, springing either from the thing itself, or from something associated with it, forms the root of the whole matter. But that which is thus engendered in the mind, is next born into practice or real life; so that we have first the love of sin in the heart, and second the practice of sin in the life, real life, practical life.

When our First Parents sinned it was because they first chose to do so, because they first thought it best for the time, all things considered. As the text aptly says, the fruit appeared desirable both for food and wisdom; and desire being once conceived it was of ready birth and speedily leaped forth into life. "She took of the fruit and did eat, and gave also to her husband with her, and he did eat." Alas! though temptation may be supposed to palliate the guilt, it could neither apologize for it nor prevent its interminable sorrows.

Now the moment our First Parents sinned, their state was changed in law from that of life, righteousness, and happiness to that of sin, misery and death. In this last state, guilt was first of all attributed; then followed misery or the influence of bin on the mind, cowardice, and shame; finally death entered.

Thus we have the whole attributes of sin before us,—the love of it, the practice of it, the state of it, its guilt, its power, and its punishment. We shall now speak of these six matters relating to sin.

CHAPTER XIX

Concerning Sin

1. OF THE DESIRE OR LOVE OF SIN:—It would suit too generally those who indulge in sin to be permitted to apologize for it—to be permitted to say, "we could not help it. We were compelled to it. We were tempted to it. We were desirous to please. We were deceived," and so forth. This was the unhappy but unavailing apology of our First Parents. "The serpent beguiled me," said she. "The woman, which thou gavest me," said he. But the Divine Father held each guilty, for they were all responsible. With his instructions or word for our guide it is equally criminal to deceive or to be deceived.

Let us not imagine, that overt sin can be atoned for by a pretended inward purity, We judge of the secret thought by the outward act: and if we commit sin it is because we love it. If it is found in our practice it is because it is first in our heart. Love it not and you will avoid it; abhor it and you will flee the very appearance of it.

Lot's wife loved sin, looked back upon its flaming abodes, and was changed into a statue of salt. Joseph abhorred it, fled from its presence, maintained his innocence, and rose to the primacy of Egypt, an honorable and providential reward of his tried virtue. If our First Parents yielded to sin it was because it was first in their hearts.

2. OF THE PRACTICE OF SIN:—To sin, or not to sin, that is the question, apology being wholly inadmissible. The scriptures demand not only that we shall do no evil, but that we shall not think it. Why do evil thoughts arise in your hearts? said our Lord Jesus. The violation of law is to be dreaded even in thought. How dangerous then in word! and how much more so in action! But to keep it out of our words and actions, it is only necessary to keep it out of our hearts. Strangle it in the birth then; it is the offspring of the serpent and worthy of death. It is in the heart that evil is conceived; it leaps forth to life at the lips; and is perfected by action; it is here the monster appears full formed and raging to destroy: for sin is dangerous to him who indulges in it, dangerous to

his fellows, and insulting to God. The practiser, like the lover of it shall never see life. If, however, it is bad to love it, it is still worse to practice it. Chase it then from the thought.

"Lord," said David, "who shall abide in thy tabernacle? who shall dwell in thy holy hill? He that walketh uprightly, and speaketh the truth in his heart. He that backbiteth not with his tongue, nor doth evil to his neighbor, nor taketh up a reproach against his neighbor. In whose eyes a vile person is contemned: but he honoreth those who fear the Lord. He that sweareth to his hurt and changeth not. He that puts not his money to usury; nor taketh reward against the innocent. He that doeth these things shall never be moved."

Law is the most majestic and controlling influence in the universe, whether we consider it physically or morally. When we sin, therefore, we insult the majesty of law and him who made it; who will not hold us guiltless; but will certainly require it at our hand. From law springs all the order we behold in the universe; disregard to it is the certain source of disorder. See the order and permanence of the natural systems, which continue to obey the laws impressed upon them at their creation; and behold the distracted fortunes of the human family, of the Jewish nation, and of the Christian church, who have broken away from original law. But its majesty cannot be compromised; its insulted honor must be appeased; on earth it demands the outpouring of the blood of the Son of God. But in Satan's case it refuses propitiation altogether. It calls for nothing short of perpetual exclusion; and his daring outrage on earth will be punished forever both in him and all who rashly espouse his fortunes.

3. OF THE STATE OF SIN:—The same thing may exist in different states. So may man. He once existed in a natural state. He now lives in a preternatural one. He was once possessed of righteousness, happiness, and life. He is now doomed to sin, misery, and death.

The earth is successively in a state of light and darkness, of elevation and depression, changes giving birth to very different phenomena. The oak is first in the acorn, and wine in the grape, and the grape in the seed. Man himself is first in the womb and next in the world, in a state of adolescence and in a state of marriage.

It is admirable to behold how suddenly a thing will change its state or condition, and clothe itself with all the advantages and disadvantages of the state into which it leaps. At night-fall the earth is merged in darkness, and only a few hours suffice to clothe her silent sphere with all the nocturnal drapery of the solemn change. Again she immerges from night, is born of darkness, arises dripping from the womb of the morning, and in a few hours again clothes herself in the garments of light.—The oak which is now in the acorn, soon appears in the forest, and finally in the fire. The seed that is sown to-day is in a state of vegetation to-morrow. The child that is this moment in the womb, is next moment in the world and living by a new mode of subsistence totally; and the youthful pair, who now stand upon the floor in a state of celibacy, by the usages of society, sit down in a state of wedlock for life, but before night may be in a state of death.

So it is in religion. The Eunuch sitting in his chariot, a Jewish proselyte, steps out, is immersed by the Evangelist, Philip, and becomes a Christian. The Jews stand on the one side of the Red Sea and are the bondmen of Pharaoh; they pass the waters, are immersed into Moses in the cloud and in the sea, and are become his disciples; on the one side they are slaves, on the other freemen. Noah was this moment in the ark and next moment on the earth. In the former a fugitive from the world that had sinned, in the latter the sole heir of the world we now inhabit, — Adam and Eve, then, were this moment in a state of nature, innocent and happy; next moment they were in a preternatural state, guilty and miserable; and as they had by the violation of law, suddenly unrobed themselves of the blessings, privileges, and honors of their original state, so they very soon felt themselves clothed with the horrors of that into which they had sunk, shame, cowardice, and recrimination.

4. OF THE GUILT OF SIN:—Is not guilt filed against that man who sins? yes, it is. Let us, therefore, remember that, in the vision of the judgment. It is said "The books were opened." It is dangerous pastime to incur debt; it is still more dangerous to incur guilt. The sins of the Jewish nation were remembered against them regularly once a year by the ministration of the High Priest, when he appeared before the Lord on the day of annual atonement: and this could have been done, only because guilt had been filed against the nation. The Lord Jesus is said to have redeemed those transgressions upon file under the first covenant. But it is obvious, that the Ruler of the world puts on file the sins of all nations, and all individuals, Adam and Eve, not exempted, and that their transgressions are borne with only in view of the one act of righteousness of the Lord Jesus Christ.

5. OF THE POWER OF SIN:—All our doings, that are not of a negative character, exert a moral or immoral influence over us according as they are good or evil. He, who voluntarily incurs guilt once, is greatly strengthened thereby to repeat it; and the circumstances of the case, which are not always understood, in all their relations, may involve him again and again.—Innocence is a clean canvass on which to delineate the portrait of life. Happy the man, who does reverence to its sacred and fair page.

The less apparently the sin, the greater in reality the danger. At all events "he that is unfaithful in the least is unfaithful also in that which is greatest." He, that for a trifle would sacrifice his innocence, and violate law, his conscience, his religion, and his sacred honor, could not easily be supposed long to resist a greater temptation. Judas abstracted paltry sums from the money with which he was entrusted, till yielding to the ascendancy, which his evil actions had acquired over him, he finally sold his master for forty pieces of silver. The politic Ahitophel, David's minister, profoundly understood the influence which evil actions sway over the guilty. In conformity with this he counseled the ambitious but unexperienced Absalom to go into his father's wives in the presence of all Israel, a deed fitted beyond others to destroy all hope of future reconciliation with his royal father, to make himself the fool-hardy villain, and to embolden his fellow conspirators. The miserable results of its influence on our First Parents were cowardice, shame, recrimination, and guilty palliation.

6. OF THE PUNISHMENT OF SIN:—Death is the opposite of life, and is, therefore, the consummation of evil. Like birth, however, it is so common among the sons of men, that as there is but little general joy for the first so there is but little public sorrow for the last.

The human family consists of about a thousand millions of souls, who die off and are renewed again in every thirty years nearly. All this amazing carnage goes on in comparative quietude and, therefore, it fails to affect us; but could we behold on some boundless plain the whole race of man, all who have lived since Adam and Adam himself, all who now live, and all who shall live from this to the resurrection, with death stalking from rank to rank, killing this immense mass of flesh and blood, mowing down successively the kings and fathers of mankind, courtiers and their slaves, and withering the flowers and dashing to pieces the glory of society, the high, the low, the rich, the poor, yea all the inhabitants of the earth, and casting them into the grave without distinction, at the rate of three thousand every hour and fifty every minute, then perhaps we should gain some adequate conception of sin and of its horrid nature, not only in its love and practice and guilt and state and power, but also in its punishment, death; for "the wages of sin is death."

Thus, then, have we glanced rapidly at sin in its different phases. And thus we see where Adam stood in the eye of the law, when his divine Creator called to him, "Adam, where art thou," after he had sinned, and fallen from innocence. He now stood all naked, divested of righteousness, and ready to be slain according to the most literal import of the law which he had violated, which said not only "Thou shalt die," but intensely, "Thou shalt surely die;" and not only so, but it marked out the time of his death. "In the day thou eatest thou shall surely die." This could not be misunderstood; it is not now misunderstood when interpreted most literally; it was not then misunderstood; for both of our ancestors surely knew it to mean precisely what it said; that they should both die on the day they violated it. What Eve answered to the seducer, and what Adam said to her, conspire to shew, that both understood the law aright; that it threatened immediate death; and their conduct virtuous and pious had, up to the day of the fall, been framed upon a literal understanding of it. Indeed if God had not meant what he said, how could angels, henceforth, have any confidence in his word? How could any of his intelligent creatures aware of this transaction ever again repose in his sayings with confidence that they would be fulfilled? The law, then, said that man should die, he should surely die, and die the day he eat of the interdicted fruit; and it meant what it said without any gloss or explanation whatever. The fear and the shame, and the recrimination, and the palliation, which succeeded, prove also, that they were dead in law the moment they sinned. Had now a thread of lightning from the clouds passed through them and laid them lower than the shades in which they sought concealment the executive would have enforced what the legislator had decreed, literally decreed, publicly decreed. "In the day thou eatest thereof thou shalt surely die."

CHAPTER XX

Of Opening the Eyes

"For God doth know that in the day you eat thereof then your eyes shall he opened and you shall be as gods, knowing good and evil."

THEN YOUR EYES SHALL BE OPENED:—To what? To the things of a new and preternatural state. They had already tasted of good; they should then taste of evil; and increase their knowledge by sacrificing their happiness, and learn the value of innocence by having lost it, and the honor of being admitted to sensible communion with the Deity by being denied it forever; while the pains they should suffer and the remorse which should consume them, would instruct them how fallacious it was to reason of a matter on which they had revelation, to prefer the word of any one to that of God, and to think of what they might become in a new state when they were so completely blest in their natural one.

When persons change their state their eyes are necessarily opened to the advantages and disadvantages of that state. But before the change occurs it is impossible to possess any thing but faith on the subject. A child knows nothing of day and night and season and change, it knows nothing in short of practical life before it is born into it. So of man in relation to the unseen world; we know nothing of it experimentally: we may have faith, but we have no knowledge of it.

This reasoning holds good of moral changes as well as physical ones, and of religious as well as moral ones. Hazael, while he was only servant to the king of Syria, felt like a man; but when he was elevated to the throne of that kingdom he felt like a usurper, and executed upon the nation of Israel his neighbors all those cruelties which it was told him by the prophet Elijah he would practise, and which at the time Hazael thought barbarity fit only for a dog. "Is thy servant a dog" said he to the prophet, who was weeping in view of the cruelties which he should practise on the daughters of Israel and their children. "Is thy servant a dog, that he should do this great thing."

It is said of Paul that those, who had witnessed against Stephen and were now stoning him, laid down their garments at his feet for care till they had accomplished their bloody deed, and that this young man was well pleased with his slaughter, that he made havoc of the congregation, entering into houses, and dragging men and women, whom he committed to prison. He himself said he had shut up the saints in prison, had voted against them in the question of life and death, had scourged them, compelled them to blaspheme, and persecuted them even to strange cities.

Yet there was but a moment between all this dread cruelty, blindness, madness, and the most unfeigned faith, reformation love. He entered Damascus, was visited by a Christian, arose, was baptized, was pardoned, and received the Holy Spirit. He had changed his state; his eyes were opened.

These things show that persons are not to be judged of in one state by what they were in a former state. A good state may give forth a bad being and a bad state may give forth a good being. The Saviour came out of Galilee and satan out of heaven; Paul came out of an evil nation and Adam out of Paradise. Sin issued from the garden of Eden, and righteousness out of Jerusalem in which was slain the Son of God.

The command to man was, that he should not change his state lest his eyes should be opened to evil and because his native state was good. The command to men now is, forthwith to change their state, because it is evil, and to obey the gospel when they will experience that their eyes have been opened to good:—

CHAPTER XXI

Conclusion

YOU SHALL BE AS GODS:—This expression perhaps implies that the Devil before this period was familiar with idolatry, and that by using the word gods here he meant not only to arouse the ambition of our First Parents, but to pave the way for that species of false religion, which more than any thing else tended afterwards to destroy from the earth all faith in the true God. Idolatry, as will be shown in another part of this work, is most of all things opposed to the true religion of the state of respite or the present state.

We have now touched upon the several points in the very general narrative of scripture relative to the state of evil, and the temptation and fall by which man was introduced into it.

It commences in temptation and ends in death; all its intermediate points are evil and only evil. It differs from the first state as happiness does from misery, as righteousness does from sin, as courage does from cowardice, as shame from self-approval, as obedience from disobedience, as weakness from strength, as death from life, as Satan from God.

It now remains for us to examine the state of respite, or the present condition of man; and to shew the principles upon which it has obtained in consistence with the law which put an end to the state in which man was created.

"In the day thou eatest thereof thou shall surely die."

In conclusion, however, we beg leave to ask those who affect to scorn the Mosaic history of the origin of evil and of man, where are the romance or lightness of which they complain? In what point of the extremely condensed narrative do they find anything inconsistent either with the possible, or the probable or even the decorous? Is there in it any thing contradictory to the acknowledged constitution of human nature? Is man's life asserted to have been originally any thing else than animal life like our own? Does it offend them, that the writer should have referred the origin of mankind to God, and said that they were created and did not make themselves, or were the work of chance, or fate, or nothing at all? Was it cruel to try their virtue in order to increase their happiness? Or to represent them as blest with sensible communion with their maker because they were innocent? Was it improper to represent the Deity as good rather than evil? Or would they have been better pleased if God had been represented as the author of both good and evil?

For my own part, I am compelled to say, that I am unable, after many years of inquiry, to discover any thing improper, indecorous, or unnatural in this history.

CONCERNING THE STATE OF RESPITE

CHAPTER XXII

Of Respite, Reprieve &c.

In every human government there is a legislative and an executive power lodged somewhere. This is the nature of the divine government also, in which the legislative power is retained by God and the executive is granted to his Son Jesus Christ; "For the Father judges no person having committed the power of judging entirely to the Son, that all men might honor the Son as they honor the Father."

It is a rule also in human governments, that with the executive shall be deposited the powers of respite, reprieve, and commutation of punishment. Respite means the suspension of punishment, reprieve the total abrogation of it, and commutation the change of it.

In despotic governments the legislative and executive powers are lodged in the same person, who consequently possesses also the powers of respite and reprieve. This was the state of the divine government at the Fall. He who made the law, was at that time clothed with the executive authority also and all the powers of respite, reprieve and commutation. This was the divine God, who enjoyed the right, even on our own plans of procedure, either to execute the punishment due to this capital misdemeanor, to change it, to abrogate it altogether, or to vouchsafe a respite.

God is a great king, the eyes of men and angels, myriads of angels and the intelligencies of all orders in all worlds are upon him and judging of the wisdom and rectitude of his ways: the general welfare of his creatures in all parts of his universe depends on good order; and good order depends upon good law and the sanctity which attaches to good law; for it is not enough that laws be good; they must be clothed also with a sanctity that shall make them be respected, make them be obeyed.—The laws both of God and man, therefore, which concern the general good, have ever been clothed with all possible majesty, that is, they have ever been accompanied and enforced by pains and penalties. Now this majesty cannot be compromised without imminent danger to the public safety. And there is abundance of instances on record going to prove that some crimes and misdemeanors are of so capital a nature that they cannot be forgiven: the party guilty of them when condemned cannot be reprieved. Nearly all England petitioned the monarch George III. in behalf of the celebrated divine doctor Dodd. The public morals, the sanctity of individual right, the public welfare, and, above all, the law judged him worthy of death and the king would neither reprieve nor respite him, nor commute his punishment.

Our Heavenly Father, therefore, could not, would not, did not reprieve the offenders in the case before us. And if it be inquired why our First Parents did not perish on the day they ate the forbidden fruit, it can be legitimately accounted for, only by saying, He respited them or suspended for a time their fate.—But he did not pardon, he did not change their punishment. He exercised the executive right and respited them for a few short years only.

The parties accordingly, the man, the woman, and Satan, under condemnation, and in a state of respite, are dismissed, after having been severally addressed as follows:

CHAPTER XXIII

God's Address to Satan

"And the Lord God said unto the serpent. Because thou hast done this, thou art cursed above all cattle, and above every beast of the field; upon thy belly shalt thou go, and dust shall thou eat all the days of thy life. And I will put enmity between thee and the woman, and between thy seed and her seed: it shall bruise thy head, and thou shalt bruise his heel."

Far, doubtless, was Satan the murderer of our race from imagining that one so feeble as she whom he had deceived, should yet triumph over him, should yet see him foiled, and caught in the net which he had spread for others; but God who is rich in mercy, and who taketh the wise in their own craftiness, saw, even in the constitution of this weak female who had been thus cruelly beguiled, the means of her own revenge, the revenge of us all; he suspended, therefore, the immediate execution of the sentence, and, on account of the "child-bearing" attribute with which she was endowed, saved her from ruin and perpetual death by a depth of wisdom transcending the most profound thoughts of the adversary, and by a generous mercy, which even the powers and principalities of heaven itself could not anticipate. "The seed of the woman shall bruise the head of the serpent, " Glory to God and to the Lamb, glory in the highest heaven.

CHAPTER XXIV

God's Address to the Woman

"And the Lord God said unto the woman, What is this that thou hast done? And the woman said, The serpent beguiled me and I did eat.

Unto the woman he said—I will greatly multiply thy sorrow and thy conception, in sorrow shalt thou bring forth children; and thy desire shall be to thy husband, and he shall rule over thee."

Although by this address the pains of child-bearing were to be increased, and child-bearing itself rendered more frequent in the State of Respite than would have been necessary or proper in the happy and virtuous condition in which they were created supposing they had persevered in their obedience till they reached puberty and had had children; although she was to lose much of the equality which she enjoyed with him to whom she had been espoused, and was now to be ruled by him, still there wants not benevolence and pity in God towards woman in this matter; for although he destined her by sorrow to be a mother and to obey her husband, it formed no part of her doom to "Earn" her "bread by the sweat of her face." This was to be supplied her by the more natural and more potent industry of the man.—Her sorrows, however, were to be sufficiently multiplied; and we may say Woe to the man, who, by his indolence or idleness, addeth to their number. Heathens, Catholics, and Protestants are very guilty of this. The true Christians, who form their manners and customs by the maxims of revealed religion, will carefully avoid it.

CHAPTER XXV

God's Address to Adam

"And to Adam he said, Because thou hast hearkened unto the voice of thy wife and hast eaten of the tree of which I commanded thee, saying, Thou shall not eat of it; cursed is the ground for thy sake; in sorrow shalt thou eat of it all the days of thy life; thorns also and thistles shall it bring forth to thee; and thou shall eat the herb of the field. In the sweat of thy face shalt thou eat bread, till thou return into the ground; for out of it wast thou taken; for dust thou art and unto dust shalt thou return."

This was a new and sad arrangement for our royal ancestor, who had now spent a whole century in dignified ease in Paradise, living on the fruits of that happy and exuberant garden, and released from all the care and pain incident to our present precarious mode of subsistence. For with all his pristine vigour he soon experienced the enfeebling tendency "of the herb of the field" on which he was now destined to feed, and, by diseases and death which they either engendered or were unable to resist, finally, after the lapse of a few hundreds of years, to return to the dust whence he was taken. "For dust thou art," said his merciful but offended God, "and unto dust shalt thou return."

BECAUSE THOU HAST HEARKENED UNTO THE VOICE OF THY WIFE.—Inasmuch as man preferred the word of woman to that of God he is here destined henceforth to provide for her; and because she refused to obey God she is, therefore, subjected from this time to a less generous lord, who, it is said, should rule over her.

CHAPTER XXVI

The Clothing of Our First Parents

"Unto Adam also, and his wife, did the Lord God make coats of skins, and clothed them."

They had already made to themselves clothing of vegetable product, fig leaves; but their offence was a capital one and their blood had been forfeited; nevertheless as the respite was granted with a view to a final reprieve as the child-bearing has proved by the appearing of Jesus Christ, and as the revealed religion of the present state was to embody bloody sacrifice till the true offering should be made to God and to law, the Heavenly Father, therefore, furnished them with garments of the more appropriate material of animal products, which probably were the skins of those animals first slain in sacrifice to him, whose displeasure was now to be propitiated and whose sparing mercy was now to be entreated. If any thing, antecedently to the fall had been offered up to God in Paradise, it could have been only the simple but natural sacrifice of thanksgiving to his name, or an offering of fruit possibly every day; but now in a state of guilty respite a new ordinance was introduced suited to the nature of the state, offerings for sin or sin-offerings, more acceptable to God in our present state, because most befitting this state.

CHAPTER XXVII

Of the Expulsion from Paradise

"And the Lord God said, Behold the man is become like one of us to know good and evil; and now, lest he put forth his hand and take also of the tree of life, and eat, and live forever, therefore the Lord God sent him forth from the Garden of Eden to till the ground from whence he was taken. So he drove out the man."

"And he placed at the east end of the garden of Eden cherubim, and a flaming sword, which turned every way to keep the way of the tree of life."

BEHOLD THE MAN HAS BECOME LIKE ONE OF US:—As the divine Father was the Creator of all things, so he understood all things; he knew what sin, guilt, misery, and death were; and that they were opposed to the good of man. All the heavenly powers also had witnessed in the fate of Satan the influence of evil, and in his daring outrages, the danger attending his immortality in a state of outlawry. Had man been permitted to eat of the tree of life now, which before was intended as a prop to his original purity and a retreat from the first approaches of temptation, he would have found himself in the condition of the traitor angel himself, in a state at once sinful and immortal; this would have been more perilous for him than his present circumstances. He had now become like the heavenly powers in knowledge; but he did not like them retain his purity; and it would have been dangerous, therefore, to admit him to a participation of their immortality.

SO HE DROVE OUT THE MAN:—This was in mercy. But still how affecting the spectacle. The sire of men, the mother of all living, divested of the purity and privileges of their original condition, and sent forth from their native home to till the waste howling earth from which they had been taken!

> The world was all before them,—
> They hand in hand, with wandering steps and slow,
> Through Eden took their solitary way.

and carried with them the recollection of their former happiness, sorrow for their present guilt, and the fear of future death.

The period of adolescence, however, soon after this expired and new feelings arose. Their youth, adolescence, and above all their sanctity and innocence had heretofore kept them unconscious of their native defencelessness; but now expelled the sacred abodes of virtue and having attained to that age which follows adolescence, they were comforted by marriage, and Eve, in the sorrow that was threatened, had a son. She thought she had obtained the promised seed, and called his name Cain, which means triumph, crying exultingly when she beheld the boy, "I have gotten the man from Jehovah."—The man who was to triumph over her adversary. Alas! how mistaken. She needed a wiser, a better, a greater than he.

"And he placed at the east end of the garden of Eden cherubim and a flaming sword which turned every way to keep the way of the tree of life."

Some think, that the text here is corrupted, and that the whole passage is intended to describe an order of instituted worship, the symbols of which were cherubim and the lighted or blazing lamp, as they would translate the expressions "flaming sword," but this emendation of the text is not supported by any critic of eminence whom we have consulted. Cherubim and the blazing lamp were very ostensible symbols in the Jewish religion; still the criticism is unauthorized.

We have now followed the scriptures in the accounts which they deliver concerning our First Parents in Paradise, their preternatural state, and state of respite till their expulsion from their primitive abode. The text now leaves us with the following items; that they had three sons, Cain, Abel, and Seth, at the age of one hundred and thirty, and after this both sons and daughters; finally Adam died at the age of nine hundred and thirty years. Consequently he must have been seen by many of his descendants. All the ten patriarchs who lived before the flood, Noah excepted, necessarily conversed with him.

We shall now feel ourselves at liberty to enter into a more minute examination of the condition of man from the fall downward, and, therefore, will submit for consideration the following chapter.

CHAPTER XXVIII

On the Revealed Religion of the State of Respite

The history of man is divided by civil historians into ancient and modern history; by religious men it is more frequently distributed into four ages, the Adamic, Patriarchal. Jewish, and Christian; and the religion of these ages is accordingly called the Patriarchal, the Jewish, and the Christian religions. However much in accessary and accidental matters these dispensations differed from each other, in two fundamentals they have all been the same, namely, as follows:

1. *There is but One Living and true God.*
2. *That this Proposition, from Abel downward, has been a matter of faith, and not of knowledge.*

The fall, then, has proved a most interesting event to man, inasmuch as it has changed the very first principle of his intercourse with the God to whom he owes his existence. This requires to be well understood, and is, therefore, most worthy of being investigated. We have finished our inquiries into that original order of things in which man was admitted to personal and sensible intercourse with his maker, and in which he enjoyed the honor and privilege of possessing knowledge on the grand fundamental proposition of all the dispensations of the true religion, that there is one living and true God; and we are now entered upon the consideration of that condition of mankind, in which this proposition is spoken of as the subject of faith exclusively. The change from knowledge to belief of a proposition so influential and fundamental as this, ought, we repeat it, to be well understood, and it is, therefore, most worthy of being investigated.

It has been observed, that the scriptures, the new and old testaments, all the parts of which uniformly harmonize with each other, never speak of Adam as possessing faith. While the whole train of Patriarchs upwards to Abel are celebrated for their noble deeds of righteousness rendered to God on this principle, Adam is passed by in profound silence.

Was then this a slight offered to our royal ancestor because he did not possess faith in the great proposition? Or because he had pursued a course of conduct contrary to the leadings and dictations of this powerful principle? Certainly it was for neither of those reasons; but because he had, by his original condition, been honored with knowledge on this point, and was consequently never called to walk by faith in regard to the divine existence. He did not believe that there was a God, he knew that there was a God. In his primitive state he was admitted to face-to-face intercourse and heard his voice; what a man sees and hears, therefore, he knows rather than believes, belief being referable to the experience of others, knowledge to the experience of one self. A life of obedience to God derived from sight and sense, began and ended with Adam. As he was the first, so he was the last in a native state, to enjoy sensible communion with the Deity. Consequently he was the first person on earth whose apprehension of the divine existence was not derived from the testimony of others. In regard to the great proposition of the Divinity he saw and heard and knew; we hear and reason and believe. We walk as if seeing him who is invisible; he walked having beheld the evident God. His obedience, therefore, was natural; our service, as the apostle says, is rational. He could not help but know; we cannot help but believe; his sin was a violation of natural goodness; ours is a violation of rational belief; ignorance in him would have been unnatural and impossible; unbelief in us is improbable and irrational. It was his to know and ours to believe; and, therefore, faith in the divine existence among men is derived from the knowledge of one and the reasoning of all.

Man has not been left to originate the idea of God; for he can originate no idea whatever, but is so constituted that things must originate in him their own ideas; God has, therefore, implanted his own idea in him by a sensible discovery of himself in person to one, Adam, and by a rational manifestation of his glorious works to all, which are greatly illustrative and confirmatory of the traditionary testimony; so that our belief in the fundamental proposition rests ultimately on the double foundation of the reason of us all and the knowledge of one.

When Abel believed, therefore, he believed first of all on the testimony of his father Adam, who had seen God. and this belief was necessarily confirmed by "the things which are made," which the reason of man from the creation of the world, the apostle says, sees clearly to be evident and unequivocal indications of the attributes of the Deity, even "His eternal power and godhead."

The question, then, would the double influence of sense and reason exerted on the works of nature and of man, ever make any one ask, Is there a maker of all that we see, is useless. Man has from the beginning of the world believed there is a maker of all that we see; and has never, in regard to this fundamental, been left vainly to seek his belief of it from the exercise of his senses on the works of nature and of man. The state of the case as it exists in the world would rather warrant this question, From God's having manifested himself in person to one and , in his works to all, can any one, from the beginning of the world, ever have rationally disbelieved his existence? No. Disbelievers then are irrational on this point which will be more fully shown as we proceed.

Faith in the one living and true God, we conclude from scripture, originated among the professors of the true religion in a primitive manifestation of the divinity to the father of mankind; and this has been subsequently confirmed to them from time to time by a succession of other particular manifestations made to other eminent and sacred persons from Adam to Moses, and from Moses to our Lord Jesus Christ. Finally the true faith has been strengthened and confirmed among its professors in all ages by the works of nature, which evidently illustrate, though they were never designed to originate the proposition that "There is a God."

At the fall, then, knowledge yielded to faith, as happiness did to misery, innocence to guilt, and life to death. Now the Christian religion, with her wonted candour, admits her own defectiveness in this particular, and grants, that even on her own principle we see things "darkly as through a veil." This is admirable in Christianity, which would rather openly avow than meanly conceal her own necessary and unavoidable deficiency; which though it cannot be cured in the present state, will, nevertheless, be fully atoned for in the perfect state, which is soon to follow. "Now remains faith," &c.

But if the first State was distinguished for knowledge, it is certain it could possess no hope. In this respect the present, and the primitive states differed from each other. And the object of our hope being so transcendently grand, even eternal life or life in ourselves, it may be problematical whether this attribute in the revealed religion does not exalt it above even Paradise and all its privileges. For the life of Adam which is animal, and the life of Christ which is spiritual, the one lying without a man and the other being essentially within him, differ surprisingly from each other; and the innate nature of the latter gives it such a splendid superiority over the former, that it can scarcely be doubted that with all our present embarrassments, the hope of the one is to be preferred even to the eternal enjoyment of the other in Paradise.

The enjoyment of the Holy Spirit by Christians and by all the faithful since the days of Abel goes also greatly to extenuate the effectiveness of the first principle of the true religion, for if we are not permitted to behold God's person, by this gift we are allowed to experience his blessedness; and by the love of God shed abroad in our hearts to wait patiently for the second corning of our Lord Jesus Christ from heaven.

The remission of sins also by the blood of Christ almost lifts up the veil through which we are compelled by faith to behold the king in his beauty, and the land that is now afar off, and fills us with more than angels' joys; while on our harps we move to the songs of redemption "a sacred chord" which their harps will not, cannot bear; for verily he laid not hold of angels, but he laid hold of the seed of Abraham. The seed of Abraham may therefore sing higher strains than angels dare.

The true faith, in its journeyings from the days of primitive man, has had to contend with powerful obstacles, and has never yet triumphed over them in such a manner as to become the religion of the world. It has suffered by foes and by friends: but idolatry and atheism have ever been its greatest enemies.

Atheism opposes it by a bold and direct denial of its proposition, and by asserting that there is no God. This, however, is a doctrine which has never been relished by a majority of mankind; though as in ancient so in modern times it has been very popular with a middle class of philosophers, and with such of the people as were unfitted by the defectiveness of their education to read the writings of profounder men, and more celebrated philosophers. The sentiment, then, is toto caeto adverse to the general proposition of revealed religion, and in its march among the people renders faith in God unnecessary by denying his existence.

Second to atheism in its birth and superior to it in influence with mankind has been idolatry, or the worship of false gods.—When man departed from the only true God he fell into a condition in which he was necessarily more exposed to that spirit which had seduced him from his original uprightness. Having become his prey we may be sure that so mighty and vile a conqueror would not easily resign his claims to that prey, but that every possible means would be put into requisition to frustrate the scheme of belief set afoot for our redemption.

The great adversary of God and man had upset the original institution. This admitted, we may well suppose, that his next effort would be directed against the remedial scheme by faith.—This was no mean enterprise, but called for a subtilty not inferior to that which was employed by him in his original design against the world. But how could faith in the general proposition of true religion be destroyed? By atheism? This was not sufficiently popular in its nature; and was moat likely to lose in practice what it promised in theory, and to be as feeble in effect as it was mighty in pretence. What was to be done?

Idolatry, and Satan is declared by scripture to be the author of it, idolatry was introduced; and this proved itself entirely adequate to the exigencies of the case, How? By substituting Polytheism for the true proposition, and knowledge for faith! Idolatry, by introducing the worshipper to sensible communion with the gods, exalted itself above the true religion, and by substituting knowledge for faith, rendered the last abortive, contemptible, and unnecessary; for the moment a man believed in an idol as God and yielded personal homage to it as such, instantly his faith in the true God evaporated and was abolished if he had heretofore held to that faith; and if he had not, then his first act of devotion sealed him idolatrous and made it impossible for him in future to participate in the blessings and rites of the true religion. Thus idolatry substituting false gods for the true God, and false knowledge for true faith, easily won upon the senses and impatience of mankind; and by its shows and fascinations marched triumphant through the world, destroying in its progress every vestige of revealed religion, and all the principles of faith and hope and love to which that religion gives birth, polluting and degrading the morals of mankind, till the benighted population of our globe were "filled with all unrighteousness."

Theological antiquaries have spent much time and great learning on the question concerning the rise and origin of idolatry; but the birth of this false religion, like the birth of its author, is hid in too high an antiquity ever to be correctly understood by the men of this generation. Whether it was begun by atheistical or interested persons, or by the devil, or devout persons, it avails not to inquire. It was introduced by some pernicious spirit, and has accomplished every thing against the faith, that a thousand devils and all the atheists on earth could have desired. It has taken possession of the world, and if not destroyed by the spread of better principles and purer morals, is likely to keep possession of the world. Perhaps it will be abolished only at the second coming of the Messiah.

Besides Idolatry the true faith has, in these latter ages, had to contend with corrupted forms of the true religion, as Catholocism, and Mahometanism. And besides Atheism it has had in our own times to struggle hard with what is styled Deism, and Scepticism. These states of mind, however, are rarely popular and have never perhaps met with a reception hearty enough to make them national. The nearest approach that ever such principles made to a national ascendancy was in France at the time of the decapitation of Louis XVI. But whether the sceptics, deists, or atheists, at that critical era formed a majority, it were difficult to determine. Some who then swayed the destinies of that ill-fated empire were avowedly atheistical; but these were the few in power and not the majority of the French nation.

Deism, or the belief in one living and true God has long been esteemed the only true doctrine of nature. This has been wrought up to a system and called Natural Theology. The natural religionist, like the believer in revelation, has also had to defend his position against the doubts of sceptics and the denial of atheists.

"The ordinary arguments against natural theology with which we have to contend," says an eminent writer[2] "are those of atheists and sceptics; of persons who deny the existence of a First Cause, or who involve the whole question in doubt; of persons who think they see a balance of reason for denying the existence of a Deity, or who consider the reasons on both sides as so equally poised that they cannot decide either way."

This eminent author has taken a new position with the antagonists of natural religion, if there he such a thing; and has written a book not chiefly to prove the truths of natural theology; but "To explain the nature of the evidence on which it rests—to show that it is a science, the truths of which are discovered by induction like, the truths of Natural and Moral Philosophy."

If Natural Theology is thus to be elevated to a science and made to rest on a basis like that on which Natural, and Moral Philosophy is founded, then the argument against skepticism and atheism will henceforth be, not that they are merely irreligious, but that they are unscientific also; and by consequence that their abettors are not only irreverent but also ignorant; but ignorance and irreverence are too much in the same person.

An objection of a very different nature, says his lordship, has sometimes proceeded, unexpectedly, from a very different quarter—the friends of revelation—who have been known without due reflection, to say that by the light of unassisted reason we can know absolutely nothing of God and of a future state. They appear alarmed lest the progress of Natural Religion should prove dangerous to the acceptance of Revealed; lest the former should, as it were, be taken as a substitute for the latter. They argue as if the two systems were rivals, and whatever

---

[2] Henry Lord Brougham, We urge upon the reader the perusal of his Lordship's book. It is titled, "A Discourse of Natural Theology."

credit one gained, were so much lost to the other. They seem to think that if any discovery of a First Cause and another world were made by natural reason, it would no longer be true that "life and immortality were brought to light by the gospel." Although these reasoners are neither the most famous advocates of revelation, nor the most enlightened, we yet do well to show the groundlessness of the alarms which they would excite.

The Chancellor next observes, that the most sincere and zealous christians have always been the greatest advocates of Natural Theology: and mentions the names of Ray, Clarke, Derham, Keill, and Paley to attest the truth of his assertion.

He states further that Natural Theology is most serviceable to the support of revelation, because all the soundest arguments in behalf of the latter presupposes the former to be admitted; and he cites the names of Butler, Bacon, Boyle, and Newton as authority for his argument, Bacon, he says, accurately taking "the distinction between Revelation and Natural Religion; that the former declares the will of God as to the worship most acceptable, while the latter teaches his existence and powers, but is silent as to a ritual."

The most extraordinary part of the section referred to, and certainly not least interesting to christians is the following:

3. "Accordingly we proceed a step further, and assert, *thirdly*, that it is a vain and ignorant thing to suppose that Natural Theology is not necessary to the support of Revelation. The latter may be untrue, though the former be admitted. It may be proved, or allowed, that there is a God, though it be denied that he sent any message to man, through men or other intermediate agents; as indeed the Epicureans believed in the existence of the gods, but held them to keep wholly aloof from human affairs, leaving the world, physical as well as moral, to itself, without the least interference with its concerns. But Revelation cannot be true if Natural Religion is false, and cannot he demonstrated strictly by any argument, or established by any evidence without proving or assuming the latter. A little attention to the subject will clearly prove this proposition.

Suppose it wore shown by incontestable proofs that a messenger sent immediately from heaven had appeared on the earth; suppose, to make the case more strong against our argument, that this messenger arrived in our own days, nay appeared before our eyes, and showed his divine title to have his message believed, by performing miracles in our presence. No one can by possibility imagine a stronger case; for it excludes all argument upon the weight or the fallibility of testimony; it assumes all the ordinary difficulties in the way of Revelation to be got over. Now, even this strong evidence would not at all establish the truth of the doctrine promulgated by the messenger; for it would not show that the story he brought was worthy of belief in any one particular except his supernatural powers. These would be demonstrated by his working miracles. All the rest of his statement would rest on his assertion: But a being capable of working miracles might very well be capable of deceiving us. The possession of power does not of necessity exclude either fraud or malice. This messenger might come from an evil as well as from a good being; he might come from more beings than one; or he might come from one being of many existing in the universe. When Christianity was first promulgated, the miracles of Jesus were not denied by the ancients; but it was asserted that they came from evil beings, and that he was a magician. Such an explanation was consistent with the kind of belief to which the votaries of polytheism were accustomed. They were habitually credulous of miracles and of divine interpositions. But their argument was not at all unphilosophical. There is nothing whatever inconsistent in the power to work miracles being conferred upon a man or a minister by a supernatural being, who is either of limited power himself, or of great malignity, or who is one of many such beings. Yet it is certain that no means can be devised for attesting the supernatural agency of any one, except such a power of working miracles; therefore, it is plain that no sufficient evidence can ever he given by direct Revelation alone in favour of the great truth of religion. The messenger in question might have power to work miracles without end, and yet it would remain unproved, either that God was omnipotent, and one, and benevolent, or that he destined his creatures to a future state, or that he had made them such as they are in their present state. All this might he true, indeed; but its truth would rest only on the messenger's assertion, and upon whatever internal evidence the nature of his communication afforded; and it might be false, without the least derogation to the truth of the fact that he came from a superior being, and possessed the power of suspending the laws of nature.

But the doctrines of the existence of a Deity and of his attributes, which Natural Religion teaches, preclude the possibility of such ambiguities and remove all those difficulties. We thus learn that the Creator of the world is one and the same; and we come to know his attributes, not merely of power, which alone the direct communication by miracles could convey, but of wisdom and of goodness. Built upon this foundation, the message of Revelation becomes at once unimpeachable and invaluable. It converts every inference of reason into certainty, and above all, it communicates the Divine Being's intentions respecting our own lot, with a degree of precision which the inferences of Natural Theology very imperfectly possess.—This, in truth, is the chief superiority of Revelation, and this is the praise justly given to the Gospel in sacred writ—not that it teaches the being and attributes of God, but that it brings life and immortality to light.

It deserves, however, to be remarked, in perfect consistency with the argument which has here been maintained, that no mere revelation, no direct message, however avouched by miraculous gifts, could prove the faithfulness of the promises held out by the messenger, excepting by the slight inference which the nature of the message might afford. The portion of his credentials which consisted of his miraculous powers could not prove it. For unless we had first ascertained the unity and the benevolence of the being that sent him, as those miracles only prove power, he might be sent to deceive us, and thus the hopes held out by him might be delusions. The doctrines of Natural Religion here come to our aid, and secure our belief to the messenger of one Being, whose goodness they have taught us to trust.

4. In other respects, the services of Natural Religion are far from inconsiderable, as subsidiary to, and co-operative with, the great help of Revelation. Thus, were our whole knowledge of Deity drawn from Revelation, its foundation must become weaker and weaker as the distance in point of time increases from the actual interposition. Tradition, or the evidence of testimony, must of necessity be its only proof: for perpetual miracles, must be wrought to give us evidence by our own senses. Now a perpetual miracle is a contradiction in terms; for the exception to, or suspension of, the law of nature so often repeated would destroy the laws themselves, and with the laws the force of the exception or suspension. Upon testimony, then, all Revelation must rest. Every age but the one in which the miracles were wrought, and every country but the one that witnessed them—indeed, all the people of that country itself, save those actually present—must receive the proofs which they afford of Divine interposition upon the testimony of eye-witnesses, and of those to whom eye-witnesses told it. Even if the miracles were exhibited before all the nations of one age, the next must believe upon the authority of tradition; and if we suppose the interposition to be repeated from time to time, each repetition would incalculably weaken its force, because the laws of nature though not wholly destroyed, as they must be by a constant violation, would yet lose their prevailing force, and each exception would become a slighter proof of supernatural agency. It is far otherwise with the proofs, of Natural Religion; repetition only strengthens and extends them. We are by no means affirming that Revelation would lose its sanction by lapse of time, as long as it had the perpetually new and living evidence of Natural Religion to support it. We are only showing the use of that evidence to Revelation, by examining the inevitable consequences of its entire removal, and seeing how ill supported the truth of Revelation would be, if the prop were withdrawn which they borrow from Natural Theology: for then they would rest upon tradition alone.

In truth, it is with Natural Religion as with many of the greatest blessings of our sublunary lot: they are so common, so habitually present to and enjoyed by us, that we become insensible of their value, and only estimate them aright when we lose them, or fancy them lost. Accustomed to handle the truths of Revelation in connexion with, and in addition to, those of Natural Theology, and never having experienced any state of mind in which we were without the latter, we forget how essential they are to the former. As we are wont to forget the existence of the air we constantly breathe until put in mind of it by some violent change threatening suffocation, so it requires a violent fit of abstraction to figure to ourselves the state of our belief in Revelation were the lights of natural religion withdrawn. The existence and attributes of a God are so familiarly proved by every thing around us, that we can hardly picture to ourselves the state of our belief in this great truth, if we only knew it by the testimony borne to miracles, which, however authentic, were yet wrought in a remote age and distant region. [3]

5. The use of Natural Theology to the believer in Revelation is equally remarkable in keeping alive the feelings of piety and devotion. As this topic has occurred under a former head, it is only to be presented here in close connexion with Revealed Religion. It may be observed, then, that even the inspired penmen have constant recourse to the views which are derived from the contemplation of nature when they would exalt the Deity by a description of his attributes, or inculcate sentiments of devotion towards him. "How excellent," says the Psalmist, "is thy name in all the earth; thou hast set thy glory above the heavens, I will consider the heavens, even the work of thy fingers; the moon and the stars which thou hast ordained."—See also that singularly beautiful poem the 139th Psalm; and the book of Job, from the 38th to the 41st chapter.

It is remarkable how little is to be found of particularity and precision in any thing that has been revealed to us respecting the nature of the Godhead. For the wisest purposes it has pleased providence to veil in awful mystery almost all the attributes of the Ancient of Days beyond what natural reason teaches. By direct interposition, through miraculous agency, we become acquainted with his will, and are made more certain of his existence; but his peculiar attributes are nearly the same in the volume of nature and in that of his revealed word."

We have now looked at the principle and the proposition of revealed religion, as affected by atheism, by idolatry, by skepticism, and by deism or Natural Theology. The Law and the Gospel come next to be

---

[3] Mr. Locke has said, upon a similar question, "He that takes away Reason to make way for Revelation puts out the light of both, and does much about the same as if he would persuade a man to put out his eyes, the better to receive the remote light of an invisible star by a telescope."—(Human Understanding, iv. 19, 4.)

considered in regard to these fundamentals. The connection between them and the gospel will be considered fully in another place, and therefore suffice to say here of the Law, that

Notwithstanding the burdensome and varied ritual with which the Mosaic economy was encumbered, at bottom it was very simple, being nothing more than a republication of the proposition of Natural Theology and the true religion, namely: that there is but one only living and true God, the maker of heaven and earth. The Jewish nation had to maintain this proposition occasionally in great afflictions; but by the use of the scriptures they finally overcame all enemies and their own disposition for idolatry.

In the Christian religion the general proposition concerning the unity of the Deity is taken for granted, or as a thing understood and believed by the Jews, to whom first of all the gospel was addressed. It is, therefore, incorporated with our religion or with the particular proposition of our religion, that Jesus Christ is the Son of God. The true Christians also have had to sustain the general proposition of Revelation as well as the particular oracle of Christianity against Jews and idolaters by a great "fight of afflictions."

Indeed those in every age who have exercised faith in the true God and manifested their attachment to his authority by keeping his commandments and ordinances, have seldom failed to have their faith subjected to the severest test; but, like gold tried in the furnace, their faith is now likely to ascend to the top of society, and to occupy the highest place both in the understanding and affections of some of the first spirits in the world.

After this rather long chapter on the things of the religion of the present state of Respite, let us turn back and take a summary view of certain other matters, the understanding of which will better prepare the reader for the gospel, which we hope to bring forward in due time. Let us, then, begin at the beginning, and notice in a general way the Mosaic account of the creation.

CHAPTER XXIX

The Mosaic Account of the Creation

"In the beginning God created the heavens and the earth." This is the foundation stone, the parent oracle in Revealed Religion. Its importance accordingly is equal to its gravity and seniority; for the person, who believes it, is instantly relieved from atheism, from the ancient cosmogony and theology of the Greeks and Romans, and from the skepticism of modern times. To know that the things that are seen, the minerals, animals and vegetables of our globe and the globe itself were not made by things that appear, the sun, the moon, and the other heavenly bodies: but, that all things, above, below, and round about us, had a common origin, one maker, the true and living God, is invaluable faith, and fits a man for other communications, without the knowledge of which, he cannot come into the possession of life eternal.

The fact that the whole visible universe with all its impressions and sentiments of beauty, order, variety, sublimity, immensity, stability, and perpetuity, issued without type, from the divine storehouse of the uncreated mind, fills us with the highest admiration of the glorious power, wisdom, and goodness of Almighty God; and unjudging and unfeeling must be that heart, which in the illimitable fields of created nature, cannot gather up by reason what has been approved or communicated by revelation, that "In the beginning God created the heavens and the earth."

As the Mosaic account of the origin of man, his trial, temptation, fall, respite, and destiny, so admirably accords with nature and reason; so the account, which the same venerable historic monuments record of the creation of the world, are equally natural and reasonable, and harmonize also with the results of the most elaborate and profound research into the phenomena of external nature relative to that kind of science which has for its object the unity, power, wisdom, and goodness of the Divinity.

What for instance can better meet our reason and wishes in regard to the creation than that it was made by one only living and indivisible God? and that he made it at one single effort with all its powers? for he made it at once and arranged it by degrees. In a moment, in the twinkling of an eye the creation, the whole creation stood forth; its suns and moons and planets, and comets, were instantly seen pendent in the concave of ethereal heaven, and their details successively arranged in six days.

The elements of matter, according to the Mosaic account are in number five, light air, earth, water, and heat, an enumeration more extensive than that of the ancient philosophers, who reckoned only four, and better suited to any general account of the creation than would be the refined analysis of modern science, which enumerates upwards of forty elementary substances.

On the first day God separated light, the most beautiful and refined species of matter, and caused it to stand forth from its sister elements in distinct vision. God said "Let there be light and there was light"—The true sublime in writing, and truly the sublime in power!

A second revolution completed and the planets are girt with a cincture of azure atmosphere, the element next in beauty to light, and separated from other matter and grosser fluids to be the *pabulum vitae* of the animal and rational beings for whom was reared this great this wondrous frame.

On the third day the water, an element next in refinement to the air, was separated from the solid land; the former to be stocked with fish and the latter now impregnated with the seeds of vegetable life.

On the fourth day the light, which on the first had been separated from the dark masses which formed the bodies of the planets, was collected around the central orbs, and the sun and stars appeared. This was a most gracious provision; for unless the light had been collected to a focus, nothing could have been seen distinctly; it would have remained as it was on the first day equally diffused throughout nature; and instead of day light we should have had universal and perpetual twilight. Thus the focus of heat became the focus of light also, the source whence in future should spring "exulting" day, the sign of seasons, of months, of years, and all the gay, and rich, and various phenomena of life, animal and rational.

As the waters were already formed into oceans, seas, rivers, and lakes, and the light and heat radiated from a common point in such a manner that animal life could through the blue atmosphere taste of their blessings, the waters were now stocked with fish and the air with fowl. Thus terminated the fifth day, and

> Thus from the deep the Almighty King
> Did vital beings frame,
> Fowls of the air of every wing
> And fish of every name.

On the sixth, the reptiles were created, and cattle and beasts of the field innumerable, sent roving o'er the earth to feed on the herbage already provided for them during the proceeding days.

This splendid and fair frame being ordered and furnished with all that was necessary for use and ornament, "God said.—Let us make man in our own image, and in our own likeness." Praised be the name of the Lord. So "God created man in his own image; in the image of God created he him; a male and a female created he them." Thus was the world gifted with its lord.

> Thus chief o'er all his works be low
> At last was Adam made,
> His maker's image blessed his soul
> And honor crowned his head.

Finally, on the seventh day God rested from all the works which he had made. "And God blessed the seventh day and sanctified it; because that in it he had rested from all his work which God created and made."

Man is a creature of body as well as spirit, he is animal as well as rational, and as he owed every thing to the Almighty, the seventh day was given him for the refreshment of his person and the religious improvement of his spirit; during this monumental day, therefore, Adam and his beautiful partner, it is very likely, during that century which they lived in Paradise, appeared at the altar of the Lord God in Paradise, and at early morn, and in the evening, as was the case afterwards among the Jews, placed a double amount of free-will, or thank-offering upon the table of the Lord on that day, praising and blessing God. To this service sin-offering, after the fall, was added.

Where now is the indecorum of this account of the creation? In what other manner would *les savants*, the wits, who object to this statement, have proceeded, if to them had been deputed the sublime task of creating the visible universe, or even of giving an account of this glorious deed? for the simplicity and propriety of the account is so extraordinary as almost of itself to prove the certainty of the fact, and the inspiration of the writer. Each of the elements according to its perfection and refinement is successively separated from the grosser and less refined with which it had been created *en masse*, receives "a local habitation and a name" and is thus prepared for the reception and sustenance of animal and rational life, light being created first and man last.

Would the sages already referred to, have described the sun to shine the first day without any light to shine with, or any order or beauty to shine upon? Of what utility would his rays have been without the atmosphere by which they required to be equally dispersed, the land and water lying *en masse* and not an eye looking from the deep or from the land to be benefitted by the light?

Or would they have created, or told that there were created fish before there were created oceans, seas, rivers, and lakes for them to swim in; birds before an atmosphere to fly in; and beasts and reptiles before the solid land to walk on; and man first instead of last, presenting him with an unassorted and confused mass instead of a creation characterized by order beauty and utility?

Those who suspect the authority and impugn the propriety and decorum of the Mosaic cosmogony should reign up a little the untamed licence of their own reasonings and reflect twice upon the matter before they speak once against it; simplicity and ignorance are too much in the same person. Those who speak against the account of the creation are like him who reckons without his host.

CHAPTER XXX

Concerning a Plurality of Worlds

But the skeptic, making a deadly thrust, says, We object not to the rationality, but to the truth of the Mosaic account of the creation, the discoveries of modern science demonstrating that there has been a succession of worlds and that this is not the first, but one made from the ruins of former worlds now no more, characterized by features differing altogether from those of our own. We acknowledge the fact; but protest that this is a thing that is admitted in the new testament and proved in the old. Peter speaks of a former world that perished: and vouches that as this is not the first so it will not be the last; but will be followed by a world in which righteousness alone shall dwell.

Notwithstanding, however, the immeasurable greatness of the material system, the deviating regularity of its parts, their uniform motion, and apparent perpetuity, there is no evidence that it is commensurate in extent with the illimitable fields of space, or that it is confined to a single point in the boundless abyss in which it has been lighted up by the great Eternal. To the motion and well-being of each part we see that space of superior extent is necessary; to the well-being of the whole, therefore, a proportionate superior space must be equally necessary, and thus the visible universe presents us with the inconceivably grand spectacle of a vast system of splendid orbs, suns, moons, planets, and comets, forever falling through space and traveling with inconceivable velocity the interminable profound—a loco-motive of fearful and prodigious extent carrying along with it the elements by which it is moved, warmed, and illuminated.

It is not necessary however to conclude, (as is too commonly done and I think without sufficient reason) that the present is the first creation and was made out of nothing. On the contrary the material of which it is made may have been employed as the elements of a succession of creations all different from each other in their identity, their properties, or relations; or they may have been analogous; or they may have been identical in these things, and the previous worlds may have fulfilled the same ends on a scale more minute, or on one incomprehensibly more vast and glorious.

At all events the holy scriptures actually favor the idea that there has been a plurality of worlds, in which the same elements formed the *prima materia*. Indeed the scriptures seem to reckon it a sin to be ignorant of this matter; for Peter, speaking of the scoffers of the last days, says: "But this willfully escapes them, that by the word of God the heavens were of old, and the earth subsisting by the water and from the water by which the world that then was, being deluged with water, perished," &c. The same sacred writer informs us that the present world is not the last, but is destined to a still more terrible consummation than that which preceded it in order to make way for a new heaven and a new earth—the abode of righteousness only.

Peter's language suggests to us the following ideas concerning the state of our earth before the general deluge, that the seas and oceans, which now appear, were then to a great extent embowelled in magazines under the surface, and not affused externally as they now are, forming a part of the superficies of our globe, much of the land in the antediluvian world being sustained above water, or as he expresses it, "subsisting from the water and by the water."

Between Adam and Noah, a period of near two thousand years, extensive local convulsions, doubtless took place in many portions of the earth; and particular incrustations of surface with all the enormous brood of animals and men upon them were precipitated to the bottom of the abyss, which had up to that time sustained them; the remains of these submerged monsters and men became in time imbedded in different strata or layers of mud, and now, as fossils, form the admiration of the modern Geologist and give birth to some of the wonderful reasonings and sublime inductions of that interesting science. But at the general deluge, when the entire incrustation of land was broken to pieces, the whole mass of entombed water rose to the surface and the populated lands and kingdoms, with all their works of art, and men and animals sunk to the bottom of the dread abyss. This, it is likely, is what is meant in Genesis, where it is said, "The foundations of the great deep were broken up."

In this catastrophe, the higher and more protuberant portions of the solid surface formerly at the bottom of the seas, now appeared and formed the earth as it at present subsists. Hence marine substances are found on the tops of our loftiest mountains; and the remains of men and land animals at the bottom of the seas imbedded in successive layers of mud.—There has been but one general destruction of this world by water then; and anterior local partial convulsions are doubtless sufficient to account for all other geological and osteological phenomena, the admirers of which are possibly led astray in some degree, by mistaking particular and extensive convulsions of nature for general and universal ones.

The accuracy of the inductive philosophy and the sagacity of modern science are in nothing rendered more striking than in the demonstration of the above fact given by these curious inquiries. What the scriptures put us in possession of by revelation, modern philosophy demonstrates by the most profound and elaborate research. "It is shown," says Henry Lord Brougham, "that animals formerly existed on the globe, being unknown varieties of *species* still known; but it also appears that *species* existed and even *genera*, wholly unknown for the last five thousand years. These peopled the earth not as it was before the general deluge, but before some convulsion long prior to that event, had overwhelmed the countries then dry, and raised others from the bottom of the sea. In these curious enquiries, we are conversant not only with the world before the flood, but with a world, which before the flood was covered with water, and which in far earlier ages had been the habitation of birds, and beasts, and reptiles. We are carried, as it were, several worlds back, and we reach a period, when all was water and slime and mud; and the waste without either man or plants, gave resting place to enormous beasts like lions and elephants, and river horses, while the water was tenanted by lizards, the size of a whale, sixty feet long, and by others with huge eyes and shields of solid bones to protect them, and glaring from a neck ten feet in length, and the air was darkened by flying reptiles covered with scales, opening the jaws of the crocodile, and expanding wings, armed at the tips with the claws of the leopard."

"No less strange, and not less proceeding from induction, are the discoveries made respecting the former state of the earth; the manner in which those animals, whether of known or unknown tribes, occupied it; and the period when, or, at least, the way in which they ceased to exist."[4]

It is possible that the distinguished author of these observations is in an error here, and with all the patrons of the science, Cuvier and others, mistakes particular antediluvian convulsions for general ones.

---

[4] The researches both of Cuvier and Buckland, far from impugning the testimony to the great fact of a deluge borne by the Mosaic writings, rather fortify it; and bring additional proofs of the fallacy which, for some time, had led philosophers to ascribe a very high antiquity to the world we now live in.

The extraordinary sagacity of Cuvier is, perhaps, in no instance more shown, nor the singular nature of the science better illustrated, than, in the correction which it enabled him to give the speculation of President Jefferson upon the *Megalonyx*—an animal which the President, from the size of a bone discovered, supposed to have existed, four times the size of an ox, and with the form and habits of the lion. Cuvier has irrefragably shown, by an acute and learned induction, that the animal was a sloth, living entirely upon vegetable food, but of an enormous size, like a rhinoceros, and whose paws could tear up huge trees.— *Dis. of Theol.*

The earth is now in regard to fire what it was before the flood in regard to water. Some countries are mere incrustations of land stretching over floods of liquid fire and ready to be engulfed. Italy, it is most probable, is of this nature, and the *malaria* of that country is possibly some distant result of an incomprehensible operation of the entombed fire acting upon the bituminous constituents of her soil. At all events, Peter informs us that this world which was once destroyed by water, is reserved for fire, "against the day of Judgment and perdition of ungodly men." Men have broken God's good covenant made with them after the flood, the token of which is the bow in the clouds. A more fatal destruction, therefore, awaits them—perdition by fire. But this will not be so extended in its duration as was the flood, which continued on the earth a whole year; seed time and harvest is not again to be confounded and interrupted; the entire destruction of the nations will occur in one day, in the twinkling of an eye; and sudden as a glance of lightning the world, with the violence of a mill-stone, shall be plunged into an ocean of fire. The Millennium, it is supposed, will then begin, and a new heavens and a new earth will arise, in which righteousness alone will dwell.

CHAPTER XXXI

Concerning Satan

The devil is described in Scripture as being originally an angel, and as others which were cast down with him are called "his angels," it follows that he was of a superior order, a ruling angel. The precise rank which he held, however, is not made known, nor the place of his domination or rule. Whether he enjoyed the supreme power of the present world, before the earth was what it is now, and ruled in a creation of matter infinitely superior to this in which the elements were wrought up to higher beauty and more ethereal grandeur, light being the grossest modification there, as it is the most refined and beautiful of matter here; or whether he was of the principalities and powers who sway scepters over particular legions and hosts of the angels of God in heaven, or sat next to the Almighty and ruled high estates and seraphic intelligences there, is not revealed in the Scriptures. For ourselves we conjecture not on the point. Suffice to say he was an angel of God in authority.

The Saviour says of this being, He abode not in the truth; and Peter, that he was cast out into the abyss.

The commandments of God, in the scriptures are called the truth. John says "I have no greater joy than to hear that my children walk in the truth." And when it is said of Satan, that he abode not in the truth, it means that he violated some law: but what that law was we know not.

He is a spirit, at least we suppose he is, and the sin which he committed, may have respected something, which, we being men, cannot understand and, therefore, it is not discovered to us by the sacred writers. Or if he inhabited a material creation, and he seems, even from the first naming of him in scripture, to have understood both matter and mind perfectly and to have been able to subject it to his own evil purposes, then the objects of that creation might be such that we could not understand them, and, therefore, the scriptures are silent on the subject.

He was cast out into the abyss. This implies that he was cast out of heaven, or out of some other place, into that eternal profound in which the present fair universe has been lighted up with all its orbs. This seems to have been the punishment of him and of the unfortunate partners of his high crimes and misdemeanors, and surely, if he fell from heaven, which is the most probable opinion, his punishment was great; for we can conceive of no greater torment for an angel of light, than to be excluded from the presence of God, and sent forth into the interminable regions of impervious darkness. What the profound was, before it was enlivened and illuminated by the sun and moon, and other heavenly bodies, we know not; and how long Satan and his crew roamed it, previous to the creation of the planetary system, we know not; and how he chanced first to settle his weary steps upon our globe, or whether our globe is the first he visited, or only the first he seduced to a state of ruin like his own, we know not; or whether he visited it because the matter of which it is composed originally formed the abode of his own dominion and throne, we know not. These are details which futurity alone will unfold to man.

It is said in scripture, however, that he is now reserved in chains of darkness against the judgment of the great day, that is the great day on which all men are to be tried. But this chain is not of God the Father, but of the Son. The devil was not chained on account of what he did in heaven, nor is he yet to be judged on account of his high misdemeanors there. His ejectment from the world of light was his punishment for what he committed in that place, and his trial on the day of our judgment is for a second offence not against God only, but against the human family, whom he has seduced from rectitude to the violation of law, and exposed to a ruin like that which will inevitably overtake himself. This difference between what Satan did in his native abode, and his crime against man on earth, should be carefully noted. The two offences totally different in regard to the places in which they were committed; in the first, man was not involved. In his last offence, which was in Paradise, man became a partner and a fearful sufferer. He first sinned against God and was expelled his original home.—Next he sinned against man and by the Son of Man will he be punished. The Lord Jesus regarded Satan in no other light than the murderer of the whole family of man. Indeed, in a certain point of view, he murdered the Lord Jesus himself; for he was the ultimate agent in that dire affair which introduced among us death with all our woes. His offence was most foul, most devilish, and most unlimited shall be his punishment; the family will yet be avenged of him for the evil he has done us; we have now a hero who has espoused our cause, and will greatly avenge our wrongs. He has seduced our family into the violation of law and made us all, without exception, obnoxious to death; and the Saviour gives no other interpretation to the foul deed but murder, ruinous, sweeping, remorseless murder. Yes, this traitor angel, in a state of outlawry from God, roaming the interminable regions of chaotic darkness into which he had been expelled, full of inveterate treason against the Almighty, and high designs against the new-born world and its happy inhabitants, is described in scripture as having been in Paradise at the fall, and as having then become the ultimate cause of that original sin, which brought death into this world, with all our woes.

It may be observed in this place, that the scripture nowhere suggests the idea that Satan is to be punished in hell fire, on account of his sin in heaven; nor that Christ prepared it for any of the sons of men. Yet both wicked men and devils will be cast into it. It would have appeared incongruous with the character of the Divine Father to have anticipated the defaults of his angels and prepared hell fire to receive them falling. This is a poetic fiction, but it was perfectly a natural punishment to put Satan out of a place which he could no longer enjoy on terms comporting with his own allegiance and the uncompromisible authority of the Almighty. Therefore he was punished merely by expulsion from the royal abodes. This also was the way in which Adam was punished. When he sinned he was merely expelled Paradise; but this involved an interdict of the tree of life by which Adam in a state of innocence might finally have lived forever. As God the Father did not create everlasting fire for the devil and his angels, so our Lord Jesus did not create it for mankind his brethren. This would have been monstrously incongruous with every idea of his being a Saviour and Redeemer. The state of the case, therefore, is as follows. The Devil by seducing us into sin became the murderer of our family to a man. God saw it, and pitied us, and knowing the character and power of our adversary and our incompetence to cope with him he laid our help upon one mighty to save, and sent us the Messiah partaking of the nature of the injured family and qualified to avenge its wrongs. But before he could avenge our wrongs it was necessary he should feel them; before he could feel them it became necessary he should put himself in our circumstances, and before this could obtain, he required to taste our nature. "Inasmuch, therefore, as the children were partakers of flesh and blood, he himself, also partook of the same, that through death he might destroy him that had the power of death that is the Devil." The author of Christianity is our hero or captain, and is now perfected as such by partaking of the family feeling through suffering. He is a son of man, and has been murdered by the Devil, like his brethren, like all the world besides; with the family vengeance, therefore, he will one day meet our adversary, and consign him to that fearful punishment which he has prepared for him, namely, everlasting fire.

It is asked why the Devil's offence in Paradise is punished with greater severity than his sin in heaven. Many things will suggest themselves to the reader as reasons for this. On earth it was foul deliberate murder, in heaven it was not. In heaven it was against God only, on earth it was against both God and man. On earth it was the strong against the weak, an archangel against an arm of flesh. An ethereal prince against an innocent and beautiful female. In heaven it might be to exalt himself to higher honor, on earth it was to drag down others to his own dishonor. In heaven it might be ambition, on earth it was envy, black envy; and if he spoke at all we may, with our great poet, conceive him speaking thus:

> O Hell! what do mine eyes with grief behold!
> Into our room of bliss thus high advanced
> Creatures of other mould, earth born perhaps.
> ————————————————Hell shall unfold
> To entertain you two, her widest gates.

It has been said, and indeed it is publicly taught from the pulpit, and even published for divinity, that God did from all eternity ordain a certain portion of the human family to perpetual punishment in hell fire, and that that number can neither be increased, nor diminished. This is very injurious to the character of God, who did never provide hell even for Satan; but on the contrary simply expelled him his former home and, when lost to all reformation and become the murderer of mankind, consigned him to the Son of Man our Saviour. As to ordaining man or any of our family to damnation, the scriptures are silent.

The Lord Jesus declares, that "God so loved the world that he gave his only begotten son that whoever believed on him might not perish but have everlasting life." If, therefore, any one is punished it will be because he has, in this life and during his mortal career, taken sides with Satan, and refused to repent, who will suffer a punishment never provided for him by the Father, even as wicked men will suffer what was not primarily intended for them by the Son, who will say to them, Depart, ye cursed, into everlasting fire prepared (not for them but) for the Devil and his angels.

CHAPTER XXXII

Of Justice Commercial, Civil, and Political

Few scripture terms have given rise to so many polemic religious discussions as the word justice employed in regard to the death of Christ, thus—

"Now we know, that whatever thing the law says, it says to them who are under the law: that every mouth may be stopped, and all the world (Jews and Gentiles) may he liable to punishment before God. Wherefore, by works of law there shall no flesh be justified in his sight; because through law is the knowledge of sin.

"But now, a justification which is of God, without law, is exhibited, attested by the law and the prophets; even a justification which is of God, through faith in Jesus Christ, for all, and upon all who believe; for there is no difference. For, all having sinned and come short of the glory of God, are justified freely by his favour, through the redemption which is by Christ Jesus, whom God has set forth a propitiatory through faith in his blood, for a demonstration of his justice in passing by the sins which were before committed, through the forbearance of God: for a demonstration also, of his justice in the present time, in order that he may be just, when justifying him who is of the faith of Jesus."

The whole passage means, that although God forbore with past sins, he himself was not unrighteous: though he delayed the infliction of capital punishment he was not unjust; but had suspended it in view of what had now occurred in behalf of mankind—the offering of the propitiatory sacrifice of our Lord Jesus Christ.

When the import of the word justice in this passage is ascertained the whole business will be seen clearly. There are several kinds of justice among men; or this word is used by us in different ways; we speak of political justice, civil or legal justice, and commercial justice; and this difference in the application of the term is proper enough; for there is a difference between a just governor, a just merchant, and a just witness; and it is from not adverting to this distinction in the nature of justice and the use of the term that so much wrangling in relation to its import in the above passage has occurred.

Some theologians confounding these uses of the word, teach that there was in the death of Christ an equivalent rendered to God for sin, and that he endured in his precious and sacred person the precise amount of vengeance, which would have been suffered by the elect supposing them to have been damned to all eternity! Had our Heavenly Father been acting commercially in this affair, this might have been asserted, though it never could have been proved, as eternal suffering cannot be redeemed by temporal more than eternity can be measured by time. But this conceit originates in the mistake, of substituting the commercial for the political use of the term, and supposing that the death of Christ occurred and is spoken of in the first sense instead of the last.

I have seen it somewhere, that Doctor Priestly asked the advocates of the commercial scheme, To whom did the Saviour pay the debt? The Doctor answered his own question thus, That he must have paid it to the devil, for it was he who held men in bondage. It is likely, however, that the Doctor put this question chiefly on account of his own smart answer; for it is certainly true that the socinianism which he espoused, was as deficient in point of a correct explanation of the justice spoken of in the passage under consideration as the scheme against which his ridicule was directed.

It has been asked by others, who themselves have overlooked the true explanation of the difficulty, If God received an equivalent, where is his mercy, exhibited in our pardon? The idea of an equivalent is not connected with the use of the word justice in relation to the death of Christ, the matter being political and not commercial.

Justice is most generally divided by civilians into two kinds, communicative justice and distributive justice, the former establishing the rules of fair dealing and commerce between man and man, the latter being the justice of magistrates and princes.

1. Civil or commercial justice obtains when one thing is bartered for another of equal value all things considered; and it equally affects both parties negotiating. The just merchant, therefore, deals with an equal regard to his own right and that of the man with whom he does business.

2. Legal justice obtains in our courts of law when justice is done to the life, property, security, liberty, character, and happiness of the citizens. In its political or most ample form it affects the whole nation and has for its ultimate end the general welfare and the security of the community at large. Into this use of the term justice enters not the idea of equivalent at all; but in communicative or commercial justice *equivalent* is the chief idea. If a man is imprisoned or slain on account of high crimes or misdemeanors against the public or the state he is not supposed thereby to render to society an equivalent for what he has been guilty of, but is punished because he deserves it, because it might still further endanger the public safety to let him live or go at large, and finally and chiefly to make the law intended for the common good respected and sacred in the estimation of the citizens.

This question, therefore, arises very naturally, Was it as a trader, or a Ruler that God acted in the great matter of the death of Christ? Surely it was as the illustrious the just Ruler of men, that he acted in this sublime affair and set his Son forth in blood. The justice of the text, then, is of a political nature, and not commercial; consequently the idea of equivalent is excluded from the explanation, and in doing this act, this strange act God purposed to demonstrate to men and angels his justice as the supreme Ruler of men. He purposed to clothe his law with a sanctity that should make it reverenced, make it obeyed. The term propitiatory, which occurs in the quotation, establishes this view of the matter. In the case of insulted majesty we propitiate. In commercial affairs we pay dues, but do not propitiate.

When the Lord Jesus, therefore, was set forth in blood as a propitiatory it was to do honor to the majesty of law and the character of God as the Ruler of the world.

It is objected that there can be no demonstration of justice in that case in which the innocent is made to suffer instead of the guilty. This is indeed a capital objection and, if just, strikes a blow at the root of the most popular doctrine in our religion, that Christ died, the just for the unjust to bring us to God.—Although I have had the objection frequently made to myself In the course of my public labors I do not remember of leading, or hearing from any one, a satisfactory removal of the difficulty.

In meeting it therefore, let it be remembered, that we are discoursing not of commercial but political justice, in which the law and the common good are the chief ideas; in civil matters it were indeed unjust to make an innocent person pay away his whole estate in behalf of twenty others who might have squandered their living. But even this, if done voluntarily, would not be called injustice in the person receiving pay, though the person purchasing the debts of the twenty others would certainty be deemed generous.

But still we are speaking of a case purely political, in which the person said to be just receives nothing; this last observation defines the case, and perhaps brings our answer one step nearer to the objection. In this matter then the just person receives nothing, gives nothing, but is acting politically and as the guardian of the public safety. His office is to take care that the law on which that safety depends, has free course and is glorified. If, therefore, ten innocent persons should voluntarily offer themselves for one guilty one, instead of one for ten, that the law may be magnified, he is not unjust; the community is only more secure.—But if said Ruler should allow ten or one to violate the law with impunity, he would be unjust?

If a public ruler for the honor of the law and the good of those who have constituted him guardian of the public safety, enforces the law in the case of one or one thousand offenders. Is that ruler unjust? No. God, then, would not have been unjust if Adam had died the day he sinned.

If the Ruler in a case *extra* accepts of the life of one instead of many, supposing the one to be more honorable than all the many, does he thereby suffer the law to be dishonored, the public safety to be endangered, or his own character, as a just ruler, to be impugned? No. Jesus, then, might be accepted for Adam, and for us in him, the greater for the less.

The objection, then, is answered, and the difficulty removed; for there can be no injustice in the ruler where the offerer presents himself voluntarily; and if it is not voluntarily, to slay him would not be injustice but cruelty, not unlawful commerce, but political tyranny.

An innocent person, therefore, may, without impugning the integrity of the ruler's character, generously offer himself in behalf of another and die in his stead. Perhaps, says one, for a good man some would even dare to die. But who would suffer this if it tended to dishonor the law, or endanger the character or the lives of the citizens? and a Ruler is not unjust as such, but when he disregards those great points.

It stands on the page of history, that the king of the Locreans published a code of laws, which he supposed would if honored secure the public safety and exalt the morals of the citizens. To clothe them with becoming majesty, therefore, he decreed that the person who dared first to violate the sacred code, should be punished with the loss of both eyes. Now, awful to relate, the prince, his son, became the first offender; and was, of course, fairly obnoxious to the punishment. The case was evidently one of the most interesting nature; as respects the king his father, most affecting, most delicate. The questions in the case were as follows, shall the law be violated with impunity? Shall the public safety, the public morals be compromised? Shall the prince lose both his eyes?

The quality of the royal offender increased the difficulty; for it is a rule in such cases that, for the honor of the law, the substitute shall excel in quality the principal; it must be the greater for the less, the just for the unjust. What then was to be done? for the prince was more noble than all the Locreans.

Love is noble in invention; it is fertile in expedient. The King his Father, therefore, devised the following memorable means for diminishing the difficulty and at the same time securing the law, the public good, and his own honor. As he alone in the nation was superior to the prince he voluntarily and greatly offered himself in this way; that the prince should lose one eye and he another, which took place accordingly.

Instead of exposing his character for injustice, when he accepts the innocent instead of the guilty a Ruler in fact more establishes his character for that virtue, and must as a public functionary, by so doing, rise to the very pinnacle of public estimation.

Here it is the author of the Christian religion enters. He comes forward to give his life a ransom for many, for the world. He presents himself instead of Adam and in him all men. He offers himself the greater for the less, the just for the unjust, the Lord of all instead of all.

The facts, therefore, on which the true religion is founded, are of the simplest and most intelligible kind. It is one man falling by one violation, and bearing downwards with him into this preternatural condition the population of a globe then in his loins; and another man of superior mould, of more ethereal temper and divine, interposing as the greater for the less, the just for the unjust, the innocent for the guilty, not his power, not his authority, but his person, that the Ruler of men, of the universe might be just when justifying or pardoning the ungodly, the guilty.

How perfectly, then, does this whole business commend itself to the understanding, and to the best affections of the human heart It is a great, a happy, a successful, a divine effort to rescue from death myriads of human beings, to rescue fallen man; and the contemplation of it is holy, and heavenly, and lovely, and glorious. We may say with the spirits justified and all other creatures in heaven, and on the earth, and under the earth, and in the sea, "Blessing, and honor, and glory, and power, be unto him that sitteth upon the throne, and unto the Lamb, for ever and ever."

If the Divine Father had not made original law his care, but suffered it to be violated with impunity, on what would the grounds of our present confidence in him have been founded? Who of good men or angels, after such inefficiency, would have fled to him for refuge from the like confusion in the present state? The universe would be over-run with mobs of men and angels; the world forever and forever would be a scene of anarchy. But any kind of government is better than anarchy. Therefore, if Christianity were founded in divine tyranny, it were better than anarchy or any other result of imbecility or inefficiency. But it is not; it is founded in a divine regard to law and the good of man.

Satan, and his infernals, then, will certainly be punished; for he is the murderer of our race; and no adequate reason can be assigned why wicked men should not partake of his fortunes. "These shall go away into everlasting punishment, but the righteous into life eternal."

Our First Parents, and in their loins all men, could have been respited only in view of the appearing of Jesus Christ our Lord, who was to magnify law and make it honorable. But the importance, and beauty, and blessedness of the respite consist in its relation to that in view of which it was granted, namely, a final reprieve, or an abrogation of punishment altogether. And this is to be the lot of such as honor the scheme of our salvation by receiving in character the Prince by whose personal suffering it has been perfected. Here men enjoy the respite of life, which we could not have done if Adam, according to the letter, had died the day he sinned; for then we should all have perished, being, as the Apostle would say, in his loins, as our original father; but he being respited, lived, and we in him. The gospel then, announces to all who will obey it, a total abrogation of punishment, and life with Christ in heaven.

But it is objected, that believers die as well as others: this is answered "by the fact, that their death is but for a moment in comparison with Adam's, for death should have held him in bonds forever; his was perpetual death without any resurrection. If he had died unrespited he would have died eternally and we in him. But now he and we and all have been respited and will be wholly reprieved, if we obey the gospel and persevere in obedience to the end of our life; and thus the favor of God, who laid our iniquity upon one mighty to save, has abounded over both his offence and ours. The Apostle discourses in this strain in his Epistle to the Romans.

"Wherefore as by one man sin entered into the world and death by sin, and so death, passed [*as a sentence*] upon all men; for that all have sinned; therefore, as by the offence of one an adjudication of condemnation came upon all men; even so by the righteousness of one an adjudication [*or respite*] to life came upon all men. For if by the disobedience of one many were [*in law*] made sinners, so by the obedience of one the many shall [*in redemption*] be made righteous."

These, then, reader, are the blessings which attach christians to the person and character of the Lord Jesus Christ; who being of the ancient, royal, and religious family of David according to the flesh, is withal clothed with a nature truly divine, and is the Son of God, who has laid upon him all royal offices and made him our Prophet, our Priest, and our King; our Mediator in heaven, where he negotiates our salvation and waits at his Father's right hand for the accomplishment of the events which are to be followed by his descent again to this world.

May we not appeal to the reader, then, that it is an honor to be permitted to obey the gospel and to pass in due season from the government of our parents and the state into that of the Messiah, now elevated to the throne of the world by the Great God himself. He is just such a governor as men require and such as they would choose if they knew him and loved righteousness. His affection for us has been demonstrated to all amount. How simple and honorable the faith, how high the hope, how pure the love, how unstained and elevated the morals he inculcates. O! how rejoicing to the heart of man is the voice of Christ. "O! it is a noble music," says one, "which he maketh to the soul of man, sweet as the breathing sonnets of lovers, and spirit-stirring as the minstrelsy of glorious war. It rouses to noble deeds like the Tyrtean song, sung on the eve of battle to noble Spartan youth, and rejoiceth the heart of sin-oppressed nature as the voice of liberty from Tully's lips rejoiced the Senate House of Rome, upon the famous Ides of March, when the godlike Brutus

——————"Shook his crimson steel
And bade the Father of his country hail."

CHAPTER XXXIII

Remission of Sins, the Holy Spirit, and Eternal Life

1. Gospel is a word employed by the sacred writers to signify good news, of a religious kind, the first element of which is remission of sins; or in the gospel Almighty God for Christ's sake proffers to forgive us all we have done, and said, and even thought, contrary to the will and wishes of himself our Creator, if we will believe and reform; or to vary it again, The sins of youth, of manhood, and of old age done against God, or done against man, or known to man, or known to God alone, shall be struck out, cut off, erased from God's recollection, and our own consciences, and buried in eternal oblivion to arise against us no more in time or in eternity, but to be forever forgiven, if we will obey his commandments by the Messiah.

"Repent and be immersed every one of you in the name of Jesus Christ for the remission of sins," said the prime minister of the kingdom "and you shall receive the gift of the Holy Spirit."—Acts 2:38.

2. A second element in the gospel is the gift of the Holy spirit, "You shall receive the gift of the Holy Spirit." If after a long sad night of sin, during which grief and fear and a spirit of desperation alternately sway the heart, sudden joy shall arise; if after the most oppressive bondage the greatest liberty of mind shall follow; if love shall supercede hatred, gentleness anger and meekness revenge, and all the graces of God's Spirit shall be transferred to the human heart again, as to their native

seat, then the promise of the Holy Spirit, as an element of the true Gospel, must be regarded as of the very essence of good news.

3. But last, though not least, Eternal Life is promised to man by the gospel. Our present animal life is burdened with mortal endurance and must terminate in the severest dissolution, total disorganization. Now, if after having "shuffled off this mortal coil" we shall be resuscitated and born from the dead, if after the most affecting separation we shall be repossessed of ancient friends, and from the solitude of the funeral vault, mount up to the society of heaven itself, and live there with God, and Christ, and all good angels, and redeemed men, by the power of a never-dying existence, the message which assures us of this must be eminently entitled to the appellation Gospel or good news.

Remission of Sins, then, past sins, all sins, the spirit of God the Holy Spirit, and life eternal, or life with God in heaven are distinguishing points of the true Gospel of Jesus Christ.

Hence the following corollaries—1st. Christians are a pardoned people; they enjoy the Holy Spirit, and they hope by Christ to receive eternal life. 2d. An unpardoned person is not a Christian; a person devoid of the Spirit of Christ is not a Christian; any man destitute of the hope of Eternal Life is not a Christian.

What immense advantages over other men, then, does the disciple of Christ enjoy for the purification of his morals and for the cultivating and maturing in himself of all those rare qualities which go to make up the true man of God!

But the inestimable privileges just mentioned are not, as the reader may well suppose, conferred on men imprudently but tendered to all only on proper principles; for, in the first instance, it would be highly incongruous to bestow them on such as do not desire to possess them; and equally so to confer them on those who, from want of principle, are incapable of turning them to that improvement and moral reformation for which they are designed; and finally, to administer them to such as do not previously recognize the goodness and authority whence they emanate, would be equally dangerous and improper. Accordingly our Creator requires that, before we are admitted to the pardon of our sins, we shall heartily believe, by the proper evidences, and with our lips confess before the world, the divine mission of the author of Christianity; also, that we shall seriously reform from those transgressions, the pardon of which we implore; and lastly, as proof positive of the state of the case, he enjoins on all to be baptized into the name of the Father, and of the Son, and of the Holy Spirit. Thus the gospel is shewn to embrace a still wider range of elements or "first principles" than merely remission, the Holy Spirit, and eternal life; men of the one part being required as a first step to believe, repent, and be baptized; while God of the other part promises the remission of sins, the Holy Spirit, and eternal life. Those six matters will be handled at length in the subsequent part of the volume.

Those things do certainly constitute the elements of the true gospel; but, before the analysis can be understood and appreciated, it is indispensable that the several items which form it shall be seen in their own separate and proper relations. In other words they must be seen related to that thing which as the gospel, they are intended to destroy, namely, sin. "For Christ was manifested to take away our sins." Or "He was manifested to destroy the works of the devil," which are sin and its adjuncts.

God has decreed the destruction of sin; he has determined to put it down; he will expurgate the universe of it. It is that thing which he hates. He will, therefore, show it no favor; but will detach it from the hearts and habits of men who are guilty of it, or he will destroy it and them by a perdition ruinous and eternal. In the mean time that it may be destroyed and men saved, pardon is freely offered, and promptly to be administered to "every one" of us who believes the gospel and obeys it. "Be baptized every one of you," say the scriptures to the penitent, "in the name of Jesus Christ for the remission of sins and you shall receive the gift of the Holy Spirit." But be it marked, that if the favor, which is here tendered, fails to win us and to slay our attachment to sin; if pardon, holy communion with God and his son, and life eternal in the heavens fail to influence our life and to make us what he would have us to be, then wrath shall be substituted for love, and force for favor; punishment shall take the place of reward and hell of heaven, and instead of meeting with a Saviour we shall be compelled to encounter the arm and omnipotence of an incensed and insulted God.

Sin is a dreadful evil and the origin of it has arrested the attention and excited the inquiries of the greatest geniuses and best men that have ever lived. It is a very font of fire, that breaks forth unceasingly, and departs into thousands of streams scorching and consuming every thing in their way. Sin, as we have seen, is contemplated in the holy scriptures under a variety of aspects; but under every view that can be taken of it, it is a dreadful evil. The violation of law is greatly to be deprecated as a thing that affects not only our own well-being, but also that of our neighbors; moreover it cannot possibly be indulged in without incurring the certain displeasure of that good but tremendous God, who will not be baffled in his designs. The Eternal ought to be obeyed; he has a right to be obeyed; he will be obeyed by all the lovers of truth and righteousness; and, therefore, he has vowed that, while his favor shall be extended to the obedient, his force shall press down to perdition all the impenitent of the earth. "The Lord Jesus shall be revealed from heaven with his holy messengers by flames of fire taking vengeance on them who acknowledge not God and obey not the gospel of our Lord Jesus Christ." II Thess.

In the holy scriptures this abominable evil is turned round, and looked at, and denounced in all its attributes and functions. The holy men of God behold it indeed as a unit—as the violation of law; but they behold it on many sides; they change the point of sight and see it under numerous aspects; they turn it round as they would a die, and comment upon it in all its forms and appearances; but whether it is in the mind, on the lip, or in the life engendering death, they uniformly denounce it as the greatest evil, fatal to man, insulting to God, and to be expiated only by the blood of our Lord Jesus Christ. In speaking of it, therefore, let us study to be correct rather than elegant, and scriptural rather than original; let us be guided by the instructions of the Apostles rather than the dictations of our own reason, and labor to attain, concerning this horrible thing, the enlightened views which these pious men and mighty ministers of Christ have committed to writing in the holy scriptures. These men shew us that sin is a fibrous root, and that like a thready cancer its several fillaments is to be eaten out distributively by a set of remedies divinely adapted to the purpose. The love of sin in the heart is not to be cured by every thing and any thing; nor is it to be taken out of the practice by any thing and every thing, nor can a man be removed and released from its state, its guilt, its degrading influence and ruinous punishment by any thing and every thing. Sin is like a distemper that is ever ready to change its seat, and is, therefore, unceasingly pointing in different directions. Now it is in the head, anon in the heart, and again in the life. It must be met, therefore, at these points accordingly.—If a man loves sin this abominable affection can be cured in him only by the exhibition of a remedy that reaches to the heart—faith, faith in God by the christian religion. One must discover to him the divine power, wisdom, and goodness in such a light as shall dissipate the dark and deadly affections of his heart, and make him hate that which he formerly loved, and love that which he has formerly hated. In brief, it is in religion as it is in nature we are presented with sets of opposites. As light and darkness in the natural world are contraries to each other, so in the religious world obedience to God and disobedience, are contraries to each other; the love of the one, therefore, must be substituted for that of the other in the heart of man as a first step. We must first either love obedience or hate disobedience. If as a first step, we hate disobedience nothing remains but that we will love obedience; or if we first admire obedience hatred of disobedience must necessarily ensue. But here at all events is the beginning place, the heart; religion begins in the heart; the word, as its Latin pedigree imports, signifies to rebind or connect again; the human family was once connected with its Maker in bonds of peace and amity; it requires to be reconnected; every man is once bound to God by many natural blessings; but he requires to be rebound to him by the bonds of Christianity; and this bond must reach the heart; it must extend from this point of life; as the heart is the point in the human body whence life first leaps forth to vivify all the other organs as they form in succession; so it is the point whence religion, the new, the blessed, the fresh life of religion leaps forth and pervades all the active powers in man, teaching him first by word to say Abba Father, and afterwards by action to keep all the divine commandments.

How then is the heart to be suitably affected; for affected it must be before any man is prepared to obey the gospel: while the gospel is in a man's head only, it maybe said it is his in word; but he himself is God's indeed only when the gospel is in his heart. It must, to be sure, be first in the head or understanding, but it is not expected nor intended of God, that it should dwell inoperative there; but, that the savour of such excellent knowledge should diffuse itself, like ointment, into the heart and over the affections of the soul, filling the whole inner man with a glowing admiration of righteousness, and love for the Righteous One.

Men may be divided according to their hearts. There are for instance, the faint-hearted, the hard-hearted, the impure-hearted, and the good and honest-hearted; and it may be well to notice this before dismissing the question How is the heart to be suitably affected, or changed,

The *faint-hearted* are those who are unable to arm themselves with the resolution necessary to obey the gospel and to aspire by confession and a life of submission, to the inheritance of immortality and life eternal. They are constantly framing apologies for their own pusilanimity. They fail to add to their faith courage; and are afraid of every thing. They affect to be afraid that they have not believed *enough*, or have not repented *enough*; they are even afraid lest they should offend God by obeying him, and trample upon the blood of the *Lamb* by seeking in it the salvation which it was shed to secure!

The *hard-hearted* are those, who beholding the goodness of God in the great dispensations of nature, social life, and the gospel, remain unaffected without any suitable convictions of the necessity of obedience, and of the infinite importance of eternal life. The words of the Great Eternal fall upon their mind light as a feather, and after all they have seen and all they have learned concerning God, like Israel in the desert, they harden their hearts, and stiffen their necks.

The *impure* in heart are such as are not single in their eye to eternal life; who have formed strong attachments to worldly pursuits and the rewards of earthly merit, money, distinction, fame, things that rest upon their minds with an undue and unbecoming weight, and press them down, with all their fancied greatness, to the base level of worldly men. They are "men of this world" exclusively, and not of the world that is to come; they are of time not eternity, of the earth not of heaven, and walk by sense or reason, and not by faith in God; they look at the things that are seen, not at the things that are not seen.

We do not say that this class of men are all faint-hearted, or that they are all hard-hearted: no, some of them are valorous and even famed for their courage; and some of them are blessed with the finest affections of the heart, and possess the kindliest sympathies, and are our men of honor and honesty and patriotism and every virtue; but it is all earthly in its character; their lives flourish with the choicest fruit, fair to the eye and pleasant to the taste; still it is mortal in its nature and rises from an earthly root. There is no fear of God before their eyes. They honor not the Eternal one; he is not their inheritance; he is not their riches, nor their wisdom, nor their power. The consequence is that they acknowledge him not in their ways, and are ignorant of his true character. Their families, if they have any, are soon initiated into the same carelessness for eternal things, and ignorance, and disregard of God. They are, therefore, the betrayers of that sacred trust that has been committed to them by the Almighty, and the destroyers of that precious circle of dearest relatives, which he has bestowed on them as their kingdom to he ruled, instructed, and exalted.

The Redeemer speaks of a class of people as "good and honest-hearted." But this class will be examined more particularly in a subsequent section. We have made the above imperfect division of men according to their hearts chiefly to fix the reader's attention upon the point before us and to assure him that religion must commence in the heart. With these observations we return to the question.

How is the heart to be affected, or changed so as that the love of God shall rule it? For the present the reader must be satisfied with the answer, that faith in God is the means provided by the Christian religion for the accomplishment of that end; the proof will be given in another section.

As faith is intended to destroy the love of sin from the heart or mind, so reformation is to cut it from the life or practice, and to purify all the active powers, that inwardly and outwardly the aspirant after eternity, may be clean before his translation from the world to the church, which being a divine institution is intended of God and of his Son Jesus Christ, to be on earth a house of holy men. When a man is thus purified internally and externally he is to be translated into the church by the ordinance of baptism, which being administered for the remission of sins, serves the double purpose of changing our state and washing away our guilt. The Holy Spirit is next granted, to remove the sad remains of sin in the soul, or to substitute joy for grief and so forth.

When sin and the gospel are understood, and their relation to each other is perceived; the adequacy of the latter to destroy the former is seen to be marvelously correct. Faith, repentance, baptism, remission, the Holy Spirit, and the resurrection, cancel severally the love, the practice, the state, the guilt, the power and the punishment of sin with admirable felicity. Hence the importance of the restoration of the true gospel, and the renewal of that good order in its several parts for which it was distinguished when first announced by the Apostles.

The definition, of sin, supplied by the Apostle John, is that it is the transgression of law. The same inspired person says that all unrighteousness is sin. We shall, therefore, collect from the face of scripture, those things which they denounce as unrighteousness, that the reader may see what it is and what has to be expurgated from the heart before a man is prepared to obey the gospel.

Covetousness, debate, deceit, maliciousness, envy, murder, malignity, whispering, back-biting, despite, hatred of God, pride, boasting, evil pleasures of every kind, disobedience to parents, masters, governors, and seniors; bargain-breaking, defectiveness in natural affection or infanticide, implacability, unmercifulness, unprofitableness to God, or a want of due care for the great work of salvation which he has set afoot on the earth, cursing, bitterness of speech, filthy conversation, blood-thirstiness, concupiscence, fornication, adultery, sodomy, incest, uncleanness, idolatry, reviling, drunkenness, wine-bibbing, wantonness, extortion, usury, exorbitancy, theft, fraud, idle words, chamberings, brawlings, bickerings, strifes, emulations, wraths, swellings, tumults, lasciviousness. witchcraft, necromancy, sedition, heresy, corrupt intercourse, perversity, murmuring, complaining, disponding, discord, scoffing, injustice, treason, deception, ungodliness, blaspheming, man-stealing, perjury, evil-surmising, the inordinate love of money, high-mindedness, irreverence for seniors or elders, itching ears, self-willedness, obstinacy, striking, grudging; eye-service, love of the world, folly, oppression, impatience in adversity, sorcery, rioting, bribery, corruption, ignorance of God, presumption, swearing, partiality, churlishness, naughtiness, backsliding from good, uncharitableness, false testimony, seduction, sacrilege, apostacy, slothfulness, dissimulation, want of hospitality and hospitality with grudging, ambition, revenge, rage, rancour, cruelty, suspicion, jealousy and resentment—Sins which if indulged in will forever debar us from the mansions on high; but which nevertheless, if reformed from, will be abundantly pardoned us through the gospel if we believe and obey it. For the faith of the gospel, is abundantly equal to the purification of the heart and obedience to the purification of the conscience.

These, then, are the things which have stained men and families, and nations, and the world, during the present state of respite; and to annihilate them from the minds and manners of men is a chief intention of the gospel of Christ; for surely it has not accomplished for any individual all the good he needs, if it has not yet purged him from these immoralities.

The abhorrent nature of sin and the utter detestation in which it is held by the Almighty is publicly evident by the punishments which he has from time to time inflicted upon the individuals, families, and nations, which have been notorious for indulging in it. Assyria, Greece, Rome, Egypt, are all sunk into heaps of national ruin; and the individuals, who formed their highest glory and by their chivalrous deeds in war carried those nations to the very pinnacle of renown, have inherited but a doubtful fame. The best judges decide equally of the greatness of their powers and the enormity of their crimes, the supremacy of their intellect and the baseness of their morals, their fame here and their damnation hereafter.

The destruction of the Egyptians in the Red Sea; and the cities of the Plain, Sodom and Gomorrah, on which in excess of wrath God poured hell out of heaven, licking up those populous towns with his lightnings, scaring their foundations with fire and brimstone, and washing the very sites which they occupied by floods of water poured from on high to the amount of a sea, are lasting monuments of his fierce indignation against sin. This is farther illustrated by the enormous streams of blood which were made to flow for the expiation of sin among God's ancient people the Jews. Besides the daily, weekly, monthly, and annual services, sometimes their kings and other dignitaries sacrificed holocausts of hundreds and thousands of sheep and oxen; even these did not suffice to propitiate the offended and insulted God; and, therefore, he broke forth upon them on various occasions and by flames of fire, by war, and by pestilence slew, as the scriptures say, "the fattest of them." Two and twenty thousand of them were slain in one day; and in forty years six hundred thousand fighting men, all the souls above age who came out of Egypt save two—Joshua and Caleb, were punished with death on account of sin.

The flood, too, though more remote, pours upon us from afar a fearful lesson of the wrath of God and the wrong of crime; and by her fatal catastrophe reflects in the distance the mournful assurance of the certain destruction of the guilty, and of the difficult but determined deliverance of the righteous.

This brings us back again to our First Parents, whose sphere was still beyond the flood, and whose fortune no less admonishes us of the dire nature of sin, and of the determination of the Almighty to expurgate and destroy it from the world either by force or favor, by gospel or by law.

Every thing depends upon preserving the elements of which we have been discoursing in their natural and scriptural order; derangement is the cause of all disorder; it is disorder; and it is the derangement of these principles that occasions much, if not all of the division that is so obvious, so dangerous, so shameful among the professors of the christian religion.

Suppose for a moment that the order, which those elements have in the scripture, was preserved inviolate by all; that all proposed first faith, then reformation, and finally obedience, that the converts might be pardoned and blessed and introduced to the hope of life eternal. What then? Why, in this manner all who are converted to God by the gospel, would become uniformly instructed first to believe, then reform, then obey the message of God by Christ The proclaimers and ministers, who labor for the Lord, would not then oppose and contradict each other as they now do in all places. The people would cease to stumble over those blocks that professors have thrown in their way, and the gospel would have free course, would run and would be exalted in society.

The Christian Religion may be divided into three parts, its faith, its church order, and its morality. Now if we all should first agree upon its faith or the gospel, which is the thing here meant, then the ground of inquiry and discussion would thereby be narrowed down one third at least; and it would remain, only to ask and determine What is the order of the church of Christ? What is the morality enjoined upon Christians? These two questions are not attempted to be settled in this volume. It is on the first of the three we are writing. What is the Gospel?

Instead of announcing the faith in the order for which we plead the ministers of all parties both contradict us, and one another. Some put repentance before faith, as if a being, who is to be affected by knowledge and motive, could reform towards a God of whom he is ignorant, and begin a new life with nothing before his eyes but old motives. Others administer baptism before both, as if an unconscious babe could derive benefit from an ordinance, which its own parents do not understand; and as if, it might in after life be recognized as the child of a Christian by a sprinkling, the impressions of which are as fugitive as the morning cloud, and in their existence evanid and short-lived as is the early dew. Others propose that, before either faith, repentance, or baptism, a man must be operated upon by the Holy Spirit. This is unchristian and wholly anomalous, having no warrant in scripture either by precept or example.—such a proposition was never made to mankind either by our Lord Jesus, or his apostles, or any other being employed in the original proclamation of the gospel.

But as the practice of sin cannot be supposed to precede the love of it, so repentance, which is to destroy it from the practise, cannot be supposed to precede faith which is to destroy it from the mind. Therefore as the love or desire to sin must go before actual commission, so faith is anterior to repentance; and in the order of nature and of the gospel a man must cease to love sin before he ceases to practice it. Again as it would be shocking and incongruous to translate from a state of sin to a state of righteousness a being, who had not previously recognised the authority by which the duty was enjoined or the benevolence by which the privilege was conferred, so baptism must, and does in the gospel, be preceded by faith and reformation. Hence the scheme, which administers baptism without either faith or repentance and which sets an idolatrous importance upon water as if it could accomplish something for a child irrespective of those principles, is chargeable with the crime and consequently the guilt and punishment of deranging the elements of the true gospel of Christ. Baptism is put first instead of third; and things are arranged thus, baptism, faith, repentance; instead of, faith, repentance, and baptism. As it would be improper to pardon before penitence, and equally so to withhold it from the truly repenting, so baptism is for the remission of sins as well as for translating us from the world into the church. Again, the Holy Spirit is intended to destroy from the mind that misery, which is so inseparable from the present state, and to replant in the human bosom again, as in their native seat, the virtues of love, joy, gentleness, meekness, and peace. It would be unnatural, therefore, as well as unscriptural to allege that the Holy Spirit is to be received before being translated from nature to grace, from the world to the church. The Christian religion, consequently, does not propose to bestow this blessing on any but those who obey the gospel. "Repent and be baptized every one of you in the name of Jesus Christ for the remission of sins, and you shall receive the gift of the Holy Spirit," Acts 2:38. Again, "Have you received the Holy Spirit since you believed?" Acts 19. Not, Have you believed since you received the Holy Spirit? Yet the modern methods of proclaiming the gospel would give birth to the latter unscriptural question much more readily than to the former scriptural one, which was put to the disciples by Paul. But the misery and power of sin must follow the guilt of it and, therefore, the gift of the Spirit which is to remove its misery, must be preceded by pardon, which is to take away the guilt of it. The last of the evangelical elements is the resurrection; and it would be as rational and not less scriptural to teach that it took place before death, as that baptism, which refers also to the resurrection, should go before faith and repentance; or remission before baptism or the Spirit before either.

These things must be preserved in their natural order, if we would preach and administer the gospel as the Apostles did.—But men began at a very early date to derange these first principles of the doctrine of Christ. Hymeneus and Phyletus had the rashness to teach, almost under the eyes of the Apostles, that in their own time the resurrection was past already and so "overthrew the faith of some." The popular faith, or rather the errors of the present time, have upset nearly the faith of all, the portion of sincere believers being surprisingly diminished. The people are boldly taught, that they cannot believe, cannot repent, cannot obey, and that "No mere man since the fall is able in this life, perfectly to keep the commandments of God; but does daily break them in thought, word and deed." Whereas, John declares, that "His commandments are not grievous but joyous, and in the keeping of them there is great reward." These order things—thus, Infant baptism, the special operations of the Holy Spirit, the forgiveness of sins, faith, repentance, and the resurrection. This is a pernicious arrangement, a destructive error, and to be rejected with disdain as a most unscriptural gospel. First because it makes faith to depend upon the operations of the Spirit and not upon the testimony of the Evangelists; and so it changes the character of true faith from evangelical and scriptural to spiritual and incomprehensible faith.

This error reflects upon the perfection of the holy scriptures, and causes men to neglect them, and to look up to God through the medium of their own frames and feelings rather than through the medium of these holy oracles, which are given as a luminary to our feet and a lamp to our path, to be read and studied devoutly, till we reach the full stature of Christians perfectly instructed.

It, moreover, represents the gospel as an assemblage of blessings which we have not the power intellectually or morally, it is not agreed which, some saying the one, some the other, and a third party both, to receive; as if the divine God had spread a feast for all mankind, which he knew they had no power to eat, and which, to consume, it would be necessary to create new powers in man. This sentiment is very objectionable; for it is in religion as it is in nature; as in the one he provides, food, drink, and the material of raiment, but leaves us to prepare and use them; so in religion he has furnished all the means of salvation and enjoins on us to apply them to their proper ends, prudently leaving us with the faith of the gospel and the power of understanding it, to use it as wise men for the great and gracious purposes for which he gave it by Jesus Christ our Lord, to whom be glory forever. Amen.

CHAPTER XXXIV

Conclusion of Section First

We shall conclude this part of our volume by reasoning with the reader on the several subjects of life and death, knowledge and faith, obedience and disobedience, trial and temptation, good and evil, and misery and happiness as discoursed of in the foregoing pages; for we deem it positive philanthropy to be urgent in the case. Silence would be criminal; and carelessness more than a fault in a matter in which such various and vast interests are involved.

It is the duty of us all to make ourselves thoroughly acquainted with the scripture scheme devised by God for our salvation. If we think otherwise and consequently neglect the scriptures, and live ignorant of God and the true religion, we deprive ourselves of the most excellent knowledge; we also render ourselves unfit company for such as differ from us on this important point, and who, by their devotion to the holy Oracles, have become learned and wise in the exalted science of eternal life. Think for a moment of the many and admirable points which must necessarily be found in a scheme like the foregoing; in which God and man, angels and demons, Messiah and satan, saints and sinners, patriarchs, prophets, apostles, and all the most renowned men are playing their respective parts. Think for a moment of what must be the richness, variety, depth and excellence of that intercourse which is founded on a unity of sentiment in regard to the topics of life and death, sin and righteousness, knowledge and duty, and all other subjects, which are treated of in that endlessly varied book the Bible. The flower of mankind, wherever this book has come, have deemed it their highest honor to become acquainted with it. For if nature cries aloud through her ten thousand halls that there exists "One only true God," Revealed Religion confirms the fact and informs all men of the ritual and the morality by which he would be served and worshipped. To be ignorant of these things, the proposition of the true religion, its ritual, and its morals, is, therefore, highly criminal and even disgraceful to any man. What! ignorant of the religion of our own country! Why we would condemn a Turk or a Heathen if he were found ignorant of the religion of his own country.

If the doctrine of the late chancellor of England in his volume on Natural Theology, is correct, and his voice may justly be deemed the adjudication, of the highest tribunal on earth in the case, then nature and revealed religion may be likened to two witnesses for God, declaring by works and words, and power and wisdom the existence and character of the Great Eternal. Shall it be conceded by the loftiest spirits among men, shall they even reason for it, "That there is one living and true God"? and will we, notwithstanding, remain wholly ignorant of the voice of nature and of religion together and turn a deaf ear to the wisdom which formed the one and dictated the other?

Not inferior to the chancellor was John Locke. Perhaps it was the former, who said of him "As for the private character of the man, it was one of the most beautiful and stainless that ever adorned human nature, and rarely has there been seen a nobler example than he exhibited of the union of high intellect and equally elevated virtue." It is no disparagement to a man, therefore, totally to dissent from those who differ on religion from John Locke. This illustrious Englishman's belief is a notable testimony of the truth and excellence of the Christian Religion; and it is not to be expected that prudent men will readily forego his pure example to follow in the path of an inferior and less celebrated man. Infidels and atheists have, in some instances, discovered great versatility of genius and a lighter wit, in the defence of their sentiments; but Atheism and infidelity can boast no such a man as John Locke. Voltaire was a wit; Gibbon was full of haughty pride; David Hume was unduly attached to worldly applause; J. J. Rousseau was capricious; and Volley insidious; but the idea we form of John Locke is, that he was learned and elevated, pure, grave, and contemplative.

"The Honorable Mr. Boyle, the most exact searcher into the works of nature that any age has known, and who saw atheism and infidelity beginning to show themselves in the loose and voluptuous reign of King Charles the second, pursued his philosophical inquiries with religious views to establish the minds of men in a firm belief and thorough sense of the infinite power and wisdom of his great Creator.

This account we have from one who was intimately acquainted with him and preached his funeral sermon.[5] "It appeared from those who had conversed with him on his inquiries into nature, that his main design in that (on which as he had his own eye most constantly, so he took care to put others often in mind of it) was to raise in himself and others vaster thoughts of the greatness and glory, and of the wisdom and goodness of God.—This was so deep in his thoughts, that he concludes the article of his will, which relates to that illustrious body of the Royal Society, in these words, wishing them a happy success in their laudable attempts to discover the true nature of the works of God; and praying that they in all their searches into physical truths may certainly refer their attainments to the glory of the great Author of nature, and to the comfort of mankind."

In another place the same person speaks of him thus: "He had the profoundest veneration for the great God of heaven and earth that I ever observed in any man. The very name of God was never mentioned by him without a pause and visible stop in his discourse."

Of the strictness and exemplariness of the whole course of his life, he says, "I might here challenge the whole tribe of libertines to come and view the usefulness as well as excellence of the Christian religion in a life that was entirely dedicated to it." The veneration he had for the holy scriptures appears not only from his studying them but more

---

[5] Burret.

particularly from a distinct treatise which he wrote, on purpose to defend the scripture style, and to answer all the objections which profane and irreligious persons have made against it.

His zeal in propagating Christianity in the world, appears by many and large benefactions to that end.

In his younger years he had thoughts of entering into holy orders; and one reason that determined him against it was, that he believed he might in some respects be more serviceable to religion by continuing a layman. "His having no interests, with relation to religion, besides those of saving his own soul, gave him, as he thought, a more unsuspected authority in writing or acting on that side. He knew that the profane had fortified themselves against all that was said by men of our profession, with this, that it was their trade, and that they were paid for it; he hoped therefore that he might have the more influence the less he shared in the patrimony of the church."

Mr. Locke, whose accurate talent in reasoning is so much celebrated even by the sceptics and infidels of our times, showed his zeal for the Christian religion, first in his middle age, by publishing a discourse on purpose to demonstrate the reasonableness of believing Jesus to be the proper Messiah; and after that, in the last years of his life, by a very judicious commentary upon several of the epistles of St. Paul.

The holy scriptures are everywhere mentioned by him with the greatest reverence; and he exhorts Christians "to betake themselves in earnest to the study of the way of salvation, in those holy writings, wherein God has revealed it from heaven, and proposed it to the world; seeking our religion where we are sure it is in truth to be found, comparing spiritual things with spiritual." And, in a letter written the year before his death, to one who asked this question, "What is the shortest and surest way for a young gentleman to attain to the true knowledge of the Christian religion in the full and just extent of it?" His answer is, "Let him study the holy scriptures, especially the New Testament. Therein are contained the words of eternal life. It has God for its author; salvation for its end; and truth, without any mixture of error, for its matter:" a direction that was copied from his own practice in the latter part of his life, and after his retirement from business; when for "fourteen or fifteen years, he applied himself especially to the study of the holy scriptures, and employed the last years of his life hardly in any thing else. He was never weary of admiring the great views of that sacred book, and the just relation of all its parts. He every day made discoveries in it that gave him fresh cause of admiration.

The death of this man is agreeable to his life. For we are assured by one that was with him when he died, and had lived in the same family for seven years before, that the day before his death he particularly exhorted all about him to read the holy scriptures; that he desired to be remembered by them at evening prayers; and being told, that if he chose it the whole family should come and pray by him in his chamber, he answered, he should be very glad to have it so, if it would not give too much trouble; that an occasion offering to speak of the goodness of God, he especially exalted the care which God showed to man, in justifying him by faith in Jesus Christ; and returned God thanks in particular for having blessed him with the knowledge of that divine Saviour.

About two months before his death he drew up a letter to a certain gentleman, and left this direction upon it, "To be delivered to him after my decease." In it are these remarkable words: "This life is a scene of vanity that soon passes away, and affords no solid satisfaction, but in the consciousness of doing well, and in the hopes of another life. This is what I can say upon experience, and what you will find to be true, when you come to make up the account."

"Sir Isaac Newton, universally acknowledged to be the ablest philosopher and mathematician that this, or perhaps any other nation has produced, is also well known to have been a believer, and a serious Christian. His discoveries concerning the frame and system of the universe were applied by him to demonstrate the being of a God, and to illustrate his power and wisdom in the creation.

This great man applied himself likewise with the utmost attention to the study of the holy scriptures, and considered the several parts of them with uncommon exactness; particularly as to the order of time and the series of prophecies and events relating to the Messiah. Upon which head he left behind him an elaborate discourse, to prove that the famous prophecy of Daniel's weeks, which has been so industriously perverted by the Deists of our times, was an express prophecy of the coming of the Messiah, and fulfilled in Jesus Christ."

"Sir Francis Bacon, lord Verulam, was a man who, for his greatness of genius and compass of knowledge, did honor to his age and country; I could almost say to human nature itself.—He possessed at once all those extraordinary talents which were divided among the greatest authors of antiquity: nor can one tell which to admire most in his writings, the strength of reason, force of style, or brightness of imagination. This great man was a firm believer, and possessed the genuine and ardent spirit of devotion and piety which reason dictates, and revelation purifies and exalts. His principal error seems to have been the excess of that virtue which covers a multitude of faults. This betrayed him to so great an indulgence towards his servants, who made a corrupt use of it, that it stripped him of all those riches and honors which a long series of merits had heaped upon him. But in the following devotional piece, at the same time that we find him prostrating himself before the great mercy-seat, and humbled under afflictions which at that time lay heavy upon him, we see him, supported by the sense of his integrity, his zeal, his devotion, and his love to mankind, which give him a higher figure in the minds of thinking men, than that greatness had done from which he was fallen.

The prayer above-mentioned, was found among his lordship's papers, written with his own hand, and is as follows:

"Most gracious Lord God, my merciful Father, my Creator, my Redeemer, and my Comforter. Thou, O Lord, soundest and searchest the depths and secrets of all hearts; thou acknowledgest the upright of heart, thou judgest the hypocrite; thou ponderest men's thoughts as in a balance; thou measurest their intentions as with a line; vanity and crooked ways cannot be hid from thee.

"Remember, O Lord! how thy servant hath walked before Thee; remember what I have sought, and what hath been principal in my intentions. I have loved thy assemblies, I have mourned for the divisions of thy church. I have delighted in the brightness of thy sanctuary; the vine, which thy right hand hath planted in this nation, I have ever prayed unto thee, that it might have the first and the latter rain, and that it might stretch her branches to the seas and to the flood. The state and the bread of the poor and oppressed have been precious in mine eyes. I have hated all cruelty and hardness of heart; I have (though a despised weed) procured the good of all men. If any have been my enemies, I thought not of them, neither hath the sun almost set upon my displeasure; but I have been as a dove, free from superfluity of maliciousness.

"Thousands have been my sins, and ten thousands my transgressions; but thy sanctifications have remained with me, and my heart (through thy grace) hath been an unquenched coal upon thine altar.

"O Lord, my strength! I have since my youth met with thee in all my ways, by thy fatherly companions, by thy comfortable chastisements, and by thy most visible providence. As thy favors have increased upon me, so have thy corrections; so as thou hast been always near me, O Lord! and ever as my worldly blessings were exalted, so secret darts from thee have pierced me; and when I have ascended before men, I have descended in humiliation before thee. And now, when I thought most of peace and honor, thy hand is heavy upon me, and hath humbled me according to thy former loving kindness, keeping me still in thy fatherly school, not as a bastard, but as a child.—Just are thy judgments upon me for my sins, which are more in number than the sands of the sea, but have no proportion to thy mercies; for what are the sands of the sea? Earth, heavens, and all these, are nothing to thy mercies. Besides my innumerable sins, I confess before thee, that I am debtor to thee for the gracious talent of thy gifts and graces, which I have neither put into a napkin, nor put it (as I ought) to exchangers, where it might have made best profit, but misspent it in things for which it was least fit; so I may truly say, my soul hath been a stranger in the course of my pilgrimage. Be merciful to me, O Lord, for my Saviour's sake, and receive me unto thy bosom, or guide me in thy ways."[6]

The examples of these celebrated men may well teach us the important lesson, to make ourselves soundly acquainted with revealed religion before we reject it; for it is unbecoming either to reject or refuse that of which we are in a great degree ignorant. This, however, is as common as it is unbecoming. Men every where reject, and receive Christianity, without investigating either its true character or its evidences. When those guilty of the former impropriety speak against it, their words, therefore, have no weight with the sensible and prudent portion of mankind; and when such as are at fault in the latter case rise up in its favor their defence is necessarily of as little weight. Both these kinds of people are to be regarded as weak men and equally dangerous to their own cause.

We have observed that "the fall of our first parents and our recovery by Jesus Christ form a great drama." Well you object to religion because this is its character; because it represents mankind as having been once in a better state; once wise, innocent, and happy; but tried, tempted, and unfortunate; and now doomed to misery and death because of the evil of another rather than their own unfaithfulness. And you startle at the idea of a Mediator, and of God appointing such an Intercessor; again you wonder that faith should be selected, and ask why repentance and obedience are enjoined: and in short you are confounded by every thing and any thing that is named christian.

Are you, then, assured that such objections are of a kind wholly unexceptionable? Are you sure that they do not involve too much to be of service to prove any thing? Religion then, for this is the argument, is not what you would have expected it to be. Well now, this is a very weak argument; for see,—what is there either in nature, or society, more than in religion, that is precisely what the wisest of us would have expected it to be? Would you, with all your reason, have expected antecedently to experience, that day and night should succeed each other at intervals of about twelve hours in one part of the globe, as at the equator, and in another at the interval of six months, as at the pole? Would you have

---

[6] Stretch.

expected that the seasons should succeed each other as they do at present, and one part of the globe be almost burnt by heat, while the other is pinched with eternal cold, and covered with perpetual snow? Would you previous to experience have expected the oak to grow from the acorn and the bird of Paradise from the yolk of an egg? The diamond is pure charcoal, water a compound of one of the most inflammable principles in nature, and a ray of light, which is white, is actually made up of all the colors of the rainbow! But again, look at society. Who would have expected virtue to suffer in any case, either by poverty, or sickness, or death? Yet it does suffer from all these. And who would have hoped to see vice triumphant and driving, even in the street, his victorious carr over the neck of peace, and truth, and righteousness? Yet all this is seen; and, therefore, the objection by standing its arms too wide loses everything; for on this plan of objecting, nature and society themselves, as well as religion aright be set aside. We cannot, therefore, reject religion because it is not what we expect it would be as a thing coming from God.

But suppose it had been deputed you to form a religion for the world, what would have been your plan? You answer, I would, when our First Parents sinned, have laid them quietly asleep and made another pair. Well, what if the last pair had done worse than the first and sinned without temptation, or refused to live because you required they should be tried? But observe, the question respects man as he is and not as he might have been. What, then, would have been your religion for the world as it is, all full of error, ignorance, iniquity and death? Would you have preferred knowledge to faith in such a state of things? and instead of making men virtuous first and shewing them God afterwards, would you have shewed them God first and made them virtuous afterwards? Instead of first illuminating them in regard to themselves and other men, and the history of creation and the existence and character of the Deity, and afterwards giving them eternal life, would you first have bestowed this gift on them irrespective of their deeds good or evil, and instructed them subsequently?

Now, are you certain that said plan would have been less liable to objections than that of scripture to which you take the exception? You are not at all certain. I could muster a host of objections to any scheme you could possibly project if you would torture your inventive powers to eternity; and so no objection warranting its rejection can be brought against revealed religion that a better one might have been formed. We see things partially and do not like God behold the end from the beginning; we cannot, therefore, tell what is best. If it is once determined that our religion comes from God we are sure that it is upon the whole the best that could be given to man in his present condition; therefore, it is important that men everywhere labor to understand it as it came out of the hands of its author, and not merely as it is retailed by those who, like wine dealers, have a profit by diluting it.

But you reply further, that I have not reached the sinew of your objection and, consequently, have not yet cut its connection with your own case; that you object not to the plan of revealed religion, but to what forms the basis of it—That there is one living and true God. Good,—let us understand your case better.—You deny the proposition that there is one living and true God. Do you deny it as forming the basis of Natural Theology, or only as it is the foundation of revealed religion? Are you deistical, or atheistical? Do you admit this proposition as a dictate of nature, and only deny the authority of religion in regard to it? Or do you deny it altogether as a sentiment even of nature, and assert that her order, system, design, and variety warrant no such belief? I deny it altogether, you reply. Well, now I understand your case. You are an atheist. You deny the divine existence altogether!

What is to be done for you? Lord Brougham, who has set the belief of one living and true God on a scientific basis, would turn from you as an ignoramus; and the scriptures would describe you as a fool. "The fool hath said in his heart there is no God." Psalm 51. We, therefore, dismiss your case as one which punishment or experience, time or eternity alone can cure.

But you exclaim "I shift my ground. I admit the proposition as announced by nature through all her works; that there is a God. I am not an atheist, but a deist."

Your case, then, is as follows.—You do believe in the divine existence and character, and would do homage to his authority, because nature and reason both dictate such a course. But you reject revelation as unnecessary; that is, the proposition is made so very clear by the testimony of one witness, namely, Nature, that the testimony of the other, namely, Religion, is rendered wholly unnecessary. This is your argument. Now see—what is not absolutely necessary may, nevertheless, be very useful. You would not like to dismiss from your table, and wardrobe, and household, every thing of a useful and ornamental nature, and retain only those things which were purely and barely necessary. Would you? Your works answer, no. Well then, Revelation, though we should grant for your sake that it is not absolutely necessary, may nevertheless, be very serviceable, very useful. Well then, In what may its usefulness consist? It is very evident that, however eloquent in announcing the being and character of her Creator, nature is at all events wholly silent as to the time when she herself was created. On this point, which is one on which men are exceedingly impatient, scripture comes into our relief and informs us that "In the beginning God created the Heavens and the earth." Again, we are equally impatient on the subject of our own origin; and here again Revelation meets us, and delivers us from all perplexity by informing us that in the beginning "God made man in his own likeness"—an oracle awarding to us so honorable a beginning as may well make all men search that Volume in which it is found, the Bible. But, moreover, nature is wholly silent as to the manner in which the divine authority would be honored. If she declares that there is a God, she is wholly silent in regard to the "ritual" by which he would be worshipped; and in this respect Revelation is exceedingly useful, if not absolutely necessary, and altogether indispensable. Again, men have differed exceedingly on the nature of virtue; but Revelation purposes to establish one morality all over the earth; and so in this again it may be as necessary as it is certainly desirable and useful.—Finally, the fundamental proposition of all religion, that there is but one God, has been greatly corrupted and departed from. To have it re-asserted by divine authority and by this means get clear of idolatry, is certainly one of the most desirable things on earth. Now Revelation does this; and so dispels the doubts which might otherwise arise from the side of nature on this point as well as those which may arise from the Polytheism of mankind sanctioned by ancient usage and rendered venerable by its great antiquity.

Are you rejoiced at the discovery which you have made by your researches into nature in regard to the existence, unity, and character of the Divinity? Then be glad; exult and be exceedingly glad, that your discoveries are all confirmed by the voice of Revelation, and that, instead of having but one witness to the truth in which you rejoice, you have two, both Nature and Revelation asserting and re-asserting the fact. Men are known by their works and words, and not by either taken separately; it is so with the Deity also. He is not to be perfectly known by his works alone, nor by his words alone, but by both taken together. I am no advocate for credulity, that is, for believing on only one half the evidence, whether that half be his works, or his word.—And I am no advocate for distrust, as if his works and word, when taken together, were insufficient for our faith to rest upon. I go for both and for that faith or belief which is produced by both, and confirmed by both.

But you say, "I again shift my ground. I am even desirous of revelation and object not to the matter of the Bible, but to its evidence; it is too scanty; it ought to have been, so full that no one could have doubted it; of course all would have believed."

This is better reasoning by far, or at least the objection is laid in against a point in which a man's doubts may be reasonably listened to. We have seen that if a revelation is once proved to have come from God no objection can reasonably be brought against it on account of its admirable, novel, or peculiar nature. If it has come from God, then God-like it must be and cannot lawfully be objected to; but its authority we confess is always the first thing to be proved; and some may, like the objector, imagine and even feel, that the proof "is too scanty," or not in a sufficient ratio to command assent, induce belief.—Now is the objector assured that the proof which accompanies Revealed Religion in general and Christianity in particular, is not of this very character and granted just in such a degree as to make every one believe it so soon as it is understood? You answer, "No; It has not made me believe." Granted; but have you thoroughly inquired? Have you impartially investigated? have you weighed, compared, and concluded? or have you concluded first, like the unjust magistrate, who designed to enquire into the case after he had decided upon it? If you have thoroughly investigated the evidences of revelation in general and Christianity in particular, How did you proceed? How were your enquiries conducted? On the plan of Locke, and with the gravity of that great man? Has your plan of procedure been that of common sense at all? Did you, when you heard that Christianity proposed innate or eternal life on a plan authorized by God, enquire first into the morals she inculcates? and when you found out that they were pure and holy, did you in the first instance improve your own by adopting those which she enjoined? If you did not, it is evident that your enquiries were not conducted with a view to the elevation and perpetuity of your own nature, which are the two main ideas in all true religion,—for the religion that does not seek to reform us and, on reformation, propose eternal life, is suited neither to the wants nor wishes of human nature as it is now circumstanced. But did the discovery and conviction of the purity of her morals take any effect upon you whatever? did they even cause you to suspend your decision against her for a moment? Or did her loveliness in your eyes diminish in proportion as she appeared pure and holy? If this was the case there was something essentially wrong in your plan of investigating Christianity. But suppose you acted thus far in a manner becoming a true man, Did you next in the spirit of an impartial jury-man, sit in all good faith and intention on the evangelical testimony, the writings of the immediate followers of the Messiah, Matthew, Mark, Luke, and John? Did you next compare the prophecies of the Jewish Religion with the facts of the Christian Religion? And then did you notice the divine agreement of the last of these things with the first of them? Finally, did you examine and see with what admirable felicity the doctrines of the latter are adapted to the wants, and powers, and desires of mankind; and how perfectly every thing in our religion accords with our natural apprehensions of the divine power, wisdom, and goodness?

But this volume is not intended to touch with the question concerning the evidences of the gospel; but to show only what that gospel is as it came out of the hands of its author. We shall, therefore, return.

1. The first feeling of surprise, when we read the history of our first parents, is excited, perhaps, by the fact of their having been put upon trial. Here, as in many other things, the mind labors for a reason, seeks for an explanation. Adam was the first of men, and necessarily required peculiar treatment. And we think to ourselves that, if we had had the guardianship over him, his fate would have been very different. This shows that God's ways do not always meet our highest reason. But what does this prove? It proves that our highest reason is sometimes folly when compared with the deep wisdom of God. We often conclude upon a very limited knowledge of things.—He ever decides from the most perfect knowledge of all things. He knows every thing; we understand comparatively nothing. He knows the end from the beginning, we neither know the beginning, middle, nor end. Had you, reader, been the disposer of all events could you have secured an equal amount of happiness by pursuing a different course In relation to primitive man? When you had showered upon him all riches, made him lord of this lower world, and crowned him with all honor till his highest gratitude was aroused, would you have afforded him an opportunity of displaying this noble feeling of the soul by overt acts done and performed under its sacred influence? For you must perceive, if you are a man, that to be commanded by such a patron to do any thing in the chapter of possibilities must under his circumstances have met the fondest desire of Adam's heart, and increased the amount of his happiness.

We are in the habit of saying that the first man was tried; but it would, perhaps, better comport with the case, to say that he had a command from God, in order that by obeying it he might relieve his soul from that burden of gratitude with which, we see, it must have been filled to overflowing. Would you, then, have given him an opportunity to run off by words and actions this fountain which your goodness had created within him? Or would you have left him to burst and perish by the agonies for freedom with which it must finally have convulsed him? But if trial was intended, could any thing excel the kind provision which was made for man under this view of the case? Here was the tree of life standing in the midst of the garden, by the side of the tree of the knowledge of good and evil, to which on the approach of temptation Adam could at any time retreat and thereby gratify his highest ambition by seizing, and not unlawfully, immortality or perpetual animal life; he could have "eaten and lived forever." Again, see the beautiful and intimate relation which his intellectual trial in the naming of the animals bore to the future trial of his heart, his moral trial. He was, by this means, greatly instructed in necessary self-respect—He had been made, by this exercise of his understanding, to feel his own dignity, his own personal worth, and fitted to guard his own innocence at all hazards and to preserve the honorable pre-eminence over the rest of created nature to which, on account of his excellent capacity, his God and Benefactor had exalted him. Indeed, the eating of the interdicted fruit by our great sire seems to have been caused rather by an exalted devotion for his lovelier, fairer, but more unfortunate partner, than by and deficiency in self-respect, or irreverence in him towards his glorious Creator. For, as the Apostle says, "Adam was not deceived but, the woman being deceived, was in the transgression" I Tim. 2:14. Though the mother of mankind could endure trial, she could not suspect, temptation. She was too divinely constituted either to be unfaithful or suspicious. In an evil hour, therefore, she yielded to the voice of falsehood to which she had never before listened, and which she could not now suspect, and unhappily broke her faith with God, whom she had heretofore honored and adored.

How exceedingly inspiring is the fact of being able, by the holy scriptures to trace our descent to so honorable an ancestry, to two distinguished individuals privileged on account of their original excellence, with the incomparable honor of standing in the presence of the great God, and of beholding his glory, and majesty, and beauty; nay to two beings created in the image of God! "For in the image of God made he them." Gen. 1. Surely the Bible, which thus awards to mankind so venerable and royal an origin, must commend itself alike to the understanding and heart of every reflecting man, who duly considers the high and important communications which it conveys to the world. Let me, then, adjure the reader of this book, to study the holy scriptures; for in them he will find revealed the most excellent knowledge, and "truth," as John Locke says, "without any mixture of error."

2. But secondly; if any thing more than another in the history of primitive man is calculated to excite our amazement it is that God should have permitted them to be tempted by the Devil.—This is a matter the reason of which cannot be so easily perceived and explained as their trial by their Creator, which obviously took place in order to enlarge the sphere of their happiness and exalt their virtue; whereas the temptation was both dangerous and degrading. Trial in their case, as we have seen, was a command with an inducement to abstain from evil; while the temptation was a command and inducement to do that evil.— They are, therefore, as completely opposites in the moral world as light and darkness are opposites in the natural world, but perhaps nevertheless, they were equally necessary, and equally reasonable in the eye of him who sees, and knows, and governs all.

Man, as has already been observed, has been endowed by his Creator with a capacity for knowledge and with a sense of duty, that is, he has been formed with intellectual, and moral attributes by which he can understand things that are, and things that ought to be. Now it was his happy and high privilege in his original condition to have made known to him just so much of duty as had an evident tendency to increase his happiness. He walked in the commandment of his God and learnt experimentally the blessedness of duty, and of honoring the things that ought to be. But there was in him also a capacity for another class of ideas and for all the misery resulting from the knowledge of that fatal class of ideas, viz: things that ought not to be or undutifulness. He had been warned by his Creator of the dangerous nature of this kind of knowledge and of the fatal consequences which would result to himself if he should, contrary to the Divine counsel, presume to possess himself of it, the knowledge of evil or of undutifulness. Satan with his compeers, was the only created being in the universe who possessed an experimental acquaintance with this. Why then let him loose upon innocent unsuspecting man? Was it because it was best for man, all things considered, that he should be possessed of this dangerous kind of knowledge? that he should have an experimental acquaintance with evil as well as with good and learn to estimate happiness by tasting of the bitterness of misery? Was it best for him, all things considered, that he should understand experimentally the things that ought not to be, as well as the things that ought to be, and learn finally the excellency of duty by tasting the woes resulting from the contrary? And was it on this account that temptation was superadded to trial, or permitted in addition to it? Satan himself must have fallen in trial alone, and not in temptation, for there was no other Devil to tempt him. This was not the case with man; he did not fall in his trial by God, but in his temptation by the devil. Satan was put upon the word or command of God, but persevered not, as our Lord said, "in the truth;" and it must have been a great aggravation of his crime that he fell without being tempted. Man was also put upon God's word or the truth, and persevered in trial, but fell in temptation.

Our Redeemer, like his prototype, Adam, was subjected both to trial and temptation—trial by God and temptation by Satan. But, unlike Adam, he came off victorious; he "was tempted in all things like unto us yet without sin." The sufferings of the Redeemer in life and in death, when we look at them as permitted by God, may be regarded as trials for his perfection as the leader of life or captain of salvation; but, when viewed as a means made use of by Satan for forcibly driving the Lord Jesus from the glorious enterprise of Man's Salvation, they are to be regarded as a temptation, by which Jesus became a High Priest all alive to our infirmities, because "in that he himself hath suffered, being tempted, he is able to succor them that are tempted." Trial alone would have left him on a footing with angels, who are tried but not tempted. But verily he laid not hold of angels some of whom had already fallen by trial, but of the seed of Abraham who stood condemned on account of a temptation; it behoved him, therefore, to be made in all things like unto his brethren, in flesh and blood, and trial and temptation, "That he might be a merciful and faithful High Priest in things relative to God, to make reconciliation for the sins of the people." Having tasted the fascinating and seducing influence of temptation, when the devil showed him all the kingdoms of the world and the glory of them in a moment of time, his personal experience enables him to put up in our behalf a heartfelt and eloquent supplication for us before the throne on high.

It is sometimes asked why God permitted Satan to tempt man; and why he permitted man to eat the forbidden fruit. There are many things that are exceedingly mysterious in the *what* and the *wherefore*. It should be remembered, however, that the prior question is alway Are things so; not What are they so; and to understand the first of these in regard to a matter is in most cases all that is necessary to enable us to make a moral, or a natural use of it. The devil did tempt the ancestors of mankind, and the ancestors of mankind did violate law, things which have given birth to the remedial scheme of the gospel whether we understand all the reasons for them or not.

But God did not permit our First Parents to violate law; on the contrary he prohibited them by an express injunction enforced by a most special penalty even immediate death. He prohibited them as much as the moral nature of the case admitted; for in such affairs it does not answer that legislators shall put physical restraints upon those whom their laws respect, and shut them up in prison or tie their hands or shut their mouths in order that the ends of the law may be attained; for the ends of the law would not in this way be attained but lost.

3. The next thing that attracts our attention, is the law concerning the Tree of the knowledge of good and evil. "In the day thou eatest thereof thou shalt surely die." We feel surprised at the intensity and definitiveness of the language in this scripture, the word *die*, and the word *surely*, which is prefixed thereto; and our minds precipitately hurry onward to these questions. Must not God have known perfectly that they would eat, and that on the day they did so they would not die? Why, then, this positiveness, you *shall* die, you shall *surely* die? It looks bad, very bad indeed. And yet any thing else would have been highly improper as the reader will acknowledge if he reflects for a moment on the fact, that although the power of respite is lodged with the executive branch of a government, the legislature never frame nor word their laws with the least reference to the exercise of that power. Though they know that such a power exists and that it may he acted upon they never recognize it in the moment of legislation; but proceed in word and deed as if no such power existed in any branch of the government. They do not decree in this manner, The person guilty of murder shall die—unless reprieved by the executive. This would be bad policy, a dangerous method of enacting laws, and infinitely beneath the dignity of the legislator. The law to Adam, therefore, was framed with reference to the crime which it denounced and not to the respite which was afterwards extended to him. In this respect the wording of it "Thou shalt die, surely

die," is perfectly legislative in its tone and intention, and in its peremptoriness harmonizes with the voice of all subsequent legislators.

The powers of respite and reprieve have been frequently exercised by God during his government of the world. The antediluvians were respited for one hundred and twenty years; Pharaoh the king of Egypt was repeatedly respited; but failing to reform he was punished with all his host and drowned in the Red Sea. The Israelites in the wilderness, having by their idolatry and contumaciousness rendered themselves justly obnoxious to death, were for Moses' sake respited for forty years; but their presumptuous crimes could not be wholly pardoned and they all save two died in forty years. Nineveh was respited for forty days and, because of her penitence and reformation, was at the end of that time reprieved and her punishment abrogated.

4. It may be asked why the scriptures, after representing Satan as the ultimate cause of sin, do not on him inflict the sole punishment, why did not the Deity punish him instead of our First Parents whom he deceived. The devil was not at this time under law to God. He was an outlaw roaming the interminable profound in which the universe had been lighted up after his revolt from God; and it was as a being under punishment and without law that he came to this world and seduced and ruined man.

God is the Ruler of all worlds. He can do nothing but in perfect righteousness. "He is a God of truth and without iniquity, just and right is He." If he had laid his hand on Satan in the present case and for doing what it had never been commanded him not to do, for it had not been said to him Thou shalt not beguile man, the divine character might have been suspected, and, therefore, the Lord God made a family matter of the whole affair, and left the adversary in our own hands whom he had abused and murdered, "I will put enmity between thee and the woman, said the Lord to our destroyer, and between thy seed and her seed; it shall bruise thy head and thou shalt bruise his heel."

It ought to be observed that it is out of this family quarrel the future punishment of Satan arises; and thus though he has in law escaped God, yet in equity, as the murderer of our family, he ought not to escape man; and therefore, the Son of Man will wreak our vengeance upon him and plunge him into eternal fire. Satan brought eternal punishment on the human family, for if our species should endure forever it would continue to die, and, therefore, his punishment shall be eternal also. He shall drink of the cup which he has filled for others. As he has rendered to us so will we render to him double, and by Jesus Christ our Lord behold our family justly avenged; for our adversary is strong, determined, and irreclaimable; but strong also is the Lord God, who judges him.

It is no doubt indispensable that this fallen seraph should ultimately be captured, for his existence may be as dangerous to angels as it has been to men. He is a being of lion-like ferocity going about "seeking whom he may devour." May God preserve his saints and all men from his wiles. His fearless courage led him to contend for the body of Moses with the archangel Michael himself, who in return only said "The Lord rebuke thee, Satan," Perhaps there is none in heaven, the Almighty and his Son excepted, who dares encounter him. It is probably on account of present safety and hope of future deliverance from the attacks, plots, and counter plots of the adversary and his myriads of demons that the angels are put in subjection to the Son of Man, the Son of God. Satan is their enemy as well as ours; but like us they are probably his inferiors in power; in God, therefore, or in God's image in power and in every other attribute and virtue, our blessed and adorable Lord Jesus Christ, they, like ourselves, depend for salvation. For, as Peter says, "Ye were as sheep gone astray; but are now returned to the Shepherd and Bishop of your souls, Jesus Christ, who is gone into heaven, angels and principalities being made subject to him."

5. It may be thought that death for the first transgression was a punishment altogether disproportioned to the offence. Weak men, in cases like the present one, are apt to confound law with the sanction of law, and to call that cruel and unjust which is only provident and indispensable. The questions in the case are What is the law? Is it just, or unjust? Does it minister essentially to the general good? If it does, it cannot be too well guarded. The next question is, Whether the appended sanction is the best in the case. When this is ascertained the matter is ended.

6. From all that has been written the reader will perceive that the condition of the human family is neither what it once was unstained uncorrupted by sin; nor is it so bad as it might have been, and indeed must have been, unless the mercy of God had interposed in our behalf. When we take a survey of the whole premises we feel that the honors and ease of the Paradisiacal state is no longer ours; the blessedness of standing in the presence of the God of the whole earth, and hearing his voice in the language of approbation and command is for ever denied to our family on this earth. But again, our condition is not wholly evil. It is not all temptation; it is not entirely composed of temptation, sin, and death. The fact is, we are prisoners respited, and by a gracious Providence are permitted to walk abroad on parole of honor; and a circumstance in this affair which exceedingly enhances the value of the divine clemency, is that the respite is granted us in view of a final reprieve; for it is the avowed design of God, by the gospel, to grant eternal life to as many as believe and obey it.

Being, in a state, which can neither be styled the best nor the worst, but one in the middle between the two, having in it much of good and much of evil, sin and righteousness, trial and temptation, happiness and misery, life and death, the ignorance of nature and false religion, the light of the gospel and the true faith, the rewards of heaven and the punishment of hell let us consider for a moment the means by which we are sustained in the midst of so many contradictories, so many counteracting and opposing influences.

7. In the first instance then, if we separate all these contradictories, we see that every good gift, life, knowledge, duty, happiness, faith, favor with all its blessings, comes down from above, from the Father of Lights, in whom there is no variableness nor the shadow of change. And that temptation, sin, guilty misery, and death are of that Wicked One, Satan, who is a sinner, from the beginning. Now while it is granted that we enjoy not the good gifts of God singly and apart from the evil things introduced by Satan, yet it is most certain, that in the very midst of those miseries we are allowed to possess them; and while by temptation, sin, and death, we are compelled to exclaim "O wretched man that I am," by the super-abounding mercy of God, we can exult and shout, "thanks be to God, who giveth us the victory through our Lord Jesus Christ." If the state of sin compels us to exclaim with the Psalmist "I was shapen and brought forth in iniquity and in sin did my mother conceive me." The state of righteousness by Jesus Christ enables us to add—we are washed, we are sanctified, we are justified, through the Spirit of our God, and by the name of Jesus our Lord.

8. We are, indeed, not admitted, to the indescribable honor of standing, like our First Parents, in the immediate presence of the Lord God, our adorable Heavenly Father, and of enjoying a sensible experience of his existence, but, praised be his name, we have a precious *Faith* in Him and in the name of his Son Jesus Christ; and if the ancients from Abel downwards accomplished glorious deeds, and rendered on this principle a lofty tribute of praise to the existence of the invisible God, may not we, who enjoy a super-abundance of revelation, if we are not permitted to see, yet "Walk as if seeing Him who is invisible?"

9. It is to be ascribed to the good mercy of our Heavenly Father that, though our state is really and truly changed from good to evil, from death to life—our nature, human nature, is still essentially the same. In Paradise it was as capable, if not as prone to sin. There it was both peaceable and fallible as facts prove; and if it did not die there, it was at least so constituted that even there it could die, and there indeed it actually did become mortal.

10. Again, the nature of our existence is still the same; that is, it is of an animal type. It is dependent on the external world, and has to prosecute a research into the things thereof on account of that dependence. This, however, is to be reckoned a blessing, for it requires all the force of a relation thus influential to cause us to become acquainted with the character and uses of things.

Blessed, therefore, be our God, who through Jesus Christ our Lord has brought to light a new species of life, life of a higher type, essential, independent, eternal. How desirable "The gift of God, which is eternal life through Jesus Christ our Lord!" How admirable a boon! How magnificent a favor! How royal a bounty! How god-like an endowment. O! let us magnify the name of our God through Jesus Christ. Let us sing praises to God and the Lamb as long as we live. God has delivered our souls from sin and our bodies from death. We will rejoice in his name. We will pursue peace. We will shake off all evil, and aspire to perfection, that we may "Behold the King in his beauty and the land that is afar off."

11. Like our First Parents, we also are gifted with a capacity for knowledge; and with a sense of duty; and no facts in their history show us that they excelled in these matters, if we except Adam's naming of the animals. If he seized upon some point in the external conformation of each, as it passed in review before him, a judgment of the highest order was unnecessary; but if in this affair he derived the style or name of the creature from its instincts, its actions, and its habits, or means of subsistence, then he must have been a man of admirable intellectual endowments and of vast compass of thought. We have seen, that it is probable they were one hundred years in Paradise; now their never having approached the tree of life during that long period, on account of its contiguity to the interdicted tree, which they were commanded neither to eat nor even touch, but having kept at a most devotional distance from both all that time, demonstrates that the tone of their moral feeling was lofty and excellent, and that they possessed the most exalted sense of duty to God their Creator.

Their descendants, however, by the lights of science and an ever accumulating literature, sustained and sanctified by the glorious and ever blessed gospel, are certainly in possession of the means, if they make use of them, of rising to an intellectual eminence not inferior to theirs, and of reaching a sense of duty not less chaste and devotional than that for which they were distinguished.

O! then, reader, turn to God. Search the scriptures. In them you have eternal life; and in them you will discover a knowledge, which surpasses finite inquiry. In them, also, you will see, unsealed your own duty, the things which our God requires of you through Jesus Christ.

We may say of the whole Bible what is said of a particular portion of it, "Blessed is he that readeth, and he that understandeth, and keepeth the sayings of this book." Amen. Salvation to our God, who sitteth upon the throne, and to the Lamb.

12. Our First Parents were gifted with a glorious capacity for happiness, and their joys, doubtless, were ample as the day, the bright, the autumnal day. But mark, O reader! the joys of the Christian are those of heaven itself, even the joys of the Holy Spirit, "which God has given," as saith the scripture, "to those who obey him." "Rejoice always," says the Apostle, "and again I say rejoice." It were impossible for men even though mortal seriously to believe in the things of Christianity without exulting, without rejoicing. Peter says, "In whom, though you see him not, yet believing on him, you rejoice with joy unspeakable and full of glory." Will the reader obey the gospel? Does he believe in the only Begotten Son of God? And will the great motives of eternal judgment and eternal life prompt him to immediate reformation? Does he believe and repent? Let him be baptized and he will be pardoned, and shall receive a new spirit, the spirit of Christ.

13. There is a difference between our First Parents and us in this respect, that they were under law; we are presented with the gospel. They were in danger of committing sin even in Paradise, we are invited to the pardon of sin even in our fallen estate, and are constantly and directly invited to receive the blessing of the Spirit through the faith.

14. In regard to trial and temptation the scriptures assure us that their condition was little different from our own. They were tried by God, and tempted by the devil. These things are also found in our lot. They persevered a while in rectitude, so do men now; and some even surmount the most violent temptations to evil, noble spirits, men like Joseph, Daniel and Job.

15. We have not in the present state the tree of life; but we have Jesus, who will reward our fidelity by yet granting us access "to the Tree of life, that grows in the midst of the Paradise of God," and by which we shall enjoy immortality; of a higher kind than the mere animal immortality, which would have been enjoyed by our ancestors had they eaten of the tree of life, which grew in the midst of the Paradise of Eden.

> Here's pardon here's peace, yes, here's more,
> Here's glory eternal at last.

16. In length of life the ancients and the primitive pair in particular greatly exceeded us, who live in these latter days; but if our life is shorter our knowledge is greater; as light increases the shadow shortens; and as

the world grows older it becomes both wiser and weaker. It was proud days for man when he lived almost a thousand years: but a short life and a good one is vastly to be preferred to a long and bad one; and the universal sentiment is "Let me die the death of the righteous and let my last end be like his." If a wish were wisdom the world would be crowded with wise men; but obedience alone is true wisdom. The best means for dying the death of the righteous is to live the life of the righteous. Practice self-denial, and mortification; no cross, no crown. He that would inherit all things must overcome all things; but he that will not contend against evil, must himself be slain by evil at last.

Reader, the Lord Jesus has said, "He that overcometh shall inherit all things." Would you then be deemed greater than Alexander and more worthy than Caesar, seek not with the latter to overcome the Gauls; weep not with the former for another world to conquer. Conquer yourself; and be assured of this, "That he who rules his own spirit is greater than he who taketh a city."

17. We have given one chapter on a plurality or succession of worlds, for this last is what we mean, and have observed that the earth is probably now in regard to fire what it was at the flood in regard to water, that is, as much of the waters of our globe were previous to the flood confined in vast subterraneous lakes, so now fire is treasured up in liquid floods under ground. Of this the many volcanoes and burning mountains in all quarters of the world, may be regarded as proof positive; for what are these craters but the vents or chimneys of those seas of fire which have been increasing in the bowels of the earth since the world began, and which are now in reserve against the day of judgment and perdition of ungodly men, "who shall be punished with an everlasting punishment from the presence of the Lord and from the glory of his power."

Europe, as the seat of bad government and corrupt religion, the seat of the hugely wicked empire of Rome and the still more hugely wicked Popedom of Rome, stands in a fearful predicament in regard to the second Advent of Messiah. Hekla in the north and Vesuvius and Ætna in the south, are perhaps the northern and southern vents to a lake of fire into which a vast proportion of that devoted country, whose soil is almost composed of human blood and human bones, will be plunged "to arise no more at all."

18. Our chapter on the Mosaic account of the creation expresses our sentiments of the grandeur of that illustrious fact and the simplicity and correctness of the record in regard to it.—When, the whole is taken in connexion with man, and the world and its innumerable tribes are regarded as his kingdom, we have a correct view of the creation and of the exalted rank of our own species.

In the beginning it stood fair and good in the eye even of its great Creator. There was neither sin, misery, nor death, till in an evil hour the Tempter came, and with him all these entered. The original empire fell. Adam with his whole animal dominion, beast, and bird, and fish, and reptile, after a short-lived existence, derived from the gracious respite of God, sunk, with all that had been put under his feet, into the ground whence he had been taken.

But a better dominion shall arise, or rather has arisen, under our Lord Jesus Christ; a kingdom that shall never end, which sin shall not pollute, and death shall not destroy, has began and will be perfected at the day of his Second Advent, when all things that give offence shall be removed, and the righteous shall shine forth in the kingdom of their Father like the stars forever and ever.

19. But we have seen the fate to which Satan is doomed. He is the first as he is greatest enemy of mankind, a murderer from the beginning, a liar, and the father of lies; when, therefore, he speaks lies he speaks of his own, as our Lord Jesus has said. He is destined to a horrible punishment, and will be damned for ever with all who yield to his suggestions or follow his example. But however dark damnation will be to him, it will prove ten-fold darker to men, from the recollection, that though not to Satan yet to them, were tendered pardon, salvation, and eternal life through a crucified Redeemer.

Do you then scorn God, O Reader? Do you cast in your lot with such as trample upon the blood of the cross and offer contempt to the Spirit of favor? Can you tempt the dangerous ocean of eternity apart from the company of the righteous, bearing along with you the intolerable burden of your own iniquities, the vengeance of an incensed God, and the fearful recollection of an insulted and despised Saviour? God have mercy upon your soul!

> Turn sinner, turn, why will you die?
> God your Maker asks you why;
> God who did your being give,
> Made you with himself to live.

It is with wicked men as it is with Satan; they wax worse and worse. He sinned first against God, then against God and man; and he will be doubly punished. He fell from heaven, ruined the world, and will be tortured in hades. He and all his are already informed of their fate; they believe and tremble. "Jesus," said they to our Lord while on earth, "we know thee who thou art, the holy one of God: Art thou come to destroy us before the time." Even they shrink from the fiery flood; they fear the boiling wave; already they hear the molten surges of penal fire, the billows roar and toss their heads on high, but they dash no shore to rest the feet of all whom they ingulf. It is perdition all, ruin and black despair.

For God's sake, O reader! for your own soul's salvation's sake, stop, bethink yourself, be wise to-day, delay not; to-day, if you will hear, believe, reform, obey, and be forgiven, "For now is the accepted time, and now is the day of salvation."

20. It is said of our First Parents, after they had sinned, that their eyes were opened. Now, reader, if this was the fact with them, be assured that it is the fact with all who obey the gospel. There is a glorious magic in the word of God—the magic of unalterable truth; and the eyes of all who obey him are opened to matters which previously were wholly hid from their eyes. Adam possibly promised himself an easy forgiveness; the antediluvians lightly esteemed the word of God by his servant Noah who preached to them. Pharaoh haughtily exclaimed, "Who is this Jehovah, that I should let Israel go?" And Israel themselves tempted him in the desert and questioned his word; but Adam and the antediluvians and Pharaoh and Israel discovered to their own fatal dismay that, however lightly they had esteemed God's word, there is no lightness with him. He means what he says. And if men obey the gospel their eyes are most assuredly opened to the propriety of the course which they have chosen to pursue; and if they do not obey it, their eyes will just as assuredly be opened finally to their own fatal mistake, the mistake of trifling with the word of so great a King as God, the Father of our Lord Jesus Christ.—Has he commanded men every where to believe in the name of his Son our Lord, to reform, and be immersed? There is no question of it. The faith, the gospel as it began to be preached at Jerusalem on the day of Pentecost, was to be preached in all the world. All then, who hear of the faith preached at Jerusalem, are bound to obey it in the form given to it there, for in no other was it to be preached to the world. Now it may seem a light matter to deviate from the primitive annunciation of the gospel by those who were inspired to speak it correctly; but all who are guilty of such a deviation, will doubtless, one day, have their eyes opened to the danger of their own unfortunate procedure. Reader, return to the primitive faith, the primitive church order, and the primitive morals of Christianity, and you will soon perceive the infinite propriety of the course which you have adopted.

Finally, it is the high office of revealed religion, to unscale the eye of man to matters of transcendent interest, to pour upon his sight the visions of creation, to convey to him the lofty intelligence of the divine origin of nature and of man, to redeem to him boundless regions of noble thought, and on her oracular page, spread forth before him the venerable form of long departed time, swift-winged time, here a moment and gone forever, like the bird of Jove stooping from the heavens to mock the glance of the eager artist, who would catch the flashings of his sun-bright eye, his regal plumage, his bright, his matchless form.

'Tis hers, also, to sweep from the arena of the mind the rubbish of a ruinous immorality, and with more than angels' joys to plant again the corner stone, and build thereon, a temple fair to God alone, to unseal the future, to steep our hopes in streams of life, to beckon away from meaner things than heaven bestows, to wash our eyes, to cleanse our hands, to cleanse our hearts, and bless our souls.

Hers also it is to bring us to the fountain of salvation, the church of Christ, and there to open to us the precious sources of holy communion with God. Like a fond mother the church takes us to her bosom and dandles us upon her knees. She feeds us upon the unadulterated milk of the word, causes us to grow, teaches us to walk, and to run in the good ways of God our Father, and when she has matured us in knowledge and strengthened us in the hope, perfected us in the love and confirmed us in the faith, and disciplined us in the obedience of the gospel she throws open before us a field wide as the world itself, saying "Hold forth the word of truth to all around." "Shine as lamps in the world."

We conclude upon the absolute necessity and the exceeding excellence of Revealed Religion. Without it we should have none of all those invaluable things which it offers to our faith; we should have no authoritative ritual by which to worship God; no hopes of a uniform system of morals all over the world; and no well defined faith respecting either the future or the past as regards eternal life.

Now to God, the Father of all mercies, the God of all grace, and to Jesus Christ our Lord, be present and everlasting honor and glory, Amen.

A DISCOURSE OF THE TRUE GOSPEL

SECTION SECOND–OF THE MESSIAHSHIP, OR THE PARTICULAR PROPOSITION OF CHRISTIANITY

"Behold my Son, the Beloved in whom I delight."

CHAPTER I

Introductory

The things of Christianity may be generalized and summed up under the three heads of "Faith," "Order," and "Morality." In such a division the first head, "The Faith," would include all the parts of our religion which are strictly evangelical. The second, namely, "The Order," would embrace whatever is ecclesiastical or belongs to the public order of the church. And the third, viz: "The Morality" of Christianity, would comprise the public and private morality and manners and customs enjoined upon its professors. The first part is intended to form or make men Christians; the second is to keep them such; and the third is intended to show what Christians are, or must become, in morals and in their public and private customs, if they would honor their profession and please God.

How important and consequently how desirable to walk and be perfect before the Lord Jesus in these, the great things of his Religion!

THE MORALITY OF CHRISTIANITY.—It commences in the heart; the lord Jesus regarded this as the fountain of evil, and said that "Out of the heart proceed evil thoughts, murders, adulteries, fornications, thefts, false-witness, blasphemy,—things which defile a man." He would, therefore, seal up the fountain, and dry up its streams by first drying up their source; he would cleanse the lips and the life by first cleansing the heart, or to cite his own figure, "first make the inside of the cup and platter clean and the outside will be clean also." In other words he purposes to purify the external powers of speech and action by first purifying that internal spirit in man, which sets these more obvious activities in operation.

His first lesson in morality, therefore, to us mortals who live in the present probationary state and are so prone to evil, is to cease to think evil, cease to indulge in vain imaginations and vain reasonings, to practise self-denial, a self-denial that shall extend itself to the very reins, to the thoughts and intentions of the heart. "If any man will come after me," said he, "let him deny himself and take up his cross and follow me; for whoever will save his life shall lose it; and whosoever will lose his life for my sake shall find it. For what is a man profited if he gain the whole world and lose his own soul? or what will a man give in exchange for his soul? for the Son of Man shall come in the glory of the Father and then he will reward every man according to his works."

ORDER OF THE CHURCH.—This is a department in the system of Christianity of vast importance, involving the interests of the whole world, Jews, Gentiles, and the Church of God. The public edification of the body of Christ depends immediately upon it, and even the very identification of the church herself as an institution distinct from all others; for now is she to be identified but by walking in the order and ordinances ordained for her during her hours of public service. Men may be known privately as professors of our religion by their faith; but if they would be recognized publicly as the church, they must adhere to the ordinances as they were delivered to that body at the beginning by the apostles of our Lord and Saviour.

But the order involves the safety and well-being of the world as well as the church, some of it having a direct bearing that way, as the prayers, supplications, intercessions, and giving of thanks which are ordered to be made for all men. Of this we may reason as follows, that as the loss of baptism would be, and has been, dangerous to the well-being of those for whom it was designed, namely, converts, and as the omission of the supper would be, and has been, unfortunate for those who have actually obeyed the gospel, so the omission of that part of our worship which is intended directly to affect the good of the Jews and Gentiles, must, by a parity of reasoning, prove equally unfortunate to those who are the subjects of those prayers.

THE FAITH.—Under this head, in said general division, would be embraced all the facts of Christianity, the things to be believed, the blessings to be received and enjoyed in submitting to the gospel, and the gospel itself in particular.

The following are some of the things to be believed, the last judgment, eternal life, and final punishment, the death, burial, resurrection, and ascension of Christ, his birth and ministry, and above all, that which forms the fundamental proposition of the whole religion, namely, that He is the Messiah the Son of God.

It will readily be perceived by the reader, that, if the proposition of the Messiahship forms the basis or foundation of our religion, it ought to be proved that it does; it ought to be shown that it is fundamental. There is a difference between the truth of a thing and its fundamentality; the question in regard to the first is to be referred to the proof; that concerning the second to the system; that is when we inquire into the truth of a proposition we examine the evidence; when we inquire into its fundamentality we examine the system; this we do for two reasons; first to find in what fundamentally consists, and second whether the proposition in question be clothed with the attributes of fundamentality. To illustrate in the case of a clock or watch, if it be inquired What is it that produces motion? The answer is, It is the power. In which of its parts is the power lodged? Ans. In the weight if it is a clock, and in the spring if it is a watch. Now here the attribute of fundamentality consists in the elasticity of the spring, and the inertia of the weight, by the superior powers of which, the weight and friction and resistance of all the other parts are overcome. In such an inquiry it is found that these parts are clothed with the article of fundamentality and that they are the moving power, without which the mechanism would cease to move; according to this illustration then, that is fundamental which is essential, or which cannot be dispensed with but at the peril of the system to which it belongs.

This is the character of the proposition, that Jesus is the Son of God, of which we come now to discourse, that is, it is essential to the Christian religion, to its authority; for if this could be proved false, all the rest might be true, but it would be without authority; for they are all published *prima facie* under cover of the fact, that the speaker of them is the Son of God. If Jesus is the Christ, though, the facts recorded of him might be true, yet the religion would be without power, for it is based on the truth of this matter viz: that he is the Son of God, which is the thing to be shown in this discourse; for, as has already been said, we write not on the truth of the Christian system, but only to show what that system is as it was delivered at the beginning. In the prosecution of our purpose we present the reader with the following.

CHAPTER II

The Recognition of Jesus by His Father

"Behold my Son, the Beloved in whom I delight."

The high importance of this oracle is to be inferred from the fact that the Divine Father in person delivered it. We shall perhaps bring our argument here within the grasp of the reader by observing that all the revelations found in our religion were not delivered by any single individual, whether it were apostle, prophet, evangelist, teacher, the Son of God himself, or the heavenly messengers. On the contrary all these, from the Son down to the simple prophet, have been employed as organs through which to communicate to man the will of the Creator. For instance Paul was the first, it may be affirmed, who imparted to the church the oracle, that Christians shall not all be dead at the second coming of the Redeemer, but shall be on the earth at that eventful era. "Behold," says he, "I show you a mystery, (a matter formerly unknown) we shall not all die, but we shall all be changed in a moment, in the twinkling of an eye, at the sound of the last trump; for the trumpet shall sound, and the dead shall be raised, and we shall be changed." Peter prophesied that another world shall succeed the present one, peopled by righteous men only. "For we look," said he, "for a new heavens and a new earth wherein dwelleth righteousness." And John foretold that the wicked should die a second death. "And death and hades," said he in the lofty style of symbolic vision, "were cast into the lake of fire; this is the second death; and whosoever was not found written in the book of life was cast into the lake of fire." Angels imparted the glad tidings of the immediate appearance of John the Baptist, and of the Lord Jesus Christ. And to Jesus himself was granted the distinguished honor of communicating to the world the most precious of all oracles intrusted to the care of God's messengers to mankind; that "God so loved the world as to give his only begotten Son, that whosoever believeth on him may not perish, but have eternal life." There was, however, an oracle, a divine oracle, that could with propriety be intrusted to no prophet, to no apostle, nor to the harbinger John, nor to angels, nor even to the Son himself, but required, from its eminently peculiar character and its vast importance, to be imparted to the world, by the great God himself. This was the proposition that Jesus, the Messiah, was his Son.

It rests with all fathers to acknowledge their own children; the first thing to be noted in this grand matter, therefore, is the decorum which distinguishes it. Any other person acting in so nice a case, would have destroyed the credibility of the proposition, human authority in an affair of so peculiar a nature being wholly inadmissible. It was unknown that God had a Son. It was unknown that any being sustained so intimate, so peculiar, a relation to the great Eternal; far less was it known that any Being clothed with flesh and blood and in the likeness and form of Man, stood in that relation to him. Necessity, therefore, as well as absolute propriety and decorum made it indispensable that God, who alone knew the secret, should himself reveal, or impart it to mankind. John the Baptist was ignorant of the existence of so high a relation subsisting between any man and God. "I knew him not." said he. And the Saviour himself observed on one occasion, that "No man knows who the Son is but the Father." And when Peter confessed the proposition in the presence of his colleagues, the Messiah reminded him of the peculiar channel through which he had derived his extraordinary illumination. "Flesh and blood hath not revealed this to thee," said he to

Peter, "but my father who is in heaven." As, therefore, God alone possessed the truth in this case and alone could reveal it, he did reveal it; he himself did make it known; and in those ever memorable terms imparted the saving mystery to mankind.

"Behold my Son, the Beloved, in whom I delight."

But, as was observed to a King, by one eminently skilled in our religion, this communication to the world was not "done in a corner," but in open day, and in the presence of innumerable witnesses, and before one in particular, chosen for the purpose, John the Baptist, a man celebrated for his integrity, godliness, and stern attachment to rectitude, and all the higher virtues of benevolence and truth.

It is well known that the Jewish nation continued for fifteen centuries, to serve God day and night, by the rites of their religion, in the hope of the Messiah's appearance. It is on the page of history also, both sacred and profane, Jewish and Roman, and mentioned by Josephus the Jew, and Suetonius the Roman, that in the days of Jesus, the nation expected their Messiah, Now this eager anxiety among all ranks, was but the workings of a traditional expectation handed down from father to child, and confirmed by the writings of their own prophets. At a moment, therefore, when expectation rose on tip-toe, John the Baptist appeared. The people were aroused; the public mind was concentrated on the person of this faithful man; the scattered and diffused hopes of the nation found a resting place for a moment and collected upon the Harbinger. "All men mused whether John were the Messiah."

The immersion by this servant of God gave things a still more focal complexity, and still further prepared the nation for the audience to which the case made it necessary they should be admitted. For he came, "preaching in the desert of Judea, and saying, Repent you, for the kingdom of heaven is at hand." This had the desired effect, and brought about the crisis; for all ranks went out to him at Jordan, "Jerusalem and all Judea, and all the region round about Jordan; and were baptized of him in Jordan, confessing their sins."

At a moment, therefore, foretold by the prophets, and much longed for by all the nation, when expectation was on tip-toe, and all the people were assembled, and had been baptized "It came to pass that Jesus also being baptized and praying, the heavens were opened: and the Holy Spirit descended like a dove upon him; and a voice came from heaven which said:

"Behold my Son, the Beloved, in whom I delight."

The scriptures, then, do not propose Jesus as the Son of God in a general and figurative, or a lax and undefined sense, but in the strictest and most literal apprehension of the terms; he is the Son of God, on the authority of his own Father. He is proposed to us as a Son on the recognizance of his own Father. This is proper; this is decorous; this renders the Christian religion unimpeachable in this important respect; and thus, if we believe him to be the Son of God, it is because this relationship was first of all acknowledged by God.

We are, therefore, led to the fundamentality of this proposition by the very fact of its peculiarity. Has God a Son? Does one clothed with flesh and blood and holding the human form, stand thus intimately related to the Deity? Does a man, as Son to the Great Eternal, share with him all the attributes of unlimited power, unlimited goodness, and omniscience?

But our argument is this, that the manifestation of the Deity at this time to Israel, for the purpose of introducing to the ancient nation his own Son, does, of itself, stamp the oracle delivered, with a divine importance. Such an appearance of the majesty of God, would be inadmissible at a crisis of only common interest; and could be admitted only on the occasion of originating an institution involving the highest interests of men.

But again, the argument is rounded and rendered doubly strong by another consideration, that this oracle of God's is the only one in Christianity communicated by the Father in person; for although we have in the sacred scriptures innumerable communications, on death, life, immortality, time and eternity, and reward and punishment, in all this abundance of revelation there is but a single oracle, a solitary proposition, uttered by God alone, namely, that Jesus Christ is his Son! Thus him, to whom God first gave the name of Jesus, (for parents name their own children) he finally recognized as his proper Son.

From the very peculiarity of the proposition, therefore, from the fact that it was originally enunciated by the Father in person, and that is the only oracle in our religion communicated by him, we infer its fundamental importance.

CHAPTER III

The Messiah's Person Identified with That of the Son of God by the Holy Spirit

Nothing that has come down to us concerning the Jews, afford us any warrant to believe, that they expected in the person of the Messiah one of such exalted quality as we have just seen our Lord Jesus recognized to be, the Son of God. They expected a Messiah nevertheless; and it was necessary, at his appearance, that first of all his person should be pointed out. This was done by the Holy Spirit, who descended upon him after his baptism in the presence of the whole nation, assembled at Jordan, as we hare just seen. Thus, Jesus was first declared as the Messiah and his quality described afterwards; he was first pointed out in person by the open and public descent of the Holy Spirit upon him, and afterwards recognized by the divine Father as his proper Son, as if one person should lay his hand upon another, for whom the public were in anxious waiting, and a third should step forward and say, Behold my Son. The Holy Spirit said, as it were, Behold the Messiah. The Father instantly exclaimed, Messiah is my Son.

Now the propriety of the Holy Spirit's pointing out to the Jewish nation the Christ, when he had come, is seen to be very great when considered in relation to the prophecies with which he had before inspired the holy prophets of that nation, concerning him. From the days of Adam down to Moses, and thence again to Malachi, and John the Baptist, the Holy Spirit had drawn out on the page of holy writ, by the ministration of pious men and prophets, an extensive chain of predictions respecting the appearance of this illustrious person, and of the immense benefits which would result to mankind from his ministrations. So that when the Holy Spirit descended upon the person of Messiah, it was not merely as if a person should lay his hand upon another, whom the public eagerly expected, but also as upon one whom he himself had repeatedly promised should appear for certain great specified purposes. The Divine Spirit, by the many predictions found in the Ancient Scriptures, had assumed the attitude of a voucher for the Messiah; that in his person and ministry certain great deeds should be accomplished by him. These predictions, filed in the Sacred Oracles of the Jewish nation, required to be redeemed, in order that the Spirit by which they were inspired, might be justified before the nation, and the world, as the Spirit of truth.

It had been foretold that Christ should be of Bethlehem, of the House of David, of the tribe of Judah, and of the seed of Abraham, The identification was of course to respect all these particulars; but beyond these there laid a series of prophecies depending for their fulfillment on the voluntary and active services of the Messiah, all of which required to be redeemed before the Spirit, by which the prophets of the Jewish nation spoke, could stand justified before the world and the nation, as the Spirit of truth, the Spirit of the true God.

The history of Jesus' descent and birth with their attendant circumstances, identified itself with the prophecies which related to the Messiah in these particulars; when he was attested at Jordan, therefore, it only remained for him to proceed in his public ministry; but how interesting the moment of his recognizance by the Spirit, and how exceedingly important that the Spirit should point out with great particularity the person who was to justify him in the many illustrious deeds which he had predicted concerning him!

The particular proposition of Christianity, then, is not merely that Jesus is the Messiah, but that he is the Messiah, the Son of God. Hence when John comes to sum up the evangelical testimony for the truth of the fundamental proposition of our religion, he does not say, these things are written that you may believe Jesus to be the Messiah merely, or the Son of God merely, but both the one and the other; not only the sent of the Father, but the Son of the Father also. "These things are written that you may believe that Jesus is the Christ, the Son of God."

The essential and fundamental importance of the proposition before us, therefore, is directly inferrable from the bearing which it has upon the character of the Holy Spirit; to impugn whose veracity, it is declared by the Redeemer, is to incur guilt of so heinous a nature, that it shall never be forgiven a man, neither in this world nor in the world to come.

Meanwhile we see, that as by the miraculous power of the Holy Spirit upon the Virgin, Jesus the son of God was originally begotten, so by the Holy Spirit he was publicly and fully attested as the Messiah of the Jews, and the Saviour of Mankind.

CHAPTER IV

The Vindication of His Divine Rank by Jesus Himself

Relationship to one's proper father is a pervading and proud idea in human society, and it was felt to be no less so by the Messiah, who most tenaciously maintained before his countrymen the relationship which God had publicly avowed. Indeed he would have died, and actually did die, rather than improperly surrender his title to that rank which was his due by the avowal of his Divine Father, made in the presence of the whole nation and of John the Baptist, a person of great dignity, of great gravity of manners, and the special witness chosen to give testimony to the certainty of this avowal. But was this to be wondered at? Let us make the case our own, and we shall better feel the argument. Suppose we had been the person attested by the Father as his Son, the beloved, in whom he delighted. Would we have lightly esteemed so sublime a recognizance, so glorious a rank? Would we, for any reason whatever, have tamely surrendered a dignity so essential, or even silently suffered our acknowledged connection with the Great Eternal, under this endearing relation, to be contradicted? No verily; verily no.

We can offer no greater dishonor to a man than violently to deny his relationship to the person, who has legitimately acknowledged himself his father. This was the abominable crime of which the Jews first of all were guilty. They, violently and in the face of God speaking to them from heaven, denied that Jesus was his Son, and dared, as scripture saith, to "make God a liar!" The Lord Jesus felt the insult, and told these presumptuous men emphatically, "You do dishonor me." John 8. The following passage on this point is clear and remarkable.

"If I honor myself, my honor is nothing; it is my Father who honoreth me, of whom you say that He is your God. Yet you have not known Him; and if I should say I know Him not, I should be a liar like yourselves; but I know him and keep his saying," namely, that he himself was his Son.

Thus it is seen that the Lord Jesus regarded this admirable oracle concerning himself, as lying at the bottom of the institution which he came to set up; and that the denial of it by his contemporaries, was as dishonoring to him, as it was insulting to God, and dangerous to themselves. "I go away," said he, "and you will seek me, and will die in your sins; whither I go you cannot come." John 8:21.

When, however, any of the Jewish nation recognized Jesus and confessed him to be the Son of God, his faith was always promptly approved and, in most instances, greatly rewarded. For example when John the Baptist bore testimony Jesus approved it, reminded the rulers of having sent to him on the subject, said to them that he was the shining and lighted lamp, and declared to the people generally, that a greater had never been born; and to his own disciples in particular, that he was the person spoken of in that famous prophecy, "Behold I send my messenger before thee who shall prepare thy way before thee;" and again in that other no less remarkable one, "Behold I send you an Elijah before the great and notable day of the Lord come; and he shall turn the hearts of fathers to their children, and the hearts of children to their fathers lest I come and smite the land with a curse." "This," said our Lord of John the Baptist, "is the Elias that was to come." When Nathaniel, the guileless Nathaniel, in transport, exclaimed "Rabbi, thou art the Son of God! thou art the King of Israel." Jesus declared he should yet be admitted to more illustrious visions, to sublimer proofs of the truth which he had believed and confessed. "I assure you, that hereafter you shall see the messengers of God ascending from and descending upon the son of man"—Perhaps, the Apostles and Evangelists going back and forward to Christ for instructions relative to the kingdom of heaven. When Peter confessed this truth the Lord pronounced him blessed; and at the same time advanced him to the primacy of the kingdom, giving him the keys thereof, and the honor of opening the door of the kingdom, first to the Jews and afterwards to the

Gentiles. When the man, whom Jesus had cured of blindness, confessed and adored him, He approved it, and said "For judgment am I come into this world, that they who see not may see, and that those who see may be made blind." Matthew and James and John, who admitted his Messiahship, and followed him at his single command, were afterwards rewarded for their faith and prompt obedience, by being advanced above his numerous disciples to the apostolic office. Finally, for the encouragement of all who had heard the Father's voice and learnt of him, that Jesus was his Son, the Redeemer declared, "Whoever confesses me before men, him will I confess before God and all the holy angels."

But if any one hesitated to confess what the overwhelming evidence of the Messiahship had compelled him to believe, his conduct received upon the spot a just reprobation. To those among the chief priests and rulers, who acted this base part, and believed in him without confessing him, he said "How can you believe in me who seek honor one of another?" For they loved the praise of men more than the praise of God. To such he declared generally, "Whoever is ashamed of me before this adulterous generation, of him will the Son of Man be ashamed, when he comes in his glory with all the holy angels."

Of demons he would accept of no confession. They knew him to be the Son of God; but he bound them over to silence; for he had not come to save but to destroy these infernals. "We know thee who thou art, Jesus thou Son of God; art thou come to destroy us before the time?" But these impure things, which, when they could no longer torment men, would destroy a herd of swine rather than not be employed in evil, were rebuked and suffered not to speak in a matter by which they were but to perish. While Christ would accept no testimony from demons he would give them none. Satan sought him to work a miracle by changing stones into bread, but he had come to convince the Devil of his divine relation to the Father by moral, not miraculous evidence, by courage and constancy, not by a display of miracle and magnificence. Adam had been foiled by lack of these virtues; Jesus was to overcome by the exercise of them; by faithfully and constantly maintaining the oracle of the Father. The devil was first to be conquered, and afterwards punished. He was first to be overcome by moral power and afterwards by physical power. The victory is won; we wait for his perdition.

What we have said might suffice to demonstrate the vast difference, which the Lord showed for that high attestation or public avowal of him which was tendered by the Father, before many witnesses at Jordan; but the reputation of our Lord, in all future ages, depended on the truth of it, and he determined, therefore, that men should receive or reject him on their belief or disbelief of this prime matter. He, therefore, built the church upon it, no person being to be received into his institution, but on the confession of it The following will probably set the matter in an attitude in which the reader will be able, both to see it, and lay hold of it as a direct argument for the primary importance of the proposition under consideration.

"When he came into the coasts of Caesarea, he asked his disciples, saying, who do men say that I the Son of Man am? And they said, some say that thou art John the Baptist; Some, Elias; and others Jeremias, or one of the prophets. But whom say ye that I am? And Simon Peter answered and said, thou art the Christ, the son of the Living God. And Jesus answered and said to him, blessed art thou, Simon Barjona; for flesh and blood hath not revealed this unto thee, but my father who is in heaven. And I say also to thee, thou art Peter, and upon this rock I will build my church, and the gates of Hades shall not prevail against it."— Matthew 16:13.

In this beautiful, interesting, and highly significant passage four things are particularly remarkable. First, the name Christ, Son of the living God, which Simon gives to Jesus. Second, the name Petros, stone, which Jesus gives to Simon. Third, the truth itself, which Simon confesses. And fourth, the word petra, rock, by which the Saviour, figuratively and in allusion to Simon's name, Petros, stone, designates this eternal truth which Peter had confessed; That Jesus was the Christ, the Son of the Living God. On this fact, then, his church is founded.

It is common with our Lord to reply in the same terms in which he is addressed, for instance the leper says "if you will." Jesus answers "I will." Thomas says "How can we know the way?" Jesus says, "I am the way." "Why do your disciples transgress?" "why do you also transgress?" says the Saviour. From want of attending to this practice of our Lord the vivacity of his reply to Simon is not felt, and the spirit of the passage, indeed, almost vanishes. "Thou art the Christ; and thou art the stone." The Lord Jesus was apt to speak in metaphor withal. He styles Herod a fox, his own body a temple, when in the temple; himself a vine when on Mount Olives among vines. He calls death a sleep; his own death a baptism, Simon a stone, *cephas*; and in the above passage the truth declared by God, that Jesus was his Son, he calls a rock, not Petros a stone, which was Peter's name, but *petra* a rock, a figure of the immovable proposition in Christianity, and used in allusion to Peter's name.

The Catholics not distinguishing between *Petros* and *petra* in the passage and confounding the figurative name of Simon, *stone*, with the figurative name of the truth, *rock*, take the one for the other, and pitch their church upon a mortal man, instead of the immortal truth. For while Peter said of himself, that he must shortly die; of the word of God, he said, "It liveth and abideth forever." And this is the word, which by the Gospel, is preached to us Gentiles, namely, that Jesus Christ is the Son of God. The gates of Hades have prevailed against Peter; but not against the truth which he confessed. Peter is dead; but the truth is still alive. Consequently the foundation of the true church stands sure. The foundation of the false church is a dead man, instead of a living Saviour, or a dead man's bones, Peter's relics, of which mother church boasts to this good hour; and it is a curious fact, that most of Catholic churches are in grave yards to this day. They even bury their dead within the very pale of their Cathedrals; as if corruption, which we have seen is the foundation of their establishment, were a thing to glory in. This is not unfrequently the practice of Protestants also, who too often bury their dead around their places of worship, as if the foundation of their church where yet in the sepulcher; or as if the mother of harlots were worthy to be imitated in so holy a custom.

But again, the Papists are at fault in this also; they suppose that the Son, and not the Father, founded the church. Jesus built the church, but he did not lay the foundation thereof; for then he would have laid himself; for he himself is the foundation of it, the person of whom the fundamental truth is asserted, "Behold my Son, the Beloved." God the Father, therefore, founded the church. Both Peter and Paul take notice of this, "Other foundation can no man lay, said the latter, (for a particular church as at Corinth) than that which is laid, (by the Father at Jordan for all churches,) which is Jesus Christ." Peter writes thus. "To whom coming as to a living stone, rejected indeed of men, but chosen of God and honorable." Again, "Behold I lay in Zion a stone, a tried corner stone, elect, precious, and they that trust on him shall not be ashamed." Those who trust in Peter have the greatest reason to be ashamed, for the good man is dead; but here is a foundation stone, which Peter, in the above scripture, says is alive. Or as Paul says in another scripture, "It is testified that he liveth."

When the Lord Jesus was called to defend his pretensions publicly before the Sanhedrim, he reminded them of this. "Did you never hear His, the Father's voice or see his form? Or have you forgotten his declaration, (namely, that Jesus was his Son,) that ye believe not him whom he hath sent forth?" The force of this passage is not felt in our common translation. On this occasion the Lord Jesus was defending the divinity of his mission, before the national senate, and for thus purpose appealed to the different particular evidences by which his mission was sustained; these are in number five.

1. His own open avowal and frank acknowledgment of it.
2. The testimony of John, whom they believed to be a prophet.

3. The marvelous works which he was empowered to perform.
4. The recognizance of him by the Father at Jordan.
5. The testimony of their own scriptures.

The whole passage is inimitable for the force of its argument and the natural simplicity of its diction.

In the new translation it reads as follows.

"If I alone testify of myself, my testimony is not to be regarded: there is another who testifies of me; and I know his testimony of me ought to be regarded. You, yourselves, sent to John and he bore testimony to the truth. As for me, I need no human testimony; I only urge this for your salvation. He was the blazing and shining lamp; and for a while you were glad to enjoy his light."

"But I have greater testimony than that of John; for the works which the Father has empowered me to perform, the works themselves which I do, testify for me that the Father has sent me. Nay, the Father, who sent me, has himself attested me. Did you never hear his voice, or see his form? Or have you forgotten his declaration, that you believe not him whom he has sent forth.

You search the scriptures because you think to obtain, by them, eternal life. Now these also are witnesses for me; yet you will not come to me that you may obtain life." John 5.

If, in the examination of testimony, there is any force in facts, the passage just cited must commend itself to the enlightened reason of every competent enquirer into the truth and divinity of Christianity. The particular use, however, to which we desire to apply it is, that the reader may see, that Jesus set the highest estimate upon it as matter of fact that the Divine Father had himself attested him publicly at his baptism in the river Jordan. The Jewish senate also, before whom he spoke, knew this; and therefore it was, that he appealed to them thus, "Did you never hear his voice, or see his form?"

But it was at the close of his ministry, that our Lord Jesus gave the highest and most sublime of all proofs of his reverence for the oracle which the Father had announced concerning him. He died because he said he was the Son of God; and he died thus in honor of the Father, who had acknowledged the relation, I honor my Father, said he on one occasion. He maintained in life and in death the great proposition on the truth of which, in future ages, depended, with all mankind, his claims to legitimacy, and glorified his Father upon the earth, by not shrinking from, but actively vouching in public, the divine veracity in regard to this cardinal point. The author of our religion fell a victim to the fury of those who gave God the lie and denied the proposition on which he had founded our religion; but at the same time he became the first martyr to the truth of Christianity, the King of martyrs. The truth of God is, therefore, further sanctified by the blood of his own Son. At the time when he was about to give this last notable and noble proof of his high attachment to the saying of his Father, he said to the contemptible Pilate, who, in violation of the laws both of God and man and contrary to the dictates of his own conscience, signed his warrant for crucifixion, "To this end was I born and for this cause came I into the world, *that I should give testimony to the truth.*" Our Lord is, therefore, styled, by way of eminence. "The faithful and true witness." Rev. He vouched the veracity of the Father unto the death.

"And the Lord turned round and looked upon Peter. And Peter remembered the word of the Lord, how he said to him, Before the cock crow, thou shalt deny me thrice; and Peter went out and wept bitterly. And they led Jesus away to the High Priest; and with him were assembled all the Chief Priests and Elders, and the Scribes. And Peter followed him afar off, even into the palace of the High Priest, and he sat down with the servants and warmed himself at the fire; and the Chief Priests and all the Council sought for testimony against him, but their witness agreed not together. And there stood up certain and bare false testimony against him, saying: We heard him say, I will destroy this temple that is made with hands, and within three days will build another made without hands; but neither did their testimony agree together. And the High Priest arose in the midst and asked Jesus, saying, Answerest thou nothing? What do these testify against thee? But he held his peace, and answered nothing. Again the High Priest asked him and said, Art thou the Messiah, the Son of the Blessed? And Jesus said, I am: and you will see the Son of Man sitting on the right hand of power, and coming in the clouds of heaven. Then the High Priest rent his clothes and said, What need have we of any further testimony? You have heard the blasphemy. What is your decision? And they all condemned him to be worthy of death."

For a son, by cowardice or inconstancy, to set his own father in the attitude of a liar, is degeneracy in the extreme. This was far from being the case of our blessed and adorable Lord, whose courage ever supported him in the maintenance of the truth dangerous as it was; and whose constancy, in this matter, never forsook him even at the moment when the confession of it was to issue in the most severe death, crucifixion. For it is evident both from his last trial before the High Priest, and what was said by his cruel enemies, while he hung upon the cross, that he died, as we have already asserted, because he confessed that be was the Son of God.

"They that passed by reviled him, wagging their heads, and saying, thou that destroyest the temple, and buildest it in three days, save thyself. If thou be the Son of God come down from the cross. The Chief Priests, and Scribes, and Elders, also mocking said, he saved others, himself he cannot save. If he be the King of Israel, let him come down from the cross and we will believe on him. He trusted in God; let him deliver him, for he said I am the Son of God. The thieves, also, who were crucified with him, cast the same in his teeth. The centurion and the Roman guard also said, Truly this was the Son of God."

But Jesus, as compassionate and forgiving as he was courageous and constants prayed "Father forgive them, for they know not what they do." Finally, he died with the word father upon his lips, leaving to his followers a most animating example of confidence in God to death, as he had become to them the purest model of courage in maintaining the truth through life.

From the time, therefore, at which, in the presence of John the Baptist and the Jews assembled at Jordan, the Father attested him as his Son, from his temptation in the wilderness till his trial and his last breath upon the cross, he suffered not the glorious oracle to depart from before his eyes. He kept the saying of the Father, till, in one last convulsive agony, he cried with a loud voice, "Father, into thy hands I commend my spirit; and having said thus, he surrendered up his spirit," leaving behind him in his death the most unequivocal testimony to the fundamental importance of that great truth for which he died, namely, that he was the Messiah, the Son of the Blessed God.

CHAPTER V

Testimony of John the Baptist to the Recognition and Identification
of the Messiah

John Baptist said that he had come in order that the Messiah, who then had come also and was existing in the nation unknown and unattested, might be made manifest to Israel. But this does not import, that John was appointed to give an original attestation of him; for this he could not do inasmuch as he was himself ignorant of him. The recognition of him as the Son of God by the Father and the identification of his person with that of the Messiah's by the Holy Spirit, could not be done by proxy, but called for the immediate presence of the Deity.

"As for me I knew him not," said John; "but that he might be made manifest to Israel, I am come immersing in water. Further, I saw the Spirit descending from heaven like a dove, and remaining upon him. For my part, I should not have known him, had not he, who sent me to immerse in water, told me, Upon whom you shall see the spirit descending and remaining the same is he, who immerses in the Holy Spirit. Having therefore, seen this, I testify, that he is the Son of God.—John 7.

This proves evidently that, like Jesus, John conceived the public attestation of Messiah by the Father, to lie at the root of the whole matter, to be essential in our religion. It demonstrates also, that, while John's mission respected the public appearance of Messiah, he, nevertheless, understood perfectly that he himself was merely a witness, and that his ministry did not reach so high as to give an original attestation to the Christ, but only to declare what he had heard and seen in relation to him. He perceived that the proposition of the New Institution was of God; and on this fundamental thought, projected on one occasion, a bold but just argument; that he, who rejected the mission of Jesus, made God a liar; and that he, who recognized his mission, attested the Divine veracity.

"Now John's disciples had a dispute with a Jew about purification. Then they went to John and said to him, Rabbi, he who was with you near the Jordan, of whom you gave so great a character; he too immerses, and the people flock to him. John answered, A man can have no power but what he derives from heaven. You yourselves are witnesses for me, that I said, I am not the Messiah, but am sent before him. The Bridegroom is he, who hath the bride, but the friend of the bridegroom, who assists him, rejoices to hear the bridegroom's voice: thus my joy is complete. He must increase; while I decrease. He who comes from above is above all. He who is of the earth is earthy, and speaks as being of the earth. He who comes from heaven is above all. What he testifies is what he has seen and heard; yet his testimony is not received. He who receives his testimony vouches the veracity of God. For he whom God has commissioned relates God's words, for to him God gives not the spirit by measure. The Father loves the Son, and has subjected all things to him. He who believes on the Son has life eternal; he who rejects the Son, shall not see life; but the vengeance of God awaits him."—John 5.

Thus John made the Christian proposition of the Messiahship a question of fact between God and man, and showed that he apprehended the new religion to rest on an oracle having God for its exclusive author.

The relation, which this great man's ministry bears to the Messiahship, was, nevertheless, most interesting and direct. He was born and sent forth to give testimony to the truth; he was selected from among all his countrymen as a special witness to be present at Jordan to see, to hear, and rehearse that which was to save the world, that which was to form the subject of belief with all mankind.

Jesus our Lord excepted, John the Baptist was the person most of all looked at by the ancient prophets of his own nation. First, the Psalmist of Israel describes him under the figure of a lamp which God was to light to lead the nation to the Son of David, thus—"I have ordained a lamp for mine Anointed."—Psalms 132:17. To this it is probable our Lord alluded when he said of John, before the national senate, that "He was the blazing and shining lamp."—John 5.

The next prophet, who spoke of the Baptist, was Isaiah. In the fortieth chapter of his prophecies he enjoins on the Priests, the teachers of the nation, to comfort God's people, and the city of Jerusalem, in particular, which had now accomplished the great purpose for which she had been preferred to other Capitals, and he adds as descriptive of the Harbinger of Messiah the following prediction:

"The voice of one proclaiming in the wilderness, prepare the way of the Lord, make for him a straight passage. Let every valley be filled, and every mountain and hill he leveled; let the crooked roads be made straight, and the rough ways smooth, that all flesh may see the Saviour sent of God."

Finally, Malachi, the last of the Jewish prophets, delivered two predictions concerning the same personage. In the first, "Behold I will send my Angel before thee, who shall prepare thy way," he describes him as an angel preceding the Messiah; and in the last, as an Elijah come to prepare the nation to receive the august one by whom he was to be quickly followed.

"Behold," he exclaims, "I will send you an Elijah. the prophet before the great and dreadful day of the Lord; and he shall turn the heart of the fathers to the children., and the heart of the children to the fathers, lest I come and smite the land with a curse."

Both these prophecies are applied to the Baptist by the Lord Jesus. John's father also, Zacharias, applies the first of them to him,—thus, "And thou, child (John) shall be called a prophet of the Most High; for thou shalt go before the Lord to prepare his way." The last of these prophecies was again employed relative to the Baptist by the angel, who announced his birth. "Moreover, he shall go before him in the spirit and power of Elias to reconcile fathers to their children, and, by the wisdom of the righteous, to render the disobedient a people well disposed for the Lord."

Thus John the Baptist was spoken of four times by three prophets. In the first prediction he is described as a blazing lamp in his own nation leading the people to the Anointed of Jehovah. In the second his public appearance in the wilderness or desert part of Judea, is noticed; and in the third he is spoken of as an Elijah, and even an angel preceding Jehovah's Anointed. These prophecies are both appropriated by the Baptist himself, and applied to him by the highest authority, Gabriel, God's messenger, and Jesus, God's Son.

The purposes of John's mission were two. First, he was to prepare the people to receive in a becoming manner, the king Messiah. Second, he was, after his attestation at Jordan, to bring those people to the king Messiah. And that all jars and party animosities and sectarian feelings might be quashed, and the nation brought to a level on which they could receive Messiah and love one another, he proclaimed, by the authority of heaven, "the baptism of repentance for the remission of sins." Those who refused to yield obedience are charged with having rejected the good designs of God in regard to themselves, while those of any rank in society, who followed John, are regarded as those alone who would meet the Messiah in his kingdom.

John was eminently distinguished for honor and integrity. In the midst of his own popularity he forgot not the designs of his mission; when the whole land from Dan to Beersheba flocked to him at Jordan, and "all men mused in their hearts whether he were the Messiah," and when even the great men of Jerusalem sent a deputation of Priests and Levites on the question of his public ministrations, he honorably confessed and denied not, saying, "I am not the Messiah." And that the end of his mission might obtain, and all flesh see the Savior sent of God, he raised his hand towards our Lord Jesus and exclaimed, to the illumination of all present and the conversion of two of his own disciples, who immediately followed Jesus, "Behold the Lamb of God, who taketh away the sins of the world." This good and great man finally fell a victim to his own official fidelity in the well-remembered case of Herod, whom he hesitated not, with his usual integrity, to rebuke.

Can we, then, suppose, that this honorable individual stooped to imposture in the scatter of the Messiahship? and that what he said he saw and heard at Jordan, was false? No, such an idea is to be rejected with scorn. He was selected from his birth as a man possessing the qualities of a faithful and true witness; and, therefore, correctly reported what he heard and saw.

Our argument then is this, that the fact of John's being chosen to give testimony to his own nation concerning the proposition under consideration, clothes it with essentiality; and we are constrained to believe it to be fundamental in our religion, till it is proved that all this prophecy, the visitation of angels and the testimony of Jesus can respect a matter of inferior importance.

We add, that, if the first appearance of Messiah called for reformation, what manner of life ought those to live, who look for his second advent!

CHAPTER VI

Moses and Elias and the Messiah

Moses and John the Baptist were like the *alpha* and the *omega* of the Law, the first and the last of that institution. It was given by the one and concluded by the other. "For" as the scriptures says "the law was till John," when the kingdom of heaven was preached. This great man, John the Baptist, stood up, the angel of two worlds, the ancient and the modern, or of two ages the Jewish and the Christian. When he raised his voice backwards, the temple, the priesthood, the law and the prophets fell from their supremacy, and lost their authority as a distinct system of religion. When he poured his voice forward into the future, a new people arose, with a new experience, new rights, a new name, and new honors; Messiah himself appeared, and came up from among the people; and with him the great Apostles of the new reign; and faith, and hope and love. Christians took the place of Jews, the gospel that of the law, and faith the place of flesh; good principle was substituted for hereditary descent, and the obedience of faith for national pride. Great was the day, the subject great, the personages great. "Verily I tell you," said our Lord, "of those who have been born of women, there has not arisen a greater than John the Baptist." Great, therefore, as Moses was, the Baptist was his superior, even as he who rescinds laws is superior to him who makes them; or as the person who hears the voice of God for the world, is greater than he who hears it only for a single nation. In this respect John must be considered greater than all men; who preceded him. Yet he was less than the least in the kingdom of heaven, even as a child born into a king's family, is greater in that family than the attendant physician, notwithstanding the eminent and peculiar offices to which he is admitted.

But it is Moses chiefly of whom we desire to speak. He was a great and honorable servant of the Most High, and ministered in a variety of ways to the introduction of the Christian Religion. In relation to the Messiah he spoke the following luminous prediction, which is applied by Peter to the Lord Jesus, in his address in the temple.

"A prophet like me, shall the Lord your God raise up for you, from among your brethren; him shall you obey in all things whatsoever he shall say to you; and it shall come to pass, that every soul, that will not obey that prophet, shall be cut off from among the people."

Here Moses foretells that disobedience to the Messiah should be punished by excision from the congregation of the Lord. But disobedience pre-supposes disbelief; and if it be inquired, what it was the Jews disbelieved, the answer is, that they disbelieved the oracle of the Father concerning the Redeemer. "Had you believed Moses," said our Lord to them, "you would have believed me, for he wrote of me; but if you believe not his writings, how shall you believe my words?" The Jews, then, rejected even the testimony of Moses to the great proposition, and consequently suffered the excision denounced against them by their own lawgiver; all which demonstrates that what they rejected was fundamental in Christianity.

There is something very extraordinary in the fact, that Moses accompanied by Elias, should have appeared on the mount during the transfiguration of the Lord Jesus, and that the oracle announced at Jordan should have been repeated in their presence during this private occurrence.

"After six days Jesus took Peter, and James, and John, brother of James, apart to the top of a high mountain, and was transfigured before them. His face shown as the sun; and his raiment became white as light. And presently appeared to them Moses and Elias conversing with him. Peter upon this addressing Jesus said, Master it is good for us to stay here; let us make here, if you will, three tents, one for thee, one for Moses, and one for Elias. While he was speaking, behold a bright cloud covered them, and out of the cloud a voice came which said, This is my Son, the Beloved, in whom I delight; hear him. The disciples hearing this fell on their faces, and were greatly frightened; but Jesus came and touched them, saying arise; be not afraid. Then, lifting up their eyes they saw none but Jesus."

Some commentators think that Elijah in this passage means John the Baptist; but to me this is by no means probable; for while John is styled an Elijah and the Elijah which was to come, he is no where in scripture called Elijah only, as if this were literally his name. Metaphorically we say of a meek man he is a Moses, and of a wise man he is a Solomon, and of a strong man he is a Samson; but we do not call them Moses, or Daniel, or Samson, unless these are literally their names. This is the nature of the case here; the person in the passage is called Elijah only, which would not have been done, unless it had actually been Elijah, the ancient prophet known by that name.

The glory of the whole scene must have been exceedingly grand; and it becomes the more remarkable, that the whole should have been withdrawn in a manner and at such a time as to leave upon the minds of the disciples the divine communication, "Behold my Son! the Beloved, in whom I delight." But the disciples were Jews, and had been accustomed to hear Moses and the prophets in religion; the words "hear him," were therefore, added. At the utterance of this, the author of the Law and the prince of the prophets, Moses and Elijah, withdrew their persons, as the moon and the stars hide their diminished heads before the rising glory of the sun.

This private attestation of the Son of God was duly appreciated by the three disciples in whose presence it took place.—Accordingly Peter speaks of it as a fact confirmatory of all the former predictions relative to the Messiah; but this he does wisely only to the disciples or brethren, who having tasted of the divine excellence of our Religion, were prepared to listen to whatever could in truth be spoken in favor of its divine origin.

"For we have not followed cunningly devised fables when we made known to you the power and coming of our Lord Jesus Christ, but were eye-witnesses of his grandeur; for when he received of God the Father, honor and glory, a voice to this effect came to him from the magnificent glory, This is my Son, the Beloved, in whom I delight." ii Peter 2.

Thus to John the Baptist and Moses and Elias, who lived and died Jews, we have added other three witnesses, Peter, James, and John, who lived and died Christians; so that we have the flower, the glory of both economies., the law and the gospel, bearing testimony to the truth and primary importance of the great proposition in handling.

Be it observed, however, that this private recognition of the Son of God, is not the point we are laboring; that which is before us, is that higher and more public, and original and more ancient attestation, which, at Jordan, in the presence of the nation assembled, vouched Jesus to be the Son of God and their Messiah.

CHAPTER VII

The Proposition Considered in Relation to Adam

When we contemplate the proposition of our Religion in connection with the Father of Mankind, the matter of it is to be considered chiefly. Adam was possessed of an animal, and consequently a temporary existence only, and forfeited even that,—When this is duly reflected upon in connection with the wants of man, the mind is necessarily led to a conclusion like that which forms the proposition of our religion; that in some splendid personage God would manifest life of a higher type, eternal life. "We show unto you" says the apostle John, "that eternal life which was with the Father, and which was manifested unto us," viz: in the person of Jesus. In the matter of the Christian creed, then, there is something exceedingly promising, "Behold my Son."

Adam, to be sure, was styled son of God; but this was because he was created by God, and made in his own image, a being capable of knowledge, duty, and happiness. The Lord Jesus, however, is called the Son of God because he was begotten by God, and consequently because of his essential nature, having in him the life and essence of the Divine Father, from whom he descended, for it is a law in the universe, that "like begets like." And thus, if the world has sunk to perdition by one styled son of God on account of his creation; there is something exceedingly proper in the restoration of the world by a personage called the Son of God on account of his original and essential nature.

Adam and Jesus are contrasted thus by the Apostle Paul.

"The first man, Adam, was made a living soul—the last Adam, a vivifying spirit. However, that was not first which was spiritual, but that which is animal, and afterwards that which is spiritual. The first man from the earth, was earthy; the second man is the Lord from heaven. As was the earthy so also are the earthy; and as is the heavenly so also shall be the heavenly. For as we have borne the image of the earthy, we shall also bear the image of the heavenly."—1 Cor. 15.

The violation of the divine law by Adam, implied the transcendant nature of him who was to honor that law. Law is not magnified by substituting the less for the greater, the unjust for the just, or the guilty for the innocent; but in such a case the greater must take the place of the less, the just be substituted for the unjust, and the innocent for the guilty. The proposition, therefore, which respects the identification of him, who is greater than Adam, yes "greater than all," must be important, must be essential.

CHAPTER VIII

The Proposition Considered Relative to Angels

Although it would have been indecorous and improper for an angel to have introduced Jesus to mankind as the Messiah and the Son of God; yet it was perfectly admissible that one should announce his nativity and his conception. Accordingly that pure, elevated, and grave messenger of the Most High, the angel Gabriel, was sent by God to declare his nativity, his conception, and his name. To Joseph he said, "Thou shall call his name Jesus, because he shall save his people from their sins;" but to Mary he said "The holy progeny shall be called the Son of God."

Angels have manifested the greatest interest in our salvation by Jesus Christ. The same Gabriel appeared to Daniel of old to instruct him in things relative to the appearance of Messiah the Prince, and noted the precise time at which he was to "be cut off but not for himself." Peter says of the angels in general that they desire "to look narrowly" into the things of our salvation. It is probable, therefore, that they do themselves derive some substantial benefit through Christ, deliverance, perhaps, from their grand enemy the apostate seraph. But whether they are subjected to the Lord Jesus on this account, is not so evident. The apostle predicates their homage to him on his superior nature, being the Son of God, and consequently the heir of all things. But, if as heir of the creation, the Holy Spirit it put in subjection to him, as he himself is to the Father, no wonder if the angels are made obedient to him. "Let all the angels of God do him homage." Heb. 1.

When the Holy Spirit was given to Jesus by the Father he poured him forth into the hearts of those who were to worship the Father, that their faith and works might be sanctified by this holy unction, and that the whole church might be "a temple of God through the Spirit." When the angels were subjected to him he did not grant to them what had been awarded the Holy Spirit in redemption, the sanctifying of the believers in mind and person; but he appointed them to minister to the heirs of salvation externally; he gave them an outward charge.

Having announced the conception, birth, and name of the Messiah, having ministered to him at his temptation in the wilderness, and his agony in the garden, they were the first at his tomb; whence they rolled away the stone. They attended him also to heaven.

> They brought his chariot from above
> To bear him to his throne;
> And with a shout exulting cried
> The glorious work is done.

The argument here is this, that the subjugation of the angels to Jesus being predicated on the fact, that he is the Son of God, it follows that his recognition by the Father must have been essential to them; but if essential to them, how much more to man!

The moral of the whole is, that if angels who excel in power and dignity subject themselves to God's Son, how reasonable, how indispensable that men promptly follow their example and yield themselves voluntary sacrifices to him, who has purchased them with his precious blood! With what infinite dismay will the disobedient behold their Saviour, when he comes attended by all the bright retinue of heaven "to be glorified of his saints and admired by all them who believe."

CHAPTER IX

The Proposition as Related to Satan

We shall now look at the Christian proposition with a reference to the great enemy of mankind, Satan. Man's inexperience, inconstancy, and undue attachment to a sublimer knowledge than was suited to his nature, for as we have seen misery is preternatural to man, made him fall a victim to the temptation of the ruined archangel. He eat and was afraid, his eyes were opened, and he was covered with shame. He hid himself from the face of his Maker, for whom he had showed so short-lived a fidelity, was rebuked, doomed by painful and fruitless toil to earn a scanty subsistence from the earth now accursed for his sake, separated from the tree of life, expelled the blessed paradise of God, and denied all sensible communion with the divine Father, till under the accumulated and intolerable burden of his iniquities and miseries he yielded to the influence of age and infirmity and, in accordance with the righteous judgment of God, sunk into the dust whence he had been taken. Alas! alas! for the lord of the world, the great sire of mankind, the King of men. Behold him stretched in death, his righteousness gone, his beauty changed to ashes, his sovereignty cut short, his crown faded from his brows, his sceptre wrested from his powerless grasp, his empire in arms, and none to avenge his cause.—All this, too, the result of malice, deadly malice; envy, black envy; fiendish envy, fiendish malice. Well did it become the God of heaven, when addressing Satan under the appropriate emblem of a serpent, to say to him "Because thou hast done this thou art cursed above all cattle, and above every beast of the field; upon thy belly shalt thou go and dust shalt thou eat all the days of thy life; and I will put enmity between thee and the woman, and between thy seed and her seed; it shall bruise thy head, and thou shalt bruise his heel."

It is certainly a fact in revealed religion, that the human family is in a preternatural condition. It is another fact, that this preternatural condition is the effect of the violation of law; and it is a third fact, that into this violation of law the original ancestors of mankind were seduced by a fallen seraph, styled, in scripture, Devil, and Satan, and figuratively lion, serpent, and so forth. Those figurative names convey to us the ideas at once, both of his intelligence and superior strength. The scriptures, therefore, reason concerning him that he is not to be put down by an inferior agent. "How can one enter a strong man's house and spoil his goods," said our adorable Lord when speaking of him, "except he first bind the strong man, and then he will spoil his house." In the original prophecy concerning him, therefore, that the woman's son should bruise him, it was, of course, implied that that son should be endowed with superior power, and superior intelligence. Eve, at the birth of her first son, seems to have thought, that in his person she had received the avenger of her wrongs referred to in the denunciation of her diabolical seducer. She called him Cain or triumph, and exclaimed, "I have gotten the man from Jehovah." But in this she was woefully mistaken. Her son was distinguished from her adversary only by his physical inferiority, he was weaker, but not less wicked; for he slew his brother, and, like the devil, became a murderer also! "And wherefore slew he him?" enquires an Apostle, "Because his own works were wicked, and his brother's righteous."

To overcome our adversary, therefore, the exigencies of the case called for a greater, and better, and wiser, than Cain; wiser, that he might know what had been done, and what ought now to be done; better, that he might apply himself faithfully and constantly to the doing of it; and greater that he might possess all the powers requisite for doing it. In brief, two things required to be accomplished. First, sin required to be abolished; secondly, the Devil was to be destroyed. The Christian religion, therefore, proposes the accomplishment of both of these by Jesus Christ; and for these reasons presents him for our faith. The devil and his works, then, are to destroyed; these by moral means or the gospel, and himself in person by a stronger than he, Jesus the woman's seed, or son. When we put our foot upon a serpent's head, it is only that we may destroy him by our superior power; so that that part of the original and prophetic denunciation which threatened the bruising of his head, fairly implied that the woman's son was to be endowed with a force superior to that of his mighty and dangerous antagonist. Righteousness, therefore, will destroy sin, the righteous one will destroy the sinner, namely, Satan, whom the Son of Man will meet prepared for that mighty and dreadful trial of personal strength, which will take place on that day, when the Devil will be taken and cast into that great lake of fire, with all who have refused to acknowledge God and obey the gospel of our Lord Jesus Christ.

Now in putting down Satan and his works by these two classes of means, moral and physical, Jesus only employs the powers which have been employed against himself by his subtle and powerful enemy. The first was used at his temptation in the wilderness; the last at his death on Mount Calvary. In the first he would have made him a sinner; in the last he murdered him, and Jesus for great purposes permitted it.

It must be acknowledged by every one who reflects on the affairs of the Jews and the popular prejudices of these people at the appearing of Christ, that it called for no inferior degree of confidence, in any being wearing the human form, to assert, even in conformity with the oracle of the Father, that he was the Son of the Eternal. And we know that no just man, no man fearing God could possibly presume to sustain so august and dangerous a proposition, if it were false. But even if true, it must be seen, that nothing but fidelity of the purest and sublimest kind, could support a being in human form while sustaining it. For what had such a person to expect of his contemporaries and countrymen, but that they would hold him to be a madman or possessed? The very idea of the fatal abuse and insult, that must necessary follow the re-assertion of the fact announced, must have operated on the mind of the person attested with the most tremendous effect. A being inferior to the Son of God must, we think, have chosen to be silent on the subject rather than incur the odium unavoidable to such high pretensions. In conformity with all rational anticipation the Jews, therefore, were inflamed to madness, by the claims of our Lord Jesus, and burst out in these impassioned interrogatories "Whom makest thou thyself?" "Say we not well, that thou are mad and hast a devil?" "For a good work we stone thee not; but because thou being a man makest thyself equal with God." "He is worthy of death." What but truth and the sternest possible attachment to it, could possibly have borne up a just man's soul under reproaches like these? Nothing. And the devil, aware of the difficulty and delicacy of the case, pitches his diabolical temptation upon this overwhelmingly interesting point, our Lord's legitimacy. "If thou be the Son of God." Satan, therefore, was the first to suggest this flagrant insult to the author of the Christian religion. "*If thou be the son of God* command these stones that they became bread." The dishonor was replied to only by a reference to the word of God, "It is written man shall not live by bread alone; but by every thing that God appoints." Satan repeated the insult at the temple, and would have betrayed the Redeemer into one act of obedience to himself, by the double influence of a garbled scripture and the delicate question of his legitimacy. But again he was victorious; again he overcame by the word of God, saying "It is written thou shalt not tempt the Lord thy God." Finally, the Fiend, with a dazzling bribe made a large but vulgar demand. "Worship me." He showed him all the kingdoms of the world and the glory of them in a moment of time, and said "All these things will I give thee if thou wilt fall down and worship me." "Get the hence, Satan," said Jesus, "for it is written, Thou shalt worship the Lord thy God and him only shalt thou serve." When the devil had left him, "lo! angels came and served him" (*with food.*)

The object of the tempter seems to have been to betray the Saviour into one act of obedience to him at all events; and to accomplish this, Satan spurred him on by assailing his appetite for food and passion for renown heightened by scripture quotation, and by dishonorable and evil suggestions respecting his sublime relationship to the divine Father. But the hero of our salvation, alike alive to what is and to what ought to be, and making all his knowledge and all his desires do homage to duty, appeals to what is written in the holy scriptures. Eve said, "The Lord God commanded," but she proved unfaithful. Jesus who was to lead us by faith, said "It is written;" and did the highest honor to the bible. Thrice he said "It is written;" a lesson to all those who aspire to eternal life, of the shortest, sharpest, and surest nature, that the bible is the book to study, and the only and exclusive guide how they ought to walk and to please God. Blessed be the name of our God and Father. Praised be the Lamb.

So much for what is called our Lord's temptation. But, to what he could not be seduced by favor, the adversary hoped he might be compelled to by force; and, therefore, by wicked men he set himself to urge his death; so when that dire event was about to take place the Redeemer said, "the prince of this world cometh and hath nothing in me." He was regarded by Jesus as the secret but prime accessory to his death. But neither the terror nor the shame, with which his passion on the cross was to be clothed, could move his constant soul, or drive him from the oracular proposition of the divine Father. "Behold my Son, the Beloved, in whom I delight." When the trial came, therefore, he confessed before Pilate and the High Priest the dreadfully contested truth, and to the confusion of Satan, answered his unrighteous judges in the affirmative, that he was the Messiah, the Son of the Blessed. Perfectly faithful, perfectly constant, Satan, it has been discovered, had no part or lot in him; he bruised his heel, but never reached his heart, except by the soldier's spear: he died with his face to his enemies, marred with an honorable wound. God Almighty be praised forever.

Is it surprising after all this, that the Son of Man should destroy this insatiable enemy? Murder is a capital offence in every civilized code. Satan is the king of murderers. If the human kind should continue to exist for ever, the murder of this lion-like angel would extend itself to eternity; he is an eternal murderer; and, therefore, he shall be eternally punished. He shall go into everlasting fire prepared for him and all his messengers.

But no ordinary power is necessary to seize an archangel, perhaps the chief of all the angels of God, perhaps the first of all God's creatures, as he was the first to sin; like Adam, in this world, the first of men, and the first to violate law divine.

Our Lord, however, is possessed of the necessary power, and he will exert that power in due time. Meanwhile he has given sufficient proof of his superior endowments by rising again from the dead. "No man taketh my life from me," said he, "I lay it down of myself." "Therefore does my Father love me, because I lay down my life, that I may take it again." Having life in himself by virtue of his filial relationship to the Father, this divestment of the mortal robes in which he was clothed, could have been effected by the violence of his enemies, only by permission. When his disciples would have offered resistance to the cruelty and oppression of those who rejected his claims, he said "Think you not, that I could pray to my Father, who would instantly send me twelve legions of angels?" But the mystery concerning the woman's seed or son, his extraordinary endowments, his unrivaled greatness, his matchless strength, and adequacy to the accomplishment of our salvation, and the perdition of our fearful murderer, are all resolvable into the paramount oracle of which we discourse. The argument is this, that if Jesus is to destroy Satan, who has murdered the whole family of man, he must be more powerful than Satan; even as he who binds a strong man must be more powerful than that man. But this superiority is derived from the fact that Jesus is the Son of God. Now the fact, which explains the destruction of our enemy by one clothed with our own form, must be important, must be essential.

CHAPTER X

The Proposition Considered in Relation to the Mother of Our Lord

Let us now proceed to the consideration of the Father's oracle as it refers to the prophecy going before concerning the seed of the woman. The first intimation of deliverance, and revenge for the wrongs we had sustained, was given not in the form of a promise to man, but of a threatening to our adversary. "To the serpent the Lord God said, Because thou hast done this—I will put enmity between thee and the woman, and between thy seed and her seed, it shall bruise thy head and thou shalt bruise his heel."

The language in this scripture is remarkable to us; though before the origin of Christianity there was no reason why it should be deemed remarkable by any who read it. The threatening limited the general term seed to a male issue "Thou shalt bruise his heel;" but, then, those who reflected on the terms of the prophecy, antecedently to the nativity of the Lord Jesus, must necessarily, from their defective knowledge in this matter, have concluded, that he was to be the offspring of woman by the ordinary laws. This was Eve's own idea of it, "I have gotten the man from Jehovah!" That, therefore, which causes the language of the text to appear remarkable to us, who enjoy the privilege of seeing it fulfilled, is that it should be literally and exclusively true of our blessed and adorable deliverer; who is, in verity, of woman, but not of man. We shall now contrast with the first prophecy the last one contained in scripture concerning the nature of the illustrious personage in question, our glorious captain. The first speaks of him as the woman's son, the last as God's son.

"Now in the sixth month God sent Gabriel his messenger to Nazareth, a city of Galilee; to a virgin betrothed to a man called Joseph, of the house of David, and the virgin's name was Mary. When the messenger entered, he said to her, Hail, favorite of Heaven! the Lord be with you, happiest of women. At his appearance and words she was perplexed, and revolved in her mind what this salutation could mean.

And the messenger said to her, Fear not, Mary, for you have found favor with God. And behold, you shall conceive and bare a son, whom you shall name Jesus. He shall be great, and shall be called the son of the Highest. And the Lord God will give him the throne of David his father. And he shall reign over the house of Jacob forever; his reign shall never end. Then said Mary to the messenger How shall this be, since I have no intercourse with man? The messenger answering, said to her, the Holy Spirit will descend upon you, and the power of the Highest will overshadow you; therefore the holy progeny shall be called the Son of God. And lo, your cousin Elizabeth also has conceived a son in her old age; and she who is called barren, is now in her sixth month; for nothing is impossible with God. And Mary said, behold the handmaid of the Lord, be it to me according to your word. Then the messenger departed.

The women of Israel, and of Juda in particular, were highly ambitious to become the mother of Messiah; the proud dames of that nation made it the theme of their frequent conversation; and to this Mary is supposed to allude in her ecstasy before her cousin Elizabeth. "My soul magnifies the Lord, and my spirit rejoices in God my Saviour; because he has not disdained the low condition of his handmaiden, for henceforth all posterity will pronounce me happy. For the Almighty, whose name is venerable, has done wonders for me. His mercy on them that fear him extends to generations of generations. He displays the strength of his arm, and dispels the vain imaginations of the proud. He pulls down potentates from their thrones, and exalts the lowly. The needy he loads with benefits; but the rich he spoils of every thing. He supports Israel his servant, as he promised to our fathers, ever inclined to mercy towards Abraham and his race."

The powerful ones in Israel, whom God had thus humbled, the rich whom he had, in this respect, sent empty away, had doubtless, like the first of women, Eve, and even Mary, never dreamt of the literal import of the saving and prime oracle concerning the woman's seed in the denunciation of Satan; but thought, certainly, that he was to be the proper offspring of man. Mary herself said to the messenger of God, "How shall this be, seeing I have no intercourse with man."

The deliverer of the human race, partakes of the nature of those whose wrongs he came to redress, and of the nature of him, the living God, who will not see the weak abused, nor the innocent trampled upon with impunity. Jesus is the son of the woman and of God. By his relation to the first he tastes our wrongs; by his relation to the last he is powerful to avenge them.

To God the only wise, to God the Father of our Lord Jesus Christ, and to Jesus Christ his only begotten, be the power and the glory, and the honor, and the victory, and the majesty, world without end. Amen.

A fine writer says, "The great object of the Prophecies of the old testament is the redemption of mankind. This redemption, at the fall of man the mercy of God was pleased to foretell. And, as the time for its accomplishment drew nearer, the predictions concerning it became so clear and determinate, as to mark out with historical precision, almost every circumstance in the life and character of infinitely the most extraordinary personage that ever appeared among men. Any one of these predictions is sufficient to indicate a prescience more than human. But the collective force of all, taken together, is such, that nothing more can be necessary to prove the interposition of Omniscience, than the establishment of their authority. And this, even at this remote period, is placed beyond doubt."

To the above we would add, that, as the object of the prophecies of the old testament, is the redemption of mankind, the object of the several narrations and evangels of the New Testament, is to reflect light on these ancient predictions, and to show that they have been fulfilled; for these two divisions of divine revelation are mutually interlinked together, the new testament depending on the old for prophecy, and the old depending on the new for fact. Of this the prophecy of the woman's seed and the facts announced to Mary by Gabriel, God's messenger, form a striking example. The Jews never can hope for any being pretending to be Messiah to afford so literal a fulfillment of the first prediction found in their scriptures concerning him, as does the fact of the New Testament; and Christians could not desire a more literal prophecy for the sublime nature of their Saviour, than is afforded them in said prediction by the Jewish scriptures.

It is not compatible with the present treatise on the gospel, that I should consider all prophecy delivered before the coming of Christ, with a reference to revealed religion in general; or even in relation to the Christian proposition in particular; for this discourse of the true gospel of Christ, is intended rather to point out to readers what that gospel is than by any array of evidence, to attempt a proof of the truth of it. Having brought into close comparison the first and last of these prophecies, which relate to the person of our Saviour alone, and having touched as with the finger, those points in which both mutually minister light and force to each other, let it suffice to speak of the intermeditate predictions relative to himself, which lay between these extremes, as follows.

We have seen, that, in the first prediction, the word seed, which is indefinite in regard to sex, is afterwards limited to male issue and called he, "Thou shalt bruise his heel." This was proper, as otherwise it would have left us to conjecture, whether we were to be ransomed by a male or a female deliverer. Nor, is it probable, that all would have arrived at the same conclusion on this point; for as the woman had been betrayed, some might have imagined that to save us and destroy our enemy by her in person would more redound to the glory of him who catches the wise in their own craftiness; while doubtless, others would have been of a contrary opinion; and so have given birth to a schism on one of the most important predictions concerning the Redeemer of mankind. God, then, from the beginning limited the current of our enquiries into prophecy relative to Messiah, to one sex; and by so doing authorized mankind to hope for a Son to deliver them out of their sore distresses.

But as mankind were to be spread over the face of the whole earth in families and to be distributed upon distinct continents, as has actually been done since the flood, it became necessary, that further limitation, in accordance with these facts, should be made to the predictions concerning Messiah. Accordingly the local limitations to these prophecies run thus, that he should be born in Asia, in Canaan, of the tribe of Judah, city of Bethlehem. In the apportionment of the three sons of Noah, Shem, Ham, and Japheth, Japheth heired and peopled Europe; Ham, Africa; and Shem, Asia. And God was to dwell in the tents of Shem, or Messiah was to be born in Asia. Subsequently, and agreeably to this prediction by Noah, God chose an Asiatic or descendant of Shem, namely, Abraham, and promised him the land of Canaan, saying "To thee will I give this land whereon thou liest;" and again, "In thee and in thy seed shall all the families of the earth be blessed." Thus a national and local limitation was made to the predictions concerning Messiah. Jacob, Abraham's grandson was also a prophet, and, by him, God chose Judah in preference to the other patriarchs, as the ancestor of Messiah, and, consequently, the Canton of Juda as the land of Emmanuel's birth. The words of Jacob are as inimitable for their beauty, as they are remarkable for the limitation which they make of the ancestry and birth-land of the personage to whom they refer.

"Judah, thou art he whom thy brethren shall praise. Thy hand shall be in the neck of thine enemies. Thy father's children shall bow down before thee. Judah is a lion's whelp; from the prey, my son, thou art gone up. He stooped down, he couched as a lion, even as an old lion; who shall rouse him up? The sceptre shall not depart from Judah, nor a lawgiver from between his feet till Shiloh come, and to him shall the gathering of the people be. Binding his foal to the vine, and his ass's colt to the choice vine, he washed his garments in wine, and his clothes in the blood of grapes. His eyes shall be red with wine and his teeth white with milk."

When the proceeding promises to Abraham were fulfilled, and his descendants were settled in Canaan, the hill country of Juda fell to the tribe of Judah, and was locally distinguished from the inheritances of the other tribes by the names of Juda, and Canton of Juda. Of this tribe

God chose David's family as the one which should give birth to the long expected deliverer, and swore with an oath that, of the fruit of the loins of this celebrated Israelite, he would raise up the Messiah to sit on his throne. The promise was thus limited to the descendants of this single famous individual. Another prophet marked out, by the will of God, the birth-city, and Bethlehem was named—thus: "Thou Bethlehem in the land of Juda, art not the least renowned among the cities of Judea, for out of thee shall come a governor that shall rule my people, Israel."

The train of prophecy, extending from Paradise to Bethlehem, issued in the following narration.

"And it came to pass in those days, that there went out a decree from Caesar Augustus, that all the world should be taxed; and this taxing was first made when Cyrenius was governor of Syria. And all went to be taxed, every one to his own city. And Joseph also went up to Galilee, out of the city of Nazareth, into Juda, unto the city of David, which is called Bethlehem, because he was of the house and lineage of David, to be taxed with Mary his betrothed wife being great with child; and so it was, that, while they were there, the days were accomplished that she should be delivered; and she brought forth her first born son, and wrapped him in swaddling clothes and laid him in a manger; because there was no room in the inn."

It only remained that he, who had come, should be made known in his proper person as the long expected one; and, therefore, God, who began the train of prophecy in Paradise, ended it at Jordan. He who at first said, The seed of the woman should bruise the serpent's head, said at last "Behold my Son, the Beloved, in whom I delight." Thus God was the beginning and the ending, the alpha and the omega in the great train of prophecy, which connected Eve with Mary, Adam with Jesus, Paradise with Canaan. Now, the fact in which such distant extremes are made to meet, must be supreme in the Christian system, must be essential.

CHAPTER XI

Of Certain Evangelical Facts Connected with the Proposition

Touching the fact of our Lord's nativity and subsequent events it may be observed, that the design of the Evangels which record them, differs somewhat from that of those prophecies which had been delivered previous to his appearing; for while these last were to show that he was to come, and to be of such a people, such a nation, such a tribe, such a family, and such a person, country, canton, and city; the former were intended to show, that he had come, and that all these accidents, limitations, and particularities are fulfilled in him, of whom God spake the special oracle on which our religion is founded.

The advent of our blessed Lord is first of all hailed by the righteous and blameless father of the baptist, in the following inimitable passage, on the natal day of his first, and only, and great son John.

"Blessed be the Lord, the God of Israel, because he has visited and redeemed his people; and (as anciently he promised by his holy prophets) has raised a prince for our deliverance in the house of David his servant;—for our deliverance from our enemies, and from the hands of all who hate us; in kindness to our forefathers and remembrance of his holy appointment, the oath which he swore to our father Abraham, to grant us, that being rescued out of the hands of our enemies, we might serve him boldly, in piety and uprightness all our days."

"And you, child, (John) shall be called a prophet of the Most High; for you shall go before the Lord to prepare his way, by giving the knowledge of salvation to his people, in the remission of their sins, through the tender compassion of our God, who has caused a light to spring from on high to visit us, to enlighten those who abide in darkness and in the shades of death, to direct our feet into the way of peace."

It would be of no use to inquire whether Zacharias apprehended the nature of the deliverance by Jesus Christ, of which he spoke through the Holy Spirit, with which, at this time, he was filled. It may, I presume, without offence, be affirmed of him what Peter affirms of the Prophets generally, who understood not, but inquired into the import of, their own predictions, "that not for themselves, but for us they ministered these things." It was not necessary, therefore, that they should understand them.

The next matter in Luke's narrative, concerning the now incarnate Redeemer, is that of the angels who said he was born, as we have seen, and was lying swathed in the manger in Bethlehem.

"Now there were shepherds in the field in that country, who tended their flocks by turns through the night watches. On a sudden the messenger of the Lord stood by them, and a divine glory encompassed them with light, and they were frightened exceedingly. But the messenger said to them, Fear not; for lo! I bring you good tidings, which shall prove matter of great joy to all people; because to day is born to you, in the city of David, a Saviour, who is the Lord Messiah. And by this you shall know him; you shall find a babe in swaddling bands, lying in a manger. Instantly the messenger was attended by a multitude of the heavenly host, who praised God, saying, Glory to God in the highest heaven, and on earth peace, and good will amongst men."

"And when the messenger had returned to heaven, having left the shepherds, these said one to another, let us go to Bethlehem, and see this which has happened, whereof the Lord has informed us. And hastening thither, they found Mary and Joseph with the babe, who lay in the manger. When they saw this they published what had been imparted to them concerning the child. And all who heard it wondered at the things told them by the shepherds. But Mary let none of these things escape unobserved, weighing every circumstance within herself. And the shepherds returned glorifying God for all that they had heard and seen agreeably to what had been declared to them."

The song of the angels of the nativity has in it a division of things which, for one particularity, ought to be remarked. *"Glory to God in the highest heavens."* This item probably refers to the joy of the angelic world, who, in becoming subject to the Son of Man, might he conceived to receive some special benefit through him. This, as has been observed, was most probably a deliverance from the frightful person and evil influence of the great adversary of God, of angels, and of men, the Devil. The angels are called the sons of God in Job, and in that book, it is said, that at the origin of the visible creation, they all shouted for joy. In the same book it is also written, that there was a certain day when the sons of God came together to present themselves before the Lord, and Satan came also among them. At another convocation of those high powers in heaven, Satan presented himself and became a lying spirit in the mouth of all the prophets of king Ahab. The angels knowing his original crime in heaven, and his history there, and also the wide spreading desolation, which he has introduced among men, and the whole history of his wiles, and witchery, and wickedness in this world, knowing also that there is but one step between the most perfect innocence and the most deadly guilt, between sin and righteousness, happiness and misery, heaven and hell, they, doubtless, feel in some measure in jeopardy from the wiles, and witchery, and wickedness of this diabolical spirit, and long for his subjection and final perdition by his calm, decisive, grave, and great royal antagonist, the Son of Man, to whom be the victory and the glory.

The following speaks of the circumcision of our Lord, the purification of his mother, Simeon's prophecies, and other matters.

"On the eighth day, when the child was circumcised, they called him Jesus, the messenger having given him that name before his mother conceived him.

And when the time of their purification was expired, they carried him to Jerusalem, as the Law of Moses appoints, to present him to the Lord; (as it is written in the law of God, "Every male, who is the first born of his mother, is consecrated to the Lord") and to offer the sacrifice enjoined in the law, a pair of turtle doves or two young pigeons.

Now there was at Jerusalem a man named Simeon, a just and a religious man, who expected the consolation of Israel; and the Holy Spirit was upon him, and had revealed to him that he should not die till he had seen the Lord's Messiah. This man came, guided by the Spirit into the temple. And when the parents brought in the child Jesus, to do for him what the law required, he took him into his arms, and blessed God and said, "Now, Lord, thou dost in peace dismiss thy servant, according to thy word; for my eyes have seen the Saviour, whom thou hast provided in sight of all the world, a luminary to enlighten the nations, and to be the glory of Israel thy people.—And Joseph and the mother of Jesus, heard with admiration the things spoken concerning him. Simeon blessed them, and said to Mary his mother, "This child is destined for the rise and for the fall of many in Israel, and to serve as a mark for contradiction; yes, your own soul shall be pierced as with a javelin, that the thoughts of many hearts may be disclosed."

There was also a prophetess, Anna, daughter of Phanuel, of the tribe of Ashur, in advanced age, who had lived seven years with a husband, whom she married when a virgin; and being now a widow of about eighty-four years, departed not from the temple, but served God in prayer and fasting night and day; she also coming in at that instant, gave thanks to the Lord, and spoke concerning Jesus to all those in Jerusalem who expected deliverance.

After they had performed every thing required by the law of the Lord, they returned to Galilee, to their own city, Nazareth. And the child grew and acquired strength of mind, being filled with wisdom, and adorned with a divine gracefulness."—Luke 2.

These are all the remarkable things recorded of our Lord Jesus before the appearance of John at Jordan, if we except the visit of the magicians, the slaughter of the children by Herod at Bethlehem, the flight into Egypt, and return thence. One thing more, however, is noticed by Luke, and on account of its interesting nature we shall give it in this place.

"Now the parents of Jesus went yearly to Jerusalem at the feast of the passover. And when he was twelve years old, they having gone thither, according to the usage of the festival, and remained the customary time, being on their return, the child Jesus staid behind in Jerusalem, and neither Joseph nor his mother knew it. They supposing him to be in the company, went a day's journey, and then sought him among their relations and acquaintances; but not finding him, they returned to Jerusalem seeking him. And after three days, they found him in the temple, sitting among the doctors, both hearing them, and asking them questions. And all who heard him were astonished; but they who saw him were amazed at his understanding and answers. And his mother said to him, Son why have you treated us thus? Behold, your father and I have sought you with sorrow. He answered, why did you seek me? Knew you not that I must be at my Father's? But they did not comprehend his answer.

And he returned with them to Nazareth, and was subject to them. And his mother treasured up all these things in her memory. And Jesus advanced in wisdom and stature, and in power with God and man."

"Why did you seek me? Knew ye not that I must be at my Father's? But they did not comprehend his answer."

Two things are indicated by these expressions; that those pious persons who lived in the days of the Messiah, and even such of them as were immediately related to him and were destined by God to be actively engaged in the events relating to our holy religion, were totally ignorant of the import of the things which were transpiring before them, and like us, depended on future facts and future revelations by the Spirit, to make them understand them. 2d that the Lord Jesus, from infancy, regarded every thing that was his Father's as being also his. In this scripture he calls the temple his Father's, and speaks of it as his home, as other children speak of the house of their father as their home. Where do we seek a child but at his father's house? and where was the child Jesus to be sought for but at his father's house which was the temple? From childhood, his descent from God Almighty seems to have been the all absorbing idea of his soul. He ever cherished in his inmost heart this transcendently sublime fact, that God was his real father. When he came of age, therefore, he said, in accordance with this truth and the law of primogeniture in his own nation, of which God his father was king, "All that the Father hath is mine." The temple, therefore, was his; and because the heir is greater than the things heired, he said to the Jews on one occasion, "Behold a greater than the temple is here." Inspired with a holy indignation on account of the abuses in the temple, and eagerly desiring that his Father's house, which had been ordained a place of prayer for all nations, should, at the approaching festival, be all holiness, he came to Jerusalem a short while before the Passover.

"And finding changers sitting in the temple, and people who sold cattle, and sheep, and doves; he made a whip of cords, and drove them all out of the temple, with the sheep and cattle, scattering the coin of the changers, and oversetting their tables; and said to them who sold doves, "Take these things hence, make not my Father's house a house of traffic." Then his disciples remembered the words of the scripture, "My zeal for thy house consumes me." John 2.

Another case and we shall return. All the Jewish youth, above twenty one, were bound by the law to contribute, for the repair of the tabernacle and afterwards for the temple, which David calls the palace of God, a dedrachma annually. The following scripture refers to that legal institute and is remarkable for a singular reflection of our Saviour in regard to himself in this matter, as being the son of the king for whom the tax was collected.

"When they were come to Capernaum the collectors came and asked Peter, "Does not your teacher pay the dedrachma? he said, yes, being come into the house, before he spoke, Jesus said to him, What is your opinion Simon? From whom do the kings of the earth exact tribute or custom? from their own sons or from others? Peter answered, From others. Jesus replied the sons then are exempted. Nevertheless, lest we should give them offence, go to the sea and throwing in a line, draw out the first fish that is hooked, and having opened its mouth, you shall find a statter; take that and give it for me and you." Math. 10.

The Saviour means that according to the usages of earthly princes, he, as Son of God, king of the Jews, had a right to be exempted from paying the tax collected for the repair of his father's house, and so forth.

Thus we have glanced hastily at all the notable things which are recorded of Jesus, from his conception to his appearing in Israel, and some few more; but we now return to the proposition before us; "Behold my Son! the Beloved, in whom I delight."

CHAPTER XII

The Law, the Prophets, and the Psalms

There is a very ostensible division of the ancient scriptures, into the law, the prophets, and the psalms. This division is recognized by the Redeemer himself, in the following remarkable passage spoken after his resurrection.

"And he said to them, This is what I told you while I remained with you, that all the things which are written concerning me, in the law of Moses, and in the Prophets, and in the Psalms, must be accomplished: Then he opened their minds, that they might understand the scriptures, and said to them, Thus it is written, and thus it behooved the Messiah to suffer, and to rise from the dead the third day; and that reformation, and the remission of sins, should be proclaimed in his name among all nations, beginning at Jerusalem. Now you are witnesses of these things; and behold I send you that which my Father has promised; but continue you in the city, until you be invested with power from above!"

1. Those prophecies which are found in the five Books of Moses, relative to the Messiah, refer principally to his descent or ancestry, without saying any thing of his public ministry. He was to be a prophet raised up in Israel, of the tribe of Judah, by the line of Jacob and not that of Esau, or Ishmael. He was to be of Abraham and Shem, not of Lot, or Japhet, or Ham. Finally, he was to be the son of woman, in an exclusive sense, and not of man. All these items of prediction were fulfilled to the letter in Jesus our Lord.

2. The Psalms further limit his descent to the family of David, and clothe him with more royal honors, speaking of him as a king exalted to the throne of the universe, and a Priest entering upon his office with the god-like endowment of life in himself, eternal life. But indeed all things relative to Messiah, from his birth to his resurrection, and thence again to his second coming, are touched with such wonderful particularity, that one would think the Psalms were penned after the Messiah had appeared, rather than one thousand years before the facts took place. They, in this respect, are a kind of prophetic gospel.

3. The prophecies which relate to the Messiah, in that division of the ancient scriptures which is styled the Prophets, further limit his descent to a virgin of the house of David. The "Lord hath created a new thing in the earth" exclaims Jeremiah, "a woman shall compass [conceive] a man."—31:22.

This were a novelty in the earth to be sure, but the prophecy is in perfect conformity, nevertheless, both with earlier predictions and with future fact. "When the fullness of time was come," says Paul, "God sent forth his Son, born of a woman, born under the law, that he might buy off those under law, and that we (Gentiles, never under law,) might receive the adoption of sons." Gal. 4.

But to enumerate all the events and facts in the birth, life, ministry, death, resurrection, and exaltation to heaven of our Lord Jesus, which go to fill up the measure of ancient prophecy, would be to write out the whole of the four gospels. This is unnecessary, and would be inconvenient. We shall, therefore, only speak of two more events as having formed the subjects of prophecy and so bring this item of consideration to a close.

We have already taken one fact from the new testament and one prophecy from the law, namely, that of the woman's seed, and the birth of our Lord Jesus, and have noticed their literal agreement with each other. We shall now take one from the Prophets, the second division of the Bible, and compare it with one fact testified of Jesus in the gospel. The prophecy is as follows:

"Behold my servant whom I have chosen, my beloved in whom my soul delights, I will put my spirit upon him; he shall give laws to the Gentiles; he will not contend, nor clamor, nor cause his voice to be heard in the streets. A bruised reed he will not break; and a dimly burning taper will he not quench, till he render his laws victorious. Nations shall trust in his name."—Isaiah 42.

The fact in the new testament, which fills up the first part of the above prophecy concerning Messiah, is recorded of our Lord Jesus, by all the four evangelists, namely, his appearance at Jordan, and his reception of the Holy Spirit on that occasion. Matthew writes thus:

"Then came Jesus from Galilee to Jordan to be immersed by John. But John excused himself, saying, It is I who need to be immersed by you; and you come to me! Jesus answering, said to him, Permit this at present; for thus ought we to ratify every divine institution. Then John acquiesced. Jesus being immersed, no sooner arose out of the water, than heaven was opened to him and the Spirit of God appeared descending like a dove, and lighting upon him; while a voice from heaven proclaimed, This is my Son! the Beloved, in whom I delight."

When the prophet and the Evangelist are brought together in this way, we learn that the public attestation of Jesus by his Father at Jordan, which forms the basis of the Christian religion, is a fact which goes to fill up one of the clearest and most remarkable predictions in the whole Bible. The ancient prophecy and the voice from heaven begin with the same word "Behold;" and afterwards coincide almost to a letter. There can be but one apology for the man, who fails to recognize their singular coincidence, that is, his utter ignorance of them; but this apology is a very doubtful one, seeing the scriptures are equally open to all.

As we have compared one new testament fact with a prophecy in the law, and one with a prediction in the prophets, we shall now compare a gospel fact, testified of our Lord Jesus, with a former prophecy found in the Psalms. That is, his resurrection from the dead, the fact in our religion, which gives vitality to, and stamps divinity upon, Christianity. Paul who had correctly studied into the evidences for the resurrection of Christ, speaks of it as follows:

"Now, I declare to you brethren, the glad tidings which I announced to you; which also you have received, and in which you stand. By which also you are saved, if you retain those joyful tidings, which I delivered to you; unless, indeed you have believed to no purpose. For I delivered to you, among the first things, what also I received first,—That Christ died for our sins, according to the scriptures; and that he was buried, and that he arose the third day according to the scriptures; and that he was seen by Cephas, then by the twelve. After that, he was seen by above five hundred brethren at once; of whom the greater part remain to this present time, but some are fallen asleep. After that he was seen by James; then, by all the apostles. And last of all, he was seen by me, as by one born out of due time. For I am the least of the apostles; and am not worthy to be called an apostle, because I persecuted the congregation of God."—1 Cor. 15.

The prophecy in the Psalms, relative to the resurrection of Messiah from the dead, to which we refer, is that found in the sixteenth, it reads as follows:

"I have regarded the Lord as always before, me, because he is at my right hand, that I might not be moved; for this reason my heart is glad, and my tongue exults; moreover too, my flesh shall rest, in hope that thou wilt not leave my soul in the unseen world, neither wilt thou permit thy holy one to see corruption. Thou hast made me to know the way of life; thou wilt make me full of joy with thy countenance."

It would be impossible for any thing to be more literally verified than the above prediction is by the resurrection of the Lord Jesus Christ. The following is the inspired Peter's conclusive and irresistible reasoning upon both the prophecy and the fact to which it pointed.

"Brethren permit me to speak freely concerning the patriarch David; that he is both dead and buried, and his sepulcher is among us to this day; therefore being a prophet, and knowing that God had sworn to him with an oath, that of the fruit of his loins he would raise up the Messiah to sit on his throne; he, foreseeing this, spake of the resurrection of the Messiah, that his soul should not be left in the unseen world, nor his flesh see corruption. This Jesus has God raised up, of which all we are witnesses; being exalted, therefore, to the right hand of God, and having received the promise of the Holy Spirit from the Father, he has shed forth this, which you now see and hear. For David is not ascended into heaven, but he says, Jehovah said to my Lord, Sit thou at my right hand, until I make thy foes thy footstool. Let, therefore, all the house of Israel assuredly know, that God has made this Jesus whom you have crucified, Lord even Messiah." Acts 2.

Paul, in the Jewish synagogue at Antioch in Pisidia, touches the resurrection of our Lord, and quotes three distinct prophecies as predicting the event. The prophecy in the 16th Psalm, now under consideration, is the last we cite; thus.

"Wherefore, also, in an other place he says, "Thou wilt not permit thy holy one to see corruption." Now David, says the Apostle to his auditors, having served his own generation according to the will of God, fell asleep, and was gathered to his fathers, and saw corruption. But he, whom God raised up, did not see corruption."

All that we have written of the predictions of the old testament and of the facts of the new, has, as must appear to the reader, either a mediate or immediate, bearing on the proposition, that Jesus is the son of God, and are proofs either direct or collateral, that Christianity professes to be based on this divine oracle,—professes that God's wisdom framed and foretold it, his goodness made it known, and his power has demonstrated it, and will defend it. Christ, we have already seen, compares the proposition to a rock, and as such has pitched his church upon it, for there can be no Christian church where this is denied, against which he says, the gates of Hades shall never prevail.— Innumerable and powerful spirits, armed with all kinds of weapons necessary to test the truth of this, have appeared in society. Kings, Priests, Statesmen, Philosophers, Poets, Historians, and Orators have reasoned, laughed, ridiculed, raged, persecuted, and failed. The church survives, and still stands secure, more than ever convinced by the various artillery played off upon her by her enemies, that her origin, her foundation, and her destiny are divine.

CHAPTER XIII

The Proposition in Regard to Miracles

We now come to the consideration of the Christian proposition as connected with miracles. It will readily be apprehended by the reader, that, if a miracle is impossible, there can be no revealed religion; because no religion, or any thing else beyond what is strictly natural, can be communicated to us by the author of our existence except by miracle. However scientific it may be to conclude from the innumerable indications of contrivance and utility found in nature, that there is a God, and that that God is worthy of our reverence; no conclusion can with any show either of science or reason, be deduced from these sources in proof of a special religion, as the Christian religion, or a particular proposition in that religion, as that God has a Son and that he like the Father, is worthy of divine honors. Christianity, therefore, professes to rest her authority upon a special interposition of the Deity, and thus, in this point she meets our most perfect conceptions of a true revelation. Had she based her scheme on any truth purely natural, no interposition would have been necessary to reveal or confirm it, and men seeing this, her claims to a divine origin must have failed to be acknowledged.

As nature makes the general revelation, Christianity, in conformity with this fact, proposes herself as a special revelation. In this point also, therefore, she is on the side of reason and propriety; for had she purposed only to divulge the great truth which is cognizable by our reason exerted on the things of nature, men would have pronounced her unnecessary and of course granted her but little courtesy. She, therefore, purports not to be the general religion of nature, or to be founded on the facts which are said to give birth to natural religion; but is a special revelation made to us on special principles, or miracles. Here, however, the mind hesitates, and sometimes goes so far as not only to doubt the reality of the Christian miracles, but the possibility of all miracles whatever; nay some have dogmatically asserted that a miracle is absolutely impossible! that is, that the author of the order of nature is incapable, even for special purposes, of interfering with this order, or he who gave laws to nature cannot for one moment suspend these laws whatever the exigency may be. If it be once admitted that there is a God, and this can be proved on scientific principles, then the reasoning that he can work miracles, is shorter than that which is necessary to prove that he cannot work miracles. But it may be answered, that this latter proposition being of a negative kind requires not to be proved; let the person, who says so, remember that as negative propositions have the mastery over positive ones in this respect, that they need not to be proved, so they not unfrequently enjoy this distinction over them also, that they are evidently more glaringly absurd. To admit that revelation must be special and founded on special miracle, and afterwards deny the possibility of miracles. It is to join together golden truth and the dross of basest assumption. It is to assert the necessity of revelation and to deny its possibility. But more of this in another place. There is, therefore, an amazing concatenation of miracles drawn out in the gospel to keep before the public the person of whom it was said "Behold my Son;" miracle after miracle follows each other in rapid succession, surprisingly diversified in manner, kind and form, till the mighty chain terminates in that amazing wonder his resurrection from the dead—a miracle which, for its transcendent peculiarities, the apostle (Eph. 1:19) singles out as affording the most illustrious display of the mighty power of God.

CHAPTER XIV

The Proposition as Related to the Jews

But as miracle was intended immediately for the Jewish nation, or those in whose hearing the Christian oracle was announced, we shall pass on to speak of this people in relation to the grand proposition. They rejected the claims of our Lord Jesus and put him to death; and in forty years afterwards, were divested of their nationality; since which time they have failed to regain it. Eighteen hundred years have elapsed and still they lie scattered as foreigners, among the nations, the graveyard their only home. In conformity with a promise made to their fathers, God had taken them from a severe bondage in Egypt by a providence of the most extraordinary kind. Moses appeals to it as such in the following energetic style.

"Ask now of the days that are past, which were before thee, since the days that God created man upon the earth, and ask from the one side of the heavens to the other, whether there has been any such thing as this great thing is, or hath been heard like it? Did ever people hear the voice of God speaking out of the midst of the fire as thou hast heard and live? Or hath God assayed to take him a nation from the midst of another nation by temptations, by signs, and by wonders, and by war, and by a mighty hand, and by an outstretched arm, and by great terrors, according to all that the Lord your God did for you in Egypt before your eyes?"

The following fond and soothing language is held of the same gracious providence. "He found him in a desert land, and in the vast howling wilderness, he led him about, he instructed him, he kept him as the apple of his eye. As an eagle[7] stirreth up her nest, fluttereth over her young, spreadeth abroad her wings, taketh them, beareth them on her wings, so the Lord alone did lead him and there was no strange God with him."

This last clause, "There was no strange God with him" is what we desired to reach. To cleanse the nation and to keep it clean of idolatry was the end of both the law of Moses and all the providential dealings of God with them from the day he took them by the hand to bring them out of Egypt to the coming of our Lord Jesus. He dealt with them like the parent eagle with its young when she teaches them to fly.—God

---

[7] Naturalists inform us, that it is usual for a certain species of the Eagle to build their aerie or nest on the edge of some lofty precipice overhanging the ocean and, when their young ones are fully fledged, to adopt the following expedient in order to teach them to fly. The old eagle takes one first, and, having roused or stirred it up, she at last pushes it from the sublime crag on which her nest is pitched. The eaglet descends towards the ocean followed by the parent bird; who fluttering over it and carefully marking the point of descent, as it approaches the surface of the sea, suddenly, in a moment, like a glance of lightning, throws herself full swoop under it, takes it on her shoulders, spreads abroad her wings, and bears it aloft into the higher regions of the atmosphere, when she permits it again to descend exercising in its fall its untaught wings upon the blue sea air. Again before it reaches the water, she receives it upon her maternal shoulders; again she soars on high to an elevation still more sublime, and again she permits it to descend, till, by this exercise, the eaglet has learnt to fly; when she returns exulting with it to her nest, the abode of her lofty repose.

It was in this manner God instructed the children of Israel to quit idolatry, and to place their confidence in him, The Most High. Jacob for a time left off his idols, and "There was no strange god with him."

made them to reside in the high places or most eminently rich portion of the habitable globe that they might enjoy the increase of the field, and suck honey out of the rock and oil out of the flinty rock. "Butter of kine, and milk of sheep, with fat of lambs and rams of the breed of Bashan, and goats, with the fat of the kidneys of wheat; and he did drink the pure blood of the grape. But Jeshurm waxed fat and kicked."

They were, perhaps, the most prone people to idolatry that ever existed, and notwithstanding they had beheld its abomination in Egypt, and were instructed in its pernicious tendency for forty years in the wilderness, and on account of it subjected to six successive servitudes to the surrounding nations and carried off to Babylon, they could scarcely be cured of this horrible evil. As the fundamental purpose of their economy was the re-assertion and establishment of the Divine unity, idolatry became the chief sin. The first commandment, in conformity with the nature of their religion, was "Thou shalt have no other God but me." And the second respected image worship which was denounced also, as a capital crime. But if we put together all the sufferings to which that nation was doomed on account of the violation of the fundamental maxim in their own religion, their slavery to the Mesopotamians, to the Moabites, to the Canaanites, the Midianites, the Amorites, and to the Philistines, and even that to the Babylonians they do not all of them make a scantling of the horrible fortunes which have followed them since their rejection of Jesus our Lord. Their rejection of him, therefore, must be considered, by all who contemplate its results, as the rejection of a proposition paramount to that of the unity of the Deity itself, the core of their own religion; and from their abjuration of Jesus as the Son of God and the dire calamities which have been consequent upon it, we learn the peerless importance of that which, we say, forms the basis of Christianity We are warranted from their fortunes to conclude, that what they rejected was fundamental, and that a people is made or unmade by their belief or disbelief of this paternal revelation in our religion.

The matter of the oracle in the Paradisiacal state was contained in this, "Of every tree in the garden thou mayest freely eat; but of the tree of the knowledge of good and evil thou shalt not eat; for in the day thou eatest thereof thou shalt surely die."

In the second revelation, namely, the law. The fundamental maxim was, "I the Lord your God am one Lord." Or, as Dr. George Campbell translates it, "Jehovah is your God, Jehovah is one."

The third institute has for its radix or root, what we have repeatedly enunciated; "Behold my Son, the Beloved, in whom I delight."

The admirable congruity of those three communications with the origin of mankind, as recorded in the archives of revelation the bible, and with the history of the world in regard to religion, will appear sufficiently evident to the reader. We shall observe, that in Paradise, man being admitted to open converse with the Deity, the word of God to him partook of the nature of a command rather than a proper revelation. But when men were no longer admitted to holy vision with their Creator; but were obliged to walk by faith; when they had erred amazingly from the one God; and all the nations had corrupted the true religion, and changed all ideas of God into the most filthy idolatry; then in the law the Divine existence or unity, was reasserted, accompanied with the maxims of a pure morality.—Finally, when the world was to be redeemed, the oracle partakes of the grandeur of the enterprise, it is commensurate in greatness with the thing to be accomplished; and God by a pure revelation gives up his Son, his Beloved Son. Praised be the name of the Lord, praised be our God.

The God of the bible, has spoken only thrice, in nearly six thousand years. Is there in this account of matters, any thing incompatible with the idea which we form of the dignity and gravity of the God of nature? A silence of two thousand five hundred years, is a solemn pause. Another pause of fifteen hundred years expired and the institution of Christianity went into operation.

CHAPTER XV

The Proposition Considered Touching Corrupted Forms of Christianity

The senior oracle of Christianity may, as has been observed, be considered in relation to modern corruptions of the truth, namely, Romanism and Protestantism.

Very unlike Romanism the primitive church engaged no arts on her side; she did not, like that harlot, seek to consecrate herself in the esteem of worldly men and the vulgar, by a meretricious display of the finest specimens of sculpture, painting, music, and so forth; but marched forth to the conversion of the world, devoid of all external ornament.

> "For loveliness needs not the foreign aid of ornament;
> But is, when unadorned, adorned the most."

Unlike Protestantism, also, she sought not to distinguish herself by an affected party prudery; but looked like a sweet, innocent virgin attired in godly simplicity, without partiality, without hypocrisy.

> "Thoughtless of beauty, she was beauty's self."

Her robes were robes of righteousness; her garments were salvation and praise. She wore for a girdle, the truth; her sandals were the gospel of peace; the oil of joy gladdened her countenance and the spirit of God was in her soul; life dawned upon her brows; the riches of Christ were in her hands—tried gold, and raiment, and eye-salve, and balm, and the water of life, and the bread of heaven. She walked the earth in the length thereof, and the haughty Roman bowed to her charms.

"Grace was in all her steps, heaven in her eye."

Alike unacquainted with the creeds of Protestants, and the idolatrous manuals of Papists, her only manual was the bible, and her creed, for the binding together of all who obeyed her, was Jesus is the Son of God. On this faith and this volume she gathered her children thick as the stars of heaven, and as the sand by the sea shore innumerable, and she fondled over them with the solicitude of the hen when, at eve, she gathers together her infant brood under her wings.

Let not the reader think, that Romanism, or Protestantism, is primitive Christianity. Let him beware of the fatal error of confounding things so dissimilar and distinct. As Popery and Protestantism are not the same, so neither of them is the religion of the new Testament. These are institutions of priests and clergymen; guides who, if a man will follow them, will devoutly fill his soul with the most perplexing doubts and troubles concerning every matter which the author of Christianity has communicated for our faith, our hope, our obedience, and perfection in morals and religion. Reader go not after them. Seize upon the holy scriptures as a gift to you from God. Believe that you can understand them, and become wiser by them, than all who live by perverting them.

Nothing can be more opposed to the simplicity and prosperity of the Christian religion, than the undue importance which its professed friends have put upon certain doctrines as they call them which, if true at all, may not belong to our religion but to philosophy; or if they form part of Christianity they, nevertheless, do not form its first principles. They merit not the rank of fundamentals; much less should they be permitted to usurp a dignity or importance commensurate with the most fundamental truth in the system, the prime article of faith, that Jesus our Lord is the Messiah, the Son of God.

"Then said the Jews to him, Who art thou? And Jesus said to them Even the same that I said to you from the beginning." John 8:25. The beginning,—When we leave behind us the many things which affect to be original Christianity and search for a beginning to our religion, we have to pass by, as comparatively modern and wholly without authority, many famous ecclesiastical establishments and their supporters. In brief, if we mount up the stream of Christian history to its source and would drink of the waters as they flowed purely from the great fountain of life, at the beginning, we have to go back to the author of our religion himself. We must reject parties and creeds, for the original church and the Bible alone; we must cease from men and their systems, and embrace Christ and the glorious proposition of His Messiahship. Paul says of our Lord, that "He is the beginning," that is, of the Christian religion.—The Christian religion, therefore, has a beginning. But it is a distinguishing feature in most corruptions or modifications of it that they have no beginning; or if they have, it is a beginning, almost in every instance, dissimilar from that which forms the beginning of True Christianity. They do not sufficiently honor or estimate the oracle so surely divine, which was spoken concerning Christ by the Father.

CHAPTER XVI

The Proposition Considered as a Creed

But we have said, that this revelation of almighty God may be contemplated relative to faith or belief. There is nothing in the Christian religion more extraordinary than that its author is the Son of God, even as there is nothing more fundamental; the man, therefore, who has surely believed this, has surmounted all difficulty in regard to becoming a Christian and an heir to the privileges, honors, and promises of the institution. This oracle is, therefore, made the subject of public, and personal confession. In short, it is the creed of Christianity, original Christianity; and he who believes the fact may become a Christian. When a sensible man sets out on a course of enquiry into the truth of our religion it will be well for him to keep this in his eye. He will thus find the field of investigation narrowed to a point. Foreign matter will be thrown off as a *caput mort*, dead matter, and a single proposition with its proof will lay before him, which he will discover calls for good sense, honorable inquiry, and honest decision rather than credulity, superstition, and base submission. As it is the most extraordinary proposition in our religion it is not wonderful, that it should form the matter of faith. The divine wisdom is in nothing more conspicuous in our salvation than in proposing for belief, a fundamental truth which, for its grandeur and peculiar character, covers all other articles in Revelation. It is wonderful that there should be a heaven and a hell; wonderful that there should be a general judgment and a general resurrection; it is wonderful that Christ should rise from the dead and ascend into heaven; but if we can once assure ourselves, by the proper evidence, that he is the Son of God, these things will be viewed by us only as different pieces in the same great gallery of revelation, of which the oracle under consideration, is the *chef d'auvre*, the master piece.

The original promulgation of the gospel was distinguished for the simplicity of its faith. All, who confessed that Jesus was the Messiah the Son of God, were freely and lovingly admitted to the rights and privileges of the Christian church. There was no difference made between the Jew and the Greek. The warlike Roman, the rude Sythian, the gay Athenian, and the grave Spartan were affectionately gathered in together under the wings of Immanuel. The slave was not excluded, nor the poor; the man of sorrows, and the grieved in spirit, the bereaved mother, and the houseless orphan were not only admitted within the walls of the sanctuary of the Lord of glory, on a footing of equality with those who enjoyed the right of primogeniture in religion, the Jews, but they and the Jews together were by their espousals to the Messiah and his heavenly cause, raised to a rank equal to that of his own, and, by the hearty belief and public avowal of the truth, which the Father announced at the Jordan when Christianity began, made sons and daughters to the Lord God Almighty. Praised be his name. Praised be his holy name.

The late restoration of the gospel was in nothing more singular than in its proposing again this faith in all its pristine singleness and simplicity. The persons who believed and confessed, were promptly and gladly admitted to fellowship, to remission. The world wondered; but the obedient rejoiced. The Pharisaical professor, who felt his self conceit wounded, blamed and raged; but those who received the truth experienced the peace and love of God shed abroad in their hearts by the Holy Spirit which was given to them. Praised be God.—Praised be the Lamb.

But this proposition must be preserved single. Nothing must be mixed with it; for this would call us to the confession of a plurality of matters; whereas we are evidently required to confess only "the truth," not truths, far less truth and error mixed, and least of all error only; as is too frequently done. The Father's word concerning Jesus, is the Truth.

This is the master revelation, the *primum mobile* of the Christian Religion, the power that gives life and motion to all the other parts of the evangelical machinery. Yes, the gospel, when detached from the rubbish of near two thousand years, the rubbish of Romanism, the impure touch of popes, and prelates, and priests, and preachers, when redeemed from the incumbrances which interest and ignorance have heaped upon it, and by which they have pressed it down to the ground, when disentangled, and elevated to a ground on which it can be seen in its original simplicity, resolves itself finally into this glorious and great oracle that Jesus is the Messiah the Son of God.

It is necessary, however, to discriminate, and to know for whom this single truth is designed. All men are not saints, all men are not sinners.

Some have already believed this and every other matter proposed by Christianity. Others have not yet believed it, and it is to them that it is to be announced.—This is the matter to be proposed for their faith. The parties have drawn up what they call their creeds and confessions in order to show what they believe, and what all others must believe if they would become members of their parties; this, however, was unnecessary; for we know that if any man is a Christian he must, of course, be understood to receive the whole of the old and new testaments as his book of doctrine, discipline, and worship. But when it is asked of these parties what God requires of the poor needy sinner to believe in order to be saved, they have no creed for him. Their systems of belief are shaped out for saints, if we could believe them themselves to be such. We write not then upon the creed of the saints; that would be to draw out every thing in the sacred writings; it is the creed of the sinner concerning which we discourse. And here God has anticipated all by announcing from heaven the matter to be believed by all. He has left no room for councils, synods, and general assemblies; but, has ordered men every where to receive Jesus as his Son. This brings the faith of mankind to terminate on a truth, of a truly divine origin, a truth promulgated by the Father, and not by men, a truth as remarkable in its nature as it is powerful in its effects in all those who believe it.

In these respects it differs surprisingly from creeds and confessions purely human. These are all of too varied a character. There is no unity in them; and if there were it would avail but little; as any thing of less force and less peculiarity of nature than the revelation in question, must necessary fail of effect, moral effect. That God so loved the world as to give his only begotten Son, that whosoever believeth on him might not perish but have everlasting life, is of a most powerful nature to reform and purify mankind.

CHAPTER XVII

The Proposition in Relation to Christ's Death

The merits of the death of our blessed Lord resides, wholly in its intrinsic excellence. It was the death of one perfectly just instead of thousands of unjust. It was the Lord of all instead of all; and, therefore, unspeakably calculated to do honor to the divine law, and by consequence to set the good God, the Ruler of the universe and of men, in the attitude of a just Governor, when in mercy he proceeded to acquit sinners of their guilt. O! it was a most precious sacrifice, a holy, spotless, stainless sacrifice, of a sweet smelling savour to God, and in its nature most saving to men. It was indeed the sacrifice of a Lamb that might well take away the sins of the world. It was a ransom which might well buy off from death the captive nations, the ruined family of man. All angels, had they stooped to death in behalf of the world, could not, would not, have thrown such an unction of majesty around the laws of the Most High; they could not and would not have enveloped in such a halo of glory, honor, dignity, grandeur, and holiness the character of the Ruler of the universe God Almighty our Heavenly Father.

In the scriptures the Saviour is spoken of under perhaps above one hundred names. He is the Lamb of God, the Lion of the tribe of Judah, and the Horn of salvation, the Root of Jesse, the Offspring of David, the Vine and Branch of Righteousness. He is the Rock, the Bright and Morning Star, the Light of the world, and the Sun of Righteousness; the Man Christ Jesus, the Second Man, the Son of Man, and the Seed of the Woman, the Bread, the true Bread, the Bread which came down from Heaven, the Stone rejected of men but chosen of God, the Corner Stone and the Head of the Corner, King, Advocate, Anointed, Apostle, Bishop, Captain, Counselor, Deliverer, Governor, Saviour, Lord of lords and King of kings, Potentate, Lord of all, Mediator, Melchisedec, Prince of Life, and of the kings of the earth, Ruler, Shepherd, Great and Good Witness, Chosen, Servant, the Amen, Alpha and Omega, the Beginning of the creation of God, the Blessed, Immanuel, Head of the Church, High Priest, our Hope, Jesus, Shiloh, our Passover, Prophet, Ransom, Redeemer, the Truth, the Way, the Life, and the Propitiatory. But above all these and in a word, he is the Son of God the Beloved, and only Begotten of the Father, heir of all and the image of the invisible God. Therefore his sacrifice in our behalf, like himself and like his illustrious Father, is infinitely worthy and to be accepted in all law human or divine. In brief nothing could excel the majesty of the offering, unless God the Father himself had died for us, which was rendered unnecessary, if it had even been possible, seeing his son, his blessed and only begotten son, presented himself in our behalf. O! to God and to the Lamb be endless honor, and salvation, and wisdom, and glory, and strength.

Whether the death of Christ be contemplated relative to God, to the Holy Spirit, or to Jesus Christ himself; whether it be considered in regard to Adam or Moses, or men, or angels, saints, sinners, or Satan and his infernals it is altogether wonderful, because it is the death of him, who is the Wonderful, the Son of God, the Son of Man.

The God of Heaven set the greatest possible merit upon the precious blood of Christ, and foretold by Isaiah that "if he should make his soul an offering for sin he should see a seed, who would celebrate his praises." Paul says of those who trample upon this blood that "it is a fearful thing to fall into the hands of the living God." The Holy Spirit tells us that all the blood shed from the beginning of the world in sacrifice was merely a shadowy type of the blood of the Son of God; and that although "without the shedding of blood there was no remission," yet the blood of animals never could cleanse the conscience;

that Christ's precious sacrifice alone reached that point in man, which indeed is a main point, for it is in the conscience that the sense of guilt resides; so that while knowledge purifies the understanding, pardon by the blood of Christ alone, can cleanse the conscience and deliver it from its troubled awakenings and dire whisperings and forebodings of punishment.

If a man were in prison for a capital crime, his blood forfeited, and under condemnation, and his fellows without were to call in at the prison window that he might take courage, that a sheep was to be offered in his stead. What might we in reason suppose his answer to be? "How much better is a man than a sheep, you mock me. The law does not admit of the less suffering for the greater." But suppose they told him that his fellow prisoner was to be taken for him. What might we suppose his answer to be? Would he not say, The guilty cannot suffer in law for the guilty, the guilty must suffer for themselves, my fellow prisoner is already dead in law, and cannot become my substitute. But suppose it were told him that the King's son had assumed his responsibility and would take his place in law, What then? He could then say, Now I am encouraged, this is admissible, it is the greater for the less, the just for the unjust. My conscience is cleansed, I shall he pardoned, I shall live.

The reason why the blood of a beast could not possibly cleanse the conscience, is that it was impossible in law to take a beast for a man. This would be to take the less for the greater, which is not admissible in such a case; the irrational for the rational, the brute for the man. Men, therefore, from the fall, came to the altar of God earning thither their cups of blood merely to show, or to (keep in remembrance, that their own blood or life, for the blood is the life, had been forfeited by an original infraction of law, till the greater, the just one, should appear, to take the place of the less and unjust. No man in his senses, could possibly think that the infraction of law could be redeemed by the blood of a beast. No man, therefore, could attain to any thing like a conscious sense of pardon by a mere animal offering.—If they had "Then," as the apostle says, "the worshipers being once cleansed would have ceased to offer:" but this they did not, but continued to sacrifice year by year, till Christ came, who by the one offering of himself, forever perfected them that are sanctified, that is, his dignity, infinite excellence, majesty, honor, and matchless grandeur, as the Son of God, inspired us with perfect assurance that as the greater for the less, the just for the unjust, the lord of all for all he is accepted by God; the substitution of his blood for ours must be honorable in law, glorious to God, and saving to man; the mind in this offering has something to rest upon, the offering of one infinitely excellent in behalf of worms of the dust. We are conscious by his resurrection that his offering is accepted; and we are conscious by the word of God that we are in him pardoned, and therefore, our conscience is absolutely in peace, "peace with God through Jesus Christ." The terrors of conscience are now dissipated by the light which has arisen from the tomb of Jesus and by the cruel suffering to the death which brought him to the tomb.

Let us then rejoice in our Saviour, the Prince of the kings of the earth. Let us exult and be glad, for salvation has been brought nigh. Let us give glory to God and sing praises. Let us sing of his love, his salvation, and wisdom, and glory. Hallelujah. Amen.

CHAPTER XVIII

Faith and Confession

Those who believe in Christ are commanded to confess him openly, to own by words before men their sacred convictions of the Saviour, and to join themselves forthwith to his body, the church, in order to their future upbuilding in the faith. It is no uncommon feeling, however, among those, who only believe the gospel without having tasted of its saving virtues and exalting joys, to imagine to themselves a plan very different from that of true Christianity, and to promise themselves that they will be able to profess it in a very domestic manner indeed. They think they will be exceedingly modest and retiring in their profession; so much so, indeed, that no one, not even their wife or husband, as the case may be, shall perceive it. They imagine that their religion will thus grow in proportion as they confine it to their own bosom, and be strengthened as they check its ardour to walk abroad, never dreaming that the sacred fire, which religion kindles up in the bosom, may, like other fires, be smothered by confinement, and that, like children, it will fail to acquire strength if it is denied exercise and the open air. Is not a taper quenched by its own burning when confined to too narrow bounds? And will not the religion, which is denied the honor of shining in the higher apartments of speech and action, by and by emit but a feeble ray, if confined to the cellar of the mind exclusively, and finally die, choked by the damps of false modesty and morbid apprehension, lest the ungodly should suspect us of piety? Away, then, with this miserably modified Christianity, which is ashamed of Jesus, and ashamed of his people in these days of wide-spreading irreligion. If you indulge in it, reader, of you will the Son of Man be ashamed before God and all the holy angels.

"If thou confess the Lord Jesus with thy mouth, and believe in thy heart that God has raised him from the dead, thou shalt be saved, for with the heart man believeth unto righteousness, and with then mouth confession is made unto salvation."

Here the Apostle connects faith and confession with salvation, as our blessed Lord before him connected faith and baptism with it. The reason of this is understood when it is known that a confession of the faith always preceded baptism.

The word saved in many parts of the scriptures has all the force and meaning of the word pardon. The above scripture speaks of faith and confession and connects righteousness with the one, and salvation with the other. Confession in the name of Christ is here assigned a very important connection and is associated with salvation itself; while belief is made to respect righteousness merely. But there is a real and important distinction between righteousness and salvation. Cornelius was a righteous man before he heard the gospel, but the messenger of God, notwithstanding, commanded him to send to Joppa for Peter who would tell him words by which he and his house should be saved. He did so and was pardoned. A person then may have such a hearty belief in God as to become perfectly upright and righteous in life and conduct, still he may not have the remission of his sins according to the Christian religion, because he may not have confessed Jesus Christ in the proper ordinance appointed for remission. He, then, who has received into his heart the saving oracle of the Father, should with all speed confess it before men, and seek pardon and the answer of a good conscience, by attending to this in the way appointed by Jesus our Lord. There be many people in the present day, however, who suffer exceedingly from their own defective acquaintance with the religion which they both profess and reverence and love. To such we would affectionately say, O! suffer the writer with all humility and brotherly affection, to aid you by this treatise in making "crooked things straight." Do you walk in darkness and see no light; do you, even with the new testament in your hand, feel that all is not right; that there is still something wanting to perfect your joys and calm your troubled breast? Do you still doubt, do you still hesitate whether you have an interest in the blood of Christ; whether you are pardoned through that most precious medium, and are a child of God and a joint heir of eternal life with Jesus Christ your Lord? Confess the truth which you have believed with your heart unto righteousness; turn to God and embrace this blessed religion in the form which was given to it by Jesus and his holy and inspired apostles. Arise: "why tarriest thou, Arise and be baptised and wash away thy sins, calling upon the name of the Lord." Surely, troubled sinner, the Lord has brought his salvation nigh; surely God has made himself known to those who were ignorant of him, and has been found of those who sought not after him. Will he then not be found of you, if you seek him in his own appointed way? "I am found of those who sought not after me," said the Lord, surely then he will be found of those who do seek after him in Christ Jesus; surely he will forgive and save all the contrite in heart, all who confess the oracle which his own lips have uttered concerning his adorable Son our blessed Saviour. As you have believed and repented, now confess and be saved; change your state; pass from the world to the church; quit sinners as you have quit sin, and join the righteous as you have espoused righteousness; and, dear friend, the Lord will bless you, and pour balm into your sin-sick soul; he will heal the diseases of your mind; he will bind up the bleeding heart; he will cure the fainting heart, and give you "beauty for ashes, the oil of joy for mourning, the garment of praise for the spirit of heaviness;" and you will be a tree of righteousness, a tree of the Lord's planting whose fruit will be glorious to God, and life to those that behold and taste of it; for men will return to God by your pious example.

CHAPTER XIX

Faith and Evidence

As our faith depends on the experience of others, and the fact in behalf of which the testimony is delivered, may or may not be pleasing to us, it becomes a question Whether in every case our faith is in proportion to the evidence? That is, Do we in all instances believe in a fact with a strength of confidence proportionate to the evidence which we have of its truth? I am persuaded we do not. I am persuaded that however it may be accounted for, we in many instances yield a stronger assent to certain propositions than the testimony warrants, and that in some cases we withhold our belief in direct opposition to very respectable evidence. It is an easy matter to believe that to be false, which we do not wish to be true; and testimony against what we desire should be false, is in many instances too readily received by us all. It is said in scripture that "As many as were determined on eternal life believed." that is, as many among Paul's auditors as had a disposition for eternal life on the principles and practices recommended by the Apostle, believed the facts of the gospel; eternal life was what they desired to possess, and they therefore gave a serious examination and ready admittance to the evidences of its truth and divine origin. While those, who sought nothing beyond the present world, and cared not about eternal life, rejected salvation and persecuted Paul who preached it. Nathaniel admitted the Messiahship very promptly, as did also several of the Apostles, as James and John the sons of Zebedee, and Matthew the Publican. Thomas, on the contrary, was very unbelieving on the subject of Christ's resurrection, and vowed he would not accept of any thing short of sensible demonstration of the fact. When the other disciples said to him "We have seen the Lord," he said, "Except I shall see in his hands the print of the nails, and put my finger into the print of the nails, and thrust my hand into his side I will not believe." The Lord granted him this proof, but said "Thomas, because thou hast seen me, thou hast believed: blessed are they that have not seen and yet have believed."

As a mirror can not reflect the image of a thing unless that thing is present, so there can be no evidence where there is no fact. Again, as it is not the fortune of every thing to be reflected from a mirror, there may be facts unknown, unascertained. Jesus might have been the Son of God and we might not have known it; because God might not have testified it.—But although there cannot be evidence without fact, yet, there may be testimony without either; for it does not follow that because men testify therefore they are to be believed, or therefore the thing is true concerning which they testify. They sometimes speak falsely, and are sometimes imposed upon by their imaginations and even by their own senses. In the case of the Messiahship, the person testifying is God; so that testimony here is the same as evidence, because it is impossible for God to lie. That Jesus is his Son must be a fact, or God could not have testified to it.

It is of vast importance to distinguish between evidence and testimony. A man may vouch a thousand things that cannot rationally be received as evidence. But here it is, perhaps, we impose upon ourselves and take the one for the other. We wish the thing to be so and on that account greedily seize upon every thing as a proof of its truth. We swallow down as evidence all that is proposed, style that proof which is only testimony, and receive as faith that which is only fancy. How gladly do we, who desire eternal life, grasp each thing that seems to make for the truth of the Christian Religion, and how eagerly do those, who like Gallic, care for none of these things, seize upon every thing in opposition to that religion! Mr. Paine, Mon. Voltaire and others were glad of every thing that militated against Revelation, because those men did not desire it to be true; while Paley, Clarke and others eagerly laid hold of every circumstance which they believed in any way calculated to illustrate and establish the credibility of our religion.

Upon the whole it may be said of Christianity, that there is abundance of evidence for its truth to every one who desires to inherit eternal life; but to such as are at ease and are contented with their lot here, testimony against it will in most instances be more acceptable than all that can or could be presented in favor of its truth.

There are many so fascinated with the pleasures of life, and so enthralled by their possessions here, that they never think either of God or heaven; who, if they could be taken thither, would doubtless have such a longing desire for the rich and fair abodes which they have created for themselves in this world that they would night and day be looking down upon them, and if it were possible would drop down again into a world where every thing from which they had been carried, had so little of heaven and so much of themselves in it. We are many times amazed at the apathy of individuals in regard to eternal life; and like fools, modern ministers apologize for their listlessness by telling them that they cannot believe unless they are wrought upon by some irresistible agency! But if those, who have such an appetite for believing every thing themselves would tell those, who desire to believe nothing that would disturb them at ease in their possessions, that they ought to bestir themselves, inquire into the truth of Christianity, and do homage to the God who made them, they would render them a much more rational and important service. There is no reason either in nature or revelation for laying the burden of such people's indolence or worldly-mindedness upon the Almighty. It is all of themselves. They love the world and the things of the world. God is not in all their ways. They do not honor him in their families. They call not upon his name. They are the men of this world, and not of the next. And it will always be best to tell them that they do not desire to inherit eternal life, that they are satisfied with the things of time, and with all their fancied greatness are little in their ambitions.

CHAPTER XX

The Kingdom of Heaven

The state of respite and the considerations out of which it has arisen, has afforded the divine mercy an opportunity of originating among us an Institution called the church; since the days of Moses the assembly of the faithful have been styled the church or congregation of God, and in the new testament the church of Christ, "My church." Since the days of our Lord Jesus, therefore, the true worshipers have been congregated on the belief of the elementary proposition under consideration, and called the church.

This establishment however, is spoken of in the scriptures under various names. It is called in some instances the fold of Christ. This is on account of the shepherd-like care which he exercises over them, and their own dependence on him for that care. They are styled the temple of God also, because God by his Holy Spirit, which it is the glory of Christianity to impart to each member, is said to be present with them and to dwell in them. They are even styled his family, which is an appellation the most honorable, all of them being his sons and daughters. But as this wide spreading family is diffused among all the nations of the earth, they are in the scriptures, also, called his kingdom; under this view of the matter, they are styled "a holy nation, a chosen race, a peculiar people" having their "citizenship in heaven" whence they look for the Saviour the Lord Jesus Christ. The person, therefore, who enters the church, is said to have entered the fold of Christ; he has been built as a lively stone into God's temple, he is also, accounted of as one who has entered God's family; he belongs to the royal house and has the great King for his father; but every man's family is his kingdom, the legitimate province of his paternal authority. It is also so with the Great God; and therefore, those who have obeyed the gospel, have entered his kingdom; they are become denizens of the heavenly reign, and subjects of the government of God. He, or his Son under him, being King.

In conformity with this varied representation of the same thing, namely, the church, those who believe and are baptized, are represented in the scriptures as having passed from condemnation to life, that is, from the present state of respite, which is a state of condemnation, to the church, in which they become the expectants and heirs of eternal life; they are said to be *married* to Christ; to have been *buried* and *raised* with him to a newness of life; they have been *ingrafted* into the good olive, another figure of the church; they have been *planted* in the husbandry or farm of God, translated from darkness to light, from the government of Satan to that of God; they are indeed, by means of belief, reformation, and immersion, said to be *born again*, *born* of water and Spirit, *born* of God; and in consequence of this are spoken of as adopted, having their *eyes opened, delivered, saved, sanctified, justified, released, purged, cleansed, washed, illuminated, circumcised, and created* after the image of God. They therefore are called the elect of God, but not before this; they are styled the faithful, the saints, the disciples, the brethren, Abraham's seed, God's heirs, joint heirs with Jesus Christ, the called, the beloved of God, and the sons and daughters of the Lord Almighty, who doeth all these things.

We ought not, however, to imagine that conversion to Christ by faith, repentance, and baptism, is in any respect changed by being set forth in scripture by these figures. Conversion is the same when called a death, burial, and resurrection, as it would have been if these figures had never been used to set it forth. Calling it a planting, a birth, a translation, a marriage, or salvation, does not altar its nature, or the means by which it is literally effected, namely, faith and obedience to the gospel. Some people like to choose figurative passages of scripture, especially the preachers; and when it happens that such do not know what conversion is in the fact, they make sad work of it in the figure. For figures can only be properly understood when we have correct ideas of the facts, which they are employed to represent. The new birth or second birth, spoken of in John 3 is a very popular figure; and when a man, who has not yet learnt what conversion is in fact or how it is accomplished, desires his audience should esteem him to be very "deep in divinity" he selects this figurative portion of sacred writ; and as an evangelical accouchier proceeds accordingly to show his audience with what dexterity he can handle the obstetrics of the gospel. But if a man once understands that conversion to God is effected by faith in Jesus Christ, reformation, and immersion, he may with much comfort to himself, shut his ears on every such an occasion, and leave the oratorical doctor to sport himself with his own deceivings. No body should attempt to teach the whole of a thing to others, who does not understand the one half of it himself, and the man who does not understand a thing in fact will not be likely to explain that thing in figure. Thousands of preachers, who do not know what they say, will tell their hearers that "they must be born again," who would not for all the blessings of the new birth, believe, repent, and be baptized themselves.

Figures have a fine effect in giving vivacity and sprightliness to the things which they prefigure; they are like a ray of light falling upon the face of a clock or watch, which shows more luminously what the time of day is without altering the mechanism. The mechanism of the gospel, therefore, is not destroyed, or changed, or even varied by being set forth as a birth, burial, &c.

The church of God is an *imperium in imperio*, a divine government in the midst of worldly governments, a moral kingdom in the midst of political ones; it is in the world, but "not of the world;" Our Lord said of it, "My kingdom is not of this world." It is a kingdom of peace; it has no arms, no ammunition, no munitions of war, its subjects do not fight. "If my kingdom were of this world then would my servants fight." Those institutions called Christianity, which have established themselves in the nations by force of arms, are therefore not the kingdom of Christ; they are not the church of Christ; their members are not the members of the church of Christ, but of the church and kingdom of the clergy. The Kingdom of Christ is founded in his own blood, not in the blood of his enemies; it is enlarged by the diffusion of the truth, not by the triumphs of war. It aspires to superior renown by the inculcation of superior principles; and would seek perpetuity and stability by the practice of eternal virtue in all those who are the subjects of it.[8]

When the Religion of Christ is contemplated and set forth under the figure of a kingdom, it is to bespoken of accordingly. Jesus is the king. Christians are the subjects. The whole globe is the territory. The new testament contains its laws. Jerusalem is its capital. It began in the days of the Caesars. It will terminate only with eternity; and men are born into it in a manner agreeably to the will of God, that is, by "water and Spirit;" in a word, men are begotten to God by hearing and believing the gospel, and born to him by obeying it. But in all this the literal gospel is not changed; it still is believe, repent, and be baptized.

The general government of God over the nations, and the special government of Christ over the church, should be better understood than they are; and the difference between both of them, and political governments of the governments of this world, should be well

---

[8] See Brother Campbell's Extra on the Kingdom of Heaven; in which our religion is treated of under this idea.

understood. I have endeavored to decipher the difference between the divine administration and that of the nations in certain points but without much success. When and for what God lays his hand on an individual, on a city, nation, and district of country to punish them, when he exalts to renown and for what, when he casts down to the ground thrones and those who sit upon them and cuts up the nationality of a people and scatters them to the winds of heaven and for what he does this, is a piece of political science which statesmen ever have left, and perhaps ever will leave, uncultivated, unimproved.

When the Lord Jesus handles an individual for his misdemeanors, when he lays his hand upon a family and for what, when he takes hold of a church or district of churches to punish them, as he did the churches of Asia, is a part of Christian science but little understood. Yet both God and Christ do punish individuals, families, cities, nations, and churches.

One thing I think is certain; that the divine administration proceeds upon the principle of virtue and vice, rewarding the former and punishing the latter.

Secondly: In the matter of rewarding virtue the divine government differs from the human; for while our law punishes the disobedient, it confers no positive reward upon the obedient. But the divine government does. "In the keeping of his commandments there is great reward."

Our cities are shockingly governed by men, and they are terribly punished by God. The magistracy generally look to the emolument, and not to the design of the office. They are generally the creatures of party policy, and not the offspring of the general virtue of the community. They, therefore, rule and make laws of monopoly and of external policy without regard to virtue and the morals of the citizens. We consequently have swellings and tumults, mobs, and murders. In fine, we think with the scriptures, that "the wicked walk on every side," because the vilest men are exalted.

The government of Christ is administered on better principles; and if a church is recognized by him to be his, every branch in it that beareth not good fruit, is loped off and burned. The present state of Christendom, however, conceals from the eyes of many this economy in the government of God and Christ, for it is not easy to say which among the different assemblies can well be recognized as a true church of Jesus Christ. It may be said of them generally that if they are not synagogues of satan, they are at least assemblies exceedingly ignorant of original Christianity both as respects knowledge and duty.

From all that has been quoted it is most obvious, that the proposition under consideration, lies at the bottom of Christianity. If this is true all things else in our religion is true; if it is false nothing else is of any authority; and the world is wholly without revealed religion. But it is true to all intents and purposes; and therefore Christianity is true, and is intended of God to be the religion of the world, the whole world.

What admirable knowledge have we here! The Son of God made known to mankind by his own Father, the great Eternal. Again, how fortunate, after the lapse of so many ages, after so much apostacy, and in the midst of so much division, to be able to throw off all rubbish from around the sacred oracle, and to seize the truth all simple and uncompounded as it came from the lips of God himself! The truth, the saving truth, the truth worthy of all acceptation, is that Jesus is the Messiah the Son of God! This is the foundation stone of the Christian church, the great matter of faith with Christians and that which is proposed to man for salvation in all the world. "He, who believes and is baptized, shall be saved; and he, who believes not, shall be condemned."

We can now, from the eminence to which we have climbed, look around us and view things in comparison. In the distance is seen Adam the first of men. At hand Jesus the Son of God. Each the head of a creation. Adam of the old, Jesus of the new. The first dominion animal, the last spiritual. The old creation defiled with sin, misery and death; the new pregnant of life, righteousness, and joy. In the one all is natural, weakness, corruption, and dishonor; in the last every thing is spiritual, stable, incorruptible, and honorable. "As in Adam all die, so in Christ shall all be made alive." In the resurrection eternal life is substituted for animal life, the knowledge of God takes the place of faith, and supreme bliss the place of misery. Man is brought back to the true God, corrected, reformed, sanctified, glorified, and made meet to inherit heaven; rich in experience, and full of reverence for the divine authority.

In the "creation of God," of which Jesus is called the beginning, there will be no temptation, no tempter, no sin, no misery, no death; knowledge, duty and happiness, will be united in man never to be severed any more; and his appetite for truth, derived from the first of these, his love of the beautiful in morals, and his thirst for joy, will be gratified to overflowing through the ceaseless ages of eternity.

But be it observed that in all the plans and means by which the divine mercy accomplishes our redemption there is nothing inconsistent with, or different from, that which is reasonable, or even our own usages. If there were it would destroy the credibility of Revealed Religion; for how should we receive as faith that which, when fully examined and fully understood, first insulted our reason? The facts of one suffering voluntarily in behalf of another, and the greater taking the place of the less, and the just that of the unjust, do not essentially differ in their nature from the case in which the richer takes the place of the poorer, and in the way of benevolence discharges his debts; or that in which one man in pity redeems another who is captive. God's plans are the very same as our own when founded in wisdom and goodness. He only proceeds on them on a more extended scale. When Sabinus the Syrian, during the siege of Jerusalem, says to the Emperor, "I choose death voluntarily for thy sake, O! Caesar," and the Lord Jesus says, "I give my life for the life of the world," in what does the difference lie? Not in the principle; but in the person and in the occasion. Jesus acts the part of Sabinus on an infinitely extended scale. Sabinus dies for one, Jesus for all. When one man, in accordance with an oracle, devotes himself in behalf of Rome, and another in behalf of Greece, and a third person in behalf of the world, the principle is the same, the persons, the occasion, and the ends to be accomplished only are different. Now, it is this heroic, and at the same time reasonable, and necessary nature of Christianity that so highly recommends it to our understanding. At bottom it is only the application of a principle to the salvation of the world which we have been in the habit of seeing applied to individuals, and nations at most. There is, therefore, nothing of the marvelous in the structure of Christianity, nothing of the unheard of at all. We all practice on its fundamental principles a thousand times in the course of our life, and history affords innumerable instances perfectly illustrative thereof; some on vast, some on minuter scales. The largeness, not the unreasonableness, of our religion astonishes us. We wonder that the whole world should be cornered and lie in a preternatural condition, and yet ten thousand arguments prove it. We wonder that *God's Son* should appear to deliver us from this condition, and yet that a greater, and wiser, and better than all, should do this, is much more reasonable than that one of ourselves or an inferior person should do it. It is the greatness of the game, the mightiness and importance of the stake alone, which appears incredible. The race is for eternal life, and not a thousand pounds; the personage is not Sabinus or Codrus, but Jesus; it is not one of the kings of the earth, but the king of kings; and the stake is not an individual or nation, but the world, the whole world from the beginning to the end of it.

The man who objects to our salvation, because of the principle on which it proceeds, does certainly, therefore, object to that which is most reasonable and common among men. He might as well object to admit it in the settlement of his own debts by a friend, when his misfortunes have disabled him from settling them for himself. But the man who receives this salvation receives something which, at the same time, can be defended rationally. Reason is not sacrificed to salvation; nor the man to the Christian; but reason is only sanctified and the man is saved. It is in the profession of false, and corrupted religion, that reason and the man disappears, and gives plate to frenzy and the fool.

There is a very general prejudice among the higher and middle classes of society, against our religion, arising from its supposed hostility to our common natural rights and liberties. I fancy, it will be very satisfactory, therefore, to such of those as may read this book—to see things in regard to this prejudice, cleared up a little.

Be it observed, then, that the question lies between the common wealth of Israel or the church, and the best government on earth; say for the present, the United States' government. Is man and his natural and inherent rights more honored by the commonwealth of Christianity or that of the United States? That is the question, for if it be shown that our religion is in equal or greater harmony with our nature than the best government on earth, then the objection is done away with; and the person who makes it is bound, on the principles of reason and good faith, to turn Christian as readily as, and more readily than, if arriving from another government, he would seek to become a citizen of these United States.

What, then, are the inherent gifts which nature bestows in common upon men?

Answer.—First life; second the love of knowledge; third a talent for duty; fourth a capacity for happiness; fifth personal and mental freedom without restraint. I say, without restraint.

What, then, is the use of society or human government?

Answer.—To impose restraints, and punish us when we will not abide by them. Some governments impose more restraints upon nature than do others. They are consequently reckoned not so good. And those governments are esteemed the best, which impose the fewest restraints; for the social system is accounted good in proportion as it approaches the natural system. But see—society confers no right; we, therefore, owe her none. It is nature that bestows all right, all liberty, all property mental and physical. God gives; man takes away. Yes, our life, our love of knowledge, our talent for duty, our capacity for happiness and right to personal freedom, are five matters which are given to us by God and not by man. They are the inherent or inherited rights of nature, and are not granted to us by any consent of man. They are not communicated to us by any human authority, and no human authority should take them away. Any limitation or any modification, of these rights and liberties, must, therefore, be of society. Government is made up of these several quantities of power, which all the citizens out of their native fullness, throw in as that which they are willing to surrender for the good of each other, and for the future security of that portion of our natural rights and liberties, which still remains. Government is, therefore, a creation by the people. In making it, we resemble rich men throwing of our abundance into the hat of a poor man, who himself has nothing; and we continue to throw in until he is richer than any one of us; but not so rich as the whole taken together. But we give it to be retained only so long as he who receives it, shall use it well. Every government, therefore, is at first as poor as Job, has nothing of itself, and depends for its power, as it does for wealth, on the voluntary contributions of the citizens. Some nations, like some individuals, are profuse rather than prudent, and surrender to their governments powers which make them lords rather than servants, and tyrants rather than rulers. These governments become like the beggar who is not satisfied with being raised to a condition of wealth superior to any of his benefactors, but he exalts himself to be the Lord of all; and they style the people their "subjects," instead of the people calling them their ministers.

But let us look more attentively at natural rights and liberties; let us see what things naturally belong to us in consequence of possessing life, freedom, knowledge, a capacity for happiness, and a taste for duty.

1st. LIFE:—From the possession of life, proceeds the right to enjoy it, and to put into requisition all those means which are proper for securing the necessaries, utilities, and ornaments thereof.

2d. KNOWLEDGE:—Our capacity for knowledge, and our love for it, gives birth to the right of free inquiry and free discussion in all that relates to nature, society, or religion. The great things of science, government, and Revelation are ours, only through the capacity which we have for knowledge; for it is certain that unless we possessed this endowment, we must for ever remain ignorant of these things. But in bestowing it upon man, the great God has signified to all that he intends we should freely inquire, and fully discuss every thing, and any thing relating to nature, social life, and revealed religion.

3d. DUTY:—From our sense of duty spring our right and freedom of choice, and the doctrine of our responsibility to God and to one another. If, therefore, we are denied the right of choice, we are in fact denied to be creatures endowed with a sense of duty, and consequently creatures of moral responsibility. All the right of choosing a possession, choosing a country, a government and governors, a wife, and a religion, is involved in this natural sense of duty with which we are endowed. It ought, therefore, to be greatly respected.

4th. HAPPINESS:—From the capacity to enjoy and be happy, arises the right of pursuing happiness by such means as knowledge and duty shall enable us to put into use for the attainment of that end. Happiness is the perfection and ultimate idea in our nature, and the end of all government human and divine; for it is certain that the dealings of God with man and his management of him, on the principles of Revealed Religion, is only to make us finally partakers of his own happiness.

5th. PERSONAL FREEDOM:—This natural gift is of the last importance; on the possession of it depends every thing; the perfection of the man of genius, the man of science, the artist, and all both rich and poor, and high and low. What were man if this were taken from him? On our free intercourse with external nature, the blue atmosphere, the spangled heavens, the green earth, and all the drapery and garniture of the globe, with trees, shrubs, under-shrubs, herbs, grains, grasses, mountains, vallies, rivers, seas, oceans, and the works of art and man, depend both life, knowledge, duty, and happiness; and it is certain that if our personal freedom is denied us, these are virtually denied us also. Rob us of the one and you rob us of the others. Grant us the one, and you secure us in all the others. This natural gift has given birth among the nations to the *habeas corpus* act, a circumstance which demonstrates its vast importance.

But let us look over these things again. Life is the indefeasible right of every man until he forfeits it by a violation of that compact to which he has set his seal as a member of civil society.

The personal freedom, which we have of nature, is that which makes life worth the having and like life itself is inalienable, that is, like our right to live, it is bestowed upon as by God, to be retained by us, not to be bartered away.

KNOWLEDGE.—Our capacity for knowledge gives birth to our right to free inquiry, without which we might sink into the most brutal ignorance, and be imposed upon by the more crafty of mankind, till our personal freedom, and the right of life whence it springs, should either be wrested from us altogether or rendered so intolerable as to make death its opposite, the most desirable of the two. From the right of free inquiry all the knowledge of the world; all that we know of the earth, the sea, the air, the skies, all that we know of Science, Mechanics, Astronomy, Optics, Mathematics, Geography, Electricity, Galvanism, Chemistry; all that we have learnt of the arts, whether useful or ornamental, Music, Drawing, Engraving, Sculpture, Painting, Poetry, Eloquence and History; all that we know of Natural History, Anatomy, Botany, Mineralogy, arises from free inquiry and from the capacity for knowledge with which our Creator has endowed us. Take away free inquiry then, and you reduce man to the level of the brute; you virtually adjudge him not to be possessed of a capacity for knowledge, and consequently injure, insult, degrade, and dishonor his nature. If we prevent a man from freely inquiring into "*What is*," we must not be surprised if he fails to know "*What might to be*;" that is, deprive him of knowledge, and you divest him of morality, that is, ignorance and immorality are inseparable, or ignorance is the parent of vice.

DUTY:—From man's capacity for duty arises all the civilities of enlightened and civilized life.—The freedom of choice, the adoption of morals, the preference which we give to the beautiful and humane in social life, the maxims of the family circle, and rules of discipline, obedience to parents, and subordination to magistrates. Take away the right of choice in these things, the right of improvement, and again you brutalize man, and virtually deny him to be created a moral agent; you insult his moral sense of duty; you injure, you degrade, you dishonor his nature, and sink him beneath the man in point of happiness, for mere animal enjoyment can never fill up the measure of his capacity for happiness.

HAPPINESS:—Man, as we observed in our first section, was created in the image of God with a capacity for happiness. But the enjoyment of this great good, after which his nature unceasingly thirsts, was laid, as we have seen, in the line of duty. For if knowledge precedes duty, duty must precede happiness.—Hence the vast importance of intellectual and moral freedom; the moment this is taken from a man the road to happiness is blocked up, and he is left a prey to ignorance and despair. Man may after this be happy indeed, but only as a brute. No rational bliss can be attained and enjoyed but through the medium of knowledge and duty. It is by enlightening the understanding with what is to be known, and disciplining the affections in what ought to be done, that the spirit of man either in social, or religious life, can taste of the happiness which it is his ambition to enjoy.

We return to the question, therefore, whether the government of the Messiah does not bear a more benevolent aspect to these natural rights of life, personal freedom, knowledge, duty, and happiness than the best government on earth? say the American government?

1. To begin with life, the chief gift. Christianity purposes to bestow upon all, who by sacred intellectual and moral culture will prepare themselves for its reception, the gift of eternal life. Her regard for life, therefore, is most sacred and cannot be excelled by that of any other government on earth. She esteems it as the most admirable of all the gifts of God; and says, "Is not life more than meat and the body than raiment?" Still she flatters not its possessors, but reminds them of the truth that "It is but a vapour that soon passes away," and strongly inculcates the necessity of fitting ourselves for the reception of immortality, which she knows to be better adapted to our desires.

2. As for our love of knowledge, she purposes to fill us with all the riches and treasures of Jesus Christ. She opens for us a field of inquiry and sacred meditation, which the literature of the nations knows nothing at all about; and by assuring us that all that we see, the world, the universe, is of God, she inspires us with an ardent zeal to inquire into his glorious works; so that she brings the works and words of God alike before us, and fills us with the most excellent knowledge. She is the patron of free inquiry, free discussion, and her motto is, "Prove all things and hold fast that which is good."

3. In regard to duty, she says, "Whatsoever things are true, whatsoever things are honest, whatsoever things are just, whatsoever things are pure, whatsoever things are lovely, whatsoever things are of good report, if there be any thing virtuous, any thing praise-worthy, think of these things."

Think of these things:—The Christian Religion begins at the proper place; she searches out the root of the evil; she probes the wound and applies the knife and the cautery, and discovers the same solicitude for the health of the mind, for the thoughts and intents of the heart, that political law exhibits for the body, the words and actions. *Think* of these things. Now if the laws of the republic are to be admired because of the virtuous direction which they would give to our words and actions, how much more to be admired is Christianity, which would seat virtue deep down into the soul; and produce the fruits of righteousness in man, by first planting the seeds of it in his mind and spirit. And if it is accounted benevolent in national law to secure the safety of the whole by taking from each the overgrowth or superfluity of natural right, is it not much more benevolent in revealed religion to carry out into the heart the good work which political law begins, and to extend to the mind and thought what the imperfection of human law could apply only to the lip and life. If the mind be allowed to be one third of the man, and his words and actions the other two thirds, then the defectiveness of human laws will appear in this, that they never touch that one third. But the mind is to words and actions what the root is to the tree and the fruit. Human laws, therefore, do not reach the root of the matter, they fail to make man happy, because they leave him impure.

Whoever therefore, docs virtuously and from principle admire the good government of the nations, must much more admire that of Christianity; and whoever would make choice of a particular political system of government because it more than all others coincides with natural right and natural liberty, must much more make choice of the Christian system of revealed religion; because it more than all others sheds a benign influence on the rights and liberties of man. In short, God's revealed system is more than all others like his natural system, that is, the political systems of men are not in such harmony with God's natural system as Christianity is.

Need I after this, say, that our Religion in connection with good government, is better calculated to produce happiness in man, than good government when acting alone? Why, to possess the privileges, honors, and principles of Christianity and the shadow and protection of such a political policy as that of the United States, is almost bliss complete. Here the man of God can sit under his own fig tree, and under his vine in the full enjoyment of life, with the right of free inquiry, the right of choice, and right through these channels to pursue happiness, none daring to make him afraid. But while we give the preference to Christianity, and have showed that it is in greater harmony with nature than any system of man's devising, yet it ought to be distinctly remarked that she exists as an *imperium in imperio*, a divine kingdom in the midst of earthly kingdoms. She is in the world, but not of the world. Her origin is from above, and she aspires only to the government of such spirits as are emulous of immortality and will conform to her pure and just and holy laws. At present her authority is but partially respected. The times allotted for the great worldly policies of Rome and others have not expired; but the glorious day is at hand when she will mount up to the supreme dominion of the world.

From the foregoing observations it will appear to the reader, that our natural rights are life, freedom, and a capacity for knowledge, duty, and happiness; and that our natural liberties consist in a freedom to gratify and enjoy all these agreeably to the laws of nature. But in entering into society, we submit to certain social restraints; and hence are created what are denominated political rights and liberties; which consist of the enjoyment of life, freedom, knowledge, duty, and happiness according to the laws of society. And the political systems devised by men will always be good in proportion as they approach the system of nature devised by God. But nothing of man's devising can approach so near to nature or so perfectly harmonize with it as docs the Christian religion.

The Christian Proposition is evidently a question of fact between God and the man who hears it; and, therefore, in judging of it every man is made to sit as a juror on his own life. He that receives the proposition "sets to his seal that God is true," and whoever receives it not "makes God a liar." Not every sin shall condemn a man at the last day; but one sin certainly will condemn him; that he "has not believed in the name of the Only Begotten Son of God." If God has identified that of his own Son with the person of the Messiah, it must be highly injurious to the divine majesty to have this contradicted. Be it remembered therefore, that it is a fearful thing to fall into the hands of the living God. Be it remembered that our God is a consuming fire.

3. But the Holy Spirit has recognized the author of the Christian Religion as the long promised and much expected Messiah of the Jews; he descended on his person and remained on him in the presence of the whole nation. What then, is to be the fate of that man, who sins against the Holy Spirit, and by refusing his testimony in this important matter, sets aside the great fact of the Messiahship on which the redemption of man is founded? Is it a light matter, can it be conceived to be a light matter, to charge with falsehood the ancient scriptures and the Spirit by which they were dictated? No. The Holy Spirit, therefore, will neither dwell in us while we live, nor raise us after we are dead, if we are found to dishonor him before men, by so violent an insult done to his veracity.

4. The denial of the Messiahship involves vast consequences. How shall that man meet Jesus in judgment, who has contemned the proposition of our Holy Religion, and the proof which goes to sustain it? Who has not deigned the Christian religion even a respectful hearing? Who instead of submitting to its wholesome restraints, accepting of its unrivaled blessings, and clothing himself with its pure morals, has trampled upon the entire institution and rejected all its claims to veracity and good faith?

See in what an attitude the man sets himself before the judge of all the earth, who questions his divine descent. Mark the dishonor which he offers to the judge of the quick and dead who denies the Messiahship. He lays in against him a proper insult truly, and commits an injury against the Lord's anointed, which by the kings of the earth would be punished with immediate death. He charges him with imposture and the most unworthy deceit; and, instead of turning to his own purification and salvation the religion which his Redeemer has consecrated by his precious blood, he makes it the medium of grosser profanity and finally dies by that by which it was intended of God he should live.

But the number of those who affect to disbelieve in Christ, is perhaps smaller than that of those who refuse to obey him after they have believed. What can be the reason, that mortal men, after recognizing at the bar of their own consciences the divine mission of the author of the true Religion, should nevertheless hesitate to obey him, refuse to accept the precious blessings sent to us from God, and set themselves in the attitude of those who are either afraid to obey or ashamed to confess the name of our great Redeemer? There is a reason for this, and therefore, we shall labor the point a little, and endeavor to discover it.

In seeking to find an answer to the above question we require to be guided. We shall, therefore, follow our Lord Jesus, who has assigned several reasons for this erratic course in some who hear the gospel and obey it not. First in relation to the men of Messiah's own day, the scriptures say: "Nevertheless many of the Chief Priests, and scribes of the people believed on him; but they confessed him not; for they loved the praise of men more than the praise of God."—To these the Redeemer said "How can ye believe on me, who seek honor one of another, and seek not the honor which cometh of God alone." Here, then, is one reason in answer to the question already asked.—Men desire the approbation of one another, and will secure it at all hazards. The explanation very readily suggests to us also, that the defect is not in the head but the heart, not in the understanding but in the affections, and that while such men have the penetration to perceive the truth of the Messiahship, they possess not the fidelity requisite to obey him; but with all their good sense, suffer themselves to be ruled by a little brief applause, the transient approbation of relatives and acquaintances. Is it to be questioned for a moment, then, that such people ought not to be gifted with immortality? My opinion is that it would be highly dangerous to render such persons independent by eternalizing them. Innate life would ill become men of such defective virtue. Metal of so base a sort ought not to be poured into the mould of immortality. God's Son says of them, therefore, that they "shall never see life." "He that believeth (obeyeth) the Son hath everlasting life; and he that believeth not the Son shall not see life; but the wrath of God abideth on him." This means what it says and calls for no explanation.

But in this love of popularity is to be taken into account the means usually employed to secure it; the fascinations of riches, the love of place, the distinctions which possession and personal accomplishments confer, and every other matter which may recommend us to men and which without obedience make us an abomination to God.

These things work upon the imaginations and worldly interests of men; and make them ashamed or afraid to join the church, which must ever be composed of that portion of society who in a degree have overcome these feelings, and who are for the most part poor or the middle class of mankind. "Has not God chosen the poor of this world, rich in faith, and heirs of the kingdom of heaven?" Not that the scripture just quoted suggests that God prefers the poor to the rich, for we are expressly informed that he indulges no personal preferences towards any man, but makes his choice on good principles and good actions alone. "With God there is no respect of persons." But the poor of this world are in more propitious circumstances in regard to the gospel and are more apt to be rich in faith and holy confidence in God. There are in the higher ranks of society matchless forms of human nature, both in body and in mind, men and women of the fairest mould, having minds enriched with every natural gift, and every social grace; and it would, and perhaps it does, make angels weep to see so much personal attraction, and so much mental power and grace thrown like a weed away, for the lack of being sanctified by faith in God. What a pity that those noble beings, and "forms excelling human," do not give audience to the sacred ministers of the Christian Religion, the apostles and prophets of Jesus Christ! How greatly is it to be deplored that such do not add to their social refinement, the consecrations of our holy religion, and that while their wealth and personal and mental superiority carry them suddenly to the summit of society, they remain there regardless of the honor that comes from God alone, and never once deign to make a single effort to secure his favour. How much it is to be regretted that in many instances, these prime images of the Deity are forgetful of the sacred oracles and wholly unacquainted with them; rich indeed in worldly lore, but perfect beggars in regard to the treasures of wisdom and knowledge, which are stored up in the Book of God.

To such we would beg leave to say, Study the scriptures. In the language of the wisest of men, we would say, "Remember thy Creator in the days of thy youth, while the evil days come not, nor the years draw nigh, when thou shalt say I have no pleasure in them. While the sun, or the light, or the moon, or the stars be not darkened; nor the clouds return after the rain. In the day when the keepers of the house shall tremble, and the strong men shall bow themselves, and the grinders shall cease because they are few, and they that look out of the window be darkened, and the door shall be shut in the streets, when the sound of the grinding is low and he shall start up at the voice of the bird and all the daughters of music shall be brought low. Also when they shall be afraid of that which is high, and fears shall be in the way, and the almond tree shall flourish, and the grasshopper shall be a burden, and desire shall fail, because man goeth to his long home, and the mourners go about the street. Or ever the silver cord be loosed, or the golden bowl be broken, or the pitcher broken at the fountain, or the wheel broken at the cistern. Then shall the dust return to the earth as it was, and the spirit shall return to God who gave it."

To such as believe the gospel and do not obey it, we read a fearful lesson in the words of our Redeemer. "Fear not them that kill the body, but are not able to kill the soul, but rather fear him who is able to destroy both soul and body in hell; yes, I say unto you, fear him." If those who believe the gospel without obeying it, and continue in sin, from fear of the rebuke and scorn and contempt of those who themselves are not Christians, would but think of the mighty power of God to protect them and of the little real importance that belongs to the good opinion of many who are opposed to God, they certainly could not for a moment hesitate to decide, but would readily say, with Joshua, "Let others do as they will, as for me and my house we will serve the Lord."

The Redeemer, however, suggests another reason why men who believe in him, do not obey. They are ashamed to profess the gospel in its simplicity. To such he says "Whosoever shall be ashamed of me and my gospel before this evil and adulterous generation, of him will I be ashamed before my Father and the holy angels!" It is a singular fact that a man, who has intellect enough to understand and believe the truth and blushes not to commit sin, shall nevertheless feel quite ashamed of the gospel, redden at the idea of obeying it, and feel as if his own pride and the pride of his giddy and godless and elegant but earthly circle of acquaintance were going to be wounded. When, however, a man believes the truth and boldly confesses it, he greatly justifies his own nature and shows himself worthy of a blessing. "Whosoever shall confess me before men," says the Lord, "him will I confess before my Father in heaven."

But besides these hindrances from the side of men, the love of popularity, the fear of men, and shame for our religion, the Lord Jesus assigns another reason why individuals do not obey the gospel, viz: that they have not the love of God in them. "I know you" said he to certain persons, "that you have not the love of God in you." Ah! this is a special reason. Many there be whose love, self-love burns with an intensity too great to be concealed. It is most obvious that they are lovers of their own selves; and like the unjust judge, "Fear not God and regard not man." Wild, turbulent, and contumacious they turn up their insolent faces to heaven as if it were unworthy of their ambition, and stalk abroad upon the earth as if the world were made for them and them alone. Such are your men in office too frequently in these days of sickly infidelity, the leaders of armies, and naval officers, professors of science, and courtiers, parasites, men of honor, and the nobles of the earth. But he who is higher than the highest will find them out, and he will humble the triumphant look of their haughty eyes. He will reach them. He will visit them in due season. God will test both the strength of their wisdom and the rectitude of their ways. He will search them as with a lighted candle, and unravel the obliquities of their course. They purchase a little "brief authority" here at the marvelous forfeiture of eternal life hereafter. They sacrifice endless eternity on the altar of passing time, and honor themselves only and not God, who made them, and for whom they were made.

To such we would say, be ashamed, you haughty ones.—Prove that you are what you would have all the world believe you to be, by substituting in your life internal virtue for external ornament; clothe yourselves with humility of mind; condescend to the poor; increase their bread; and know that true excellence consists in doing good to others. Do you judge the God of heaven to be altogether such a one as yourselves? Does he admire what you admire? And does he approve what you so eagerly pursue? He is the God of truth and righteousness, just and upright is he. He loves all the meek of the earth, and listens to the cry of the poor man. He looks down from heaven on high. His face lightens the path of the upright in heart, and he comforts those who mourn. Go, then, and learn of him, haughty scorner, go and gather grandeur and personal nobility by imitating God. Let the princely ornaments of uprightness, and truth, and peace, and condescension, and meekness, and purity, be the objects of your ambition; adorn yourself with these, and begin to speak of true greatness, when you have possessed yourself of real goodness.

Perhaps I cannot close this discourse, with greater interest to the reader than by adding the following letter from a Christian. In it he will see two things at least; that good sense is not sacrificed, and that the finer feelings of the human heart are not crushed, by becoming a Christian; but on the contrary that the former of these is directed into a proper channel, and the latter towards an object infinitely suitable and all-worthy of being loved, the Redeemer of the world.

MY DEAR WALTER:—

There is no theme so dear to my soul as our Blessed Lord and Saviour Jesus Christ. To him I look at all times and for all things, and in him all my most ardent wishes and earnest expectations and hopes are centred. To me he is all things. He is my God, my Lord, my life, my preserver and the uplifter of my head. I love him, adore him, worship him. I live in him, hope in him, rejoice in him. To be found in him clothed upon with his righteousness, see him as he is, and be transformed into his glorious image, constitute my highest ambition. What are all the honors of this world, all the gaudy trappings of the highest earthly dignitary—the loudest notes of the trumpet of fame, the highest respect claimed by, and paid to the most haughty of the sons of men! To be made a king and priest unto Jesus Christ, surpasses all that can be imagined or enjoyed by mortals here as far as the heavens are higher than the earth—there is no comparison. The contrast is the brightness of eternal glory as beheld by John exhibited in the person of our blessed Jesus and the dullness of all objects with which this favored apostle had ever before been conversant. To be immortal, clothed in light, crowned with glory, our faces as the sun shining in his strength, our mouths filled with praises to our God, our voices as the sound of many waters, and our hearts dilated with unalloyed joy and gladness; to mingle in social, and loud and hearty songs, with all the excellent of the earth to Him who has redeemed us by his blood; to behold the beauty of the Lord, contemplate his works, to admire the magnificence of a universe without bounds; in short, to have every power of the mind immeasurably enlarged and made to dwell in an immortal, a spiritual, a glorious, a *powerful* body and then to be feasted to overflowing with every thing grateful to these purified and enlarged senses, constitute all that can be enjoyed.

I like to think about heaven, it is my home. It is that rest which remains for the people of God, and into which I hope to be introduced by a greater Joshua than he who led the children of Israel into Canaan. I long for, and anticipate the second coming of my blessed master. Come quickly, Lord Jesus. O! how my soul would bound if I should hear the last summons from the trump of God, and see the Lord Jesus coming in the clouds of Heaven, with power and great glory, attended by ten thousands of his saints! Farewell world—welcome, thrice welcome, my change. I have no deep-rooted affections in this earth, and I desire to become daily more and more indifferent to all its fascinations, that my spirit may be purified as the spirit of my master is pure, and that I may thus be transformed into his likeness even while tabernacling in clay—I can conceive of no higher enjoyment than to be like Jesus—He is the personification of infinite excellence—He is perfection—He is God. To be like him, therefore, is to be excellent, perfect, god-like. Who would not see thee, thou King of Saints? There is none that I desire beside thee. O! when shall I come and appear before God. I feel, Walter, enthusiastically fond of my Lord and my God, Jesus Christ. He has done great things for me, whereof I am glad. He has given to us great and precious promises whereon I rely. He has awaked in my breast, hopes which reach far, far beyond the utmost stretch of imagination. He has made me to rejoice in hope of the glory of God, and be filled with joy when looking beyond the valley of the shadow of death. I by faith, distinctly view the resplendency of the New Jerusalem, having the glory of God, and being lighted up by the Lamb. The Jerusalem of the Jews was nothing—the temple was nothing—the visible presence nothing— when compared with our Jerusalem, our temple, and the Lord God, and our visible presence the Lamb—Glory to God in the highest. Hallelujah to the Lamb! for such enriching prospects. Let us go up into the house of the Lord. Our feet shall stand within thy gates, O Jerusalem!—they shall prosper that love thee. Walter, let us go up to this Pentecost. We shall never know what joy is until we get there, and as for enthusiasm, that is the place where we can allow it to flow with unrestrained impetuosity from hearts bursting with fullness of love to him who has washed them in his own blood, raised them to glory, honor, and immortality.

S. C——.

ANSWER

MY DEAR S:—God bless you; the Son of God preserve you; the communion of the Spirit of God be with you:—I will confess to you that your sentiments concerning our Saviour, are those which the holy scriptures have imprinted, I hope indelibly, on my mind, respecting him.

I do believe him to be that adorable Being whom you describe, the Son of God and our Redeemer. I have listened to many great men speaking and writing on science. I have read some, and heard much of politics and government; but after eighteen years patient study into the sacred oracles, I am persuaded that the Bible contains the most excellent knowledge. This book has the advantage over all others in this, that it is perfect in regard to the matter of which it discourses. It is not so with books of human science whether natural or moral. The wisest of philosophers and the most exalted of our statesmen have deplored their own blindness, and the defectiveness of science; but here is a book, the Bible, in which all that needs to be known in this life and is necessary for salvation, is contained. There is no defect here. So that although religion has been little attended to by great men, yet we find it perfected in spite of their neglect of it; while that which they have most of all cultivated and cherished is still very inexplicable in some important points; which shows, I think, that the book which contains our religion must be of God.

If the sense of guilt which rests, and has rested, upon the nations generally, since the world began, is felt to be intolerable by an individual, Christianity says, "Come unto me all you that toil and are burdened." The precious blood of Christ, like that of an unspotted and unblemished lamb, has been shed for the remission of sins. "Be baptized for the remission of your sins and you shall receive the gift of the Holy Spirit." If a man becomes satisfied of the fleeting nature of all earthly things and of the unprofitableness of mere human intercourse, here is the church, the Lord's house, and the house of all who love God and work righteousness. If we are anxious for the future and deplore the shortness and uncertainty of life, here is revealed life eternal; and if we mourn over the sins of mankind and our own in particular, here is righteousness in abundance and the most certain directions for a holy life.

Now Christ is made unto us the medium of all this knowledge and consolation; and his ministrations, therefore, as well as his exalted and divine nature and excellence, presents him to us as the personage most worthy of our confidence, reverence, and affection. Those best acquainted with him have always loved him most. I would instance the evangelists, and prophets, and apostles by whom we have the holy scriptures; I would instance the holy angels, and the Holy Spirit, and above all the Divine Father, who calls him his beloved in whom his soul delighteth. If any thing in a man can please God, it must be the loving of his Son Jesus Christ; but this love to him can be manifest only by the keeping of his commandments. For the Lord himself has said "If you love me you will keep my commandments."

I do rejoice that the work of mediation has been awarded to one so dear to the Father; I do bless God that he has laid our help upon one so mighty to save; I do greatly accord with God Almighty in giving the government to one so venerable for his wisdom and so worthy of possessing power. The intellectual incapacity and especially the moral defectiveness of human Rulers, are very obvious and greatly to be deplored on account of the unhappy and destructive results which they have given birth to. But Jesus is perfect every whit; there is no deficiency in him. His official capacity, like his real nature, is without a fault. How are we blessed who come to the knowledge of God by such a prophet! how highly honored to obtain forgiveness through the intercession of such a High Priest! how greatly are we blessed in being governed by such a prince! My attachment for him is not a blind attachment; but one that grows out of a long and patient inquiry into the Christian Religion, and serious meditation upon what they say, of the human family and of Him in particular, the Redeemer of that family. He is precisely what we need; and if he had not effected our salvation, my own reason, I confess, is unable, all things considered, to invent one better, or half so good, so wise, so just, so rational, so glorious to God, so honorable to his Son, and so fortunate and saving to man.

> O Jesus the Giver of all I enjoy!
> My life to thy honor I wish to employ,
> With praises unceasing I'll sing of thy name.
> Thy goodness increasing thy love I'll proclaim.

The Lord Jesus, My dear S. is transcendently excellent. I only need to touch this string to be wholly inspired with love and delight and glory. Are we enraptured with the qualities of each other because we both love Christ; how great and excellent then must that love of Christ be! How glorious and ravishing is his person and offices even in the eye of faith! which is nevertheless but a veil through which we look at the king; but when this shall be rent asunder, when it shall yield and give way to knowledge, and we shall be admitted to sensible communion with him, O how ineffable our joys! how unspeakable and full of glory! We shall follow in his train through all eternity. Pure as the Spirit, who shall raise us from the dead, his saints shall join the angelic retinue of heaven and traverse boundless and trackless eternity under the eye of one Lord, who alone and already has sounded its depths and traveled it all over, and is ever the same at all times and in all places.

The following piece from Mr. Simpson's Plea for Religion, will show you that holiness of life and victory in death are the legitimate results of faith in our Redeemer. It describes the case of Janeway.

At the age of twenty he was admitted a fellow of his college. Still, however, he went on with his religious contemplations, and became so mighty in prayer, and other sacred exercises, that he forgot the weakness of his body, and injured his health. He studied much, prayed much, and laboured much in every way he could contrive to be of use to mankind, and to promote the honor of the Divine Being. Sickness coming on, he was never permitted to preach but twice. His disorder, which was of the consumptive kind, increased rapidly upon him, but yet with some intervals of relief. During the greatest part of his sickness, however, he was so filled with love, and peace, and joy, that human language sinks under what he saw and felt. During the greatest part of his illness, he talked as if he had been in the third heavens; breaking out every now and then into ecstasies of joy and praise. Not a word dropped from his mouth but it breathed of Christ and heaven. He talked as if he had been with Jesus, and came from the immediate presence of God. At one time he said;—"Stand and wonder; come, look upon a dying man and wonder. Was there ever greater kindness? Were there ever more sensible manifestations of rich grace? Why me, Lord? why me? Sure this is akin to heaven. And if I were never to enjoy more than this, it were well worth all the torments men and devils could invent, If this be dying, dying is sweet. Let no Christian ever be afraid of dying.—Death is sweet to me! This bed is soft. Christ's arms, his smiles, and visits, sure they would turn hell into heaven! Oh! that you did but see and feel as I do! Come, and behold a dying man, more cheerful than ever you saw any healthful man in the midst of his sweetest enjoyments. Worldly pleasures are pitiful, poor, sorry things, compared with one glimpse of his glory which shines so strongly into my soul. Why should any of you be so sad, when I am so glad! This is the hour that I have waited for."

About forty-eight hours before his dissolution he said again:—

"Praise is now my work, and I shall be engaged in that sweet employment for ever. Come, let us lift up our voices in praise. I have nothing else to do. I have done with prayer, and all other ordinances. I have almost done conversing with mortals. I shall presently be beholding Christ himself, that died for me, and loved me, and washed me in his blood.—I shall in a few hours be in eternity, singing the song of Moses and the song of the Lamb. I shall presently stand upon mount Zion with an innumerable company of angels, and the spirits of just men made perfect, and Jesus the mediator of the new covenant. I shall hear the voice of much people, and be one amongst them who say—Hallelujah! salvation, glory, and honour, and power unto the Lord our God! And again we say, Hallelujah! Methinks, I stand as it were one foot in heaven, and the other on earth. Methinks I hear the melody of heaven, and by faith I see the angels waiting to carry my soul to the bosom of Jesus, and I shall be forever with the Lord in glory. And who can choose but rejoice in all this?"

In such a rapturous strain as this he continued, full of praise, full of admiration, full of joy, till at length, with abundance of faith and fervency, he cried aloud: "Amen! Amen!" and soon after expired.

The following is the note appended to Janeway's case by the author, who was certainly an excellent man and a lively and zealous professor of the Christian religion.

"Janeway arrived at these high attainments in the divine life, by a constant perusal of his Bible; a frequent perusal of Baxter's Saints Everlasting Rest, a book for which multitudes will have cause to bless God for ever; and by spending a due proportion of every day in secret prayer, and devout contemplation.

Mirandola, who died in the flower of his age, after he had for some time quitted all his great employments under Charles the fifth, was esteemed the most beautiful person of that age, and a man of the most exalted genius; and yet, after having read all that could be read, and learnt every thing that could then be learned, he wrote to his nephew, an officer in the army: "I make it my humble request to you, that you would not fail to read the holy scriptures night and morning with great attention; for as it is our duty to meditate upon the law of God day and night, so nothing can be more useful: because there is in the holy scriptures a celestial and efficacious power, inflaming the soul with divine fear and love."

Spencer, though a man of dissipation in his youth, in his more advanced years entered into the interior of religion, and his two hymns on Heavenly Love, and Heavenly Beauty, hath expressed all the height and depth of Janeway's experience:

> "Then shall thou feel thy spirit so possest,
> And ravisht with devouring great desire
> Of his dear self, that shall thy feeble breast
> Inflame with love, and set thee all on fire
> With burning zeal, through every part entire,
> That in no earthly thing thou shall delight,
> But in his sweet and amiable sight.—
> Then shall thy ravisht soul inspired be
> With heav'nly thoughts, far above human skill,
> And thy bright radiant eyes shall plainly see
> Th' idea of his pure glory present still
> Before thy face, that all thy spirits shall fill
> With sweet enragement of celestial love,
> Kindled through sight of those fair things above."

Spencer's religion was "a religion of feeling;" which is unquestionably the religion of the Bible. "Whom having not seen ye love; in whom, though now ye see him not, yet believing, ye rejoice with joy unspeakable and full of glory."

This same devout and heavenly spirit breathes strongly in all the old authors. Augustine is famous for it; so were several others of the ancient fathers of the church. Thomas A. Kempis is excelled by none in this way. Bernard is very pious. His hymn on the name Jesus is in a high strain of this kind.

The religion of Christ is indeed a religion of feeling as well as of faith; for though it be first faith and fact, yet certainly no man can possess the knowledge of its facts without feeling their moral influence and rejoicing in their greatness, glory and design. Dear S., let us hold by the Scriptures and hold fast to what we have attained; but let us not be contented with present attainments, but aspire to perfect purity of manners by transferring into our life the virtues of our Redeemer. Let us take him and no other for our model. May the God of peace be with you; may Jesus Christ preserve you; the Holy spirit bless you; and to God, and to the Lamb be present and everlasting praise, Amen.

THE AUTHOR.

A DISCOURSE OF THE TRUE GOSPEL

SECTION THIRD–FAITH

"This is my Beloved Son, in whom I am well pleased, Hear you Him."

CHAPTER I

Introductory

In conformity with our nature, Christianity divides itself into knowledge and duty. This division extends itself even to the fundamental proposition itself, the first part of it being intellectual, "Behold my Son;" the second moral, "Hear you him."

On the intellectual part of the divine oracle we have expatiated at length; and we trust that our readers, by what has been written, are sufficiently convinced that if a man would become a Christian he must, as a first step, believe Jesus to be the Son of God and the Messiah. But we now come to the settlement of a very different question, a question not of knowledge but of duty, not intellectual but moral, not of the head but of the heart, not what shall we know but what shall we do, not what has God revealed but what has he commanded, not what has he done for us but what has he ordered us to do for ourselves. We repeat it, we are now come to the settlement of a question of a very different nature from that which was bandied in the preceding discourse; not the "*Quid est,*" but the "*Quid oportet,*" the duty and not the knowledge of the gospel. It is not "Behold my Son," but "Hear you him." In fine we are come to the momentous question, "What shall we do to be saved?"

"Hear you him." This is the Father's answer to the question, and it is exclusive. At the delivery of it, Moses and Elias, the author of the Law and the prince of the Prophets, and the Law and the Prophets themselves were withdrawn, and the true worshipers were left with Jesus before them, as the sole teacher of mankind. As, therefore, all the revelations in our religion depend for their authority upon the truth and certainty of that revelation communicated by the Father, so all the teachers in the Christian institution depend for their authority upon the authority of that one teacher sent forth by the Father. We have, therefore, no Father but God; no teacher but Christ. We hold of the one for knowledge, and of the other for duty, as we hold of the Spirit for happiness. "Joy by the Holy Spirit."—There is nothing human in our religion, it is all of God, and of his Son, and of the Holy Spirit. Those, therefore, who embrace it, have these names put upon them, "Go, convert the nations, baptizing them unto the name of the Father, and of the Son, and of the Holy Spirit."

It is very important to be correct here. Error here is error in the premises. Men have thrust themselves between us and the Father, between us and the Son, between us and the Holy Spirit; and have proposed for knowledge that which was not of God, that for duty which was not of the Son, and that for joy which was not of the Spirit. They have made creeds, invented ordinances, and framed experiences. They have also, misplaced things; they have put enjoyment before duty, and duty before knowledge, they have happiness without obedience, and obedience before faith; and have given precedence to the work of the Son over that of the Father, and the work of the Spirit over that of both. The consequence of this has been, that a people has arisen, whose joys are not of the Spirit, whose duty is not of Christ, whose knowledge is not of the Father; so that in all the matters of knowledge, duty, and happiness, they are *toto caelo*, a different people from those who were named christians in the days of the apostles.

Be it observed, therefore, that Christ alone is the called and sent of God. The apostles do not in any of their writings, affect to be sent of God, but through Jesus Christ. But Jesus himself was sent directly from the Father. He said to them, therefore, "As my Father sent me into the world; so send I you into the world." Whoever, therefore, says he is called and sent of God to preach the gospel, presumes upon a higher honor than was enjoyed even by the apostles, every one of whom was called and sent by the Son, not one of them by the Father.—Hence, there are two missions recognized by our Lord Jesus, his own, and that of the apostles; the former holding for its authority of God, the Father; the latter, of Christ, the Son.

But seeing Christ was deputed to publish Christianity, why were any substitutes admitted instead of himself the principal.—The case is this. It was among the mediatorial duties of the Messiah, after having effected our redemption, "to appear in the presence of God for us;" it was also in the economy of the scheme, that he should ascend to heaven before receiving the Holy Spirit. On these accounts his absence was unavoidable. Hence, the necessity for the apostolic mission, holding of him immediately for its authority.

It is of supreme importance, therefore, that we understand the gospel as it came from the lips of Christ and his apostles; the pretensions of papists and protestants, are a mere farce; they are absurd;

they bring to us no new knowledge; they enjoin upon us no new duty from Christ, they communicate no additional joy by the Spirit. On the contrary, they have taken away the key of knowledge, the one styling it "a dead letter," the other closing it altogether; these wide spread schisms have invented ordinances, and framed experiences which are neither of Christ nor of the Holy Spirit. Christ then, and the apostles alone are to be devoutly listened to on the great question, "What shall I do to be saved?"

As for the present teachers of Christianity, they are abroad at their own risk; and we shall be fools if we inquire not especially into both what they preach, and by whose authority they preach. The scriptures pronounce a most solemn anathema upon the man or angel, who would usurp the rights of Christ and his apostles, and teach for gospel, that which is purely human. "If I or an angel from heaven preach any other gospel unto you than that which we (Paul) have preached unto you, let him be Accursed." From this state of the case, the reader will readily perceive that we may render the modern teachers of our religion, an essential service by turning away from them wholly.—By affording them no opportunity of leading us astray, we may both save ourselves and preserve them from the anathema which Paul has announced against those who differ from him in the gospel; for they do not, and will not enunciate and administer the it as they have the apostles for an example.

CHAPTER II

Of the Person Appointed by Christ to Answer the Important Question,
"What Shall We Do to Be Saved?"

By throwing aside Greek, and Roman, and Protestant teachers, we are left to seek an answer to the question in the caption of this chapter from the holy scriptures alone. In them we have an infallible instructor, a teacher whose words are the same in every age, the same to every people, the same to the Jew as to the Gentile. This is a noble character of the divine oracles. They never vary in their language. Parties and partisans may, and do change their dialect and the technicalities of theology, but the good and holy word of God is ever the same. "It liveth and abideth for ever," unchanged and unchangeable.

When, therefore, we assume this noble stand, when we do take the Bible as our sole guide, To whom does Christianity direct us first to look? To God first? To whom does God direct us? To His Son our Lord and Saviour, "Hear you him." These are his words. To whom does Christ direct us? The Apostles. "As my father hath sent me unto the world, so send I you into the world. He that heareth you, heareth me; and he that heareth me, heareth him that sent me."

Are we then to listen to the entire twelve, for an answer to the question "What shall we do?" No. Many of these twelve have not left behind them a single word on the subject. Andrew, Philip, Thomas, Bartholomew, and Simon Zelotes, have not written one word in the scriptures, and not one word is said in the scriptures concerning any thing they ever spoke in answer to the question, What shall we do? This holds good of John, James the greater, and James the less, and of Judas, and of Matthias, of whose preaching not a single specimen is left on record; we cannot from the scripture learn what one of all the eleven I have named, said in answer to the question "What shall I do to be saved?"

Peter is the only one of the original twelve whose answer to this interesting question is on record. What he said to the Jews, and what he said to the Gentiles, how he answered the question of duty on the day of Pentecost, and at the house of Cornelius, is still preserved; but the preachings of all the rest are lost, unrecorded. Hence the scriptures throw us right upon this man for an answer. "He that heareth you, heareth me; and he that rejecteth you, rejecteth me."

Let us then look at Peter for a moment. Is it merely because the scriptures put it out of our power to consult any of the other original apostles, in regard to this all absorbing question, that we turn to Peter for an answer? Is our appeal to him and to what he said, a matter of mere necessity, or of decorum and choice? Certainly with every Jew and every Gentile it must, after what Christ said to Peter, be a matter of choice and decorum, to listen respectfully to what Peter said; because he was appointed by Jesus Christ, to be the first one who should answer the question of Salvation to both people, Jews and Gentiles. Yes, of the entire twelve, Peter was the one appointed by Christ to answer this question, first to the Jews and afterwards to the Gentiles.

The elevation of this apostle to the primacy in this business is expressed by Jesus himself, thus: "And I will give to thee the keys of the kingdom of heaven; and whatsoever thou shalt bind on earth, shall be bound in heaven; and whatsoever thou shalt loose on earth, shall be loosed in heaven." *The Keys*:—Keys are used for opening doors; and the scriptures speak of opening the "door of faith," or the faith, that is the door of the church. Who then opened the door of faith to the Jews and to the Gentiles? Peter. If, therefore, we explain the Saviour's figure, by facts, he intended that Peter should be the first to announce the gospel to all people.

Did the other apostles recognize and honor this appointment of Jesus their Lord? Most assuredly they did; for although they stood up on the day of Pentecost, in connection with the first apostle, not a man of them presumed to open his mouth till Peter had discharged the duty of that office to which he had been elevated by his Lord and Master Jesus Christ. He spoke, and not they. "But Peter, standing up with the eleven, lifted up his voice, and said, "Ye men of Judea, and all you that dwell at Jerusalem, be this known unto you, and hearken unto my words," &c. When Peter had laid before his vast audience, what God desired, they should know, he next disclosed what remained for them to do, and in answer to their question, "Men and brethren, what shall we do" he said, "Repent and be baptized every one of you, in the name of Jesus Christ, for the remission of your sins and you shall receive the gift of the Holy Spirit," &c. Under covert of this original annunciation of the gospel, all the other apostles commenced their evangelical labors in Jerusalem and among the Jews; but till it was made, none of them presumed to open his mouth.

Paul, who was to be the apostle to the Gentiles, was turned to God, and the ninth chapter of the Acts describes his conversion. In the tenth chapter the Gentiles were converted; and, if it would have comported with previous arrangements, Paul might have been employed to perform this important business. The other apostles also were still alive, and James, or John, or Thomas, could have been found as readily as any other. But Jesus had given the keys to Peter. He had appointed him to the distinguished honor of being the first to preach the gospel to the Gentiles and of telling them what to do to be saved.—When they were to be converted, therefore, the deference which was due to his appointment by Jesus, was not withheld; for the angel, which appeared to Cornelius, did not say to that favored person, send for Paul, or James, or John, or Matthew; but send for Peter. "And now send men to Joppa, and call for one Simon, whose surname is Peter. He shall tell thee what thou oughtest to do."

The reader will perceive that Peter's duty was perfected when he had told men what to do to be saved. When he had converted the household of Cornelius, then Paul, and after him any and all others, commenced, under covert of Peter's proclamation, to labor among the nations; but till this was performed, neither Paul nor any other, was permitted, to mouth the gospel to the Gentiles. The two people then are wholly independent of a set of men to invent answers to the saving question. Christ has anticipated all human wisdom here, by appointing the holy apostle to this important business.

It is not intended by this, to limit to Peter the power of loosing from their sins, the Jews and Gentiles; for, after his resurrection, and before he ascended to heaven, Jesus empowered the apostleship with this extraordinary authority, saying to all the twelve, "Whose sins soever you remit, they are remitted; and whose sins soever you retain they are retained;" but precedence was given to Peter in this affair, and he, first and before all the others, answered to all people, Jew and Gentile, the great question, "What shall we do?"

Might not then, some other one of the apostles have presumed upon this distinguished appointment?

Might not John or James, the Boanerges of the kingdom, have stepped forward on the day of Pentecost, and when the Jews cried "Men and brethren what shall we do," have answered the people, and so have discharged the sublime office of opening the kingdom to them? Might not the Holy Spirit himself, have with propriety, bid the Gentile Cornelius send for Paul, who was then converted, or for John, or Matthew, or James, and caused any one of them to speak the gospel to that pious personage and his household? No. The apostles and even the Holy Spirit were now all in subjection to Jesus.

To the Jews, therefore, who asked, and to the Gentiles, by whom he was sent for to tell them, Peter, by the authority of his Master, showed them words by which they both might be saved. He proclaimed to them the oracle of the Father, concerning Jesus, and commanded them to repent, and be baptized for the remission of sins. This is the apostolic answer to the question, and not only so, but it is the answer of that man among the apostles, who of them all was advanced to the great honor of doing it. It confirms us further in the propriety of his answer, when we know from the word of God, that he spoke as the Spirit gave him utterance. The author of the Christian Religion, knowing that this required to be done, determined it should be done for both people by the same person, and also that it should be well done. He, therefore, suffered neither him nor his colleagues to appear in public, or to put themselves in an attitude to give birth to the question, till he was able to return an answer to it, with infallible certainty. "Tarry you at Jerusalem until you be endowed with power from on high." Acts 1.

Does any one then inquire, not what God has done to save him, but, knowing this much, what he himself shall do to be saved? We answer not, read Doddridge, or Luther, or Wesley, or Calvin, or other men equally celebrated with them; no, these famous worthies never were appointed to give an original and infallible answer to this momentous question. They themselves were Gentiles, none of whom ever partook of the honor of the apostolic office, far less was any one of them advanced to the primacy in this matter, or like Peter styled *princeps*, the chief. But suppose that a man either by mistake or design, and Protestants have done it by mistake and Catholics by design, should be guilty of returning an answer of his own framing, to this question, What does he do? He substitutes fallibility for infallibility, himself for the holy apostle Peter, his own authority for that of the Son of God, and finally he ends in uselessness, what was commenced either in ignorance or presumption, by returning a wrong answer to a great question, which Christ had appointed a person to answer aright, long before he was born. I might here set down the names of a vast number of modern ministers, who have written either ignorantly or presumptuously, and at all events erroneously, on this subject; but we will defer this, till we reach a more advanced post in our march to the end of our subject.

The first part of this volume is intended to contain the facts to be believed, the last the things to be done by the person who would become a Christian; the former is derived from that part of the divine oracle which says, "Behold my Son," the latter from that which says, "Hear you him;" the first speaking of the things that are, the second of the things that ought to be; the wholly ultimately consisting, like the gospel, and like the paternal revelation itself, of knowledge and duty, or of the things which God has been pleased to do in order to save us, and what he has ordered, we should do in order to save ourselves. And again, to show that Christ did answer to the Jews, and ordain the apostles, and Peter in particular, first to answer to all, both Jews and Gentiles, the great questions of both knowledge and duty, "What shall we do to be saved?"

After some preliminary chapters, we shall show that the apostles in conformity with the element of Christian belief delivered by God, taught first, that men should believe in Christ, and second, that they should obey him.

In the mean time, the reader will perceive, that the writer proposes nothing in this book more new than that of showing that neither he or any other person, pope, priest, or preacher, has the least shadow of authority to propose any thing new either under the head of knowledge or duty, but that in the Christian religion, all men hold of God the Father, immediately for the former, and of the Son immediately for the latter; Peter of Jesus, and the Jews and the Gentiles of Peter.

CHAPTER III

Faith and the General and Special Propositions

A Deist believes that God exists; a Christian believes that God has spoken. Deism asserts that God is good; Christianity, we think, is an additional proof of his goodness. Deists say we are credulous; we know that they are inconsistent. They allege that we believe without evidence; we are sure that him in whom they believe they do not worship. They think it impossible the Deity should speak; we deem it improbable he should be silent; they, if they worship at all, worship a dumb Deity; we the eloquent, the living God. They think the author of nature grand, we think him condescending also. They think he fills the universe; we believe he fills the hearts of men who love him, also. They believe him to be in the vast; we believe him also to be in the minute. With the Deist, God numbers all the stars; with the Christian he also numbers all the hairs of our head; so, that of two sparrows, which are sold for a farthing, one cannot fall to the ground without his knowledge.

The proposition of the Deists that there is one living and true God, we name the general proposition, because it is believed by all men, Jews, Gentiles, and the church of God; and with the author of the Discourse of Natural Theology, we admit its credibility, even on scientific principles.

The Christian proposition, that Jesus is God's Son; we style the particular one, because it is believed only by a portion of mankind, who depend for their belief of it on a special proof, differing in many points from the universal evidence, which the works of nature every where supply of the divine existence and character.

The first of these propositions is received by Deists, and both of them by Christians. The former is proved by the works of nature; the latter by the words of revelation. And as Revelation does not say the first is false, so nature does not assert the last to be impossible. For if nature show that there is a God, Revelation may show that there is also a Son of God, experience demonstrating, that where there is one being there may be another of a like nature. While Adam stood alone in Paradise, creatures of limited knowledge permitted to behold him, might have deemed it highly improbable, if not absolutely impossible, that from him should proceed another being of the same nature, the same personal conformation, and same powers of mind and body, but of a different sex. They might have supposed such a variety improbable, impossible: but what would their reasoning have proved? That they were foolish in listening to it, instead of waiting patiently on the dictates of experience. Eve's appearance would have put all their conjectures and probabilities to the blush. It is so in the case before us; if nature shows there is a God, Revelation proves that there is a Son of God; and therefore, rational conduct in a Deist is this; *First*, that believing the general proposition of the Divine existence, he hold in the first instance, to the possibility and probability of a particular Revelation. *Second*, that he investigate the particular proposition of Christianity, and, on believing it on its proper evidences, obey it. This will make his pretensions to piety and sincerity pass current with those who play the part of men in the matter, and he will be numbered with such spirits as Paul, and Isaiah, John Locke, Newton, Fenelon, Brougham and others of like excellence.

But perhaps you hesitate, perhaps you fear to render homage to the author of our religion. Quiet your apprehensions on such a point. No one ever dishonored a father by honoring his son; on the contrary, in honoring one we honor both. It is even so in religion also. If you honor the Son you honor the Father who sent him forth; for in both nature and character he is such a son as becomes such a father.

Has the Father life in himself—the divine and inscrutable attribute of a never-dying existence or immortality? Well, he has granted to the Son to have this same life or immortality in himself also. Does the Father, by his innate vitality, make alive whatever he pleases? then the Son by the same vitality, does the very same thing. Do the dead hear the voice of God? They also hear the voice of the Son of God. Does the Father enjoy the native right to try all men for their actions in this life? Then He has deputed all this right to the Son. So that, with propriety, he could say, I and the Father are one. But there is the magic of divine simplicity, beauty, and excellency in the holy Scriptures, in which these things are set forth, and we, therefore, give them in the Redeemer's own words. The Jews sought to kill him because he had healed, *on the Sabbath day*, a man who had been diseased thirty-eight years.

"But Jesus answered them. My Father works until now; I also work. For this reason the Jews were the more intent to kill him, because he had not only broken the Sabbath, but, by calling God his real father, had equaled himself with God. Then Jesus addressed them, saying, Most assuredly I say to you, the Son can do nothing of himself, but as he sees the Father do: for whatsoever things he does, such things does the Son likewise. For the Father loves the Son and shows him all that he himself does: nay, He will show him greater works than these, works which will astonish you. For as the Father raises and quickens the dead, the Son also quickens whom he will: for the Father judges no person, having committed the power of judging entirely to the Son, that all might honor the Son as they honor the Father. He that honors not the Son, honors not the Father who sent him. Most assuredly, I say to you, he that hears my doctrine, and believes in him that sent me forth, hath eternal life, and shall not suffer condemnation, having passed from death to life. Most assuredly, I say to you, the time comes, or rather is come, when the dead shall hear the voice of the Son of God; and hearing, they shall live. For as the Father has life in himself, so has he given to the Son to have life in himself; and has given him even the judicial authority, because he is a Son of man. Wonder not at this; for the time comes when all that are in their graves shall hear his voice, and shall come forth. They that have done good, shall rise to enjoy life; they that have done evil, shall arise to suffer punishment. I can do nothing from myself; as I hear I judge; and my judgment is just, because I seek not to please myself, but to please him who sent me." John 5.

The faith of a Christian terminates on the special proposition of our religion. He believes that the author of Christianity is God's Son.

No man under heaven, can believe a divine revelation to be either impossible or improbable without exposing himself to the charge of indiscriminately confounding two things wholly distinct; viz: faith and opinion. Hume might have an opinion that God would not, could not, or did not address men on the subject of eternal life; but he had no evidence, and consequently could have no faith; for faith depends on evidence, and opinion on the absence or uncertainty of evidence. But he could not hold this rationally, even as an opinion, because for every reason that God would not, there are two reasons that he would, communicate with men in regard to their future destiny. God, we all see, can bring light out of darkness, the flashing diamond from the dull charcoal, and immortality from the tomb; to say, therefore, that the original element of Christianity is impossible, is very preposterous. With God nothing is impossible. God may exist, and so may his Son, and it is equally probable that for certain great purposes, God would himself introduce this Son to the notice of mankind. Still we grant, that it is wonderful there should be a Son. But the man, who devoutly believes the former proposition, may and, in most instances, will believe the latter. There are some people, however, who are absolutely incredulous in regard to revealed religion, and may be styled enthusiastic unbelievers; that is, they lay, by their weak-headedness, more stress upon their conclusions than their premises warrant, and rave away about the incredibility of Christianity, as if it had never been seriously believed by a sensible man on earth. These are the unbelieving bigots, the invincibles in the army of the infidels. Bigotry is fast passing from the ranks of those, who believe Christianity, to the ranks of those who disbelieve it; and if it was intolerable on the one side it is ten-fold more intolerable on the other; for there it is wholly unmodified by any thing like reverence and godly fear; so that of all the bigots in this world the unbelieving bigot is the most insufferable for imprudence, impiety and religious ignorance. Faith to such, is worse than ashes; yet if his own mental acquisitions were deciphered and analyzed they would in most instances he found to consist of faith chiefly and not of knowledge. It is found upon enquiry, that men of the most profound knowledge of the works of nature, like the great philosophers whom we have already mentioned, are generally possessed of the most sincere and grave belief in God and in the Christian Religion; while socialists and creatures of easy belief in human affairs, are generally altogether void of the solemn and solid principle of faith in the Eternal. It requires no labor to be ignorant of the Christian Proposition and the proof which goes to sustain it. The greatest fool in Christendom can boast a superiority of this nature. But to believe both the proof and the proposition, has been deemed not unworthy of the talents, power and genius of Selden, Chillenworth, Boileau, Hale, Boyle, Milton, Cowper, Brown, Bacon, Romaine, Littleton, Paley, Locke, Cudworth, Clarke, Doddridge, Lardner, Robertson, Butler, Watts, Campbell, McKnight, Addison, Beattie,

Boerhaave, Burnet, Collins, Erskine, Euler, Fenelon, Tillotston, Grotius, Sir Humphrey Davy and others.

CHAPTER IV

Diverse Observations Concerning Faith

It has already been noticed, that the scriptures are wholly silent in regard to the faith of Adam. This, doubtless, is to be traced to the fact that our great ancestor was not called to walk by this principle alone. Like the angels, and all who have kept their first estate, Adam was privileged to behold God, and, consequently, to enjoy a sensible apprehension of his divine existence. Like other rational natures, he may have been indebted to the works of God for the character of God, but for his knowledge of God's being or existence alone, he had a sensible rather than a rational proof. He heard his voice.

In this respect, therefore, he differed essentially from other men; who depend upon a rational proof for the divine existence as much as for the divine character. We have to reason from His works to the one as well as to the other; never, in this life, being permitted to behold the Divine presence.

The first of "the men of faith," therefore, was his son Abel, who is declared to have offered sacrifice to God on this principle. There is an expression in the end of the last verse of the 4th chapter of Genesis, namely: "Then began men to call upon the name of the Lord," which might imply, that the worship of God by faith, did not commence till after the birth of Enos, Adam's grandson by Seth, about one hundred and thirty-five after the expulsion from Paradise; but the clause should have been rendered differently; because, as it now reads, it contradicts the fact, that, in the days of Abel, who had been many years dead, God had been called upon through an instituted order of worship, of which also he had testified his approbation, in the days of the first martyr, Abel. It is well known to those critically acquainted with the text of scripture, that verbs of the infinitive active, have many times a passive signification and that their explanation is to be given according to the sense rather than the syntax. Commentators, therefore, render the verse thus, "Then men began to be called by the name of the Lord." The Polyglot has it thus, "Then began men to call themselves by the name of the Lord," that is, the men of faith began to call themselves the sons of God, which is the name they get in the next chapter but one, thus, "It came to pass when men began to multiply upon the face of the earth, and daughters were born to them, that the 'sons of God' saw the daughters of men, that they were fair; and they look them wives of all whom they chose. And the Lord said, my spirit shall not always strive with man," &c.

There are, as we have seen, two ways by which men can be assured of the divine existence, knowledge and belief. To Adam, it was a matter of knowledge; to other men it is a matter of belief. Hence the importance of the principle of belief in revealed religion, the fundamental idea of which is the being or existence of the Deity. The next is that of his Divine character, as the creator, preserver, and governor of the universe. In every dispensation of religion, therefore, whether Patriarchal, Jewish or Christian, the divine character and divine existence have been indispensable, as facts to be believed.

Hence it is, the apostle, in his notices of faith, has said, "He that cometh to God, must believe that he is the rewarder of those who diligently seek him." And he cites the deeds of the ancients as the legitimate effects of true faith.

These, however, are not the matters proposed ostensibly for belief in the Christian Proposition; but they are included in it most assuredly; for we cannot believe in the Son, without believing in the Father and, as the apostle John says, "Whoever denies the Son, does not acknowledge the Father." But the reverse of this is certain, that whoever acknowledges the Son acknowledges the Father also.

It is the glory of the Christian Religion, that it commences by enlisting on the side of righteousness, one of the most powerful and universal principles belonging to human nature, belief. When the gospel was first proclaimed to the nations, they were wholly devoid of faith in the true God. His very idea was lost amid the rubbish and pollutions of idolatry; and belief, the only principle by which his existence and character could be realized, and on which it is possible to found a true system of morals, was unknown, so that the wisest of the Grecian sages was compelled to say that "It was equally difficult to discover the parent of the universe, and dangerous to make him known to the common people." For centuries, God had permitted the nations to follow the devices of their own imaginations, and many were their expedients to supply the lack or absence of faith in the true God. But they all availed nothing, and at the coming of Christ, the kingdoms were returned back again into the hands of God by the kings of the earth, the statesmen, philosophers, and rhetoricians of this world, in a condition, which at once proved the horrible danger of forsaking God, and the utter inability of man to purify himself, when in a state of idolatrous apostasy. The doctrine of Christ being founded on faith in the only living and true God, and being alike distinguished for the excellence of its morals, and the supremacy of its motives, accomplished in a few years for society, what the wisdom of the learned had failed to produce in as many centuries; and the boasted wisdom of both Greece and Rome, was seen to be arrant folly. Paul holds the following language in relation to this state of things.

"For this doctrine, (the doctrine of the cross) is, indeed, foolishness to the destroyed; but to us who are saved it is the power of God. Therefore, it is written, 'I will destroy the wisdom of the wise, and will set aside the knowledge of the prudent.'—Where is the wise man? where is the scribe? where the disputer of this world? Has not God shown the wisdom of this world to be folly. For when, in the wisdom of God, the world through wisdom knew not God, it pleased God through the foolishness of this proclamation to save them who believe. And although the Jews demand a sign, and the Greeks seek wisdom; yet we proclaim a crucified Christ: to the Jews, indeed, a stumbling block, and to the Greeks foolishness: but to them who are saved, both Jews and Greeks, Christ the power of God and the wisdom of God."

Every thing here, is said to be accomplished by good principle; but without good principle, the history of the kingdoms loudly declares nothing can be accomplished in that which most of all vitally affects man, namely: righteousness and permanent happiness. It is a truth that happiness follows righteousness as the shadow does the substance and is as inseparable from it.—And misery, baleful misery, so preternatural and injurious to man, is equally a concomitant of sin. How, then, could the nations be happy when separated from the true God, and wholly uninfluenced by the great controlling and saving principle of belief so indispensable to a proper apprehension of his existence and character? How could they be happy when plunged into the lowest abyss of idolatry and sunken in the mire of manners and customs shameful and polluted beyond the endurance of Christian ears? for it is a shame to mention the things that were done by them both in private, and in their public assemblies, and their assemblies for worship. How could they be happy where sense and the flesh had usurped the place of faith and righteousness, and where the bulwarks of all purity had been swept away by the overwhelming current of unrestrained lust? It was impossible, and, therefore, the nations, at the original proclamation of the gospel, were as deplorably miserable as they were shamefully unrighteous; and the apostle says, "they were filled with all unrighteousness."

Does not the Christian religion then commend itself to our highest reason when it proposes, first of all things, to impart good principles to those whose morals it would correct and elevate? Is not good principle the only sure foundation on which to build good practice? Is this not first to make the tree good? Its sagacious author owned, that a bad tree could not produce good fruit; and that a good tree could not produce bad fruit, and that every tree is known by its fruit.

His entire scheme of salvation is, therefore, constructed on these maxims. He purposes to make men what God would have them to be, and what their own happiness and interests require them to be, by inculcating, chief of all things, a principle of action, without which nothing can be attained in relation either to God, or our own purification and perfection. The history of the Romans, the Greeks, the Persians and Assyrians and of all the nations in the ancient and in the modern world also demonstrates the fallacy of all attempts at righteousness and happiness, when good principle is overlooked or disregarded. The first letter, therefore, in the divine alphabet of Christianity, is belief in God and in his Son Jesus Christ; this is *Alpha*. Among the numerals of our religion this is the figure one. It signifies but little when taken alone; but when connected with the other things, with which it has been associated by its author, it becomes surprisingly, momentously significant, and the abjuration of it is perdition to the guilty. "He who believes not shall be condemned." And let not the reader falsely imagine, that this condemnation is arbitrary and absolute. No, it is necessary and unavoidable; for the person who repudiates the faith of the gospel repudiates that principle, the absence of which let down from the righteousness necessary to the enjoyment of God and heaven the whole ancient world, a principle necessary to prepare himself and make him meet for God and heaven; for heaven will be granted only to those, who by proper principle and proper practice, shall be fitted for it. The rejection of this principle, therefore, is the rejection of heaven and eternal life; for he who believes not in the Son shall never see life.

The gospel, it will be seen by the reader, is comprehended ultimately in one external fact, that Jesus is the Son of God; and one internal principle, namely, faith; to the truth of the first, therefore, all the other facts in our religion are for their authority to be referred; and into the operation of the last, all the righteousness of our religion is to be resolved. The Christian Religion is, therefore, a system of great simplicity as well as originality, and on that account is admirably adapted to the capacity of those for whom it is intended. It is the greater dying for the less, the just for the unjust, that, by faith in the fact, we might be brought back to righteousness and to God; it is the prime proposition, however, to assure us first of all, that he who died is the greater, is the holy, is the just. In the simplicity of its structure, Christianity is surprisingly analogous to the systems of nature.

It is in a high degree interesting, that, to the operation of a few simple agencies—perhaps finally to one, we should be able, agreeably to the philosophy of nature, to refer the lovely forms, the graceful attitudes, the beautiful colors, and all the motions, tastes, and odors by which the vegetable kingdom is so eminently characterized; the stems, stalks, and trunks are exalted; the branches, props, or arms, and foliage are evolved, and all the buds, flowers, and fruits thrown forth, successively, in groups so gay, so rich, so various, that our reason is confounded, and we readily conclude, that a creation so fair, so lofty, or so rich, as is the rose, the cedar, or the vine, must needs be the offspring of combined innumerable principles. But the certain and sober dictates of experience abundantly assure us, that, to the combined operation of only one or two vital and non-vital forces, the whole of vegetable phenomena, however brilliant, lovely, or impressive, is ultimately to be referred.

And it is not in the vegetable world alone, that diverse vast and minute phenomena are alike controlled by the same all-pervading principle; throughout inorganic nature also, this obtains; the tear that descends from the eye of afflicted beauty, the dew-drops resting like beads on the downy leaf, as well as the mightiest spheres,

> "The moon, that now meets the orient sun, now flies
> With the fixed stars, fixed in their orb that flies,
> And the five other wandering fires, that move
> In mystic dance, not without song."

are alike influenced by the same all-pervading force.

Now it is, as we have seen, in religion as it is in nature; a few principles, perhaps only one ultimately, accomplishes every thing. The hand, that raised 'the potent rod of Amram's on in Egypt's evil day,' and hers, who stretched forth her all, her only mite, the widow's mite, and cast into the treasury of the Lord, were equally inspired by the same principle of faith; she too who sat at Jesus' feet, Mary who loved the better part, and old Elisha doubly portioned with his master's spirit, when with his mantle he smote asunder the swellings of Jordan, and Paul on Mars' hill, when like Maia's son he stood amid the crowd of curious and gay Athenians, and raised his head on high, and from his lips poured light and life divine into the souls of Damaris and Dionysius the Areopagite. Behold, the great apostle of the Gentile world, whose single labors could out weigh those of a thousand of us modern pigmies, and a dozen even of his own compeers with Cephas at their head; behold him raise himself on high amid the Areopagus—his mighty spirit stirred within him by the huge apostacy from God and faith that lay around in Athens. O, who can tell the measure of his soul, when to that grave, and learned, and venerable assembly he cried aloud "You men of Athens," and shook the bulwarks of the heathen world.

But whether it be in Paul temperance, or in Apollos and Cephas spirit and eloquence, whether it be love like John's, or the joy of Mary, when she cried, "My soul doth magnify the Lord," or peace, or long suffering or the gentleness of Christ, the goodness of Barnabas, or fidelity in Pergamenian Antipas, the poverty that repines not, the riches that exalt not themselves, the mourning that sucks at the breast of the Bible heavenly consolation, the mercy that shows to others what it supplicates for itself, or the purity whose boldness is all divine, the spiritual hungering, the spiritual thirsting that eats and drinks heavenly things and rich in the name of the Lord, all Christian ornaments, all godly graces are referable ultimately to faith and on this principle as on a sure foundation the entire superstructure of Christian character is reared.

CHAPTER V

Faith and Corrupted Religion

The evil of substituting any thing in the room of faith is monstrous. It was this principle which threw off the Jews who believed not. "They were broken off because of unbelief;" and it was this principle which kept off the idolatrous Gentiles. It was this principle, which, of the believing of both people, made a new church, a new man, and clothed the profession of revealed religion with the purest, the most exalted morals. In brief, it was faith that eminently distinguished the gospel from the law and from all other religions in the world; and because of the fundamental nature of this principle, the Apostle, by a very bold figure, styles the whole institution of Christianity, the Faith. The absence of this principle was sufficient to debar all men, Jews and Gentiles, from the privileges of the Christian church. Circumcision and the observance of the law availed nothing without faith in Christ. Nothing could exalt a man to discipleship but a hearty and avowed profession of the great proposition that Jesus was the Son of God; and faith in this was a ready passport to all the riches of Christ. One of the most dangerous errors in modern exhibitions of the gospel, is the fatal practice of substituting other things for faith. One party substitutes the sprinkling of children; another, the operations of the Spirit; a third, feeling, &c.

But the moment, that a child is sprinkled in the name of Christ, that instant is the principle of Christianity changed from *faith* to *flesh*; and the member is added to the body, not on account of any personal fitness either to be blessed of God by the remission of sins, or comforted by the impartation of the Holy Spirit, or influenced by the faith, or hope, or love of the gospel; the gospel, indeed, is instantly transformed into the law; and the Christian church is secularized, and made a worldly sanctuary, instead of a habitation of God through the Spirit given to those only who believe. The gospel could no more travel the world around, burdened with this surreptitious and intolerable ordinance, than a man could climb the Andes with a millstone slung around his neck.

To substitute the operations of the Spirit for faith is equally dangerous and not less absurd. It is as if a man should put cause for effect and effect for cause; or as if one in planting trees should insert the top instead of the root and raise into the atmosphere what should be sunk into the ground. For the Spirit is not given to make men believe;

but because they do believe. This however, like the practice of sprinkling, is a modern error, and the Scriptures furnish no reasoning against it, but what arises out of the stubborn fact, that the Holy Spirit was never given to men in order to make them believe the gospel; but because they had already believed it. This preposterous error, of putting the Spirit before faith, besides bewildering those who believe it, and it is the first idea in all modern systems, flies in the face of the most express sayings of God, contradicts one of the most obvious maxims in society, that faith comes by evidence or hearing, breaks down the whole evangelical testimony concerning the Son of God, and inculcates the most criminal disregard for the holy Scriptures. It was, doubtless, introduced to account for certain phenomena in supposed opposition to the schemes of those great men, who led the way in the Protestant Reformation.

To substitute feeling for faith is also a modern error, it is not recognized in the scriptures, and, therefore, they furnish no intended argument against it. At the restoration of the true gospel, the common objection to immediate obedience was "I do not feel as I ought to feel, in order to obey the gospel." The non-professing portion of present society have been trained to this mode of speech by those who meet in classes, conventions, and companies to tell what they call their Christian experience, which consists generally, of a history of those intervals and moments of mental misery and happiness, for which the lives of the faithless and secular professors of modern times are distinguished, being occasionally exalted to the heights of enthusiasm, and again sunken to the depths of despair.

The practice of sprinkling infants, therefore, the doctrine of spiritual operations, and the absurd and uncertain custom of waiting for frames and feelings, must all be thrown out from before faith or belief, and this principle be brought into the very front, and be made stand forth in bold relief in the grand master-piece of the gospel, the preacher announcing to his hearers what Jesus has announced to all. "He, who believes and is baptized, shall be saved; and he, who believes not, shall be condemned."

But sometimes repentance itself has been put in the place of faith, as if it were possible for a man to reform his life towards that God, of whose existence and character he has had no previous apprehensions by belief. This is absurd; for though we can easily conceive the possibility of a man's reforming relative to a God, whose supremacy is already recognized, yet it transcends the utmost stretch of human conjecture to imagine how any one should reform relative to an existence and supremacy which has not yet been recognized. Without faith, however, it is impossible to please God. The apostle has said so; therefore it is impossible to repent without previously possessing belief. In the gospel belief precedes repentance; and this last must, therefore, be thrust backward into its proper natural place in the proclamation of the gospel.

How marvelously abused has been the gospel of Christ! from being the most potent and pointed organ of reformation among mankind, it has, in the hands of its professed friends, become the most powerless and inefficient instrument of good that can be named. Is it not surpassed by a temperance society? What is effected by that thing called the gospel now preached from every pulpit in Christendom? Are not ninety-nine out of a hundred of those who listen to it, left precisely where it finds them, in their sins? There is no possible manner of accounting for this, but by protesting that the things preached are not the true gospel of Christ, or they are the things of Christ deranged. This is the fact. The gospel has been deranged, inverted, contaminated, maimed, confounded, and misrepresented. It can, under these circumstances, therefore, accomplish comparatively nothing; it does accomplish nothing comparatively. This is not to be wondered at; for how should a man make music on an instrument, a flute for instance, whose parts are all misplaced? Till, therefore, the preacher of Christ put all the facts of the gospel, the commands and the privileges of the gospel in order, and preach them arranged, defined, and applied to their proper ends and purposes, he will never effect any thing comparatively. He may hold the attention of his ignorant auditors in play, and live by those whom he fails to enlighten and save, but this is a miserable consummation and greatly to be deprecated by the servants of Jesus Christ, who is glorified by seeing much fruit resulting from the labors of those who serve him in the gospel. When faith is contemplated in relation to the other elements of the gospel, therefore, it is seen to occupy the first place; it goes before repentance, before baptism, before remission, before the enjoyment of the Holy Spirit, before the resurrection of the dead. It is in fact the first of all these six articles in the true gospel of Christ.

CHAPTER VI

Faith and False Religion

The true religion wears a very singular aspect touching the origin of false worship or idolatry. There are, as has been already observed, only two means by which man can enjoy an assurance of the divine existence, knowledge and faith. It was the glory of the Paradisiacal state, that in it man was permitted to enjoy a sensible knowledge of the Deity; and it is one of the deficiencies of the preternatural condition into which he fell, to be denied this honor, and to walk by faith. Thus the true religion recognizes two states, under which man has been fated to exist, a natural, and preternatural, or a state of innocence and happiness, and of sin and misery. In accordance with these he was granted first to walk by knowledge, last by faith. This was a most important change in the religious condition of man; and he must have felt it, and felt the deficiency of his new state most sensibly and with infinite regret.

What was it, then, that gave birth to idolatry? This is a question that has greatly vexed the learned and the theological antiquarian of modern times; but image-worship is so ancient and idolatry so buried in the depths of antiquity, that but little of a satisfactory nature has been discovered concerning their origin. Our answer to this question, is, that it originated in the defectiveness of the state in which we now exist, and into which man was translated at the fall by his violation of law. Idolatry, it is most probable to me, was invented to supply the deficiency of a state of belief, and to bring man back again, if possible, to a natural and sensible acquaintance with their God; a privilege of which his Creator had now deprived him, on account of his own delinquency. It may occur to some who have not reflected maturely on this matter, that a state of belief is not so defective, a state. To this we answer, that belief is sometimes very lively, and in the Christian religion, it is exalted almost to knowledge; still, however, belief is not knowledge, and it is the boast of Christianity, to assure us that faith shall ultimately yield to sight; that God's people shall yet behold his face, and that all their hopes shall be realized by fruition. "Blessed are the pure in heart," said our Lord, "for they shall see God." The true religion, therefore, inculcates the defectiveness of the present state of faith, and denounces as the greatest sin, any attempt to supply this by image-worship. Idolatry on the contrary encourages every effort to raise man by false means above his present condition; it is, itself, originally, an effort of Satan, and ignorant devout people, to seize upon honors and privileges, which belonged to man only in his primeval condition of righteousness and innocence. "Make us gods to go before us," exclaims the voice of the idolater. The true religion says, "Thou shalt not make unto thee any graven image or any likeness of any thing that is in heaven above, or on the earth beneath, or that is in the waters under the earth; for I the Lord thy God am a jealous God, visiting the iniquities of the fathers upon the children to the third and fourth generation of them who hate me, and showing mercy to thousands of them that love me and keep my commandments." While, therefore, Christianity boasts of her principles of faith and hope, as being of a victorious and triumphant nature, that has regulated the course of all the people of God since the beginning of the present state, from Abel downward; yet in this respect she speaks relatively, and admits that, a more perfect state of things is approaching, in which both hope and faith will be rendered unnecessary by the immediate presence of God and the Lamb, the object of both our faith and hope.

While idolatry attempts to supply the defects of a stale of faith and trial, by a sensible communion with the gods, revealed religion in general, or Christianity in particular, is to be honored for its admirable fidelity in the case, and inconquerable attachment to the truth, by both acquainting us with our real condition, declaring its defects, pointing out to us the true remedy, and seasonably warning us against all surreptitious and unauthorized means of improving it.

CHAPTER VII

God's Benevolence in Selecting Faith as the Religious Principle

God's benevolence as well as his wisdom, are singularly displayed in selecting the principle of belief, as that on which to build the future character of his people and on account of which to confer on them eternal life; had he pitched on appetite, passion, genius, talent, relationship, or distinction personal, professional, or official, the ground-work of our religion would then have partaken of the partiality, weakness, and inefficiency of those things, and men would have had very plausible, if not very potent reasons for complaint; but the power of believing is incident to all mankind. The rich have no advantage over the poor here: the prince and the peasant, the king and the beggar, here find themselves on a level: all are equally capable of that principle by which they may be made immortal. The man of state talents, the man of genius, the discursive historian, the philosopher, the mathematician, the artist, the soldier and the scholar, with all the less heroic and less distinguished among the sons of men, are equally capable of believing facts when proved, and of being influenced by them as they feel them related to their own safety, and their own interest. Why then should we indulge in envy? Has not God humbled both the philosopher and the scribe, the proud reasoner, and the subtle disputer among the nations? It is far from being certain that Homer, Virgil, and Socrates, and Demosthenes, and Cicero, and Bonaparte, and Pitt, and Nelson, and Jefferson, and Voltaire, and Fredrick, and Peter, will be gifted with immortality at the judgment; though it is most certain that the thief upon the cross will, because he believed and repented of his deeds. We know not whether Agripina, Isabel, Joan of Arc, Mary Stewart, Elizabeth of England, Catharine, Gourney, Maintenon, Dacier, Lambert, Rowe, Graffigny are in heaven; but we are assured that Mary Magdalen, and Tabitha, and Priscilla are there; because these less celebrated women believed in the true God and clothed themselves with his righteousness accordingly. Those, therefore, who have shone as stars of the first magnitude in the firmament of worldly society, may emit a very inferior splendor in the heaven of immortality, if they be at all permitted to shine there in a sphere for which they discovered so little attachment while shining or rather scorching here.

It is a proud characteristic of Christianity, therefore, that its principle of belief is equally adapted to men in all ranks, of all professions, and all kinds of talents; and that her master and saving proposition is equally interesting, because equally related to all, Jesus our Lord being the Saviour of all. He "gave himself a ransom for all."

It is this property of universality in its principle of belief, that so eminently qualifies Christianity to become the religion of the world; for men universally can believe that which is proved to be true. And what is not less declarative of the benevolence of our Creator, men every where have, in their powers of body and mind, a higher disposition for truth than for falsehood, for good than for evil; for happiness than for misery; for reward than for punishment; for error, and evil, and misery, and punishment are all preternatural to man, and belonged not to him in his original condition. These considerations should inspire us with philanthropy, or give a fresh impetus to it in those who already possess it; and cause them to sound abroad the true gospel; to assail error in every form; to level its walls with the ground; to trample falsehood underfoot; and to erect the standard of truth in proud pre-eminence over all that is evil in the world.

There is, I imagine, a true and sound argument for the truth of Christianity, to be found in this very fact; that its first principle is of a universal nature. Had it pitched itself on a less extended basis, had it proposed its blessings on a more limited and partial principle, it would not have answered the condition of all men, and consequently only some could have been saved; but now every soul, who has a taste for eternal life, may believe, and the evidence of Christianity is of a kind that accommodated itself to such as desire immortality, rather than those who do not; for it is not to be denied that there are some men, who do not desire to enjoy eternal life, who are gorged or satisfied with their fortunes in this world so much as fairly to have destroyed within them, all anxiety and care about that world which is to come.

CHAPTER VIII

Faith and Flesh or Abolished Religion

During the early ages of the world and under the preceding and introductory economy of the law of Moses, now abolished, men were associated in an ecclesiastical connection on the partial accident of family descent, without immediate respect to better principle. As preparatory to the introduction of a religion adapted to the exigencies of the world, this was unavoidable. But when the universal religion appeared, it rendered all former institutions unnecessary, and the law was annulled. It is wonderful that the Jews in general, and their sages in particular, did not perceive the defectiveness of the law; but of such a gross texture was the veil thrown around their hearts, that even to this day they cannot discern the end and intent of the economy that is abolished; but believe in their own ancient order of things, as if it were of universal obligation, not judging, that love, and not law, must save the world, that faith, and not flesh, is necessary to the elevation and perfection of the morals of mankind. Paul pours forth his sympathies for them in regard to this judicial blindness in the following touching terms.

"I speak the truth in Christ, I do not speak falsely, my conscience bearing me witness, in the Holy Spirit, that I have grief and unceasing anguish, in my heart, for my brethren, my kinsmen according to the flesh; (for I also was, myself, wishing to be accursed from Christ;) who are Israelites; whose, are the adoption, and the glory, and the covenants, and the giving of the law, and the rites of service, and the promises; whose, are the fathers; and from whom the Messiah descended, according to the flesh; who is over all, God blessed for ever. Amen."— Romans 9.

To associate believers in the true God with unbelievers, is as if one should attempt the union of incongruities, or to unite light and darkness. It is as if we should tie a dead man upon a living man's back. There is no fellowship between him who believes, and an infidel; yet it is certain that, in Israel, the true believers were, at divers periods, fearfully in the minority. In the day of our Lord Jesus, many of them seem to have believed neither God nor Moses, and were equally ignorant of the writings of the one and the power of the other. "If you had believed Moses," said Jesus on one occasion, "you would have believed me, for he wrote of me; but if you believe not his writings, how will you believe my words." Again, he said to the Sadducees, "you do greatly err not understanding the scriptures nor the power of God." Yet, these men enjoyed all the privileges of the law, the temple, and the synagogue.

The Christian Religion lays the axe to the root of the tree here, and cuts down, or lops off, every tree and every branch, that produces not fruit, the fruit of faith; nor is any one to be associated in church membership under the Messiah, who has not previously attained to faith in the only living and true God, and to the confession of the special proposition of our religion; that Jesus Christ is His Son and our Savior. This popular attribute in the gospel must greatly commend itself to the understanding and heart of such men of sense and philanthropy as desire to enjoy the benefit of a revelation. Christianity pays no regard to family pride, and family descent. Her preferences are all on the side of good principle in the first instance; because according to one of her own maxims, she knows, that nothing else will produce good practice. "Make the tree good and the fruit will be good also."

This thing of descent, had taken a most impure and improper hold of the public mind in Jewry in the days of the Caesars; and to correct the national sentiment in this point, was a special business of both John the Baptist and our Lord Jesus Christ.

"Presume not," said the former in his address to his countrymen, "Presume not to say within yourselves, We have Abraham for our father; for I assure you, that of these stones God is able to raise children to Abraham. And even now the axe lies at the root of the trees; every tree, therefore, which produces not good fruit, is cut down, and turned into fuel. I, indeed, immerse you with water, into reformation; but he who comes after me is mightier than I, whose shoes I am not worthy to carry away. He will immerse you in the Holy Spirit and fire. His winnowing shovel is in his hand, and he will thoroughly cleanse his grain; he will gather his wheat into the granary, and consume the chaff in unquenchable fire."—Math 3.

Our Lord Jesus in relation to this change that was to pass on the principles of the revealed religion; asked the Jews if they had not read in their prophets, that in the new institution they were all to be taught of God; he declared to the president of the Sanhedrim, that, in order to enter the kingdom of Messiah, a man must be born again, strongly implying, that descent, even from Abraham, would be of no avail in the kingdom, that was about to be set up. The privileges of his reign, indeed, are all of a nature that forbids them to be conferred on any but one endowed with the principle of belief in his name. Of what avail were it to baptize for the remission of sins, an infant even if descended from Abraham? Of what use were it to introduce it to the church of Christ, in which men are fed only by faith and hope, on the objects of faith and hope? Without the possession of these principles a man cannot possibly have administered to him the blessings of the new economy. It was not so in the former divine institution; the blessings in that were, in many cases, of an animal nature and adapted to animal men; the milk, the honey, the wine, and the oil of Canaan, were as necessary and as useful to the member in the Jewish church of eight days old as to the member of eighty years old; old and young alike lived by those products of the land and they were equally guaranteed to both if descended from Abraham by Isaac and Jacob, and circumcised upon the eighth day, if males. Circumcision extended not to females.

"Now there was a Pharisee, called Nicodemus, a ruler of the Jews, who came to Jesus by night, and said to him, Rabbi, we know that you are a teacher sent from God; for no man can do these miracles, which you do, unless God be with him. Jesus answering, said to him, most assuredly, I say to you, unless a man be born again, he cannot discern the reign of God. Nicodemus replied, How can a grown man be born? Can he enter his mother's womb anew, and be born? Jesus answered, most assuredly I say to you, unless a man be born of water and Spirit, he cannot enter the kingdom of God,"—John 3.

The language employed by the Saviour, in the above passage, is of the most positive kind; and imports, with unequivocal certainty, the truth that a great change was to pass upon the very fundamentals of revealed religion, that the ground of admission into the kingdom of Messiah was not to be fleshly descent, that membership was to be the natural birth-right of no man, not even of a Jew, that a man must be born again before he could enter the kingdom or church of God. The principle of admission into the church, then, is not flesh, but faith; it is good principle, not honorable, not religious descent.

The modern profession of Christianity has grievously erred by changing the principle of faith into that of fleshly relationship, and making it the natural birth-right of the children of believers to have a membership in the church by baptism without faith. This is to throw the church back again upon first principles of a worldly nature; or as the apostle says upon "beggarly and meager elements," or first principles which have no other tendency than to bring the children of faith into bondage to the children of the flesh; there is nothing of an exalting and abiding nature in the accident of kindred blood. Ishmael, who partook of the blood which ran in the veins of the Patriarch Abraham himself, was a wild marauder; and Esau, who proceeded from the loins of the child of promise, was an ungodly and profane person. The man who believes in God and in Jesus Christ may become pure, and holy, and lovely, and glorious; because he is possessed of the principle of belief by which it is possible for him to please God; but the person devoid of this principle cannot please God; the Scriptures have said it. "But without faith it is impossible to please God."

The great plea for this corruption of the new Institution is, that "the Jews were commanded to circumcise their children." This is not a fair statement; the Jews were never commanded to circumcise all their children; they were commanded to circumcise only some of them. In every state the females are the most numerous part of the children; males are most generally, if not always, in the minority; and it was this minority only who were to be circumcised. The incongruity between circumcision and the practice of sprinkling infants is so flagrant in this point, that nothing but blindness of the most inveterate nature can keep any one from perceiving it the moment it is mentioned. Who can rationally infer, that, because the Jewish parent good or bad, must by divine authority, circumcise his son and servant, therefore, I, a Christian, without any other authority, must baptize both my son and daughter? It would be equally good reasoning to say, that because the Jews eat the Passover once a year, therefore we will eat the Lord's supper twice in that time. Our religion does not command us to baptize, but to be baptized. The Jewish religion commanded to circumcise, not to be circumcised. They were to do something for their children on the eighth day; but we are commanded to have something done to ourselves when we believe, without respect to days. "Be baptized every one of you in the name of Jesus Christ for the remission of sins." &c.

But what is our Apostle reasoning for, in his various Epistles concerning the Law, the Romans, and the Galatians in particular? Does he speak against the law? No; he extols the law, as a matter most holy, most wise, most good. He shows it was too holy, just and good for those who lived under it, proving them all to be sinners. Therefore he reasons to show his readers, that in the new religion the blessings were still higher and better, and that the children of the flesh were not the heirs of these things.

What good does a child derive from sprinkling? Its sins are not remitted thereby; it does not thereby receive the Holy Spirit; it is not by this means introduced to the hope of eternal life; it does not celebrate the death of Christ; nor take any part in the institutions of God's house; prayer, praise, the reading of the scriptures, the teachings, the exhortations, and fellowship are all equally unknown to it. These institutions are intended for those, who can discern their use, and who are able to apply them to their proper purposes; to crowd the children of believers into the church, therefore, merely because they are such, without respect to the fundamentals of Christianity, is to level all differences, to do away the most important distinction which God has been pleased to make between faith and infidelity, between the children of the flesh, and the children of the faith. God knows, that, even upon the fact of admitting people to membership on a confession of the faith, we have enough ado to preserve, by all vigilance, the church pure and holy; we have enough ado to keep her chaste and godly as beseemeth a divine institution.—To throw upon her the burden of our children, as they come into the world, is to press her down to the ground, and to reduce her to a level with general society; for it is in this way human society receives its members, it receives them from the loins.—But the church is not a natural society, but a preternatural and divine one, and therefore she receives her members on the preternatural principle of belief in God, and his Son Jesus Christ our Lord.

The proclaimers of the true gospel, ought to avail themselves of every proper occasion to expose infant baptism, in as much as it operates more fatally on the principles and purity of true practical Christianity than any other error abroad. In the heap of rubbish that lies incumbent on the ancient gospel this presses with the most sensible and certain weight.

CHAPTER IX

Faith,—Its Indispensable Nature

For his mental acquisitions man is wholly dependant upon his own experience and on that of others. The sum of his acquirements, therefore, is knowledge and faith. His own experience is his knowledge, the experience of others is his faith. As it was indispensable that we should be acquainted with those facts on which our redemption is founded, as it was absolutely necessary in religious learning that we should know something of primitive man, his fortunes and fall, and something of Christ, his death and resurrection, and as we all could not possibly enjoy a personal and sensible experience of these matters, faith became indispensable. There was indeed, no other power in man, by which he could obtain an acquaintance with those facts. The first principle of our religion, the principle of acquisition, that by which we acquire the knowledge, the organ of illumination, the means by which we gather into the storehouse of the mind, the riches of revelation, the riches of Christ, is therefore faith.—Thus it may be seen that faith has a primary respect to the understanding.

When the illuminations, which it conveys into the mind, are allowed to influence the affections or, as we sometimes say, changes the heart, this change of heart is called repentance *"meta anoeo,"* or a change of mind; and when repentance changes the conduct, this change of conduct is styled obedience; and when obedience leads to baptism this is called a change of state, "translation from darkness to light;" this change of state again, leads to a change of feelings, innocence is substituted for guilt; the Holy Spirit for misery of mind. So that the gospel purposes to change successively our mind first in regard to knowledge, then in regard to duty, then in regard to happiness; and finally to present the whole man internally and externally, in mind and practice, faultless before God.

Now, as the heart can be brought to repentance, as it can be brought into that state of change, which the scriptures call *"metanoeo,"* or repentance, only by becoming acquainted with the facts of our religion, and as it can know these only by faith or belief, therefore, we have another argument for the indispensability of faith derived from the nature of repentance. The argument is this—in a change of mind, knowledge or faith must effect this change; but we cannot enjoy knowledge; we can, however, possess faith; faith, therefore, must produce repentance; and because it is indispensable for this, it is indispensable in our religion in which repentance is a chief matter. "Unless you repent you shall all likewise perish."

We have observed somewhere that knowledge must precede duty; when, therefore, faith is substituted for knowledge, it the substitute like its principle, must precede duty; so that if we would perform vows to God; if we would feel any obligation to our maker and do what he bids us, we must first recognize his existence and character and right to command. Here, then, we derive an argument for the indispensable nature of faith in Religion, from obedience in general, as well as from repentance in particular as above. When this principle by its illuminations has changed the heart, when it has produced repentance, *"metanoeo,"* then the disciple can commence the profession of Christianity by baptism and proceed onward during life in the performance of every duty, in "the obedience of faith," as the scriptures express it.

From the foregoing it will appear very obvious that faith is neither repentance nor obedience. It ought, therefore, neither to be substituted for them nor confounded with them. A man may believe, and not repent, he may repent and not obey; and be it observed, that it is of much use for those who proclaim the gospel to be assured of this difference, and in their labors to make allowance for it; for it is no uncommon error of preachers to charge with the guilt of impenitence those who are only ignorant, and to call that disobedience which is the mere result of error. Belief is "the confidence," which we have in the unseen object concerning which the testimony is given; repentance is the good effect which this object by its attributes and character takes upon the mind; and obedience is that course of conduct resulting from repentance, regulated by God's authority. Thus repentance and obedience, are the internal and external effects of the things believed, which in revealed religion are, first that "there is one living and true God;" and in Christianity "that Jesus Christ is his Son."

CHAPTER X

The Congruity of Faith with Man's Capacity for Knowledge

When God formed man with the powers of sensation and reflection, he formed him with a capacity for knowledge; for this is that in which a capacity for knowledge consists—the power of acquiring ideas by sensation, and of reflecting upon them when acquired. Now these powers of sensation and reflection are bestowed upon all men, and, therefore, it is predicated of mankind universally, that they are every where endowed with a capacity for knowledge. Where is it that men are not gifted with the senses of seeing, hearing, smelling, tasting, touching? Where is it that men do not reflect upon the external things transferred to the mind by these senses? In their powers for acquiring knowledge, therefore, men are every where the same. But see—if God gave man a capacity for knowledge, he gave him at the same time a capacity for faith also; for faith differs from knowledge only as other people's experience differs from our own; ours is the result of our observations, and reflection and experience is the result of their observations and reflections; and as their powers for experience; or their senses, are the same as our own, in order to believe what they know, or in order to make their experience ours, it is only necessary for them to report it, or to testify to us what they saw and heard. "Faith cometh," then, as the apostle says, "by hearing." That doctrine, consequently, which says a man cannot believe the gospel, virtually denies that we can avail ourselves of the experience of others; and consequently it makes the gospel, which is reported to us as true upon the experience of others, or of those who were chosen by God as witnesses and sent forth to testify it first to the Jews and afterwards to the gentiles, a matter ulterior to human nature; or it represents the gospel as a matter which a man has not the capacity from God to believe. Thus, also, it represents God as sending to man a message to be believed, which he cannot believe; which is absurd. In bestowing on man a capacity for knowledge, therefore, God bestowed on him a capacity for faith also; but faith is the principle on which all the blessings of Christianity may be received, therefore men every where have a capacity for receiving the blessings of Christianity; or in other words, the gospel, in its principle of faith or belief, is adapted to human nature universally.

Out of this state of the case arises an argument enforcing upon the ministers of Christ the absolute necessity of understanding the nature of evidence in general, and of the evidence of our holy religion in particular, in order that they may with success instruct others also. For what man is sufficiently prepared to teach to others that which he does not well understand himself. In regard to the evidences of our religion, it may be worth while to make the following observation; that they are divided into the internal and external. In regard to internal evidence a thing may be of such a mould as to prove of itself that its origin is divine. When we look at man, for instance, and enquire into his origin, the evidences of his creation by God, are so many and striking, that we immediately arrive at his divine origin from the tenfold greater difficulty of believing the contrary.—We cannot believe man made himself, or that the world made itself; they prove their own origin; and, therefore, we believe that God made them both. It is so with the bible and new testament; the internal congruity of their several parts, the admirable agreement of the facts of the one, with the prophecies of the other, the felicity with which the oracle gradually develops itself, the perfect adaptation of the whole scheme in doctrine infinite honor which it brings to the great Creator, all demonstrate that the author of nature is the author of revelation. But then, to be able to handle all this weight of internal evidence a man must be eminently skilled in the word of God; he must give his days, and weeks, and months, and years to the study of it, for unless men are publicly and privately and soundly instructed in the evidence of revelation in general and of Christianity in particular, it is not to be expected that they will ever arise and render a rational and enlightened obedience to the gospel, how much soever it be adapted to their necessities, and their powers to receive and enjoy it.

To stand up in the great congregation, in the midst of weak believers, sceptics, deists, and atheists, and, irrespective of all external evidence for either the authenticity or genuineness of the several books which compose the Bible, to prove by its own natural structure that that book is divine, to so handle its contents, to so compare and deduce, tractate and resolve, state, define, and illustrate, as shall cause it to become its own proof, its own defence, is a work that might well become the most prodigious genius on earth.

CHAPTER XI

A Definition of Faith in Word and Fact

We have repeatedly observed that the mental acquisition we make by the experience of others is called faith. Accordingly the term faith is derived from a Latin word *fides* signifying trust, and that again from a Latin word signifying to trust or put confidence in another, because, in believing that which we have not seen ourselves, we are compelled to trust to the testimony of others. As the Latin *fides* signifies truth, so the Greek *pistes* signifies persuasion, and is derived from the verb *peitho* to persuade, because in faith we are persuaded to trust to the experience of the witnesses for the truth in the case.

The word faith, then, is descriptive of the state of mind which it represents; that is, the mind that believes is in a state of trust, or confidence, as the Apostle says, in regard to something of which it has heard, but which it has not seen. Noah heard of the flood by direct communication with the Deity; he believed, or trusted the declaration, and carried himself accordingly; for he "made an ark to the saving of his family by which he condemned" the unbelieving part of men, who trusted not the oracle; and he is, therefore, said by this to have "become an heir of the righteousness which is by faith." "Faith," therefore, as the apostle defines it "is the confidence of things hoped for;" that is, when the things believed lies in the future, the mind reposes in the testimony of God concerning it. If he has said it exists and will be granted, as eternal life for instance, the mind confides in the truth of the saying, and believes that there is such a thing as eternal life and that it will be granted on the terms prescribed by him, who has the power and right to bestow it, and who has promised it. But the object of our faith or the matter of faith, or the thing to be believed may lie in the past, and then it cannot form an object of hope. The apostle, therefore, besides saying that "Faith is the confidence of things hoped for," adds that it is also "the evidence of things not seen." See Heb. 11:1. Thus, when the thing spoken of as the matter of faith, lies in the past, as the creation, the fall, the flood, the call, Messiah's resurrection, faith is called evidence or conviction, like that which is produced by a demonstration; and when the matter of faith lies in the future, as the second advent, the general resurrection, the judgment, and reward and punishment, then faith is confidence in these things as hoped to occur. We need not then wander out of the sacred oracles for a definition of faith; for here it is in the first verse of the eleventh chapter of Hebrews described as—confidence and *elenghos*, evidence or conviction.

If that state of mind which reposes with confidence in the testimony of another is described by the word faith or trust, this is a proof that "Faith comes by hearing" as the apostle vouches. But now, if this state of mind were brought about by an operation of the Holy Spirit, as modern Christendom teaches, then the word which would have described it, is *inspiratio* and not *fides*; and it would in Scripture be called inspiration and not belief. The apostolic commission also would have read, "He who is inspired and is baptized, shall be saved; and he who is not inspired shall be damned," which indeed, is the very doctrine or down right absurdity, taught by the parties of the present day. Faith, then, human or divine, is trust or confidence in the testimony or experience of another. Let us apply the foregoing remarks to some Christian matter. For instance, What is *christian* faith? *Ans.* It is confidence in the testimony of the apostles concerning Jesus Christ, that he did rise from the dead, that he was recognized at Jordan by the Father as His Son. In conformity with this scriptural use of the term the Lord Jesus in his prayer for the disciples, (John 17) prays also "for all those who should believe in" him "through their, the apostle's word," or testimony. The man then who has got his faith by inspiration and not by the word or testimony of the apostles, has no part nor lot in the Lord's prayer; John 7; while he who believes on him by the scriptures, which contain the apostolic testimony, is lifted up, in this prayer, upon the palms of the hands of our great High Priest before the throne on high.

Does the reader, then, trust the apostles of Jesus in regard to the great, the matchless oracle of the Father concerning him? Their integrity, like their morality, is unimpeachable; and the design of their enterprize is befitting such an oracle, such witnesses, such integrity, and such morality; for it was no less than the enterprise of turning the world, the whole world, from false religion to the one living and true God, and from the basest and most terrible immorality to a purity all heavenly, all divine.

But terms may be defined by facts as well as by words; and, therefore, we shall show the reader from scripture what faith is in fact or deed. When the spies of old were sent to speculate on the condition of

Jericho, they were received and entertained by the harlot Rahab. In return for her hospitality, they promised that in the destruction of her city, she should be spared; and for this purpose she "bound in her window a line of scarlet thread," as a symbol of her own confidence, and of their oath; for she made them swear to her that they would spare her. Well, the woman, in the confidence of true belief, reposed in the oath of the spies, and was saved; for "Joshua had said to the two men that had spied out the country, Go into the harlot's house, and bring out thence the woman and all that she hath, as ye swear unto her." And they did so. Thus the religious principle of faith may be exercised by a harlot without any spiritual operation. Accordingly both Paul and James make honorable mention of this woman's faith, as being of a genuine kind. "By faith the harlot Rahab perished not with them that believed not, when she had received the spies in peace."—Abraham was peculiarly distinguished for the lofty confidence which he reposed in the divine word. He left his own country beyond the flood and on this principle wandered in Canaan, the promised land, "dwelling in tabernacles with Isaac and Jacob, the heirs with him of the same promise." He even offered up his own son in confidence of the Divine veracity "Accounting that God was able to raise him up even from the dead; from whence also he received him in a figure." Heb. 11. Who is this that rushes from the heavens like the forked lightnings! that seizes the patriarch's uplifted arm! that exclaims "Abraham, Abraham! lay not thy hand upon the lad?" It is the swift winged messenger of Jehovah's presence—it is Abraham's shield and Isaac's Savior. Behold he cometh from on high to reward the well tried faith of our father; behold he cometh bearing from heaven the joyful tidings of the oath of God! 'Now I know, saith Jehovah, that thou fearest me, seeing thou hast done this thing? and hast not withheld thine only son from me; by myself have I sworn, saith the Lord, because thou hast done this thing, and hast not withheld thy son, thine only son, in blessing I will bless thee, and in multiplying I will multiply thy seed as the stars of heaven, and as the sand which is upon the seashore, and thy seed shall possess the gate of his enemies, and in thee and in thy seed shall all the nations of the earth be blessed, because thou hast done this thing?' Seest thou, saith James, how faith wrought by his works, and by works was his faith made perfect! By faith, saith the apostle, Abraham, when he was tried, offered up Isaac, and he that had the promises, offered up his only begotten son, of whom it was said, that in Isaac shall thy seed be called, accounting that God was able to raise him up, even from the dead, from whence, also, he received him in a figure.

Behold the symbol of divine mercy! the ark, riding upon a world of waters—a sea without a shore! who is its inmate?—whence is he? and whither does he go; It is the child of faith—the patriarch Noah; he escapes from a world that had sinned.—The foundations of the great deep have been broken up—the windows of heaven have been opened, and the world is dissolved. The mighty, which were of old, men of renown, with all their power, and pomp, and glory, have gone down to the bottom of the mountains—the whole earth and its inhabitants—their works of art—their elaborations of science—their trade—their commerce, and all their mirth, and pomp, and revelry, are forever overwhelmed; he alone is escaped, a monument of divine grace. "By faith, Noah being warned of God of things not yet seen" says Paul, "moved with fear, prepared an ark to the saving of his house, by which he condemned the world, and became an heir of the righteousness which is by faith."

Is it not presumable from the above, that faith is comprised simply in believing as we are told, and in doing as we are bid by God, our heavenly Father?[9]

Enoch, it is written, walked with God, and was not found, for God took him. How sublime the principle that keeps a man forever in the presence of him that is invisible! How affecting, also, to behold this venerable and famous ancient so eminently inspired with it at that early age of the world; raising himself on high amidst the antediluvian apostacy, and warring against the spirits of the mighty now in prison! With what noble enthusiasm does he declaim against the sinners of his time; 'Behold the Lord cometh with ten thousand of his saints, to execute judgment upon all; and to convince all that are ungodly among them, of all their ungodly deeds which they have ungodly committed, and of all their hard speeches which ungodly sinners have spoken against him.' Methinks I see the pomp of heaven, the chariot of the Almighty and the horsemen thereof descending to bear aloft the "*First Reformer.*" The Lord took him, and in his translation what unbounded encouragement has God afforded to all, who subsequently dare to make a stand for the truth in the earth! Awake, O Christians! awake and emulate the enthusiasm of this noble ancient; labor to please the Lord; but without faith it is impossible to please him, for he that cometh to God, must believe that he exists, and that he is the rewarder of those who diligently seek him.

And thou, O righteous Abel! first of the martyrs! though we have beheld a more excellent sacrifice, and blood that speaketh better things than thine, think not thou art forgotten before God, or that the faith which inspired thee, is wholly evanished from the sons of men; by the same principle by which thou laidest thine excellent and sweet smelling sacrifice upon the altar, we, on whom the ends of the world have come,

---

[9] Peter makes the ark by which Noah was saved and separated from the condemned a type of our baptism, by which disciples are separated from the unbelieving and disobedient; speaking of the ark, 'the antitype to which, baptism, says he, does now save us,' &c.

behold it consumed by the all approving fire of heaven, and we rejoice; with equal pity, also, we deprecate the black envy that seized thy brother; that filled his infuriated eyes; that raised his murderous arm, and poured out thine innocent blood upon the earth, which opened her mouth wide to receive it from a brother's hand. 'By faith Abel offered more excellent sacrifice than Cain,' &c.

"Through faith we understand that the worlds were framed by the word of God, so that things which are seen, were not made of things which do appear." It was by lives formed on this principle, that the ancients obtained great renown. In a word, faith is the substance of things hoped for; the evidence of things not seen; i.e. in internal thought it is a hearty persuasion that the objects of our hope will be given to us by God, and in external action it is obedience; or the evidence which we afford to ourselves, to others, and to God, that we hope for the unseen things which he has promised to us. Finally, is it not presumable from the above, that faith, take it all in all, is comprised in believing what we are told, and in doing what we are bid of God?

The history of the world has afforded ample opportunity for the development of all that is great in man; we have seen him in the arts; we have seen him in philosophy; we have seen him at the bar, and in the Senate-house:—in peace and in war we have seen him, and in all these things we have seen he can be great—great in war, like the rapid, and terrible, and winged Macedonian; thundering like Achilles, or powerful and pleasing as Hector—strong as Manoah's son, and in conquest rich as Caesar, like the mighty Stagyrite profound and various in wisdom, and harmonious as the sage of Crotona; like Homer too, we have seen him, like Bacon, and Newton, and Locke, we have seen him; but it is only when humanity is sustained by faith in the Eternal perhaps, that we see it clothing itself with all the sublimity of which it is capable—it is only when it is brought to act in great and hazardous enterprises on a simple confidence in the unseen God, that it reaches the summit of that moral grandeur, for which it is distinguished.

Behold Moses at the sea of Edom with the burden of the elect nation on his soul: he had gone down to Egypt; he had seen her royal lord; his eyes had beheld Pharaoh; and he asserted the rights of his brethren; he claimed for the Most High his people; 'shewed his signs among them and wonders in the land of Ham; he sent darkness and made it dark: he turned their waters into blood, and slew their fish; their land brought forth frogs in abundance in the chambers of their kings; he spake and there came divers sorts of flies and lice in all their coasts; he gave them hail for rain and flaming fire in their land, he smote their vines, also, and their fig-trees, and broke the trees of their coast; he spoke and the locusts came and caterpillars, and that without number, and they did eat up all the herbs in their land and devoured the fruit of their ground; he smote also all the first-born of their land, the chief of all their strength: He brought the people forth also with silver and gold, and there was not one feeble person among the tribes;' but now he stood with the beloved of the Lord in charge—Israel with all his bands—the terrors of the Red sea before, and the arms of Egypt behind!—The nation fainted at the scene, they would have returned to the oppressor's yoke.

But lo! the *man of faith* elevates his hand; he stretches the rod of God over the mighty deep; the winds blow; the waters flow; the waves are divided; the sea is dried and Israel on the shores of deliverance sings a temporal triumph in the song of Moses; 'I will sing unto the Lord for he has triumphed gloriously—the horse and his rider hath he thrown into the sea; the Lord is my strength and song and he has become my salvation: He is my God and I will prepare him a habitation; my father's God, and I will exalt him; the Lord is a man of war, the Lord is his name! Pharaoh's chariots and his horses hath he cast into the sea; his chosen captains also are drowned in the Red Sea.—The depths have covered them; they sank unto the bottom as a stone; thy right hand, O Lord, has become glorious in power, thy right hand, O Lord, has dashed in pieces the enemy.'

Is it not developed in the above case that faith is comprehended in believing what we are told, and in doing, *promptly* doing, what we are bid of God? undoubtedly it is, and this is the manner taken by the apostle to instruct the church in the nature and power of true faith:—By faith, says he, they passed through the Red sea as by dry land, which the Egyptians assaying to do without faith, were drowned. It was on this principle he kept the Passover, and sought salvation for the first born of his people in the sprinkling of blood: he forsook Egypt also on this principle and refused to be called the son of Pharaoh's daughter. The same faith operating in his parents, inspired them with a noble contempt of the commands of Pharaoh, and they hid Moses three months, because they saw he was a proper child. Joseph, and Jacob, and Isaac, and Abraham, all afford examples of the principle and practises which constitute the entire of a true faith in God.

Those alone, who have labored in the Ancient Gospel, know how many objections, difficulties, and excuses, are to be removed, overcome, and rebuked in those with whom they have to do. Some conceive it too inconsiderable a matter merely to believe that Jesus is the Christ—object to its novelty, and say all the world believe it! some cavil at the ordinance, despise immersion, and ask whether there is any thing in the water: others think that the preacher does not sufficiently reverence the sacrifice of the blessed Redeemer; and most are willing by any excuse to avoid obedience: This one says 'I have no faith,' that one 'I have no feeling;' one is afraid, another ashamed, a third careless, and a fourth profane; while those who have made a profession of religion in some party form, have a series of objections to be removed, of a nature wholly *sui generis*—they hope every thing—they hope they have faith, hope they have repentance, hope they have remission of sins, hope they have the Holy Spirit, nay, they even hope they have been baptized—nothing at all being with them a matter of certainty—having no confidence that they are the possessors and heirs of any positive or immediate blessings.

Now, here is the field for the man of God, who labors publicly and from house to house in the True Gospel; and in order to clear away the rubbish, his mind must be richly furnished with the history of the men of faith from Abel downward. If the objection is 'I have no feeling' then separate faith from feeling and ply the sinner with the case of Abraham sacrificing his son Isaac by faith, without regard even to the finest of all human feeling, viz: the parental feeling. If he asks whether there is any thing in the water, answer his question by asking another; ask whether there was any thing in the rod of Moses, or the mantle of Elijah, with which he smote asunder the swellings of Jordan, or the rams' horns that blew down the wall of Jericho, or in the red thread that saved Rehab, or in the sprinkling of the blood that saved the first born on that night when the destroying angel cut off all the first-born of Egypt.

The restoration of the True Gospel gave birth to the most singular phenomena: If the reader has ever practised fishing at night, if he has ever lifted the light over the pool, or has seen any other person do it; if he has watched subsequent appearances and looked at the crowd of fishes which approached the flambeau, swimming carelessly and lazily under the light, some, however, active and suspicious, some near to hand and some further off, and all confused; then he has seen a matter which may give him a kind of image of the scenes which occurred when according to the True Gospel we began to urge men by revealed truth and argument to accept of an immediate acquittal or pardon of their sins in baptism. Truth and error, and their effects on the mind are clearly seen by the presentation of the Gospel as administered by the Apostles.

CHAPTER XII

The Figurative Use of the Word Faith

The nouns and verbs of every language are subject to two uses, a literal and a figurative. The great Shepherd says of himself "I am the *door.*" Herod is styled a *fox.* Unstable men, who depart from the faith, are compared to wandering *stars* and *clouds* carried about by the winds. The nation of Israel was styled a *vine* which God had brought out of Egypt and planted in the fertile and richly watered soil of Canaan. Ephraim on account of his unsavory conduct, is compared to an unturned *cake*; Babylon to a lofty *cedar*, and the Gentile nations to a *wild olive*. The Christian church is called the *good olive tree*, the *bride* the Lamb's wife, the *fold* of Christ, and the *body* of Christ. The Law, on account of receiving its members by fleshly relationship, is styled the *flesh*; and the gospel, because it receives its members by faith, is, therefore, styled *the Faith*. Thus faith, from being used for the first and essential principle of our religion, by a very natural transition, is put for the religion itself. For instance:—

"Wherefore the law was our schoolmaster till Christ, that we might be justified by faith; but after that the Faith is come, we are no longer under the schoolmaster." Gal. 3. "Examine yourselves, whether you be in the Faith." 2 Cor. 13. "Him that is weak in the Faith receive ye" Rom. 14. "By grace are you saved through the Faith, and that matter, *the Faith or the gospel*, is not of yourselves; it is the gift of God." There are many passages the force of which is greatly enfeebled on account of the word not being translated with a regard to this tropical use of it by the inspired writers.

But inasmuch as faith is an assent of the mind to certain things which others, by their own experience, know to be true, it is sometimes put for these things, or for the truth. John the Baptist is said to have borne witness to the truth, because he testified that God recognized Jesus as his Son; and Jesus in his prayer calls this revelation the truth; "thy word is the truth," but this truth is also styled in various instances the Faith. "A great company of the Priests were obedient to the Faith." "Felix heard Paul concerning the Faith." "The word of the Faith which we preach." "And now preached the Faith which once he denied," namely, that Jesus was the Christ, the son of God. It is likewise used to describe the attribute of faithfulness in the divine character, "Shall their unbelief make the faith (*faithfulness*) of God without effect;" and for the same quality in Christians, "the fruit of the Spirit is faith, (*faithfulness*;) and for their profession of the gospel, "Your faith is spoken of throughout the whole world." Thus we see, that a word used in its literal sense for the fundamental and most important of all the principles of our religion, that principle or power, by which we lay hold of the facts which is intended to save us, is also used figuratively, a circumstance which shows us that the most essential terms in our religion are not exempted from that use to which all other words of the same class are liable in all languages and by all sorts of writers, the figurative and the literal. This should teach us also to discriminate between the use of language, and never to suppose that because a term is employed figuratively, it may not also be employed literally, and so cause the trope to destroy the fact, and the figurative use to confound, darken, and perplex the literal import as is done with regeneration.

CHAPTER XIII

The Design of Faith

Faith is designed to serve, as near as possible, all the purposes of knowledge, and to cause us "to walk as if seeing him who is invisible." What would we desire our behavior should be, supposing we were admitted to sensible communion with God? Externally, in word and deed, we could wish only that it should be unspotted, wholly unstained by evil; that we should say nothing, and do nothing that did not meet the approbation of God, in whose majestic presence we were honored to stand. But these activities of speech and action are clean only when the mind, which puts them in operation, is clean; and therefore it would be most important that no evil thoughts should be admitted into the mind during the personal presence of the great God of heaven and earth. We would of course make a conscience of excluding all evil from our thoughts during such high communion, and would labor to be holy. Enoch, Noah, and Moses walked as if seeing him who is invisible, and thus, in a moral point of view, the faith of these exalted worthies, served all the purposes of knowledge or sensible communion with God. It is said to Christians that they "are come to mount Zion, the heavenly Jerusalem, and the city of the living God, to an innumerable company of angels, to the general assembly and church of the first born, whose names are written in heaven, to God the Judge of all, and to the spirits of just men made perfect, and to Jesus the Mediator of the New Covenant, and to the blood of sprinkling that speaketh better things than that of Abel."

To understand this, it is necessary to keep in mind that we walk by faith, not by sight. At the fall, then, sight yielded to faith; and again, at the resurrection faith shall yield to sight, and man shall be admitted to the presence of his God. But faith now does not alter the nature of things; and, therefore, we are just as certainly come to the glory mentioned in the above scripture as if we had sensible communion with it. To illustrate this. If the United States were to bestow the right of citizenship on a foreigner in Great Britain, it might be said that he was come to Columbia, to the capital of the United States, to the innumerable officers which minister in the Republic, to the whole assembly of the American citizens and to the President and the celebrated spirits of the Revolution, and so forth. The distinguished foreigner, might not, at the time of receiving the honor, see all the grandeur of the commonwealth of which he had become a citizen; still it was in existence and he was a member of it although he had not yet crossed the Atlantic and taken actual possession of the honor and riches voted him. In belonging, therefore, to the commonwealth of Israel, to the church of Christ, we are really come to mount Zion and to the city of the living God, &c. And as the foreigner above referred to, would really find his faith give way to sight the moment he landed on the American shore; so, the moment we rise from the dead, our faith will yield to personal experience and we shall know by unveiled communion, the truth of the glorious scripture above quoted.

The moral of this exalted revelation is added by the apostle. "See that you refuse not him that speaketh, for if they escaped not who refused him that spake on earth (Moses) much more shall not we escape if we turn away from him who speaketh, from heaven (the Father, at Jordan and at Sinai.) Whose voice then shook the earth; but now he has promised, saying, Yet once more I shake not the earth only but heaven also. And this once more signifies the removal of those things that are shaken as things that are made, that those things, that cannot be shaken, may remain. Wherefore, we receiving a kingdom that cannot be moved, let us have grace whereby we may serve God acceptably with reverence and godly fear; for our God is a consuming fire."

Nature is rich, and beautiful, and splendid, and various; but O what boundless regions of glorious thought have been redeemed to man by the elevation of Jesus to the throne of God! Youth, immortal youth, beauty, loveliness and eternal life, the kingly ornaments, of wisdom, greatness, dignity, veneration, crowns, the imperial pomp of powers, virtues, dominations, principalities, thrones, the social glory of the general assembly and congregation of the heirs in heaven, of angels innumerable, spirits perfectly just, and God, and Christ the Mediator of the New Covenant: Hallelujah. Blessing, and glory, and wisdom, and thanksgiving, and honor, and power, and might, and dominion be to our God and to the Lamb forever and ever. Amen.

Faith is a proper substitute for knowledge, and serves all the purposes of it when it keeps these things before us, and causes us to walk as if seeing God, who, during this state, must be invisible to us.

CHAPTER XIV

Faith and Favor or Grace

There are two predicaments in which man may receive favors at the hand of his maker. In belief and in unbelief; that is, God may vouchsafe favors to a man on account of good principle, and he may bestow them on him irrespective of principle. Many of the blessings of life are holden by us irrespective of principle; we come into the world and enter a circle of numerous and kind relations the moment we are born; the breast of the mother and the bosoms of all are open to receive us; we eat, drink, sleep and are refreshed, and cherished by a thousand caresses during the whole period of childhood. But during all this time and amid all those favors, we are wholly without the knowledge of God.

Even religious blessings are not withheld from us. God has anticipated us even with them, and has provided for us a Redeemer in the person of his Son, has given us the word of life, the Bible, Christians to teach and proclaim it, and parents to illustrate it by their example and pious reverence for God. And so if there are other blessings of a nature to be received on the footing of good principle only, he has, by all these precursory favors, fairly put it into our power to possess ourselves of good principle and of all the blessings and enjoyments appended to it. We consequently, in many instances, find ourselves in possession of good principles before we are aware of their immense value, and sometimes even believe in God and in his Son Jesus Christ, before we know the inestimable account to which this most precious faith may be turned.

While, therefore, God bestows many things on good and bad indiscriminately, and gives to all men life and breath and all things richly to enjoy; there are certain goods or favors which are disposed of by him only on proper principle; that is, they are granted only to such as by good principles are able to appreciate them and turn them to their proper purposes. Many of the blessings of Christianity are of this nature and cannot be used and enjoyed, and of course need not be bestowed, on any but such us are prepared for their reception by faith in God. Such are the remission of sins, church membership, and the innumerable honors and immunities consequent upon this membership. Still this throws no man at a distance from his Creator; for by the Holy Scriptures we can be brought into his presence and learn of him the fundamental oracle of Christianity; we can learn of him that Jesus Christ is his Son and our Savior, and so by faith enter into a personal enjoyment of all the distinguished favors of the Christian Religion. "None are excluded here but such as do themselves exclude." Christians ought, therefore, in obedience to the divine commandment, to "Bring up their children in the nurture and admonition of the Lord," and masters should instruct their servants, teachers their pupils, and magistrates the people, till violence and deceit, and blasphemy and outrage are wholly done away from the community.

CHAPTER XV

Faith and Love

Love is of two kinds special and general, or benevolent and complacent. The love of benevolence is that affection in God which leads him to bestow all things necessary to life on all the creatures which he has made; man tastes of this feeling when he entertains a care for the inferior tribes and for his own species universally, irrespective of those personal regards which arise out of the particular relations of social life. "The righteous man, the bible says, is merciful to his beast," and of God it says, "his tender mercies are over all his works;" that is, traces, nay, evident tokens of his benevolence towards his creatures, are visible every where.

But there is a fitness in things nevertheless; and therefore, there is also a preference for things. The lower tribes or brute-beasts, though the objects of every good man's benevolence, are never like our own species, the objects of our complacency. We feed them, protect them, and nourish them; but we have no rational delight in them, such as we experience and cherish for our sons and daughters. The reason of it too, is this: their fellowship is not meet for us, they are animal without being rational, and consequently are incapable of the rational reciprocity which gives birth to the love of complacency. Adam admired and no doubt felt a real benevolence for his whole animal dominion as it passed before him, for like ourselves, he was created capable of this general feeling; but among them all, it is written, "there was not found a help meet for Adam." There was not one of them for whom he felt a personal preference or could love with delight and look upon with soul-mixing complacency. There was nothing in them which he could identify with what he most of all admired in himself, knowledge, duty, and rational happiness. Eve appeared, whose form, attitude, grace, beauty and dignity, meeting his eye, filled his soul to overflowing and caused him with new born delight to exclaim, "This is now bone of my bone and flesh of my flesh." Charmed with the glorious gift, he put his own name upon her and called her woman, because she was taken from man; thus testifying that not good will merely but complacency, not general benevolence but personal preference and infinite delight inspired his soul and his tongue in regard to the matchless person to whom God had now espoused him.

God is said in scripture to love mankind and so to love them too, as to give his Son Jesus Christ for them. It behooves us then to know whether this gift proceeds from benevolence merely, or from a personal delight which he entertained for mankind at the moment he granted it.

If we look at the world at the time God's Son appeared to take our place in law, and consider the political condition of men under the governments which they had framed and adopted, then it was a scene of unmixed tyranny, iron, Roman, imperial tyranny on the side of the rulers; and on the side of the people base submission and prostitution of all political equality and manly right.

If we look at mankind as they then existed, in regard to religion, polytheism was substituted for the true God and impure converse with images for faith; the people every where inflaming themselves with idols and indulging in licentiousness unfit for Christian utterance. Their morals of course were insufferably abominable. As one who beheld them said, "They were filled with all unrighteousness." It could not then be on account of any delight that God took in the sons of men, that he gave his Son our Lord for them; for it is impossible for the Deity to entertain complacency for a man all defiled and unclean, ignorant of God, without faith, devoted to idols, inflamed with lewdness. A righteous man cannot love with delight his fellow mortal thus defiled, thus degraded. If, therefore, he should feel for him, it could only be good will: he could not make him his companion; he could not indulge towards him complacency. God then did not give his son for us because we were the objects of his delight, but because he saw that by this means we could become the objects of his delight. Before we believed the gospel and before he gave his Son for us, we were the objects of his gracious benevolence merely, but when we believe and obey the truth as it is in Jesus, we change our attitude in the affections of the Father, we are made his children and become the objects of his real complacency; he delights in us as he did in his Only Begotten, of whom he said "Behold my Son, the Beloved, in whom I delight." All mankind are of course equally the objects of this general benevolence; for all, when considered in relation to their origin, their state in law, their condition in religion, and their morals, are on a level; as the apostle, when arguing this point, says, "We have before proved both Jews and Gentiles to be all under sin;" again, "All have sinned and come short of the glory of God being justified freely by his grace through the redemption that is in Christ Jesus." Accordingly Jesus said that "God so loved the world as to give his only begotten Son, that whosoever believeth on him may not perish but have everlasting life." Now it was not for the Jewish world, or the Gentile world, or the elect world, but for all these that God gave up his Son. "He is the propitiation not for our sins only;" says the apostle John, "but also for the sins of the whole world." Who then are the objects of God's benevolence? The world, the whole world,—and nothing less than the whole world.—Who then are the objects of God's delight? those who obey the gospel. Thus the Scriptures divide men into saints and sinners. The first class, including all men, are the objects equally of God's benevolence and those for which he gave his Son; the second class are those who accept the salvation which his blood has bought, and are styled the saints. He then that would advance himself in the divine affection must believe and obey the gospel; and, from being the object of God's benevolence merely, he will thus become that of his complacency. God will become his Father and he shall be called God's son. "Come out from among them and be ye separate, says the Lord, touch no unclean person and I will receive you. And I will be a father unto you and you shall be my sons and daughters saith the Lord Almighty."

Let no man imagine or teach, nevertheless, that because God loved the world and gave his Son for us, that, therefore, all the world will be saved. This is the silly and dangerous doctrine of universalism; which has its origin in ignorance, and its issues of course in immorality; for the vile thing is as distinguished for its wickedness as it is for its errors. It begins with confounding the objects of benevolence with those of supreme delight, or saints with sinners, the world with the church; it then proceeds to demolish the distinctions of sin and righteousness, and ends with the abrogation of all punishments, and the binding of devils and condemned spirits upon the backs of the saints through all eternity!

But see—the Saviour on one occasion, healed ten lepers; they went to show themselves to the priest; on their way they all were cleansed. Yet none of them returned to thank him but one. When he saw it, he said, "Were there not ten lepers cleansed, but where are the nine? Has none returned to glorify God but this Samaritan." Still they all had been equally the objects of his gracious benevolence; but in the Samaritan alone could he delight. In him alone was gratitude found. I may show a favor to a man, who will in the sequel, prove himself very unworthy of it and of my complacency. This is the way with men for whom Christ died; the favor does not affect their heart or their life; they are ungrateful; they love the world, they love the things of the world; they put God far away from them. Like Festus they say, "Go for this time and at a more convenient season I will send for you." To such the Lord with righteous indignation will say, Because I have called, and ye refused; I have stretched out my hand, and no man regarded; but ye have set at nought all my counsel, and would none of my reproof: I also will laugh at your calamity; I will mock when your fear cometh when your fear cometh as desolation, and your destruction cometh as a whirlwind; when distress and anguish come upon you: then shall they call upon me, but I will not answer; they shall seek me early, but they shall not find me: for that they hated knowledge, and did not choose the fear of the Lord: they would none of my counsel; they despised all my reproof: therefore shall they eat of the fruit of their own way, and be filled with their own devices. For the turning away of the simple shall slay them, and the prosperity of fools shall destroy them. But whoso hearkeneth unto me shall dwell safely, and shall be quiet from fear of evil.

CHAPTER XVI

Faith and Election and Sovereignty

There are two great systems in which the sovereignty of God appears, Nature and Religion. By his sovereignty he made the universe what it is, and by the same sovereignty he made the Christian Religion what it is. Now the questions are frequently asked, in regard to his natural doings, Why did he make man what he is, and place him originally in a state of trial as the Scriptures represent and the history of our own life proves? To this it may be answered that unless he had made us what we are, the objector or person who asks these questions, never would have enjoyed either the person, nature, or existence which he now possesses; and if he had not put us under trial, he would not have suited his treatment to our nature; for by granting us rational knowledge and a sense of duty, he made us responsible beings, and his system of trial is only adapted to our nature as such. In the first case then appears his sovereignty, in the last, his benevolence.

Again: It is asked why he framed the gospel such as it is, and then called man to obey it? We answer, If he had not given his Son to death, then man never could have known the character of the Divinity as he now does; and if he had not pitched this thing upon the all-pervading principle of Faith, then it would not have been adapted to man in his present condition; for in revealing his character by the Christian system, and offering its blessings on the universal principle of Faith, he only suits his salvation to our wants and capacities. In the first of these points he displays his sovereignty absolutely; in the last, his sovereignty relatively or in connection with his goodness bending to our necessities and nature.

Great evil has arisen to Christianity from confounding his sovereignty in nature with his sovereignty in religion, and from substituting the one for the other; and reasoning about it, as if man were as physically a lump of clay when he is to be saved, as he was when God formed him out of the dust of the ground and first created him. But God used physical means in the first of these cases and he employs moral and verbal means for the second.

The following, written a few years since by the author, will set election and the sovereignty of God, in a proper attitude before the reader.

When the apostles preached the gospel they gave commandment to retain it as it had been delivered to them, anathematizing man and angel who should dare to disorder, alter, or corrupt it. The whole New Testament was written either to establish or defend it, or to detach it from the corruptions of Jews and Gentiles, to whom it was either a stumbling block or an institution of manifest foolishness.

The epistle to the Galatians is directed against the conniptions of the former, who, under the mask of affected zeal for the law of Moses, eagerly desired, like some modern zealots, to superadd it as "a rule of life." But "If I or an angel," says the Apostle, "preach anything else to you for gospel, let him be accursed," and he repeats the anathema. The four Evangelists, the great bulwarks of Christianity, are for the purpose of supporting its reality on the principle of the conformity of its author's birth, life, offices, death, resurrection and glorification to the predictions of the ancient oracles and the great power of God. The acts are a history of it publication; and as there were not wanting among the Greeks those who sufficiently abhorred the resurrection, the reader will find this part of the gospel sufficiently defended and illustrated in the 15th chapter of 1 Corinthians. Besides perverting, and maiming the glad tidings, some would have circumscribed its entire influence to the Jewish nation, and "forbid it to be preached to the Gentiles."

The gospel proposes three things as the substance of the glad tidings to mankind—the remission of sins, the Holy Spirit, and eternal life; and the Apostles every where, in conformity with their mission, plead for reformation towards God and faith in our Lord Jesus Christ, as the state of mind adapted to the reception of these inestimable blessings. In the proclamation of the gospel, therefore, these high matters were ordered thus—faith, reformation, baptism for the remission of sins, the Holy Spirit and eternal life; but how this order has been deranged, some things added, some subtracted and others changed, must be manifest to all who know, and, alas! who does not know this, that even now whole bodies of worshipers deny the resurrection of the body; some would, to this day, superadd the law as "a rule of life;" others deny the gift of the Holy Spirit; the Socinians, totally object to the sacrifice; and almost all who do embrace it reject, nevertheless, the remission of sins in baptism, which the sacrifice has so greatly secured to all who believe and reform.

Some have substituted sprinkling, some the mourning bench, for the baptism of remission; and even those who most of all affect to be orthodox, publicly preach in direct contradiction to God's most universal commandment, that a man can neither believe nor repent; they publish that faith comes by the Spirit, and not by the word, "thus making the word of God of non-effect," and contradicting the apostles, who every where speak of the Spirit as a "Spirit of promise" to those who should receive the gospel. Others will immerse, but not for the remission of sins; and others preach the gospel maimed, disordered, changed and corrupted, in connexion with a scholastic election, which not only retards the progress of the glad tidings, but also opposes itself to Christian election—to political election—to all rational ideas of election, and causes the entire gospel to smell in the estimation of all unprejudiced men.

The Apostles never preached election to unconverted people as the Calvinists do; and the disciples themselves were never spoken to on this matter as persons who had believed, because they were elected, but rather as those who were elected because they had believed—"formerly you were not a people, but now you are the people of God:" "you are an elect race;" "make your calling and election sure." After preaching the ancient gospel for a long time, I am finally convinced that nothing, not even the grossest immorality, is so much opposed to its progress, as the scholastic election; which, indeed, is no better than the fatalism of the Greeks and Romans.

Every election necessarily suggests to us six things—the elector or electors—the person or persons elected—the principle on which the election proceeds—the ends to be accomplished by it—when the election commenced, and when it shall cease. Let us peep at the scripture election, in this order; and, first, in regard to the elector. No one, I presume, will dispute that God is He. 2d. As for the person or persons elected, I would just observe, in accordance with the ancient oracles, that, although there were in the world, previous to the days of Abraham, and even during the life of that patriarch, many who feared God and wrought righteousness, yet till then none but he ever worshipped the true God in the character of an elect person. Elect and election are words which do not occur in scripture with a reference to any who lived before Abraham; previously there were no elect head, no elect body, no elect principles, no ends to be accomplished by an elect institution; and therefore the scriptures speak of none of his contemporaries as they speak of Abraham: "Thou art the God who didst choose (i.e. elect) Abraham." This patriarch, therefore, is positively and Scripturally the first elect person mentioned in the divine oracles; consequently the history of the doctrine of election commences with the fact of God's having chosen, for general and magnanimous purposes, this ancient worthy. But the choice of Abraham was accompanied by the following promise, which at once reflected the highest praise on God and honor on the patriarch: "In you and in your seed shall all the nations of the earth be blessed." Now the Apostle, in Galatians 3 says, "The seed is Christ." Substituting, therefore, the definition for the term itself, then the promise would read, "In you and in Jesus Christ, or the Messiah, shall all the families of the earth be blessed," God here, then, has set forth two persons in which a man may certainly be blessed: for let it be attentively noticed that it is in Abraham and Christ, not out of them, that the blessing is to be obtained. Christ and Abraham only are here represented as being strictly and primarily elect persons; for it is said of Christ, "Behold my elect." All other persons must be found in them before they are elect, and as a person can be related to Abraham and Christ only in one of two ways, i.e., by flesh or faith, it follows that if any one, from the patriarch's time to the present, has enjoyed the blessings of an elect person or worshiper of the true God, he must have been a child of Abraham by one or both of these principles. He must have been a Jew or a Christian.

The election taught by the Protestants contemplates all the righteous, from Abel to the resurrection of the dead, as standing in the relation of elect persons to God; than which nothing can be more opposed to fact and scripture: for though Abel, Enoch, and Noah, were worshippers of the true God, they were not elect men; nay though

Melchisedec himself, king of Salem, was at once priest of the Most High God, and the most illustrious type of Messiah; though he received tithes of Abraham, blessed him, and, as Paul informs us, was greater than he; yet neither Melchisedec nor any of the numerous worshipers for whom he officiated in the quality of God's priest, did ever stand in the relation of elect worshipers in the scripture-sense of the word elect. Abraham was the first elect man; and it remains for those who assert the contrary of this, to prove their proposition—a thing they never can do by scripture.

The elect institution reared upon the patriarch Abraham, and which has been made the deposit of covenants, laws, services, glory and promises, is quite distinct, from the general righteousness of the world, whether that righteousness may have been derived from revelations made to men before the commencement of the elect institutions, or afterwards from traditions, or from an apprehension of God's existence derived from the face of nature, the currency of events, and the nature of human society among Gentiles, ancient or modern. I say the election is a *sui generis* institution, in which the worshiper does not, with the uncertainty of a Mahometan, idolater, a Chinese or Japanese, ask the remission of sins; but in which this blessing is stable and certain, secured to him by the promise and oath of God, two immutable things, by which it is impossible for God to lie, that the man may have strong consolation, who has fled into this institution for refuge to lay hold on the hope set before him in the gospel; which is the second apartment of the elect building, as Judaism was the first,—"In thee shall all the families of the earth be blessed"—a promise made to no other institution.

In the above we ascertained two of the six things suggested to us by the term election, viz. that the living *God* was the *elector*, and that *Abraham* was the *first elect person*; and now if we ask when it began and when it shall end, I answer, first, that election will close at the end of the world—all the gracious purposes of the institution will be accomplished at that time—false religion and bad government—the domination of political and trading influences—and every thing which opposes itself to the religion and authority of this institution—shall have been put down; and angels and men shall behold this truth, that the God of Abraham is the true God, and Jesus the Messiah his Son; and that Mahomet, and Confucius, Zoroaster, and Brahama, were self-created apostles.

As for the commencement of the election, if Abraham was the first elect person, as we see he was, it follows this must have been when God called that patriarch from his native country to be the head of the elect people: "Now the Lord had said to Abraham, Get you out of your country, and from your father's house to a land that I will show you, and I will make of you a great nation; and I will bless you, and make your *name great*, and *you shall be a blessing*; and I will bless them that bless you, and curse them that curse you; and *in you* shall all the families of the earth be blessed." Gen. 12. Here, then, is the commencement of that institution which is finally to triumph over imposition and falsehood.

It only remains for us to speak of the great and illustrious purposes for which God has set up this institution in the earth, and finally of the principle on which a man of any nation may be admitted to the privileges of it, viz. the remission of sins, &c. &c. First, then, in regard to the end of the election, I say, it is the blessing of mankind—"In you shall all the families of the earth be blessed." This is God's declared purpose in regard to mankind by the institution called "the election;" consequently its purpose is not (like the election of Edwards, Calvin, and others,) to exclude, curse, and destroy; but to gather, to bless, and to save! "In you shall all the nations of the earth be blessed"—"I will make you a blessing." Abraham, Isaac, and Jacob, then, were not chosen for the mean partial purpose of being *dragged* into heaven, will or no will, on the principle of final perseverance; but for the general and benevolent purpose of saving mankind by an institution of which they were made the root or foundation. While the pulpit election represents the God of heaven both partial and cruel, the scriptural election furnishes us with the fairest specimen of his peerless impartiality and philanthropy: the lineaments of the divine character are in nothing more effulgent than in the blessing of the nations on the principles of an election, because it represents the Most High as anticipating the alienations and apostasies of his self-willed and unhappy creatures, running into all the idolatries and consequent immoralities of Assyria, Persia, Greece, Rome, &c. &c. and then providing for their redemption from those things by this elect institution, in which he had deposited a correct theology and the principles of a pure morality to be preached to the world in the fullness of time, i.e. after the wisdom of this world, viz. philosophy, government, and idolatry had been sufficiently proved incompetent to the purification and elevation of the human family.

I am sure our Heavenly Father in all this has shown the wisdom and prudence of one who hides a piece of leaven in three measures of meal until the whole be leavened. He has treated the rebellious and refractory nation of the Jews as a woman would a bowl of meal set down by the fireside, with the leaven in it, and turned, and warmed, and tended it, until the leavening process has commenced, in order that the whole mass may be more speedily and certainly transformed; yet, after all, it would scarcely work in them, so dead were they to heavenly things. Nevertheless the principles of this establishment, the church, must prevail—idolatry must be put down—the knowledge of God must cover the earth—the saints must obtain the government of the world—righteousness run down like a river, and peace like a flowing stream.

Having ascertained, in a summary way, the elector, the *person* elected, the ends of the election, the time when it began and when it shall end, I shall speak of the principle on which it proceeds, and also on the sovereignty of God, and where it obtains in our religion, in the subsequent pages. I only observe here, that Calvinistic election exhibits the divine sovereignty in a point in which it by no means obtains in Christianity. It is not exhibited in a capricious choice of this, that, and other persons, and passing by others, as Calvinism would and does have it; but in the justification of sinners of all nations on the principle of faith, as will appear by and by, an act of God's sovereignty, which was very displeasing to the Jews.

I shall close this point with an observation or two for the reflection of the reader, until the handling of the next item.—First, then, it ought to be observed that scriptural election is managed entirely on the plan of political election, the ends thereof being the general welfare of the nations—"In you shall all the families of the earth be blessed."

Second. Whether a man can believe, i.e. imbibe the electing principle, is never answered in the Holy Scriptures—for this substantial reason, that in them it is never asked. This is an unlearned question of Modern divinity, (altogether unworthy of primitive Christianity) and could be agitated only by fools and philosophers; all the world knowing that we must believe what is proved. Whether we will always act according to our rational and scriptural belief, is another question which the reader may answer by making an appeal to his own conscience. If we would, how many would immediately be baptized into Jesus Christ!

The following sentence is found in our last topic: "Having ascertained in a summary way, the elector, the person first elected, the ends of the election, the time when it began, and when it shall terminate, I shall speak of the principle on which it proceeds," &c. Let us then speak of the principle on which a person may, at any time, be admitted into the elect institution, or church of God and Christ.

1. This election divides itself into two great departments, the Jewish and Christian churches, the first receiving its members on the gross, limited, and partial principle of the flesh, i.e. relationship to Abraham by the line of Isaac and Jacob. The second admitting its members on the exalting, universal, and impartial principle of faith in Jesus Christ.

2. The election of individuals to church privileges by the first of these principles, viz: Fleshly relationship, can be justified only by the fact, that in the infancy of the world, the rudeness of the age, &c. rendered the introduction of the higher and more refined principle of faith, if not impossible, at least altogether impolitic, in regard to the ends to be accomplished by the institution.

I need not observe that the change of principle from *flesh* to *faith* occurred at the coming of the Lord Jesus Christ, and that many of the Jews, who stood in the first apartment of the election, failed to be received into the second for want of the proper principle of faith in Jesus. But the limited nature of family descent, the extent of belief as the first principle of Christianity, the degradation of the infidel Jews, and the elevation of the believing Gentiles, are all set forth by the apostle, in the following beautiful allegory, in his letter to the Roman disciples: "Now if some of the branches were broken off, and you, who are a wild olive, are ingrafted in instead of them, and are become a joint partaker of the root and fatness of the olive, boast not against the branches, for if you boast against them you bear not the root but the root you."

"You may say, however, the branches were broken off, that I might be grafted in."

"True—by unbelief they were broken off, and you, by *faith*, stand; be not high minded, but fear—For if God spared not the natural branches, perhaps neither will he spare you. Behold then, the goodness and severity of God: towards them who fell, severity; but towards you, goodness, if you continue in his goodness, otherwise, you also shall be cut off; and even they, if they abide not in unbelief, shall be grafted in, for God is able to graft them in. For if you were cut off from the olive, by nature wild, and contrary to nature were grafted into the good olive, how much rather shall those who are the natural branches be grafted into their own olive?"

The Magna Charta of the whole elect institution is the covenant made by God with Abraham; from the superior and inferior branches of which are derived what the apostle, in Heb. 8. calls the new and old, the first and second, the inferior and better; or, in other words, the Jewish and Christian covenants, i. e. the law and the gospel—the one enjoyed by the Jews on the footing of *flesh*, the other by men of all nations on *faith*. It is thus the apostle, by a metonymy of principle and privileges, styles the law *flesh*, and the gospel *faith*. The infancy and rudeness of the age of law, is indicated by the apostle in the following metaphor: "So the law was our *school master* until Christ, " Again allegorically—"Now I say, as long as the *heir* is a minor he differs nothing from a bondman, although he be lord of all; for he is under tutors and stewards, until the time before appointed by his father." The grossness of fleshly relationship and the spirituality of faith, together with the substitution of the last for the first of these principles, is thoroughly enforced upon the Galatians, in the allegory of Sarah and Hagar: "Cast out (says the scripture) the bond maid and her son; for the son of the bond maid shall not inherit with the son of the free woman. Well then, brethren, we (christians) are not the children of the bond maid, but of the free woman:" i.e. not of flesh but of faith. It must be manifest, therefore, from what has been written, that the entire election has been managed, first and last, upon these two principles, and that, the one has now superseded the other.

I shall close this paper with two or three remarks upon *faith* and family *relationship*: It is on this limited and partial principle of birth or blood, that the old world has obtained its chiefs, judges, dictators, kings, sultans, emperors, priests, &c. and the consequence has been that an alarming proportion of such officers has proved the worst of tyrants and knaves. The fact is, that, in the old world, a man may, by family connexion, become the heir both of religious and civil offices, to which neither his talents nor character at all entitle him. Yet this was just the principle on which the Jews obtained their kings and priests; nay, it was the principle, also, on which they were introduced into the church. Their priests, therefore, were most corrupt. Nadab and Abihu were slain of the Lord, and the two sons of Eli also perished in their immorality and presumption. The arrogance of Rehoboam issued in the dismemberment of the kingdom; and but few of his successors were famous for piety. Religion flowing from family pride went on apace until the appearing of John and Jesus, the first of whom told the people not (now) to say "We have Abraham for our father;" and the last that they must be "born *again*" if they would enter into the reign of Messiah; not that the new birth and faith are the same thing, for they are not. The new birth is a thing proposed to the believer in Jesus—Nicodemus believed, and to him it was said, "You must be born again." i.e. of water and the Spirit. Preachers are very apt to mistake here, and to tell the unbelieving man that he must be born again; but it is a fact that no unbelieving man can be born again. The Scriptures expressly assert that "to those only who received him he gave the power of becoming the sons of God, even to those who believe upon his name; who are born not of blood, nor of flesh, nor of the will of man, but of God;" i.e. by water and the Spirit—the way which he wills his children to be born to him on the principle of faith. The apostle defines faith, in general, to be "the confidence of things hoped for, the evidence of things not seen;" of course Christian faith, in particular, must be an assent to the evidence of the existence of the Messiah, though we do not see him, and a confident reliance on God as one who means what he says, and who will perform what he has promised. Thus true belief engages both the head and heart of a man. "He that comes to God must not only believe that he exists, but that he is a rewarder of those who diligently seek him." This definition is illustrated in the 11th chapter of Hebrews, by the faith of Abel, Enoch, Abraham, Isaac, Jacob, Sarah, Moses, and his parents, Gideon, Barak, Samson, David, Samuel, and the prophets. But as Cain believed in the existence of God, without, exercising any confidence in him, as a rewarder of his worshippers; so, many now have only the one half of the true faith, and believe that Christ exists, without having the least confidence in either him, his words, or his institutions. Hence they won't be baptized, they won't be born again, neither ought they, until they can trust his words. Sinners, look to the history of his faithfulness.

I would observe that the teachers of Christianity ought never to go out of the Bible for a definition of faith. In regard to the origin of faith, I would just state, that, like our affections, it is not dependant upon the will but upon evidence.—Other powers of the mind, as recollection, imagination, &c. are dependent on the will in their exercise, while the *will* itself is solely under the direction of that law which governs all animated nature: viz. the desire of happiness.

Man is possessed of other powers of acquiring knowledge besides the power of believing; for he is a creature of sense and reason, as well as of faith: but while for the propagation and education of mankind, God has laid hold of appetite, passion, reason, &c., rather than faith, yet it must be granted that we cannot see how our gracious Father, in bestowing on our fallen family a system of morals, should make the practice of it to proceed upon any other principle than that of belief.— Faith and sense act with supreme power among mankind, and are the two most universal principles of our nature:—they are very closely allied to each other; and it is not easy to say where the one begins and the other ends. Had the Divine Father predicated our salvation upon a fine imagination, a strong memory, a piercing intellect; military, philosophic, and literary talent; upon high birth, or even good morals; then we should have seen coming up to the Christian altar our Homers, Virgils, and Miltons; our Lockes and Newtons; our Washingtons, Alexanders, &c., and men might have complained. But so long as it is written, "He who believes and is baptized shall be saved," no one, who has ears to hear, and feet to carry him to the water, has the least ground of complaint. The principle then on which Christian election proceeds, is faith, a power of action in human nature alike distinguished for its utility, purity and universality.

We now come to speak of the sovereignty of God, and the point of our religion at which it appears.

In order to arrive at our conclusions with effect, I would observe that the following phrases are used in scripture to mean the same thing: "justification from sin," "righteousness of God," "righteousness of faith," "forgiveness of sins," "remission of sins." If the reader will bear these phrases in mind, I shall show him shortly how the same sentiment comes to be varied into five different expressions by the writers of scripture.

Meanwhile, let us peep at the history of the remission of sins among the Jews. The Jewish religion was exceedingly comforting to the man of God in this respect; much more so, indeed, than modern Christianity; for if a man sinned, the Lord had appointed five different sorts of animals, as the mediums of remission. These were calves, lambs, kids, turtle doves and young pigeons, any of which the man of God could carry to the altar, and by confession at the sanctuary obtain forgiveness of the God of Israel.

If a man feared God, he would have been very poor who could not muster a pair of young pigeons. But if he could not, the Lord had appointed what was styled "the poor man's offering." "If," says the law, "he (the sinner) be not able to bring two turtle doves, or two young pigeons, then he that sinned shall bring for his offering the tenth part of an ephah of fine flour for a sin offering; he shall put no oil upon it, neither frankincense; for it is a sin offering." Again—"Then the priest shall make an atonement for him as touching the sin that he hath sinned in one of these (sins specified in the beginning of the chapter,) and it shall be forgiven him." Lev. 5. As rich and poor were liable to commit sin, these different animal offerings were evidently appointed with a reference to the different degrees of wealth among the worshippers— while the very poor and destitute were permitted to present what we have seen was called "the poor man's offering," stript of every article, of oil, wine, and frankincense, which could render it expensive. Thus our heavenly Father, in giving a law, made all possible provision for the comfort of the worshiper, by instituting the above means of forgiveness.

In Christianity the institution for forgiveness is baptism, which is not to be repeated, a real superiority over the law remission: the Lord Jesus, by his precious blood, sanctifying in this way the believer once for all (his life.) "Be baptized every one of you, in the name, (i.e. by the authority) of Jesus Christ for the forgiveness of your sins." Thus the symbol of remission in the true religion is changed from animal blood to water; while the blood of Christ, between them, like the sun at the equator, reaches to the ends of the earth, and forms the real cause of pardon to all who ever shall be forgiven, from Abel to the resurrection of the dead.

Now, I say, it is just here that the sovereignty of God appears in Christianity, in forgiving sins of men in the institution of baptism upon the principle of faith in the blood of Christ, as the great and efficacious offering for all. And hence we shall see how the same sentiment came to be expressed in five different ways by the scriptures. While the phrase "forgiveness of sins" was the expression used among the vulgar of the Jewish nation, the doctors and teachers of law, more affected and technical, varied from the civil style, for the more learned and juridical expressions, "justification from sins," "remission of sins." The Doctors, then, in speaking of the offerers at the Temple, pronounced them "justified," and again they said they were constituted "righteous" according to law, i.e. in offering they had done just what the letter of the law demanded; for had they not done so, the Lord ordered that every such person should be cut off from among the people.

Now, the apostle being a Jew, and infinitely skilled by his education in the *technia* of the Jewish lawyers, adopts their own phrases in discoursing with them on the subject of forgiveness, e.g. he says in the synagogue of Antioch in Pisidia, "Be it known to you, therefore, men and brethren that through this man is preached to you the forgiveness of sins; and by him all that believe are justified from all things from which you could not be justified by the law of Moses," And as the lawyers made use of the word "righteousness" in reference to remission or to describe a person whose sins had been forgiven: so the apostle, speaking of the baptized believer whose sins had been forgiven, and was justified, in the language of the law calls this "the righteousness of God;" because it was a righteousness granted by God; and "the righteousness of faith," because it was on the principle of faith in the Son of God, that any one was allowed to approach baptism. I pertinaciously keep baptism in view in this matter, both because the scriptures make it the institution of forgiveness, and because it is altogether unusual both in law and religion, either to forgive or condemn on account of a latent principle. Faith is not justification; forgiveness or remission is justification; and faith is the principle, and the only principle too, on which remission can be obtained. Now both faith in Jesus, and baptism for remission, were novelties to the Jews; and it was in the promulgation of these things that they took offence; and God's sovereignty is exerted in the changing of the righteousness by law for the righteousness by faith, and in offering the last not to Jews only, but to Gentiles also, and in degrading the former from their ancient standing for not embracing the good message of favor.

When we consider the display of God's sovereignty in the introduction of Christianity, it appears both immense and absolute: absolute, because he consulted no one among men or angels; immense, because it swept away at one stroke all that the world of both Jews and Gentiles accounted holy and venerable. The law was a ponderous and imposing establishment.—Its theology and morality distinguished it from, and rendered it superior, infinitely superior to, all the systems of the Gentiles.

The sanctuary and its inestimable furniture, the altar, the priesthood, and the services, consisting of offerings, sacrifices, washings, meat and drink offerings, &c., their tithes, feasts, fasts, synagogues, and books of law, with their psalters and books of prophecies, that these, all these, founded upon divine authority, most flattering to the senses, and handed down to them from the most remote antiquity, should be abandoned for the sake of Christ and the remission of sins, with the other remote advantages held out by Christianity, was what the Jews could not contemplate but with amazement mingled with abhorrence. Yet did the Divine Father, in his absolute and uncontrolled sovereignty, command all the Jews every where to do this, and to do it too on pain of incurring his highest displeasure: but the same sovereignty which withdrew authority from the law of Moses, denounced at the same time the superstition of the whole world besides, and ordered all men every where to repent and believe the gospel; and here it is that the sovereignty of God appears in our religion in all its sublimity. What! denounce the religion of the world, and introduce a new one!! Yes, all, all was condemned and withdrawn, and the aspirant after immortality left with nothing before him to save and encourage him in the thorny road through which he followed his Master, but the flesh and blood of Jesus Christ; every thing now called for spirit instead of letter, and love instead of law, until righteousness should be established in the earth, and Christianity become the religion of the world.

This exhibition of the divine sovereignty, gave birth to many questions between the Jews and Christians, the management and settlement of which devolved chiefly on the apostles. Of these questions, the following are a few; the Christian method of remission made them ask, "What profit there was in circumcision," i.e. the law of Moses? and the admission of the Gentiles to this remission on the same footing with the Jews, made them inquire, "What advantage then has the Jew?" These two questions are answered by the apostle, in the 3d chap. of his epistle to the Romans. The third question, was leveled at the very vitals of Christianity itself; for the remission being granted on the principle of faith, and consequently by a favor, and neither by works of law, or righteousness, which men had done. The Jews, from an ignorance of human nature, and the true character of God, mistook the tendency of the apostolic doctrine, and asked thirdly, whether Christianity was not essentially this, "Let us sin that favor may abound?" In reply, the apostle shows that it was by faith and favor, that both Abraham and David were saved, and that law had originally issued in the death of the first of men, and in all who came from his loins, while the law of Moses, which they all knew, was good only for showing how severely and universally sin had taken hold of mankind.

The casting off of the infidel Jews, gave occasion finally to the question—Whether God had not departed from his former character, and violated his promise to Abraham? This question is answered in the famous ninth chapter of the same Epistle, a portion of Holy Scripture which some sectaries have most shamefully abused, but which I hope this view of the matter will ultimately redeem from their partial and limited systems—Here the apostle shows them that they considered it no infringement on the divine character when, for popular purposes, he preferred their fathers, Isaac and Jacob, to Ishmael and Esau; and roused up Pharaoh upon the throne of Egypt by whom he wished to make his power known, and who on account of his own bad character, should have been condemned long before he was either drowned, or even made monarch of the land of Ham; but both Ishmael and Esau and Pharaoh, and even they themselves, when cast off were treated by God in the only way their abominable character merited; and, therefore, God dealt with them as the potter does with a dishonorable vessel; he dashed and would dash them in pieces—Moreover, the apostle lets them know that the blessings of Christianity, were never held out or promised indiscriminately to Abraham's seed, but only to so many of them as believed. Justification from sin is a blessing, which, indeed, it were folly to offer to an unbelieving man, whether Jew or Gentile.

Having given the reader a clue to the question of God's Sovereignty, I shall now review some scriptures which have been quoted as opposing the doctrine of Christian Baptism and the nature of a true faith.

1. It is said, Romans 8. "Whom he foreknew, he also predestinated to be conformed to the image of his Son, that he might be the first born among many brethren.—Moreover, whom he did predestinate, them he also called: and whom he called, them he also justified; and whom he justified, them he also glorified."—Now what is this, but that God, as may be seen from fact and from the ancient writings of the prophets, foreknew, that the Jews and Gentiles, indiscriminately, would believe on his Son, and for that, had predestinated or appointed them to share in his honors; he therefore, in the fullness of time, called them, remitted their sins, and glorified them, as his only worshippers, by making to rest upon them, the Spirit of God and of glory.

But it is said: "Well then, he has mercy on whom he will have mercy, and whom he will, he hardens." This is true—and blessed be his holy name, that he will, if the scriptures mean what they say, have mercy on all who believe, not of the Jews only, but of the Gentiles also; and the unbelieving wretch who will not accept of pardon on the gospel plan, will be hardened and heated seven times in a furnace of fire; Romans 9. The ancient idolaters were hardened, and the case of the modern Jews illustrates this verse. Again it is said, Eph. 1st chapter, "According as he has elected us in him, before the foundation of the world." This is also very true, and means just what it says; but, observe that it is one thing to elect us in him, and quite another to elect us to be in him. It would be one thing to elect a citizen, and another to elect a man to be a citizen; the one would be to make him a citizen, and the other to elect a citizen to some other matter; but then it was "Before the foundation of the world." We many times determine who shall fill certain offices, so soon as we have succeeded in the election of a superior officer. Many citizens were marked out for offices long before the President was inaugurated; and so the disciples of the Messiah, were chosen to love and purity, before the foundation of the world—while the disciples of Mahomet, Confucius, and others have been appointed to no such distinction.

But again, "No man can come to me unless the Father draw him." How common is this form of speech, even among ourselves! Who has brought you here, and what has drawn you here, are phrases which are current every where, and yet, who ever thinks that the charm or power by which one person is drawn after another, is a physical one. The power of drawing is moral, not physical, and so the Saviour, in the 5th John, says that no man could come to him, unless, the Father draw him, because the political mob which he addressed, had followed him, from the gross and animal reason of having got themselves filled the night before with the loaves and fishes; paying no regard to the divine power which wrought the miracle, "Verily, I say to you, you followed me not because you saw the miracle, (Father in the miracle,) but because you did eat of the loaves and were filled."

CHAPTER XVII

Faith and Justification, &c.

Faith, in a very many scriptures, is associated with the remission of sins; but the remission of sins also, in a very great many scriptures, is declared to be a grace, a favor of God. Faith, therefore, is something which is opposed to merit, or in other words, faith has nothing in and of itself meritorious. This accords admirably with the accounts of faith, which have been delivered in this discourse; for what merit can any one have, when he believes facts, the knowledge of which has been conveyed to him by the testimony of another? None. It may be kindness in a neighbor, who sees my house on fire, to inform me of the fact, but there can be nothing meritorious in my believing it. But though there is nothing meritorious in my faith; in the case adduced, there may be, and certainly is something exceedingly useful in it. It is thus in religion, in which faith opposes itself to merit, but not to religious and moral utility. When regarded merely as an organ of knowledge, the means or channel by which it conveys into the mind the experience of others, it is wholly without merit.

But the object of our faith may take a moral effect upon the mind; and then it or faith is said to purify the heart. "Purifying their hearts through faith." Now the different effects of faith on the mind and practice of the believer are set forth in the scriptures by various names and designations. When the love of God in Christ, for this is the thing set forth in the gospel, so affects sinners estranged from him by wicked

works, as to make them love him, they are said to be *reconciled* to God.—
When it so affects us as to cause us to detest sin, this is called
sanctification of spirit. When we are so influenced by it as to turn to God,
this is styled *conversion*; and when it gives us a filial disposition towards
God, this is called the spirit of *adoption*. Thus by reconciling,
sanctifying, and converting the soul, faith delivers us from the influence
of sin.

There is nothing theoretical in the faith recommended in the
scriptures. It is wholly of a practical nature, and demonstrates its
genuineness by its effects. In purifying the heart, and reconciling us to
God and by means of these virtues enabling us to overcome the world,
faith is most triumphant and victorious. "This is the victory by which
we overcome the world, even our faith." It is when the principle of faith
takes this moral effect upon the mind that we are fitted for justification
or remission of sins and not before it; for I imagine it would not be
approved by any to say that God justifies the unreconciled, the
unconverted, the unsanctified.

But though faith does all these things and works in us those several
states of mind and feeling yet does it clothe us with no merit in the
presence of God. What it effects it effects for ourselves, not for him, and
all those several modes of mind are internal, and consequently are not
to be ranked or classed with works or any external action of the believer.

When faith takes effect upon the outward conduct, that effect is not
called reconciliation, or purification, or sanctification, but *reformation*
and *obedience, good works, righteousness*, and so forth. Thus the effects of
faith are either *internal* or *external*. Its internal effects are reconciliation,
conversion, purification or sanctification of spirit. Its external effects are
reformation, obedience, good deeds, and general righteousness.

But besides this *internal* and *external* effect of faith upon the mind
and manners of the man, there are attached to faith, by the sacred
writers, some things which are not effects of it. These are the things
given to a man by God on account of being fitted by this principle to
receive them. They are first *justification* or the *remission of sins*, or, which
is the same, *salvation, redemption*, and the *Holy Spirit*. These are called the
gifts of God; the favors of God; the mercies of God; and the blessings of
the gospel.

Here, then, we have three classes of things, every where in scripture
appended to faith. Its internal fruits are what it works *in* us; its external,
what it works *by* us; and its blessings are what it brings *to* us. So, then,
faith works *in* us, *by* us, and brings *to* us the blessings of the gospel of
peace.

But as we must not confound the internal and external effects of faith, with each other, nor substitute the one for the other; so we must not substitute either of them for the blessings of the gospel granted to us through faith; that is, we must not confound reconciliation with justification; and imagine that because faith has produced in us that blessed peace of mind which is indicated by the word reconciliation, therefore we have received the justification, or pardon of sin which the Christian religion bestows. We must not substitute conversion for salvation, or purification for redemption, or sanctification with the Holy Spirit, for if we do we confound the internal effects of faith upon the mind with the gifts and positive blessings conferred upon us on account of faith.

But this is precisely the error into which protestantism has led many excellent people. It has caused them to mistake reconciliation to God for actual justification, and to believe that the sanctification of mind, which they experience through faith, is positively the forgiveness of their sins; and that the purity which results from faith, is actually the Holy Spirit. But it is a fact, that, while such people believe the gospel and experience all the blissful effects of faith in reconciling, purifying, converting, and sanctifying their souls, they have not received an acquittal from their former sins in the way and by the ordinance of baptism, which the great head of the church has appointed for the remission of sins. So that they are reconciled but not justified, converted but not pardoned, sanctified but not adopted, purified but have not received the Holy Spirit.

Now all this may obtain, all this may be positively true without doing any violence to the case of any one. For, though it may seem strange that a person should be purified without having the Holy Spirit, yet this is perfectly possible; nay, it is absolutely a doctrine of the holy Scriptures, that we must be purified before we receive the Holy Spirit; for this gift of the Spirit is not given to a man to make him pure, but because he is already pure. The heart is to be cleansed by faith and the word of God, before the Holy Spirit takes up his abode in it. I do not think that in any passage of the New Testament the work of purification is ascribed to the Holy Spirit; but only to the word of God, and to faith which comes by hearing that word. Indeed the original gospel purposes to fit us for the reception of the Holy Spirit by first purifying us through the belief of the truth. But suppose the contrary of this and then the Holy Spirit must be sent into an unpurified heart, into an unclean abode!

Again, it may seem strange that a soul should be converted to God and not justified; reconciled to him and not pardoned. And yet nothing is plainer on earth than that the soul must be both converted, and reconciled to God before the man can be justified from his past sins. But suppose the contrary, that he were justified before being converted and pardoned before he was reconciled to God; would not this be highly dangerous? What! pardon a man before he is reconciled to the pure and holy God, who grants this pardon! What! justify him from his past sins before he is converted from the love of sin! monstrous! Justification, then, or pardon and the gift of the spirit are subsequent to faith and to both its internal and external effects upon the man who possesses it.

But let us review these things. The internal effects of Faith are susceptible of being divided; that is, they are either intellectual or moral, or it affects the understanding, and the will. Its intellectual effects are indicated in Scripture by the terms "illumination," "opening the eyes," "opening the eyes of the understanding;" "turning from darkness to light," "the knowledge of God," "the knowledge of Christ," &c. Now then we have in Scripture the above set of terms denoting the internal intellectual effects of Faith, or its effects on the understanding; and have "reconciliation," "conversion," "purification," and "sanctification," indicative of its internal moral effects, or its effects upon the will, the heart, or the affections.

When its intellectual illuminations influence the affections then will appear in the life and manners of the man its external results, viz: "Obedience," "good works," "righteousness," &c. These words have a greater or less extended signification; for instance, "good works" is never used to denote our attendance upon any particular ordinance, as prayer, reading the scriptures, baptism, the Lord's supper, &c. But obedience comprehends both what is meant by good works and our attendance upon these ordinances also. Righteousness and good deeds may be attended to by a man, who has no regard to the law of Christ; but obedience cannot; for obedience is the actual honor which we render to law. In baptizing an infant, for instance, there can be no obedience, because Christ has not delivered any law on such ordinance. However good a work it may be therefore, it includes no religious obedience. Obedience thus has a more extensive signification than the expression "good works," except when "good work" includes infant baptism and then the import of the expression stretches itself beyond all religious obedience. Baptism then and other positive ordinances are never, in the Scriptures, classed with *good works* and deeds of *righteousness*, but is a part of the particular obedience of Christianity. Consequently when the man whose faith has affected him internally and externally, is pardoned, or granted remission of sins in baptism, upon the principle of faith in the atoning blood of Christ, we are not to imagine that he is justified from sins by any good deed done in this ordinance, but only on or by or through the faith, which influences him thus to accept of forgiveness. The beggar who lifts from my hand the charity which I reach out to him, has no merit; but takes it, because I warrant him to believe, I will give it to him. Baptism then is Christ's hand to distribute pardon to such as by a true and living faith are prepared to accept it.

Forgiveness of sins which is what is meant by justification, is posterior to faith and its internal and external effects of reconciliation and righteousness on a man. Is it asked now whether a person can experience all the blessedness of faith in his soul, reconciliation to God, conversion, and sanctification of spirit, and not be pardoned; I answer yes. How so? Because these things precede and go before remission; and he may not have this by the particular means, which Christianity employs for conveying to him this blessing. But the effects of justification or forgiveness is peace with God. Granted, I answer that the first Christians who were all baptized for pardon, had peace with God. But it is said they had peace with God through faith, not baptism. Just so. Therefore although their sins were pardoned them in baptism, yet we are not allowed to think that they were pardoned for or on account of baptism; but on account of the faith which they had, and which had influenced them thus to accept it. I do not give the beggar my charity on account of taking it out of my hand, but because he needs it, and has the disposition to receive it from me. We are forgiven then, not because we are baptized, but because we need forgiveness, and are by faith prepared to receive it through the merits of Christ alone.

But the reader objects, That there are many who enjoy peace with God, who have not received the remission of past sins in baptism. How do you dispose of their case? I answer, that this is very true; there are thousands and I hope tens and hundreds of thousands, on whom true faith in the merits of Christ's most precious blood, has had all its blissful and happifying and purifying effects, both internally and externally. This I recognize with unaffected, unfeigned joy. These people also rejoice in God and in the Lord Jesus Christ their Saviour, yet I grant that their joy springs not from an actual acquittal from sins through baptism. No; they do not rejoice because they are forgiven; but think they are forgiven because they rejoice, that is, because they rejoice in the sacrifice of Christ, whom they now believe in, and honor, and adore as their Lord, their Saviour and their All. But how can they have peace without pardon? They are made to believe that the internal effects of faith viz: reconciliation, purification, and sanctification of mind, are the signs of pardon, are proofs that God has forgiven them their past sins; and they are thus, by a defective Christianity, made to mistake reconciliation for justification, and conversion of soul for the actual forgiveness of sins.

Is there any thing dangerous in this mistake? Yes; it throws the mind back upon itself instead of outward upon the word of God, and causes professors to give heed to their own frames and feelings rather than to the order and ordinances of the gospel. This is exceedingly dangerous to their virtue and perseverance in true holiness. Frames and feelings are very variant and fugitive; and if these folks do not feel in their soul at all times the liveliest unction of reconciliation, conversion, and sanctification, they immediately suspect the genuineness of their own faith, and of course their forgiveness. This has a natural tendency to destroy their peace and lead to apostacy. To ward off apostacy, therefore, and to keep alive those feelings, which they imagine to be the best proofs of faith and forgiveness, they meet in bands, classes, and monthly conventicles, to tell their ups and downs of feeling, their doubts and fears, their happiness and misery, and joys and sorrows. Have those of them, who are most distinguished for a walk and conversation becoming the gospel, always the best feelings, and do they always tell the most splendid or most affecting experience? No; they, like all modest people, very frequently, say least of themselves, while those, who are less distinguished for piety and righteousness, have most to say of themselves, and are enabled one way or another, to tell the most surprising things of religion and the forgiveness of their sins. Far from obtaining this blessing in Baptism on an enlightened confession of the faith, these can show you, if you only have the credulity to believe without proof, that they got the remission of sins in a dream, on a seat, at a bench, while reclining under a hickory bush, or in riding to the city, or in crossing the ocean, or in escaping from a wolf, or in leaping over a fence, or while returning from church. How then do you account for the joy of these people at the times and minutes to which they refer? I account for it thus:—that their minds were in a religious train of thought either at the time or previously; and that at the moment of their ecstasy, they were enabled to take such a view of the love of God by Jesus Christ, that they felt reconciled to him, and converted to the necessity, propriety and beauty of a religious life; this, soon, in a moment, filled them with joy and they believed themselves justified when they were only reconciled, and pardoned when they were only converted.

Well, sir, if a man can be converted without being pardoned, can he be pardoned without being converted? No. Faith must perform its internal and external work on him before he is fitted for pardon. Are these people all by their state prepared for pardon by baptism? Yes; all of them at least, on whom the work of reconciliation and righteousness has obtained. Such of them as love God and work righteousness are permitted to enjoy the great privilege of remission of sins by baptism.

But some, who are guilty of the error which you have pointed out, and mistake the effects of faith upon their mind for justification or pardon, have been immersed on their faith in Christ. Well they were pardoned in baptism of course. But they say they were not. Their say-so will not alter the nature of things. The ordinance was instituted for this purpose; and if reconciled, converted, and sanctified, men who are baptized are also forgiven at the same time. Their ignorance or error cannot destroy God's faithfulness. Baptism is for the remission of sins; and they need pardon, and desire pardon when they are baptized; they have got it, therefore, according to God's appointment, whether they think so or not.

I see, you will say, that the comfort of a Christian may be marred, and his righteousness endangered by not receiving justification or pardon of sins in an ordinancial and positive shape; but again you ask, does the Christian Religion itself suffer any thing from our neglect of this ordinance of remission? Yes. By abjuring it we destroy the integrity of Christianity; we fracture the gospel, and present for a whole that which is but a part.—We leave out the one third of the gospel, and preach righteousness and reconciliation only, while we ought to preach the christian justification at the same time, and baptize the converts for the remission of their sins that they might receive the Holy Spirit.

In conclusion; seeing justification or remission of sins is allowed to have an excellent tendency to promote our peace, for the scriptures say "Wherefore being justified by faith, we have peace with God," and to confirm us in holiness, we ought to secure it by the very means which the scriptures appoint. It is not for theory or correctness' sake, but for its moral influence and its influence in promoting righteousness of life and peace of mind, permanent peace of mind, that we argue for remission of sins by baptism. He, who is baptized on a true and living faith in the blood of Christ, is no longer troubled with his former or past sins. God has forgiven them. He has washed them away; and the disciple of Christ, instead of trusting the great and weighty matter of forgiveness to his own feelings and frames of mind, looks out of himself to the stable and ever-living word of God. The future is now all before him; he has dropt for ever the burden of his former iniquities, and the past troubles him no more. In fact, he is now translated into the church of God, and into the glorious liberty of the sons of God, and is permitted, in rest from the burden of past offences, to rejoice in hope of the glory of God: and this hope maketh not ashamed for its the love of God shed abroad in the heart through the Holy Spirit who is given to us. Washed in the blood of the Lamb the convert is clean every whit, and tastes the truth of that saying that the kingdom of God is righteousness and peace and joy in the Holy Spirit. Amen.

CHAPTER XVIII

Primitive Preaching

As God had proposed Jesus for the faith of mankind, and as the Spirit had pointed him out as Messiah, as Jesus himself had sustained the proposition to the death, sanctified it by his blood, and proved it by his resurrection, in brief, as he had decreed that the church should be reared upon the belief of this great truth as on a rock, so the Apostles, who were commissioned to convert the nations, did, in accordance with the example of God, and Christ and the Holy Spirit, do the highest honor to the proposition of the Father, and in all places whithersoever they went, proclaimed this as the matter of faith, the thing to be believed in order to salvation.

The terms in the Apostolic mission in regard to local order in the proclamation of the gospel, are these, as uttered by our Lord; "You shall be my witnesses in Jerusalem, in Judea, in Samaria, and in the uttermost parts of the earth." *the Gentiles.* Now, had the Apostles, instead of beginning at Jerusalem, gone first to the Gentiles, would they have obeyed Christ? No. Suppose they had addressed themselves first to the Samaritans, would they have kept his commandments? No; because they were to proclaim first to the Jews. But suppose again that they had commenced first in Judea, would they not have followed the directions of their Lord? No, They were to begin at Jerusalem. It had been foretold by the Spirit, and the prediction required to be redeemed by fact, that "The Law should go forth from Zion and the word of the Lord from Jerusalem." Had they disobeyed Christ in this particular, they would have insulted the prophetic word and the Spirit by whom it was spoken; they would have insulted prejudices and persons, which the local order in their commission was intended by their Lord to respect and honor; and they would have proved themselves wholly unworthy of the distinguished rank in the kingdom of God, to which they had been raised by their royal master.

But these faithful men followed to the letter the directions, which were graciously given them by their Lord. Essentials and Non-essentials were unknown to them. The nice and dangerous distinctions of modern times, were not then invented. With them every thing was essential to be done, which Jesus had enjoined and they proved their love for him, only by doing whatsoever he had commanded them. They began therefore at Jerusalem, wicked but highly favoured Jerusalem.

Nothing can be more false, more full of insult to fact and to the holy scriptures, than the claims of primogeniture of which the apostate church of Rome has every boasted over other churches. Our religion began at Jerusalem, not Rome; Jerusalem, therefore, as the apostle Paul says, in his epistle to the Galatians, "is the mother of us all." The church of that city is the parent institution, and had the honor of being set up by Jesus Christ himself. What then is Rome. She is a harlot, and is described as such in the word of God, a detested and an accursed institution, that has committed spiritual whoredom with the kingdoms of this world, and brought such disgrace and scandal upon our religion and the Christian name, as thousands of years would not serve to wipe away. The stains and blots which she has imprinted on the seamless garment of Christianity cannot be erased, cannot be washed off; but must be burnt out by fire.

Those, then, who follow the apostles, those who hold to the True Gospel, who walk in the ordinances delivered to the church of Jerusalem, the parent institution, and keep the morality of Jesus Christ purely, have an ancienter and more honorable origin than Rome, filthy Rome. We are of the "free woman," says Paul, the legitimate spouse of Jesus Christ, Jerusalem, the church of Jerusalem, who never was accused in the scripture for having departed from the faith of Jesus; but on the contrary is there described as having maintained the faith once delivered to her saints in a great fight of affliction, even after her Lord had been crucified, after Stephen had been stoned, Peter imprisoned, and James slain with the sword. In the midst of unspeakable afflictions she maintained her perilous station, as the mother of Christian churches, till the destruction of Jerusalem; when agreeably to the prophetic instruction of her Lord and Master, she fled from the abodes of the wicked, whom she could not convert to the faith, and from the city which was now, on account of its sins, destined to a protracted desolation.

As some folks think Christianity began at Rome, and, therefore, call her *Mother Church*, so some other good folks suppose that it began at mount Sinai and accordingly wander about in a wilderness of error to this good day. But others again carry the birth-day of the divine institution backward to the days of Abraham, and reason, that, because our religion was spoken of to that Patriarch, and laid in embryo among the promises made to that great man, therefore, they must do as Abraham did, circumcise their children, or instead of it, baptize them. But as well might Rebecca, who married Isaac, have reasoned, that because her husband was once in the loins of Sarah, therefore, she ought to do as Sarah did, give her handmaid to Isaac, that by her he might have a child; and when this was done, turn both the child and her into the deserts of Arabia!

Others fond of venerable matters, and not distinguishing between fact and prophecy, carry up the origin of Christianity to a still higher antiquity, and find its beginning in Paradise, and in the denunciation which was uttered against the Serpent there. Others again, willing to outstrip all the rest, and the scriptures themselves, and even the common sense of mankind also, carry the beginning of Christianity beyond the beginning of the world, and lay the corner stone of the institution in eternity, abounding in all that kind of wisdom, which would cause a man to lay his foundation stone in Europe, and build in America, or found it in the ocean, and rear his house on the land!

Shall we then follow such into eternity and strive to find the beginning of Christianity there? Shall we suppose ourselves in Egypt and then with the Israelites figure to ourselves a "slough of despond" as big as the Red Sea, and after passing it at the peril of our own souls, find the gospel at mount Sinai? Or shall we go still farther back and discover it among the antiquities of Abraham and of Paradise? No, no.

The scriptures speak more soberly, more sensibly of this matter, "Behold I lay in Zion a chief corner stone;" "Beginning at Jerusalem;" "which is the mother of us all." "The law shall go forth from Zion, and the word of the Lord from Jerusalem."

But the church of Jerusalem, the parent church, will yet be restored to her right of primogeniture, and shall become the glory of all churches; and, when the harlot institution and her daughters are burnt in fire, "She shall arise and shall shine forth bright as the morning sun."

The birth place of Christianity being thus determined by fact and scripture, it being on the page of holy writ, that Jerusalem was the cradle of Christianity, and the city in which the gospel was first preached, and the true church first organized, we are thereby brought to a point exceedingly favorable for determining what the original gospel is, and in what way and manner it was first announced.

Let us then follow the apostles in the local order which the terms of their commission prescribed for their evangelical labors. Let us with them begin at Jerusalem, and when we have determined what was proclaimed for gospel and proposed for faith first in that city, then let us follow them "to Judea, to Samaria, and to the uttermost parts of the earth." Let us, in short, ascertain what *they* preached to the Jews, to the Samaritans, and to the Gentiles, for faith and gospel, and then we have ascertained, both what the true ancient and original gospel is, and the manner in which they preached it, and that in which we ourselves ought to receive and obey it.

The first question to be answered in relation to the original preaching is, did Peter and his compeers follow the example of the Father and the Holy Spirit, the latter of whom identified Jesus with the Messiah and the former with his Son? In other words did the apostles in Jerusalem propose for the faith of their audience, Jesus as the Christ, the Son of God? We answer, yes: and refer the reader for authority to the history of the first discourse as contained in the second chapter of the Acts of the Apostles.

But we shall here set down the very words of the apostle, which contain the matter to be believed. They are found in the conclusion of his address, the preceding parts of his discourse being merely a preamble in order to bring in the faith with more certain effect; in order to infix in their souls, and understandings, the fundamental idea of the Messiahship.

"Therefore, let all the house of Israel know assuredly, that God hath made that same Jesus, whom you have crucified, both Lord, and Messiah." Acts 2:36.

The word Lord, as all understand it here, means the heir of all things, or Son of God. So that we see, the matter of faith in Jerusalem, or the thing to be believed in Christianity, was that Jesus is the Son of God and the Messiah. Behold, reader, the above verse which contains the truth; it is the word of God; it lives and abides for ever; it cannot be erased; it has thus read, and thus spoken, for near eighteen hundred years; and it will continue to speak thus till time shall be no more; it maybe overlooked, it may even be scorned when seen; still it cannot be blotted out; it will maintain its position for ever, and calmly as now to us, so to ages yet unborn, will preach with unerring certainty, the true faith which was first preached in Jerusalem.

What then is predicated of this faith? What is vouchsafed the man who believes the sacred oracle of the Christian Religion? We answer, favor, divine favor. Three thousand who received it the moment it was announced by the apostle, were all pardoned, freely, fully pardoned, on the spot, and added to the church that very day. "Repent and be baptized every one of you in the name of Jesus Christ for the remission of sins," exclaimed Peter to his convicted auditors, "and you shall receive the gift of the Holy Spirit." Here is the *faith* and here is the *favor* that accompanies it, pardon and the Holy Spirit, through the Messiah, the Son of God.

Is there, then, any difficulty in apprehending either the faith proposed, or the favor conferred in the above proclamation?—Yes; it is replied; the faith is too little, and the favor too great. We cannot think it to be enough to believe that Jesus is the Messiah the Son of God; and we think it by far too much for men to receive the incomparable blessing of remission of sins by a simple immersion on such a faith. You think the one too little, and the other too much? good; but observe, that I am not inquiring into any one's thought, but into that which formed the matter of faith or belief in the original gospel as promulgated by the apostles of Christ. And having ascertained that in Jerusalem they preached only what God had revealed concerning Jesus Christ, we now go with the true ministers of the true gospel down to Samaria.

Philip was the person, who first preached the gospel to the Samaritans; "and when the apostles who were at Jerusalem heard that Samaria had received the word of God, they sent unto them Peter and

John." Acts 8. But what did Philip propose for faith to the Samaritans? Let the following verse of scripture declare the answer. "Then Philip went down to the city of Samaria, and preached Christ unto them." Now we have seen how God preached Christ at Jordan, that he was his own Son; also how the Holy Spirit preached him, that he was the Messiah; and also how the apostles preached him at Jerusalem, that he was both the Lord and the Messiah. In preaching Christ, therefore, Philip showed by the proper evidences, by the word of God at Jordan, by Christ's resurrection, by prophecy and by the miracles which he himself wrought in Samaria, that Jesus was both Lord and Christ. Like those of Jerusalem, the people of Samaria received the "saying of the Father," and "they were baptized both men and women." Acts 8.

The faith and the favour which composed the gospel as preached to the Samaritans were, therefore, the same as those which were preached to the people of Jerusalem. And Philip's course of proposing Christ as the Son of God for the faith of the people, and of baptizing such as believed it, was approved both by the Apostles and the Holy Spirit; for the former sent down to Samaria two, Peter and John, and the latter descended from heaven upon them and filled the converts with the gift of tongues &c. as he had done the Jews.

Philip, immediately after this, was ordered to the south "unto the way that goeth down from Jerusalem, unto Gaza, which is desert," to meet the eunuch, a grandee of the court of queen Candace, of Ethiopia. Here again, it is recorded, he "Preached unto him Jesus." Whereupon the eunuch desiring to be baptized, Philip called upon him for a confession of the faith.—The Eunuch "answered and said I believe that Jesus is the Christ, the Son of God." The matter of faith, and the favor conferred here are again the same as at Samaria and Jerusalem. The Spirit caught away Philip, and the Eunuch went on his way rejoicing. Blessed be the Lord God, the Father of our Lord Jesus Christ.

The ninth chapter of the book of Acts, details the conversion of Paul, he received the matter of belief from the lips of the Lord Jesus, and on his way to Damascus, learned the essential and fundamental proposition of our religion by the Voice of the Son of God himself. "Who art thou Lord?" he exclaimed, "I am Jesus whom thou persecutest" said the Redeemer. The Lord then instructed him to proceed to Damascus where he would be informed what to do in order to partake of the blessings and favors which attached to the faith which he had received. He went accordingly, was baptised for remission, and received the Holy Spirit. Here again, the matter of faith is the same as at the conversion of the Eunuch, the conversion of the Samaritans, and the original proclamation in the city of Jerusalem.

Is it surprising, then, if Paul preached what he himself had believed? surely no; it is added, therefore, "And straightway he preached in the synagogue, '*that he, Jesus, is the Son of God.*'" "Further; Saul increased the more in strength and confounded the Jews that dwelt at Damascus, proving that this is the very Christ." Peter in the next, the 10th chap, unlocks the door of faith to the Gentiles or the house of Cornelius. How then did he commence? What was the matter of faith here? The great oracle again, the word of the father at Jordan. "That word you know was published throughout all Judea, and began from Galilee after the baptism which John preached: how that God anointed Jesus of Nazareth with the Holy Spirit" &c. Here Peter goes back to the very moment of the Recognition; and proposes Jesus as the anointed of Jehovah and the Lord of all. While he was informing his auditors of the blessing which attached to this faith, and while the words "remission of sins" were yet on his lips, the Holy Spirit descended on the Gentiles, testifying to Peter and those Jews who accompanied him, that God had purified the hearts of his hearers by faith, and had accepted them. He commanded them, therefore, to be baptized.

Peter, to whom the keys of the kingdom of heaven were given by the Lord Jesus, or to drop figure for fact, Peter, to whom was granted the high honor of first preaching the gospel to the Jews and the Gentiles, having now performed what he had in charge from the Messiah, and the Gentiles being received, the narrative proceeds with the history of the labors of Paul the apostle. The Helenistic Jews at Antioch received the gospel next. "Then tidings of these things came to some of the church which was in Jerusalem, and they sent forth Barnabas, that he should go as far as Antioch." Barnabas preceded thence, "to Tarsus to seek Saul," whither he had been sent from Caesarea by the Brethren on account of the Jews who fought to kill him. Barnabas returned with Saul to Antioch, and the two together were intrusted with the bounty of the church to bear it to the Capital of Judea for the relief of the brethren there. On their return they were separated from the other teachers in the church of Antioch, by the command of the Holy Spirit, to promote the conversion of the Gentiles, for which they had been ordained. "And when they had fasted and prayed they laid their hands on them and sent them away. So they being sent forth by the Holy Spirit departed unto Selcucia" &c. It is said they "preached the word" first at Salamis, that is, they preached the word of the Father concerning Jesus. They then proceeded to Paphos and Paul preached the faith to the Deputy there; after which they came to Perga and finally to Antioch in Pisidia and there they entered the Synagogue, and, after the reading of the law, addressed the Jews and all present on the question of the Messiahship of Jesus Our Lord. The matter of faith preached in the Synagogue at Antioch, is precisely what had been preached to the Jews in Jerusalem, to the Samaritans, to the Eunuch, to Paul himself, and to Cornelius, viz: that Jesus was the Jewish Messiah. The blessings appended to the belief of this matter are shown to be the same here also as in all former cases, viz: "remission of sins" immediate remission. "Be it known to you, therefore, men and brethren, that through this man is preached unto you the forgiveness of sins." This is enough. Those who listened on this occasion spurned both the faith and the favors appended to it; and the two preachers turned to the Gentiles. "It was necessary that the word of God (*concerning Jesus*) should first be preached to you; but seeing you put it from you, and judge yourselves unworthy of eternal life, lo, we turn to the Gentiles; for so hath the Lord commanded us." Acts, 13.

Paul and Barnabas next preached in Iconium, and Lystra, and Derbe, whence they returned to Iconium, and to Antioch in Pisidia; and after having passed through Pamphilia, Perga, and Attalia, they sailed to Antioch in Syria, "from whence they had been recommended to the grace of God for the work which they had fulfilled." Thus ended Paul's first mission to the Lesser Asia.

During his second journey the Apostle, in addition to the places in which he had preached when accompanied by Barnabas, visited the regions of Galatia, Phrygia, Assyria, also Troas, and afterwards Macedonia, touching at Samothracia and Neapolis, and finally landing at Philippi, "the chief city of that part of Macedonia: and a colony." Here were converted Lydia, her house, and the jailor and his house. In searching for the matter of faith in the addresses of Paul at Philippi, we come to these words, spoken to the keeper of the prison, "Believe on the Lord Jesus Christ, and thou shalt be saved and thy house; and they spake unto him the word of the Lord, and to all that were in his house." Here Jesus Christ and the word of the Lord which had attested Jesus to be the Christ, again form the matter of *faith*. But what was the *favor* appended to the reception of this word? The same as before, "remission of sins." "They were all baptized, he and his, straightway." 16 Cor. Paul and his associate Silas next visited the Synagogue in Thessalonica, where he proposed the question concerning the Messiah, and said, "this Jesus whom I preach unto you, is the Christ," or the Messiah. The same faith was announced at Berea, Athens and Corinth, where Paul was "pressed in spirit, and testified to the Jews that Jesus was the Christ." At Ephesus the same matter of faith was proposed, and recurrence made to John's testimony concerning Jesus. After many labors the Apostle returned to Syria, and finally Jerusalem, in which city he was taken a prisoner by the Romans, and sent to Rome to the Emperor, to whose judgment he had been compelled to appeal. Here, the book of Acts informs us, he preached Christ, in chains, persuading them (the Jews) both out of the law of Moses, and out of the prophets, from morning till evening. And Paul dwelt two whole years in his own hired house, and received all that came in unto him, preaching the kingdom of God, and teaching the things which concerned the Lord Jesus Christ with all confidence, no man forbidding him. Thus ends the Acts of the Apostles, the only book under Heaven from which any man, pope, prelate, priest, papist, protestant, preacher or layman, can learn with divine certainty what was originally preached for faith, and what originally preached for favor. But from it we learn, by every fragment, specimen, and remains of apostolic preaching which it embodies, that the matter of faith was *one*, and uniformly *one*, vis: that "Jesus was the Messiah, the Son of God." So that what was revealed by the Father at Jordan, confirmed by the Holy Spirit, sanctified by the blood of Christ, was also preached by the apostles, and made the foundation of the church.

The some blessings also were attached to the matter of faith in every place in which it was preached and received; it was still baptism for the remission of sins and the Holy Spirit. It was this in Jerusalem, this in Samaria, this in the case of the eunuch, of Paul, Cornelius, Lydia, the jailor, at Antioch, at Ephesus and at Corinth. It was, in short, what Jesus ordered in his commission to the apostles—"He that believeth and is baptized, shall be saved."

By ascertaining the primitive creed of the gospel, and the blessings which originally attached to the reception of it, we obtain a rule by which all subsequent preaching can be measured, and determined to be either true or false, pure or corrupted, evangelical or unevangelical. The true gospel therefore proposes to mankind as a first step, the remission of past sins in baptism, supposing the following oracle of the Father to be received. "Behold my son, the beloved, in whom I delight." How beautiful for simplicity, then, is the true gospel of Christ! A single proposition to be examined, and heartily received in the manner God directs, and having appended to it the most inestimable blessings.

Has then, the Father recognized Jesus of Nazareth as his Son, and may men with impunity deny his recognition? Has the Holy Spirit identified him with the Messiah of the Jewish nation, and may men, without danger reject him? Let the fate of the Jews themselves, who were guilty in this point, be at once an answer to these questions, and an awful warning to all other people. But shall it be deemed a light matter that Jesus died in confirmation of the divine oracle, and that God raised him up again from the dead in proof of its eternal certainty?—Shall we give the lie to God and to his Son and to the Spirit of God and be faultless? Impossible. The man thus guilty has made himself obnoxious to death, and in the judgment cannot possibly escape the most fearful condemnation.

But if we turn from the heavens to men, and look to our own flesh and blood, to John the Baptist, to the apostles, the Evangelists, and original professors of Christianity, who both heard the voice of God speaking from heaven, and witnessed the resurrection of the Messiah, and eat and drank with him, and were taught by him after he had risen from the dead, what is the state of the case? It is this and nothing more, that they were permitted to enjoy a sensible proof of those things, and appointed to communicate them to the world. Their knowledge is proposed for our faith; their testimony for our evidence. Do we receive or reject the facts which they state; do we receive or reject the testimony they deliver. The reader may do this last; he may reject their proposition and their testimony both, and turn away from them as unworthy of his regard, but I know that in a capital offence the evidence of such men as Paul, and John, and James, and Matthew, and Peter, and Luke, would execute him in any enlightened country in Christendom if it were against him, and it would save him if it were in his favor.

But see the innumerable items of collateral proof for the proposition, arising from its relation to Moses and the prophets and to the things contained in the sacred books of the Jewish nation, its relation to Adam, to the first of men, and the world of angels—to all angels and to all demons and to all men, to the Ruler of the universe and the majesty of law, to defective, corrupted, and false religion, to the purification of the conscience, and the pardon, and salvation of men, and to the final judgment of the world, the reward of the righteous and the condemnation of the wicked, and then say whether there be any thing incredible or useless or unnecessary in the great oracle that forms the element of Christian belief. "Behold my Son, the Beloved, in whom I delight."

Turn then, reader, to God, search the scriptures; believe the gospel; and obey it; and all its honor and privileges are yours. That you may speedily do this, is the prayer of the author. To God and to Jesus Christ be present and everlasting honor.

A DISCOURSE OF THE TRUE GOSPEL

SECTION FOURTH–REPENTANCE

"Then Peter said unto them. Repent, and be baptized every one of you in the name of Jesus Christ, for the remission of sins, and ye shall receive the gift of the Holy Spirit."

CHAPTER I

Repentance Defined

By understanding that man is a creature capable of having the experience of others transferred to his mind, we learn that he is a being of faith; by the same means we learn what faith is; namely, the experience of one or more transferred to the mind of another; or, as the Apostle says, *confidence* and *conviction*;—*confidence* in relation to the speaker; *conviction* in relation to the fact.

Let us then endeavor to approach repentance in a prudent and scriptural manner; and first, when ideas of things are received into the mind either by our own experience or that of others, the mind is capable of reflecting upon them in their various attributes, relations, and uses. For instance when one has deposited in his mind the oracle, that "Jesus is the Messiah," he has the power of contemplating the proposition in its different extraordinary complexities, connections, and designs; he reflects upon the idea of Sonship, which is predicated of the extraordinary personage in question, and upon his relation to the great God indicated by the term; by this means he arrives at his infinite excellence, and the fact that he must share with his divine Father in all the attributes of infinite power, infinite goodness, and unlimited wisdom; also, that in partaking of human nature, he must feel both with us and for us in our present sore distresses. These qualities and characteristics in the Redeemer being ascertained, the mind naturally proceeds to the different relations in which Christ is said to stand to all who are in any manner concerned in his public ministrations and finally it arrives at the relation which he bears to one's self and to the advantages or disadvantages, the goods or evils, indicated by that relation.

Things thus examined and reflected upon, have the power of affecting the mind and of changing its condition both intellectually and morally, both in regard to its views and its feelings. When, therefore, the things of religion take such a permanent intellectual and moral effect on the mind as to affect both our sentiments and actions, it is called in scripture *metanoea*, a change of mind. This is the etymological and primary import of the Greek term translated repentance. In this sense John seems to use it in his address to his countrymen, when he enjoins on them to bring forth fruits meet for repentance, that is, works declarative of a change of mind. He wished, by this repentance which he preached, to bring about a mental change, as a first step, telling his prejudiced and erring countrymen to suppress their family pride and no more to say *within themselves* "We have Abraham for our father," but to repent, change their sentiments, and give proof positive of this by their works.

Thus, in the Christian religion, we have two fundamental terms, both of them relating primarily to the mind, faith and repentance, the first denoting the means by which the things of our religion are conveyed into the mind, the second denoting the effect which these things have upon the mind.

Words, however, seldom long retain their primary import, but being subject to secondary and figurative uses, are sometimes so much employed in these last senses as to have their etymological sense merged in them altogether. This seems to have been the fate of *metanoea*, which from being used to signify a change of mind, came by an easy transition to denote that change of conduct which was the natural result of it. This is the sense in which it is frequently used in the New Testament; so that in the sacred oracles it has all the force of the English word *reformation*. Now there is a substantial reason for this too; because a change of mind, even for the better, is of but small value unless it gives birth to a change of manners; and, therefore, the word is understood in its best and most comprehensive meaning when it is understood to signify a renovation of both mind and conduct effected by the objects of our faith deposited in the mind and acting deeply and permanently on both the understanding, will, and affections.

When, therefore, John the Baptist gave an explanation of repentance in practice, he said, "Let him, who hath two coats, impart to him that hath none, and him who hath meat do likewise:" he bid the revenue officers exact no more than was due, and the soldiers to be content with their wages, avoiding all violence and false testimony.

But the objects of knowledge and faith may have an immoral instead of a moral influence on the mind; there is, therefore, another

Greek word translated I repent, in the New Testament, namely, *metamelomai*, and it is used to signify a change for the worse.

Among those who have criticised on the world *metanoeo* and *metamelomai* the most worthy of regard is the learned and celebrated Presbyterian, doctor George Campbell. Of these two words he says, "I shall now offer a few remarks on two words that are uniformly rendered by the same English word, in the common version, between which there appears, notwithstanding, to be a real difference in signification. The words are *metanoeo* and *metamelomai*, I repent. It has been observed by some, and I think with reason that the former denotes properly a change to the better; the latter barely a change whether it be to the better or worse; that the former marks a change of mind that is durable and productive of consequences; the latter expresses only a present uneasy feeling of regret or sorrow for what is done, without regard to the duration of its effects; in fine, that the first may be translated into English, *I reform*, and the second, *I repent* in the familiar acceptation of the word."

Agreeably to the above criticism *metanoeo* or I repent, will stand in scripture for that moral reformation which should distinguish those who desire to obtain the blessings of the gospel; it will appear in generosity, liberality, charity, good faith, honor, honesty, contentment, as explained by the Baptist; but it will not stand for *obedience* to the ritual of the gospel. The word obedience comes in after repentance in the proclamation of the good news and includes both repentance and submission to the ritual and positive institutes of Christianity. Thus, "Repent and be baptized," said Peter, to those who had believed and inquired for instruction.

Thus we have three words in sequence; faith conveying into the mind the knowledge of facts; repentance indicating the effects of these facts on the mind and moral conduct of the individual; and obedience denoting the apprehension which the mind has formed of God's authority in the special and particular dispensation of the gospel.

This difference between the moral reformation, which Christianity enjoins on all men, and the obedience which it demands of all who do thus reform, ought to be well understood. Those, who have labored in promulgating the true gospel, will understand me perfectly when I say, that there are many whom the schemes of the day have brought to moral reformation, who, from prejudice, fake teaching, and error, cannot, nevertheless, by all the labor imaginable, be brought to see and recognize Christ's authority, in the apostolic proclamation of the gospel, in such a manner as to obey the positive institute of baptism intended for the remission of their past sins.

When, therefore, a man reforms because of the facts of which he has heard and which he cannot help believing, he shows by his reformation a deference for the facts; but if at the same time he refuses to obey the gospel he rejects the authority of God and is not to be numbered with the faithful.

CHAPTER II

Repentance in Regard to the Scriptures

In order to bring the unbeliever to faith, repentance, and obedience, we shall now turn to him and address him on the important particular in the caption to this chapter, the holy scriptures. With Bollinbroke, Hume, Voltaire, Gibbon, Rousseau, Chesterfield, Godwin, Hobbes, D'Alembert, Diderot, and the other celebrated leaders of the crowd of infidels you have heretofore joined in denouncing the Bible. Reader! this precious volume never since the days of Jesus Christ ascended so high in the understanding and affections of sensible, unprejudiced and disinterested inquirers till assailed by these pompous and arrogant philosophists. They meant it not, but in fact, they only served the cause which they labored to destroy. The artillery of sophistry, ill-founded premises, insidious argument, and illegitimate conclusions, which they fired off against the citadel of the truth which stood upon the rock of ages, took effect indeed upon the base and combustible materials of wood, hay and stubble, which had been heaped upon it by the lapse of years, and the lapse of those who professed themselves its friends, a vile, hireling, immoral, papistical clergy; but the church herself, it is seen, has gloriously escaped the weapons of these sophists, and is absolutely beautified by being unhooded of the caps and cowls and beads and baubles with which a gloomy, and dark, and dangerous priesthood had deformed her. Since the days of the French revolution, when hades itself seemed to be let loose upon Christianity, there has arisen a host of the most excellent men, the flower of human kind, who have received the Christian Religion on its proper evidences, and to whom the Bible is the most precious of all books. By these men the arguments of the noted infidels, which you, O thoughtless creature! affect to admire and foolishly follow, have been severely sifted, and gloriously and publicly exposed as vain, insolent, and profane sophistry. What then is the weight and value of their example, who have insulted the Bible and God who gave it? With such as have taken pains to inquire before they decided, the example of Thomas Paine, of notorious memory, the Scottish and English historians, Hume and Gibbon, Voltaire, Peter, and all both great and small of those who were so great in word and little in deed; so wise in theory, and foolish in practice; so great in fact and little in effect; does not weigh one scruple, or derogate from the intrinsic excellence of the Bible to the value of a feather. You then look at the Bible through the glasses, which these vain men have imposed upon your eyes, and you are amazed at the discoloration, and deformity, and disfiguration, and every thing else, of the object which they affect to describe! Why, sir, you may as well hope to find the beauty of Paris and Absolem, and Helen, and Mary Stewart among the caricatures of Hogarth, as to find the true Bible in the accounts which Paine and his compeers have delivered of it; These earthly beings had not the patience to inquire into its contents. They knew comparatively nothing at all about it. They cared nothing at all about it, and they confessed this. They wanted to be famous; they would be notorious for something, and for every thing and any thing, rather than for nothing. But they knew that to touch with a religion, the whole of which every body believed without understanding the one half themselves, was the proper road to notoriety.—"Verily they have received their reward." These gentlemen now without doubt reap the benefit of the infidelity in which they indulged, and eat the cake of their own preparing; but I can tell you that before leaving the stage of this world, on which they played such marvelous buffoonery, some of them felt when it was too late, and confessed when it was of no value either to themselves or others, the extravagance and wickedness of their own blasphemous lives, and the enormity of their huge apostacy from God and Revelation. I shall here transcribe some impressive anecdotes of these miserable beings called infidels, who lived and died without God and without hope in the world.

Voltaire, during a long life, was continually treating the Holy Scriptures with contempt, and endeavoring to spread the poison of infidelity among the nations. In his last illness, he sent for Tronchin. In the greatest agonies, exclaiming with the utmost horror—"I am abandoned by God and man." Doctor, I will give you half of what I am worth, if you will give me six months life. The doctor answered, sir, you cannot live six weeks. Voltaire replied, then I shall go to hell, and you will go with me! and soon after expired;

This is the hero of modern infidels! Dare any of them say, Let me die the death of Voltaire, and let my last end be like his? That he was a man of great and various talents, none can deny, but his want of sound learning and moral qualifications, will ever prevent him from being ranked with the benefactors of mankind. If the reader have felt himself hurt by the poison of this man's writings, he may find relief for his wounded mind by perusing Findlay's Vindication of the Sacred Book from the Misrepresentations and Cavels of Voltaire: and Lefans' Letters of certain Jews to Voltaire. The hoary infidel cuts but a very sorry figure in the bands of these sons of Abraham. During Voltaire's last visit to Paris, when his triumph was complete, and he even feared that he should die with glory, amidst the acclamations of an infatuated theatre, he was struck by the hand of providence, and fated to make a very different termination of his career.

In the midst of his triumph, a violent hemorrhage raised apprehensions for his life. D'Alembert, Diderot, and Marmontel hastened to support his resolution in his last moments, but were only witnesses to their mutual ignominy, as well as to his own. Rage, remorse, reproach, and blasphemy, all accompany and characterize the long agony of the dying atheist.

On his return from the theatre, and amidst the toils he was resuming to acquire fresh applause, Voltaire was warned that the long career of his impiety was drawing to an end.

In spite of all the sophisters drawing around him, in the first days of his illness, he gave signs of wishing to return to God whom he had so often blasphemed. He called for the priest. His danger increasing, he wrote the following letter to the Abbe Gaultier:

"You had promised me, sir, to come and hear me. I intreat you would take the trouble of calling on me as soon as possible."

(Signed) VOLTAIRE.
Paris, 26th February, 1778.

A few days after he wrote the following declaration, in the presence of the Abbe Gaultier, the Abbe Mignot, and the Marquis de Villevieille, copied from the minutes deposited with Mr. Mornet, notary at Paris:

"I, the underwriter, declare that for these four days past, having been afflicted with the vomiting of blood, at the age of eighty-four, and not having been able to drag myself to the church, the Reverend the Rector of Lulpice, having been pleased to add to his good works that of sending me the Abbe Gaultier, I confessed to him; and if it pleases God to dispose of me I die in the church in which I was born, hoping that the divine mercy will deign to pardon all my faults.

Second of March, 1778. (Signed) VOLTAIRE.

In presence of the Abbe Mignot, my nephew, and the Marquis Villevieille, my friend."

After the two witnesses had signed the declaration, Voltaire added these words, copied from the same minutes,—"The Abbe Gaultier, my confessor, having apprised me that it was said among a certain set of people that I "protest against every thing that I did at my death; I declare that I never made such a speech, and that it is an old jest, attributed long since to many of the learned, more enlightened than I am."

This declaration is also signed by the Marquis de Villevieille, to whom, eleven years before, Voltaire wrote, "Conceal your march from the enemy in your endeavors to crush the wretch!"

Voltaire had permitted this declaration to be carried to the Rector of Sulpice, and to the Archbishop of Paris, to know whether it would be sufficient. When the Abbe Gaultier returned with the answer, it was impossible to gain admittance to the patient. The conspirators strained every nerve to hinder the chief from consummating his recantation, and every avenue was shut to the priest, whom Voltaire himself had sent for. The demons haunted every access; rage succeeded to fury, and fury to rage again, during the remainder of his life.

D'Alembert, Diderot, and about twenty others of the conspirators, who had beset his apartment, never approached him but to witness their own ignominy; and often he would curse them and exclaim: "Retire! It is you that have brought me to my present state! Be gone. I could have done without you, but you could not exist without me! And what a wretched glory you have procured me!"

Then would succeed the horrid remembrance of his conspiracy. They could hear him, the prey of anguish and dread, alternately supplicating or blaspheming that God against whom he had conspired, and in plaintive accents would he cry out, "O Christ! O Jesus Christ!" and complain that he was abandoned of God and man. The hand which had traced in ancient writ the sentence of an impious and reviling king, seemed to trace before his eyes, "Crush then, do crush the wretch!" In vain he turned his head away; the time was coming apace when he was to appear before the tribunal of Him whom he had blasphemed; and his physicians, particularly Mr. Trouchin, calling to administer relief, thunderstruck, retired, declaring the death of the impious man to be terrible indeed. The pride of the conspirators would willingly have suppressed these declarations, but it was in vain. The Mareschal de Richelieu fled from the bedside, declaring it to be a sight too terrible to be sustained, and Mr. Tronchin that "the pains of Orestes could give but a faint idea of those of Voltaire."[10]

Here, reader, is the last of this present life of the prince of infidels, Voltaire—the man who despised the Bible, and cursed God and Jesus Christ. Had he consummated his recantation, who would have had the least faith in it? It would have been base hypocrisy. Voltaire knew of what importance it was to the future repose of his bones to die in mother church, and that if he refused this he was likely to be denied a funeral altogether. He died as he lived, therefore, abandoned of God. Heavens! what a contrast does this man's death form with the noble

---

[10] Simpson.

death of that admirable man, John Locke, who, after having long studied the scriptures, declared them to be "truth without any mixture of error;" and died in the highest state of Christian resignation, and comfort of the Holy Scriptures.

But, unhappy reader, in being ignorant of the Bible, you are ignorant of the book which of all in the world, alone has within itself the marks of its own divine origin. The Bible trusts not the cause of man's salvation, and the genuineness and authenticity of its several books to extrinsic and foreign evidence, as history, chronology, geography, and natural history, but like the works of God in nature, so it, the word of God, contains within itself proof positive of its own heavenly inspiration.

Mark its congruity with right reason; touching as with the finger the great subject of creation, it informs us that the order which at present exists among the elements is of God, who, when his hand separated them successively according to their comparative beauty, took the first of them, the light, and threw it around the centre planet, the sun, to give light as it now radiates from a common centre; next he took the second element, the air, and stocked it with fowl; then the water, and stocked it with fish; and finally the land with beasts of every name—till the palace being completed, the king was introduced in the person of our common ancestor, Adam, to whom God gave a partner whom he called Eve, because she was the mother of all living. Ah reader! you may in the greatness of your ignorance, in your consummate folly you may repudiate this oracle; but it forms a base for those who are in search of eternal life, to rest their faith upon, of more than Doric strength, of more than Tuscan simplicity. How shameful to be ignorant of the Bible! and yet a man's ignorance of it is his best apology for being opposed to it. There can be no doubt, therefore, sinner, that you speak against the Bible for the best reason which can urge any man forward in so dangerous a course, namely, ignorance of it, total ignorance of its contents. But if you are well versed in the scriptures, and at the same time are opposed to them, then you are a rare person. But this I cannot believe.

Next follows that succinct account of things relative to primitive man, without which it is impossible for any man satisfactorily to account for the origin of the evil, misery, and death which afflict the world.

Then again follows the line of ancestry for the Messiah, running like a cord of gold through a web of silver, from Adam to Noah, from Noah to Abraham, from Abraham to David, and from David to Jesus, the ancient prophecies concerning whom form a proof most admirable and absolutely irresistible. How uncalled for, if they are false, were many of them, considered in regard to the circumstances under which they were uttered!

When Moses busily marshalling the affairs of his own nation, told the Israelites that the maker of heaven and earth would raise them a leader, how uncalled for was the prediction by the then circumstances of that truly great and good man! No Israelite demanded of him to prophecy either this or any other prediction; the circumstances of the case called not for it. If it had been a guess, reason said most certainly "Be silent, for to speak is unnecessary and will be dangerous." Why then did he thus stake his reputation with future ages. He knew that posterity would try him by the rules which he had delivered to the nation for trying others, and that if no such person appeared he must be set down, by his own rule, as an impostor; than which there is no viler man.

But again; look at the identical nature of the prediction. Moses clothed his prophet with authority which was to supersede his own; and destines to excommunication from the congregation the man who shall refuse to hear him. Now to set up a national worship to-day and tell those for whom it is designed that another man after him, who might arise to-morrow, shall come with all the authority of God to change it and introduce others, would have been a degree of folly in Moses wholly incredible by any but an infidel or the weakest of men in regard to right reasoning.

Why did he foretell that this prophet should be of Judah, of Jacob, of Isaac, of Abraham, of Shem, of Seth, of woman and not of man, rather than of Levi, and Esau, and Ishmael, and Japhet, and Cain, and of both the woman and the man? Why was he to be of Asia, and Canaan and Judah, and Bethlehem; rather than of other places? Particularity of this kind is highly dangerous in cases of fraud and imposition. Why does the same volume tell us that Messiah should be a prophet, a priest and a king, be put to death as the first of them, raised from the dead to be the second, and exalted to heaven to be the third, namely, a king? Why did they foretell that he should receive the Holy Spirit, as Jesus did at baptism, that the fundamental proposition of his religion should be taught to the world by God speaking from heaven, that he should perform the duties of his ministry chiefly in the tribes of Zebulon and Napthali, and die at Jerusalem, that he should be gifted with the power of miracles and be crucified with transgressors, that he would be poor, rejected and disrespected by the proud of his own nation, that he should be preceded by a forerunner as John the Baptist, that he should be tried, condemned by an unrighteous judgment, executed, die with thieves, pray for them, be presented with vinegar and gall at his death, have his garments parted by lot, be pierced in the hands and feet with nails, mocked and spit upon, be buried in, the tomb of a rich man, be raised from the dead in three days, settle the affairs of his kingdom, and ascend to heaven! Finally why did Moses foretell his own people that if they rejected this prophet, or refused to hear what he had from God to communicate, they should loose their nationality, and be scattered to the ends of the earth, a hissing, a by-word, and a proverb among the nations; that after a long dispersion they should be restored to their own land? This, on the part of those who spoke, was wholly gratuitous, altogether uncalled for. Now, impostors generally exercise a little more prudence in regard to futurity and posterity. Mahomet for instance acted more warily; you will find a surprising difference between the Koran and the Bible in this respect. The writers of the Bible have indeed surprisingly and unnecessarily committed themselves if there is no connection between Jesus and their predictions. The force of prophecy is not felt in the delivery but in the fulfillment of it, Moses therefore, could not have delivered his predictions concerning the Messiah and the disorganization of the state at his appearance, in the belief that they would be of the least use in establishing the divinity of his own mission with the people to whom he spoke; and he must have known that with posterity, if they were false, they would be worse than useless; that they would wholly disprove it, and set him in the attitude of an impostor with all mankind. Did he then, unjudging man, purpose to set himself in the attitude of a knave with his contemporaries and of a fool with posterity? This is the dilemma to which infidels are brought; thus is their argument reduced to the truly absurd.

But to turn to Christianity. How gratuitous and dangerous it was for Paul to prophecy that a man of sin, the Pope of Rome, should arise in the Christian church; that he should exercise all the authority of a God, and should exalt himself even above God. How dangerous, how unnecessary to condescend upon the following particularities, the distinguishing characteristics of Catholicity, and predict of its lents, its saint-worship, and the celibacy of its clergy! "Now the Spirit says expressly that in future times some will apostatize from the faith, giving heed to deceiving spirits and to doctrine concerning demons: through the hypocrisy of liars, who are seared in their own conscience; who forbid to marry, and command to abstain from meats, which God has created to be received with thanksgiving by the faithful, who thoroughly know the truth; that every creature of God is good:"—How unnecessary, and uncalled for, that the new testament should foretell that this same pope should attain to temporal power, should be clothed with purple and scarlet and adorned with gold and precious stones and pearls; that the city in which he should appear and reign was built on seven mountains, that he should lord it over the kings of the earth, that ten of them would bow their necks to him for a season and give him their power, finally that the abominable establishment of which he was the head, should be drunken with the blood of the saints, that six hundred and sixty six years old it should give birth to the monstrous inquisition after which time the kings should turn upon the old bird and his foul cage as England, Switzerland and the Netherlands did, and as France did, and as Spain and Portugal are now doing, and that the whole of his former adherents should make him desolate, and naked of dominion, and eat his flesh, his revenue and church lands, and burn his religious houses with fire! Now to foretell all this was wholly unnecessary to Paul and John. Nobody demanded this of them, or any other prophecy. They contributed it voluntarily, gratuitously; and must either have spoken by the Spirit of God, or must have intended to destroy with posterity what they built up with their contemporaries; to make themselves fools with the one, and knaves with the other, and must have been ambitious to set up in one age what they wished to have destroyed in the next.

This O reader, is the nature of your argument; this is the absurdity to which it is reduced. Surely you have a vast appetite for the marvelous, and must possess the development of credulity in a very eminent degree.

Before leaving the Law and the Gospel, or rather the subject of prophecy as connected with their divine origin, it will be proper perhaps to let you see, O man of the earth, the power which this branch of Divine Revelation exerted over some spirits, who for mental excellence and all the wit and manners, which form the ambition of the crowd, cannot well be supposed inferior to you, whosoever you are. The first of these is John, Earl of Rochester; the second the great Lord Lyttleton. The former of whom was converted from the basest and blackest infidelity by that singular chapter of predictions concerning the appearance, rejection, trial, death, burial, resurrection and ascension of the Messiah, the 53d of Isaiah. The latter, Lord Lyttleton, by reading and studying the conversion of the Apostle Paul. So that in the cases of these distinguished individuals you may see what, God grant, may be a type of your own future history, that is, your future conversion to God and Jesus Christ your Saviour.

"John, earl of Rochester, was a great scholar, a great poet, a great sinner, and a great penitent. His life was written by Burnet, and his funeral sermon was preached and published by Mr. Parsons. Dr. Johnson, speaking of Burnet's life of this nobleman, says, "The critic ought to read it for its elegance, the philosopher for its argument, and the saint for its piety."

His lordship, it appears, had advanced to an uncommon height of wickedness, having been an advocate in the black cause of atheism, and an encomiast to Beelzebub. He had raked too in the very bottom of the jakes of debauchery, and had been a satirist against religion itself. But when, like the prodigal in the gospel, he came to himself, his mind was filled with the most extreme horror, which forced sharp and bitter invectives from him against himself; terming himself the vilest wretch that the sun ever shone upon; wishing he had been a crawling leper in a ditch, a linkboy, or a beggar, or had lived in a dungeon, rather than offended God in the manner he had done.

Upon the first visit of Mr. Parsons to him on May 26th, 1680, after a journey from the West, he found him laboring under great trouble of mind, and his conscience full of terror. The earl told him—"When on his journey, he had been arguing with greater vigor against God and religion, than ever he had done in his life-time before, and that he had been resolved to run them down with all the argument and spite in the world; but like the great convert, Paul, he found it hard to kick against God." At this time, however, his heart was so powerfully affected, that he argued as much for God and religion, as he ever had done against them.—He had such tremendous apprehensions of the Divine Majesty, mingled with such delightful contemplations of his nature and perfections, and of the amiableness of religion, that he said,—"I never was advanced thus far towards happiness in my life before; though upon the commission of some sins extraordinary, I have had some considerable checks and warnings from within; but still I struggled with them, and so wore them off again. One day, at an atheistical meeting in the house of a person of quality, I undertook to manage the cause, and was the principal disputant against God and religion; and for my performances received the applauses of the whole company.—Upon this my mind was terribly struck, and I immediately replied thus to myself —"Good God, that a man that walks upright, that sees the wonderful works of God, and has the use of his senses and reason, should use them to the defying of his Creator!—But though this was a good beginning towards my conversion, to find my conscience touched for my sins, yet it went off again: nay, all my life long, I had a secret value and reverence for an honest man, and loved morality in others. But I had formed an odd scheme of religion to myself, which would solve all that God or conscience might force upon me; yet I was never reconciled to the business of Christianity; nor had I that reverence for the gospel of Christ, which I ought to have had."

This state of mind continued till the fifty-third chapter of Isaiah was read to him, together with some other parts of the sacred scriptures; when it pleased God to fill his mind with such peace and joy in believing that it was remarkable to all about him, upon which he used to enlarge in a very familiar and affectionate manner, applying the whole to his own humiliation and encouragement.

"O blessed God," would he say, "can such a horrid creature as I am be accepted by thee, who have denied thy Being, and contemned thy power? Can there be mercy and pardon for me? Will God own such a wretch as I?"

In the middle of his sickness he said still farther:—"Shall the unspeakable joys of heaven be conferred on me? O mighty Saviour, never but through thine infinite love and satisfaction! O never but by the purchase of thy blood"—adding—"that with all abhorrence he reflected upon his former life—that from his heart he repented of all that folly and madness of which he had been guilty."

He had a strong and growing esteem for the sacred scriptures, and evidently saw their divine fullness and excellency:—"For, having spoken to his heart, he acknowledged, all the seeming absurdities and contradictions fancied by men of corrupt and reprobate judgements, were vanished; and the excellency and beauty of them appeared conspicuously, now that he was come to receive the truth in the love of it."

During his illness he had a hearty concern for the pious education of children, wishing "his son might never be a wit, one of those wretched creatures who pride themselves in abusing God and religion, denying his Being or his Providence; but that he might become an honest man; and of a truly religious character, which only could be the support and blessing of his family."

One of his companions coming to see him on his death-bed, he said to him:—"O remember that you contemn God no more. He is an avenging God, and will visit you for your sins; and will, I hope, in mercy touch your conscience, sooner or later, as he has done mine.—You and I have been friends and sinners together a great while, therefore I am the more free with you.—We have been all mistaken in our conceits and opinions; our persuasions have been false and groundless; therefore I pray God grant you repentance."

When he drew towards the last stage of his sickness, he said, "If God spare me yet a little longer time here, I hope to bring glory to his name, proportionable to the dishonor I have done to him in my whole life; and particularly by my endeavors to convince others, and to assure them of the danger of their condition, if they continued impenitent; and to tell them how graciously God hath dealt with me."

And when he came within still nearer views of dissolution, about three or four days before it, he said,—"I shall now die: but, Oh; what unspeakable glories do I see! What joys, beyond thought or expression am I sensible of! I am assured of God's mercy to me through Jesus Christ! Oh how I long to die, and to be with my Saviour!"

For the admonition of others, and to undo as much as was in his power, the mischief of his former conduct, he subscribed the following recantation, and ordered it to be published after his death:

"For the benefit of all those, whom I may have drawn into sin by my example and encouragement, I leave to the world this my last declaration: which I deliver in the presence of the great God, who knows the secrets of all hearts, and before whom I am now appearing to be judged; That from the bottom of my soul I detest and abhor the whole course of my former wicked life; that I think I can never sufficiently admire the goodness of God, who has given me a true sense of my pernicious opinions and vile practices, by which I have hitherto lived without hope, and without God in the world: have been an open enemy to Jesus Christ, doing the utmost despite to the Holy Spirit of grace: and that the greatest testimony of my charity to such, is to warn them, in the name of God, as they regard the welfare of their immortal souls, no more to deny his Being or his Providence, or despise his goodness; no more to make a mock of sin, or contemn the pure and excellent religion of my ever-blessed Redeemer, through whose merits alone, I, one of the greatest of sinners, do yet hope for mercy and forgiveness. Amen."

The following is the case of Lord Lyttleton.

"Lord Lyttleton, author of the History of Henry the Second, and Gilbert West had both imbibed the principles of unbelief, and had agreed together to write something in favor of infidelity. To do this more effectually, they judged it necessary to acquaint themselves pretty well with the Bible. By the perusal of that book, however, they were both convinced of their error: both became converts to the religion of Christ Jesus; both took up their pens and wrote in favor of it: the former his Observations on the conversion of St. Paul; the latter, his observations on the resurrection of Christ; and both died in peace."

Whether, therefore, we look at the Old or the New Testament, the religion of the Jews or that of the Christians at Moses or Jesus, the prophecies delivered by the former, and fulfilled by the latter, or the influence which they have had on thousands of the human family, and on such men as Rochester and Lyttleton in particular, we see that they are most orderly and correct in fact, and powerful and precious in effect.

But leaving the subject of prophecy, see O man, the pure Theology of the Jewish Scriptures. Look at it as it existed in Canaan alone for fifteen hundred years in the midst of innumerable nations devoted to idolatry all around! Behold it rearing itself on high in the centre of the civilized world, a flaming beacon to keep the Polytheists of Assyria, Egypt, Greece, and Rome, in perpetual remembrance of the point of safety and divine religion from whence they had gone so shockingly astray. See it towering to the skies in the presence of these abominable and apostate nations, a monument to the Divine unity, and the doctrine of the One Only Living and True God; and then say whether the Bible be altogether the object of that scorn with which you would affect to treat it. Unthinking, unjudging man! What resemblance in this point do the ancient scriptures bear to any other religious document of antiquity? What resemblance is there between the theology of the Bible and that gross and mad Polytheism into which the ancient nations above named, run headlong? It differs from them as much as light from darkness, and is as wide apart from it in nature and effect, as the God of the Jews differed in character from the base immoral phantasies of Jupiter and Titan. What comparison can you institute between the King the Lord of Hosts, and Belial, or "Osiris, Isis, Oris, and their train of bestial gods?" What likeness was there between the idol Bull and crocodile of Egypt and the living but invisible God of the Holy Scriptures? Shame upon the man and his boasted reason also who would name the comparison. It is brutish to do so. And you reader, who indulge in a reasoning so perverse, so do damning in its nature, are on the brink of perpetual ruin; read in the following the fate of Altamont; and say whether with him you would live, with him you would die.

"The sad evening before the death of the noble Altamont, I was with him. No one was there but his physician, and an intimate friend whom he loved, and whom he had ruined. At my coming in he said, "You and the physician are come too late. I have neither life nor hope. You both aim at miracles. You would raise the dead." Heaven, I said, was merciful, "Or I could not have been thus guilty. What has it not done to bless and to save me? I have been too strong for Omnipotence! I plucked down ruin!" I said, the blessed Redeemer—"Hold! hold! you wound me!—This is the rock on which I split—I denied his name." Refusing to hear any thing from me, or take any thing from the physician, he lay silent, as far as sudden darts of pain would permit, till the clock struck. Then with vehemence; "O time! time! it is fit thou shouldst thus strike thy murderer to the heart. How art thou fled forever! A month!—O for a single week! I ask not for years, though an age were too little for the much I have to do." On my saying that we could not do too much: that Heaven was a blessed place—"So much the worse. 'Tis lost! Heaven is to me the severest part of hell!" Soon after I proposed prayer. "Pray you that can. I never prayed. I cannot pray; nor need I. Is not Heaven on my side already? It closes with my conscience. Its severest strokes but second my own." His friend being much touched, even to tears at this—who could forbear? I could not—with a most affectionate look he said, "Keep those tears for thyself. I have undone thee. Doest weep for me. That's cruel. What can pain me more?" Here his friend, too much affected, would have left him. "No, stay, thou still mayest hope. Therefore hear me. How madly have I talked! How madly hast thou listened and believed! But look on my present state, as a full answer to thee, and to myself. This body is all weakness and pain; but my soul, as if strung up by torment to greater strength and spirit, is full powerful to reason, full mighty to suffer. And that which thus triumphs in the jaws of mortality, is doubtless immortal. And, as for a deity, nothing less than an Almighty could inflict what I feel." I was about to congratulate this passive involuntary confessor, on his asserting the two prime articles of his creed, extorted by the rack of nature, when he thus said very passionately: "No, no! let me speak on. I have not long to speak. My much injured friend! my soul, as my body, lies in ruins; in scattered fragments of broken thought; remorse for the past, throws my thoughts on the future. Worse dread of the future, strikes it back on the past. I turn, and turn, and find no ray. Didst thou feel the mountain that is on me, thou wouldst struggle with the martyr for his stake, and bless heaven for the flames:—that is not everlasting flame; that is not an unquenchable fire." How were we struck! Yet soon after still more. With what an eye of distraction, what a face of despair, he cried out; "My principles have poisoned my friend; my extravagance has beggared my boy; my unkindness has murdered my wife! And is there another hell? Oh! thou blasphemed, yet most indulgent Lord God! Hell itself is a refuge if it hides me from thy frown."

Soon after his understanding failed. His terrified imagination uttered horrors not to be repeated, or ever forgotten. And ere the sun arose, the gay, young, noble, ingenuous, and most wretched Altamont expired.

It is not easy for imagination itself to form a more affecting representation of a death-bed scene than that of this noble youth."

Again: look at the theology of the New Testament. The same Living and True God, who had brought from afar, from the Beginning of the world, the men of faith, who served and loved him in all preceding ages, appears to found a new institution; he bows the heavens and comes down; he lays the foundation of a new temple, the temple of Christianity; he introduces to mankind by far the most illustrious person that ever trod our earth, the Lord Jesus Christ. He announces him in a glorious voice; he attests him, and marks him out by a peculiar signal, the descending Spirit, filling the Redeemer of our fallen race with powers and virtues all divine, and sending him forth to heal the brokenhearted, to preach glad tidings to the poor, to loose the prisoner, to unbind his fetters, to open the blind eyes, and unstop the deaf ears, to sanctify the unclean, to raise the dead, to die for the whole human race and to establish among the benighted nations, the light of immortality and eternal life. O, what a just and pure theology has Revealed Religion brought in among the Gentiles! No longer the slaves of "gods many and lords many," "to us there is but one God, even the Father; and one Lord, even Jesus Christ." Yet, you, O man of the world, despise or neglect this, or presume to confound or compare it with the mummery of priests. Do you indeed deny this doctrine, do you deny the existence of one Living and indivisible God? Then you deny the doctrine of universal nature as well as that of the Old and New Testaments; for nature proclaims in ten thousand voices by ten thousand tongues the existence, character, and unity of God. And what, if after all your petty reasonings, the Bible should turn out to be true, and all your own imaginations fake? There are some mistakes, you must know, that can never be corrected, some errors that can never be put right. The future state, into which you are fast hastening, is not the place to adjust the matters of religion. Time is the day allotted to man for making up his views on the superlative topic of life eternal. What then is your taste for this? Have you any appetite for divine Revelation, and the meal it provides? You will eternally and unavailingly regret jour own guilt and naughtiness, if you be careless of religion and the things that concern your own everlasting welfare. Read in the following the narrow escape, which men with the most enviable qualities, make at death, who seek the praise of men and forget God.

"A gentleman, whose name is concealed from delicacy to the connections, was descended of a noble and religious family. His life was extremely irregular and dissolute, but his natural parts and endowments of mind so extraordinary, that they rendered his conversation agreeable to persons of the highest rank and quality. Being taken ill, he believed he should die at the very beginning of his sickness. His friend, with whom he had frequently disputed against the existence of God, and the truths of revealed religion, visited him on the second day after he was seized. He asked him how he did, and what made him so dejected?

"Alas!" said he, "are you so void of understanding, as to imagine I am afraid to die? Far be such thoughts from me. I could meet death with as much courage as I have encountered an enemy in the field of battle, and embrace it as freely as I ever did any friend whom I entirely loved: for I see nothing in this world that is worth the pains of keeping. I have made trial of most states and conditions of life. I have been rich and poor. I have been raised to honor and reversed in a high degree. I have also been exposed to scorn and contempt. I have experienced the difference between virtue and vice, and every thing that was possible for a man in my station; so that I am capable of distinguishing what is really good and praise-worthy, and what is not. Now I see with a clearer sight than ever, and discern a vast difference between the vain licentious discourse of a libertine, and the sound arguments of a true believer: for though the former may express himself more finely than the latter, so as to puzzle him with hard questions and intricate notions, yet all amount to no more than the fallacy of a few airy repartees, which are never affected by sober Christians, nor capable of eluding the force of solid reason. But now I know how to make a distinction between them; and I wish from the bottom of my heart I had been so sensible of my error in the time of my health; then I had never had those foretastes of hell I now have. Oh! what a sad account have I to give of a long life spent in sin and folly! I look beyond the fears of a temporal death. All the dread that you perceive in me arises from the near approach I make to an eternal death; for I must die to live to all eternity."

He continued in this manner to bewail his past folly, atheism and infidelity for forty days, and then expired. His friend, however, took large pains with him to encourage his repentance, faith, and return to a proper state of mind. At last, however, he was brought to entertain some hope, that the Redeemer of mankind would take pity on his deplorable condition, pardon his sins, and rescue him from that everlasting destruction which awaits all such characters. He told his friend, that if he departed with a smile, he might hope for the best concerning him; but if he should be seen to give up the ghost with a frown, there would be reason to fear the worst.

This was about three o'clock in the afternoon, and he lived till four the next morning. A little before he expired he was heard to speak these words softly to himself—"Oh! that I had possession of the meanest place in heaven, and could, but creep into one corner of it." Afterwards he cried out four several times together—O dear, dear, dear, dear,—and, near a minute before he expired, his friend perceived him to look full in his face, with a smiling countenance.

There we leave him till the resurrection-morn."

The Christian Religion, in the circumstances attending its origin, is not less wonderful than the Mosaic. Who but the Deity, in the days of Moses, could have given birth to a theology so pure as that of the law? None; unless we can suppose that, when all the nations had gone astray from the true God, and adopted Polytheism; when they had ceased to walk by faith, and embraced image worship; when they had lost the knowledge of the true God, and invented idolatry; when they had declined from pure morals, and sunken into the depths of iniquity; when they had no intercourse with God, and all vision and revelation failed or was withdrawn; a man arose, a most wonderful man truly, Moses arose, and shook himself free from the entire rubbish of irreligion, Polytheism, image worship, and their consequent immorality, and asserted the existence, character, and unity of the divine essence. This, reader, you must believe, if you deny the inspiration of the Bible. There is no alternative. The one or the other of these propositions must be true. You most either believe that Moses was just such an astonishingly great person as to do all this, or you must believe that God did it by him. Choose then, on which horn of the dilemma you will be pleased to hang your cause. If you yield the point and admit the divinity of revelation, our dispute is ended. If you deny it, and assert the power of Moses to do all this of himself exclusively, then you admit him to be a wiser and greater man than Socrates, the Athenian, who, although he arrived by his inquiries to the doctrine of the Divine Unity, confessed nevertheless it was both difficult to attain, and dangerous to promulgate it among the common people of that idolatrous age. He died, therefore, an idolater, offering a cock to the god Esculapius. Moses on the contrary, publicly taught this theology and founded the whole of his simple, pure, and natural system of morals upon its truth. Yes, the whole of the morality in the law is founded upon the fact, that there is but one living and true God. The nation's responsibility to him is made by Moses, the moral code. Now, can any thing excel the decalogue in religion and morals? for the one half is religious and the other moral, the first table of these commandments relating to God, and the second to the people. It is the moral part of it, we desire to reach by these preliminary observations.

The morals taught by this ancient legislator, are most pure and holy; and when considered with a reference to the times in which they were given to the Jewish nation, demonstrate their own divine origin; for no man can be supposed to have possessed in his own person and of himself alone, the prodigious wisdom which was necessary to compile a thing so simple and correct, and pitch it upon a theology so true, but at the same time so perfectly contradictory of every other existing system of religion then in the world.

Let me tell you, O false reasoner! that if you imagine Moses to have compiled the Pentateuch, and invented the religion and morals therein contained, you cause to unite in this man the wisdom of God and the duplicity of the Devil; you bring together in one person, the most distant extremes, you unite heaven and hell; and while denying God and the Devil, you in fact create to yourself in the person of Moses, a being that is equal to both!

But you reply that Moses admitted war, and exercised great cruelty towards the enemies of Israel. Do not now confound the national policy of that people, with their code of private morals. I am speaking of the morality of the Bible, not of the national policy practiced by the Jews who were entrusted with the Bible. To avoid war, was as impracticable with them as it is with ourselves, and if they exercised cruelty towards their enemies, it was because their own safety and the preservation of the True Religion made it necessary.

Now from viewing the morals of the first economy of Revealed Religion, turn to the morals of the second, those of Christianity. How pure and wonderful! They descend into the heart, and a look and word are rebuked and denounced as the external signals of internal default! "Why do evil thoughts arise in your hearts?" The Jews, at the appearing of our Saviour, had become shockingly delinquent in regard to virtue. Forgetting justice, mercy, and the love of God, they had strongly attached themselves to the Mosaic ritual and given a preference to that which was merely ceremonial and positive over that which was necessary and moral in its nature. The blessed author of Christianity said to them, "These you ought to have done and not have left the other undone." But I need not discourse to you of the extraordinary purity and elevation of the morals of Christianity. The system is reputed by both friends and enemies to be the best in the world. Take J. J. Roseau's views of it in the following:

"I will confess to you," says he, "that the majesty of the scriptures strikes me with admiration, as the purity of the gospel hath its influence on my heart. Peruse the works of our philosophers with all their pomp of diction: how mean, how contemptible are they, compared with the scripture? Is it possible that a book, at once so simple and sublime, should be merely the work of man? Is it possible that the sacred personage, whose history it contains, should be himself a mere man! Do we find that he assumed the tone of an enthusiast or ambitious sectary! What sweetness, what purity in his manner! What an affecting gracefulness in his delivery! What sublimity in his maxims! What profound wisdom in his discourses! What presence of mind, what subtilty, what truth in his replies! How great the command over his passions! Where is the man, where the philosopher, who could so live, and so die, without weakness and without ostentation? When Plato described his imaginary good man, loaded with all the shame of guilt, yet meriting the highest rewards of virtue, he describes exactly the character of Jesus Christ; the resemblance was so striking that all the fathers perceived it. What prepossession, what blindness must it be, to compare the son of Sophroniscus to the son of Mary? What an infinite disproportion there is between them? Socrates dying without pain or ignominy, easily supported his character to the last; if his death, however easy, had not crowned his life, it might have been doubted whether Socrates, with all his wisdom, was any thing more than a vain sophist.—He invented, it is said, the theory of morals. Others, however, had before put them in practice; he had only to say, therefore, what they had done, and to reduce their examples to precepts. Aristides had been just before Socrates defined justice; Leonidas had given up his life for his country before Socrates declared patriotism to be a duty; the Spartans were a sober people before Socrates recommended sobriety; before he had even defined virtue, Greece abounded in virtuous men. But where could Jesus learn, among his contemporaries that pure and sublime morality, of which he only hath given us both precept and example. The greatest wisdom was made known among the most bigoted fanaticism, and the simplicity of the most heroic virtues did honor to the vilest people upon earth. The death of Socrates, peaceably philosophizing with his friends, appears the most agreeable that could be wished for; that of Jesus expiring in the midst of agonizing pains, abused, insulted, and accused by a whole nation, is the most horrible that could be feared.

Socrates, in receiving the poison, blessed indeed the weeping executioner who administered it; but Jesus in the midst of excruciating tortures, prayed for his merciless tormentors. Yes, if the life and death of Socrates were those of a sage, the life and death of Jesus are those of a God. Shall we suppose the evangelic history a mere fiction? Indeed, my friend, it bears not the marks of fiction; on the contrary, the history of Socrates, which nobody presumes to doubt, is not so well attested as that of Jesus Christ. Such a supposition, in fact, only shifts the difficulty, without obviating it: it is more inconceivable that a number of persons should agree to write such a history, than that only one should furnish the history of it. The Jewish authors were incapable of the diction, and strangers to the morality contained in the gospel, the marks of whose truth are so striking and inimitable, that the inventor would be a more astonishing character than a hero."

But now, O reader! if Jesus was not what we most assuredly believe him to be, the Son of God, how, pray, do you account for all these grand things in the New Testament, the works of his Evangelists or preachers? How do you account for a scheme that excites the admiration of the whole world, the deists themselves not excepted? How is it that among a nation who hated all the world so much that the meanest of them accounted it an unlawful thing to come into one that was of a different nation, one should arise and with a benevolence altogether supernational, and we may say superhuman, propose to save all the world, and instruct it in the most unstained purity and morality? Account, account, friend, for this inexplicable singularity. This you cannot do. Your infidel proposition is absurd, and time or eternity will certainly prove it to you. Reform yourself, correct your sentiments in regard to the Holy Scriptures. They are not what you have imagined them to be. In prophecy, in religion, and morality, they are the admiration of all good men.

"Grotius possessed the brightest genius ever recorded of a youth in the learned world, and was a profound admirer, and a daily reader, of the sacred writings; yet after all his attainments, reputation, and labor in the cause of learning, he was constrained at last to cry out, "Ah! I have consumed my life in a laborious doing of nothing?—I would give all my learning and honor for the plain integrity of John Urick!"

You do not look at the old Bible as to a pregnant grape ready to burst into new wine at the appearance of Jesus Christ; you do not see it as a woman in travail, who had arrived at her full time, and ready to be delivered. You never consider it as it presented itself like a flower that had been budding and blossoming till when Jesus appeared, it burst into bloom and reddened with the glory of a full blown rose. You never think that the dark night had then come to an end, and that from the womb of prophecy the Son of Righteousness, as was expected, arose. No, no,

Thomas Paine, the shrewd and insolent Thomas Paine, has had the audacity to style Moses a coxcomb, and you with the credulity of a child that has not yet cut its second teeth, have believed him! The Novum Organum, the Essay on the Human Understanding, and the Principia, must all give way to Paine's farthing rush light; or rather the authors of these mighty monuments of human genius, science, and rectitude, must all hide their diminished heads before the superior glories of the author of the Age of Reason! And a book, the size of Robinson Crusoe, with double the quantity of romance and not half its decency, must annihilate the very Bible itself! I should think a man, who had read "The Babes in the Wood," might have more sense than to propose a contest between the Bible and Mr. Paine's Age of Reason. It looks like a boy firing off a pop-gun at the fortress of Gibraltar, or a child reaching with a broom-stick to take the sun off the nail on which he supposes it to hang.

Having quenched the moon and her attendant stars by the flashings of a farthing rush light, having disposed of Moses and the prophets by means of Mr. Paine, you next turn to Christianity, and threaten the sun himself by bringing forth at noon the spermaceti flambeau of a French sophist, Mon. Voltaire! This is the man whom with his disciples you would have to take the place of the Redeemer of your own soul and his Holy Apostles; and his ribaldry and immoral sophistry, you would substitute for the simple, beautiful and unstained virtue of the New Testament!

When you think of our religion you never dwell for a moment on the expansive philanthropy on which it professes to be founded; you never hang for a second on that unlimited and unrivalled affection which its unstained author entertained and expressed and manifested for all mankind, and even you, your own self. No, no; you never think of the good that Christianity has accomplished whenever she has been permitted to speak out; you look at Catholicity and see that it gave birth to that portentous institution the Inquisition, and that her popes, priests, and prelates have been the most arrant villains that ever existed under heaven; and all this you imagine is the Christian Religion! Why, sir, these impostors and miserable sinners had more real wit than to believe this themselves; and durst not for the soul of them let the books in which Christianity is written, be seen by the people! Do you know this much of the whole matter, that the Catholics are forbidden by a papal Bull from reading the scriptures. These Italian priests, sir, saw, it would appear, what you with all your republican *sense* and *reason*, do not seem to see, that Paul and John had anticipated them and pre-described their wickedness and huge hypocrisy to a shaving, and therefore they closed the unpolluted Bible, and opened their own idolatrous Manuel.

But if you desire to know what Catholicism did do, and what true Christianity never could perform, I will tell you. It produced Voltaire. Yes, sir, your teacher was one of a thousand from the bosom of Mother Church. It was indeed, sir, this shocking establishment that gave birth to Voltaire and to those other monsters of infidelity and profanity, D'Alembert, Diderot, Rousseau, Condorcet, and the disgusting and licentious Pigault le Brun. These, with the whole brood of impious murderers, who figured in the French Revolution, are the immediate offspring of Mother Church. But what else had she to expect of such nurslings, seeing she had in her own practice set them such a horrid and rabid example of blood-thirstiness? For as the scriptures say, "In her was found the blood of the saints;" and her merchandize was "the souls of men." In her blind zeal for supremacy, Mother church has at different times, it is said murdered no less than fifty millions of Protestants! Of the Indians, besides those who fell in the islands, the Catholics butchered twelve millions on the continent of America. But, my friend, it would be as preposterous to blame the Bible with this, as it would be to blame the sun for shining while they performed these cruelties. Though armies rush to battle in the day, though murder, and rapine, and bloodshed are practiced in the face of the world, shall we deny the excellence of the sun, and abjure his light, because men and armies pervert it, and abuse it to the destruction of one another? on such oblique reasoning we might repudiate the use of nature's best and choicest gifts; we might, as we have seen, shut our eyes to the lamp of day itself, and say that we scorned to look by the light of a sun that had shone on such men. The Bible is not to be rejected because it has been abused. Reform your sentiments, then, in regard to this holy book.

"When Struensee, prime minister of Denmark, had been disgraced and imprisoned for certain misdemeanors of which he had been guilty, he was brought from a state of infidelity to a serious sense of his situation. He then declared, "The more I learn of Christianity from scripture, the more I grow convinced, how unjust these objections are with which it is charged. I find, for instance, that all which Voltaire says of the intolerance of Christians, and of blood-shedding caused by Christianity, is a very unjust charge laid upon religion. It is easy to be seen, that those cruelties, said to be caused by religion, if properly considered, were the productions of human passions, selfishness and ambition, and that religion served in such cases only for a cloak.—I am fully convinced of the truth of the Christian religion, and I feel its power in quieting my conscience, and reforming my sentiments.—I have examined it during a good state of health, and with all the reason I am master of. I tried every argument, I felt no fear, I have taken my own time and I have not been in haste. I own with joy, I find Christianity the more amiable the more I get acquainted with it. I never knew it before. I believed it contradicted reason, and the nature of man, whose religion it was designed to be. I thought it an artfully contrived and ambiguous doctrine, full of incomprehensibilities. Whenever I formerly thought on religion in some, serious moments, I had always an idea in my mind how it ought to be, which was, it should be simple and accommodated to the abilities of men in every condition. I now find Christianity to be exactly so; it answers entirely that idea which I had formed of true religion. Had I but formerly known it was such, I should not have delayed turning Christian till this time of my imprisonment. But I had the misfortune to be prejudiced against religion, first through my own passions, but after wards likewise by so many human inventions, foisted into it, of which I could see plainly that they had no foundation, though they were styled essential parts of Christianity. I was offended when God was always represented to me as an angry, jealous judge, who is much pleased when he has an opportunity of shewing his revenge, though I knew he was love itself; and am now convinced, that though he must punish, yet he takes no kind of delight in it, and is rather for pardoning. From my infancy, I have known but few Christians that had not scandalized me by their enthusiasm and wickedness, which they wanted to hide under the cloak of piety. I knew indeed that not all Christians were such, or talked such an affected language; but I was too volatile to inquire of better christians after the true spirit of religion. Frequently I heard sermons in my youth, but they made no impression upon me. That without Christ there was no salvation, was the only truth which served for a subject in all sermons, and this was repeated over and over again in synonymous, expressions. But it was never set in its true light, and never properly proved. I saw people cry at church, but after their tears were dried up, I found them in their actions not in the least better, but rather allowing themselves in every transgression, upon the privilege of being faithful believers.—He said, he observed in Paul a great genius, much wisdom and true philosophy. The apostles write extremely well, and now and then inimitably beautiful, and at the same time with simplicity and clearness.—The free-thinkers extol the fables of Æsop, but the parables and narrations of Christ will not please them: notwithstanding they are derived from a greater knowledge of nature, and contain more excellent morality. Besides they are proposed with a more noble and artless simplicity than any writings of the kind, among ancient or modern authors."

Brandt, the companion of Struensee in guilt and misfortunes, with great freedom owned that his imprisonment was the means of setting his soul at liberty; and he found his chains so little troublesome to him, that he would oftentimes take them up and kiss them."

What Struensee says of popular preaching, is very correct.—The clergy seem to think that there is a charm in the expressions, "Without Christ there is no salvation;" and they therefore, repeat and repeat and repeat again, till the whole population yawns. The first principles of the gospel are never arranged by them; they have by their corruptions anticipated the gospel and cannot and do not administer it as directed by Christ and his Apostles; they chime away on a few points, which serve as so many bells by which they lull the people into a most sinful repose, and cause them to put an undue estimate upon certain doctrines of election, reprobation, free will, ordination, and other things as the system may inculcate; so that their ignorant and superstitious people would die for these phantoms and false doctrines of their preachers' systems, while they would and do be guilty of neglecting justice, mercy and the love of God. Now, infidel reader, this also offends you; you see this; you have, I grant, wit enough to see it. But what then? What does this prove? Struensee saw this also; but he acknowledged that this made nothing for the certainty of infidelity and against the cause of Christianity. Christianity will ever remain the same pure, unpolluted, and heaven-descended thing whether professors be vicious or virtuous, and whether you believe it or not. In the scriptures she stands all undeformed and holy, and to-day looks as pure and fresh from the pages of the Bible as she did seventeen hundred years ago.

But your great objection to the scriptures is, that they were compiled after the time at which they profess to have been written. This has been a thousand times asserted, and as often confuted. For this proposition there does not exist the shadow of a proof: it is a base assumption. And to set it aside, the arguments are so numerous that one scarcely knows which of them to use first.

Do you really assert with Celsus, that Daniel's prophecies were written after the facts which they describe had occurred? Now how could this be? Many of these prophecies refer to Christ and his religion; but if they were invented and written after Christ came, how is it that Christ spoke of them and quoted them to his disciples, naming the prophet himself, as you may see by referring to the 24th chapter of Matthew? But in regard to the truth of the scriptures, which you doubt or deny, and which we say bear in their own bosom infallible proofs of their divine origin, let me exhort you to the careful consideration of the following from the pen of one of the ablest and most accurate reasoners on this subject, Mr. Leslie. Against deism he says as follows:

"The method I shall take, is firstly to lay down such rules, as to the truth or matters of fact in general, that, where they all meet such matters of fact cannot be false. Then secondly to show that all these rules do meet in the matters of fact of Moses, and of Christ; and that they do not meet in the matters of fact of Mahomet, and of the heathen deities, nor can possibly meet in any imposture whatsoever.

II. The rules are these, 1st. That the matter of fact be such, that men's outward senses, their eyes and their ears, may be judges of it. 2. That it be done publicly in the face of the world.—3. That not only public monuments be kept up in memory of it, but some outward actions be performed. 4. That such monuments, and such actions or observances be instituted, and do commence from the time that the matter of fact was done.

III. The two first rules make it impossible for any such matter of fact to be imposed upon men at the time, when such matter of fact was said to be done, because every man's eyes and senses would contradict it. For example; suppose any man should pretend that yesterday he divided the Thames, in presence of all the people of London, and carried the whole city, men, women and children, over to Southwark, on dry land, the waters standing like walls on both sides; I say it is morally impossible that he could persuade the people of London that this was true, when every man, woman and child, could contradict him, and say that this was a notorious falsehood, for that they had not seen the Thames so divided, nor had gone over on dry land. Therefore I take it for granted, (and I suppose with the allowance of all the Deists in the world) that no such imposition could be put upon men at the time when such public fact was said to be done.

IV. Therefore it only remains, that such matter of fact might be invented some time after, when the men of that generation wherein the thing was said to be done, were all past and gone; and the credulity of after ages might be so imposed upon, as to believe that things were done in former ages which were not.

From this the two last rules secure us as much as the two first rules in the former case; for whenever such a matter of fact came to be invented, if not only monuments were said to remain of it, but likewise that public actions and observances were constantly used ever since the fact was said to be done, the deceit must be detected by no such monuments appearing, and by the experience of every man, woman, and child, who must know that no such actions or observances were ever used by them. For example; suppose I should now invent a story of such a thing, said to be done a thousand yeas ago, I might perhaps get some to believe it; but if I say that not only such a thing was done, but that from that day to this, every man at the age of twelve years had a joint of his little finger cut off; and that every man in the nation did want a joint of that finger; and that this institution was said to he part of the matter of fact, done so many years ago, and vouched as a proof of it, and as having descended without interruption, and been constantly practised in memory of such fact, from the time that such fact was done; I say it is impossible I should be believed in such a case, because every one could contradict me, as to the mark of cutting off a joint of the finger; and that, being part of my original matter of fact, must demonstrate the whole to be false.

Let us now come to the second point, to show that the matters of fact of Moses, and of Christ, have all these rules or marks before mentioned; and that neither the matters of fact of Mahomet, or what is reported of the heathen deities, have the like; and that no impostor can have them all.

I. As to Moses, I suppose it will be allowed me that he could not have persuaded 600,000 men that he had brought them out of Egypt through the Red Sea; fed them forty years with bread by miraculous manna, and the other matters of fact recorded in his books, if they had not been true. Because every man's senses, who was then alive, must have contradicted it. Therefore he must have imposed upon all their senses, if he could have made them believe it when it was false. So that here are the first and second of the above mentioned four marks.

For the same reason it was equally impossible for him to have made them receive his five books as truth, and not to have rejected them, as a manifest imposture; which told of all these things, as done before their eyes, if they had not been so done. See how positively he speaks to them, Deut. 11:2-8—"And know ye this day, for I speak not with your children, which have not known, and which have not seen the chastisement of the Lord your God, his greatness, his mighty hand, and his outstretched arm, and his miracles, and his acts, which he did in the midst of Egypt unto Pharaoh, the king of Egypt, and unto all his land; and what he did unto the army of Egypt, unto their horses, and to their chariots; how he made the water of the Red Sea to overflow them as they pursued after you; and how the Lord hath destroyed them unto this day; and what he did unto you in the wilderness, until ye came into this place; and what he did unto Dathan and Abiram, the sons of Eliab, the son of Reuben—how the earth opened her mouth and swallowed them up, and their households, and their tents, and all the substance that was in their possession, in the midst of all Israel. But your eyes have seen all the great acts of the Lord, which he did," &c.

Hence we must suppose it impossible that these books of Moses, if an imposture, could have been invented, and put upon the people who were then alive, when all these things were said to be done.

The utmost therefore, to which even supposition can be stretched, is, that these books were written in some age after Moses, and published in his name.

To this I say, that if it were so it was impossible that these books should be received as the books of Moses, in that age wherein they may have been first invented. Why? Because they speak of themselves as delivered by Moses, and kept in the ark from his time. "And it came to pass when Moses had made an end of writing the words of this law in a book, until they were finished, that Moses commanded the Levites, who bare the ark of the covenant of the Lord, saying, take this book of the law, and put it in the side of the ark of the covenant of the Lord your God, that it may be there for a witness against thee."—Deut. 31:24, 25, 26. And a copy of this book was to be left with the king. "And it shall be, when he sitteth upon the throne of his kingdom, that he shall write him a copy of this law in a book, out of that which is before the priests the Levites; and it shall be with him, and he shall read therein all the days of his life; that he may learn to fear the Lord his God, to keep all the words of this law, and these statutes to do them."—Deut. 17:18, 19.

Here then you see that this book of the law speaks of itself, not only as a history or relation of what things were then done; but as the standing and municipal law and statutes of the nation of the Jews, binding the king as well as the people.

Now in whatever age after Moses you suppose that this book was forged, it was impossible it could be received as truth; because it was not then to be found, either in the ark, or with the king, or any where else. For, when first invented, every body must know that he had never heard of it before.

Therefore they could less believe it to be the book of their statutes, and the standing law of the land, which they had all along received, and by which they had been governed.

Could any man at this day invent a book of statutes for England, and make it pass upon the nation as the only book of statutes that ever they had known? As impossible was it for the books of Moses (if they were invented in any age after Moses) to have been received for what they declare themselves to be, viz: the statutes and municipal law of the nation of the Jews; and to have persuaded the Jews, that they had owned and acknowledged these books all along from the days of Moses to that day, in which they were first invented; that is, that they had owned them before they had ever heard of them. Nay more, the whole nation must in an instant forget their former laws and government, if they could receive these books as being their former laws; and they could not otherwise receive them, because they vouched themselves so to be. Let me ask the Deists one short question: was there ever a book of sham laws which were not laws of the nation, palmed upon any people since the world began? If not, with what face can they say this of the book of the laws of the Jews? Why will they say that of them which they confess impossible in any nation, or among any people?

But they must be yet more unreasonable. For the books of Moses have a farther demonstration of their truth than even other law-books have. For they not only contain the laws, but give an historical account of their institution, and the practice of them from that time; as of the passover in memory of the death of the first-born of Egypt; and that the same day all the first-born of Israel, both of man and beast, were by a perpetual law dedicated to God; and the Levites taken for all the first-born of the children of Israel. That Aaron's rod, which budded, was kept in the ark, in memory of the rebellion and wonderful destruction of Korah, Dathan and Abiram; and for the confirmation of the priesthood to the tribe of Levi. As likewise the pot of manna, in memory of their having been fed with it forty years in the wilderness. That the brazen serpent was kept (which remained to the days of Hezekiah, 2 Kings 18:4) in memory of that wonderful deliverance, by only looking upon it, from the biting of the fiery serpents. Numb. 12:9. The feast of Pentecost, in memory of the dreadful appearance of God upon Mount Horeb, &c.

Besides these remembrances of particular actions and occurrences, there were other solemn institutions in memory of their deliverance out of Egypt in general, which included all the particulars. As of the Sabbath; their daily sacrifices and yearly expiation; their new moons, and several feasts and fasts. So that there were yearly, monthly, weekly, daily remembrances and recognition of these things.

Not only so, but the books of the same Moses tell us that a particular tribe was appointed and consecrated by God, as his priests, by whose hands, and none other, the sacrifices of the people were to be offered, and these solemn institutions celebrated; that it was death for any other to approach the altar; that their high-priest wore a glorious mitre, and magnificent robes of God's own contrivance, with the miraculous Urim and Thummim in his breastplate, whence the divine responses were given; that at his word the king and all the people were to go out, and to come in; that these Levites likewise were the chief judges, even in all civil causes, and that it was death to resist their sentence. Now, whenever it can be supposed that these books of Moses were forged in some ages after Moses, it is impossible they could have been received as true, unless the forgers could have made the whole nation believe that they had received these books from their fathers, had been instructed in them when they were children, and had taught them to their children; moreover that they had all been circumcised, and did circumcise their children in pursuance of what was commanded in these books; that they had observed the yearly passover, the weekly sabbath, the new moons, and these several feasts, and fasts, and ceremonies, commanded in these books; that they had never eaten any swine's flesh, or other meats prohibited in these books; that they had a magnificent tabernacle, with a visible priesthood to administer in it, which was confined to the tribe of Levi, over whom was placed a glorious high priest, clothed with great and mighty prerogatives; whose death only could deliver those that were fled to the cities of refuge; and that these priests were their ordinary judges, even in civil matters; I say, was it possible to have persuaded a whole nation of men, that they had known and practised all these things, if they had not done it? Or, secondly, to have received a book for truth, which said they had practised them, and appealed to that practice? So that here are the third and fourth of the marks above mentioned.

But now let us descend to the utmost degree of supposition, viz; that these things were practised before these books of Moses were forged; and that these books did impose upon the nation only in making them believe that they had kept these observances in memory of such and such things, as were inserted in those books.

Let us then proceed upon this supposition, however groundless, and will not the same impossibilities occur as in the former case? For, first, this must suppose that the Jews kept all these observances in memory of nothing, or without knowing any thing of their original, or of the reasons why they kept them.—Whereas, these very observances did express the ground and reason of their being kept; as the Passover, in memory of God's passing over the children of the Israelites in that night wherein he slew all the first-born of Egypt, and so of the rest.

But, secondly, let us suppose, contrary both to reason, and fact, that the Jews did not know any reason why they kept these observances; yet was it possible to put it upon them, that they had kept these observances in memory of what they had never heard of before that day, whensoever you will suppose that these books of Moses were first forged? For example; suppose I should forge some romantic story of strange things done a thousand years ago, and in confirmation of this should endeavor to persuade the Christian world, that they had all along, from that day to this, kept the first day of the week in memory of such a hero, as Apollonius, Barcocibas, or Mahomet; and had all been baptized in his name; and sworn by his name, and upon that very book (which I had then forged, and which they never saw before) in their public judicatures; that this book was their gospel and law, which they had ever since that time, these thousand years past, universally received and owned, and none other. I would ask any Deist, whether he think it possible, that such a cheat could pass, or such a legend be received, as the gospel of Christians; and that they could be made to believe that they never had any other gospel? The same reason is applicable to the books of Moses, and to every matter of fact, which has all the four marks before mentioned; and these marks secure any such matter of fact as much from being invented and imposed in any after ages, as at the time when such facts were said to be done.

Let me give one very familiar example more in this case. The Stonehenge in Salisbury plain is known by everybody; and yet none knows the reason, why those great stones were set there, or by whom, or in memory of what.

Now suppose I should write a book tomorrow, and affirm that these stones were set up by Hercules, Polyphemus, or Garagantua, in memory of such and such of their actions; and for farther confirmation of this should say in this book that it was written at the time when such actions were done, and by the actors themselves, or by eye witnesses; and that this book had been received as truth, and quoted by authors of the greatest reputation in all ages since. Moreover that this book was well known in England, and enjoined by act of parliament to be taught our children, and that we did teach it to our children, and had been taught it ourselves, when we were children. I ask any Deist, whether he thinks this could pass upon England; And whether, if I should insist upon it, I should not, instead of being believed, be sent to Bedlam?

Now let us compare this with the Stonehenge, as I may call it, or twelve great stones set up at Gilgal, which is told in the fourth chapter of Joshua. There it is said, that the reason, why they were set up, was, that when their children, in after ages, should ask the meaning of it, it should be told them; and the thing, in memory of which they were set up, was such, as could not possibly be imposed upon that nation, at that time when it was said to be done: it was as wonderful and miraculous, as their passage through the Red Sea.

But to return. The passage of the Israelites over Jordan, in memory of which those stones at Gilgal were set up, is free from all those little carpings before mentioned, that are made as to the passage through the Red Sea. For notice was given to the Israelites the day before of this great miracle to be done. It was done at noon day before the whole nation; and, when the waters of Jordan were divided, it was not at any low ebb, but at the time, when that river overflowed all its banks; and it was done, not by winds, or in length of time, which winds must take to do it; but all on a sudden, as soon as the "feet of the priests, that bare the ark, were dipped in the brim of the water, then the waters, which came down from above, stood and arose up upon an heap, very far from the city Adam, that is beside Zaretan; and those, that came down towards the sea of the plain, even the salt sea, failed, and were cut off; and the people passed over right against Jericho. The priests stood in the midst of Jordan, till all the armies of Israel had passed over. And it came to pass, when the priests, that bare the ark of the covenant of the Lord, were come up out of the midst of Jordan, and the soles of the priests' feet were lift upon the dry land, that the waters of Jordan returned unto their place, and flowed over all his banks, as they did before. And the people came up out of Jordan on the tenth day of the first month, and encamped in Gilgal on the east border of Jericho; and those twelve stones, which they took out of Jordan, did Joshua pitch in

Gilgal. And he spake unto the children of Israel, saying, when your children shall ask their fathers in time to come, saying, what mean these stones? Then shall ye let your children know, saying, Israel came over this Jordan on dry land. For the Lord your God dried up the waters of Jordan from before you, until ye were passed over; as the Lord your God did to the Red Sea, which he dried up from before us, until we were gone over. That all the people of the earth might know the hand of the Lord, that it is mighty; that ye might fear the Lord your God forever."

If the passage over the Red Sea had been only taking the advantage of a springtide; how would this teach all the people of the earth, that the hand of the LORD was mighty? How would a thing, no more remarkable, have been taken notice of through all the world? How would it have taught Israel to fear the LORD, when they must know that, notwithstanding all these great words, there was so little in it? How could they have believed, or received a book, as truth, which they knew told the matter so far otherwise from what it was!

But the passage over Jordan, which is here compared to that of the Red Sea, is free from all cavils, that are made as to that of the Red Sea; and is a farther attestation to it, being said to be done in the same manner, as was that of the Red Sea.

Now to form our argument, let us suppose that there never was any such thing, as that passage over Jordan; that these stones at Gilgal were set up on some other occasion, in some after age; and that some designing man invented this book of Joshua, and said that it was written by Joshua at that time, and gave this stonage at Gilgal for a testimony of the truth of it. Would not every body say to him, "we know the stonage at Gilgal, but we never heard before of this reason for it; nor of this book of Joshua? Where has it been all this while? Where and how came you, after so many ages, to find it? Beside, this book tells us that this passage over Jordan was ordained to be taught our children from age to age; and therefore that they were always to be instructed in the meaning of that stonage at Gilgal, as a memorial of it. But we were never taught it, when we were children; nor did ever teach our children any such thing. It is not likely that could have been forgotten, while so remarkable a stonage did continue, which was set up for that, and no other end."

If for the reasons, before given, no such imposition could be put upon us as to the stonage in Salisbury plain; how much less could it be to the stonage at Gilgal?

And, if where we know not the reason of a bare naked monument, such a sham reason cannot be imposed; how much more impossible is it to impose upon us in actions and observances, which we celebrate in memory of particular passages? How impossible to make us forget those passages, which we daily commemorate; and to persuade us, that we had always kept such institutions in memory of what we never heard of before; that is that we knew it before we knew it!

And, if we find it thus impossible for an imposition to be put upon us, even in some things, which have, not all the four marks, before mentioned; how much more impossible is it, that any deceit should be in that thing, where all the four marks do meet!"

Well, unhappy man, you have read the argument of Mr. Leslie for the absolute truth of the things contained in the books of Moses, and I hope you do at least see that believers in revealed religion are not wholly without mind and argument; and that unbelievers do not engross all the reason in the world. How do you meet this? Can you nullify his argument? No, indeed; facts are stubborn things, and the method Mr. Leslie has chosen to establish the truth of them when existing only in record, is equally stubborn. It is said "that Charles Gildon, author of a book called the Oracles of Reason, was convinced of the fallacy of his own arguments against religion, and the danger of his situation, by reading Leslie's book. He afterwards wrote a defence of revealed religion, and died in the Christian faith." But listen to the case of a nobleman who was awakened on his death-bed, and then say whether you are prepared to entertain in life and in death your present views of the scriptures, concerning which we pray God you may change your mind.

"DEAR SIR:—Before you receive this, my final state will be determined by the Judge of all the earth. In a few days at most, perhaps in a few hours, the inevitable sentence will be past that shall raise me to the heights of happiness, or sink me to the depths of misery. While you read these lines, I shall be either groaning under the agonies of absolute despair, or triumphing in fullness of joy.

It is impossible for me to express the present disposition of my soul —the vast uncertainly I am struggling with! No words can paint the force and vivacity of my apprehensions.—Every doubt wears the face of horror, and would perfectly overwhelm me, but for some faint beams of hope, which dart across the tremendous gloom! What tongue can utter the anguish of a soul suspended between the extremes of infinite joy, and eternal misery? I am throwing my last stake for eternity, and tremble and shudder for the important event.

Good God! how have I employed myself? what enchantment hath held me? In what delirium hath my life been past? What have I been doing, while the sun in its race, and the stars in their courses, have lent their beams, perhaps, only to light me to perdition!

I never awakened till now. I have but just commenced the dignity of a rational being. Till this instant I had a wrong apprehension of every thing in nature. I have pursued shadows, and entertained myself with dreams. I have been treasuring up dust, and sporting myself with the wind. I look back on my past life, and but for some memorials of guilt and infamy, it is all a blank—a perfect vacancy! I might have grazed with the beasts of the field, or sung with the winged inhabitants in the woods to much better purpose, than any for which I have lived. And oh! but for some faint hope, a thousand times more blessed had I been, to have slept with the clods of the valley, and never heard the Almighty's fiat, nor waked into life at his command!

I never had a just apprehension of the solemnity of the part I am to act till now. I have often met death insulting on the hostile plain, and, with a stupid boast, defied his terrors; with a courage as brutal as that of the warlike horse, I have rushed into the field of battle, laughed at the glittering spear, and rejoiced at the sound of the trumpet; nor had a thought of any state beyond the grave, nor the great tribunal to which I must have been summoned;

> "Where all my secret guilt had been reveal'd;
> Nor the minutest circumstance conceal'd."

It is this which arms death with all its terrors; else I could still mock at fear, and smile in the face of the gloomy monarch. It is not giving up my breath; it is not being forever insensible, that is the thought at which I shrink: it is the terrible hereafter, the something beyond the grave at which I recoil. Those great realities, which, in the hours of mirth and vanity, I have treated as phantoms, as the idle dreams of superstitious beings; these start forth, and dare me now in their most terrible demonstration. My awakened conscience feels something of that eternal vengeance I have often defied.

To what heights of madness is it possible for human nature to reach? What extravagance is it to jest with death! to laugh at damnation! to sport with eternal chains, and recreate a jovialancy with the scenes of infernal misery!

Were there no impiety in this kind of mirth, it would be as ill-bred as to entertain a dying friend with the sight of an harlequin, or the rehearsal of a farce. Every thing in nature seems to reproach this levity in human creatures. The whole creation, man excepted, is serious: man, who has the highest reason to be so, while he has affairs of infinite consequence depending on this short uncertain duration. A condemned wretch may with as good a grace be dancing to his execution, as the greatest part of mankind go on with such a thoughtless gaiety to their grave.

Oh! with what horror do I recall those hours of vanity which we have wasted together! Return, ye lost neglected moments! How should I prize you above the eastern treasures! Let me dwell with hermits; let me rest on the cold earth; let me converse in cottages; may I but once more stand a candidate for an immortal crown, and have my probation for celestial happiness.

Ye vain grandeurs of a court! Ye sounding titles, and perishing riches! what do ye now signify! what consolation, what relief can ye give me? I have a splendid passage to the grave; I die in state, and languish under a gilded canopy; I am expiring on soft and downy pillows, and am respectfully attended by my servants and physicians: my dependants sigh, my sisters weep, my father bends beneath a load of years and grief; my lovely wife, pale and silent, conceals her inward anguish; my friend, who was as my own soul, suppresses his sighs, and leaves me to his secret grief. But, oh! who of these will answer my summons at the high tribunal? Who of them will bail me from the arrest of death? Who will descend into the dark prison of the grave for me?

Here they all leave me, after having paid a few idle ceremonies to the breathless clay, which perhaps may lie reposed in state, while my soul, my only conscious part, may stand trembling before my Judge.

My afflicted friends, it is very probable, with great solemnity, will lay the senseless corpse in a stately monument, inscribed with,

Here lies the Great———

But could the pale carcass speak, it would soon reply:—

False marble, where?
Nothing but poor and sordid dust lies here!

While some flattering panegyric is pronounced at my interment, I may perhaps be hearing my just condemnation at a superior tribunal; where an unerring verdict may sentence me to everlasting infamy. But I cast myself on his absolute mercy, through the infinite merits of the Redeemer of lost mankind. Adieu, till we meet in the world of spirits."

****

Nothing is so well calculated to convince us of the vast importance of living wholly under the power of the gospel, as seeing great and valuable men dying in such a low and unworthy manner, as many of the first characters of our world have been known to do. The cases of Grotius and Salmasius, of Johnson and Haller, are mortifying instances. Great talents, great learning, great celebrity, are all utterly insufficient to constitute a man happy, and to give him peace and confidence in a dying hour. We know the promises of God are all yea and amen in Christ Jesus: but if the promises be sure, and strongly animating, to the proper objects of them, the threatenings of God are not less infallible, and at the same time are extremely alarming to the proper objects of them. Nothing within the compass of nature can enable a man, with the eyes of a mind properly enlightened, to face death without fear and dismay, but a strong conscious sense, founded on scriptural evidence, that our sins are pardoned, that God is reconciled, and that the Judge of the world is become our friend.

Oh sinner! such is the case of the above unfortunate nobleman. To you I would say, mourn over your aspostacy from God and the scriptures; weep and howl for the misery that is coming upon the world for its transgression; and for the punishment that shall most certainly overtake yourself, if your sentiments in regard to the holy scriptures are not reformed and corrected. The time, the awful time will come, when you will lament that that holy book is now no more; that the salvation which it contains is no longer proclaimed for your acceptance; that the gates of Heaven which it would have opened to you, are now forever barred against you; and that for the light which it imparted, you are now compelled to have your portion in the blackness of darkness forever.

"Sincerely pitying, and ardently praying for the whole generation of those unhappy persons, who have forsaken the only fountain of living waters, and hewn out to themselves broken cisterns, that can hold no water; with the great Bacon we declare, "There was never found in any age of the world, either philosophy, or sect, or religion, or law, or discipline, which did so highly exalt the public good as the Christian faith." With Brown, "We assume the honorable stile of Christian, not because it is the religion of our country, but because, having in our riper years and confirmed judgment, seen and examined all, we find ourselves obliged by the principles of grace, and the law of our own reason, to embrace no other name but this, being of the same belief our Saviour taught, the apostles disseminated, the fathers authorised, and the martyrs confirmed." With Mirandula we rest in the Bible "as the only book wherein is found true eloquence and wisdom." With Robinson, we say, "The scriptures of the Old and New Testaments, contain a system of human nature, the grandest, the most extensive and complete, that ever was divulged to mankind since the foundation of nature." With Grew we profess, that "The Bible contains the laws of God's kingdom in this lower world, and that religion is so far from being inconsistent with philosophy, that it is the highest point and perfection of it." With Hartley we say, that "No writers since the invention of letters to the present times, are equal to the penmen of the books of the Old and New Testaments, in true excellence, utility, and dignity." With Boileau, we say, "Every word and syllable of the Bible ought to be adored: it not

only cannot be enough admired, but it cannot be too much admired."
With Hale, we are clearly of opinion, that "There is no book like the
Bible, for excellent learning, wisdom, and use." With Boyle, we consider
it as "a matchless volume," and believe that "it is impossible we can
study it too much, or esteem it too highly." With Newton, "we account
the scriptures of God to be of the most sublime philosophy." With
Milton we are of opinion "There are no songs comparable to the songs
of Zion, no orations equal to those of the prophets, and no politics like
those which the scriptures teach." With Rousseau, every ingenuous man
may say, "I must confess to you that the majesty of the scriptures
astonishes me, and the holiness of the evangelists speaks to my heart,
and has such strong and striking characters of truth, and is moreover so
perfectly inimitable, that if it had been the invention of men, the
inventors would be greater than the greatest heroes." With Selden, after
having taken a deliberate survey of all the learning among the ancients,
we solemnly profess "there is no book in the universe, upon which we
can rest our souls in a dying moment, but the Bible." And we therefore
boldly declare, before the face of all the unbelieving and disobedient
world, in the words of Chillingworth, "Propose to me any thing out of
the Bible, and require whether I believe it or not; and seem it never so
incomprehensible to human reason, I will subscribe it with hand and
heart; as knowing no demonstration can be stronger than this—"God
hath said so, and therefore it must be true."

But it is not the mere belief and reading of the scriptures which we
would inculcate upon the reader; this is a sort of reformation which he
may indeed stand in need of; but what will the reading of the sacred
oracles avail him if not accompanied by obedience. Change both your
mind and your behavior; turn you from the evil of your way, as the
scriptures command. Let the love of God prevail with you to reform
your life; let the death of Christ influence you to obey the gospel; let the
offers of forgiveness constrain you to become what God would have you
to be; let the immortality which a risen Saviour has brought to light,
inspire you with the love of Heaven; let the judgment which is
predicted, and the awful and eternal fate which awaits every sinful man
on that day, fill you with self-abasement, lest you miss of eternal life,
and be driven away in your iniquity, and share in a punishment which
was not intended originally for any of the sons of men, but for devils
only. Ah! miserable and careless sinner, you stand on the brink of a
precipice, over which, if you fall you will be broken to pieces. You are
like a man walking blindfolded among red hot plough-shares. Your
murderer, the enemy of God and man, waits but to devour. Do you run
all naked and unarmed into the lion's mouth? Do you throw your soul
into the jaws of the crocodile? Will you voluntarily cast yourself into a
den of asps and dragons? Do you of yourself repudiate the Bible, and
put God far from you? Your duty here, as in all matters, may be to you
as medicine; not very sweet in the mouthing; but eat the book, for if

bitter to the taste, it is sweet in the bowels, and like a proper medicament, will heal all the diseases of your soul. Read often, and read till you understand; and read in order to understand. Read to obtain good, not to make and multiply objections, or to pamper your appetite for infidelity. And when you have struggled awhile to break the in crustation which ignorance has thrown over your mind, it will give way at last, and the shell in which your imprisoned mind has been entombed, will burst, and you will find yourself gloriously liberated. Immortality is a noble feast; it is a prize worth contending for; it is a crown worthy of your ambition. Pursue it therefore. It is most certainly attainable through the Christian religion; but this religion must be understood, and it can be understood only by attention to the book in which the Divine God has deposited it. If you are young it will throw around you a veil more precious than a golden veil; if you are in manhood it will give a special and noble direction to all your strength; if you are old it will sanctify all your veneration, and make your gray hairs a crown of glory; for it will direct your steps into the way of peace, and hand you down in joy to the grave. Then when Christ shall appear; when the last trump shall sound the retreat of the universe, and all the stars shall begin their march, and heaven and earth shall flee away, and be no more at all, you shall survive the ruin, "the wreck of matter, and the crush of worlds."

CHAPTER III

Reformation Towards God

It must be taken for granted here that the reader believes there is a God. If he is merely deistical we can reason with him; but if he is atheistical we deem him wholly incorrigible and not to be reasoned with at present. The difficulties, at least a few of them, which atheism has to encounter will be found in the following paragraph, by Doctor Godwin, which being read we shall proceed with our discourse.

"The following may be considered as a brief sketch of what is demanded of any hypothesis which excludes a Creator. It has so much to explain, with reference to the human race, to show us, from the mere properties, how man is what he is, in his body and his mind. The elements of his material structure have nothing peculiar in them; they are just the same as exist in other bodies, in different proportions and combinations. The bones, the muscles, the blood, may all be reduced to their primary elements, and every particle of the human frame may again enter into the composition of other bodies, organized, or unorganized. And yet these elementary bodies make a structure, composed of a number of distinct machines and chemical operations, pervaded by that mysterious principle which we call vital power, and all working to one end. It has, then, to show how, from the earths, the acids, the alkalies, and other substances which abound in nature, such a being as man could be first originated; by what relations, affinities, analogies, such combinations and selections should be made as constitute each particular organ, or limb, or eye, or ear, or hand, for instance—and how all the muscular and glandular formations, with the secretive, digestive, and circulating apparatus, should happen to unite in one individual, and form a system of numberless adaptations, without the interference of any intelligent being, with wisdom to plan and power to execute. It has also to account for the mental phenomena, exhibiting wisdom as great as those which external nature presents, if not surpassing them all; and to show how, from material properties, could result the power of consciousness, memory, imagination; the capability of soaring above thought in nature and beyond time; of generalizing, abstracting, and reasoning in a manner the most acute and profound. Nor is this all; it has to account for the existence of a pair of human beings, coeval with each other, without which there could not have been a second generation.

In addition to this, the atheistic philosophy must explain, without reference to thought or plan, the existence of innumerable tribes of creatures, in the air, and earth, and seas; all professing the most wonderful adaptation of parts, and properties, and instincts, to their peculiar mode of living, and all existing by pairs.

It must also furnish a solution to all the fitting up, and furniture; all the provisions, conveniences, and embellishments of this place of man's abode; how it came to pass so marvelously, that the soils, the minerals, and the plants; the air, the water, the seas, the tides, the dews, and rains; that the days, the nights, the summers, and the winters, are just what a wise and powerful being might have made for man, though no one made those things, or planned them, that there was no design at all in them!

It has, moreover, to expound to us, how all the planets and their secondaries came into being and were arranged into one System; how their forces were adjusted with a precision so marvelous as to assure the most astonishing regularity; and how, in a word, without any design or plan, ten thousand wonders of beauty, order, and utility exist, just as though they were produced by the most benevolent and wise intention. This is but a very brief sketch of what atheism has to perform."

What a prodigious, what a Herculean labor, lays before the atheist before he can reach the fact which goes to explain the philosophy, that the universe, man not excepted, made itself! And that it once did what it never has been able to do again; and though it became its own parent, it never could propagate a single son or daughter; or give the least sign that it lacked a companion by which it might enjoy the pleasure of domestic bliss and see arise a whole progeny of young universes; to the eldest of whom might be given the literary appellation of Athesia Universa, or Athesius Universus, as the case might demand. That any man plunged into a world of order, beauty, and utility like the present, where all above, below and round about us, teams with those works of intelligence, and mind and matter, in all their modifications, attributes, and relations, exist and act for wise and beneficent purposes, should imagine that the whole and its parts has had neither inventor nor maker, but is the work of chance, or fate, or of an innate disposition for the order, beauty, and sublimity which characterize it, residing in it long and forever prior to the time at which it acquired these attributes and was framed into its present state and appearance, is most unaccountable and can be cured in any man, only by the wisdom that comes to him by experience here, or the punishment which shall overtake him hereafter in hades.

Where such good argument abounds against atheism, we add no great names. When facts fail to enlighten and convince, reason is thrown away in the use of it.

But, reader, we suppose you to believe at the very least that there is a God; that he lives who made the heavens and the earth, and that he takes cognizance of the ways of man. The question to be settled with you is this. Do you hold this theoretically—as a bare-naked abstraction, wholly divested of morality, and apart from that course of sobriety, righteousness, and godliness with which it connects itself as a matter of the highest and holiest faith? If you do, your case is still more deplorable than that of the atheist. His defect is in the head, yours is in the heart, and with the faith of a saint or an angel your life is that of a devil, unrighteous, ungodly, dissolute! "You believe that there is one God," say the scriptures? "The devils also believe and tremble!" But you believe it without either fear or love and differing from all devils and angels also, you neither tremble nor obey. Your life is distinguished only for ingratitude and uselessness, and you are in the hand of him who made you as a caries tooth or an ankle out of joint, or a broken reed, or a vessel marred in the hand of him who makes it. Yet you hold to the point of honor and would be esteemed a true man. Ah! friend, be you rich or poor, believe me that when your honor and true manhood comes upon the carpet, those who admit them as sterling, however current in the market of the world, are but poor judges truly. Are you willing to have them tried by the Judge of all the earth? Would you have your reins and heart scrutinized by him whose eyes are flames of fire? Are you willing to be judged by the God in whom you believe and to hear his adjudication of the proposition, that you have recognized his existence and treated him with contempt or neglect?

See the fortunes of the Jews when they became unprofitable to God and failed to answer the moral and religious purposes for which he selected them from among the nations. Where is the noble pillar to his name and his fame, which they once formed in the land of their fathers? Where is that monument of praise, which shone like a pillar of fire in the midst of the surrounding and benighted nations? Its glorious entablature has been smitten and shattered into ten thousand atoms by a thunderbolt launched from the hand of heaven. Its capital has been rent in pieces, and hurled with fury to the ground. He has broken its shaft. He has razed its pedestal and base from the solid ground. Its once more than Corinthian beauty has availed it nothing. It became subservient to evil purposes; or failed to subserve the ends for which he erected it; and now it lies in ruins around the world, the pity or the scorn of all who behold it! Take warning, then, O reader! for if God spared not them, neither will he spare you.

The apostle says of the idolatrous nations, that "When they knew God they glorified him not as God, neither were thankful; but became vain in their own imaginings; esteeming themselves wise, they became fools; and changed the glory of the incorruptible God into an image." &c. This is your case partly. When you know God, you do not glorify him as God. You are unthankful. This is enough. If you are unthankful, your honor, your manhood are contraband, let men praise them as they may. Your character is not good in law, God's law, let the world admire it every so much. You may not, like these nations, change the incorruptible God into an image. But your course is precisely that of those who introduced image worship, and all its train of disgusting and licentious morals. The difference between you and the ringleaders of idolatry is that the times and circumstances do not afford you what they afforded to them, viz: a favorable opportunity of lending your influence to polytheism and image worship. But to make this plain to you, miserable man, I ask what barrier your feeble faith would oppose to any attempt to introduce polytheism and idolatry?—You do not deem your God worthy of that gratitude which you possibly would render to a worm, were it to subserve your purposes. The leach that sucks your blood and thereby renders you a momentary service, you praise and spare; but the God whose existence you acknowledge, partakes not in any degree, even with the leach of this your kindliest feeling. You play the insensate part of the man who praise the works of Reubens, Angello, and Reynolds, without ever once paying a direct tribute to the sublime genius of those spirits to whom they owe their origin. Yet perhaps you praise your reason and decry revelation. Shame upon such reason. It is as blind as a bat, and unworthy of being followed the one eighth of an inch. It cannot discern the connection between the most glorious faith and the most obvious morality; between the belief of one living and true God, and the gratitude that is due from you to his name. What would you think of the man who, like yourself, had learnt by faith the name of his own mother, and held this piece of information irrespective of the filial piety due to that dear name? We reason, then, only from the greater to the less when we say, "Thou art the man;" for if you forget God, you would forget your own mother who bare you. The ancients were wont to say that if we styled a man ungrateful we styled him every thing that was bad. The reason of this maxim is found in the experience of mankind; for the man who is guilty here, is prepared to become guilty of every other immorality: and if you are wandering in the mists of error and impurity, we pray you to halt, review your course, and perhaps you will discern that your deplorable fortunes, or your criminal conduct, is referable ultimately to nothing beyond this that you know God and glorify him not as God; neither are thankful."

Are you aware of the infinite price that has been paid by the best men on earth to preserve to you the faith which fills your head but never touches your heart, that you hold in word, but honor not in deed, which you profess in theory, but deny in practice; which, like an instrument, you hold in your hand without applying it to the purposes for which it is designed?—"They were tortured not accepting deliverance; others had trials of cruel mockings and scourgings, yea, moreover, of bonds and imprisonment. They were stoned, they were sawn asunder, were tempted, were slain with the sword: they wandered about in sheep-skins and goat-skins; being destitute, afflicted, tormented, (of whom the world was not worthy,) they wandered about in deserts and in mountains, and in dens and caves of the earth: these all obtained a good report through faith." The world was unworthy of them, but the world is not unworthy of you; in the grandest point of view, you are unworthy of it. You know your duty and you do it not. If you know it not, you are only the more guilty; you should have known it long ago. The will of the Eternal, in whose existence you believe, has been in letter for seventeen centuries; and as your own legislators make no allowance for ignorance, in cases of high crimes and misdemeanor, neither does God.

Prepare, therefore, to meet your God, Oh sinful man! And learn from the following, that the faith which you hold so lightly and irreligiously, has not been so miserably dealt with by men of nobler mould than yourself:

"Soon after Adam and Eve were driven from the celestial paradise, the spirit of persecution began to make itself known in the world. Of this we have a lamentable account given us by Moses. Abel, a man much approved of God, was the first martyr who fell a sacrifice to the envy and cruelty of his brother Cain. Afterwards commenced the persecution of Noah by his son Ham; the persecution of Lot at Sodom; and of Joseph by his brethren. Thus do we see the very first ages of the world marked with the blood of those who loved God and righteousness.

In these early ages, the first general persecution may he deemed that of the children of Israel by Pharaoh. This inconsiderate tyrant not only afflicted both sexes of all ages by means of the most cruel task-masters, but even ordered the new-born infants of the Hebrew women to be put to death. He was, however, overtaken in his mad career, and severely punished for his persecutions; first by ten dreadful plagues, and afterwards by being swallowed up with all his host in the Red Sea. After the destruction of Pharaoh and his army, the children of Israel, it is true, were happily freed from their oppressor's yoke; but were successively persecuted by the Philistines, Ammonites, Egyptians, Ethiopians, Arabians and Assyrians; and many of the holy ones of God were persecuted by several of the kings of Judea and Israel. The three holy children were thrown into the burning fiery furnace by Nebuchadnezzar. Daniel was by the order of Darius thrown among the hungry lions; and Mordecai was persecuted by the malicious Haman; but these were all freed by the hand of the Almighty, and their persecutors punished for their perfidy.

The Jews were persecuted by their idolatrous neighbors during their building and fortifying the city of Jerusalem, till that much famed work was finished by the care of Nehemiah; but after the city was finished, they were frequently disturbed by the Persians and the successors of Alexander the Great, though that monarch himself had granted the most unlimited favors.

Antiochus Epiphanes now reigning in Syria, and having some success against the Jews, went to Jerusalem, where he ordered Eleazer the priest to be put to death, in the most cruel manner, for refusing to eat swine's flesh. Then seizing on a family of Maccabees, consisting of a matron named Salamona, and her seven sons, he carried them all to Antioch. He would fain have persuaded them to embrace his idolatry, which they nobly and unanimously refusing, he ordered them all to be put to death.

Maccabeus, the eldest son, was accordingly stripped, stretched on a rack, and severely beaten. He was next fastened to a wheel, and weights hung to his feet till his sinews cracked. Afterwards his tormentors threw him into a fire till he was dreadfully scorched; then they drew him out, cut out his tongue, and put him into a frying-pan, with a slow fire under it, until he died. As long as he had life and power of expression, under these exquisite torments, he fervently called upon God, and exhorted his brothers to a similar perseverance.

After, the second son, had his hands fastened with chains, with which he was hung up, his skin flayed off from the crown of his head to his knees. He was then cast to a leopard, but the beast refusing to touch him, he was suffered to languish until he expired, with the excruciating pain and loss of blood.

Machir, the third son, was bound to a globe until his bones were all dislocated; his head and face were then flayed, his tongue cut out, and being cast into a pan, he was fried to death.

Judas, the fourth son, after having his tongue cut out, was beat with ropes, and then racked upon a wheel.

Achas, the fifth son, was pounded in a large brazen mortar.

Areth, the sixth son, was fastened to a pillar with his head downwards, slowly roasted by a fire kindled at some distance; his tongue was then cut out, and he was lastly fried in a pan.

Jacob, the seventh and youngest son, had his arms cut off, his tongue plucked out, and was then fried to death.

They all bore their fate with the same intrepidity as their elder brother, and called upon the Almighty to receive them into Heaven.

Salamona, the mother, after having in a manner died seven, deaths in beholding the martyrdom of her children, was, by the tyrant's order, stripped naked, severely scourged, her breasts cut off, and her body fried till she expired.

The tyrant who inflicted these cruelties was afterwards struck with madness; and then his flesh became corrupted, and his bowels mortified, which put an end to his wicked life."

In nature you see and recognize the divine power, wisdom, and goodness, in the scriptures you must search for his will.—These excellent spirits, of whom you have just been reading, all sacrificed themselves for the reverence which they entertained for his glorious authority. Do you imitate them. Do you become emulous of their renown. You see to what exalted fame they have been raised. Their names stand upon the pages of the Bible, monuments of praise to that faith which you hold; that there exists one, living, and true God. But you argue that his will is not so easily discerned; that the scriptures have been doubted, denied, abused; and that, therefore, the eternal life and future judgment, which they inculcate, are difficult of comprehension.

"It is said that God created man of the dust of the earth, and that he formed Eve of a rib from Adam's side. This, as it stands is a sublime lesson of God's power and our humble origin, and of the common incorporate nature of man and woman; But if you go to task your powers of comprehension, you are punished for your presumption by the arid scepticisms and barrenness of heart which comes over you. Make man of dust? we soliloquize, How is that? Of dust we can make the mould or form of man, but what is baked clay to living flesh and conscious spirit? Make it in one day?—These thousand fibres, more delicate than the gossamer's thread—these thousand vessels, more fine than the discernment of the finest instruments of vision—these bones, balanced and knit and compacted so strongly—these muscles, with their thousand combinations of movement—this secret organization of brain, the seat of thought, the eye, the ear, the every sense, all constructed out of earth, and in one day? This stately form of manhood, which requires generation and slow conception, and the milky juices of the mother, and ten thousand meals of food, and the exercise of infinite thought and actions, long years of days and nights, the one to practise and train, the other to rest and refresh the frame, before it can come to any maturity— this is to be created in one day out of primitive dust of the ground? Impossible! unintelligible! And if we go farther into the thing, and meditate that seeing there was no second act of God, this creation out of dust was not of one man and one woman, but of all men and all women that have been and are to be for ever; that it was virtually the peopling of all nations and kingdoms of the earth in one day out of inanimate dust —who can fathom the work? It is inconceivable, idle, and not worthy a thought. Thus the mind becomes the dupe of its own inquisitiveness, and loseth all the benefits of this revelation.

Not less out of the comforts of Providence have I seen the wisest men beguiled by the nicety and importunateness of their research. They have reasoned of the multitude of God's avocations throughout the peopled universe, in every star imagining the centre of some revolving system, in every system, the dwelling-place of various tribes of beings, until they had the Almighty so occupied as neither to have time nor care for our paltry earth. And if you can fix their attention upon the earth, they do straitway so overwhelm themselves with the myriads who dwell thereon, and their own insignificant place amongst so many, that they cannot see the small part of his providence which can be afforded unto them; and thus, from prayer, from trust and hope of future bliss, they escape into a heartless indifference and a wreckless independence towards their Creator; all which ariseth from their subdividing, by accurate calculation, the great work which God hath to do, without, at the same time, multiplying the power of the Almighty to discharge it all, untroubled and undisturbed. I could show equally fatal results wrought by the same unrestrained appetite for speculation in the great work of redemption, but it would lead me away too far from the scope of the argument.

Now as in creation I pretended not to unfold the methods of bringing all things into being and harmonious action, neither in providence to disclose the means for dealing out to them day by day, those supplies of nourishment and power by which their being and their action are sustained; no more do I undertake to unfold the forms of process, by which, in the last dread day, the Almighty Judge will deal out to each mortal the measure of his deserving or delinquency; being convinced that from any such attempt there would come up over my mind a mist thicker than that which covered the land of Egypt, in the midst of which I should wander like the sinful men of Sodom. But will I therefore abide from skeptical men any derision or scorn to be cast upon this solemn affair? Never. The mole who worketh his little gallery under the ground, may as well pretend to understand the minings and counterminings of a mighty army; the New Holland savage may as well pretend to understand the noble forms of a British Assize by his own club-law administration, as may vain man, though educated in these enlightened times, pretend to understand the forms of the Almighty procedure of judgment. Nor are these perplexities to be resolved by any supply of intelligence, for we shall never be able to understand any of the works of God; but they are rather to be carried off by meditating upon the magnitude of the Almighty's power and wisdom to do all the pleasures of his will. As to founding skepticism or disbelief upon this incompetency of our conception, it is the height of weakness and ignorance; seeing there is not one single case in which conception does not suffer the same eclipse, and calculation the same confusion of their powers when they would essay to contend with any other doings of the Lord. Let them endeavor to reckon up the number of mouths which he sustains in the various animal tribes; or the number of organs which go by their healthy operation to continue the well-being of each,—the fibrous sinews, the cellular folds, the pipes and channels through which life's fluids are diffused. Let them reckon up the number of seeds which he generates every year for their sustenance, or the many-webbed structure of one single plant. Let them tell the number of imaginations which the indwelling soul can conceive, the rate at which they speed through the provinces of time and space, the number of past impressions, which lie treasured in the mind, and the number of hopes and wishes which it sendeth scouting into the portentous future. Let them fathom the depth of space, and circumnavigate the outward bounds of creation, and bring home the number of stars through all the glorious galaxies and the milky way of heaven,—and sum the number of living things, vegetable, animal and rational, which are found under the dominion of God; and they shall find how utterly unequal is the task when the powers and faculties of man would cope with any one of the works of Almighty God.

Now, if by one word of his mouth he could create the subtle and pervading light, and by another carpet the chaotic earth with green and fragrant beauty, and by a third replenish all its chambers with living, creatures, and by a fourth beget the winged fancy and creative thought of man; since which day of wondrous birth-giving, creation hath stood strong and steadfast, and procreation gone on successive, and will continue so to do, the astronomers demonstrate and the naturalists declare, until the same powerful word interfere to shake and overthrow it all—who, can misgive of the ability of God in one day of judgment to review all the effects which one day of creation did originate and to organize a new constitution of things which shall be stable and everlasting as this in which we have our present abode. It seemeth to me, that what we call the day of judgment, we shall thereafter call the day of second creation, on which God launched our being anew, and furnished our voyage of existence, the second time; and it may be recounted by us in one short chapter, at the beginning of the sacred annals, even as our creation is recounted in the Bible; and prove to us, when it is past, as incomprehensible a work as it now doth seem to us, looking forward, or as creation seemeth to us, looking backward; and, though, incomprehensible, be as present to our feelings and our observations as the objects of creation are, and as demonstrative of God's justice as creation is demonstrative of his power."[11]

In our former chapter, we reasoned with you for the scriptures; must we again reason with you for the matter of the scriptures? Must the Divine God not only prove his revelation, but prove it also to be just what your unenlightened sagacity would have it to be? Be assured, and in this assurance rest contented, that Revealed Religion is precisely what your own condition, and that of all men required it to be. It is a religion of facts, and pitches itself and prefers its blessings to men on the best of principles, and the only principle on which any thing can be accomplished in regard to man with his Maker. All its blessings also, are what you need. You stand in great need of forgiveness; for unless you are wholly unlike all other men, you are a miserable sinner. I beg you not to be deceived on this point; let not your education good, bad, or indifferent, impose upon you the cheat, that you do not require to be pardoned.—Let not your profession, whether learned or vulgar, literary or mechanical, fool you on so cardinal a point. Let not property, let not riches, or mental superiority, or domestic or political worth and distinction deceive you in regard to the paramount necessity of the remission of your sins. Let not the praise of men and your success in the business of life, inflame your imagination and deceive your heart. Forgiveness is promulgated by the command of the Everlasting God, for the faith of all nations, and you are a fool if you believe it not, and doubly so if you receive it not.

---

[11] Irving.

But a spirit of grace is offered in the Bible, and this also yon need. Doubt it not; you most assuredly need it. Your present earthly ambitions are not eternal; and your lust of fame, and wealth, and power, is unworthy of immortality. It is not the vicious scions of corrupted trees that are to be transplanted into the Paradise of God. Here is the place for culture and improvement. If the gospel and the church of God in the present life fail to exalt your character, never, never will you flourish and bear fruit hard by the oracle of God and streams of life in Heaven. "Now is the accepted time; now is the day of salvation." "To day if you will hear my voice," says God, "harden not your heart."

Have you no desire for immortality? Is the doctrine thereof unsuited to your gust? Is it vapid and without taste to you? Surely you need it, if you understand the first principles of human nature and have any turn for observation, you must see that you need it. Is not the present life a mere fleeting show, an illusion, a dream, fugitive as the plastic dew-drop that hangs on the thorn and glitters under the influence of the sun that lends it light only to die, and fills it with a glory and beauty which it is unable to sustain?

Now God speaks to you by a book containing all these excellent and necessary doctrines. The holy scriptures are the source whence flows this life, and light, and joy.

"Madam Dacier in the preface to her translation of Homer, assures us that, "the books, of the Prophets and the Psalms, even in the vulgate, are all full of such passages, as the greatest poet in the world could not put into verse, without losing much of their majesty and pathos."

"Next to astronomy, few subjects expand the human mind more than the view which prophecy opens to us of the government of the great King. To see the vast mass of materials, kingdoms and countries, in motion, only to the accomplishment of his purposes: to see refractory man employed to preserve the harmony of his designs; and the disorderly passions, while apparently working solely in their own narrow circle, ignorantly advancing the fulfillment of his determinations! This is a study delightfully interesting, and which, in common with the contemplation of all the Great Creator's doings, elevates the mind above the oppression of human cares and sorrows, and seems to leave her in that serenity of admiration, which one may imagine an imperfect foretaste or part of the employment and happiness of angels."

Cowley tells us, that "all the books of the Bible are either already most admirable and exalted pieces of poesy, or are the best materials in the world for it."

Blackmore says, that "for sense, and for noble and sublime thoughts, the poetical parts of scripture have an infinite advantage above all others put together."

Prior is of opinion that "the writings of Solomon afford subjects for finer poems in every kind, than have yet appeared in the Greek, Latin, or any modern language."

Pope assures us, that the pure and noble, the graceful and dignified simplicity of language is no where in such perfection as in the scripture and Homer; and that the whole book of Job, with regard both to sublimity of thought and morality, exceeds beyond all comparison the most noble parts of Homer."

Howe, after having read most of the Greek and Roman histories, in their original languages, and most that are written in English, French, Italian, and Spanish, was fully persuaded of the truth of revealed religion, expressed it upon all occasions, took great delight in divinity and ecclesiastical history, and died at last like a Christian and philosopher, with an absolute resignation to the will of God.

There are few anecdotes of our English poets which give more pleasure than that of Collins, who in the latter part of his mortal career, "withdrew from study, and traveled with no other book than an English Testament, such as children carry to school." When a friend took it into his hand, out of curiosity to see what companion a man of letters had chosen—"I have one book only," said Collins, "but that is the best."

This knits my heart to Collins more than all the excellencies of his poetry. Sick and infirm, in the spirit of Mary, he sits at the divine Redeemer's feet, listening to the words of eternal life. In such a state of body and mind, one single promise, from his gracious and infallible lips, is of more real value and importance, than all the pompous learning of the most celebrated philosophers. This will never be properly felt and understood till we are in similar circumstances."

But why did Hervey, and Collins, and Rowe thus esteem the scriptures? Because they believed them to be of God, and they felt their salvation and impressiveness on their own souls. They perceived that nothing but Deity could give such weight and ponderous significance to an oracle which disclaimed all connection with the philosophy and philosophers of this world, and recognised none but the feeblest of men as instruments of its delivery. The Bible has God for its father. It has been born of Him by the ministrations of the feeblest of men, the apostles and prophets; and these excellent moderns, named above, discovered this. They had sense and fidelity enough to discern it. But you cannot discern, or will not avow it; you plead weak-headedness as an apology for not acknowledging the Bible as the word of God.

Will you now barter away your interest in this book? Are you willing to part with it as voluntarily as you would part with the Koran of Mahomet? You say no. Heaven bless you! It is possible there still lurks in your soul the indelible elements of maternal instruction; perhaps the sad remains of the golden lessons of a dear mother are yet there. Will you labor to extinguish the sacred spark? Heaven forbid it. Let it rather kindle into a flame, a sacred flame, that shall burn up all things within you contrary to God and righteousness.

Is there, then, O fellow man! is there in existence a God, infinite in power, infinite in wisdom, and of unlimited goodness, and you have failed to improve the fact? Does he live who laid the foundations of the earth, and meted out the heavens with a span, and are you regardless of his authority? "Do you not know, have you not heard, hath it not been told you from the beginning, have you not understood from the foundation of the world, that it is he who sitteth upon the circle of the earth, and the inhabitants thereof are as grasshoppers; that stretcheth out the heavens as a curtain, and spreadeth them out as a tent to dwell in; who bringeth princes to nought, and maketh the judges of the earth as vanity?" O miserable man! you have slighted the most excellent wisdom; you have put far from you the sublimest knowledge, if you are without the knowledge of God and his son Jesus Christ. What are all your acquisitions in the things that are made, if you are still ignorant of their peerless Maker? "The fear of the Lord is the beginning of wisdom; and the knowledge of the Holy One that is understanding." What would be your judgment of him who, on being admitted to the presence-chamber of an earthly prince, should occupy himself wholly with gazing on the riches of the apartment, without once deigning even a respectful homage to the monarch in whose presence he had the honor to stand? Would you not condemn his vulgarity, and arraign him as utterly destitute of the sensibility of a man? You are the man. You have been admitted to the very footstool of the Almighty, for "the earth is his footstool." But you have not yet even beheld the throne, nor God that sitteth thereon. The "table," which his bounty has spread for you, has become "a snare and a trap" to you; you have not recognised "the hand that feeds you;" you have not given God thanks. "God is not in all your ways." Miserable sinner! You have been admitted to the palace of the King of Kings, and but the carpeting beneath, with its endless garniture, and the star-spangled canopy above, with its boundless amplitude, alone have attracted your gaze. You have had no admiration to bestow upon the monarch himself. You have not even recognised his presence. Your ways have been as those of a brute before him. You have stretched your inquiries to the heavens upward, and pried into the heart of the earth, and to the bottom of the deep downwards, and forgotten God your

Maker. Vain man! You have not yet learned the first letter in creation's alphabet; the most obvious knowledge, which the viable things of him from the beginning of the world have clearly taught, "even his eternal power and Godhead" you have failed to discern. Your eyes, like those of a fool, "have been in the ends of the earth." Unjudging man! It is with you "as when a hungry man dreameth and behold he eateth, but he awaketh and behold his soul is empty; or as when a thirsty man dreameth and behold he drinketh but he awaketh and behold he is faint and his soul hath appetite." This will be your portion on the resurrection morn. You will be faint; your soul will be empty.

Ignorance of God is a heinous sin. It is said, therefore, that at the revelation of our Lord Jesus Christ, with his holy angels inflames of fire, he will execute vengeance on "those who know not God."

Nature with ten thousand voices chants the praises of the Almighty. She speaks to us concerning the great Creator by ten thousand tongues. She whispers to us of his love in every gale that blows; she murmurs to us his beauty in every brook that flows. She beckons us away from meaner things by every tree that waves its top in Heaven; and by every hill that heaves its shoulders broad on high would lift us up to God. She has set our light by day in the heavens, and our lamp by night in the skies, that we might stand upright and look upward, and seek the Father of light, if happily he may be found, "though he is not far from every one of us, for we are his children." But you, miserable man, are deaf to the voice of nature when she speaks and praises him who made her; whether she whispers his love in the gale, or thunders his power in the seas, you are deaf; whether she beckons you away to the heavens, or would exalt you to the stars, you are obstinate. When God thunders in the heavens—when his lightnings enlighten the world, you see him not, you hear him not. When he rends the heavens, and comes down and flies on the wings of the wind, you are yourself, you are alone. When he drives full upon us with all the riches of the year, and the horn of plenty is emptied around the land, your heart is untouched. Insensate man! When he gives you the rest of winter, and gladdens the tedious day by his innumerable dainties, you are still ungrateful. Your bite and your bed are unblest. You have prided yourself in possessions, and the number of your acquisitions, "and know not that you are wretched, and miserable, and poor, and blind, and naked." You have boasted of your discernment, and the pride of letters has been upon you; not knowing that "he taketh the wise in their own craftiness, and renders vain the wisdom of the wise." You have established yourself in the land, and raised your head on high like a tree. You are full of blossoms. You shine like the starry chestnut among the trees of the forest; but He whom you know not will reach you. He will lop off your boughs, and cut you down, and hew you in pieces, and burn you as fuel in the fire. What iniquity have you or your fathers found in God, that you should flee from the knowledge of him? Has he not been their Father, and your Father? Yes; he has made you, and sustained you in life, and blest you, and been a blessing to you? Yet you question his existence; thoughtless man! Ungrateful man! "Who knoweth not the Most High, who turneth away from following the God of his fathers. What has he not borne with in you and in them since the day he took us from the slough of idolatry in which we wallowed? Good God! the Most High has suffered infinite insult! We Gentiles have made ourselves as vile as the dirt of the street before him. Methinks if the bed of the Atlantic were emptied, it could not contain the horrible insults which have been offered to the Almighty by the modern world. From Rome the centre of sin, to the Lybian desert south, to the Euphrates eastward, to the North Cape northward, and to the Andes westward. Christendom has poured forth heaven-ward a flood of shameful blasphemy that would disgrace hades itself. O man, who read my book; if you be a man, and not a brute like other men, go to your knees, fall upon your face, prostrate yourself before God your Maker, humble yourself in the dust, be clothed with self-abasement as with a garment, to think yourself a man living in a Christian land ignorant of the God who made you. Tell him you are ashamed; that you are pained with your own ingratitude; that your sins have gone over your head; that while the true light shines you have been walking in gross darkness; take with you his own words, and he will have mercy upon you; plead with him by his own terms, and he will abundantly pardon. Say I have been "wicked," but I turn from my "ways," I have been "unrighteous" but I turn from my "thoughts." Lord have mercy upon my soul, and cut me not off in the midst of my days.

But no, you "refuse the knowledge of the Most High, and will none of his ways." You promise yourself that the ignorance of God which you cherish, shall yet fill the earth; that all men will yet be equally brutish with yourself; that your darkness will yet cover the earth, and that your own obstinacy and impenitence will fill the world!

Vain man! read the following and mark the vanity of all natural and literary greatness when unsanctified by faith in God and the Christian religion.

"The account which the celebrated Sully gives us of young Servin is uncommon. "The beginning of June, 1623," says he, "I set out for Calais, where I was to embark, having with me a retinue of upwards of two hundred gentlemen, or who called themselves such, of whom a considerable number were really of the first distinction. Just before my departure old Servin came and presented his son to me, and begged I would use my endeavours to make him a man of some worth and honesty; but he confessed he dared not hope, not through any want of understanding or capacity in the young man, but from his natural inclination to all kinds of vice. I found him to be at once both a wonder and a monster; I can give no other idea of that assemblage of the most excellent and most pernicious qualities. Let the reader represent to himself a man of genius so lovely, and an understanding so extensive, as rendered him scarce ignorant of any thing that could be known; of so vast and ready a comprehension, that he immediately made himself master of what he attempted; and of so prodigious a memory, that he never forgot what he had once learned; he possessed all parts of philosophy and the mathematics, particularly fortification and drawing: even in theology he was so well skilled, that he was an excellent preacher whenever he had a mind to exert that talent, and an able disputant for and against the reformed religion indifferently; he not only understood Greek, Hebrew, and all the Languages which we call learned, but also the different jargons of modern dialects; he accented and pronounced them so naturally, and so perfectly imitated the gestures and manners both of the several nations of Europe, and the particular provinces of France, that he might have been taken for a native of all or of any of these countries; and this quality he applied to counterfeit all sorts of persons, wherein he succeeded wonderfully; he was, moreover, the best comedian and greatest droll that perhaps ever appeared; he had a genius for poetry, and had written many verses; he played upon almost all instruments, was a perfect master of music, and sung most agreeably and justly; he was of a disposition to do, as well as to know, all things: his body was perfectly well suited to his mind, he was light, nimble, dexterous, and fit for all exercises; he could ride well, and in dancing, wrestling, and leaping, he was admired: there are not any recreative games that he did not know; and was skilled in almost all the mechanic arts. But now for the reverse of the medal: here it appeared that he was treacherous, cruel, cowardly, deceitful; a liar, a cheat, a drunkard and glutton: a sharper in play, immersed in every species of vice, a blasphemer, an atheist; in a word in him might he found all the vices contrary to nature, honour, religion, and society; the truth of which he himself evinced with his latest breath, for he died in the flower of his age, in a common brothel, perfectly corrupted by his debaucheries, and expired with a glass in his hand, cursing and denying God."

It is evident from this extraordinary case, that "with the talents of an angel a man may be a fool."—There is no necessary connection between great natural abilities and religious qualifications. They may go together, but they are frequently found asunder."

Hear, now, reader, the words of Him that is holy, of Him that is high, the Lord of Hosts is his name; he spreads out the heavens as a curtain in the night, and fills the day with glory; there is no God besides him; hear, I pray you, his words to his people of old. "Say ye to the righteous that it shall be well with him,—Woe unto the wicked, it shall be ill with him; for the reward of his hands shall be given him." Harken to his words, you covetous ones, who live that you may eat, that you may increase your stores and heap up to yourselves riches, and feast your hearts. This is the word of the Lord to you, "Woe unto them that join house to house, that lay field to field till there be no place, that they may be placed alone in the midst of the earth."

Hearken to this, you drunkards, against whom God has a controversy that shall end but in your destruction; "the Lord of Hosts is his name;" and this is his word to you, "Woe unto them that rise up early in the morning, that they may follow strong drink, that continue until night, till wine inflame them, and the harp and the viol, the tabret, the pipe and wine are in their feasts; but they regard not the work of the Lord, neither consider the operation of his hands. The mean man shall be brought down, and the mighty man shall be humbled, and the eyes of the lofty shall be humbled, and the Lord of Hosts shall be exalted in judgment, and God, who is holy, shall be sanctified in righteousness.

There are many miserable sinners among the people; who call out for evidence of the truth of the Christian Religion; who are full of pride and vanity; who snuff at the Christian salvation as at an unwholesome odour, and speak of redemption as if it were condescension in them to listen to the words of the Most High. Hearken unto His message to such and to those who provoke God. "Woe unto them that draw iniquity with cords of vanity and *drag after them* sin as with a cart rope! that say let him make speed, let him hasten his work, that we may see it, and let the counsel of the Holy One of Israel draw nigh, and come to pass that we may know it!" Ungodly men! How long will you insult the Lord that bought you? How long will you provoke the Father of our Lord Jesus Christ? Your conduct causes the land to mourn. It trembles from the one end of it to the other on account of your rebellion and transgression.

There is amongst us a class of men with pretentious to science, a *mungrel literati* who have divorced religion from knowledge, and the fear of God from all their wisdom; who search the earth and the sea for their hidden stores, and forget the most obvious wisdom and the most excellent knowledge, the fear of God and the salvation of their own souls. To such then is the word of the Lord. "Woe unto them that are wise in their own eyes, and prudent in their own sight!!" Yes, this is the word of Him that is true, of Him that is just, for he taketh the wise in their own craftiness.

"Woe unto them that are mighty to drink wine, and men of strength to mingle strong drink, who justify the wicked for a reward and take away the righteousness of the righteous from him; therefore, as the fire devoureth the stubble, and the flame consumeth the chaff, so their root shall be as rottenness and their blossom shall go up as dust. Because they have cast away the law of the Lord of Hosts, and despised the words of the Holy One of Israel."

You immoral magistrates, you plaintiff-men, who take away the righteousness of the righteous and justify the wicked for a reward, read your own doings in the word of the Eternal above quoted, and listen to the fruit of your iniquity; for you the land trembles and is convulsed; by you the anger of the Lord is kindled against us, and his hand is stretched out against us.—Judge righteous judgment, you that occupy the seats of judicature, and know that there is one Judge that is able to save and to destroy.

There be also among us, those who "sell the righteous for silver and the poor for a pair of shoes; who pant after the dust of the earth on the head of the poor, and turn aside the way of the meek, and a man and his father will go in unto the same maid to profane my holy name," saith the Lord. Can it be long well with a people, who practise those profanations, and provoke to anger the Lord by such enormities? No, as God overthrew Sodom and Gomorrah, and poured hell out of heaven upon their polluted abodes, so will he render to all lands the reward of their evil doings.

There be among us also, an indolent and inefficient ministry, who have departed from the wholesome words of the gospel, and who delude the people with their own jargon and the technicalities and subtleties of a systematic theology; who seek to other books than the Bible for their knowledge, and teach the people righteousness by precepts merely human. They are a curse to the land in which they live. They feed upon the people and the sins of the people as men feed upon bread. And you, O man, associate their doings with the truth and authority of our religion. You do greatly err not knowing the scriptures. The Bible is the constant reprover of all such; and is the patron of righteousness, honor, and all fair dealing only. The word of the Lord is clear, enlightening the eyes. To these wicked ministers God says, "What hast thou to do, to declare my statutes or that thou shouldst take my covenant in thy mouth seeing thou hatest instruction, and castest my words behind thee?—When thou sawest a thief then thou consentedst with him, and hast been partaker with adulterers. Thou givest thy mouth to evil and thy tongue frameth deceit. Thou sittest and speaketh against thy brother; thou slanderest thine own mother's son.—These things hast thou done, and I kept silence. Thou thoughtest that I was altogether such a one as thy self; but I will reprove thee and set them before thee. Now consider this, ye that forget God, lest I tear you in pieces, and there be none to deliver. Whoso offereth praise glorifieth me: and to him that ordereth his conversation aright will I show the salvation of God."

Hear this you who "speak vanity every one with his neighbor, with flattering lips and a double heart." The Lord shall cut off all flattering lips and the tongue that speaketh proud things. You say, "With our tongues will we prevail: our lips are our own; who is lord over us?" Now know that "the Lord trieth the righteous; but the wicked and him that loveth violence his soul hateth. Upon the wicked the Lord will rain snares, fire, and brimstone, and a horrible tempest shall be the portion of their cup. For the righteous Lord loveth the righteous; his countenance doth behold the upright." Guard the door of your lips, you who would enjoy the light of God's countenance. Let your conversation be upright, chaste, and holy; cultivate that prolific power in man, the power of speech, in such a manner that it shall bring forth fruit excellent and beautiful. The abominable conversation of the men of these times, is so profane and impure, that their throats and the opening of their mouths are like an opened sepulcher. "With their tongues they use deceit. The poison of asps is under their lips. Their mouth is full of cursing and bitterness. The way of peace they have not known. There is no fear of God before their eyes." Shall they escape then the righteous indignation of God? No verily; He who made you will have no mercy upon you. He will meet you with the sword of vengeance in his hand; he has said, he will rend and tear you where there is none to deliver you out of his hand. Stand in awe, therefore, O sinner, and sin not, commune with your heart upon your bed and be still; these are his injunctions to you. Offer the sacrifices of praises and righteousness and thankfulness, and put your trust in the Most High. Say with the Psalmist, I will love thee, O lord, my strength. The Lord is my rock, and my fortress, and my deliverer; my God, my strength in whom I will trust, my buckler, and the horn of my salvation and my strong tower.

Go to God by Jesus Christ and make confession in his name; acknowledge your evil deeds, your evil words, your evil thoughts. Say that you will reform; that you now cease to do evil; that you now, this instant, stand prepared to do his will; you now feel determined to understand his revelation; and will henceforth from this moment, seek to find it. Lay yourself in the dust before him and acknowledge his high right to command. Say, O Lord, I am the clay; thou art the potter; I have been in thy hands as a vessel marred in the making; cast me not away for my sins. Be not wroth, O, Lord; remember not iniquity; forgive the sins of my youth, I beseech thee. O Lord, hear; O Lord, forgive; O Lord, hearken and save. I have abjured thy word. I have dishonored thy name. I have contemned thy salvation. My days, and weeks, and months, and years have been thrown like a weed away. My childhood has run to waste; cut me not off in the midst of my days. I have drank down the pleasures of life like water. I have feasted myself with the dainties of time. I have brutalized myself before thee by the things of sense, and wholly forgot those of eternity. Be merciful, O Lord; and seeing thou hast brought me to know my own misery and guilt, receive, O Lord, receive the prodigal returned. I cast myself in the dust before thee. I put my finger upon my lips. I say with the leper of old, unclean, unclean, unclean! Is there not forgiveness with thee, that thou mayst be feared; and plenteous redemption that thou mayst be sought after? I now come to thee in prayer. I will go to thy Son in duty. I will obey thy heavenly order. I will hear thy Beloved. At his lips will I learn thy law. Like Mary will I sit down at his feet; for like her have I chosen the better part, the one thing needful, the knowledge of thee the Most High. O Lord, accept thy penitent creature, and cast me not away for mine iniquities: so will I speak thy praises as long as I live. I will publish thy saving mercy by a life void of offence towards God and towards man. All the people shall see it, and shall praise thy redeeming grace. Those who have beheld my wickedness shall rejoice, and extol thy marvelous name: My acquaintances also shall return under covert of thy saving power. My neighbors shall see it and return.

O Lord, hear my prayer, which I proffer to thy great name through Jesus thy Son, wash me in his blood; cleanse me from mine iniquity; by the blood of the Lamb remove from me my sins; for I will not return again to my folly. I will hang by the horns of thine altar; for I am dead in law. O Lord, thy loving kindness is better than life. O Lord, our fathers have told us that in thee are the issues of life; thou hast been the hiding place of thy people in all generations; the fathers trusted in thee and were never put to shame. O Lord God Almighty, have mercy on my soul: Amen.

Then he addressed this similitude to them: what man, amongst you, who has a hundred sheep, if he lose one of them, does not leave the ninety-nine in the desert, to go after that which is lost, till he find it? And having found it, does he not joyfully lay it on his shoulders, and when he is come home, convene his friends and neighbors, saying to them, Rejoice with me, for I have found my sheep which was lost? Thus, I assure you there is greater joy in heaven, for one sinner who reforms, than for ninety-nine religious persons, who need no reformation.

Or what woman, who has ten drachmas, if she lose one, does not light a lamp, and sweep the house, and search carefully, till she find it? And having found it, does she not assemble her female friends and neighbors, saying, Rejoice with me, for I have found the drachma which I had lost? Such joy, I assure you, have the angels of God when any sinner reforms.

He said, also, A certain man had two sons. And the younger of them said to his father, Father, give me my portion of the estate. And he allotted to them their shares. Soon after, the younger son gathered all together, and traveled into a distant country, and there wasted his substance in riot. When all was spent, a great famine came upon that land, and he began to be in want. Then he applied to one of the inhabitants of the country, who sent him into his fields to keep swine. And he desired to appease his hunger with the husks, on which the swine were feeding; for no person gave him any thing. At length, coming to himself, he said, how many hirelings has my father, who have all more bread than suffices them, while I perish with hunger! I will arise and go to my father, and will say to him, Father, I have sinned against heaven and you, *and* am no longer worthy to be called your son. And he arose and went to his father.—When he was yet afar off, his father saw him, and had compassion, and ran, and threw himself upon his neck, and kissed him. And the son said, Father, I have sinned against heaven and you and am no longer worthy to be called your son. But the father said to the servants, Bring hither the principal robe, and put it on him, and put a ring on his finger, and shoes on his feet: bring also the fatted calf, and kill it, and let us eat and be merry; for this my son was dead, and is alive again; he was lost and is found. So they began to be merry.

Now his elder son was in the field, walking home. And as he drew near the house, he heard music and dancing. He, therefore, called one of the servants, and asked the reason of this. He answered, Your brother has returned, and your father has killed the fatted calf, because he has received him in health. And he was angry and would not go in; therefore his father came out, and entreated him. He answering, said to his father, these many years I have served you, without disobeying your command in any thing; yet you never gave me a kid, that I might entertain my friends; but no sooner did this your son return, who has squandered your living on prostitutes, than you killed for him the fatted calf. Son, replied the father, your are always with me, and all that I have is yours: it was but reasonable, that we should rejoice and be merry; because this your brother was dead, and is alive again; he was lost and is found."

Friend, do you fear the God of heaven? There, there is the music and magic of his Son's voice. Do you invoke his tender care, behold it in the parable of the lost sheep. Do you desire to know his estimate of your recovery? See it in the woman and her piece of silver. Do you repent and return, do you cast yourself upon his mercy and gracious parental affection? Behold him in the father of the prodigal. He is all prepared to meet you, to pardon, to embrace, to kiss, to receive, to bless you, and to rejoice in your reformation. Never, never, was there given, by all the wisdom of the world, ancient or modern, so touching, so transforming and reforming a picture of the Divine mercy and love of men as is here given in these simple parables by Jesus Christ our Lord.

Methinks I see the prodigal in the field, all seated on the ground; humbled by the employment into which his poverty has driven him, and exhausted by hunger, he casts a desperate look towards the husks, on which his voracious charge are feeding, and in shame and weakness hides his face between his knees:—at this moment he comes to himself! his guilt in abandoning the family mansion—his father, mother, and kindred dear—his prodigality in wasting his family fortune, his former rank, and present degradation, the former plenty with which his youth was crowned, and his present starvation and exhaustion flash upon him and gall him to the quick. He shudders, and, in the agony of shame and grief that rests upon him, sighs forth, "How many hired servants of my father's have bread enough and to spare, and I perish with hunger!" Tears rush to his relief, and gathering up his noble but enfeebled frame, he clothes himself with a desperate resolution and exclaims, "I will arise! I will go to my father! I will say to him Father I have sinned against heaven and in thy sight: I am no more worthy to be called thy son: make me as one of thy hired servants."

O! I am touched also with the other side of the picture, Behold, the father, the heart-broken father! He leans by the door, and gazes down the lonely avenue of trees which leads to the family mansion; his aged locks stream to the last breezes of the falling year, under whose keen touch the leaves rush thickly to the ground. He is ready to say "Thus passes away the beauty of this world and all things fair below, these leaves once lived—my son also!" when, lo! his attention is arrested by a form uncouthly dressed shrouded in rags. Who is the distant stranger? His excellent form though emaciated with disease and hunger, his noble and well remembered port though in the rags of a swine-herd, tell the father it is his prodigal son returning. He sees him coming; he compassionates him; he runs, he falls upon his neck, he kisses him. "And the son said unto the father, Father, I have sinned against heaven and before thee, and am no more worthy to be called thy son, make me as one of thy hired servants; but the father said to his servants, Bring forth the best robe, and put it on him, and put a ring on his hand and shoes on his feet, and bring hither the fatted calf and let us eat and be merry, for this my son was dead and is alive again; he was lost and is found." Glory to our God, the Father of our Lord Jesus Christ.

But, there is another point of light in which the case of the prodigal is beheld in a still more affecting form; this may be called its divinity or religion, and consists in the design for which it was spoken by the Saviour, viz: to set forth the mercy exercised by God towards penitent and reforming sinners.

Yes, this is the unction of the parable, the inimitable ointment which sanctifies and enhances it in the estimation of the man of God.

> "Man's inhumanity to man
> Makes countless thousands mourn,"

But God, whose name be forever praised, is full of mercy: When there was no eye to pity nor arm to save, in his love and in his pity he redeemed us; he has borne with his people, he carried them all the days of old. His mercy, his tender mercy descends upon us unconstrained from heaven as rain upon the mown grass, and as showers that water the earth: it rests upon the sons of men lovely as the dew upon the tender herb; and is over all his works; praised be his holy name through Jesus Christ our Priest, our Great High Priest.

> His coming like the morning is!
> Like morning songs his voice!

With the mother of my Lord I say, "My soul doth magnify the Lord! My spirit doth rejoice in God my Saviour!" Our fathers were Gentiles: they forsook the God that made them, and worshiped idols—idols of gold, and silver, and wood, and brass and stone: they sunk themselves into the depth of immorality and were full of all unrighteousness; but the Lord in the greatness of his mercy admitted them to a place with his people, and granted them repentance unto life: praised be the name of the Lord, through Jesus Christ our Saviour.

CHAPTER IV

Reformation in Regard to Our Lord Jesus Christ

It is very certain that the Jews were in possession of the Holy Scriptures before the days of Jesus Christ, for before that time the Gentiles themselves were acquainted with them, Ptolemy, one of the Egyptian kings, having caused them, long before that period, to be translated into the Greek tongue by seventy men sent to him by request, from Jerusalem, and to be deposited in the Library of Alexandria. The Christians therefore, did not invent the Bible! In other words the ancient scriptures were in the world before the commencement of the Christian Religion. Thus if the present condition of the Jews does not prove the divinity of their scriptures, these scriptures prove that they themselves, once, and at, and before the beginning of Christianity, were a people enjoying a political rank and name among the nations of the earth. This they do not enjoy now, but are scattered to the four winds of heaven divested of all national rank and even political existence. Do you then, reader, believe that it once was not with the Jews as it is at this day? Do you believe that in the days of the Caesars and of Christ, the Jews lived in Canaan, had Jerusalem for a capital, the temple thereof for their seat of worship, and the scriptures as the book on which that worship was founded? O Yes! you answer, I have the strongest faith in the former nationality of the Jews, and of the Bible being in their possession, long before the commencement of Christianity. Good! This admission will save me the trouble of proving to you two or three things, which otherwise would have needed to be attended to.

First, that if the Bible be a cheat, the Jews, and not the Christians, were the people that imposed it upon the world, as a book containing divine oracles; or they imposed it upon themselves as such before the Christian religion came into existence. This will relieve your mind of one half its burden at least, in regard to Christianity, by assuring you that, if they have imposed the New Testament upon themselves as a book containing divine oracles, this is nothing more than had occurred in the world once before in the case of the Jews, who imposed, as you acknowledge, upon themselves the Old Testament. This will divide your irreligious displeasure between the Jews and the Christians; the latter being obnoxious for their having assumed the New, the former for having assumed the Old Testament as divine Revelation.

Secondly, Your admission of all this proves also, that like all the world besides, you are quite capable of believing a thing when it is proved to you; and not a thing lying immediately before you, or at your feet neither; but a thing which obtained at the distance of nearly half the world's circumference from you, and nearly two thousand years in the past—for it is very nearly that number of years since the Jews enjoyed their own government, and worshipped in Canaan. Perhaps you are already alarmed at the extent of your own admission; perhaps you tremble lest I show that you are very credulous after all your ravings against belief? No wonder; for by your admission, your faith has carried you up the stream of time, and redeemed to you facts long anterior to the appearing of the person on whom my faith terminates. I stop in my Christian belief about the days of the Caesars, and terminate it on the person of the author of Christianity; but you bound onward and upward in your political faith far beyond us, and admit that before, long before the days of our Redeemer, the Jews lived in Canaan, and worshipped God by their Bible in the temple of Jerusalem! But how far beyond us does your historical political faith really stretch itself? Do you believe that the Jews like the other nations were conquered by Alexander; and that they were once captives in Babylon; if you do not admit their prior and more ancient captivity in Egypt? I know you will answer, yes, I admit there is sufficient historic testimony that the Jews were captive in Babylon. Good! Then you admit that there was in existence, nearly three thousand years ago, and flourishing in all the triumphs of war and the riches of commerce, a city named Babylon? Yes. You do not at all doubt this, do you? No, I entertain not the least doubts of this matter. Your faith then reaches beyond ours, you see, one thousand years, or nearly; or, if you will allow us to compare time with extension, as far beyond ours, as Babylon is beyond Jerusalem! Did our Lord Jesus minister in Judea two thousand years ago? Babylon shone in Assyria three thousand years ago. Do you believe the latter of these propositions? Then we believe the former. And there is nothing different in our belief, observe you. Yours is the same as ours; for belief, real belief, is the same in all. The object, the evidence, and the witnesses may differ, but not the faith. The object of your belief, in the case suggested, is a city; ours a person; yours is Babylon; ours is the author of the Christian religion. Here then are two cases, *yours* and *ours*; the one political, the other religious; but both of them known to us only through belief. All that we know of them is but the experience of others transferred into our minds, by the written testimony of those who were eye-witnesses of the subjects in which we believe.

Let us now in a few words compare the two cases in their most striking points—the objects, the witnesses, and the testimony. Of Babylon, not a trace of her existence is left. Her walls, said to be three hundred feet high, are not only crumbled to the ground, but sunk into it, if they ever existed at all, so that the most curious and rational traveler has not been able to pick up a single stone, and say, This was once in the walls of Babylon! The same holds good of her towers and temples, her brazen gates and hanging gardens, her royal palaces, and all her meaner abodes, of which not a trace remains to tell the present generation, or you, "Here stood Babylon." You believe then in a thing that is now a nonentity, and a nonentity too, of whose former existence not one single solitary sensible proof remains. Now if our Lord were in the grave, the object of a Christian's faith would not be less tangible than the object of your faith. If he were yet in the bowels of the earth he could not be less an object of knowledge than is Babylon; for she is as completely lost to present experience, and all human knowledge, as is the person who was entombed two thousand years ago. This then throws you entirely on testimony for what you believe, human testimony. So that you see, for political and historical facts, you are equally dependent on others for their experience and testimony, as the man who believes the gospel.

Observe, reader, I draw no parallel between the city of Babylon and the Redeemer of the world, except in point of identity merely, they are both testified to have existed. Babylon has gone down to hades with all her pollutions, and there let her slumber, till God shall bid her idolatrous millions awake to judgment. To believe that she once lived and shone among the nations with the lustre and resplendency of gold, is not worth one cent to any body; but it is far otherwise with our belief and the object of it; the immediate effects of this is unstained, unspotted, heavenly purity, and in the end eternal life and joys unutterable and heaven and glory. Yes, all this is involved in our faith; and I reason with you only to show you, that no difficulty encumbers the faith which saves the soul, that does not also press with greater weight on any other belief which respects a fact equally distant. You believe in a fact far more distant when you believe in the former existence of the proud city in question.

But to come to the testimony. What are the memorials of the life and death, the rise and fall of Babylon? And where are these memorials to be found? They are to be found on the pages of history. For the portrait of her character, her origin, her decline, and fall, we are indebted entirely to history. Now, we have all this in our case also. For the origin, character, life, and death of the Lord Jesus, is as definitely and distinctly recorded as those of Babylon were by any or all the historians that ever employed a pencil in the delineation of her grandeur and renown. But we have more than this kind of book evidence, for the existence of Jesus Christ. We are not exclusively dependent even on the New Testament for the fact of his having lived and acted the part, which the scriptures say he did. The certainty of his existence is written upon our own manners and customs. We see our own fathers and mothers sitting around a board covered with bread and wine. We ask them what this means. They tell us "It is the Lord's table." We ask who the Lord is. They tell us. We ask again if this custom, of eating bread and drinking wine in memory of his death, was practised by the preceding generation, and by all the generations between the present and the time when Christianity began. They answer in the affirmative. We are incredulous, and more so, as we become older; therefore, we inquire at the voice of history as you do in regard to Babylon, and lo we find the words of our parents and instructors to be true; and that the people called christians have, from the time their religion was first published, publicly eat bread and drank wine in memory of their Master's death. The Lords' Supper then is like a pillar of proof for that which we believe.

"Trajan ascended the throne of the Caesars in the year 98, and soon afterwards conferred the government of the province of Bithynia upon his friend, the ingenious and celebrated Pliny. The character of the latter is one of the most amiable in all pagan antiquity. In the exercise of his office as proconsul, the christians, against whom the severe edicts which had been issued by preceding emperors seem to be still in force, were brought before his tribunal. Having never had occasion to be present at any such examinations before, the multitude of the criminals, and the severity of the laws against them, appear to have greatly struck him, and caused him to hesitate how far it was proper to carry them into execution, without first consulting the emperor upon the subject. The letter which he wrote to Trajan upon this occasion, as well as the answer of the latter, are happily preserved, and are among the most valuable monuments of antiquity, on account of the light which they throw upon the state of the Christian profession at this splendid epoch. The letter of Pliny seems to have been written in the year 106, or 107, and is as follows:

C. PLINY, to the EMPEROR TRAJAN, wishes health. SIRE! It is customary with me to consult you upon every doubtful occasion; for where my own judgment hesitates, who is more competent to direct me than yourself, or to instruct me where uninformed? I never had occasion to be present at any examination of the Christians before I came into this province; I am therefore, ignorant to what extent it is usual to inflict punishment or urge prosecution. I have also hesitated whether there should not be some distinction made between the young and the old, the tender and the robust; whether pardon should not be offered to penitence, or whether the guilt of an avowed profession of Christianity can be expiated by the most unequivocal retraction—whether the profession itself is to be regarded as a crime, however innocent in other respects the professor may be; or whether the crimes attached to name, must be proved before they are made liable to punishment.

In the mean time, the method I have hitherto observed with the Christians, who have been accused as such, has been as follows. I interrogated them—Are you Christians? If they avowed it, I put the same question a second, and a third time, threatening them with the punishment decreed by the law; if they still persisted, *I ordered them to be immediately executed; for of this I had no doubt, whatever was the nature of their religion, that such perverseness and inflexible obstinacy certainly deserved punishment*. Some that were afflicted with this madness, on account of their privileges as Roman citizens, I reserved to be sent to Rome, to be referred to your tribunal.

In the discussion of this matter, accusations multiplying, a diversity of cases occurred. A schedule of names was sent me by an unknown accuser, but when I cited the persons before me, many denied the fact that they were or ever had been Christians; and they repeated after me an invocation of the gods, and of your image, which for this purpose I had ordered to be brought with the statues of the other deities. They performed sacred rites with wine frankincense, and execrated Christ, none of which things, I am assured, a real Christian can ever be compelled to do. These, therefore, I thought proper to discharge. Others, named by an informer, at first acknowledged themselves Christians, and then denied it, declaring that though they had been Christians, they had renounced their profession, some three years ago, others still longer, and some even twenty years ago. All these worshipped your image and the statues of the gods, and at the same time execrated Christ.

And this was the account which they gave me of the nature of the religion they once had professed, whether it deserves the name of crime or error; namely, that they were accustomed on a stated day to assemble before sunrise, and to join together in singing hymns to Christ as to a deity; binding themselves as with a solemn oath not to commit any kind of wickedness; to be guilty neither of theft, robbery, nor adultery; never to break a promise, or to keep back a deposit when called upon. Their worship being concluded, it was their custom to separate, and meet together again for a repast, promiscuous indeed, and without any distinction of rank or sex, but perfectly harmless; and even from this they desisted, since the publication of my edict, in which, agreeably to your orders, I forbade any societies of that sort.

"For further information, I thought it necessary, in order to come at the truth, to put to the torture two females who were called deaconesses. But I could extort from them nothing except the acknowledgment of an excessive and depraved superstition; and, therefore, desisting from further investigation, I determined to consult you, for the number of culprits is so great as to call for the most serious deliberation. Informations are pouring in against multitudes of every age, of all orders, and of both sexes; and more will be impeached; for the contagion of this superstition hath spread not only through cities, but villages also, and even reached the farm houses. I am of opinion, nevertheless, that it may be checked, and the success of my endeavours hitherto forbids despondency; for the temples, once almost desolate, begin to be again frequented—the sacred solemnities, which had for some time been intermitted, are now attended afresh: and the sacrificial victims, which once could scarcely find a purchaser, now obtain a brisk sale. Whence I infer, that many might be reclaimed, were the hope of pardon, on their repentance, absolutely confirmed."

TRAJAN TO PLINY

"My dear Pliny,

You have done perfectly right, in managing as you have, the matters which relate to the impeachment of the Christians. No one general rule can be laid down which will apply to all cases. These people are not to be hunted up by informers; but if accused and convicted, let them be executed; yet with this restriction, that if any renounce the profession of Christianity, and give proof of it by offering supplications to our gods, however suspicious their past conduct may have been, they shall be pardoned on their repentance. But anonymous accusations should never be attended to, since it would be establishing a precedent of the worst kind, and altogether inconsistent with the maxims of my government."

It is an obvious reflection from these letters, that at this early period, Christianity had made an extraordinary progress in the empire; for Pliny acknowledges that the pagan temples had become "almost desolate." Nor should we overlook the remarkable display which they afford us of the state of the Christian profession, and the dreadful persecutions to which the disciples of Christ were then exposed. It is evident from them, that by the existing laws, it was a capital offence, punishable with death, for any one to avow himself a Christian. Nor did the humane Trajan and the philosophic Pliny entertain a doubt of the propriety of the law, or the wisdom and justice of executing it in the fullest extent. Pliny confesses that he had commanded such capital punishments to be inflicted on many, chargeable with no crime, but their profession of Christianity; and Trajan not only confirms the equity of the sentence, but enjoins the continuance of such executions, without any exceptions, unless it be of those who apostatized from their profession, denied their Lord and Saviour, and did homage to the idols of paganism.

These letters also give us a pleasing view of the holy and exemplary lives of the first Christians, For it appears by the confession of apostates themselves, that no man could continue a member of their community whose deportment in the world did not correspond with his holy profession. Even delicate women are put to the torture, to try if their weakness would not betray them into accusations of their brethren; but not a word nor a charge can be extorted from them, capable of bearing the semblance of deceit or crime. To meet for prayer, praise, and mutual instruction; to worship Christ their God; to exhort one another to abstain from every evil word and work; to unite in commemorating the death of Their Lord, by partaking of the symbols of his broken body and shed blood, in the ordinance of the supper—these things constitute what Pliny calls the "depraved superstition," the "execrable crimes," which could only be expiated by the blood of the Christians!"[12]

According to history, Paul the apostle, was put to death in the twelfth year of the reign of Nero, or the sixty-sixth of the Christian era; and Pliny's letter was written in 106, or 107 according to like authority. The difference between these two dates is 40 years; so Pliny's letter carries the Christian supper back to that period from Paul's death. But the apostle John did not die till the beginning of the reign of Trajan, Pliny's patron, that is, he did not die till about the time said letter was written. Thus, the epistle of Pliny carries us fairly down into the age of those men from whom we received the custom of eating bread and drinking wine in memory of Christ's death. But observe that some of the witnesses examined by the governor, confessed that they had been Christians twenty years before the date of the letter; and so we learn from the same document that the rite or institution in question, is that number of years older than Pliny's letter. This goes quite into the centre of the college of apostles, and shows that from their time to the present, the Christians have been attending to this commemorative institution.

But we find our fathers in possession of other institutions, as the Lord's day, baptism, prayers, psalm-singing, teaching, the New Testament, reading the scriptures, and collections for the poor; nay, we see themselves the members of this body of people called the church, and we put the same questions to them in regard to all these things, which we put to them in regard to the commemorative institution, and they answer the same in regard to them all, telling us that they were

---

[12] Jones' Church History.

handed to our fathers by the apostles; And see—Pliny's letter recognizes the existence of the first day of the week. Those whom he examined not only testified, that the Christians eat bread and drank wine, but that they did these things publicly on a certain day; also that they had our custom of singing hymns to Christ; and of pledging themselves to do no unrighteousness. Now here is the existence of the church herself with her most remarkable points of worship, singing to Christ, the Lord's supper, the Lord's day, the public assembling of the brethren on that day, and their doctrine of strict morality, literally recognized.

By this singular letter of the governor of Bithynia, all our remarkable church ordinances are at once carried back to the apostolic age, and thus traced to their proper source, the twelve apostles.

The supper is intended to commemorate our Lord's death, the first day of the week his resurrection.

Now, as that and the other Christian ordinances mentioned, did not originate at a time anterior to the apostles, and the letter and the christians of that age and of all succeeding ones show that they did not originate at a time posterior to the age of Pliny and the apostles, it follows that these apostles are the persons who delivered to the citizens of the Roman Empire, the Christian manners and customs on which we are now attending every first day of the week.

If then the Christians of Pliny's day and for twenty years before it and consequently the apostles themselves among them, were attending to the Lord's supper on the first day of the week, keeping the one in memory of their Master's death, and the other in memory of his resurrection, the only remaining question now is, whether they received them from Christ, or invented them themselves, and wickedly imposed them on the people. Their pure, unstained, and heavenly behavior in all other things shows, that of imposition in this particular, they were morally incapable. The consequence, or other remaining conclusion, is that they, as they said, received them and all other matters of the Christian religion from Christ.

The final question is, whether they could be imposed upon in the matters of his *death* and *resurrection*. To determine this, make the case your own. Could you be imposed upon in regard to the crucifixion of a man, if you saw him nailed to the cross, and a spear thrust into his side, till the blood of his heart poured forth down upon the ground? You answer, no. Well neither could they; for they were men like yourself. Could you be mistaken in regard to the resurrection of the same person, if after three days' interment you should see him again, supposing that for three years previous to his death, you had attended on him day and night? You say, no. Well neither could they; and so the matter ends.

Jesus has arisen from the dead, and consecrated the first day of the week a perpetual memorial of that great event, as before his death he had instituted the Supper in memory of that event; and these two Christian ordinances are with us to this day, pillars, monumental pillars, of the facts which they were intended to commemorate—whose base and summit connect together the first and second coming of their author; for his command is to "*do this*" until he comes again.

The existence of the Lord Jesus, then, is not only determined by the voice of history, as is the case in regard to the former existence and glory of Babylon, in which you believe; but his death and resurrection are established by sensible ordinances, living and speaking forth these events throughout all ages. Now this sort of proof you have not to sustain you in your belief concerning Babylon; which shows, that though your proposition is of an elder date, and lying farther round the world, and thrust into the depths of antiquity almost a thousand years beyond the date of the Christian proposition; yet you have less proof for the truth of it than we have for the truth of our proposition. Now is it thus with you, unhappy sinner, that of the two propositions, you will receive the most ancient, useless, and difficult of belief, on the least evidence; while you reject that one which involves your eternal salvation, and is established by the most, yea, I may say overwhelming evidence; for the moral, miraculous, historic, prophetic, and commemorative proofs of our religion, when taken together, are absolutely overwhelming, and forced faith upon the very masters of science and of the improved philosophy themselves.

And now, reader, who is he whom you oppose, in spurning from you the Christian Religion? He is the God of your fathers, the Eternal God, who has been the refuge of the righteous in all ages, and has spoken to us by the mouth of all the holy prophets, which have existed since the world began. What then will you do in the day of his fierce wrath? He is long suffering and not willing that any should perish, but that all should come to the knowledge of the truth, which he has published concerning Jesus Christ and the day of judgment. Look at God and tremble, be you even one of the great ones of the earth. "Who is this that comes from Edom, with dyed garments from Bozrath? this that is glorious in his apparel, traveling in the greatness of his strength? I that speak in righteousness mighty to save. Wherefore art thou red in thine apparel and thy garments like him that treadeth in the wine-vat? I have trodden the wine press alone, and of the people there was none with me: for I will tread them in mine anger, and trample them in my fury; their blood shall be sprinkled upon my garments and I will stain all my raiment, for the day of vengeance is in my heart, and the year of my redeemed is come. And I looked and there was none to help; and I wondered that there was none to uphold: therefore my own arm brought salvation to me [mine] and my fury it upheld me; and I will tread down the people in mine anger; and make them drunk in my fury, and I will bring down their strength to the earth." Such, rebellious man, whosoever you are, is the protection which will be extended to the lovers of God on that great day; and such are the blood-stained symbols of God's eternal vengeance upon those who trample upon the blood of the great Redeemer. "Their blood shall be sprinkled upon my garments, and I will stain all my raiments, says God, who can destroy and is mighty to save." Turn you, therefore, at his reproof, reader, and acknowledge that he is God alone. Repent you of your evil deeds, and flee from the wrath that is to come. Behold your Redeemer cometh upon the clouds, and every eye shall see him, and they also who pierced him, and all the tribes of the land shall wail because of him. His reward is with him and his work before him, to give to every man according to his works. He will separate the righteous from the wicked, as a shepherd separates the sheep from the goats; a flaming angel shall hew the unprofitable to pieces and cast them into outer darkness there shall be weeping and gnashing of teeth. O how tenfold more dark will the abodes of damnation be to you if you have let the day of God's tender mercy pass away unimproved!

Hear the lamentation of such. The harvest is past and the summer ended, and my soul is not saved. Woe is me! for there is given me to eat the bitter fruit of my own doings: I despised God, mocked the bible, and slighted my Saviour. Undone, undone, undone forever! O! the endless import of the word I utter, forever! long, long, long ruin, misery and ceaseless despair! Gone forever! My soul is shipwrecked. I am broken on a fatal shore, and there is none to Save me. O memory forget the life I once enjoyed! cease to kill me with the reminiscence of a crucified Redeemer! Why torment me with the recollection of knowledge which I despised, and duty which I could not be induced to perform? Why ply me vulture-like with the horrible word pardon, and the multitude of arguments ineffectual to reform? These are more poignant woes than the outward hell I suffer. They are arrows in my soul more sharp and poisonous, than the ruffled flames that beat against my ruined person. Have mercy, and let the recollection of the past be dead forever. But, no, you speak and pierce me through and through without end. Cursed be thy cruelty. Cursed be my folly. Cursed be the day I was born. But there is no day now; my birth-day, like all other days, is gone. The business of the world and time is long ago summed up, and all the saints are home. O the greatness of eternity, the dread and darkness of despair!

What is that I see, blood? No, it is but the phantom of my sleepless imagination. Ah! it is blood; it is the blood—hold, of what? atonement? Good heavens! there is no atonement for me; the day of grace is o'er. I have sinned it away, and am damned forever. O atonement! atonement! atonement! I have trampled upon the blood of atonement and done despite to the spirit of grace, which it was shed to secure. Alone, all alone, on the ocean of eternity! how vast a flood! a sea without a shore! Alone! without the solace of a companion in anguish, tribulation and stormy wrath! Where are those kindred spirits in sin, those equally abominable, and wretched, and abandoned with myself? Is it solitude all? and can he whose justice I have disregarded, whose mercy I have slighted, and whose vengeance I have incurred, appoint so ample a prison-house to every other wretch, as that he has allotted to me? O prison, prison, where are thy bounds? pit of the damned where is thy bottom? shall I thus sink and fall through the blackness of darkness forever? In this element that burns and stings and sifts me through and through, while thus I drive along with a comet's flight and a comet's fierceness, what a mighty storm pursues me! In what a gulf of horror and dismay am I pursued! Is this, then, *outer darkness*? and do such boundless wastes lie beyond the limits of created nature? Surely here is ample space for another universe with all its spheres, even though they wheeled in bulk huge as the sun himself, that once did gladden with his beams these bursting eyes. O that the Almighty would grant me death! but that may never be. I shared in crime with him who cannot die, the apostate angel; and with him must now in endless misery share. He ruined man, and was a murderer; and I, Oh! I approved the deed in scorning him, who came to save us. I have murdered Christ; my abjuration of his all-atoning blood has twice murdered him. I have crucified again the Lord of Glory, and must dying live, and living die through all eternity. Hush! hush! O desolate spirit, list! What is that which comes upon the blast doubling the darkness of hell? It sounds, as if the waters of a globe were poured through the dark profound in which I drive along. What flood-like melancholy! O who can bear it! It overwhelms all other pains besides. But, hold. Is it not fancy all? Surely it was weeping and wailing and gnashing of teeth! but then, so ocean-like, as if the breath of all the damned were on the breeze; the breeze? the storm; the tempest; the stormy tempest of damnation. O Lord! I am affrighted beyond despair, but cannot die. This affrights me more than existence, or pain itself. No gateway; no narrow gate; no exit; but bars of eternal mould are everywhere the bounds and centre of my prison house; for centre and circumference are the same in this abode infernal. Away, away, I fly lightning-like upon the thundergust of wrath, the everlasting punishment prepared for the Devil and his angels. O Lord, have mercy upon my soul!

Who is that, O sinner, that stands at Pilate's bar? Grief and pain extreme have blighted his once excellent form. His face is so marred more than any man, and his form more than the sons of men. They gaze upon him as a worm, and no man. He is the reproach of men and despised of the people. They laugh him to scorn; they shoot out the lip; they shake their heads and say, "He trusted in the Lord that he would deliver him; let him deliver him seeing he delighted in him." Many bulls have encompassed him, the strong bulls of Bashan have beset him round about. His soul is among the lions; they gape and roar upon him with their mouth as a ravening and roaring lion, and his soul is melted like wax in the midst of his bowels. He is poured out like water, and all his bones are out of joint. His flesh is dried up like a potsherd. His tongue cleaveth to his jaws; and he is brought to the dust of death. Dogs have compassed him, the assembly of the wicked have inclosed him.

O sinner, pray that his soul may be delivered from the sword, his spotless person from the power of the dogs, for it is God's Son, and your Saviour traveling with the burden of our iniquities upon him. It is the just agonizing for the unjust, the greater for the less; the Lord of all for all, the Redeemer of the human soul, the judge of the quick and the dead, the Omnipotent to save, the Mighty to destroy! They smite the Judge of Israel upon the check with a rod; they spit in his face, and mock him. To the Prince of Life they say, Prophecy to us who is it that smote thee? They scourge him; the bloodthirsty soldiers of Rome plat a crown of thorns and crush it down upon his sacred temples: they throw upon his sacred shoulders the purple of an unjust tribunal and of him who sat thereon. The soldiers make a spectacle of him to angels and to men; his furious countrymen call aloud in multitudes with the voices of lions, "crucify him. We have a law, and by our law he ought to die, because he made himself the *Son of God!* His blood be upon us and our children!"

He has been seized by the petty officers of a degenerate people, whom his holy instructions had failed to reform; he has been saluted with a kiss by his own disciple, while sold for thirty pieces of silver; he has been denied by his particular friend, and the man whom he exalted to the supremacy in his kingdom. A succession of false witnesses have deposed against him, who by falsehood and contradiction have destroyed their own testimony. He stood before the princes and judges of the people, to use the words of the prophet, like a blighted weed, like a shrub out of a thirsty soil. He had no form nor comeliness in their eyes, and when they looked upon him, his beauty failed to excite their admiration, and they turned their faces from him. "He is despised and rejected of men, a man of sorrows, and acquainted with grief. Surely! he hath borne our griefs, and carried our sorrows; yet we esteemed him stricken, smitten of God and afflicted. But he was wounded for our transgressions; he was bruised for our iniquities. The chastisement of our peace was upon him; and by his stripes we are healed. All we like sheep, have gone astray; we have turned every one, to his own way; and the Lord has laid upon him the iniquities of us all. He was oppressed and he was afflicted, yet he opened not his mouth. He is brought as a lamb to the slaughter, and as a sheep before the shearers is dumb, so he opened not his mouth." Yet was he the plant of renown, the heir and beloved of the Father. He has been before the national Senate. The High Priest of the nation has condemned him: or, to use the words of the prophet, "by an unrighteous judgment his life is cut off from the land of the living." Harken to the words of the High Priest, when all legal inquiry failed to fasten one stain upon his immaculate character:

"I adjure thee by the Living God, that thou tell us whether thou be the Christ the Son of God."

He answered, "Thou hast said. Nevertheless, I say to you, hereafter shall you see the Son of Man sitting on the right hand of power, and coming in the clouds of Heaven." Now they rail upon him with their lips; they spit in his face; they smite him with the palms of their hands; and consign him to the Roman power, where in Pilate's presence you behold him arrayed in purple, with a reed for a sceptre, in his hand! O God of all justice, have mercy; for thy darling is given to the lions, and his soul to those who are ready to devour. "And they were instant with loud voices, requiring that he might be crucified; and the voices of them and of the chief priests prevailed. And Pilate gave sentence that it should be as they required. And he released unto them him who for sedition and murder had been cast into prison, whom they had desired, Barabbas; but he delivered Jesus to their will."

How dreadful to see a fellow mortal, even when an offender, delivered up to the vengeance and fury of an enraged multitude, their tumult roaring like the voice of many waters, and their strained voices filled with death, "away, away, away with him from the earth!" But how much more oppressive to the heart, when reflecting on the case before us—we see the unspotted, the holy and the just, thrown all undefended upon the violence of such a furious mob. Methinks I see them rushing from the judgment-seat with the fury of a tempest the moment the governor's sentence is pronounced. His enfeebled frame, incapable of bearing his own cross, as malefactors were compelled to do, they rudely impose the burden on the farmer Simon; then drive along to Calvary, and Golgotha the place of sculls.[13] O Jerusalem, what a burden of guilt passed through thy gates at this dire moment! What burning flaming iniquity was filed against thee in Heaven, by Heaven's eternal King, when thou stretchedst out thine arm against the Lord's Anointed! who would have purified thy temple; who healed all thy sick; who blessed thee while alive; who felt even for thy impenitence; and with tears of deepest affliction for thy apostacy, exclaimed, "O Jerusalem! Jerusalem! how often would I have gathered thy children as a hen gathereth her

---

[13] The daughters of Israel are touched at the scene, and wail and lament his fate. But he says: "Daughters of Jerusalem, weep not for me; but weep for yourselves and for your children; for the days are coming when they shall say, happy the barren, the wombs which never bare, and the breasts which never gave suck! Then they shall cry to the mountains, Fall on us; and to the hills, Cover us for if it fare thus with the green tree; how shall it fare with the dry?"

brood under her wings, and ye would not! O that thou hadst known in this thy day the things that belong to thy peace; but now they are hid from thy eyes. Henceforth thou shalt not see me again, till thou sayest, Blessed is he that cometh in the name of the Lord:"

Methinks I see the cross thrown down upon the ground, and the great substitute for man racked to the dimensions of its cursed limbs! Exhausted and forlorn, the hands that aye were filled with blessings and deeds of love and charity, are rudely seized by the iron-handed Roman, and nailed to the murderous wood; the feet, those feet that ever trod the path of peace, are spiked and barred to make the offering sure! Death! death! horrible in every shape! but in this, clothing thy terrors with pains tenfold more terrible than flesh and blood dare encounter. Good God, 'tis violence all to crucify a man; and murder infinite to crucify thy Son; for who has lived to tell the pain extreme he felt, when all his sacred person on the uplifted cross came down upon the nails and spikes that pierced him?

But unsubdued he puts aside the stupefying draught that was offered him by those who part his garments; the ministers of religion smile, (I feel ashamed) and shake their heads; and all his honor scorn, and all his sufferings too; and say, "he trusted in God"—noble testimony from murderers—"let him deliver him now if he will have him; for he said, I am the Son of God." The thieves also cast the same in his teeth! Blessed be Heaven, who in pity to general man, veiled such a scene in darkness even though terrible. "Now from the sixth hour there was darkness all over the land till the ninth hour; and about the ninth hour Jesus cried with a loud voice, saying Eli, Eli, lama sabacthani—my God, my God, why hast *thou* forsaken me? Again he cried with a loud voice, and yielded up his spirit. And behold the veil of the temple was rent in twain from the top to the bottom, and the earth did quake, and the rocks rent, and the graves were opened, and many bodies of the saints which slept arose, and came out of the graves after his resurrection, and went into the holy city, and appeared unto many.

"Then the centurion observing what had happened, gave glory to God, saying, assuredly this was a righteous man. Nay, all the people who were present at this spectacle, and saw what had passed, returned, beating their breasts. And all his acquaintance, and the women who had followed him from Galilee, standing at a distance, beheld these things."

Reader, you also, like the writer, have a soul to be saved. Is it precious in your own eyes? or are you regardless of your condition, and the future fortunes of your immortal spirit? If you long to be saved, know then that the dreadful scene, described to us in the scriptures in such impressive and solemn language, is preserved alive that you and all ages might know the price of our Redemption. This same Jesus gave himself a ransom for our sins. He poured out his blood as one instead of all; for he is "the propitiation for the sins of the whole world." Now observe also, that the facts of which we have been speaking, his betrayment by Judas for thirty pieces of silver, his unrighteous condemnation, the mockery of his enemies, the smiting of him on the cheek, his rejection by the Jews, and delivery by the Romans, his crucifixion without the gate of Jerusalem, his death with thieves, and his burial in the rich man's tomb, his tasting of the gall and vinegar, the parting of his garments, and the casting of lots for his vesture, together with the very words which came from his blessed lips, My God, my God, why hast thou forsaken me, and his intercession also for the Jews, while he was upon the cross, "Father forgive them for they know not what they do," are all minutely deciphered on the page of ancient prophecy by the unerring pen of inspiration, and that too, seven hundred, if not one thousand years before these facts occurred. Think of this, reader, and consider the God with whom you have to do, and the nature of that salvation which you are invited to receive.

"His blood be upon us and our children." Dreadful imprecation! and answered by sufferings the most wonderful both in kind and duration. What have not the Jews suffered since the age of our Lord Jesus Christ? It is well known that polytheism and idolatry which was forbidden in the first and second commandments were the highest crimes of which the Jewish nation could be guilty, and that for these they were subjected to six successive bondages to the surrounding nations and once carried away captive into Babylon for seventy years; but what is seventy years to nearly 1800? Surely the Jews have been guilty of some sin even more heinous than polytheism and idolatry, or never could they have been so degraded by God and punished and afflicted, not by men merely, but by the Deity whom they adored. What then was their crime? They crucified the Lord of Glory. But this was not their greatest sin, they enlarged the bulk of their enormity thus. When God raised their prince from the dead they refused to reform and scorned his forgiveness. This is their great, their greatest sin. From the beginning to the conclusion of the war, which followed their rejection of the Messiah, there perished of them 1,357,490.

With this dreadful spectacle of a kingdom of people ruined and scattered by the God of heaven into all the world, and made a hissing, and a by-word, and a curse among the nations, for their rejection of Christ, we leave the reader to reflect upon his own duty, in regard to his Mediator and Saviour; for if his blood thus pursue men on earth, what will be the fate of those whom it pursues into eternity? Repent, therefore, O sinner; change your mind in regard to the holy Scriptures; change your mind in regard to God; change your mind in regard to Jesus Christ your saviour, and in regard to all these, change your behavior; listen to God the Father, who directs you to his Son; listen to his Son, who directs you to the scriptures; listen to the scriptures, which direct you to righteousness, salvation, and eternal life through God and through Jesus our Lord. Be baptized in the name of the Lord Jesus for the remission of sins and you shall receive the gift of the Holy Spirit.

CHAPTER V

Reformation in Regard to the Holy Spirit

As the Christian Religion proposes God as the Father of light, and author of the great mystery of Sonship on which it is founded; as it proposes Jesus our Lord for our lawgiver and director in all duty: so it proposes to perfect our joys by the Holy Spirit, to consummate our happiness by the impartation of glorious gifts, strength and power and soundness of mind.

But you ask my meaning; you say, "What would you teach?" I answer I can teach nothing here, that is not already taught; but I would inform you that if you will obey the gospel, "You shall receive the gift of the Holy Spirit." This is the language of an inspired apostle. But you reply. "In speaking of the remission of past sins, I can understand you, and perhaps I need this, but what do you mean to convey by this, "You shall receive the gift of the Holy Spirit?" I mean precisely what I say; that you shall receive the gift of the Holy Spirit. "You mean that I shall taste of the Spirit of the Deity?" Yes; and of his Son Jesus Christ. "But I am weak and wholly without strength, I feel so feeble that were I willing to accept the forgiveness which God offers me, I could not walk to the water."—Is this weakness in regard to God and Christ and the salvation of your own soul, in your body or in your mind? "It is certainly in my mind, but it so affects my person that I should tremble to obey." Behold then the love of God, "In that while we were yet without strength, Christ died for the ungodly." Accept then of the pardon, which his blood has secured, and you shall be abundantly strengthened. God will "strengthen you with all might by his Spirit in the inner man to comprehend the height and depth and breadth and length, and to know the love of Christ that passeth knowledge." "Does the religion of our Redeemer purpose to forgive us for the past, and grant us the Spirit of God during all time to come?" Yes. "But why should I feel so weak now when I believe the gospel and feel reconciled to God and converted to his Son, seeing that while without God I felt so strong and courageous?" What is the reason that a man, who was never in the presence of his Prince in his whole life, feels weak when he has to appear before him as a criminal? "Certainly it is because he feels conscious of guilt." Precisely so; this is your own case then; Christianity has enlightened your eyes; it has made you conscious of having lived in sin; and you begin to feel by faith that you are not unseen by the omniscient God, but are in his presence and under the piercing glances of His all-seeing eyes. "And would you have me obey the gospel in this miserable weakness?" I would. "Would not remission of past sins strengthen me sufficiently, irrespective of what you name the gift of the Holy Spirit? for this is a part of the gospel which I cannot understand, and the utility of which I cannot discern. To illustrate would not that man of whom you speak as trembling to appear before his prince, feel sufficiently strong again by being pardoned his offences, and restored to the standing of an honest man?" Here it is the figure is weak or defective; for the man was in the presence of the Prince in fact; the Christian is in the presence of God only by faith. To the one, therefore, forgiveness is a matter of fact; to the other it is a matter of faith only. Now the blessed religion of Christianity, with the candor and sweetness which attaches to it in all instances, admits that faith is inferior to knowledge or sensible experience, and that by this principle we see things darkly and only as through a veil. He, whom she recommends to us as our Redeemer, and whom our souls adore, has gone away; he has left this world and his people. Well it becomes a question whether faith, which is indeed intended to supply as far as possible the place of knowledge, is really capable of answering all its purposes, or of being a proper substitute for it in every point and particular. What do you think? "Why, I should say no; that in the very first instance, faith leaves you alone in this world, or by it you can worship but an absent Lord." You are correct. The Lord Jesus has gone away. In regard to personal presence he has left us alone. But here comes in the Christian doctrine of the Holy Spirit; for it is his decree that we shall not be left alone in the world; but believing and obeying him, we shall rejoice in him by the presence of the Holy Spirit with joy unutterable and full of glory. "Well, sir, you begin to make the matter a little more intelligible. Am I to understand you, that the Holy Spirit is intended to supply the defectiveness of the principle of faith on which Christianity is founded, and to become a substitute by his presence in the church to you for your absent Lord?" Precisely; "I will pray the Father and he will give you another comforter that he may abide with you forever, the Spirit of truth, whom the world cannot receive because it seeth him not, neither knoweth him; but ye shall know him, for he will dwell with you and shall be in you. I will not leave you comfortless, I will come to you."—These are the words of our absent Lord on this cardinal point. "And very sensible and sweet words they are. I would understand from the citation then, that what the scriptures name the Holy Spirit is to be received by the church and not by the world." Precisely. He is intended by his presence to supply the place of our dear Lord to those who love him, his disciples only. "Then if I should desire to partake of the Holy Spirit, I must believe, reform, and be baptized for the remission of past sins?" Yes; and God having thus enlightened your understanding in the knowledge of Christ by his holy word alone, or by the truth, and having reconciled the inner man and purged from your external walk and conversation all unrighteousness, Jesus will acknowledge you for his by his Holy Spirit. You shall be clean every whit by the forgiveness of sins; and the temple of your soul and body being thus sanctified, God will descend into it, he will fill it with his glory; "for we are temples of God through the Spirit."

"I had thought that the Holy Spirit was given to establish the Christian Religion as a true system." Many others think so; but the Christian religion was proved true before the disciples received the Holy Spirit. The Spirit had proved Christianity to be true when he raised our Lord Jesus Christ from the dead and showed him to the proper witnesses, the Apostles, who were chosen for this special purpose; but he was not sent to dwell with them till forty-seven days after this. "Then we believe in the resurrection of Christ on the testimony of those who saw him after he had arisen, and not ultimately upon the signs, miracles, and wonder afterwards done by the witnesses?" You are correct; the signs were a confirmation of their testimony, but their testimony is that which sustains and forms our faith in the fact, and proves it. "I perceive then that we must believe the gospel on the evangelical testimony alone at last?" Yes; His disciples inform us by their writings that they saw him after his resurrection, looked upon him, handled him, cat and drank with him, were instructed by him how to act in his kingdom, and commissioned to proclaim the good news of forgiveness in his name to all nations beginning at Jerusalem. Do you then believe that he arose from the dead on the testimony of the holy apostles and prophets; this is the question. If you do, you have a part in the last intercessory prayer of Christ on earth—John 17, where he says to God "I pray not for these, the apostles, only; but for all those who shall believe on me through their word." "But theologists tell us we must believe by the Spirit." Never mind theologists in so great a question; read the scriptures: learn of Christ that you are to believe on him through the "word" of the apostles, and you will have a share in his prayers; if you believe or seek to believe by any other method, know this, that you are not mentioned in that prayer, "Seeing, sir, that the Spirit himself is not immediately intended to prove the gospel true, are we by the testimony of the apostles alone, supplied with the only evidence of its truth." Yes. "Can Jewish, Pagan, and Christian philosophers and historians not prove it to be true?" No. None of them saw Jesus. God showed him not openly, but to witnesses chosen before of God for this purpose; which proves that he did not desire to have Jews, Pagans, or even all or any of his own people the Christians testify to the truth of it. The church was chosen or appointed to believe, and to suffer for her belief; the apostles were elected to know and to suffer for their knowledge. The church testifies to faith, the apostles testifies to the facts on which that faith terminates. "But are not books of evidence of use in proving the truth of the gospel." No. Books of evidence, written by any but the original witnesses, can establish the history or fortunes of the fact, which indeed may corroborate in some measure the original testimony; but the proof of the Christian proposition lays exclusively and absolutely in the sacred writings. The world is entirely independent of Jewish and Gentile philosophers and historians for this proof as they also are for the proposition itself. "You distinguish, then, between the proof of the Christian proposition and the history of it?" Yes. Any one may be a historian of it; but the witnesses alone can supply the testimony necessary to believe it. Matthew, John, and Paul, Peter, James and Jude are witnesses to us of its truth. Luke and Mark are historians of its origin and fortunes; so that even these two last men do not occupy the same rank precisely with the former six who were chosen to be eye witnesses. The last two wrote what they certainly believed, and what was delivered to them from "the beginning by those who were eye witnesses and ministers of the word;" but the first six wrote what they not merely believed, but what they absolutely knew to be fact, and which they had not to trust for to the experience of others; or the first six wrote what they knew; the last two what they believed. The first were witnesses, the last historians. The chief value of the histories or evangils by Luke and Mark, therefore, is, that they coincide with the original testimony of Matthew, John and Paul, Peter, James, and Jude. But in regard to the proof and the proposition, and its primitive history down to the settlement of Christianity among the Gentiles and the imprisonment of the apostle Paul at Rome, the world have to trust to the scriptures, all else being of little value in point of proof, I had almost added in point of history too.

"I am greatly satisfied with your idea that Christianity embodies in her sacred books, the proof of her own proposition, and leans not upon extrinsic testimony for evidence of her divinity. In this respect she seems, like her author, to possess life in herself, and like him consequently to live through all ages. This, indeed, must be one of the very highest marks of her divinity; and it delivers us at once from all dependence upon Jewish, Pagan, and Christian history beyond what is found in the sacred oracles. But, seeing you have cleared up this point to my satisfaction, tell me what the scriptures lay down as proofs of the baptized person's having received the spirit of Christ."

You complain now of feebleness, and consequently unhappiness; for to be weak is to be miserable. The Holy Spirit will remove this weakness, and strengthen you with all might in the inner man. This strength will render you perfectly blessed; for to be strong in the Lord is to be happy. This in scripture is called joy in the Holy Spirit. From this superhuman strength then will flow joy, love, peace, gentleness, and every divine grace, as water flows from a fountain. "You mean me then to seek this great good by obeying the gospel, and to go to Jesus Christ with all my feebleness, imperfections, fears, and transgressions about me?" Yes; Come to me, he says, all you who toil and are burdened, and I will relieve you. "I am happy to see that the doctrine of the Holy Spirit is capable of so happy and easy a solution. That faith is inferior to knowledge, and that the Lord of Christians is absent in person, are two very obvious facts; and that the scheme will certainly be perfected only when faith yields to knowledge, and the indwelling of the Holy Spirit to the presence of Jesus; but that in the mean time the Holy Spirit should remain with the disciples, is a most reasonable doctrine, and very comforting withal. I am greatly delighted in view of the fulfillment of what the gospel promises. I will seek the remission of sins in God's appointed way. I will be baptized, and hope for the promised Spirit."

Reader, let this be your happy resolution. Suffer yourself to be reformed in regard to God's Holy Spirit. Obey the gospel, and you shall taste of his strength and glory.

A DISCOURSE OF THE TRUE GOSPEL

SECTION FIFTH–BAPTISM

QUESTION.—Men and brethren what shall we do to be saved?
ANSWER.—Repent, and be baptized every one of you in the name of Jesus Christ for the remission of sins, and you shall receive the gift of the Holy Spirit, &c.—Acts 2:37-38

CHAPTER I

Introductory

We have already seen that Peter was raised by his Master, our Lord and Saviour, to the honorable office of first answering the question of salvation to the Jews and the Gentiles. We have seen also that the other apostles honored their master's authority in this appointment, and remained mute till Peter had delivered the gospel, and fulfilled the duties of his special office.

In answering the question, What shall we do; did the apostle on the day of Pentecost speak properly or improperly; that is, with authority or without authority? If he spoke without authority, he spoke improperly: if he spoke with authority, he spoke properly. But let us transcribe the question put to him, and his answer, into this chapter. On the day of the original promulgation of the gospel, he announced to a vast assemblage of people the Messiahship of Jesus, and his elevation to Heaven. It is added that after doing this, the people addressed him and his colleagues thus:—

Question. "Men and brethren, what shall we do?"

Answer. "Repent and be baptized every one of you, in the name of Jesus Christ, for the remission of sins, and you shall receive the gift of the Holy Spirit;" &c.

Here now is the question of salvation put to the original preachers by a people, who certainly needed a true answer as much as any that ever existed; for they had crucified the Lord of glory, and were the chief of sinners.

Here also is Peter's answer all unalloyed as it came from his inspired lips. Is it good, or is it bad; is it proper, or is it improper; did he make it with authority or without authority; with the consent or without the consent of Christ; by his command or irrespective of his command? Is it to be reckoned good money or counterfeit? Shall it pass in the religious markets of Christendom for bullion, or is it base dross? It will not, it does not pass current in the market. It has been condemned and nailed to the counter as base coin. Religious teachers will not offer it to the public. The Protestant ministry do not employ it for its proper purposes; they will not use it with its original design. And they must, therefore, either reckon it base coinage, or the money of a different reign and kingdom from that of their own, and consequently antiquated, obsolete, and useless.

But the discourse, by which the kingdom of Heaven was opened to the Jews, deserves to be investigated: we shall, therefore, embody it in this chapter, as a most memorable document, worthy of all distinction, worthy of all acceptation.

"And when the day of Pentecost was fully come, they were all unanimously assembled in the same place: and, on a sudden, there was a sound from heaven, as of a rushing violent wind; and it filled all the house, where they were sitting. And there appeared to them tongues resembling fire, distinctly separated, and it rested upon each of them: and they began to speak in other languages, as the Spirit gave them utterance. Now there were sojourning in Jerusalem pious men, Jews from every nation under heaven: and when this report came abroad, the multitude assembled, and were confounded; for every one heard them speaking in his own dialect. And they were all astonished, and wondered, saying one to another, Behold! are not all these that speak Galileans? And how do we every one hear in his own native language; Parthians, and Medes, and Elamites, and those that inhabit Mesopotamia, and Judea, and Cappadocia, Pontus and Asia, Phrygia, and Pamphylia, Egypt, and the parts of Africa which are about Cyrene; Roman strangers also, both Jews and Proselytes; Cretes and Arabians; we hear them speaking in our own tongues the wonderful works of God! And they were all in amazement and perplexity, and said one to another, What can this mean? But others, mocking, said, Surely these men are filled with sweet wine.

But Peter standing up with the eleven, raised his voice, and said to them,—Jews, and all you that sojourn in Jerusalem, let this be known to you, and attend to my words; for these men are not drunk, as you suppose; since it is the third hour of the day: but this is that which was spoken by the Prophet Joel, "And, it shall come to pass in the last days, says God, I will pour out a portion of my Spirit upon all flesh; and your sons and your daughters shall prophesy; and your young men shall see visions, and your old men shall dream dreams. Yes, in those days I will pour out of my Spirit upon my servants, and upon my handmaids; and they shall prophesy: and I will give prodigies in heaven above, signs on the earth beneath; blood and fire, and a cloud of smoke: the sun shall be turned into darkness, and the moon into blood, before that great and illustrious day of the Lord come. And it shall come to pass, that whosoever shall invoke the name of the Lord, shall be saved." Israelites, hear these words: Jesus the Nazarene, a man recommended to you by God by powerful operations, and wonders, and signs, which God wrought by him in the midst of you, (as you yourselves also know;) him you have apprehended, being given up by the declared counsel and foreknowledge of God, and by the hands of sinners have crucified and slain; whom God has raised up, having loosed the pains of death, as it was impossible that he should be held under it. For David says concerning him, "I have regarded the Lord as always before me; because he is at my right hand, that I might not be moved: for this reason my heart is glad, and my tongue exults; moreover too my flesh shall rest in hope that thou wilt not leave my soul in the unseen world; neither wilt thou permit thy Holy One to see corruption. Thou hast made me to know the ways of life; thou wilt make me full of joy with thy countenance. Brethren, permit me to speak freely to you concerning the patriarch David; that he is both dead and buried, and his sepulcher is among us to this day; therefore, being a prophet, and knowing that God had sworn to him with an oath, that of the fruit of his loins he would raise up the Messiah to sit on his throne: he, foreseeing this, spoke of the resurrection of the Messiah, that his soul should not be left in the unseen world, nor his flesh see corruption. This Jesus, God has raised up, of which all we are witnesses: being exalted, therefore, to the right hand of God, and having received the promise of the Holy Spirit from the Father, he has shed forth this which you see and hear. For David is not ascended into Heaven, but he says, "The Lord said to my Lord, sit thou at my right hand, until I make thy foes thy footstool." Let, therefore, all the house of Israel assuredly know, that God has made this Jesus whom you have crucified, Lord and Messiah.

Now when they heard *these things* they were pierced to the heart and said to Peter, and the rest of the apostles, Brethren what shall we do? And Peter said to them. Reform, and be each of you immersed in the name of Jesus Christ, in order to the remission of sins, and you shall receive the gift of the Holy Spirit. For the promise is to you, and to your children, and to all that are afar off; as many as the Lord our God shall call. And with many other words he testified, and exhorted, saying, Save yourselves from this perverse generation. They, therefore, who received his word with readiness, were immersed; and there were added to *the disciples* that very day about three thousand souls.

And they continued stedfast in the teaching, in the fellowship, in the breaking of the loaf, and in the prayers of the apostles. Fear also fell upon every soul, and many miracles and signs were wrought by the apostles. And all that believed were together, and had all things common. They also sold their possessions and effects, and distributed them to every one according to his necessity. Moreover, they continued unanimously in the temple every day; end breaking bread from house to house, they partook of their food with joy and simplicity of heart, praising God, and having favor with all the people; and the Lord daily added the saved to the congregation."—Acts 2.

Such is the first discourse of the prime minister of our kingdom, the first of the apostles; and such were its glorious results. "As many as gladly received the word were baptized; and there were added to the church that very day, three thousand souls."

But let the reader bear with me, while I once more separate from the body of Peter's address the great question of salvation, and its great answer.

"Now when they heard these things they were pricked to the heart, and cried out:

Ques. "Men and brethren what shall we do?"

Ans. "Repent and be baptized every one of you, in the name of Jesus Christ, for the remission of sins, and you shall receive the gift of the Holy Spirit; for the promise is to you and to your children, and to all that are afar off, even to as many as the Lord our God shall call."

Men and brethren what shall we do? Human nature is still what it was on the day when this interrogatory was put to the chief ministers of our religion. How often have we heard this question put by poor convicted sinners in our own age and country! How often does every zealous and faithful minister of the Redeemer, hear this question! Such indeed are the point and impressiveness of the truths of the gospel, that no being uttering them for salvation, with the gravity and earnestness becoming his profession, can fail to arouse the contrition of men. They are all-powerful to enlighten, awaken, convict, and save; and to this day penitent mortals still inquire, Men and brethren what shall we do? If, therefore, the ministers of our religion would meet such cases; if they would improve to the salvation of those whom they address, the convictions which their own discourses have carried home to the hearts and consciences of their awakened auditors. Why do they not investigate and understand the real value and proper application of the answer to this absorbing question, returned by Peter to the miserable but convicted sinners of his day? Is Peter's answer to be forever deemed error, and bad in law; or shall it be regarded as a thing merely theoretical, proper only for the apostolic day; but unnecessary, or dangerous, or inapplicable in our own? Are not sinners the same, the same in their guilt, in their awakenings, in their faith and penitence, and godly sorrow; do they not put the same question, and seek for the same relief, by the same blessing, viz: the remission of sins? Undoubtedly. Men are in all ages the same; and on the men of all ages the gospel is intended to confer the same blessings. Why then do we presume upon a change of means, which God has ordained, for conveying to them these blessings? Why, when they put the great question of salvation, do we not follow the holy, and inspired, and infallible example of the chief apostle, and say gladly, "Repent and be baptized, every one of you in the name of Jesus Christ, for the remission of sins, and you shall receive the gift of the Holy Spirit?" Why do we, for this unerring doctrine, substitute in so nice a case, our own inventions, and torture by protracted sufferings the returning prodigal?

Was not Moses to make every thing in the tabernacle according to the pattern shown him in the mount? Will we then depart from the pattern shown us by one who is as much greater than Moses, as he who builds the house is greater than the house? Will we risk his displeasure in this grand case; and substitute our own wisdom for his words and ordinances? Moses is praised for his fidelity; and we ought like him to be ambitious to please the Lord. If the truth has been suppressed, if it has been trodden down to the ground by the apostate church, if she has changed some ordinances and corrupted others, this ought not to scare us from the truth. She has indeed greatly abused the doctrine of remission, and by her sordid Priesthood has sold for money the blood of Christ to all comers; and her corruptions seem to have alarmed the protestants to so frightful a degree that their leaders have left out of their schemes the ordinance of forgiveness altogether; so that in their churches and gospels it has no tangible, no positive, form whatever, not a man, in answer to the question, What shall we do, daring, even when prompted by the most serious and poignant convictions in the sinner, to say, "Repent and be baptized every one of you in the name of Jesus Christ for the Remission of sins, and you shall receive the gift of the Holy Spirit." Do those who thus treat Jesus and his ministers, hope to be pardoned for so great an insult offered to his majesty? Or do they hope that the truth will be thus unrighteously suppressed for ever? that it will always and by all others of the ministers of Christ, be suffered to slumber in concealment for evermore? If they do, they err, for the answer of the holy apostle has been resumed; it has been called up again to answer the great design for which it was originally intended; the convinced, the convicted, the awakened sinner has been told in the language of Peter, what to do to be saved; and the result has been as glorious as the answer is scriptural; for those who have obeyed the gospel, according to the primitive form of sound words, have tasted all its blessings; have been pardoned, comforted, purified and made to rejoice, like those of old, "with joy unspeakable and full of glory, receiving as the reward of their faith the salvation of their souls." There is no charity in concealing or in suppressing the truth; the person guilty of so unworthy a deed, gives but poor proof of his fidelity to Christ and love to poor sinners.

CHAPTER II

The Apostle Peter

This splendid man and celebrated Apostle, was born in Bethsaida, a city of Galilee, on the shores of the lake Genesareth. His father's name was Jona, by profession a fisherman.—Peter with Andrew his brother was raised to the same enterprising mode of life, and was prosecuting the duties of his profession at the moment the Messiah called him to share in the trials and dangers and honors of the gospel. His original name was Simon; but at the period of his introduction to the prince of life, which occurred at Jordan, Jesus honored him with a new name, and said that henceforth he should be called Cephas; in English stone, and in Greek Peter, which is the appellative by which the apostle is now generally known.

Peter returned from Jordan, where he had been so highly honored by the Messiah, and resumed on the banks of the "dark Galilee" the arduous labors of his proper employment, little anticipating the illustrious office which he was destined to fill, or the fame which one day was to attach to the name which he had just received from his royal master. Little did he then think that Peter should become a watch-word to loose the nations from the bands of sin, to free captives, and to bind Princes in fetters of iron. Little did he imagine that among the names of the twelve apostles of the Lamb, the name of Peter should first be emblazoned on the jasper-flashing walls of the holy city, the New Jerusalem, and that he should sit with his compeers on twelve thrones, ruling all the excellent of the earth, the twelve tribes of Israel. But no profession, however humble, can crush a noble nature; true excellence and the fear of God are immortal, and when God decrees honor to the possessor of them, no man may negative it. The Son of the Eternal has honored this apostle, yea, and he shall be honored.

Peter was a person of great elasticity of feeling, sometimes stretching out to the sublime, and again shrinking backward to a dimension which caricatured rather than delineated the mental and moral excellence of which he has proved himself most certainly possessed. The extremes and varient tone of his passions could not possibly be better adumbrated than it is in a scene in which he himself was a chief actor, a man boldly walking upon the sea as upon the solid land and again sinking through fear at the moment when all would have expected him to feel most resolute and secure. Here we have him praying devoutly, "Depart from me, O Lord; for I am a sinful man;" and there he curses and blasphemes. At one time he swears eternal loyalty to his Lord, and anon he denies him with oaths. Now he would build three tabernacles and dwell with Christ forever, and then he forsakes him, leaves him to the mercy of his enemies, and secures his own safety by flight. Here he is designated the first apostle, there stigmatized as Satan. Now he refuses to let his Master wash him; again, he calls out, "not my feet only but my head also!" Here he is commissioned to preach the gospel to all creation, and to become a fisher of men, when, lo! he seeks again his nets and goes to the sea for fish. Here he smites off the ear of the High Priest's servant and there a female domestic of the palace overpowers his courage, and again he denies his master. A woman's voice fills him with alarm; his master's glance smites him with despair; he stands within and curses; he retires to without and weeps bitterly! Notwithstanding this, however, of the twelve, Peter was honored with the first sight of his risen Lord, and blessed with the last of his precious instructions, "Feed my sheep."

It is not, however, in the extremes of rashness and alarm that we are to look for the true character of this admirable man. His intellectual and moral excellence lay between these widely separated points; and is to be sought for in the Acts of the Apostles, and in his own epistolary writings rather than in the four gospels. While his master was on earth, the prejudice concerning a temporal reign common to the whole nation, blinded his eyes and rendered the most obvious teachings of the Redeemer, a perfect riddle to him. He could understand nothing at all of his death and resurrection, his being delivered into the hands of sinners and ascending to Heaven; and this mysteriousness of what he listened to, carried him beyond himself; so that while he loved, and honored and adored his Lord to distraction, of his kingdom he was utterly ignorant, and consequently unstable. But see him after the descent of the Spirit, marshalling the affairs of the kingdom. Look at him in the streets of Jerusalem, clothed with authority, and full of power, correcting the public sentiment, interpreting the prophets, charging upon the people the blood of the cross, preaching Jesus, convicting myriads, opening the kingdom, exhorting to obedience, baptizing thousands, remitting sins, and promising the gift of the Spirit, and then you have a peep at the majesty, enterprise, and talents for business, of this truly celebrated man.

Again, behold him in the temple, after healing by the divine power the lame man, who lay daily at the gate called Beautiful. The scene would have disarmed and exanimated a thousand of ourselves. The lame man leaps, gives glory to God; and in an instant Peter is surrounded by ten thousand of the worshippers. The magnitude, the splendor, and perilousness of the moment affect him not; the mighty crowd, and prejudiced withal; the peculiar sanctity of the place in which he stood; the presence of the temple officers, the vicinity of the priesthood, the splendor of the temple itself, and the amplitude and greatness of the whole scene affect him not. Phoenix like, from the ashes of his former character he rises by the power of Christ, triumphant over the glory and glitter of the whole temple service, and, with the thunder of a fisherman when he roars across the deep, shouts in the midst of the temple—"Ye men of Israel, the God of Abraham, and of Isaac, and of Jacob, the God of our fathers has glorified his Son Jesus, whom you delivered up and denied in the presence of Pilate, when he was determined to let him go. But you denied the Holy One and the Just, and desired a murderer to be granted to you; and killed the Prince of Life, whom God hath raised from the dead, whereof we are witnesses!" There, there was Peter in light and might. In the same mighty voice he urges upon their senses the case of the lame man, who stood all sound in their presence: now he soothes their excited feelings, and proffers as an apology for their execrable murder, that they had done it ignorantly, as did also their rulers; then he tells them that the sufferings of Messiah had been predicted; urges them to reformation, and cites the scriptures, plying them with the most obvious and popular prophecies concerning Jesus and his resurrection, till the whole mass of his audience, chained by his eloquence, and astounded by facts, stand before him in all the muteness and stupor of self-condemnation. The tones of his glorious voice reach the most distant apartments of the temple, and pierce the ears and consciences of the guilty priesthood like the knell or trumpetings of the angel of the great judgment day. They are aroused, and with bands of soldiers, and the captain of the temple, and the Sadducees, and the rulers, and elders, and scribes, and Annas, and Caiaphas, and John, and Alexander, and the whole kindred of the High Priest, gather together, and act upon the case of Peter and his associates. Undismayed amid the warlike glitter of the temple guard, unawed by the pomp of the High Priest, unsubdued by his imprisonment on the preceding night, and fearing not the whole counsel, Peter, filled with the Holy Spirit, addresses them, "Ye rulers of the people, and elders of Israel;" and with the frankness of a noble nature, and the dignity of a man inspired by the truth, turns their astonished eyes towards the cause, the innocent cause of all their alarm —the lame man who had been cured standing by the side of the apostles! They marveled, they could say nothing against it "for the man was above forty years old on whom this miracle of healing was showed!'

But who can number the pangs they felt, when the Apostle referred this to the power of Christ, and thrust in upon their consciences the blood of the Son of God! "You have crucified Jesus Christ; God has raised him from the dead. This is that stone which you builders rejected; it has become the head of the corner. There is none other name given under Heaven or among men, whereby we must be saved, but the name of Jesus Christ, and whether it be right in the sight of God to hearken unto you more than unto God, judge you."

The darkness was now past, the strength of the Spirit of Christ now rested upon the man. He felt himself almighty in the inner man, and by inspiration was able to comprehend the height, and depth, and breadth, and length of the new religion. He was filled with all the fullness of Jesus Christ, his glorified Lord and Saviour, and no opposer might stand before him; he, therefore, with John his associate, retired in triumph from the Sanhedrim. All his brethren praised the Lord for the glory of his power; and the house in which they extolled his great name trembled under the descending Saviour.

Clothed with power to kill as well as to save, the great prime Minister of the Kingdom of God, enters into the very secrets of the soul, and Ananias and Sapphira die under the majesty of his fearful rebuke—the congregation tremble, and all the people are filled with awe, and signs and wonders and mighty miracles rouse to amazement the whole city, "insomuch that they bring forth the sick into the streets, and lay them on beds and couches, that at least Peter passing by may overshadow them!" Glory to God, and to Jesus our Lord for the excellent dignity with which he clothed the man to whom he gave the keys and appointed to let into the royal kingdom the Jews and Gentiles.

Again he is imprisoned, but the angel of the Lord opens the prison door, and by the dawning of the day, the apostles stand in the temple and teach to the people all the words of this life. Again they are before the council; and again Peter, with redoubled success, cuts his opposers to the heart; they are inflamed to madness and pant for blood, but in vain: the apostles again retire in triumph from the council; rejoicing that they are accounted worthy to suffer shame for his name.

Here then are the outlines of Peter's history in the Jewish capital at the opening of the kingdom. It is of a marvelous nature, and proves him to have been a man of an admirable nature, even as he was the chief and most illustrious of the apostles. It shows also that when our blessed and adorable Lord gave to him the keys of the kingdom of heaven, and the precedence in proclaiming the gospel to the Jews and the Gentiles, he was not mistaken in his man.

Having fairly established our religion in the Jewish capital, having filled the city with the gospel, it became the duty of this apostle, in accordance with the appointment of his master, next to open the door of faith to the Gentiles. He was therefore sent for by order of heaven, and encouraged and emboldened to perform this extraordinary and ever memorable deed, by visions from the Holy Spirit. He went, doubting nothing, preached the gospel, the people believed, and the Spirit descended, to the amazement of all the Jews who accompanied him; for they heard the Gentile converts speak with tongues and magnify God. Peter was not embarrassed. He had been sent for to answer the great question of salvation, and he acted decidedly; for notwithstanding the converts had already received the Spirit, there was still one thing which they required, viz: to be loosed from past sins according to the way appointed by Jesus our Lord and the Christian religion. In strictest conformity with his mission from Jesus, and with the greatest self-possession, this transcendent apostle calls out to the brethren present, "Who can forbid water that these should not be immersed who have received the Spirit as well as we? And he commanded them to be baptized in the name of the Lord Jesus."

For the beauty and excellence of the intellectual and moral nature of this truly great man, we refer the reader to his holy epistles; which for tenderness, candour, depth, purity, and affectionate care, are not surpassed by any of the sacred writings of the same class.

His steady and fearless carriage in Jerusalem, and his decided procedure in the baptism of the Gentile converts, together with his apostolic authority and inspiration all conspire to make him the proper model for a minister of Christ to follow, and to assure those who do this, that the gospel which he preached and as he preached it, is the true gospel of Christ, and never to be departed from either in matter or form.

CHAPTER III

Doctor Doddridge's Answer to the Question, "What Shall I Do to Be Saved?"

The answer of the apostle Peter on the day of Pentecost to the question of penitents, may be considered in regard to the following matters, 1st. The immense audience to whom it was given. 2d. The great number who received it, and were baptized for remission. 3d. The joyful and spiritual effects with which it operated in those who obeyed it, 4th The different answers, which have since been given to the same question, by those who were never appointed by Jesus to this vastly responsible business.

This last item, viz: the different answers which have since been given by men who never were appointed to the office of doing so, may very properly be considered first, as the examination of it will bring up every thing concerning the other items necessary to be known.

Among the religious productions of modern times, few works have attained to greater popularity than that of the Rev. Philip Doddridge, titled "The Rise and Progress of Religion in the Soul." This excellent and pious author describes the plan of his own book in an introductory chapter, thus:

"In forming my general plan I have been solicitous, that this little treatise might, if possible, be useful to all its readers, and contain something suitable to each. I will therefore take the man, and the Christian, in a great variety of circumstances. I will first suppose myself addressing one of the vast number of thoughtless creatures, who have hitherto been utterly unconcerned about religion; and will try what can be done, by all plainness and earnestness of address, to awaken him from his lethargy, to a care, an affectionate and immediate care about it. I will labor to fix a deep and awful conviction of guilt upon his conscience, and to strip him of his vain excuses and his flattering hopes. I will read to him, Oh! that I could fix on his heart, that sentence, that dreadful sentence, which a righteous and an Almighty God hath denounced against him as a sinner; and endeavor to shew him, in how helpless a state he lies under this condemnation, as to any capacity he has of delivering himself. But I do not mean to leave any in so terrible a situation: I will joyfully proclaim "the glad tidings of pardon and salvation by Christ Jesus our Lord," which is all the support and confidence of my own soul. And then I will give some general view of the Way by which this salvation is to be obtained; urging the sinner to accept it, as affectionately as I can, though nothing can be sufficiently pathetic where, as in this matter, the life of an immortal soul is in question.

Too probable it is that some will, after all this, remain insensible; and therefore that their sad case may not incumber the following articles, I shall here take a solemn leave of them, and then shall turn and address myself, as compassionately as I can, to a most contrary character; I mean to a soul overwhelmed with a sense of the greatness of its sins, and trembling under the burden, as if there were no more hope for him in God. And that nothing may be omitted, which may give solid peace to the troubled spirit, I shall endeavor to guide its inquiries as to the evidences of sincere repentance and faith, which will be farther illustrated by a more particular view of the several branches of the Christian temper such as may serve at once to assist the reader in judging what he is, and to shew him what he should labour to be. This will naturally lead to a view of the need we have of the influences of the blessed Spirit, to assist us in the important and difficult work of the true Christian; and of the encouragement we have to hope for these divine assistances. In an humble dependence on which, I shall then enter on the consideration of several cases which often occur in the Christian life, in which particular addresses to the conscience may be requisite and useful.

As some peculiar difficulties and discouragements attend the first entrance on a religious course, it will here be our first care to animate the young convert against them. And that it may be done more effectually, I shall urge a solemn dedication of himself to God: to be confirmed by entering into the full communion of the church by an approach to the sacred table. That these engagements may be more happily fulfilled, we shall endeavor to draw a more particular plan of that devout, regular, and accurate course, which ought daily to be attended to: and because the idea will probably rise so much higher, than what is the general practice, even of good men, we shall endeavor to persuade the reader to make the attempt, hard as it may seem; and shall caution him against various temptations, which might otherwise draw him aside to negligence and sin."

The reader will perceive from the above sensible statement of the plan of his book that the Reverend author, in the first part of it, purposes to fit the sinner for salvation, or the remission of sins, and secondly, to give some general view of the way by which this is to be obtained. This is perfectly rational, and adapted to nature; for it proposes to impart knowledge, before it states duty and invites to a compliance with it. It purposes to enlighten the eyes of the sinner in regard to his own character and condition, and to what God has done to change the one and reform the other, before it informs him what God has ordered he should do to save himself. In fine, the author purposes nothing less in this latter case than, after having brought the sinner to a sense of his guilt, to answer to him the great question of salvation, What shall we do to work the works of God? What shall we do? Or what shall we do to be saved? Accordingly in his 9th chapter, headed "A more particular account of the Way, by which this Salvation is to be obtained," Mr. Doddridge actually supposes the sinner to put the question; thus, "I consider you, my dear reader, as coming to me with the inquiry, which the Jews once addressed to our Lord; *What shall we do that we may work the works of God?*"

The development of knowledge is long; the statement of duty is short. The development of facts by the apostle Peter on the day of Pentecost, fills twenty-three verses, as found in the second chapter of the Acts. His statement of duty occupies only one verse. Mr. Doddridge's book has seven chapters on the awakening, urging, cautioning, arraigning, convicting and sentencing the sinner; and but one chapter stating to him his duty in order to obtain the great salvation. Peter's discourse, and that of Dr. Doddridge, therefore, are in the general modeled alike. They both treat of knowledge, or of the facts to be understood largely; and state duty succinctly. Doddridge's attack upon the sinner occupies seventy-two pages; Peter's about one page in the New Testament. The Doctor's answer to the question of duty fills almost nine pages; Peter's answer only one verse, the 38th, "Repent and be baptized, every one of you, in the name of Jesus Christ for the remission of sins, and you shall receive the gift of the Holy Spirit." This is decided, short, intelligible, apostolic, inspired, and saving. It is but fair, however, that Dr. Doddridge should be allowed to speak for himself, that if the reader prefer his instructions to those of the Apostle, he may here enjoy the benefit of them.

"I now consider you, my dear reader, as coming to me with the inquiry, which the Jews once addressed to our Lord; "What shall we do, that we may work the works of God?" What method shall I take to secure that redemption and salvation, which I am told Christ has procured for his people? I would answer it as seriously and carefully as possible; as one that knows of what importance it is to you to be rightly informed, and that knows also, how strictly he is, to answer to God, for the sincerity and care with which the reply is made. May I be enabled to "speak as his oracle," that is, in such a manner, as faithfully to echo back what the sacred oracles teach!

And here, that I may be sure to follow the safest guides, and the fairest examples, I must preach salvation to you, in the way of "repentance towards God, and of faith in our Lord Jesus Christ:" That good old doctrine, which the apostles preached: and which no man can pretend to change, but at the peril of his own soul, and of theirs who attend to him.

I suppose, that you are, by this time, convinced of your guilt and condemnation, and of your own inability to recover yourself. Let me nevertheless urge you to feel that conviction yet more deeply, and to impress it with greater weight upon your soul; that you have "undone yourself, and that in yourself is not your help found." Be persuaded, therefore, expressly, and solemnly, and sincerely, to give up all self-dependence; which, if you do not guard against it, will be ready to return secretly, before it is observed, and will lead you to attempt building up what you have just been destroying.

Be assured, that if ever you are saved, you must ascribe that salvation entirely to the free grace of God. If, guilty and miserable as you are, you are not only accepted, but crowned, you must lay down your crown with all humble acknowledgement before the throne. No flesh must glory in his presence; but he that glorieth, must glory in the Lord: for of him are we in Christ Jesus, who of God is made unto us wisdom, and righteousness, and sanctification, and redemption. And you must be sensible, you are in such a state, as, having none of those in yourself, to need them in another. You must therefore be sensible, that you are ignorant and guilty, polluted and enslaved; or, (as our Lord expresses it, with regard to some who were under a Christian profession,) that as a sinner, "you are wretched, and miserable, and poor, and blind, and naked."

If these views be deeply impressed upon your mind, you will be prepared to receive what I am now to say. Hear, therefore, in a few words your duty, your remedy, and your safety; which consists in this that you must apply to Christ, with a deep abhorrence of your former sins, and a firm resolution of forsaking them; forming that resolution in the strength of his grace, and fixing your dependence on him for your acceptance with God, even while you are purposing to do your very best, and when you have actually done the best you ever will do in consequence of that purpose.

The first and most important advice that I can give you in the present circumstances, is, that you look to Christ, and apply yourself to him. And here, say not in your heart, Who shall ascend into heaven to bring him down to me? or who shall raise me up thither, to present me before him? The blessed Jesus, by whom all things consist, by whom the whole system of them is supported, forgotten as he is by most that bear his name, is not far from any of us: nor could he have promised to have been wherever two or three are met together in his name, but in consequence of those truly divine perfections by which he is every where present. Would you therefore, Oh sinner, desire to be saved? Go to the Saviour. Would you desire to be delivered? Look to that great Deliverer: and though you should be so overwhelmed with guilt, and shame, and fear, and horror, that you should be incapable of speaking to him, fall down in this speechless confusion at his feet; and behold him, as the Lamb of God, that taketh away the sin of the world.

Behold him therefore with an attentive eye, and say, whether the sight does not touch, and even melt thy very heart! Dost thou not feel, what a foolish, and what a wretched creature thou hast been; that for the sake of such low and sordid gratifications and interests, as those which thou hast been pursuing, thou shouldst thus "kill the Prince of life?" Behold the deep wounds, which he bore for thee. "Look on him whom thou hast pierced, and surely thou must mourn," unless thine heart be hardened into stone. Which of thy past sins canst thou reflect upon, and lay, "For this it was worth my while, thus to have injured my Saviour, and to have exposed the Son of God to such sufferings?" And what future temptations can arise so considerable, that thou should say, "For the sake of this, I will crucify my Lord again?" Sinner, thou must repent; thou must repent of every sin; and must forsake it: but if thou doest it to any purpose, I well know it must be as at the foot of the cross. Thou must sacrifice every lust, even the dearest; though it should be like "a right hand, or a right eye:" and therefore, that thou mayst, if possible, be animated to it, I have led thee to that altar, on which Christ himself was "sacrificed for thee, an offering of a sweet smelling savor." Thou must "yield up thyself to God, as one alive from the dead." And therefore I have shewed thee at what a price he purchased thee, "for thou wast not redeemed with corruptible things, as silver and gold, but with the precious blood of the Son of God, that Lamb without blemish and without spot." And now I would ask thee, as before the Lord, What does thine own heart say to it? Art thou grieved for thy former offences? Art thou willing to forsake thy sins? Art thou willing to become the cheerful, thankful servant of him, who hath "purchased thee with his own blood?"

The reader has now before him apart of that chapter of Dr. Doddridge's book headed, "A more Particular account of the Way, by which this salvation is to be obtained." He is of course better able to judge of the correctness or incorrectness, the propriety or impropriety of the observations which we are about to make upon it.

First, then, the question is one which, it never was deputed Doctor Doddridge to answer; or it is one which had been answered *ex-cathedra*, with authority, by Jesus before, almost seventeen hundred years before the Rev. gentleman was born. When the Jews enquired "*What shall we do that we may work the works of God,*" The Saviour gave them this direct, immediate, and decided answer. "*This is the work that God requires of you to do, that you believe in him whom he hath sent.*" Doctor Doddridge, at the distance of four pages from where the question is put, cites this answer to his supposed penitent, and says that what is here inculcated is the great act of saving faith. He even says it is "the *first* grand work of God." The Scriptures represent the Saviour as giving his answer immediately on having the question put to him by the people. Peter did the same on the day of Pentecost, but Doctor Doddridge does not cite the Saviour's answer to his question until he has first filled up four pages. What then is the matter of these four pages. 1st. The sinner is directed in general to repentance and faith. 2d. Urged to give up self-dependence. 3d. To seek salvation by free grace. 4th. With abhorrence of former sin, and a firm resolution of forsaking them. 5th that he solemnly commit his soul into the hands of Christ by the great vital act of faith." Such is the matter of said four pages as written by the author himself in his argument to his 9th chapter. I hope, therefore, that no violence is done to the intentions of the good man, or the matter of his chapter, when we say that his answer to the question of pardon put by the penitent sinner is substantially this, that he believe in the Son of God and repent, exercising the feelings of self-abasement, and of strong reliance for mercy on the pardoning grace of Christ alone, with a final resolution to follow him through life whithersoever he leads; but baptism for remission of sins, and the gift of the Holy Spirit form no part of the doctor's directions to his penitent, and was not intended to form any part of his directions.

The reader will be able to judge of the perfect fairness of my statement. The apostle's answer to those who had already believed, enjoins in one compact verse *Repentance* and *remission*, and states with clearness and decision the ends of that internal penitence and external obedience which it does enjoin to be remission and the gift of the Spirit; but the doctor's entire nine pages contain only the one half and far less than the one half found in Peter's verse; for he does not get a hair's-breadth beyond faith and repentance in his attempt to secure the sinner in the possession of pardon; and of receiving the Holy Spirit he says not one word. "This," says the doctor, "so far as I have been able to learn from the word of God, is the way to safety and glory, the surest the only way you can take." It must be admitted, however, that in proposing faith and repentance, Mr. Doddridge so far accords with the chief of the apostles. But why dissent from him at the very crisis of the answer; why be silent on the ordinance of remission; why say nothing of the promised Spirit; why suppress this part of the holy scriptures; why in so important a question not even allude to Peter, or to the answer that he was empowered by Jesus Christ our Lord and by the Holy Spirit, to give to the question; why not say to the penitent, "Repeat and be baptized in the name of Jesus Christ for the remission of sins, and you shall receive the gift of the Holy Spirit"? Did the doctor mean to slight the man whom the King, our Lord, was pleased to honor? Did he think himself superior to him, who had once been a fisherman? No; by no means; that is certainly not the reason why he omitted to speak of or even allude to, the distinguished apostle, in his chapter of answers to his penitent. There is a reason, however, and we shall state it. The doctor had anticipated himself. He had baptized the penitent whom he addressed, while he was yet an infant; and could not now speak of baptism again, without violating the whole scheme of Protestantism, of which he was a determined teacher. But there was another reason why the doctor must necessarily pass over this part of the scripture answer; and that is, he, with all other protestant ministers, had conceived the idea, which is so prevalent at the present day, that a sense of acquittal was to be acquired by the penitent believer through that frame of mind with which regeneration inspires the convert; and not that by which faith, repentance, and baptism for remission of sins inspires him. These two reasons may have formed the doctor's apology for not having directed his penitent to do as Peter had commanded those to do who sought to be loosed from their sins.

But again; the Rev. author might, with many others, have thought, that the repentance and remission, which was preached by the apostles on the day of Pentecost, was not intended to be preached in all the world. This also might have been preferred by him as an apology. But why did he fall into this mistake? Did not the Lord Jesus say, that the repentance and remission, which the apostles were to preach in all the world, they were to begin to preach first at Jerusalem? Whatever then was the nature and kind of the repentance and remission preached by the apostles and by Peter in particular there, that was the repentance and remission, which they were to preach "in all the world," in Asia, in Africa, in Europe. Now that repentance, was repentance through faith in the person and blood of Christ; and that remission was remission through baptism into the name of Jesus Christ. These, then, are to be published "in all the world." But remission by baptism into the name of Christ, upon the confession of faith in the person and blood of Christ, is that part of the apostolic gospel which Dr. Doddridge has omitted in his answer to the question of salvation in his "Rise and Progress." So that in fact he has left out the positive and practical acquittal of his penitent altogether.

The doctor uses the following strong language in regard to faith and repentance, "And the reasons that now recommend repentance and faith as fit and as necessary, will continue invariable, so long as the perfections of the blessed God are the same, and as long as his blessed Son continues the same." On this plan of reasoning may we not add, The reasons that now recommend remission by baptism into the name of Christ as fit and as necessary, will continue invariable, as long as the wants and sinfulness of man are the same, and as long as the gospel preached at Jerusalem continues to be the same. "Be assured" says the author, "that if ever you are saved, you must ascribe that salvation entirely to the free grace of God." We add that if it was gracious and merciful in God to publish faith and repentance as the principles on which he would bestow remission of sins, it was equally gracious and merciful in him to institute baptism by which to convey to sinners this remission. His grace appears as much in the one case as it does in the other.—But it is the offering and out-pouring of Christ's precious blood, and neither baptism, repentance, nor faith, that form the procuring cause of forgiveness. Yet God's grace appears and is resplendent in all these things; for as the death of Christ procured pardon; these things bring it home to such as by them are fitted to receive it.

"Go to Him, the Redeemer, O sinner, this day, this moment, with all thy sins about thee. Go just as thou art, for if thou wilt never apply to him, till thou art first righteous and holy, thou wilt never be righteous and holy at all." This is most excellent, and accords precisely with the example of Peter, who received in one day to baptism and the bosom of the church, her honors, and all her privileges, three thousand souls with "all their sins about them." The only difference between Peter and Mr. Doddridge is, that the former, by baptizing his converts, showed what "*coming to Christ*" means; while the instructions of the latter on this point are very indefinite and obscure, and do not agree with those of the inspired apostles.

"But know, that to reject it, *this way of salvation,* is thine eternal death. For as there is no other name under heaven given among men, whereby we can be saved, but this of Jesus of Nazareth, so there is no other *method* but this, in which Jesus himself will save us." *Method*—The doctor then admits that Christ has a method by which to save us; and that method is one. If it be one, then it must be invariably the same; the same now as on the day of Pentecost. Eighteen hundred years have elapsed since Christianity began. Peter stood at the beginning of that period and doctor Doddridge at the end of it. Which of these two, then, was the more likely to know and teach the *one* invariable *method,* which Christ has appointed for the remission of our sins? Peter has it faith, repentance, and baptism; Doddridge faith and repentance only. I humbly deem it my duty to believe Peter to be correct, and Doctor Doddridge to be in an error. I will, therefore, teach and follow the instructions of the former, and not those of the latter, but only so far as they agree with those of the former. But no disparagement to the piety of Mr. Doddridge. I am satisfied he had no official and original authority to answer the question agitated in his ninth chapter. But the apostle had authority. I am satisfied that while he had liberty with all other Christians to answer this question as the holy apostle did, he had no liberty to answer it in his own way.

"May I be enabled to *speak as his oracle,* that is, in such a manner, as faithfully to echo back what the sacred oracles teach." The desire which the pious author here breathes, was probably granted him to the full extent of the doctrines of his own church; but beyond those he has not gone, and it is very probable that his religious prejudices, like those of many other men, were such that beyond these doctrines he could not go, even with the holy apostle to guide him. The Reverend doctor was esteemed a zealous and very devout Christian in his day; but in a question which so vitally affects our salvation, we have to give the preference to inspiration and authority in the apostle over those excellent qualities in the doctor.

It is allowed then, that the Reverend author prescribes faith and repentance as the means for attaining salvation; but it is most evident at the same time, that he falls short of Peter's answer to the question of salvation by the mighty difference of the sin-remitting ordinance of baptism. But we have not got at the root of the matter yet. As the doctor left out of his annunciation of the gospel something, viz: remission that should have been added to faith and repentance; so he has in it something, namely: special operations of the Spirit which should not have been put before faith and repentance; and by these means he neither began nor ended his gospel as Peter did the true gospel. Those who believe in the word of God being a dead letter, and incapable of "converting the soul that lies in sin," without a special and preparatory operation of the Spirit, have discovered that sinners and infidels have made what they call a bad use of the doctrine, that is, they have said that it destroyed all responsibility to God; for he never could punish them for doing what the almighty power of the Spirit alone could effect. Some preachers, therefore, deem it prudent, when on the actual business of converting sinners, to say but little of the preparatory operation of the Spirit; this may account for the author's silence on this point in the chapter which has been quoted from the "Rise and Progress." We are not to imagine, nevertheless, that Mr. Doddridge did not with all the orthodox, among whom he shone as peculiarly orthodox, believe like them in the special and preparatory operation of the Holy Spirit in order to make the sinner will his own salvation. While, therefore, he invited, and exhorted, and reasoned, and remonstrated with the sinner to repent and believe, he still held to the fact or at least the protestant doctrine, that men could not even by the word of God, either believe or repent, unless that word, which he held to be a dead letter, was first "made fruitful by the infinite power of the Spirit." Thus we make the word of God of none effect by our traditions. But that the doctor did really, after all his preaching, believe true faith and true repentance were wrought in the mind by the Spirit, is manifest from his making sinners pray thus, "Save me, O Lord, who earnestly *desire* to repent and believe!" Again: "Speak, Lord, by thy blessed Spirit, and banish my fears!" I am bold to say, that in the archives of Christianity, in the whole New Testament, the most orthodox professor in Christendom would be unable to find one solitary instance of a sinner, who like the doctor's one had neither faith nor repentance in Jesus Christ, calling upon him to give him these principles by the Holy Spirit. "*Speak, Lord, by thy blessed Spirit!*" What an insult to the Holy Spirit! What contempt is here offered to the holy scriptures if the doctor could have seen it! The blessed Redeemer thought that the Jews having Moses and the prophets, had all that was necessary to keep them from hell, and guide them to heaven; and represents the very Father of the Faithful himself saying to Dives, that if his brethren would not hear them, they would not hear "if one should arise from the dead." But in the case before us, the sinner is taught to look away from the word which the Spirit has already spoken, to something else which he may yet speak! Now in the name of all that is right in religion, did the doctor imagine that the Holy Spirit would speak and answer the great question of salvation by Peter and the other apostles in one way, and to his sinner in a different way? "*Speak, Lord, by thy blessed Spirit.*" Did not the Lord do this by the apostle on the day of Pentecost? It is written, if the person who reads this book cares for what is written, it is written that Peter spoke "as the Spirit gave him utterance." "*And banish my fears.*" If the Spirit would speak again, could he be supposed to describe a better means for quieting the fears of the sinner than what he proposed on Pentecost? The converts on that day were in an agony of alarm; their fears were aroused to the highest pitch of terror, being pierced to the heart with the madness and murderousness of their own doings; for they had crucified the Lord of glory. Now did the Spirit speak to them? Yes; he spoke to them by Peter. Did what he said quiet their fears? Most assuredly. It filled them with gladness to hear from the Spirit, by the apostle, that the forgiveness of their enormities was so nigh to hand. They *gladly* received the word, and were baptized, were pardoned, and received the Spirit of Christ. What would Peter and others have thought of that man among the converts, who, like the doctors' sinner, should have hesitated and prayed, "Speak, Lord, by thy blessed Spirit, and banish my fears?" This should teach the reader that no uninspired person, such as doctor Doddridge, however pious his style, and warm his exhortations, and rational his remonstrances, is at all to be trusted for an answer to the question, the all important question, What shall we do to be saved? This has been fairly and fully answered already; and to repudiate the written, living, quick, and pregnant oracle of the Eternal God, for the vagaries and romance of a systematic Divinity, is impious and profane.

The theologists of the Protestant Reformation, have summed up ultimately in the term *regeneration* every thing of a saving nature. We shall endeavor, therefore, to bring before the reader in the following chapter their views of this matter.

In the mean time, beloved reader, let me exhort you to be not at all discouraged by the mistakes of the Rev. gentleman whose book we have been examining. He was, with all his errors, a man of unfeigned devotion to God, and in this point of view, is worthy of your admiration and imitation. Let me exhort you, therefore, to improve every admonition of his and of the holy scriptures most particularly to your own salvation. Draw near to God and he will draw near to you. Cleanse your hands from all injustice, your tongue and lips from all evil and profane language. Be humble, and reform. Your opposition to Christianity will never in the smallest degree intercept its march to the dominion of the world. The disciples of the Son of God have in thousands, and in tens of thousands, returned to the scriptures, and many of them are men whom you could never subdue. They are men profoundly and variously skilled in the question of Revealed Religion, and if you think yourself secure and standing upon the rock of truth, while you contemn God and the Holy Scriptures, you greatly deceive yourself. You have only to come in contact with those to whom I refer, to be made to feel this too. Infidelity towards God is a hollow thing; and can boast of victory and wear laurels only in the presence of those who are ignorant of the scriptures. Its crown soon withers before the majesty of truth and the power and point and glory of those who are able to handle it. Though I have conversed with sceptics, infidels, and even atheists, I never, I protest, have found one of either of these classes of men, who could lay in a truly weighty argument against the scriptures. There was a flaw either in their proposition, their proof, or their conclusion. But there can be no error in reforming as the scriptures enjoin, or in serving God who created you. This is an obvious obligation; ten thousand arguments impose this upon you. Return, therefore, in the name of God. Seek him who is mighty to save, who is omnipotent to kill. Fear him who after having killed the body, is able to cast both soul and body into hell fire. Yes; I say unto you fear him. These are the words of your Saviour and Lord, and we leave them with you. May you be suitably impressed with their tremendous significance.

CHAPTER IV

Doctor Beecher's Answer to the Question, "What Shall I Do to Be Saved?"
Regeneration, the Scriptures, &c.

VIEWS IN THEOLOGY, BY LYMAN BEECHER, D. D. &C.

This is the title of a volume from which we purpose making some extracts illustrative of the doctrine of regeneration as held by Presbyterians in general, and Dr. Beecher in particular, with his views of the holy scriptures.

This gentleman's orthodoxy having been suspected by some of his brethren in the ministry, his chapter on regeneration is written to show that he has ever taught on this matter those things which were in perfect "accordance with the bible, the confession, and the generally received opinion of the orthodox church."

In our chapter on Faith and Justification, Sanctification, &c. we observed, as the reader will possibly recollect, that faith, being the primary element of salvation as regards mental principle, operated upon its possessor by fruits both internal and external. The internal effects of faith, its influences on the mind, are indicated in the scriptures by the words "purification," "reconciliation," "sanctification," "conversion," &c. Its external, effects, by "righteousness," "good works," "obedience," "work of faith," "works," &c. We observed also, that there is a third class of words indicating not any thing done in us or by us by faith, but something done for us on account of it; these are "justification," "forgiveness of sins that are past," "righteousness of faith," "righteousness of God," "gift of righteousness," "gift of the Spirit," "forgiveness of all trespasses," "not imputing unto them their trespasses," &c. &c. Will the reader please keep in mind the effects of faith upon the believer, and the rich blessings of pardon, the Holy Spirit, &c. which are granted to him by this while we further premise a few things still necessary to be understood before he can fully perceive the value of that part of Doctor Beecher's book now to be examined? If he does, we shall perhaps, by the blessing of God and the guidance of the holy scriptures, be enabled to relieve his mind in regard to what the holy scriptures mean by regeneration. But observe Doctor Beecher is a man of intellect and literature far above contempt. He is, indeed, a piece of heavy metal; and it is neither easy to get the leaver under him, nor to pry him up from the ground which he occupies even when all is fixed for doing so. Still the word of God is powerful. It is truth; which, the ancient said, is mighty above all things and must prevail.

The state of respite in which mankind have existed since the Fall, is still a state of condemnation. The death, which was threatened, is still inflicted; and the scriptures positively declare, that the wrath of God abides upon that man, who does not believe in the only begotten Son of God. This is the present state of universal man.

But the Divine Benevolence has since the Fall originated a New Institution called the church; which is not natural but supernatural in its origin and purposes. It is of God, and is of grace and not of nature. Now the man, who has entered the church, has passed from one state to another, that is, he has passed from a state of respite into one in which eternal life is granted; or he has left the world and joined the church; or, as we sometimes express it, he has passed from nature to grace; from a state of sin, misery, and death, to one of righteousness, peace, and joy in the Holy Spirit. Now this transfer from nature to grace required to be accomplished by some visible means. Every party, then, who practises Baptism admits it to be this visible means. It is that ordinance, therefore, by which we pass from the world to the New Institution and by it receive remission.

Since the restoration of the true gospel, great efforts have been made to clothe certain religious principles, as faith and repentance, with the important office of translating men "from darkness to light; from the government of Satan to that of God." But faith and repentance being internal invisible things of the mind; cannot possibly be identified with an external visible ordinance for changing man's estate. When Adam changed his condition from innocence to guilt, it was by one bodily, external visible act, viz: the infraction of divine law. "He took also, and did eat." He was translated from his natural into the present preternatural state by a well-defined act of disobedience. His change could be seen. Well, did he fall into this visibly, and by obvious means? Yes; and shall we be taken out of our condition invisibly, and without means? No. When any thing in nature or society changes its state, it is by obvious visible means, as a child at birth, persons at marriage, and all men at death. Faith and repentance are things whose existence can be known only by their works. "Show me your faith without works," said the apostle James, meaning that those errorists whom he addressed could not do this, and therefore he adds, "I will show you my faith by my works." Not faith or repentance, therefore, is seized on to translate us from the world to the church, but obedience flowing from these mental matters. Obedience has respect to law. Christianity, therefore, must deliver a law for the accomplishment of our translation. Well, what is that? Baptism. The law of baptism. Every believer is to be baptized. "Be baptized every one of you." This, which began in Jerusalem, has to be "preached in all the world."

Man fell through law, he is restored to law; he fell by one act of disobedience, he is raised by one act of obedience. He changed his condition by neglecting the word of God, he must now improve it by attending to that word. He misimproved his knowledge, he must now improve his faith. He yielded to temptation, he must now submit to instruction. He listened to Satan he must now hear God. He perhaps thought God did not mean what he said, he now knows he meant what he said. He perhaps thought that the Divinity could compromise law, he now perceives that this is impossible. Let every one of us then improve our experience by yielding obedience to the gospel, that our sins may be taken away; for the remission of sins is the prime element in the gifts conferred by the gospel.

But again, we have said in the preceding part of this treatise, that sin may be considered in the love of it, the practice, state, guilt, power, and punishment of it. Well, as faith is to destroy it from the heart, repentance from the practice, and baptism to translate us from the state of it, so it required that something should erase it from the conscience also. When a man has incurred debt, what is it that will destroy from his mind the consciousness of that debt, and the regret consequent upon it? Nothing so perfectly as the payment of it; the liquidation of the debt is the annihilation of his sense or consciousness of it, and of his fears concerning it. His alarms are quieted when his debts are paid. Men, therefore, require to have their sins pardoned; first, because they are guilty of sin; secondly, because they cannot serve God acceptably with an evil conscience; thirdly, because it would be abhorrent to enter a divine institution, as the church, carrying along with us all our former transgressions; this would be to make her the store-house of iniquity; and finally it was, that we might be pardoned our Lord and Saviour died.

This transfer of the converts then, from the world to the church, enables us to understand another set of scriptural words, phrases, and figures which could not possibly be explained by any other fact in our religion. The change, which obtains at death, is a very obvious one; as is that also which passes upon the person, who is raised from the dead. Well, these two great changes, of a death and a resurrection, are employed by the apostle to denote that through which he passes who is translated into the church. Our faith realizing Christ as our substitute in law, we are said to be crucified with him; and being by this belief become dead to the world and sin, we are taken and "buried with him in baptism." Thus we are put out of the world. How are we received into the church? By being raised up in this ordinance, "wherein also," says the apostle when speaking of baptism, "ye are risen with him," through faith in the strong working of God, who raised him from the dead. Thus our translation from the world to the church is illustrated or shadowed forth by a death, burial, and resurrection. But the matrimonial state sometimes interposes between the cradle and the grave; and this civil change is employed by Paul as figurative of Christ and the church. She was living among the Jews and Gentiles all defiled by sin; still "Christ loved her and gave himself for her that he might sanctify and cleansed her with the washing of water by the word, that he might present her to himself a glorious church." Eph. 5:25, 26, &c. Here the church, passing from her state of celibacy and sin to that of righteousness and marriage with Christ, is cleansed by a "bath of water," as McKnight translates the above passages, which all allow to be baptism. But again; before men can either die or be married they must be born; a birth is, therefore, employed in the Scriptures to describe the translation of the believer from the world to the church. "Unless a man is born again or regenerated:" "born again;" "born of water and the Spirit;" "born of God;" "washing of regeneration," are some of the expressions found in Scriptures relative to this transfer. Here then we have three figures, a death, burial, and resurrection as one, a marriage as a second, and a birth as the third and last, all intended to describe or illustrate the translation of the convert from the world to the church. Now as a man must be dead before he can be raised; so the believer in Christ must be dead to the world and buried in baptism before he can be raised in that ordinance to serve Christ in newness of life. Again, as a man must love his partner before he is married; so the convert believes in Christ and loves him before he is baptized. Lastly, as a child must be begotten before it is born; so a man must be begotten to God before he is born to God, or, which is the same born of water, or baptized. These figures of a burial, marriage, and birth, give origin to an extremely metaphorical style of writing, which is kept up all through the sacred volume. In accordance with the first Paul says to the Romans and Colossians "for you are dead." To the Corinthians, in harmony with the figure of marriage, he says "I have espoused you to Christ," and in accordance with the last, viz: a birth, we are styled the children of God, his sons and daughters, heirs of God, born of God, that is, in a manner agreeable with the will of God, which is by the waters of baptism, children of the Kingdom, of the family of God on earth, &c.

We have now gathered up from the face of scripture four distinct matters, the internal and external effects of faith, our translation to the church, and the blessings granted to us on the occasion of this translation. We have also collected separately four distinct classes of words. The first denoting a change of mind by faith; the second importing a change of conduct by the same principle; the third denoting a change of state by baptism; and the last class indicating those blessings and gifts bestowed upon us on believing and obeying the gospel. We shall now sum up those classes of words under four distinct heads, that the reader may see which class relates to the mind, which to our behavior, which to our translation from the world to the church, and which to those mercies bestowed upon the translated convert.

Class 1: Words which relate to a change of the mind produced by faith, "illumination, opening the eyes, opening the eyes of the understanding, enlightening, knowledge of God, knowledge of Christ, reconciliation, conversion, purification, hope, sanctification of spirit." These are the internal results of faith upon the soul.

Class 2. Words which relate to the change in our outward behavior. "Obedience, good works, righteousness, justice, mercy, truth, goodness, reformation, benevolence, charity, holiness, pity, condescension, long-suffering, patience, diligence, zeal, fidelity," &c. These are external symbols of faith.

Class 3: Words referring to the changing of our state from the world to the church by baptism. "Washed, bodies washed with pure water, purged from his old sins, be baptized for the remission of your sins, engrafted, arise and be baptized and wash away your sins, planted in the likeness of his death, arisen with Christ, married to Christ, I have espoused you to Christ, dead to the world, alive to God, raised to newness of life, the washing of water, born of water, born again, washing of regeneration, bath, *loutron* of regeneration, the regeneration, Your life is hid with Christ by God's authority, Seeing ye are arisen with Christ," &c.

Class 4. Words describing the blessings which are granted to us on obeying the gospel. "Justified from all sin, justified by faith, salvation, redemption, the forgiveness of sins, gift of the Holy Spirit, spirit of glory, spirit of adoption, Holy Spirit, he has made us to sit together in Heavenly places, the church, gift of righteousness, gift of grace," &c.

These four classes of words, and phrases, and figures, describe respectively a change of mind, a change of conduct, a change of state from nature to grace, and the blessings granted subsequent to this change of state. The reader will please observe to which of these classes of words *regeneration* belongs. The word itself means born again, and belongs to the third class, all of which refer to baptism, or the change of state, which obtains in that ordinance; born of water is the same in signification with bath of regeneration. From what has been said, the reader will be able to discern the nature of Dr. Beecher's error, when he defines regeneration. He places it in the first of the above classes of words, instead of the third, and errs "by defining it to be a change of mind, instead of a change of state, thus:—

1. THE NATURE OF REGENERATION.—By this I mean the nature of the change which is produced in the subject by the Spirit of God. This, according to my understanding of the Bible, is correctly disclosed in the doctrine of effectual calling as taught in the Confession of Faith and Catechisms, as including 'the enlightening of the minds of men spiritually and savingly to understand the things of God, taking away their heart of stone, and giving a heart of flesh—renewing their wills and determining them to that which is good, and effectually drawing them to Jesus Christ—yet so as they come freely, being made willing by his grace—in his accepted time, inviting and drawing them to Jesus Christ by his word and spirit—so as they, (although in themselves dead in sin) are hereby made willing and able truly to answer his call, and to accept and embrace the grace offered and conveyed therein;' or as the Shorter Catechism teaches, more concisely and with no less correctness:

'Effectual calling is the work of God's Spirit, whereby, convincing us of our sin and misery, enlightening our minds in the knowledge of Christ, and renewing our wills, he doth persuade and enable us to embrace Jesus Christ, freely offered to us in the gospel.'

The substance of what is taught by this various phraseology is, that a change is effected in regeneration in respect to man's chief *end*, in turning from the supreme love of self, to the supreme love of God—from gratifying and exalting self, to gratifying and exalting God—a giving up and a turning from the world in all its pomp and vanities as the chief good, and returning to God as the chosen portion of the soul —withdrawing the affections from things below, and setting them on things above—ceasing to lay up our treasure on earth, and laying it up in heaven—and so grieving for and hating our past sins, as that we turn from them all to God, purposing and endeavoring to walk with God in all the ways of new obedience.

This, it will not, I think, be doubted, comprehends correctly the moral change which takes place in regeneration."

The Doctor appeals for his definition of regeneration to the Confession and Catechism exclusively. The Bible is not cited as authority. This however is not very astonishing inasmuch as having been charged with a declension from the standards of his own church, he wrote his book not to prove that he was a sound Christian but a sound Presbyterian. Having mistaken the true import of the word, and its relation to the transfer of a converted man into the church by baptism, the reader will not be surprised that the Doctor, in the following attempt to prove the spirit to be the efficient cause of regeneration, should entirely fall, and close his demonstration without adducing one single passage with the name Holy Spirit in it.

"THE AUTHOR OR EFFICIENT CAUSE OF REGENERATION IS GOD. By efficient cause I mean that power without which all other influence is vain, and, by which, means otherwise impotent are made effectual. The power then, which in all cases is the immediate antecedent and effectual cause of regeneration, is the special influence of the Holy Spirit. It is called the Holy Spirit, not by way of preeminent personal excellence, but as the divine agent to whom is commuted the work of commencing and perfecting holiness in the hearts of men.

That God is the efficient cause of regeneration, is plainly taught in the text, and throughout the bible, in the various forms of metaphor, direct testimony, and multiplied implications. Is moral pollution in the way—'I will sprinkle clean water upon you, and ye shall be clean.' Is stupidity and insensibility the impediment to be removed—'I will take away the stony heart and give a heart of flesh.' Is the condition of man represented by the battle field, a capacious valley whitened with bones— it is, God who says unto these bones, 'Behold I will cause breath to enter into you, and ye shall live.' Is it the helplessness of infancy abandoned in the open field—with no eye to pity or arm to save—it is God who 'passes by and bids us live.' Is it darkness which impedes our salvation— it is 'God who commanded the light to shine out of Darkness, who shines in our hearts.' Is death the calamity, a resurrection is the remedy —'You hath he quickened who were dead in trespasses and sins, and raised us up to sit together in heavenly places in Christ.' Is it the annihilation of spiritual life, regeneration is a new creature—'created anew in Christ Jesus unto good works.' Is it the old man who makes resistance to the claims of God—the regenerated are said to be 'born again, not of blood,' i. e. not by natural descent, nor of the will of the flesh, the striving and efforts of sinners to save themselves, 'nor of the will of man,' the efforts of men to save their fellow men, 'but of God; WHOSOEVER LOVETH IS BORN OF GOD."

But the Doctor is desirous to save the scriptures notwithstanding all that he says of the Spirit; and, therefore, to the efficiency of the one he adds the effectuality of the other, and teaches that the two combined are necessary to the accomplishment of regeneration, thus:—

"THE EFFECTUAL MEANS OF REGENERATION IS THE WORD OF GOD. By effectual means, I understand the means which God employs and renders efficient in producing the change. That he accomplishes the change by his mighty power associated with means, is the unequivocal testimony of the Bible and the Confession of Faith. Chosen to salvation, the Elect of God are, through sanctification of the Spirit and belief of the truth whereunto he called them *by the Gospel.* The Gospel is denominated 'the power of God and the wisdom of God unto Salvation.' 'The law of the Lord is perfect, converting the soul.' 'The word of God is quick and powerful.' 'The seed is the word.' 'Being born again, not of corruptible seed, but of incorruptible, by the word of God;—and this is the word which by the gospel is preached unto you.' 'Ye shall know the truth, and the truth shall make you free.' 'Sanctify them through thy truth. Thy word is truth.' 'Seeing ye have purified your souls in obeying the truth through the Spirit.' 'They shall be taught of God.' 'I drew them with the cords of love.' 'No man can come unto me, except the Father which hath sent me draw him.' 'Every one, therefore, which hath heard and learned of the Father, cometh unto me."

The author proposes to shew that to the accomplishment of this one effect, regeneration, two causes are necessary, the word and Spirit, the one efficient and the other effectual! But this distinction is arbitrary, the two words meaning the same thing, thus:—*Efficient,* the cause which makes effects; *Effectual,* productive of effects. Accordingly, the doctor drops his distinction and, in the beginning of the last paragraph quoted, says that by effectual means, he understands efficient means, or means that God renders efficient! Reader look at the sentence. Here it is "By *effectual* means I understand the means which God employs and renders *efficient* in producing the change." He had already told what his efficient means were, the Spirit; now he has another means made efficient, namely, the word! But, again; the Rev. gentleman does violence, unintentionally I hope, to the confession and catechism, by the distinction which he would establish. We were brought up a presbyterian as well as himself, and like the Doctor claim to understand the oracles of the party. If the reader will look back to Mr. Beecher's definition of regeneration taken from these books, he will see there, that the Spirit is made the *effectual* not the *efficient* means of salvation. I will quote the words, "*Effectual* (not *efficient*) calling is the work of God's Spirit;" "and effectually (not efficiently) drawing them to Christ." Thus the Doctor both departs from the distinction which he established and from the standards of his own church.

The following sentence in the last quotation, ought to be understood. The Rev. minister seems to quote scripture on account of its sound rather than its sense, and to pitch forth his authorities from the common translation of the New Testament, wholly irrespective of the standard critics and commentators of his own church.

"But we are bound to give thanks always to God for your brethren beloved of the Lord, because God hath from the beginning chosen you to salvation, through sanctification of the Spirit and belief of the truth."

Now here, it is readily admitted, is an election, for we believe in scriptural election; and it is here said to be effected by two things, sanctification of the Spirit, and belief of the truth. Well, agreeing with Mr. Beecher on the belief of the truth, we differ from him wholly in regard to what is meant by "sanctification of the Spirit." He means by it an operation of the Holy Spirit assisting to believe the truth. But a learned doctor of his own church, McKnight, renders it "sanctification of spirit" or mind or soul; and consequently shows that it is the spirit or soul of the believer and not the Holy Spirit of God that is named in the verse. If the reader will look at the above quotation, he will perceive that the Thessalonians, to whom Paul wrote it, are said to be chosen to salvation. This word salvation, according to the classification, which we have already taken notice of, means the forgiveness of sins, or pardon, "He shall save his people from their sins." They were chosen to forgiveness then, and not to "damnation" like some others, spoken of in the same chapter, "who believed not the truth." But how were they chosen, or on what account? because they had believed the truth, and the truth had taken a sanctifying effect upon their mind or spirit, and led them to obedience.

The apostle Peter uses similar language in the beginning of his second epistle, where he salutes the disciples as elect "by a sanctification of spirit, in order to obedience and sprinkling of the blood of Jesus Christ." But what interpreter understands this of an operation of the Holy Spirit upon the mind of the sinner! By rendering the expression as I have quoted it, Doctor McKnight shows us that the Greek text imports by "a sanctification of spirit," one of the immediate and internal effects of faith on the soul. The sinner believes the gospel on its proper evidence, this most precious faith takes a sanctifying effect on his soul or spirit; he next obeys the gospel; and so receives salvation by the forgiveness of his sins, and now stands ready to receive the Holy Spirit from Christ after having obeyed the truth.

If the doctor had even proved from scripture, that an assistant operation of the Spirit was granted in order to make or enable sinners to believe the gospel, he would not have demonstrated his proposition after all. He ought first to have shown that *regeneration* is a word of that kind which relates to the mind and not to something else, as baptism; and secondly, that the Spirit accomplished it, but he takes for granted the first of these propositions—that regeneration relates to the mind—and fails to apply the scriptures to sustain the last. However the case did not call on the doctor to be correct in the use of the word of God. He had to prove himself a Presbyterian, and if his colleagues and accusers were satisfied, sound was just as good as sense, and the doctor had attained his purpose, for he wrote to "justify himself before men."

Having made a mental something of regeneration, instead of referring it to its own class of words; having mistaken the confession and catechism, and made the *word* the effectual cause, while they make the *Spirit* the effectual cause, the Reverend gentleman next adduces the orthodox and standard writers, as supporting him in his ideas of the whole business.

The Doctor quotes from Knapp, Calvin, Synod of Dort, Whitsius, Witherspoon, Owen, and Howe, as follows:

"In accordance with these views of the proper instrumentality of the word in regeneration, is the testimony of Augustin, as quoted by Knapp.

'With respect to the manner in which saving grace operates, Augustin believed, that in the case of those who enjoy revelation, grace commonly acts by means of the word, or the divine doctrine, but sometimes *directly*; because God is not confined to the use of means. On this point there was great logomachy.' *Knapp's Theology*, vol. ii. p. 57.

To the same purpose is the exposition by Calvin, of Hebrews 4:12 —"For the word of God is quick and powerful, and sharper than a two-edged sword, piercing even to the dividing asunder of soul and spirit, and of the joints and marrow, and is a discerner of the thoughts and intents of the heart."

It is to be observed that the apostle is here speaking of the word of God which is brought to us by the ministry of men. For these imaginations are silly, and even pernicious, to wit, that the internal word indeed is efficacious, but that the word which proceeds from the mouth of man is destitute of all effect. I confess, truly, that its efficacy does not proceed from the tongue of man nor reside in the word itself, but that it is owing entirely to the Holy Spirit; nevertheless, this is no objection to the idea that the Spirit puts forth his power in the preached word. For God, since he does not speak by himself, but by men, sedulously insists on this, lest his doctrine should be received contemptuously, because men are its ministers. Thus Paul, when he calls the gospel the power of God, purposely dignifies his preaching with this title, because he saw that it had been slandered by some, and despised by others. Moreover, when he calls the word *living*, its relation to men is to be understood, as appears more clearly in the second epithet; for he shows what this life is, when he calls it *efficacious*: for it is the design of the apostle to show what the use of the word is in respect to us.' The words rendered *living* and *efficacious* in the above paragraph, are in the English version translated *quick* and *powerful*."

The Synod of Dort is unequivocal also, in the doctrine of effectual calling by the word and Spirit.

What, therefore, neither the light of nature nor the law could do, that God performs by the power of the Holy Spirit, through the word, or ministry of reconciliation; which is the gospel concerning the Messiah, by which it hath pleased God to save believers, as well under the Old as the New Testament. *Scott's Synod of Dort*, p. 137.

Witsius, a standard writer in the church, says, "Regeneration is that supernatural act of God whereby a new and divine light is infused into the elect—persons spiritually dead—and that from the incorruptible seed of the word of God made fruitful by the infinite power of the Spirit."

Witherspoon—one of the best standard writers in our church, and whose treatise on regeneration is the best written and the most judicious, scriptural, copious, accurate, and experimental dissertation upon that subject in the English language, speaking of the nature of regeneration says: "As, therefore, the change is properly of a moral, or spiritual nature, it seems properly and directly to consist in these two things, 1. That our supreme and chief end is to glorify God, and that every other aim be subordinate to this. 2. That the soul rest in God as its chief happiness, and habitually prefer his favor to every other enjoyment."

The authority of Owen is among the best orthodox authorities: His language is as follows:

"We grant that in the work of regeneration, the Holy Spirit towards those that are adult, doth make use of the word, both the law and the gospel, and the ministry of the church, in the dispensation of it, as the ordinary means thereof; yea, this is ordinarily the whole external means that is made use of in this work, and an efficacy proper unto it, it is accompanied withal."

Howe is equally express on this subject, he says—

"And whereas, therefore, in this work there is a communication and participation of the divine nature, this is signified to be his power. If you look to 2 Peter 1:3, 4, compared, "According as his divine power has given us all things appertaining to life and godliness, through the knowledge of him that hath called us to glory and virtue; whereby are given to us exceeding great and precious promises; that by these you might be partakers of his divine nature." Here is a divine nature to be communicated and imparted in this great and glorious work. How is it to be communicated? It is true it must be by apt and suitable means; to wit, by the great and precious promises given us in the gospel. But it must be by the exertion too of a divine power."

This appeal to the above writers shows that the proposition to be proved by the author was that his views of regeneration were strictly Presbyterian. But the reader will observe that Dr. Beecher has gone backward in the orthodox church only to Calvin; and into the heterodox or papal church as far only as Augustin. I do not say that he made this stride into the Roman territory, to show whence Calvin, and the Synod of Dort, and Whitsius, and Witherspoon, and Owen, and Howe, and himself, first obtained their doctrine of *spiritual regeneration*; but I will say this, that if he had pleased to march up the stream of Christian history beyond the days of St. Augustin, and desired to be Christian rather than Presbyterian, he would have found that not a man of the orthodox church, from the apostles downwards, did, for four hundred years, ever assert that *regeneration* meant any thing but *baptism*. Now if the Doctor doubts this, he can find ample proof of it by looking into the writings of the early fathers; and lest he should not do it, I shall here set down a piece in which he can hear the well known voice of Dr. Wall, the Episcopalian, on this point.

Mr. Wesley, whose tract on baptism is before me, says; "Dr. Wall has largely shown that the word *regenerating* does positively in the writings of Irenaeus, and in the usual phrase of those times, signify baptism. He mentions some places, which expressly declare that Christ was *regenerated* by John, meaning that he was *baptized* by him.

Near the time that Irenaeus wrote the above treatise, Clemens Alexandrinus wrote his *Pedagogue*, wherein he expressly says, "the word *regeneration* is the name of baptism."—Coll. of Tracts, page 376, by J. Wesley.

Brother Campbell interrogates Dr. Wall on this point in the following manner:

"Pray, Doctor, have you examined all the primitive writers, from the death of John to the fifth century?

W. Wall.—I have.

And will you explicitly avow what was the established and universal view of all Christians, public and private, for four hundred years from the nativity of the Messiah, on the import of the saying, "Except a man be born of water, and the Spirit, he cannot enter the kingdom of God?"

W. Wall.—There is not any one Christian writer, of any antiquity, in any language, but who understands it of *baptism*; and if he be not so understood, it is difficult to give an account how a person is born of *water*, any more than born of *wood*.

Did all the Christians, public and private, and all the Christian writers from Barnabas to the times of Pelagius, as far as you know, continue to use the term *regenerate* as *only* applicable to immersion?

W. Wall.—The Christians did, in all ancient times, continue the use of this name, *regeneration* for *baptism*, so that they *never* use the word *regenerate*, or *born again*, but they mean, or denote by it, *baptism*. And almost all the quotations which I shall bring in this book, shall be instances of it."

Did they not also substitute for baptism and baptise, the words, renewed, sanctified, sealed, enlightened, initiated, as well regenerated?

W. Wall.—For to baptize, they use the following words most commonly, *anagennan*, to regenerate; sometimes, *kainopoien*, or *anakainizo*, to renew; frequently *agiazein*, to sanctify. Sometimes they call it the seal; and frequently *illumination*, as it is also called; and sometimes *teliosis*, initiation. St. Austin, not less than a hundred times, expresses baptized by the word *sanctified*."

It is not, however, merely that we may be correct in the use of language that we labor to expose this thing of spiritual regeneration, as held by Protestants, and explained by the respectable gentleman whose volume is just before us. To be sure, even this were well worthy of our labor; for it is of infinite value to Christians that they employ sound words, that their language and technicalities be all scriptural, and used in the sense given to them by the sacred writers; but we argue against it on another account. By teaching that regeneration is that change which is called conversion, and that the Holy Spirit effects this by an undefinable influence on the sinner's mind, we render the word of God of none effect. We make it a dead letter, and absolutely blaspheme it. With all its excellencies, we stamp *tekel* upon it, and declare its inefficiency; we say it can accomplish nothing. I shall now quote the Doctor's views of this matter, by which the reader will see that I have not overrated the destructive effects produced by spiritual regeneration, that it has condemned the Bible as full of darkness, mourning and terror to man. The following are the Rev. Minister's words:—"It is all dark to the sinner, and mournful and terrible, till the Spirit make the gospel a reality instinct with life."

The gospel was to be good news to all people and the angels sang for joy when they made, the communication, but now the book, which contains it, is to all, "dark, and mournful, and terrible, till the Spirit makes the gospel a reality instinct with life!" Its glorious facts, the love of God and of Christ Jesus, the offers of pardon by his precious blood, the immediate salvation of the soul which it holds out, the fellowship of the saints and of the Father and the Son and the Holy Spirit to which it invites the resurrection of the dead, and eternal life in heaven, with all the glories of the New Jerusalem and a never ending eternity in the vales and by the streams of life in heaven; the wickedness of unbelief, the misery of sin, the wrath of God, the eternal judgment, the damnation of the soul with the Devil and demons and hades and the blackness of darkness for ever, are all so much dead matter, a *caput mort*, mere unintelligible jargon, to all for whom they are designed, "till the Spirit makes the gospel a reality instinct with life!" In this affair it is very difficult to say whether Dr. Beecher holds that the Spirit operates on the mind or on the word. He certainly teaches that it does both. Hark!

"While the sinner reads with darkened mind the sacred page, the Spirit makes it luminous and quick and powerful—it is as if written upon transparencies with invisible ink—unseen unfelt, till the illuminations of the Spirit throws it out in letters of fire."

"*Letters of fire!*" How greatly it is to be deplored that a person writing on an element of Christian doctrine so important as that of the intelligibility of the holy scriptures, should indulge in such bombast; *letters of fire!* The great Irving saw well, the destructive error pled for by Doctor Beecher, and, therefore, wrote the following just rebuke for all who promulgate such extravagance.

"Oh! I hate such ignorant prating, because it taketh the high airs of orthodoxy, and would blast me as a heretical liar, if I go to teach the people that the word of God is a well-spring of life, unto which they have but to stoop their lips in order to taste its sweet and refreshing waters, and be nourished unto life eternal. But these high airs and pitiful pelting words are very trifling to me, if I could but persuade men to dismiss all this cant about the mysteriousness and profound darkness of the word of God, and sift their own inward selves to find out what lethargy of conception or blindness of prejudice, what unwillingness of mind, or full possession of worldly engagements hath hitherto hindered them from drinking life into their souls from the fountain of living waters. But if I go about to persuade my brethren against the truth of experience, against the very sense and meaning of revelation, against my own conviction, that they may read till their eye grows dim with age without apprehending one word, unless if should please God, by methods unrevealed, to conjure intelligence into the hieroglyphic page; what do I but interpose another gulf between man and his Maker, dash the full cup of spiritual sweets from his lips, and leave him as lonely, helpless and desolate, as he was before the lion of the tribe of Judah did take the book of God's hidden secrets, and prevail to unloose the seals thereof.

Therefore, I cast off their ignorant and scholastic methods, and expound to my brethren, for whose regeneration I travail as one in birth, and if they will but approach this book of the Lord's in a reverent, humble, and teachable disposition, it will correct, reprove, and instruct them in righteousness, and everlasting life which we have undertaken in the strength of God to disclose. This book is the voice of the Spirit of God, which, if we disrespect, we cut ourselves off from all further communings. They talk as if a stroke of the Spirit were needed before the word can be perused. I say, no. The Word, which is the legible Spirit, must be had in reverence, and perused and thought on, and altogether treated as it deserves, or else God will give no further inspirations. What, in the name of divine wisdom and of common sense, will God allow all the visitations of his Spirit to prophet, priest and seer, which were committed to writing, that men might know and stand in awe of him—will he allow all the visitations of his own Son, his doctrines, his death, his resurrection, and his salvation—will he allow the legacy of spiritual gifts and graces promised and pressed upon the children of men—will he allow all this record and testament of divine gifts to go into a kind of desuetude, to die into obscurity and death, to be misused, neglected and spurned, and to one that is so holding them in contempt and neglect, come with a divine and masterful effusion of his grace, and enforce upon his unwilling soul that understanding and regard of his Word which heretofore he had not nor cared not to have? I say not. But upon the other hand, he will honor his Word by testimonies of his Spirit, the residue of which he retaineth in order to honor the record which he hath given. He will give us his Spirit just in proportion to our reverence and use of his Word. The Word is the first thing, the Spirit is the next thing, or rather they are two things which should never be parted. Keep aloof from the oracles of God, keep aloof from the places where they are discoursed of, from the companies which obey them, and you are not far from the kingdom of Satan. Come to the Word and meditate thereon; go where its truths are proclaimed, watch at the gates where divine wisdom speaketh, and look upon the men whose lives she adorneth, and you are not far from the kingdom of God. Think you not, that because the Ethiopian eunuch read in Isaiah that Philip was ordered to join himself to his chariot, and preach to him Christ, so if you read as he read, seeking intelligence, God will send an interpreter of what is dark to your hand, or send the unction and teaching of the Spirit over your very bosom."

Seeing Doctor Beecher holds such views respecting Regeneration, the operation of the Spirit, and the holy scriptures, the reader will not think it strange that he should err also when he attempts to answer the great question of salvation, and actually intrude himself upon the office of the Apostle Peter. This great scholar preached some years ago a sermon, in which he purposed to show a person the way into the kingdom of heaven, or how to be saved. I published some notes of it, which will show the reader how dangerous it is to leave the first principles of the Christian institution, and how bewildering to attempt an answer, irrespective of the good guidance of the scriptures, to the vital question, What shall I do to be saved?

The Dr. chose for his text the following admonitory portion of Holy Scripture, "*Enter ye in at the strait gate &c.*" and commenced by reading the story of a young lady who had felt great excitement on the subject of her soul's salvation. In her extreme anxiety she was induced to make known her case by letter to a friend, and after many explanations, concluded by saying, that if he, her friend, had nothing to communicate but "*repent and believe the gospel,*" an answer to her letter would be unnecessary—faith and repentance being to her either impossible or incomprehensible!

The object of the Doctor's discourse, then, was to show a different way—was to put the young lady, and all such, upon a different route into the kingdom—to bring the salvation of God near to them, and to make it more accessible to all, than it is by faith and repentance!

Any person, whose mind is not wholly abused on the subject of the Christian religion, may easily know how to enter the kingdom, if he will only condescend to let Peter and the other Apostles and evangelists be his directors. Hear, now, Acts, 2 chap, what Peter said when he opened the kingdom—"Repent and be baptized every one of you, in the name of Jesus Christ, for the remission of sins, and you shall receive the gift of the Holy Spirit," &c. To believe "Jesus to be Christ," to repent and be baptized for remission, is the way, and the only way, into the kingdom of heaven, proposed by the original preachers.

The first way into the kingdom described by the Doctor, was, "that his hearers should abandon the world, and" said he "the moment you cease to be attracted by the world, that moment are your souls in the kingdom!"

But as this might be considered more difficult than faith and repentance themselves, he lowered the terms, and was willing to bring the kingdom as near to his audience as ever he could, and nearer. "Give up your idol, then, said the Doctor, and this done your souls are in the kingdom!"

"Love to God," was then proposed as the terms, and the hearers might meet him at any point in his providence, law, or gospel! but if they could not love him supremely, he would accept them on the footing of a simple preference, "give him a bare preference," said the Doctor, "and he will receive you and your idol too!"

The love of enemies was next plead for as a way into the kingdom, and if this were too hard, the love of friends would do; at any rate we should be accepted: finally, works were proposed, as the last and easiest way into the kingdom, and then *"a cup of cold water"* was to do the business! this, however, ran the gentleman foul of the Catechism and justification by faith, and here he had to warn us that he did not mean exactly what he said, and, therefore, would *"labor a little."*

The Doctor then exhorted us to enter the kingdom, never dreaming that he himself was as certainly out of it as the veriest sinner present, if the Messiah were right when he said "unless a man be born of water and spirit, he cannot enter into the kingdom of God." Again the Doctor stretched himself like a Colossus to unite the doctrine of the confession and the divinity of the new school, and declared that although he enjoined us to come into the kingdom, he did not mean to say that *special spiritual operations* were unnecessary, for the Lord would make his people willing in the day of his power;" the Scriptures said it: who then was to blame thought I, but before I knew what I was thinking about, the Doctor exclaimed—"You resist the Spirit," so that the Spirit which was to make all willing in the day of his power, was now fairly foiled by those whom the Doctor would have a willing people!

The Doctor added, that such was the accessibility of the city, (for the word gate in his text, of course implied to him the existence of a city, though if the Doctor had looked the parallel passage in Luke 13:24, 25 he would, with common folks, have perceived that the gate of a *house* and not a *city* was alluded to) no matter, however, the Doctor added, that such was the accessibility of his city that no man could lift his eyes upon it from any point but he might behold one of these strait gates, so that if the Saviour had strait gates, the Doctor was determined to have plenty of them! nay, lest a single difficulty should be suggested to the audience, the preacher, in order to show the very contrary of his text, exclaimed in an agony of animation "It is all gate together;" that is, as I protest I understood the Doctor, that the wall of the city was all gate!

This shows that the speaker, thought there was a difference between the world and the church, and that something was absolutely necessary to introduce people into the kingdom of heaven and change their state from nature to grace. The first thing proposed for this end by the doctor, was, as we have seen, "abandonment of the world;" the second "giving up one's idol;" the third "a simple preference for God;" fourth, "the love of enemies;" fifth, "the love of friends;" sixth "works;" seventh "faith;" till the wall of the doctor's city became full of gates and finally dissolved into one entire gate, "It is all gate together."

This sermon of the doctor's, is to be prized as a true specimen of the preaching of the day; which, when it happens to awaken any of those who listen to it, feels itself wholly incompetent to farther instruction. It cannot, it does not propound translation into the kingdom of God by baptism. The speakers have anticipated themselves, and have, like doctor Beecher, to contradict themselves and utter the grossest absurdities. For instance, why did the doctor preach to the audience about entering the kingdom of heaven, when, being sprinkled in their infancy, every one before him was, according to the Catechism and the Confessions of his church, already ingrafted into Christ, and members and citizens of that kingdom? The church and the kingdom of heaven in this point, mean the same thing. Now are we to be introduced into the church or kingdom when eight days old by baptism, and to be re-introduced to that kingdom when eight, eighteen, or twenty eight years old, by some other means; such as faith, works, the love of enemies, and the other matters mentioned by doctor Beecher? This is absolutely absurd. We agree with him, however, that something, some ordinance is necessary to change our state. This, the doctor's Catechism, in accordance with scripture, admits is baptism.

We regret exceedingly that persons, so eminent for their learning, piety, and talents as Dr. Doddridge and Doctor Beecher, should be deficient in any Christian matter. Their zeal for the conversion of the world is undisputed; but they have certainly erred in regard to the selection of the means; they have assuredly departed from the apostle's *method* of preaching and administering the remission of sins; and for this reason have we introduced them in this part of our book, that the reader may see that no attribute of piety, talent, or learning is to be substituted for authority and scripture in this important question.

We add, moreover, that, however much they and others may be in error, however much they may have encroached upon the exclusive rights of the apostle, and proposed answers to a question which has not of Christ been intrusted to them, their mistakes can form no apology for any one in the presence of God, for neglecting the scriptures, or for refusing to hear the Lord Jesus Christ on the great subject of salvation. These gentlemen are ardent admirers of their Redeemer, and the most zealous of ministers, their deficiencies should only embolden us to lay aside the authority of party and the prejudices of education, and to search calmly and dispassionately the word of God for that knowledge which surpasses finite inquiry. We beseech the reader, by the tender mercies of God, by the sufferings of his crucified Redeemer, and by his love of eternal life, to inquire, and decide, and to obey God. Is the remission of all past sins an unimportant matter, is the death of the Son of God, an every day fact, is the divine authority to be disregarded, or the sanctions which enforce obedience in this matter to be lightly esteemed? "It is a fearful thing to fail into the hands of the Living God." Cast not away your immortal soul redeemed by such precious blood. Seek salvation through the Lamb's redeeming blood. O let the pains he bore, the shame he suffered, turn you and lead you to the throne on high. "Seek you the Lord while he is to be found; call upon him while he is near." Bow before the Lord, your Maker. Repent, obey, and be forgiven; and you shall receive the Holy Spirit, the gift of the Holy Spirit.

CHAPTER V

Mr. Hannam's Answer to the Question, "What Shall I Do to Be Saved?"

The PULPIT ASSISTANT, or *Three hundred Skeletons of Sermons* is the name of the book which lies at present before me. This work greatly facilitates the task which we have assumed in this part of our volume, as it is a standard work, and by the discourses which it contains, explains to us not only the art and mystery of sermon making as communicated from one to another, but supplies us at once with the answer of the whole orthodox world to the great question of salvation, What shall we do to be saved?

The following commendatory note, from Howard Malcom, of Boston, Mass., is prefixed to the work, and describes the design of the Pulpit Assistant.

"I regard the PULPIT ASSISTANT as an excellent work for young ministers, and such as have access to but few books. The skeletons are skillfully extracted from the standard sermons of Tillotson, Watts, Walker, &c. and put the purchaser in possession of the happy plans and leading thoughts of a mass of approved discourses, which could not otherwise be had without great expense. Mr. Hannam's selection of sermons has been so made as to make his work comprise a tolerable body of Divinity, as will be seen by a glance at the index. The copious and correct references to scripture constitute, of themselves, a sufficient inducement to purchase the book at its present low price. By this method of giving merely the frame work of discourses, the student not only has multum in parvo, but is exempted from the temptation to plagiarism and indolence, which is presented by whole sermons made ready to the hand,

The copious *index* gives this edition a great superiority over all those which have preceded it.

HOWARD MALCOM.
Boston, Hayward Place, Jan. 30, 1830."

The following are the two rules delivered by Mr. Hannam, for the selection of a text.

"There are in general five parts of a sermon; the exordium, the connection, the division, the discussion, and the application; but, as connexion and division are parts which ought to be extremely short, we can properly reckon only three parts; exordium, discussion and application. However, we will just take notice of connection and division, after we have spoken a little on the choice of texts, and a few general rules of discussing them.

1. Never choose such texts as have not a complete sense: for only impertinent and foolish people will attempt to preach from one or two words, which signify nothing.

2. Not only words which have a complete sense of themselves must be taken, but they must also include the complete sense of the writer, whose words they are; for it is his language, and they are his sentiments, which you explain. For example, should you take these words of 2 Cor. 1:3, "Blessed be God, the Father of our Lord Jesus Christ, the Father of mercies, and the God of all comfort," and to stop here, you would include a complete sense; but it would not be the apostle's sense. Should you go farther, and add, "who comforteth us in all our tribulation," it would not then be the complete sense of St. Paul, nor would his meaning be taken in, unless you went to the end of the fourth verse. When the complete sense of the sacred writer is taken, you may stop; for there are few texts in scripture which do not afford matter sufficient for a sermon; and it is equally inconvenient to take too much text or too little; both extremes must be avoided."

That the reader may have a specimen of this systematic mode of handling the word of God, and see the example which Mr. Hannam has set ten thousand young ministers, of presuming upon the letter of the sacred oracles, we shall insert the following Skeleton Sermon.

It is styled the Indissoluble Connection between faith and salvation. The text is, "He that believeth shall be saved," and Mark 16 and 16th verse, is referred to as containing it. But I for one here file my disclaimer of the Scriptures that contain the reading; and protest that the text is not to be found in the present copy of the scriptures. Mark xvi. and 16th reads not he that "believeth shall be saved;" but as follows. "He that believeth and is baptized, shall be saved; and he that believeth not, shall be damned." These are the words of a great King, the last words spoken on earth by our holy Redeemer; and the system of things which makes it necessary to leave the one half of them out, when answering the saving question, is not, cannot be, of Jesus Christ. Men may labor and be zealous for the conversion of souls, but if their plans and schemes of divinity make it indispensable to suppress the words of him who bought them, their labors will be of small account.

"*He that believeth shall be saved.*"—Mark 16:16.

"In order to illustrate this subject, consider,

I. What is faith? In answer, it is a firm persuasion of the truth of the gospel, accompanied with a deep sense of its importance, and a cordial acceptance of its gracious proposals; and so producing the genuine fruit of love and obedience.

1. The real Christian believes the pure unadulterated gospel; the substance of which is this, "God is in Christ," 2 Cor. 5:19.—The ground on which he believes, is the testimony of God. 1 John 5:10. He yields not a faint, feeble, wavering assent, but agreeable to the clearness, strength, and energy of evidence. He may be assaulted with doubts, nor does he wish to remove them by unlawful means, ever ready to follow where truth shall lead. His doubts, having this effect, serve in the end rather to confirm than weaken his forth.

2. The gospel which he thus believes, he believes to be most important. It rouses his attention and calls all the powers of his soul to action. Like a man whose house is on fire, and is at his wit's end, till he has found means to extinguish it—or like one who has a large estate depending, and uses every effort to get his title confirmed.

3. This belief of the gospel is accompanied with a cordial approbation of its gracious proposals. He readily falls in with the scheme of salvation which divine wisdom has contrived, and almighty power carried into effect—at the altar of propitiation he is disposed to sacrifice both pride and pleasure, and at the feet of the adorable Saviour, to "cast down imaginations." 2 Cor. 10:5.

We have heard the gospel—Have we believed it? Have we received it in the love of it? Are our hearts and lives influenced by it?

II. The salvation promised to them that believe.

Here a scene the most delightful and transporting opens to our view. A scene the contemplation of which fills the Christian with admiration and wonder.

1. It is a salvation from moral evil.

The soul of man is the workmanship of God, but alas! this temple of God is now laid in ruins, sin has darkened the understanding. It has dethroned reason, brought a load of guilt upon the conscience, created a thousand fears in the breast, and spread universal anarchy through the soul.

Now from all these evils we are saved by our Lord Jesus Christ. He procures for us the free pardon of sin. Sends down his good Spirit into our hearts to renew our nature—illuminates our mind—restores peace to our consciences. What a blessed change!

2. From natural evil.

Many and great are the mercies of an outward kind to which human nature is liable in the present life. Proofs of this fact arise from every quarter; if we look into history we shall find a great part of it employed in recording the calamities which have befallen nations; war, fire, tempest, earthquakes, pestilence, famines. If we go abroad in to the world, our attention will be arrested by scenes of distress. Job 14:1.

Now from all these miseries, the sad effects of sin, Jesus Christ came into the world to save us. Not that good men are exempt from the common afflictions of life; poverty, sickness, and death, they are liable to. But these few curses are converted into blessings. Rom. 8:28; 1 Cor. 15:55-57.

But if we extend our views to heaven, the promise, as it relates to natural evil, shall receive its full accomplishment. Heb. 4:9. There is no acting hand, as the stones that composed the temple, were hewn and prepared before they were brought thither, that the noise of the hammer might not be heard, so the painful exercises of the present life have had their full effect, only the voice of joy shall be heard, and at the resurrection, the body shall be raised "and fashioned like unto Christ."

3. ———— penal evil.

Indeed the above may be properly called penal, as they are the effects of sin, but I have here in view the punishment of the wicked. The scriptures, in order to awaken the attention of mankind, give us the most alarming description of the punishment prepared for the impenitent. Deut. 29:20; Dan. 12:2; Matt. 8:12; 25:46; Ps. 90:11. But from all these miseries, our great Emmanuel saves us. Rom. 3:25; Gal. 3:13.

To these miseries are to be opposed the joys of heaven, but oh! what tongue can describe. Ps. 16:11.

III. The connection between faith and salvation, it is necessary in order to our being saved that we believe.

1. It is the divine appointment. John 3:16; Mark 16:16. It is not a mere arbitrary command, but the result of infinite wisdom and goodness.

2. There is a fitness or suitableness in faith to the end of its appointment, so that the necessity arises out of the nature of things. The blessing of the gospel cannot be enjoyed without the medium of faith. Sin is atoned for—heaven opened—but the actual possession of the good thus procured is as necessary as a title to it. How is that good to be possessed without a suitable temper? How is this to be acquired but by believing?"

Mr. Hannam might have added "How is this faith to be known or manifested but by obedience?" and then his sermon would have admitted a complete answer to the question of salvation. He would then have quoted the Redeemers own words, without mutilating them as he has done, and as, by his example, he has taught thousands of others to do. This scripture then does not read "He that believeth shall be saved;" but "He that believeth and is baptized shall be saved, and he that believeth not shall be damned," which is a scriptural answer to the question, the great interrogatory of which we are discoursing.

CHAPTER VI

Mr. S. Deacons's Answer to the Question, "What Shall I Do to Be Saved?"

An attempt to answer the important question, What shall I do to be saved? A poem in three dialogues. Between Prudens and Evangelicus. By S. Deacon:—

The author of the volume bearing the above title, differs from Doddridge, Beecher, Hannam, and Romain, in his answer to the question of Salvation. He indeed teaches faith and repentance as necessary to forgiveness; but then he does not like them think that any special or preparatory operation of the Spirit is necessary to produce these in the mind. On the contrary he pleads for the all sufficiency of God's word to enlighten the eyes, to convert the soul from sin, and to direct our feet into the paths of life. This author then had actually, like Edward Irving, discarded the abominable doctrine of the scriptures being "a dead letter," "dark, mournful, and terrible," as Dr. Beecher has it; and perceived, if not distinctly at least in a good degree, that the Holy Spirit is not given to make men believe, but because they do believe. We shall here set down the argument of the Book, from which the reader will see, that if the author did not perceive and appreciate the apostles answer to the question of which he treats in his poem, he at least offers no violence to the power and glory of the word of God. He leaves this untouched, unsullied, untraduced.

"Prudens takes a walk one summer evening, and contemplating the beauties of creation, falls into a soliloquy on his own state as a sinner.—Evangelicus happens to hear him, and inquires the cause of his trouble.—Prudens acquaints him, that dreadful thunder brought him to serious self-examination, and he found himself lost, and wants to know what he must do to be saved.—Evangelicus tells him that he had been in a similar state and found rest in believing on Jesus; and advises him to the same expedient.—Prudens fears he may not on account of his long delay.—Evangelicus shews him, by many arguments, that his fears of this sort are groundless.—Prudens starts several objections, and asks questions concerning the extent of the death of Christ, repentance, wrath of God, &c. which Evangelicus endeavors to obviate and answer.—Prudens concludes to go home, and meditate on the discourse and to come again the next day.—Evangelicus approves of his proposal, and advises him to act accordingly.

Prudens censures vain compliments—Evangelicus concurs, and asks the state of his mind—Prudens is unsettled, and inquires if Evangelicus be so—Evangelicus allows he is when he lives by sense, and not by faith—Prudens wants to know the difference—Evangelicus explains and illustrates it—Prudens is still unhappy—Evangelicus tells him the cause is unbelief—Mutual discourse concerning faith, divine and human—Means by which it is obtained—Evangelicus recommends the Bible as the great means—Prudens approves in part; acknowledges his mind convinced, yet cannot believe—Evangelicus charges him with absurdity, points out his mistake, and proposes a respite for meditation—Pause—The subject resumed—Prudens declines disputing, and wants enjoyment—Evangelicus directs him to Jesus, and to the scriptures, as giving him encouragement—Prudens objects their insufficiency, as being a dead letter—Evangelicus maintains the contrary—Prudens chides Evangelicus, for not referring him to the Spirit's influences—Evangelicus replies, and convicts him of treating God as a liar—Prudens, self-condemned, concludes the discourse, and invites Evangelicus to dine with him on the morrow—Evangelicus accepts his invitation, and charges him to adhere to the gospel, as his only hope—Prudens thanks him, and withdraws.

Prudens cannot think the scriptures sufficient, because professors differ so much in opinion.—Evangelicus observes that others differ as much in opinion as these.—Prudens allows it, yet wants the reason of this difference in those who profess to be led by the same Bible.—Evangelicus points out the different sorts of readers, and the ends they have in view, as reasons of this.—Prudens is satisfied, but adverts again to the Holy Ghost.—Evangelicus agrees with him, but shows that the

Holy Ghost continually calls by the Bible—Prudens wants something more.—Evangelicus illustrates the nature of grace, and of believing, by several similes; and recommends a simple dependence on the Lord Jesus Christ—Prudens finds much hesitation, but at last, encouraged by arguments, promises, and scripture examples, he ventures to place his dependence on Jesus, and find rest to his soul. Evangelicus congratulates him, and gives advice with respect to his duty and privilege, temper and conduct.—After mutual expressions of gratitude and praise, they sing a hymn, and part."

They sing a hymn and part! Not one word of pardon! Not one allusion to the apostolic answer to the great question which the book is written to solve! Faith or dependence on the Lord Jesus is very properly recommended; but when the convert is brought to this, what has he received? nothing, absolutely nothing. He has believed, and his belief has taken effect upon his mind and behavior; but his state is never spoken of. He remains where he was found, in the world, an unpardoned believer; reconciled but not justified, converted but not saved, sanctified in mind but not having received "redemption through the blood of Christ, viz: the forgiveness of sins."

Prudens is represented in such a light as leaves no doubt that he was educated with the notion, that he was to be converted by the direct operation of the Holy Spirit. He chides Evangelicus therefore, for not speaking to him of this matter when answering the great question of salvation. Evangelicus replies in such a manner as to show that the author of the Poem had formed very just conceptions of the word of God although he was by no means clear of the rubbish of corrupted Christianity, and erred exceedingly in presuming to answer this question in any other way than that in which it was answered by the great Apostle.

We have only to add, that Mr. Deacon not having been appointed to the office of answering the question of salvation, which he selected for the subject of his Poem, we have to abandon him with all his good intentions to save; and must turn to Peter, whose right alone it was to open the door of the church and let in both the Jews and the Gentiles.

CHAPTER VII

John Bunyan and the Question of Salvation

John Bunyan's Pilgrim's Progress has set the popular doctrine of Conversion or Regeneration in its proper light, that is, in the light of a riddle; and the author, by so doing, has rendered himself so famous with those who love mystery, and think with Dr. Beecher, the scriptures to be "dark, mournful, and terrible," that Thomas Scott has thought this singular performance worthy of both his learning and piety, and has actually written Notes on the Pilgrim's Progress.

Mr. Bunyan does not begin with his man precisely at where the Rev. Doctor Doddridge commenced with his. The doctor's sinner was supposed to be perfectly careless, "one of those thoughtless creatures who heretofore had been wholly unconcerned about religion." But the Pilgrim presents himself in the commencement, with the Bible in his hand, all alarmed, "the night troublesome to him as also the day." Sometimes he is in the field, at one time reading, at another praying, bad at night and worse in the day.

At last, to the pilgrim a modern preacher in the person of Evangelist appears, and with characteristic sagacity gives such directions to the poor man as brings him in a very short time into what the author descriptively designates the slough of despond. He is styled Christian though he carries upon his shoulders the burden of his past iniquities and is evidently an unpardoned man, which is very unscriptural; for in the Testament Christians are a pardoned people. But this to the contrary notwithstanding, the Pilgrim unforgiven is styled Christian, and by a single saying of Evangelist is induced to set out to seek religion in company with neighbor Pliable, with whom he holds the following confabulation.

PLI—.And do you think that the words of your book are certainly true?

CHR. Yes, verily; for it was made by Him that cannot lie, Titus, 1:2.

PLI. Well said; what things are they?

CHR. There is an endless kingdom to be inhabited, and everlasting life to be given us, that we may inhabit that kingdom forever, Isaiah 45:17; John 10:27, 29.

PLI. The hearing of this is enough to ravish one's heart.—But are these things to be enjoyed? How shall we get to be sharers thereof?

CHR. The Lord, the governor of the country, hath recorded that in this book, Isaiah 55:1, 2; John 6:37; 8:37; Revelations, 22:6; 22, 17; the substance of which is, If we be truly willing to have it, he will bestow it upon us freely.

PLI. Well, my good companion, glad am I to hear of these things: come on, let us mend our pace.

CHR. I cannot go so fast as I would, by reason of this burden that is on my back.

Now I saw in my dream, that just as they had ended this talk, they drew nigh to a very miry slough that was in the midst of the plain; and they being heedless, did both fall suddenly into the bog. The name of the slough was Despond. Here, therefore, they wallowed for a time, being grievously bedaubed with dirt; and Christian, because of the burden that was on his back, began to sink in the mire.

PLI. Then said Pliable, Ah, neighbor Christian, where are you now?

CHR. Truly said Christian, I do not know.

PLI. At this Pliable began to be offended, and angrily said to his fellow, Is this the happiness you have told me all this while of? If we have such ill speed at our first setting out, what may we expect between this and our journey's end? May I get out again with my life, you shall possess the brave country alone for me. And with that he gave a desperate struggle or two, and got out of the mire on that side of the slough which was next to his own house: so away he went, and Christian saw him no more.

Wherefore Christian was left to tumble in the Slough of Despond alone: but still he endeavoured to struggle to that side of the slough that was farthest from his own house, and next to the wicket-gate; the which he did, but could not get out because of the burden that was upon his back: but I beheld in my dream, that a man came to him, whose name was Help, and asked him "What he did there?"

CHR. Sir, said Christian, I was bid to go this way by a man called Evangelist, who directed me also to yonder gate, that I might escape the wrath to come. And as I was going thither I fell in here.

HELP. But why did not you look for the steps.

CHR. Fear followed me so hard, that I fled the next way, and fell in.

HELP. Then said he give me thine hand: so he gave him his hand, and he drew him out, Psalm 40:2, and he set him upon sound ground, and bid him go on his way.

Then I stepped to him that plucked him out, and said "Sir, wherefore, since over this place is the way from the city of Destruction to yonder gate, is it, that this plat is not mended, that poor travelers might go thither with more security?" And he said unto me, "This miry slough is such a place as cannot be mended: it is the descent whither the scum and filth that attends conviction for sin doth continually run, and therefore it is called the Slough of Despond; for still as the sinner is awakened about his lost condition, there arise in his soul many fears and doubts, and discouraging apprehensions, which all of them get together, and settle in this place: and this is the reason of the badness of this ground.

It is not the pleasure of the King that this place should remain so bad, Isaiah 35:3, 4. His laborers also have, by the direction of his Majesty's surveyors, been for above these sixteen hundred years employed about this patch of ground, if perhaps it might have been mended: yea, and to my knowledge," said he, "here have been swallowed at least twenty thousand cart-loads, yea, millions of wholesome instructions, that have at all seasons been brought from all places of the king's dominions, (and they that can tell say they are the best materials to make good ground of the place,) if so be it might have been mended; but it is the Slough of despond still and so will be when they have done what they can."

John Bunyan, a faithful servant of Jesus Christ, was a Baptist, and during his life suffered a severe and protracted imprisonment at the instance of the very parties, who are now his warmest admirers, and who have written commentaries upon his ingenious and far famed performances. O that all those who affect to understand the true Gospel better than he, would show for it the same zeal and faithfulness which this holy man and excellent minister showed for his ever blessed Redeemer. His memory will descend to posterity, and live in the affections of thousands yet unborn; and thousands yet unborn may love to trace backward the dawning of their first religious feelings to the early converse which they were wont to hold with the Pilgrim in his Progress from the city of destruction to Mount Zion and to the Holy Land.

To John Bunyan's Slough of Despond may all the gospels different from that, which the apostle Peter preached, be speedily and finally consigned without the hope or possibility of making their escape by the help of any one whatever, man, angel, or demon; and may every one who believes in God and hates unrighteousness, may every one who loves Christ, and desires redemption through his blood, seek the forgiveness of sins by being baptized into his name. "And now, why tarriest thou? arise and be baptized and wash away thy sins, calling on the name of the Lord." Acts 22.

Beloved reader, you now see what is the course of safety; you now perceive, we hope, that the holy scriptures alone must guide you; that they and only they furnish an infallible answer to the all-important question, What shall I do to be saved. Forget, then, the errors and mistakes of Christians, and even their positive faults; and seek from the sacred oracles, the truth on this question. Go to the apostles and prophets and to their Master, the Lord Jesus Christ. He is all-merciful and condescending, and has by his servants given us the instructions necessary to save us. Read the Bible and obey its commands; and, when you have obtained the remission of your sins, go on in the ways of holiness to life eternal, and the God of peace be with you.

CHAPTER VIII

The Subject of Baptism Put in Train for the Investigation of the Reader

The question of baptism can all be argued under these three states, viz:

1. What is the meaning of the word baptize?
2. On what principle is it to be administered?
3. For what is it to be administered?

We propose, then, in this chapter, to show first that baptism literally means to immerse. 2d. That it is to be administered only to penitent believers, or to such as believe and reform; and, 3d. That it is to be administered for the remission of past sins.

Reader, have you ever had your attention called to a set of words in the Bible, which may be called the *inexplicati* of that volume? You possibly answer, I do not know, for I understand not what your Latin term *inexplicati* means. Well, I will tell you; it means *untranslated*, and so if we put the one for the other, my question will be this—has your attention ever been called to a class of words in the Bible which are termed the *untranslated?* It has not. Well, let me do it now. The following are some of them: bishop, deacon, deaconess, church, baptist, baptizing, pentecost, evangelist, apostle, &c. These are all Greek words. Bishop means overseer; deacon, male servant: deaconess, female servant; church, house of the Lord; baptist, immerser; baptizing immersing; pentecost, fifty days; evangelist, messenger of good news; apostle, a person sent. Now unless you understand Greek yourself, you must trust for the meaning of these words to those who do. Well; we want in the present instance to know what baptize or *baptizo* means. We must then appeal to scholars who understand Greek. Who shall they be? They shall be scholars of the first eminence, Luther, Calvin, Beza, Vitringa, Ranchius, Bossuet, Venema, Dr. Wall, Stillingfleet, Mead, Salmasius, &c., &c.

"Calvin.—'The word *baptizo*, signifies to immerse, and the rite of immersion was observed by the ancient church.' Beza.—'Christ commanded us to be baptized, by which word it is certain immersion is signified.' Vitringa.—'The act of baptizing is the immersion of believers in water. This expresses the force of the word.' Ranchius.—'The proper signification of *baptizo*, is to immerse, plunge under, or overwhelm in water.' Bossuet. 'To baptize, signifies to plunge, as granted by all the world.' Venema.—'The word to baptize, is nowhere used in the scripture for sprinkling.' Dr. Wall.—'This (immersion) is so plain and clear, by an infinite number of passages, that as we cannot but pity the weak endeavors of such Pedobaptists, as would maintain the negative of it, so also, we ought to disown and show a dislike of the profane scoffs which some people give to the English Anti-pedobaptists,' &c., &c.

Stillingfleet.—'Rites and customs apostolical are altered, as dipping in baptism.' Mead.—'There was no such thing as sprinkling used in baptism in the apostles' days, nor many ages after them.' Salmasius. —'Baptism is immersion.' Pool's Continuators.—'To be baptized is to be dipped in water.' Witsius.—'It cannot be denied that the native signification of the word baptize, is to plunge, or to dip.' Dr. Campbell. —'The word baptize both in sacred authors, and in classical, signifies to dip, to plunge, to immerse, and was rendered by Tertullian, the oldest of the Latin fathers, *tingere*, the term used for dying cloth, which was by immersion. It is always construed suitably to this meaning.'

The text, in German, and in Dutch, the Danish catechism, the Syrians, the Armenians, the Persians, and all Eastern Christians, employ the word in the sense of dipping.

But why did these great and good men profess one thing and practice another? We cannot tell. They have not told us themselves. We leave their reasons with themselves. Perhaps some, who at the present day are dissatisfied with their sprinkling, and yet remain Pedobaptists, can assign the reason.

Again, sir, look at ecclesiastical history. Dr. Mosheim, describing the rites and ceremonies of the church in the first century, says, "The sacrament of baptism was administered, in this century, in many places appointed and prepared for that purpose, and was performed by the immersion of the whole body in the baptismal font.' Writing of the second century, he uses this language: 'The persons to be baptized, after they had repeated the creed, confessed and renounced their sins, and particularly the devil and his pompous allurements, were immersed under water.'

Tertullian says—'It is all one, whether we are washed in the sea, or in a pond; in a fountain, or in a river; in a standing, or in a running water: nor is there any difference between those that John baptized in the Jordan, and those that Peter baptized in the Tiber.' Gregory, in his Ecclesiastical history, says, 'Baptism was, in the first century, publicly performed, by immersing the whole body in water.' Venema.—'It is without controversy, that baptism in the primitive church was administered by immersion into water, and not by sprinkling.' Dr. Sharp.—'Whenever a person in ancient times was baptized, he was not only to profess his faith in Christ's death and resurrection, but he was also to look upon himself as obliged to mortify his former carnal affections, and so enter upon a new state of life; and the very form of baptism did lively represent this obligation. For what did his being plunged under water signify, but his understanding, in imitation of Christ's death and burial, to forsake his former evil courses, as his ascending out of the water, did his engagement to lead a holy spiritual life.' Wolfius.—'That baptismal immersion was practised in the first ages of the Christian church, many have shown from the writings of the ancients.'

Calvin.—'Here we perceive how baptism was administered among the ancients; for they immersed the whole body in water. Now it is the prevailing practice for a minister only to sprinkle the body or the head.' Wesley.—'Buried with him alluding to the ancient manner of baptizing by immersion.' Bishop Taylor.—'The custom of the ancient churches was not sprinkling, but immersion.' Curcelloeus.—'Baptism was performed by plunging the whole body into water, and not by sprinkling a few drops, as is now the practice. Nor did the disciples that were sent out by Christ, administer baptism afterwards in any other way.' Whitby. —"Immersion was rigorously observed by all Christians for thirteen centuries.

These were all Pedobaptists in practice, but Baptists in principle; and their testimony is of great value in the decision of the question before us."[14]

Here then, reader, is the meaning of the word baptize, given to you by the great fathers of the Protestant Reformation. It is true they all sprinkled; but they allowed at the same time, as you see, that immersion was the meaning of the Greek word, and this is correct; for the Greek church, like our Baptists, dip or immerse to this day all whom they baptize.

2. The next proposition is, Who are to be baptized, or immersed, one who believes, or one who does not believe? The Catholics and the Protestants say, those who do not believe; that is, the infants of professed Christians are to be baptized. But of this the scriptures are absolutely silent. There is not one word enjoining it on any person to baptize his children. The command is not baptize your children; but be yourself baptized for the remission of your sins. The commission is not,

[14] Mr. Lynd

he that is baptized and believes, but "he that believes and is baptized;" accordingly the apostles, and prophets, and evangelists, and first ministers of our religion, baptized only those who had previously believed the gospel. This leaves those who sprinkle children, wholly and absolutely without any scriptural authority for what they do, having neither example nor commandment for their human ordinance of infant baptism. The question with the reader then, is this—Will he practise, or countenance those who practise a matter that has no divine support; that is absolutely a corruption of the original ordinance?—for as immersion has been changed into sprinkling, so the unbelieving child has been substituted for the believing child.

3. We now come to the next item of inquiry, namely: What is the believing man, woman, or child, (for little ones may and do believe in Jesus) to be immersed for; that is, are men, women, and children, who believe in Christ, to be immersed for the remission of sins? The scriptures say they are, as the reader has had sufficiently proved to him in the preceding pages. It only remains to be shown that this is believed in by all parties of Catholic and Protestant professors of our religion. We differ from them only in this, viz: we practise what they preach. They have written what they do not preach, and have in this instance departed both from the scriptures and their own books. The Restoration of the True Gospel of God laid a fair foundation for free inquiry on all the matters of faith, repentance, baptism, the remission of sins, the Holy Spirit, and the resurrection; and since the occurrence of this event, many beautiful pieces of criticism, and expositions of the principles, commandments and privileges contained in it, have been made by the ministers and brethren of this reformation. These are widely scattered over an extensive field of books and periodicals, as the Christian Baptist, Millenial Harbinger, Messenger, Christianity Restored, Advocates and other papers, as the Disciple, Christian, and Preacher, more recently come upon the carpet, all of which contain many pieces of most inestimable matter. If the reader desires proof that the Catholics and Protestants teach that baptism is for the remission of sins, we refer him to the creeds of all, and to those parts of them in particular which treat of baptism.

CHAPTER IX

Modern Preaching

The parties of the day,—Emancipators, New-Jerusalemites, Quakers, Shakers, Moravians, Seventh-day Baptists, Free Communion Baptists, Tunkers, Cumberland Presbyterians, Associate Presbyterians, Mennonites, Dutch Reformed, Freewill Baptists, Methodists, Episcopal Methodists, Protestant Methodists, Wesleyan Methodists, Associate Methodists, Radical Methodists, Calvinistic Baptists, Presbyterians,

Congregationalists, Protestant Episcopalians, Universalists, Destructionists, Roman Catholics, Lutherans, German Reformed, Unitarians, Southcotonians, and Mormonites, are the names of a few of those who pretend, within the bounds of Christendom, to teach the gospel.

Doctrines taught by the above parties:—

Eternal election, effectual calling, initial justification, special operation, general atonement, irresistible grace, free-will, final perseverance, special grace, common operations, special call, reprobation, appropriation, trinity, unity, universal salvation, restoration, annihilation, consubstantiation, and transubstantiation, dead faith, dead letter, spiritual regeneration, sprinkling, pouring, crossing, predestination, eternal decrees, eternal justification, free grace, special grace, general call, call to the ministry, Christian experience, faith by the spirit, and spiritual faith, sacraments, application of the word by the Spirit, act of faith, direct acts of faith, reflect acts of faith, feeling pardon, &c. These are a few of the technicalities of modern and schismatic Christianity, words and phrases equally unprofitable to the people and disgraceful to those who make use of them.

A word to preachers:—

Ah! dear Sirs: you cruelly abuse your office, deceive the people, and disgrace our religion when you publicly meddle with the worse than useless doctrines shadowed forth by the unsound, unwholesome, and unscriptural phrases above enumerated. These are the things which have divided and polluted the temple of Christianity, in which you would be esteemed servants of the Redeemer. These visionary theories are the bones of contention which you have thrown among the people, and which cause professors to "bite and devour one another." Amid all the religious bustle that is abroad in your societies, what estimate do you put upon the life-giving and light giving voice of the Divine Father, "Behold my Son! the Beloved, in whom I delight."

In your Bible societies, tract societies, Missionary societies, Education societies, schools, seminaries, colleges, universities, churches, classes, conventions, associations synods, presbyteries, conferences councils, assemblies, what honor is done to this word of God concerning Jesus of Nazareth? In your sermons, lectures, orations, proclamations, do you, after the example of God, and the Holy Spirit, and Jesus and the holy apostles, and evangelists, ever proclaim and strive to prove most fairly, most emphatically, most honestly, by the proper evidences, that Jesus is the Christ, the Son of God? Or have you overlooked this grand essential in the apostolic gospel, and taken it for granted that all the world believes it; that we are a Christian people as you very frequently and very foolishly style us; that we need not to have this paramount element of the Christian faith demonstrated; and that, if you only speak an oration on the first of the week, the spell of evil will be dissolved, and we shall believe and turn to God?

Believe me, sirs, there is a current of skepticism running through the land that your procedure can never stem. You, yourselves, the ministers of the gospel, are the chief causes of the infidelity, which, perhaps, you deplore. You do not propose the master oracle to the people for faith. You throw it on the back ground in your systems of theology, and although it stands bound like frontlets on the forehead of Christianity, and is written and recorded on the first leaf of the New Testament, yet you do not see, you do not appreciate it.

How can protestants be anything but divided, how can the people be any thing but religious partisans when each man must thrust forward into notice a creed, a matter of faith different from that of all the rest, and in almost every instance different from the Bible too. You are at fault in this grand matter.—Review your premises. I say review your premises. Get you down out of your pulpits, stand among the people, go abroad into the land; propose as "the matter of faith" to the people what the Divine Father proposed both to you and the people; labor to show them that it is true, that it is the word of God, that he did say this of Jesus, that he did recognize him as his Son, that the Spirit did identify him with Messiah, that the apostles did preach him both as Christ and as the Son of God, and that you also will do the same. And when you have spoken this with success and have by proper proofs carried the proposition to the hearts of the people, when you have by the truth pricked their hearts, and dying to sin they cry, as the people on the day of Pentecost cried "Men and brethren, what shall we do." Tell them what Peter told his auditors, "Repent and be baptized, every one of you in the name of Jesus Christ for the remission of sins, and you shall receive the gift of the Holy Spirit." If you will do this; if you will propose to the people the word of the Father, the matter of faith intended for us all, and if you attach to the reception of it the same blessings of remission and the Spirit, which belonged to it of old, when handled by the apostles, you will speedily see a change; counteraction, schism, and sin will soon be dissipated, the Christians will come together on one faith, one Lord, and one baptism, as of old, and the parts and shreds, of the body of Christ, which now defile the land will come together and become one body in Christ.

Have you no pity, have you no bowels of compassion? Do you not perceive, that ninety-nine out of a hundred are dying in their sins, ignorant of the very first principles of our salvation, and falling from the midst of your assemblies into the grave wholly unilluminated, wholly unsanctified, unpardoned? Is it possible that you do not perceive that your divisions and oppositions have driven the most sensible portion of society to seek for pleasure in every thing but our holy and delightful religion.—You are wrong in telling the people, that the word of God is a dead letter, that they cannot believe, they cannot repent, they cannot obey without a special and preparatory operation of the Spirit. You do err, you err egregiously when you preach, that the Spirit must make men believe, repent, and obey. It is the office of the word of God to do all this; and you greatly dishonor it by thus thrusting it backward and downward as a dead letter, incapable of quickening and making men alive to religion and to God.

I have conversed with hundreds of the youth of this country, and of your congregations. They are full of infidelity and skepticism; and believe with Paine, and Hume, and Voltaire, and Volney, and Gibbon, and Rousseau, and other American, French, and British sceptics; they feel that you have taken for granted the very thing to be proved; that you have neither stated the Christian proposition, nor argued it in their presence; that what you propose to them of eternal election, eternal decrees, eternal justification, is eternal nonsense and cannot and ought not to be proved. I exhort you once more, begin at the beginning, take the Father of mercies for your example, and not John Calvin; take the Holy Spirit and not Luther; take Christ and not John Wesley; and the book of God, the scriptures, and not the other systems of divinity with which your libraries abound. And may God direct you by his holy word, and comfort you by his Holy Spirit in all things. To Him be the glory through all ages.

To those preachers who have professedly received the original gospel, we would say, It will be a long time before the mighty masses of men, to which you address your proclamation, will sufficiently understand the elements of Christianity of which we have been discoursing, it will be long before you can supply the public with more than a bare sufficiency of proof that God recognized Jesus as his Son. If, however, you do this, if you prove this proposition, you do well, and will have but little time to prove any thing else. But see, the resuscitation of the true gospel is of recent date and perhaps you do not yet perceive in what this proof lies, Can you decipher numerically the several branches of evidence for the oracle of the Father? Do you know whether they are internal or external, or mixed; whether they are antecedent, or consequent in their nature, or both; moral, or miraculous, prophetic or evangelical, or all of these kinds taken together? Do you know which class of proofs are most in number, which most forcible, which of them direct, which indirect, which collateral, immediate, or remote? Believe me, however, that the internal evidence of our religion is that to which you ought chiefly to apply yourself. All beyond the book is of small value, or at least cannot establish one saving fact in it.—We are wholly dependent on the original witnesses for the faith that saves us. But have you schooled yourselves in the nature of proof at all? Do you know that a thing may be in testimony and not in evidence, or that a thing may be advanced as proof which in reality is no proof? Do you know that a proposition may be supernatural altogether, and consequently superlatively more difficult in the proof; and that this is the very nature of the proposition of our religion of which you are the promulgators? Brethren leave off your popular imitation; descend into the arena where the people sit; and you will there find your match among them, at the noble game of *proof* and *proposition*. Do not assume in this great affair the undue advantages of clergyman, regardless of that which God and Christ, and the Spirit of God and the holy evangelists, and holy prophets and apostles labored to establish in the earth! Look at this oracle again, brethren. See its matchless beauty, "Behold my Son, the beloved, in whom I delight." Was there ever such an introduction— did ever father on earth so speak of his son; did ever the most polished times, the most kingly manners, or royal dignity, inspire any authority, emperor, king, or potentate, to vouchsafe an introduction of like import in like terms? No; Louis *le Grand* never graced his court with an oracle at once so noble in expression, so pregnant of affection. Charles, who presented his whole empire to his son Philip, was incapable of such dignity, and no introduction, that he ever gave of his son, to his high estates and thrones and princedoms ever reached in simplicity and dignity of word, and beauty and feeling of thought the royal oracle of our royal Father. Of all the pearls in the ocean of divine revelation, this is the one most precious; among the gems of God this is to mortals the most invaluable; this is the diamond; among the precious metals of the Bible this is the gold, fine gold, tried gold, seven times tried in the furnace of a world, run off through the side of the Messiah and the blood of all martyrs. Away then, with all inferior, with all meaner things, and let the voice of the Father be heard in our religion; let him appear on the foreground of the picture; let him debate it with men; and let men debate it with him. Allow the Father's voice to be heard by men; call on men to say whether they will abjure that; and then you will know how to estimate their characters; then you will know whether they are infidel.

Men have praised general science, and the science of Mathematics in particular, on account of its relation to the improvement of the rational man; but the Christian religion calls us to a still higher exercise of our rational powers than Mathematics itself. The demonstration, which accompanies the truths of this science, are indeed so obvious and vulgar that the weakest being on earth may perceive them; but the proposition and the proof of our religion invite us to the careful review of many parcels of distinct testimony, to the reconcilement of many seeming contradictories, and to draw the most important conclusion from numerous trains of distinct proof all connected indeed, and all bearing upon the same facts: but some of them remote and indirect and others immediate and direct, but all of them scattered over a wide field, capable nevertheless, of being gathered up into a focus, and of being made to act upon the public mind with the most tremendous effect, dashing down infidelity, scattering skepticism to the winds, expurgating atheism, and turning the whole population of a land to God, and to the love and practise of righteousness through Jesus Christ our Lord.

But our argument on the whole of modern preaching is this: it fails in moral effect, because God's words are not sufficiently honored by it. "If they had stood in my counsel," said God to the teachers of Jeremiah's day, "and had caused my people to hear my words, then they would have turned them from their evil way, and from the evil of their doings." But this they did not, but substituted their own word, for those of God, and taught the people righteousness by precepts merely human. This is the character of modern preaching, which in general aims only at approved maxim and elegance in composition, leaving untouched, unproved, and unbelieved, the great oracle of the Father, which he intended to be laid by all true builders as a sure foundation stone in the mind of every son of man; the people, therefore, are not "turned from their evil way, nor from the evil of their doings." It is then on account of its absolute moral tendency that we wish you, brethren, to allow the Father to stand on the foreground of the picture, when you could portray the gospel in full form and improve the world. You can, I protest, do nothing in establishing a permanent morality in any city, town, or neighborhood, unless you do this. Do you then want your work to remain when you are dead and gone? Preach what was delivered at the beginning, that "Jesus is the Messiah the Son of God."

A DISCOURSE OF THE TRUE GOSPEL

SECTION SIXTH–REMISSION OF SINS

"Without the shedding of blood there is no Remission."

CHAPTER I

Introductory

Sacrifice may be considered in relation to five particulars: first, the person offering it; second, the person to whom it is offered; third, the necessary nature of the thing offered; fourth the end for which it is offered; fifth and lastly, the law violated.

The person offering it is man, man dead in law, according to that original statute, "In the day thou eatest thereof thou shalt surely die," or as enunciated afterwards in Israel, "The soul that sinneth it shall die." A man may be dead in law and not in fact. When the sentence of decapitation is pronounced against a criminal convicted of a capital offence, that moment his life is lost in law; but in fact, he may not die till some time afterwards. He may even be respited and not die for months or years after his adjudication to death. This was the case of primitive man, Adam, and with all men in him. The moment he became guilty of an infraction of the divine law, he was dead in law; for death was the sanction by which it was guarded and the punishment to which the violation of it made him obnoxious.

But again; property, both personal, and real, may be forfeited in law, judgment confessed, and the property enjoyed at the will of the claimant. This was the case of our first parents; for having forfeited their life in law, in the way of recognizance or of confession of judgment, they appeared at God's altar with blood, which is the life. The bloody ritual, which has distinguished the true religion since the world began, is, therefore, founded on the fact, that man at the Fall forfeited his blood; and it was intended for the purpose, as the law expresses it, of "bringing sin to remembrance." The state of the case was this: When man sinned, the statute pronounced death. The clemency of the executive, however, vouchsafed a respite, but demanded a recognizance to justice of the forfeiture. Animal blood, a lively symbol of the human, was ordained and accepted; and the men of faith, from Adam to Jesus, came to the altar of God bearing in their hands cups of blood; made confession; poured it out at the bottom of God's altar; and departed with their life in their hand as a loan. There is something exceedingly admirable in all this; and yet it obtains on principles with which we are perfectly acquainted and which distinguish frequently the policy of every government on earth. I have in my possession and at hand just now the history of a case of respite, supplied me by a beloved brother, in which the person closed in with the terms of the Executive only at the awful moment in which he was about to be launched into eternity, and when thousands of his fellow citizens were in attendance to witness his disastrous execution. He had, up to that thrilling instant, rashly dared the terrors of the law. When about to drop into the abyss he whispered to the officer in attendance, Is it yet not too late? the officer answered in the negative; on which the culprit pulled the instrument of respite from his bosom, appended to it his signature, left the scaffold, and survived. The justice and saving mercy of the government were singularly displaced in the above instance; and the people, doubtless, were pleased to behold mercy rejoicing over judgment in the case. Yet it is but an instance in kind, of that mercy and justice which were displayed by God in the case of the first of men.

But though men will admit readily in word that God is both just and merciful, yet when he would prove himself to be such in fact, they are suddenly and with singular inconsistency too startled into alarm, and would have it proved to them that their Maker can appear either to be a just God or a Saviour by such an administration of law, or respite! To bring home to them the hollowness of their own reasoning, let the case be varied a little; and instead of justice and mercy, let us instance in the Divine character those attributes of benevolence and munificence by which he feedeth every thing that lives. Suppose that it were only theoretically and not practically true that God was benevolent and munificent. Would such a theory fill these objector's mouths. But it would be just as valid in such to startle at the indications of God's benevolence and munificence afforded by the teeming autumn when God empties the horn of plenty around the land, and to seek for other reasons of his riches than the fields afford as to cavil at the respite of Adam and the absolute forgiveness of sins by Jesus Christ as the most unequivocal indications of both God's justice and mercy. If the facts displayed in Scripture, are not admitted as illustrative of the justice and mercy of the Divinity, how can any man assert that He is distinguished for these attributes at all. He is known to possess power, wisdom, and goodness only by the things of nature which are visibly indicative of these qualities; but if these were not apparent in nature we could know nothing at all certainly about them in him. But we do not theorize on the power of God. We look at the vastness of the Universe and admit it promptly. We do not theorize on the wisdom and goodness of God; we behold the uses and designs of nature, and taste of the riches of his benevolence and admit that facts demonstrate the Divinity to be possessed of these attributes. But now, in religion, we have before our eyes not a physical and natural, but a moral and political case; and justice and mercy would demonstrate that they have an existence and name among the characteristics which go to make up the Divine Nature. But here it is we hesitate; and when the facts which illustrate these are adduced for saving and moral purposes, that is, when they are proclaimed to us for belief, reformation of life, and obedience to God, we first doubt, then cavil, and finally reject them.

But there is no theory to be admitted in regard to the Divine character. If God displays eternal power we admit he possesses that attribute; if he unfolds his goodness by deeds of munificence we are safe in admitting that goodness; and if by acts of justice and mercy he displays these attributes, then and then only are we warranted in saying that he is a God of justice and mercy. Then are we warranted in saying that he is the just God and the Saviour.

Well then, if the case of Primitive Man, as described in the scripture, is admitted, we have God's justice and mercy displayed on a scale infinitely extended, a scale commensurate with the greatness of his name, and on a plan and in a case intensely interesting to man. While those who deny the account, and yet assert these attributes in the Divinity, reason for a conclusion without a premise.

CHAPTER II

Sacrifice Considered in Relation to Man in General

It has been repeatedly observed that man is a creature gifted with a sense of duty. From this attribute of his nature, then, is derived his responsibility to his fellow men, and finally to his God. Accordingly God has held him responsible to him for his actions since the world began. The word duty implies knowledge and freedom; for where there is no knowledge there can be no apprehension of duty, and where there is no freedom, there can be no performance of it. To speak of duty, where there is neither knowledge nor freedom, or where there is only knowledge without freedom, is like talking of beholding an object which does not exist, and that too, by a man who has no eyes. We might as well speak of the deaf hearing sound where no sound is made. This is not the case with man. He has knowledge to perceive and freedom to act as his history from creation demonstrates. For as then so now, and as now so then, God has treated him as a responsible being and will bring into judgment every evil thought, word and work.

Inasmuch, then, as man is responsible he is at the same time a creature of duty; and inasmuch as he is a creature of duty, he is consequently possessed of a previous knowledge, and freedom of will to choose the good, or refuse the evil; or choose the evil and refuse the good.

He is possessed of free will, then, or an ability to choose the good and consequently to practice it. But this last proposition is denied by many, who teach that though he is free to choose the better part and follow it, he has not the will to do this, being so depraved by nature, or the fall, that he wills only to choose evil and do that continually, and this they style Moral Inability. From this moral inability flows the doctrine of spiritual operations to make him willing and able to believe and obey the gospel. These interpreters of human nature, set man in the attitude of him who, with abundance of strength to carry it, refuses to take home that which is necessary to his starving family, and scorns all motives of life and death by which the case is characterized; or they represent him as a man who, with all appetite and all capacity to eat, refuses every inducement internal and external to sit down to table, and dies the same!

NATURAL INABILITY is illustrated by doctor Beecher thus:—

"NATURAL INABILITY.—'Thou canst not see my face and live.' Moses desired the full orbed vision of the glory of God; but he is answered that it would destroy his life, his natural powers could not sustain the overpowering manifestation. David said of his child, after its death, 'can I bring him back again?' and Solomon, 'can a man take fire in his bosom, and his clothes not be burned?' And God demands, 'can any hide himself that I shall not see him?' 'The Chaldeans answered, there is not a man upon the earth that can show the kings matter—tell his dream and its interpretation.' 'They which would pass from hence to you cannot; neither can they pass to us that would come from thence.' These are evidently specimens of natural inability, which no willingness or effort on the part of the agent could surmount.

Moral Inability is illustrated by the same gentleman as follows:—

Let us now look at the same terms as implying inability from disinclination or contrary choice—'aversion of will.'

'With God all things are possible:' i. e. his natural power is equal to any act which is not in its own nature an impossibility. 'God who cannot lie'—'by two immutable things in which it was impossible for God to lie.' Is God's omnipotence so limited that for want of power he could not utter falsehood? Is it not the infinite aversion of his holiness which constitutes the inability? 'The strength of Israel *will not lie*. Your new moons, and Sabbaths, and calling of assemblies, I CANNOT away with; it is iniquity, even the solemn meeting.' The *cannot* is explained to mean his aversion to hypocrisy in worship: therefore it follows, 'when ye make many prayers *I will not* hear.'

It is said of our Saviour, that 'he must needs go through Samaria.' Was he compelled to go through Samaria; or did he simply, for sufficient reasons, choose to go that way?

'He could not do mighty works there, because of their unbelief.' Did the unbelief of man overpower divine omnipotence, so that Christ had no ability to work miracles; or did it furnish to his divine wisdom such reasons against it as made him *prefer* not to do it, expressed by the phrase *could not*, i. e. chose not to do it?

'Can the children of the bride chamber fast while the bride groom is with them?' Doubtless they possess the natural ability. But the meaning is, will they choose to do it? Can they—i. e. will they?

'Can ye drink of the cup that I drink of?' It was the cup of suffering and of ignominy, and he meant not whether they could feel pain, and persecution, and shame, (for he told them that they should,) but whether they were willing, and believed that they should continue willing to suffer with him—'can ye,' i. e. are you and shall you be willing?

'If it be possible, let this cup pass from me.' Did our Saviour doubt whether God had the power to deliver him instantly from suffering? He knew he could do it; and only, as man, was not certain whether the agony he had already suffered might suffice, or the expiation demanded more. The phrase, if it be *possible*, means therefore, if it be wise and seem good in thy sight—if thou art satisfied and willing, let this cup pass, &c.; but if otherwise, not my *will*, but thy *will* be done. 'Lord, if thou wilt, thou canst make me clean:' i. e. thou canst do it, if thou art willing, implying as in the case before, that he could not cleanse him, if unwilling, calling unwillingness inability."

The doctor concludes his piece on moral inability as follows.

"But it is said, if men, as free agents, are in reality able to obey the gospel—how does it happen, that under such a pressure of motive, no one of the human race should ever have done it? and suppose we could not tell, and should admit that it is wonderful, as God does—would it follow, that the reason is the natural impossibility of evangelical obedience? How could it be wonderful, that men do not of themselves obey the gospel, if the reason of it is that it is a natural impossibility? Is it wonderful, that men do not create worlds, or uphold or govern the universe? and why should the non-performance of one impossibility be more wonderful than another? Can there be no uniformity of character without a coercive necessity producing it? Is not God of one mind, immutable, yet free? Are not the angels free who kept their first estate? And are not the fallen angels, though immutably wicked, as voluntary in their opposition to God, as the holy angels are voluntary in their obedience? As to the uniform disobedience of fallen man until renewed by the Holy Ghost, we have only to say, it is a matter of fact, well authenticated, that free agents do so—that it is a part of the terrific nature of sinful man to baffle all motives, and be voluntarily but unchangeably wicked—persevering in rebellion, amid commands, prohibitions, promises, and threatenings, and the entreaties of the whole universe, and the weeping and wailings of the damned."

There is taken for granted in this concluding paragraph two important items. First; "That no one of the human race, with all the commands, prohibitions, promises, and threatenings which are found in the book of God, ever obeyed the gospel till first renewed by the Holy Spirit." This is a large and violent assumption, alike degrading to man and contradictory of the holy scriptures. Man is altogether a creature of persuasion by motive, and the holy scriptures furnish innumerable instance of men being persuaded to obey the gospel.

I believe the only reason for this inability assigned by the advocates of a scheme, which at once libels human nature and contradicts the scriptures, is, that man is in a fallen state. Their reasoning, then, is this. Man is in a sinful state, and, therefore, no motive of life or death, time or eternity, can induce him to obey God in any matter whatever, even the smallest. Farther, God himself, it would appear, speaks, and reasons, and remonstrates, and reproves, and rebukes and exhorts in vain; words, and facts and deeds of benevolence, and redemption and grace, and nature and all argument even in the hands of God himself and argued by himself, are all in vain, and wholly useless, and ineffectual, to convert. But man it is allowed by those who teach this absurdity, was not always in his present state. He was once holy and strong to do good and to keep God's commands. He was once in Paradise and wholly unstained by evil. Now, would it not be as good reasoning to say, that because man was then in a good state he could not be moved to evil, as to say because he is now in a sinful state he cannot be moved to do good? I think it would, the reasoning is the same. But it is false; for we know that man in a state of innocence could be, and actually was moved to sin. And we know also that he can, and actually is moved to good by proper motives; the scriptures furnish innumerable examples. The question is not whether man can change his own heart, but whether God can change it by his word without a special operation of the Spirit? While we admit and teach that we cannot change ourselves, yet we boldly assert it to be the doctrine of Christ that God can and does change us both in soul and behavior by his word, the truth of the gospel without any operation of the Spirit, also that the Spirit is not granted to change the heart, but in the Christian system is given to a man because his heart is already changed by the belief of the truth. Man being in a state of innocence and holiness, did the Devil succeed to make him a transgressor? Yes. And man being in a state of sin, shall God fail by all the truth he can speak to make him righteous? Absurd. The devil in this manner is made more potent than God, and a lie by the one more powerful than the truth by the other!

This is to make devils and not sinners of mankind, and to set Satan above the Almighty!

The Devil has not one inducement to do good because his crime is such as shall never be forgiven; and he knows it; therefore, he always sins. But man has physically and intellectually the highest disposition for good. Sin, misery, and death, are all preternatural to him, and belonged not to him in his original state. This disposition for knowledge, duty, and happiness, which is the good to which his physical and mental nature is adapted, is what he is thirsting for all over the world; and it is this which the gospel purposes to convey to him on the principles of belief, repentance, and baptism. But to show that he is capable of obeying the gospel, when that gospel is proclaimed by one who understands it, I refer the reader to the conversion of three thousand people on the day of Pentecost; also to the case of the Samaritans; Paul, whom Jesus converted by his own words; the eunuch, and every other soul spoken of in the Acts of the Apostles as having obeyed the gospel. They are all said to have believed when they heard and saw; but not one of them to have been operated upon by the Holy Spirit till after they believed. And Dr. Beecher has not, and cannot produce one solitary case in which any man is said to believe by a secret and special operation of the Spirit.

The second matter assumed by the Doctor then, is this, that man being in a sinful state, incapable of good, even when all motive is presented by God himself, the operation of the Spirit to do away his inability is indispensable, and is, therefore, a doctrine of the New Testament; for it would not be given if it was unnecessary. This is the Doctor's sentiment in substance. The gospel as announced by the Rev. gentleman and his colleagues in the ministry, I regret to say, is not entirely the same as that proclaimed by Peter; and, therefore, having mistaken their own gospel for Peter's, they may have, and doubtless do think, that it is as difficult to obey the one as the other. I only add that if men were unable to believe and obey the gospel as announced by Peter, he never told them so. In no specimen of his preaching which has reached us, is there the least hint of such inability; but several matters to the very contrary are obviously apparent. When facts settle a case reasoning is rendered unnecessary. We see that man in a state of sin has, on hearing the gospel and the miracles which established its truth, believed and obeyed it. And we see that man in a state of holiness and innocence when tempted, yielded to a falsehood and sinned against God. These facts ought to make us lay aside our own reasonings, and cause us to proceed according to the word of God, and the example of the holy apostles.

But we shall say a few things of primitive man. He sinned and was respited; facts, however, show us that the Divine Father decreed at the time, that this original forfeiture of blood and life, should never be forgotten by man. In perpetual memory of this sin and forfeiture, therefore, animal sacrifice was introduced; and from Adam to Jesus, our Lord and Saviour, men have appeared at the altar of God with blood. Thus, the sacrificing of animals in the true worship is seen by us to have been introduced originally as a commemorative institution of the fall of Adam. If then our Lord's day is a memorial of the resurrection of Christ, and the supper of his death; if the passover was a memorial of the exodus of Israel out of Egypt, and the sabbath, of God's having made the world in six days, then sacrifice is a memorial of the original fall of man; so that this ancient event is rendered as certain to us by that bloody rite, as the resurrection of Christ, his death, the departure from Egypt, and the creation of the world are by the ordinances which respectively relate to them. This is an application of Mr. Leslie's celebrated argument on commemorative institutions, which that gentleman seems to have overlooked. But it is certainly as applicable to the sanctification of the seventh day, and the offering of sacrifice from the fall as to the ordinances of the Christian and Jewish religions. That sacrifice, animal sacrifice, was intended to keep "sin in remembrance," is certain, from the fact that it was incapable of taking it away. "For it was impossible for the blood of bulls and calves, and goats, to take away sin." Thus speaks Paul. The sins of the Jews, then, like those of all nations, and of Adam, were not purged by all the blood that was spilled; but only kept in remembrance before God till Christ.

CHAPTER III

Sacrifice Considered in Regard to the Jews in Particular

The grand features of the Old and New Testaments are the fall of man, and his redemption by our Lord and Saviour, Christ. But the law, as the apostle expresses it, "supervened, that offence might abound," and consequently that the whole business might be better understood by mankind universally, for whom redemption was designed. Now as the Jews were not only in a state of sin in common with all other men, but were also under sin to the law, in particular, and there being no blood in their economy capable of expiating it, in fact, as the sins of the world from Adam downward were filed against men, so the sins of the Jews were filed against that nation; and required to be redeemed by the blood of Christ, before they could stand even on a footing with the rest of mankind. Christ had not only to die for them and all others in common, but he required to die for them in a particular manner to redeem them from the law. He required, in taking their place in law, to become a curse for them; but how was this to be done? I answer by dying on a tree; for it is written, "Cursed is every one that hangeth on a tree."

The curse of Adam was death without any specification of the manner in which it should be inflicted; but the person cursed under the law was to be hanged on a tree. As, therefore, the Jews had violated their law, and had become obnoxious to the curse, of hanging on a tree, and as Adam had exposed himself and mankind to death, Christ, who took in law the place of all, required to die for all, and on a tree, for the Jews in particular. He is, therefore, said to have given himself for the whole world, and for the Jews in particular, that he might redeem the "transgressions that were under the first covenant:" that he might by his blood take them from the file and let the guilty nation off from their former covenant in order to be married to himself by the new or christian covenant.

The animals offered under the law were of five sorts, bullocks, sheep, goats, turtle doves, and young pigeons. The offerings were burnt-offerings, sin-offerings, trespass-offerings, peace-offerings, meat and drink offerings, wave and heave-offerings, and meat-offerings. It will doubtless gratify the reader to learn the manner in which the burnt-offerings were offered under the Law, as described by the accurate and learned Mr. Brown.

"The reason of their name is given in Lev. 6:9; and the Hebrew word for them is *Ouluth*, or sacrifices which ascend in flame or smoke. It is disputed among the Jews concerning the occasion of burnt-offerings, and when they became due: but the following appears to be the general opinion; viz. that they were either intended to expiate the evil thoughts of the heart, by the faith of the offerer looking to the Messiah as the great antitype; or to expiate from the breach of affirmative precepts. Burnt-offerings might be offered of any of the five kinds of animals just mentioned; and the manner of offering them was as follows:

1. The offerer brought his burnt-offering to the door of the Tabernacle before the Lord, while the tabernacle stood; but when the Temple was erected, this phrase "before the Lord" was interpreted to mean—from the gate Nicanor inward, or in any part of the Court of Israel, but especially of the priests, which was inclosed within the court of Israel. This part of the injunction, concerning the appearance of the offerer, was considered so indispensable, that even women, who were

forbidden the Court of Israel at all other times, were obliged to enter it when they offered a burnt-offering.

2. The owner of the sacrifice, after having brought it, laid his hand upon its head while it was yet alive. This was intended as a solemn transfer of sin from himself to the animal; and in its death he acknowledged his own liability to suffer. Who does not see in this transaction a striking type of the atonement, when Christ, our sacrifice, bore our sins, and graciously became our great propitiation? It was commonly at the place of rings, on the north side of the altar, and with his face directed towards the Temple, that this transaction took place; and the words made use of were as follows: "I have sinned: I have done perversely: I have rebelled, and done thus and thus (here specifying, either mentally or audibly, the specific cause of his offering.)—But I return by repentance before thee, and let this be my expiation."

3. The next thing commonly done was the bleeding of the animal, which was performed by tying it to one of the rings if large, or by the feet if small; its head lying towards the south and its face towards the west, while he that killed it stood on the east side of the animal with his face to the west, or to the Temple. During the Tabernacle, the bleeding of the animal was often performed by the offerer himself; but in the time of the Temple it was transferred to the priesthood, because they were then more numerous, and better skilled in the right manner of doing it. The blood was received in a sacred vessel, and taken by the priest to be sprinkled on the altar; which sprinkling, during every period of the Mosaic economy, was exclusively the prerogative of the priesthood. But as this was deemed a very important part of the service, the Jews especially after the introduction of traditions, were very anxious to have it done aright.—Accordingly, no priest that was a mourner, by having a person dead in his house that day,—nor one who was unclean in any way,—nor one who had not on all his priestly garments,—nor one who sat or stood on anything but the bare pavement while he was receiving the blood,—nor one who received it with his left hand, might carry the blood to sprinkle it on the altar. But if they had a mixture of precept and tradition in the requisites for the priest, so had they also in their manner of sprinkling. For having established the rule, that it was essential to the merit of the sacrifices that the blood should be sprinkled either above or below the red line which encircled the altar, and divided it into two equal parts; the priest, in the present case, had to go with the blood, first to the north-east corner, and then to the southwest, and throw a part of it against the altar, below the red line, in such a manner as that it spread on both the sides of the corners equally, forming the figure of the Greek letter gamma; and if any blood remained in the vessel, it was ordered to be poured out upon the foundation of the altar on the south-west corner, where the two holes were, which we formerly mentioned when treating of the altar, and through which the blood that remained was conveyed

to the brook Kidron. It was in consequence of the blood making atonement for the soul, and thus typical of the blood of Christ, that the Israelites were forbidden to eat it.

4. In the next place, the person whose office it was to flay and divide the animal, proceeded as follows: he hung it on the hooks near the place of rings; removed the skin; opened the heart to let the remaining blood escape (notice how accidentally, to human appearance, this happened to Christ, our great sacrifice, although the express subject of prophecy;) took out the fat; and, dividing the animal into its several parts, gave them in succession to the priests in waiting; first, the head, then the shoulders and foreparts, and lastly, the hind quarters. The Jewish treatise *Tamid* is very particular with respect to all the pieces, but such an enumeration would be here unnecessary.

5. Having each received their allotted portions, the priests carried them to the ascent of the altar, where they laid them down to salt them, according to the law, which said—"With all thine offerings thou shalt offer salt." Indeed, no injunction in the whole law was more sacredly observed than this; for the Jews themselves tell us, that "nothing came to the altar unsalted but the wine of the drink-offering, the blood sprinkled, and the wood for the fire." And in three places they used salt, namely, in the salt chamber on the north-west corner of the Court of Israel, for salting the skins; upon the rise of the altar, for salting the sacrifices, to season them, and to take away the smoke; and on the top of the altar, for salting the handful of flour, oil, and frankincense. It was to this typical law that our Saviour referred in Mark 9:49, 50, when he says, concerning the effect of the gospel on those who embrace it, "Every one shall be salted with fire, (for the fire of God's altar, as a spiritual sacrifice, holy and acceptable) and (or rather, as) every sacrifice shall be salted with salt. Salt is good: but if the salt have lost its saltness, wherewith will ye season it? Have ye salt then in yourselves, and have peace one with another." For as salt, when plentifully applied, preserves meat from putrefaction, so will the gospel keep men from being corrupted by sin. And, as salt was indispensable to sacrifices, in order to render them acceptable to God, so the gospel, brought home to the hearts of men by the Holy Ghost,[15] is indispensably requisite to their offering up of themselves living sacrifices, holy and acceptable, which is

---

[15] Mr. Brown in common with all Protestants, believed that the Holy Spirit required to bring the word home in order to make it effectual to salvation. He thinks that the salt used in sacrifices was typical of this. But it is the word that kills and not the Spirit. The knife of the priest let out the blood of the sacrifice, before salt was used, and so the word of the gospel must kill a man to the world before the Spirit seasons him for God. He must be slain and washed in baptism, before he is sanctified by the Holy Spirit, or salted with the salt of the gospel.

their most reasonable service. Perhaps the heathen derived their salted cakes from this Jewish practice.

6. The next particular concerning the burnt-offerings was, that he, whose office it was to lay the pieces on the altar, having received them from those who brought and salted them, cut out the sinew that shrank, threw it among the ashes, and when there was no reason for haste, laid the pieces in order upon the altar, or as near their natural position in the animal as possible: but when numbers were offered at the same time, and, consequently, when haste was required, and the largeness of the fire made delay insupportable, this rule was dispensed with, and the different parts were thrown carelessly upon the altar, yet so as to be completely consumed. Thus were the burnt-offerings properly called *holocausts*, or whole burnt-offerings, for the priesthood received no part of them but the skin."

Animal offerings, from Adam's day to that of Christ, may, therefore, be considered as a recognizance of sin, or a confession of judgment on the part of the worshipper.

CHAPTER IV

Sacrifice Considered in Relation to God

When considered in relation to God who appointed sacrifice, it has a triple import.

Memorial.—First it was a memorial bringing sin to remembrance. This was its original import, and, doubtless, the first purpose for which it was introduced into the true religion, and continued in it till Christ.

Ordinance.—Touching ordinance, anything may be used as such that God is pleased to appoint. The brazen serpent was the ordinance or symbol of cure to the Israelites who looked at it; the waters of Jordan to Naaman the leper; the fleece to Gideon; the pillar of fire was the symbol of rest or removal as it ascended from or descended upon the ark during the journeyings of Israel in the wilderness. The inimitable oil of the sanctuary, the symbol of induction to the priestly, prophetic, and kingly offices; and circumcision the symbol of the covenant with Abraham and induction to the particular economy of the Law; immersion, not sprinkling, is the symbol of the remission of sins and initiation into the Christian church; the first day, of Christ's resurrection; the bread and wine, of his flesh and blood; the passover of the exodus from Egypt; the rainbow of the covenant with Noah; sacrifice, of the original sin by Adam; and the sabbath, of the rest after the creation, &c.

Type.—But many things in religion were types as well as symbols; and so looked beyond the present into the future. Sacrifice for sin or sin-offerings being clothed with a triple signification, looked to the past, the present, and the future. In regard to the past, it was a memorial "bringing sin to remembrance." In regard to the present, it was a symbol of pardon. Touching the future it was a type of Christ shedding his blood in behalf of the world. Thus it was a commemorative institution; a permanent ordinance for the actual remission of sins, and a typical symbol of the blood of Christ.

Of the last import of the shedding of blood, it is possible, it is even probable that the ancient worshippers of God had no knowledge. It is common, I confess, for divines to teach that all the godly from Abel downward, looked at Christ through the sacrifices which they offered; but of this there is not one word in scripture. It does not appear that one soul of them ever attached this typical attribute to any animal that ever was offered; for it is of the nature of a type not to be understood till the antitype appears. This was the mysterious import of the sacrificial ordinance, understood by none till the appearance of Christ, and made known by revelation to his holy apostles and prophets, to whom exclusively we are indebted for our knowledge of this secret, by which we understand that the shedding of Christ's blood was not a fortuitous thing to the great God; but a matter ordained by him before the foundation of the world; and set forth in types through the offering of the blood of beasts, till Messiah appeared.

This ought to fill us with the profoundest reverence for the Omniscient God, and cause us to obey him, and honor his Son Jesus Christ, seeing he looks through all time and spans a thousand years as he does a day, and a day as a thousand years. O that men would consider their latter end, and the infinitely holy character of that God with whom they have to do! O that they would consider their ways, and turn to God before these things be forever hid from their eyes!

But to this view of the matter it may be objected that the prophets, and Isaiah in particular, spoke of the Messiah as a sin-offering. This indeed might show us that the prophet himself looked for a suffering Messiah; but it would not prove that all the other worshippers of the true God had attained to the same knowledge. We overrate the knowledge of the prophets, however, when we think that because they spoke these things, therefore they understood them. Peter assures us they did not; and Paul says of the Jewish doctors of his own day, that had they known this mystery of the cross, "they would not have crucified the Lord of glory." There were many things in the ancient scriptures which eye had not seen, nor ear heard, nor heart conceived; and the doctrine of the cross was one of these, prepared indeed for those who loved God, but at the same time requiring to be revealed by the

Spirit who first spoke them; "for the Spirit searches all things," said the apostle, "yea the deep things of God. For what man knoweth the things of man, save the spirit of man that is in him?—even so the things of God knoweth no man save the spirit of God." The apostles, therefore, received the Holy Spirit in such a measure, and after such a nature, as enabled them to understand both types and prophecies, and parables which had been kept secret of old, even from the foundation of the world. Peter's language is remarkable, and shows that the prophets were impatient of their own ignorance in regard to the import of the predictions which they delivered, searching accurately for what time and for what people those things, which they spake by the Spirit, were designed. By the same spirit, however, they were informed that they spoke of matters which related not to the dispensation in which they ministered, but to us who received the gospel.

"Concerning which salvation, the prophets inquired accurately, and searched diligently, who have prophesied concerning the favor bestowed on you; searching diligently of what things, and what kind of time; the Spirit of Christ, who was in them, did signify, when he testified before, the sufferings for Christ, and the glories following these:—to whom it was revealed, that not for themselves, but for us, they ministered these things; which have now been reported to you, by them who have declared the glad tidings to you, with the Holy Spirit sent down from heaven: into which things angels earnestly desire to look attentively."

The very angels seem to have been ignorant of the mystery of the cross, until revealed by fact; they were, therefore, represented on the propitiatory in the temple and tabernacle, which was a type of the Messiah, as looking downward to it, and toward the blood which the High Priest sprinkled upon it on the day of annual atonement. If then the prophets who spoke predictions of the sacrifice of Christ, and the angels, were ignorant of it, it was not wonderful that all others understood it not. As for the godly of the Redeemer's own day, they do not seem ever to have conceived such a thought; and though John spoke of Christ as a Lamb, who was to take away the sins of the world, and Jesus expressly informed his apostles that he came to give his life a ransom for many, yet so remote from their thoughts was the doctrine of their Messiah's becoming a sacrifice for sin, that they do not seem to have formed one correct idea on the subject. They did not even know from all he said, that he was to arise from the dead even after he had arisen. The death of Christ then is the antitype of all the sacrificial blood that was spilt, from the first lamb to the last that ever was slain on God's altar; and the relation which his high, and holy, and admirable work bears to the divine character, deserves to be spoken of.

We shall now endeavor to bring before our readers the relations which the death of Christ bears to God the Father:

First, then, the death of Christ does not sustain the same relations to the Father that it does to the Son. For instance it deprived the Son of his life, but it did not deprive the Father of life. It did not change the state of the Father from mortality; but it changed the condition of the Son in this respect. It did not perfect the moral nature of the Father; but it did that of the Son, and was intended to fit him for those high offices for which he arose from the dead. In short it is not the life or state, but the character of God that is affected by the death of Christ.

Let us then enquire how the character of God the Father is affected by the death of his Son, our Lord Jesus.

The nature of the Deity as described in scripture, is physical, intellectual, and moral; or which is the same, he is possessed of power, wisdom, and goodness; for the word power refers to his physical, wisdom to his intellectual, and goodness to his moral nature; we have to inquire, therefore, how the character of God, in the different departments of his nature, was affected by the splendid fact under consideration.

To begin at the moral nature of our Heavenly Father:—All must confess that "to give up his Son Jesus Christ to death for us all" was most good; and furnished heaven and earth with the most illustrious proof of his philanthropy, or love of men. In Titus, indeed, it is described as the shining forth of his philanthropy, all former indications of benevolence being comparatively the mere twilights, or dawnings of that sun-bright regard for men which blazed forth when God set forth his Son in blood that through faith we might have the remission of sins that are past. Our Lord Jesus enunciated this goodness of God in terms the most affecting, in his conversation with Nicodemus, when he said contrary to the prejudices of all Jews that "God so loved the world, that he gave his only begotten Son that whosoever believeth on him might not perish but have everlasting life."—The death of Christ, in short, is every where in scripture spoken of as the brightest and most unequivocal manifestation of the love of God. "Herein," says John, "is the love of God manifested, not that we loved God but that God loved us and sent his Son to be the propitiation for our sins." Nor could the moral excellence of the Divine Father, perhaps, have been brought before men by any other means.

There subsists then, between the death of Christ and the moral nature of the Divinity, a relation like that which subsists between any two things the first of which can never be fully known without the last. To illustrate; The vegetable force can be seen in the production of the trunks, stems, and straws of grasses, flowers, and trees; its energies are rendered still more evident or are further known by the branches, or twigs, and leaves; but we understand the ultimate and highest energies of which the vegetable forces are capable only when we see the buds, flowers, and pericarp or fruit and the seed which they contain for the re-production of their species. Thus is it with God, our Father; his goodness is over all his works his benevolence is seen and felt every where in life and in the things necessary to life, and in religion also; but the unmodified discovery of his moral excellency is known only through the death of his Son, our Lord Jesus Christ.

But to come to the intellectual nature of God as affected by the death of Christ—the wisdom exhibited in this affair. While every one will say that to give up his Son to death was most good, the question arises was it wise? It was good. Was it wise?

To give up his Son to death for us all was in God most good, still the question arises, and it deserves to be answered, Was it wise? Are the goodness and the wisdom of the eternal alike evident in this great affair? Was this unparalleled philanthropy the result of weakness, or did it grow out of the necessity of the case and the unrivalled wisdom of the Almighty?

The wisdom of God as related to the death of Christ may be seen from many points; but when viewed in connection with the constitution of man and his moral elevation by the Christian religion, it appears exceedingly obvious. Two of the most active powers in human nature are, it is well known, those of *faith* and *hope*; in perfecting the morals of the disciples, therefore, it was indispensable that both these powers should be enlisted; it was necessary for the accomplishment of his moral designs that the author of our salvation should bring over to his aid these active powers of faith and hope.

The object of our hope, therefore, is set before us in the splendid and inspiring fact of a future resurrection; but it is founded on the promise of the Almighty and derived immediately from the resurrection of the Lord Jesus: nay the general resurrection is so inseparably connected with that of Christ, that if the one has not taken place the other never will; if Christ the first fruits has not been reaped and offered to the Lord of the harvest, the whole harvest is unsanctified, and will never be reaped; those who have died in Christ have perished; and we are yet in our sins: the argument then is this; first our morals required to be purified and elevated; secondly this could not be done without bringing over to the side of righteousness the active principle of *hope*, thirdly hope could not be established, but by being placed on an immovable basis, and like faith required to be sustained by facts; that our hope like our faith might be in God, God raised our Lord Jesus from the dead; finally he could not have been raised, unless he had first died. He died, and the splendid results of his death fully justify the wisdom of God in permitting, in ordaining it; for he gave himself by the will of God for our sins.

The wisdom of God as related to the death of the Lord Jesus may be seen in the following, also. God is the great Ruler of men, and as such he put them originally under law which he himself framed and promulgated: It would be incongruous with all our ideas of a righteous governor, the majesty of law, the general welfare, and the common maxims of good order, to suffer the laws to be violated with impunity. The death of Christ has demonstrated to men and angels what the wisdom of God is in this respect, and that his character as the Governor of the Universe cannot be compromised.

But we dare not enter into detail on the various points by which the death of Christ holds of the wisdom of God; from what has already been offered, the reader must perceive that as it was most good in God to give up his beloved Son for our sins, so it was most wise; yes it was most wise, and has resulted in the redemption of our souls from sin in all its debasing influences; it has resulted in the settlement of both our faith and hope, and has laid a foundation for a succession of reformations which can issue in nothing but the perfection of our moral nature, and our final glorification in Heaven.

But how is this event, the death of Christ, related to the power of God? As the resurrection of Jesus was brought about by the power of God, it will be obvious to every one that the power of God must be related in some way to his death; for without his death how could he have been raised? The death of Christ then led to the most surprising development of his power who claims to be the God of the bible, the true God; and the Apostle Paul refers to it as such, and designates it the "greatness of his power which he wrought in Christ Jesus when he raised him from the dead and set him at his own right hand in the heavens, far above all principalities, and powers, and might, and dominion, and every name that is named not only in this world but also in that which is to come, and gave him to be head over all things to the church which is his body, the fullness of him that filleth all in all."

Thus we may see in general that the death of Christ is an event which involves the Divine character in all its departments physical, moral, and intellectual, or is related most intimately to the power, wisdom, and goodness of the Divinity.

CHAPTER V

Sacrifice in Relation to Christ

We have in our second discourse spoken of Christ merely as the Son of God and Son of Man; but this account of him stops short of Scripture by a wonderful odds; for besides the things that relate to his descent from man and God, as a person born into our world, there are many passages of the sacred writings which speak of this adorable person in a wonderful manner, and set him in a most mysterious attitude before the sons of men. Such are the following. "In the beginning was the word, and the word was God, and the word was with God. All things were made by him, and without him was not any thing made that was made. In him was life and life was the light of men." Again, "No man has ascended into heaven but he who descended from heaven even the Son of Man whose abode is in heaven;" and "What and if you shall see the Son of Man ascend up to where he was before." "Father glorify me with that glory which I had with thee before the world began." "Before Abraham was I am." "God manifest in the flesh." "God over all, blessed forever." "By whom he, God, made the worlds." "And thou Lord hast laid the foundations of the earth &c." "Why does David, speaking by the Spirit, call him his Lord," "By him were all things made that are in heaven and upon the earth," &c. These are a few of the marvelous sayings of the sacred oracles concerning him who was made flesh and tabernacled in human form and human nature, the only begotten of the Father, full of grace and truth; and the noblest purpose to which they can be applied, is the improvement of our own nature. They may well fill us with self-abasement and all humility and lowliness of mind; they may well clothe us with reverence and godly fear towards him with whom we have to do; and inspire us with the most mysterious and sublime conceptions of the infinite value of that blood which was shed for the redemption of the world.

The Socinians are a set of idealists, who make it a part of their religion to denounce the proper divinity of our Lord and Saviour, and to assume, in the presence of the ignorant, the arduous task of showing from Scripture that he was the Son proper of Joseph and Mary. That such may better understand the impertinence and profanity of such a doctrine, and that no person preaching the original gospel or teaching the Scriptures as they read, can with any show of fairness or propriety hold such a sentiment, we subjoin the following piece. We wrote it originally for the Christian Baptist: but as some assert that we deny the divinity, of our Lord, it will be very well, I apprehend, to insert it at this point of our discourse, seeing we have come to speak of that surplus of Scripture, which relates not to his birth by flesh and blood, but to his existence before the world was.

The Socinians very improperly call themselves Christians, thoughtless men! they are rather philosophers. The polite and unjudging may, indeed, suppose that on their heretical paradox these professors reason divinely. Well, be it so. "Jesus," say they, "is the son of Joseph." Excellent Christians! If these gentlemen interpret nature as they do religion; if they unlock the mysteries of the material world with the same adroitness and perspicacity with which they usher into open day the spiritual abortions of their own disordered minds, indeed they are divine philosophers. I have always thought the paradox of the Socinians a little too barefaced even for the vulgar.

Let us hear them in religion. "Jesus," say they, "is the son of Joseph." Now the twelve apostles, and all whom they taught the religion, worshipped Jesus; ergo, the apostles and all whom they taught worshipped the son of Joseph; ergo, the apostles and all whom they taught were idolaters!

But now, suppose that we should show that the Socinian sect fails of a peculiarity which distinguished the first Christian church, and those by whom it was gathered and instructed, the apostles, from all other worshippers besides, even from those who held many other things in common with them, what then? Again, if we should show that it was this very peculiarity which the Socinians have wiped from their creed that procured the disciples of Jesus the name of Christians at Antioch; and, lastly, if we should make it appear from reason and scripture that the Socinian paradox is a mere quibble, what then? Will it not inevitably follow that these professors act very fondly when they assume the name of Christians?

To our first proposition, then. But let not the reader suppose that I go out of my way to break my lance over the steel cap of the poor Socinians. I compassionate their temerity—and would not, the Bible being in my hand, rush into the presence of the Judge of quick and dead with their sentiments, for twice the value of the universe. But this only by the way.

And now to discover that peculiarity in the sentiments of the first Christians, which then distinguished them from their own infidel countrymen, the Jews, and now from our own countrymen the Socinians; let us away to the New Testament and rummage it in search of the mighty cause of that dreadful persecution which commenced with the death of Stephen. Acts 7.

To find out this, let it be noted that the two great prevailing parties in Jerusalem, at the moment of publishing the new institution were the Pharisean and Sadducean. Now what were the more prominent doctrines of these two sects? The scriptures, and I desire no better authority, the scriptures inform us that the Sadducces denied the resurrection, and the existence of angels and human spirits; but that the Pharisees maintained both. These two sects divided between them the inhabitants of the capital; and, as the Pharisaic party was at all times vastly more numerous than the Sadducean, it follows that a very large proportion of the citizens of Jerusalem held the resurrection of the dead and the existence of angels and spirits. Now what aspect did the apostles' doctrine bear to the respective sentiments of these sectaries? Why it confirmed, in the most illustrious manner, the dogmas of the Pharisees; it set the doctrine of the resurrection on an entire new footing; and, at the same time covered with shame and contempt the sentiments of the Sadducean materialists. The apostles, first delivering with great power of miracles their testimony concerning the resurrection of Jesus, immediately grounded the general doctrine of a resurrection on that splendid and well attested event, and gave such a blow to the pretensions of the Sadducees, as completely excited the *odium theologicum* of these incomparable doctors. But here it is but reasonable to suppose that the apostles' doctrine would irritate. This supposition, indeed, agrees well with the fact, for the chief priest (Caiaphas) and all his party, the sect of the Sadducees, were filled with zeal, and laid their hands on the apostles and put them in the common prison. Acts 5. The reader may perhaps wish to know why the Sadducees liked the doctrine of a resurrection so ill from the mouths of the apostles, and yet made this tenet a matter of forbearance in the case of the Pharisees. St. Paul says that we suffer fools gladly when we know that we ourselves are wise. The Sadducees well knew that the doctrine of a resurrection was not appended to the law of Moses, and these five books were all that these men held sacred; consequently, the Pharisaic arguments in proof of a resurrection must always have appeared very impotent and unsatisfactory to the Sadducees, because they were drawn chiefly from the lesser prophets' writings, which that party did not recognize as canonical. But the apostles grounded the general resurrection on the specific certainty of Christ's resurrection, and this was what irritated the Sadducees; they were grieved that the apostles preached "through Christ" the resurrection from the dead, Acts 4:2. But now as this particular in the apostles' doctrine incurred the resentment of the Sadducees, whose sentiments it condemned; so it is but reasonable to suppose that it would conciliate the favor and protection of the Pharisees, whose sentiments it confirmed. This in fact was the case; for when the Sadducees, who had imprisoned the apostles, consulted about putting them to death, as the sharpest and surest refutation of their hated argument for a general resurrection, there stood up a man in the Sanhedrim, a Pharisee, named Gamaliel, a teacher of the law, in great esteem among all the people, (Acts 5) and this divine plead the cause of the Christian teachers with such moderation and eloquence, that "to him they agreed." The apostles were dismissed, but charged by the Sadducees to teach the doctrine no more by the resurrection of Jesus, though, indeed, they had already filled the city with it. Now here it is wonderful and entertaining to behold the workings and contortions of religious bigotry! The Sadducees thought they saw in the apostles their last worst enemies, and they could have worried them. On the other hand the crafty Gamaliel saw in the apostles' doctrine the most certain argument for a resurrection, the favorite tenet of his own party, and with what art does he procure them their dismission. However, all this had occurred at the moment of publishing the new religion, before either party, Sadducean or Pharisaic, could well determine what was the grand peculiarity. I dare say that both these sects, in the first instance, were induced to think Christianity nothing more than some modification of Pharisaism; for the great tumult and conversion which the new doctrine at its first appearance excited in the city, together with the confusion of feeling caused by the preaching of the resurrection of Jesus, which was always very prominent in the public addresses of the apostles, had prevented these sectaries from inquiring more minutely into the faith and practice of the apostles.

The church must have already consisted of many thousands by this time. The first address of Peter on the day of Pentecost, proselyted three thousand; and we are told that the Lord continued to add to the church daily the cured. Afterwards it amounted to five thousand, and still multitudes both of men and women, were the more added to the Lord; myriads of priests were obedient to the faith, and the word or doctrine of the Lord increased mightily in Jerusalem. Now all these had hitherto enjoyed the favor of Gamaliel and his sect, and had been, perhaps, chiefly Pharisees themselves. We have seen how the Sadducees opposed them, and how artfully Gamaliel procured the release of the apostles who were at the head of the church, Those things bring us to the end of the fifth chapter. The death of Stephen and a horrible persecution of the church generally, are the very next events which follow in the order of the Acts of the Apostles. And here a reader awake to what the author of this treatise recounts, must pause in astonishment—must be confounded at the fickleness of religious favor. Stephen is murdered by the sectaries, and the disciples of that very Gamaliel, who had but this moment, employed all his eloquence in the defence of the Nazarenes, are now imbruing their hands in their blood, entering into houses and dragging out both men and women. Paul, the scholar of Gamaliel, committed them to prison. What was their crime? by what unheard of practice did the brethren forfeit the favor and protection of the people, for hitherto they were in favor with them all? Were they still only the Sadducees who persecuted the disciples? Alas! the Pharisees were turned against them also, and had now discovered a peculiarity in the Christian doctrine, which made them as much the enemies of the Apostles as the Sadducees had been before. But did not both parties just now agree to let the Christians go on unmolested? Did not Gamaliel say, "let them alone?" resolving all into this pious conclusion, that if this counsel, or this work, were of men, it would come to nought; but if it were of God it could not be overcome. What had the Christians done? Why all this horrible persecution? It was not because they had violated any legal institute—any of the external Mosaic observances. For though the word of God increased mightily in Jerusalem, though multitudes of men and women were the more added to the Lord, and myriads of the priests were obedient to the faith; yet were they all zealous of the law. The new doctrine, however Pharisees and Sadducees may have rated it, seemed only to make those who received it better men, for they were daily with one accord in the temple praising God and having favor with all the people. Now if the brethren were not persecuted for abandoning the law, for this they carried with them into the new religion, then they must have been persecuted for the apostles' doctrine, and yet not for all the several points in that doctrine; for we have seen that the Pharisees favored their method of preaching the resurrection and protected them on account of it from the outrages of the Sadducees. Indeed, it was formally agreed by both these parties to let the christians alone; to let them proceed unmolested, as long as nothing worse than the doctrine of a resurrection marked their religious creed. But this they did at a time when they had not as yet thought that the apostles' doctrine merited a more minute investigation. Still, however, the question returns, what had the christians done to excite the united fury of these two sects? Is there no scriptural answer to this important question? Is there nothing which might serve as a clue to bring us to the bottom of this persecution? We have seen who inflicted the punishment, and who had to endure it. But the cause—what was that? Not the doctrine of the resurrection. What then?

Let us follow the scholar of Gamaliel to Damascus; let us accompany this pious student of divinity to the place of his destination; the place whither he was commissioned by letters from the High Priest for the godly and religious purpose of hunting up the poor innocents of the Lord of Glory. The time was come when those who slew them thought they offered an acceptable service to God. Alas! mistaken men! they shall give an account to Him who is ready to judge the quick and the dead. Paul tells us that in this affair he carried with him to Damascus letters of authority from the high priests, but he does not himself mention the very crime which characterized a Christian; the peculiarity which distinguished a follower of Jesus from other Jews, that made him obnoxious to the persecutors, and liable to be carried off by Paul to Jerusalem. And this leaves us as much in the dark as ever concerning the particular point in the apostles' doctrine, which lay at the root of this persecution. However, the apostle was converted on his way to Damascus, and the surprising phenomena which accompanied his conversion were obvious to these who accompanied him. The whole party was struck to the earth by the splendor of the Saviour's glory. And the change in Paul's sentiments—his conversion from Judaism to

Christianity, was soon blazed throughout the city. Paul (Acts 9) immediately associated with those whom he had come to persecute and to carry bound to Jerusalem; and had even the courage to enter the Jewish synagogue, and to preach Jesus that he was the "Son of God;" at which all the Jews and proselytes of Damascus who heard his address, who listened to his arguments and were as yet unsuspecting of the change, were surprised, were confounded? The young scholar of the great Gamaliel, the famous zealot, who had carried it against the Christians with such a high hand at Jerusalem, was now an abettor of the supposed heresy of the Nazarenes—in short, was, in the pious estimation of the synagogue people, lost! an apostate! an idolater! What were the reflections of those who witnessed all this—who heard him speak, who heard him argue, who knew the tenor of his commission, and the particular crime of those whom he persecuted in Jerusalem and had come hither to seize? Reader, attend! the following are their very words: "Is not this he who made havoc of them at Jerusalem who call on (invoke) this name, and came hitherto carry such bound to the chief priests?" Surprising sentence? "Carry such." Carry whom? All who invoked the name of "the Son of God." We have hit at last then on the particular point in the apostles' doctrine which made the church so obnoxious to the Pharisees and Sadducees after they had discovered it. The brethren, then, it was found, lived in the idolatrous practice, as the Socinians would call it, of "invoking the Lord Jesus." Now, then, we can see the full import of that passage in the ninth chapter, where Ananias manifests such reluctance to visit Paul, even after the Lord Jesus bade him. Ananias, poor man, was guilty; he was one of those who invoked the name of Jesus, who was probably doing so at the hour of prayer, when the Lord Jesus vouchsafed him this vision. Reader, hear his own words. When the Lord desired him to go to visit Paul in the house of one Judas, "Lord," says he, "I have heard from many concerning this man, how much evil he has done to your saints in Jerusalem, and he is here with authority from the chief priests to bind all who invoke your name."—Acts 9:13.

Now, in these two quotations, the church in Jerusalem, and the brethren in Damascus are alike obnoxious, and are guilty of the same crime—the invocation of Jesus. Yet the church of Jerusalem was gathered and instructed by the apostles; nay, it was the first of all Christian churches, and is to be imitated by all. Is Christianity really a system of idolatry? Is the Son of God, whom Christians have been taught by the apostles to adore, the son of Joseph the carpenter? Take these words of the apostle John, 1st epistle, v. 13. "These things have I written to you who believe in the name of the Son of God, that you may know that you have everlasting life," &c. "This also is the confidence which we have in him, that if we ask any thing according to his will, he hearkens to us. Now, if we know that he hearkens to us in whatever we ask, we know that we obtain from him the petitions which we have asked." This a very odd sort of sentence on the Socinian scheme. John says that he had entire confidence in being heard: perhaps the reader does not know what the apostle alludes to in this expression. The allusion, reader, is to an express declaration made by the Saviour himself whilst on earth. (John's gospel, chapter 14.)

The apostles were dreadfully alarmed at the idea of his leaving them, being ignorant of the nature of his kingdom; so, in order to comfort them, he tells them that though he must leave them, yet he would return, and then whatever they would ask in his name he would do it for them—I am going away, i. e. to heaven; but, reader, mark the Lord's own words—"but whatever you ask in my name that I will do." Again, "that the Father may be glorified in the Son, if you ask any thing in my name I will do it." Amen! It was this promise that made John confident that Christ would hear us. Thus Jesus corrupted the apostles, and they corrupted the church of Jerusalem, and all others who would wish to shape their faith and practice by their example and teaching in the New Testament. And thus we see the origin of Stephen's dying prayer. "Lord Jesus receive my spirit—Lord, lay not this sin to their charge." And now the Socinians may themselves query whether this characteristic of the first of all Christians, and Christian churches, belongs to them.

CHAPTER VI

Sacrifice in Relation to the End to Be Attained by It

The ends for which animal sacrifices were introduced, were, as we have seen, three: first, they were commemorative institutions bringing sins to remembrance; and second, symbols of pardon, or rather respite for the time being; which two significations the ancients seem to have understood very well; thirdly, they were types of Christ; which was an import belonging to them, of which all the ancients were necessarily ignorant; for, as has already been observed, it is of the nature of a type not to be understood until the antitype, makes its appearance. Abraham, however, may form an exception in this case, and may have understood something of this typical import of sacrifice inasmuch as it is said of him by the Saviour, that he "rejoiced that he should see my day; he saw it and was glad." It is probable that this patriarch had asked God to unfold to him the nature of our redemption by the Messiah; and that the Almighty had promised to grant his request; for it is said he rejoiced that *he should see it*. God, therefore, did fulfill his promise to him, and permitted him to behold it; it is, therefore, added, "he saw it and was glad." He is said to have received Isaac from the dead in a figure or parable, that is, of the death of Christ. But we are not to suppose that any other of the ancients were thus highly favored; but were for proper reasons kept ignorant of this typical import of the sacrifices which they offered.

As for the offering of Christ, it is perhaps unnecessary to quote any thing to show for what he died. *Anti* is the proper Greek word for *instead of,* and is used in the New Testament in regard to his death. "The Son of Man came not to be ministered to, but to minister, and to give his life a ransom *anti polon,* instead of many." Blessed be the name of the Lord. Christ, therefore, is our great substitute in Law, the antitype of all the blood that was spilt from the fall to the time of his death.

CHAPTER VII

Necessary Nature of the Thing Offered

The reader has seen in the case of burnt offerings that the owner of the sacrifice, after having brought it, laid his hand upon its head while it was yet alive, and made confession of his sins: thus solemnly importing a transfer of them from himself to the animal. It becomes a question, therefore, whether the blood of the animal could in fact, expiate the sins of the offender. The apostle is voucher for us that it could not; and he assigns as a proof of it, that there was a remembrance made again of sins every year; that is, all the sins for which sacrifice had been offered during the year, were again brought into remembrance on the day of annual atonement, which shows that the animals offered for the people at confession, did not in reality take away sins.

But why this? Why could not the blood of bulls, and calves, and goats take away sins? The apostle says they could not make the comers thereunto perfect as pertaining to the conscience. But why could they not perfect the conscience? The reason is this that in all cases of infraction the law requires to be magnified and made honorable by the greater taking the place of the less, or the innocent the place of the guilty. But how much greater is a man than a sheep! Animals, therefore, never could really and truly stand as substitutes for man in law; and the offering of them, therefore, could only have been admitted till the times of reformation, as the apostle says, when Christ, the proper substitute for man, came, and as the greater for the less, the just for the unjust, offered himself without spot to God.

In cases of forfeiture and votive-offerings under the law of Moses this principle of magnifying the law was abundantly illustrated; for when any thing was to be redeemed one fifth of its real value was added as the price of its redemption before the owner could take it away. In the case of the first born also, although God accepted the tribe of Levi in their stead, still it was considered a redemption, and that the law might be magnified and appear great, a certain sum of money was demanded over and above, before the child could be redeemed.

But nothing is more obvious than that in the redemption of man the greater required to die instead of the less.

CHAPTER VIII

Of the Sacrifice of Christ in Regard to Law

If it be asked why man died; we can answer readily that it was because he sinned; but if we go a step beyond this and ask why sin should be punished with death, we can only say that so God willed. He was pleased, for reasons known to himself, to decree that the soul that sinned it should die; and the reason of the law, perhaps lies beyond our highest conception.

But, although we may not be able to say certainly what all or even any of the reasons of the law may be, yet the whole matter sets divine law itself before us in a most peculiar attitude, and shows us that it is one of the most wonderful and majestic objects ever submitted to man for consideration. It shows also that the great Governor of men will be obeyed at all hazards, that on the matter of submission to his rules of order and morality and worship, he will compromise nothing, even to the eating of forbidden fruit; that ignorance and inexperience are no apology; that apparent insignificance in the thing inhibited or enjoined avails not for an excuse; but that every sin and all sin shall be punished with death.

And it is not evil works merely that come within the wide spread influence of the divine judgments, but idle words also. "For every idle word shall men render an account in the day of judgment," said our Redeemer. Nor is this carried beyond, or even to the extreme limits of God's legislations: for in that day he will try even the secrets of men's hearts. And as Christ has died with a reference not only to the first of men, who was under law, and to the Jews, who were also under law; but also to the Gentiles, who were without written law, no human being can have any just ground to hope for exemption; but must assuredly give an account of himself to God who made him, and made him also to serve him, and to glorify him forever.

Now, that Jesus died in relation to law, is one of the most obvious matters in the scriptures, although some have failed to see this, and have even spoken against it. Such have taught that his death had no reference to law, and the character of God as the Ruler of the world; but this is absurd, for he was made under law with a reference to this very thing. "When the fullness of time was come, God sent forth his son, made of a woman, made under law, to redeem those who were under the law, that we, the Jews, might receive the adoption of sons." If, then, he died with reference to the law of Moses, why not with reference to the law delivered at the beginning of the world? Man universally stood in relation to this precisely as the Jews did to their law. They had all become obnoxious to the curse or penalty due to the violation of theirs, which was hanging on a tree. Well, the world stood in no other relation to the original law. But that he became the Saviour, or substitute of the Jews, in this point is very certain, from what is said in Gal. 3:13, viz: "Christ has bought us off from the curse of the law, having become a curse for us." But this was not in a mere moral point of view neither, or to reform them in a political or legal point of view; that is, he died with an immediate reference to their political deliverance from the death to which they became obnoxious in law; or he bore death in their stead, that they, being freed from the law, might be justified, or forgiven their sins through faith in his name. Those, therefore, who refused to accept of the deliverance, which his blood had bought, had the curse executed upon them, and they were slain by millions, till they were scattered abroad, far from their native home, upon the face of all the earth, as it is at this day. This was according to another penalty or curse, threatened by the same law, which said that those who would not hearken to the voice of the Messiah, should be cut off from being the people of God; and it becomes a question whether they will ever be permitted to return to their own land, till they put themselves in such an attitude towards the Messiah, that this curse or dispersion may be removed. They are to return to the Lord, and when they do so the veil which is around their hearts shall be taken away, and they then may return according to faith, through the mercy of the Gentiles; but then, whether they can return while the curse still remains in force, is exceedingly problematical. When the curse fell on Satan he did not, and could not, return to Heaven; and when it fell on man, he did not, and could not, return to Paradise. So of Babylon, Nineveh, Sodom and Gomorrah; and so will it be with Rome; when the curse lights upon her it shall never be removed. With God it is in law curse or substitution; but no substitute can take the place of the Jews in regard to faith. They must, therefore, suffer the curse till they return to the Lord, and the veil be removed from around their hearts. There may, therefore, be something entirely erroneous in the present views of the Christian world, in regard to their going back to Canaan and Jerusalem. For the curses, like the gifts and callings of God, are without change, a fearful truth, verily. "I say unto you fear him." And there are cases in which substitution will not be accepted. Indeed this can be admitted in law, only where there exist some extenuating circumstances, as in the case of man, who fell by temptation.

Here, then, dear reader, is a new and living way opened for us into the presence of the Great God. Through the rent veil of your Redeemer's flesh you may find forgiveness and an entrance into the holiest of all. We beseech you, therefore, not to risk your soul's salvation by offering contempt to the blood of the covenant. God will not hold you guiltless if you receive this grace in vain; but will certainly inflict on you the severe and terrible punishments which is threatened against all offenders in this matter. Instead of law here is favor; instead of sin here is righteousness; instead of misery here is joy unutterable and the pleasures of the Spirit of God forever more.

But you say did Christ die for me? The Scriptures aver that he "died for all;" not only those who already believe, or have in any age believed, but "for the sins of the whole world." If therefore, you are in the form of flesh and blood, you are included in the great reconciliation by Jesus Christ.

But it is said that "I lay down my life for my sheep." Granted; all who now believe, or have believed, or shall believe are of the family of man; and when he gave his life for the world, he gave it for them among the rest; for when he redeemed the whole he of needs redeemed all the parts, even as the man who purchases a flock of sheep purchases those who know his voice as well as those who know it not.

But if Christ died for all the world, and part of it will never be saved, will he not have shed his blood to a certain degree in vain? This is mere partisan cavilling. But see:—It is in religion as it is in the natural world; many of God's best gifts are neglected, many abused, and many of them absolutely despised. If Christ had foreseen that none would have believed, he would, doubtless, have died for none; but foreseeing that many would, he gave himself "a ransom for all," that none might perish, or complain; and so by this means whosoever believeth are his flock and heirs of his pastoral care. But to dispute about this matter and found separating doctrines upon it, constitutes the height of absurdity, and is as dangerous as it is unreasonable; it is as if men would quarrel with each other about whether a river was made for the whole world or only for so many as choose to quench their thirst at it; or whether the products of the field and orchard and garden were intended for all mankind or only for so many of them as choose to cultivate them; but the river might run dry, and I suppose it will run dry, and the summer be ended, before such foolishness is settled.

But again; You say "I cannot keep the commandments of God; I cannot obey of myself." Well who is to obey for you? "I must be enabled and caused to obey." Hear the state of the case. To obedience three things are necessary; first, authority; second, law; third, free agency, or knowledge to discern and freedom to act. Now in the Christian religion all this is found. God appears, who is certainly clothed with all right to command, and his commands are not grievous but joyous, and they are written with such plainness that he who runs may read. Well, what is necessary but that you who feel yourself a free agent, with a capacity to understand and freedom to act, do forthwith submit to his authority and obey the gospel call?

Again; you say, I admit his authority and right to command; but naked right, arbitrary authority is that from which my whole nature revolts; and while I recognize the divine supremacy and the legitimacy of his claim to be obeyed, I feel a law in my members warring against the law of my mind, so that I am weak and wholly without strength in the affair.

Now here it is you are both right and wrong; I grant the neutrality of your abhorrence to law, when that law contains in it nothing but a display of authority without any mixture of benevolence or moral motive to obedience: But this is not the nature of the law of faith or the law of the gospel. "You surprise me. Is it not law proceeding from the mere authority and will of God without respect to our necessities as lost sinners, and out nature as moral agents affected and moved by motive?" Not at all; you are altogether in an error. Authority in this case clothes itself with the most unbounded and divine benevolence and legislates for us with the tenderest regard to both our wants and our capacity. The Ruler approaches us through the pierced side of his well-beloved Son, and in our case, which is one of dire necessity, freely gives him up to death for us all; adding that with him he will freely give us all things. "Sir, these words quicken every power in my soul. Is the Ruler thus good?" Most assuredly he is. "Proceed, sir, in your instructions. Is he as good in law as he is in fact?" O yes; His law is law with a promise; obey the gospel and you shall be pardoned, you shall receive the Holy Spirit; you shall inherit eternal life. This is the nature of the law of faith. "And most capital law it is; you have aroused every good feeling in my heart; for from my childhood I have desired to serve God. Is it so then that the authority of God in the gospel clothes itself, with deeds of such eternal benevolence! and his laws with sanctions so bountiful and kind! O I have been blind, I have been a fool not to see this; but I will arise and go to my Father, I will confess in the name of his Son my Saviour and turn me from all iniquity. What hindreth me from being baptized?" If you believe with all your heart you may. "I believe that Jesus Christ is the Son of God." Then, sir, I will immerse you.

A DISCOURSE OF THE TRUE GOSPEL

SECTION SEVENTH–THE HOLY SPIRIT

I will not leave you comfortless, I will come to you.

CHAPTER I

Introductory

One of the sweetest and most endearing ideas which our beloved Lord communicated concerning the Holy Spirit, is that he would, when he came, be a substitute for him in the church, and comfort his people throughout all ages while they mourned for the world, and worshipped an absent Lord. This is the tender sentiment which introduces the blessed Spirit to us in the Christian Religion. He was to be a substitute for our all-merciful but absent Saviour. "I will pray the Father and he will give you another comforter, who shall abide with you for ever." This original and all-gracious intent of the Holy Spirit, was not overlooked by the apostle Paul; who observed that, while in this mortal and painful pilgrimage, we knew not what to pray for as we ought, but the Spirit supplied the deficiency of our supplications, and made intercessions for us with groanings that could not be uttered, and that "He, who searches the heart, knoweth the mind of the Spirit, because he maketh intercession for the saints according to the will of God." With me it is a serious belief that if the church had been left with but faith and forgiveness and the effects of them upon the souls and lives of the disciples, excellent and precious though they be, she should still have felt forlorn; "I will not leave you forlorn;" but receiving this inestimable gift, if it lifts her not on high to that happy holy place honored and glorified by the personal presence of our God and his Son, it at least brings God and his Son down to her and fills her bosom with joys unutterable and full of glory. "If a man love me, he will keep my sayings; and my Father will love him, and we will come in unto him and make our abode with him." O that men would come and taste and see that the Lord is gracious! that they experimentally knew what he has done for our souls! "Your hearts shall rejoice," said he, "and your joy no man taketh from you." "Peace I leave with you; my peace I give unto you; not as the world giveth, give I unto you, let not your heart be troubled, neither let it be afraid." O the unutterable blessedness of this knowledge of God and of his Son Jesus Christ! Is our Redeemer on high? By his Holy Spirit he is also in our hearts. Is he infinitely great? he is also infinitely condescending, and while he fills heaven, and the heaven of heavens, he dwells also in these poor bosoms of ours! Do the myriads of heavenly angels behold him? by his Spirit we more than behold him, we taste of his blessedness; we feed on him as on the bread of heaven, and feel that he is in us as a well of water springing up unto everlasting life.

"And now, I go my way to him that sent me; and none of you asks me, Whether goest thou, but because I have told you these things sorrow has filled your heart." The departure of the Lord Jesus was a matter too painful to speak about, perhaps they had never once dreamt of it, at all events they carefully avoided speaking concerning it as a matter too mournful for them to contemplate; when he came to mention it, it opened a vein of sorrow which nothing could close. Our adorable Redeemer having been with them hitherto, it was unnecessary to reveal to them by prediction the miserable persecutions which they were to endure for his sake, so soon as he should depart.—But to give them a proof of his divinity and keep them from being stumbled he foretold them of this, and said of the Jews, "They shall put you out of the synagogue; yea, the time is at hand that whosoever kills you will think that he does God service."

He assures them, however, that the wickedness of their persecutors would be caused only by their ignorance of God and the Messiah. "And these things they will do unto you because they know not the Father nor me." This, however, could not console them; his absence was intolerable; they dared not to think of it: nor risk themselves even to ask whither he was going; they were absorbed in grief, in view of what he told them. But he added as a last reason, that it was indispensable that he should go; for otherwise the Spirit, to whose bosom the whole divine institution was to be committed till his second advent, would not, could not come. "Nevertheless, I tell you the truth; it is expedient for you that I go away; for if I go not away, the comforter will not come unto you; but if I depart I will send him to you."

I will send him to you:—Here then is a promise of a great missionary from on high, the Holy Spirit, to whom was committed the cause and comfort of the saints in all ages.

CHAPTER II

The Subject Divided

Whom the world cannot receive.—John 14—New Version

Christianity, as developed in the sacred oracles, is sustained by three divine missions;—the mission of the Lord Jesus; the mission of the Apostles; and the mission of the Holy Spirit; these embassies are distinct in three particulars, namely: person, termination, and design. Like the branches, flowers, and fruit of the same tree, they are, indeed, nearly and admirably related; still, however, like these, they are distinct,—not one, but three missions, connected like the vine, its branches and clusters of grapes.

Of the person sent on these missions: It may suffice to observe, that although the scriptures give to Jesus, the Apostles, and to the Holy Spirit, the attitude of missionaries, i. e. speak of them as persons sent by the Father, they never speak of the Father himself in such style. God is said in the New Testament to send the Lord Jesus, the Lord Jesus to send the Apostles, and the Holy Spirit to be sent by the Father and the Son, but the Father himself is not said to be sent by any one.

Of the termination of these missions:—Every embassy political or religious, must and does end somewhere; hence we have political embassies to Spain, Portugal, the Court of St. James, St. Cloud's, Petersburgh, Naples; and we have religious missions to Japan, the Cape, Hindoostan, to the Indians, and the South seas. If it be enquired then in what other respect these three divine institutions differed from each other. I answer, they had distinct terminations. Our Lord Jesus was sent personally to the Jewish nation and his mission terminated on that people.

The Apostles were sent to all the nations, and their mission terminated accordingly: but the Holy Spirit was sent only to the church of our Lord Jesus Christ, and so far as his gifts were enjoyed, his mission terminated in that institution.

Of the design of these missions:—In every embassy there is something to be accomplished. We do not send out political and religious ambassadors for nothing; but for the high purpose of negotiation; and therefore, it will be seen in the following discourse, that God in sending forth *His* Son, the Apostles, and the Holy Spirit, had a great design: also, that the ends or designs of the embassies of these functionaries, were all distinct from each other.

In fine, it will be shown in regard to the Holy Spirit, that he was not sent to dwell in any man, in order to make him a Christian, but because he had already become a Christian; or in other terms it will be proved that the Holy Spirit is not given to men, to make them believe and obey the gospel, but rather because they have believed and obeyed the gospel.

The propositions of the discourse are as follows;

PROPOSITION 1. *Jesus Christ was personally a missionary only to the Jews; his mission terminated on that people; and the designs of it were to proclaim the gospel, and to teach those among them who believed it.*

PROPOSITION 2. *The Apostles were missionaries to the whole world; their mission terminated on mankind and its design was to proclaim the gospel, and to teach those among men who believed it.*

PROPOSITION 3. *The Holy Spirit was a missionary to the church: His mission terminated on that institution, and the designs of it were to comfort the disciples, glorify Jesus Christ as the true Messiah; and to convince the world of sin, righteousness and judgment.*

These are the main propositions of the following discourse, but in the settlement of them, some other points of intense interest to Christians are necessarily introduced; and if neither these or indeed the chief propositions themselves, are treated in much detail; the reader will find an apology for this in the circumscribed limits in which they are contained. There is, I apprehend, enough said to conduct the reader into the truth of the scriptures on this all engrossing topic of the Holy Spirit; and to annihilate in his mind the absurd doctrines still too generally taught: these are the two designs contemplated immediately by the editor in the original publication of this discourse; and he prays, that where ever they obtain, they may operate in reforming and purifying the reader;—may they make him more sober, more righteous, more godly: for it is impossible for the Holy Spirit to dwell with the ungodly, unrighteous and intemperate; these are times, moreover, when the professors of Christianity are but little solicitous of enjoying the consolations of the Spirit of God and Christ, a matter which certainly is much to be regretted by all who know his name in truth and very deed.

CHAPTER III

Christ's Mission

PROPOSITION 1. *Jesus Christ was personally a missionary to the Jews; his mission terminated on that people; and the designs of it were to proclaim the gospel, and to teach those among the Jews who believed it.*

1st. *Of the Messiah considered as a Missionary or Ambassador:*—One world, and but one was to be negotiated for; and, therefore, strictly speaking, there is in the Christian religion but one ambassador from God the Father—Jesus Christ our Lord: He is the only personage in the divine institution who has been *called* of God and *sent* to the sons of men in this high capacity; it may be inquired, however, whether the apostles were not *called* and *sent?* I answer they were not called and sent of God the Father; Jesus alone enjoyed this distinction, and these were called and sent of Jesus: hence he says, "So send I you into the world." But again it may be asked, "was not John sent of God?" Is it not written, "there was a man sent of God whose name was John?" I answer it is written; but this objection is obviated by the consideration that John was confessedly not of our dispensation; he was not of the kingdom of heaven, but came that it might be introduced, and, therefore, it is said, that though the most distinguished of men, the least in the kingdom of Heaven is greater than he. The immense importance of Christ's mission to the Jewish nation, may be inferred from the divine and august character of the royal personage sent, Jesus the Son of God; and the pre-eminent regard of the Father for that nation may be learnt from the same consideration. Christ was a minister of the circumcision, says Paul, to confirm the promises made to the fathers:

2. *Of the termination of Christ's Mission:*—Be it observed that for an ambassador to extend the sphere of his negotiations beyond its prescribed limits, and so transcend his authority, is wholly incompatible with the grave responsibility of such a functionary; the ambassador to St. Cloud's, if his instructions restrict him to this court, must not and cannot negotiate with the court of St. James; if one of our statesmen is sent in this high capacity on a special embassy to the Sublime Porte, his commission to that power will not warrant him to negotiate with the Czar of Russia; and an officer of this rank may be sent to Spain with no authority at all to transact national business with the authorities of Naples, or Rome.

It is so in the Christian religion also: Jesus was sent to the *Jews*; and the apostles to the *world*, and the Holy Spirit to the *Church*; we do not, therefore, in any instance behold them transcend the bounds of their missions, or do violence to the authority with which they were clothed; all is decorous here, nothing is out of keeping in the *modus* of these high functionaries.

Jesus did not conceive it in accordance with the solemn reverence, which on every occasion he discovered for the Father, to overleap the limits of Canaan and to preach to the Gentiles; he would not permit this liberty to be assumed even by his disciples, while they aided him in his personal mission; he was sent only to the lost sheep of the house of

Israel, and his instructions to them in regard to this matter, therefore, are couched in the most intelligible language; "Go not," said he to them, "into the way of the Gentiles, and into any city of the Samaritans enter ye not; I am not sent but to the lost sheep of the house of Israel."

3. *Of the design of Christ's Mission:* The elevated affairs of law and empire—the affairs of right and liberty, of peace and of war, are of high consideration in the kingdoms of this world; but Jesus stood in the court of Israel with a great design; the purposes of his high negotiations were pardon, reconciliation, and life eternal. Oh! that Jerusalem had known in this the day of her merciful visitation! He would have gathered her as a hen gathereth her chickens under her wings, but she would not, and He wept over her. Jesus, in the synagogue at Nazareth, declares the benign purposes of his mission in the following inimitable expressions: 'The Spirit of the Lord is upon me, for He has anointed me to preach the gospel to the poor, He has sent me to heal the brokenhearted; to proclaim deliverance to the captives, and recovering of sight to the blind; to set at liberty them that are bruised; to proclaim the acceptable year of the Lord.' The sermon on the mount presents him in the attitude of teaching his disciples; so that we may in this manner perceive the great ends or purpose of his mission to be comprehended in preaching the gospel to the poor, and in teaching such as admitted his divine authority.

CHAPTER IV

The Apostles' Mission

PROPOSITION 2. *The Apostles were missionaries to the whole world; their mission terminated on mankind; and the designs of it were to proclaim the gospel, and to instruct in all the will of God those who obeyed it.*

1. *Of the Apostles considered as missionaries:* Besides that of witnesses to the ministry, miracles, death, burial, resurrection and ascension of the Saviour, the apostles were to discharge the functions of ambassadors to the nations in the stead of Christ: and if the divine wisdom is most apparent in selecting as witness of the resurrection, men with their sense of vision, &c., washed all their days in the seas of Genezareth, it is no less so in sending abroad to immerse the nations, those who all their lives long had, by the nature of their civil profession, been constantly habituated to the water and the roaring of the deep. It was in coincidence with this fact, the Redeemer said to Peter: "Fear not, henceforth you shall catch men!" Blessed be his precious name!

But though the Apostles were intrusted with the ministry of reconciliation, endowed with power and clothed with the authority necessary to order all things aright in the kingdom of Christ, yet they were not ambassadors in the highest sense of that word, but only vice-ambassadors in the absence of him who elected them to officiate in his stead, and who himself was the original and sole ambassador in the Christian institution, called and sent of God the Father.

To this observation it may be objected, that Paul calls himself an ambassador; in answer I admit he does according to our English version; but the Greek original does not necessarily inculcate this idea: in Eph. 6:20, we read *huper hou presbuomen en halusei*, 'For which gospel I discharge the functions of ambassador in a chain;' but be it observed that in 2 Cor. 5:20, the apostle gives us explicitly to understand, that the duties of this high office devolved on him only in a secondary sense, and that he was an ambassador only in the stead of Christ; "*huper Christo presbuomen.*" Instead of Christ we discharge the functions of ambassadors. It was in the room of Christ then, and not in the capacity of original ambassadors, the Apostles[16] negotiated for God with the world to be reconciled.

2. Of the Termination of the Apostolic mission:—What a splendid field for holy enterprise was laid open to the Apostles when Jesus said to them: 'Go ye into all the world, proclaim the glad tidings to the whole creation!' Before his death, and while they aided him in his personal mission, the commandment was, 'Go not into the way of the Gentiles, and into any city of the Samaritans enter ye not' but now having consummated his mission and arisen from the dead, the sphere of their mission was to be extended to the utmost bounds of the habitable world, 'Go ye into all the world!' Great was the field, and we do not read that these illustrious ministers, who alone enjoyed the distinction of being ambassadors instead of Christ, ever addressed to angels or demons the word of reconciliation. Their mission was glorious and extensive, but it was limited to the children of men; and, like their master, they

---

[16] Now if the Apostles themselves were not ambassadors; and I say they are not in scripture called such; what are modern Ministers in the kingdom of Christ? are they ambassadors? I answer no; what are they, then? are they the servants of Satan? God forbid that I should even insinuate such an idea concerning them with all their errors? But can a man serve God in no other capacity than that of ambassador? Are all the functionaries of our own general government ambassadors, and can the United States be served by a man in no other capacity but this? are our magistrates, city and state officers, congressmen and senators, ambassadors? Surely no. Well, it is agreed at least that the Evangelists and primitive pastors of the church were not ambassadors; and yet they served God in the kingdom of his Son, and serve him well too; why then should the pastors and teachers of the present day arrogate to themselves this distinction, and pompously call themselves ambassadors?

discovered no desire to transcend the limits to which in his instructions he had restricted them.

3. *Of the design of the Apostolic mission:*—The purposes for which the apostles were sent missionaries to the nations are stated in their commission. 'All power, says Christ to them, is given to me in heaven and upon the earth;' go ye therefore, *disciple* the nations, immersing them in the name of the Father, and of the Son and of the Holy Spirit, *teaching* them to observe all things whatsoever I have commanded you; and lo! I am with you to the conclusion of this state.—Amen." To preach and to teach, then, formed the business of the apostles; and the end of their mission was the reconciliation of the world by the administration of pardon in the name of Christ.

CHAPTER V

Mission of the Holy Spirit

PROPOSITION 3. *The Holy Spirit was a missionary to the church: his mission terminated on that institution; and the designs of it were to comfort the disciples, glorify Jesus, and to convince the world of sin, righteousness, and judgment.*

1. *Of the Holy Spirit as a missionary:*—The idea of the Holy Spirit's being a missionary may seem a little odd; still it will be found perfectly scriptural. 'If I go away' said the Lord Jesus, 'I will *send* him to you.' He is said, like Christ, to proceed from the Father, and is called the paraclete or advocate or monitor: however much, therefore, the disciples may repudiate the subtleties of foolish theologists, on the work, divinity and personality of the Holy Spirit, they must not be stumbled at the language and doctrine of the Holy Scriptures: when God speaks, reason should learn to be observantly but reverentially silent. The Hebrew word for Spirit is *Ruach*, the Greek *Pneuma*, and the Latin *Spiritus*; it is of very frequent occurrence in the Holy Scriptures and is found in the beginning of Genesis and the end of Revelations. This discourse is intended to treat of that Holy Spirit into which we are immersed, and which came to the disciples on the day of Pentecost, and is now in the church in this world.

2. *Of the Termination of the Spirit's mission:*—The idea of the Spirit's being a missionary to the church, affords a new and striking argument against that immoral and fatal maxim in popular theology, namely, that special spiritual operations are necessary to faith! In this discourse it is shown that the church was formed before any of her members received the Spirit; that after the church was formed the Spirit was sent into her on the day of Pentecost; finally, that men did not and do not receive this

Spirit to make them disciples, but because they were or are disciples; in a word it is shown, from the express words of Christ himself, that no man that does not first of all believe the gospel, can receive the Holy Spirit. If any man thirst, says Christ, let him come unto me and drink, and out of his belly shall flow rivers of living water. Now what does this mean; that the Holy Spirit will be given to unbelievers? No; John the Apostle explains it as follows: 'This he spake of the Spirit which was to be given to those who believed, for the Spirit was not yet given (*to believers*) because that Jesus was not yet glorified.'

Concerning the Holy Spirit, the Redeemer said further. 'It is expedient for you that I go away, for if I go not away, the comforter will not come; but if I go away, I will *send* him to you;' again, 'whom the world cannot receive.' *I will send him to you: to you*, my disciples; now the number of disciples must have been at this time very great, for Christ made and baptized, it is said, more than John; there were 120 present on the day of Pentecost, and 500 brethren beheld him at once after his resurrection, and all these were reckoned disciples without having received the Holy Spirit! but if the Holy Spirit had been necessary to make men repent and believe the gospel, then he must have come to them before Jesus left the world, and consequently when he went away he could not send him, from the fact that he had already come—*I will send him to you*. The mission of the Spirit then was to those whom the Redeemer designated *you*, the disciples—the church which he had gathered; and this institution is distinguished from the world by nothing so much as that of receiving the Spirit through faith: for, a prime reason why the world does not receive the Spirit, is that it has no faith in God. 'Whom the world cannot receive because it seeth him not.' The Spirit then being received by them who believe, and the world being endued with sense, and having no faith, it is impossible that he should be received by the world, or that his mission should be to unbelieving men. He came to the church: and there is no instance on record of the Holy Spirit transcending the limits of his mission, or of operating in a man before faith to produce that principle in his soul.

The doctrine then, alas! the too popular doctrine, which extends the mission of the Spirit beyond the bounds of the church, and teaches the world, which, the Saviour says, *cannot receive him*, to sit and wait for his internal special operations to produce faith, is monstrously absurd and impious; *absurd*, because it makes the Holy Spirit to transgress, by overreaching the limits of his embassy, which is to the church—and *impious*, because it makes him give the lie to the Lord of Glory, who says, the world cannot receive him. Jesus said, 'when he is come he will glorify me;' would it glorify the Redeemer's character before either angels or men to make him a *liar*, as the Spirit would and must do, were he, according to the maxims of party theology, to be received by sinners for the purpose of originating in them either faith or repentance. Let ministers reflect on this; let all professors reflect on this.

That those who obey the gospel, that is, believe, repent and are baptized, do and must, by the very nature of the New Covenant, receive the Holy Spirit, is made certain by a *'thus saith the Lord;'* but that men, who hear the gospel, cannot believe and obey it, is wholly human and is supported by nothing but a *'thus saith the man'*—the preacher—the Episcopalian, the Presbyterian, the Methodist, the Baptist, the Quaker; for, however these parties differ in other matters, they are all alike here; in this doctrine they are one! And judge for yourself, reader, whether such among us, as are charged with the office of public instructors in the Christian religion, are not chargeable with the grossest perversity, when we refuse to announce the great things of salvation in the *sound words* of the New Testament, and cry aloud with brazen insolence, that our audience cannot believe and obey the gospel, on the testimony of the Holy Scriptures without special operations from the Holy Spirit, when Almighty God has caused it to be written in living characters on the intelligible page of his never dying word; 'Repent and be baptized every one of you in the name of Jesus Christ for the remission of your sins, *and you shall receive the gift of the Holy Spirit!'*

3. *Of the Purposes for which the Spirit was sent:*—These are couched in the following Scriptures: When the comforter is come, whom I will send unto you from the Father, even the Spirit of truth which proceedeth from the Father, He will testify of me,—He will guide you into all the truth,—He shall abide with you forever,—He will reprove, convince the world of sin, of righteousness and judgment. Take notice reader, of sin, because they *believe not* on me; of righteousness, because I go to the Father, and ye see me no more; and of judgment, because the prince of this world is judged. He will glorify me, for he will take of mine and show it unto you—all that the Father hath is mine.

Thus Jesus gives to the Spirit the attitude of a missionary to come from heaven with the three fold design of comforting the disciples, convincing the world, and glorifying Jesus: and as this is the day of missions, the day when missionaries are running to and fro upon the earth increasing knowledge, we conceive ourselves fortunate in having it in our power to present this important subject to the reader under so popular an aspect.

The Spirit's mission then is briefly comprehended in three words, *comfort, glorify, convince*; and it differs obviously from the first of the three divine missions; for it was no part of Jesus' embassy to glorify himself. I seek not mine own glory, said the Redeemer; the Spirit was to glorify him. 'He will glorify me.'

The mission of the Spirit differed also from that of the apostles in this very nice but important respect,—that while they were to preach to the world, the Spirit was to convince the world: and mark, reader, there is a very significant difference between the two offices of preaching and convincing; it is one thing to proclaim a matter to the world as divine, and quite another to prove to the world that it is divine: preaching and convincing are two distinct words, and be assured, reader, they stand for two very distinct ideas: believe me, they do. Any priest may preach that I cannot believe the gospel without special spiritual operations, but all the priests in Christendom could not make me believe it. The apostles, then, were to preach the gospel, and the Holy Spirit was to confirm the truth of it and so convince the world: thus the third mission is shown to differ materially from the first two in regard to person, termination and design.

CHAPTER VI

Of the Spirit's Mission More Particularly

At the advent of Messiah, the world, in regard to religion, was divided into Jews and Gentiles. When the church appeared as a third party, she came forth between the former two like a ship from between a rock and a whirlpool. Danger menaced her on every side, and it became indispensable that those by whom she was to be steered should be filled with the Spirit of him who launched her on the stormy ocean of time. Accordingly *"the Holy Spirit was sent from heaven."*

But as no embassy can be instituted with immediate reference to any establishment, political or religious, until that establishment is first brought into existence; as no tent nor temple can be occupied until it is reared; and no body can receive a spirit until it has been previously organized, for God first made Adam, and afterwards breathed into him the breath of life, so the Spirit of Christ could not come to the church till that church was first formed.

It becomes important, then, to determine with accuracy the precise date of the church of Christ. Every institution, civil political, or religious—every establishment of peace or war—of arts or arms—is based upon some prime, some fundamental maxim. The American Republic, for instance, stands on this maxim, that *"all men are born free and equal;"* and into this the whole superstructure of law and government may be resolved. If the foundation is sure, the building will stand, if the materials are in accordance with the foundation; if it be false or inferior, it must give way to the pressure of time, and the superstructure be destroyed together with the foundation.

But it is on Christianity we are writing. Now, then, our holy religion, when contemplated as a unique and distinct institution, resolves itself ultimately into this fact, and is based upon it, viz: *"Jesus of Nazareth is the Son of God."* If this be false, Christianity is false; if this be true, Christianity must prevail, and earth and hell in vain assail it: for great is truth and mighty above all things, and must prevail. "Upon this rock," said Jesus to Peter when he publicly confessed this truth—"Upon this rock will I build my church, and the gates of hell shall not prevail against it." It was for confessing this truth that Jesus was condemned by the Jewish Sandhedrim—he died for this, and became the first martyr to it. The Apostles died for confessing this—men were pardoned of God for confessing it—and congregations which held it were styled the churches of Christ, whether they were in order or no; whether they had ordinances, oracles, or officers, or no; and it is on the confession of this fact that the church within these few years, has begun, according to the true gospel, again to admit sinners to baptism for the remission of their sins. Glory to God and to Jesus Christ!

Besides this, that Jesus is the Son of God, there are many great and invaluable truths in Christianity—such as that he died for sinners; that he is now in heaven; that there will be a resurrection of the just and unjust, and a general judgment. But mark reader, that while for the revelation of these and other things, God has employed prophets, evangelists, apostles, and his Son Jesus Christ: yet the great fact on which the church is based, viz: that Jesus is his Son, was not left to flesh and blood to be made known, but God the Father revealed it publicly himself at Jordan to the nation of the Jews assembled there, when, on that famous day, the heavens opened over the head of the baptized Messiah, and the Spirit from the Eternity beyond was seen descending like a dove, and remaining on him, accompanied with the greatest and most wonderful of all the revelations of God, "Behold my Son, the Beloved, in whom I am well pleased!" "Flesh and blood," said the Lord on one occasion to Peter, "has not revealed this too thee, but my Father who is in heaven." The great fact on which the church is reared was made known to the sons of men, then by God himself; and in doing it he proposed Jesus as the first person of a new institution—the chief foundation stone of a new religious building, temple, tabernacle —"BEHOLD MY BELOVED SON, IN WHOM I AM WELL PLEASED."

The church is contemplated under various figures in the Holy scriptures—as a sheepfold, a nation, a priesthood, a temple—"Ye are the temple of God, and the Spirit of God dwelleth in you." But the temple was built before the glory of God filled it, and the origin of the Christian church must be dated anterior to the day when it was filled with the Spirit of God—the day of Pentecost. Some date the origin of the church in eternity; some, at the beginning of the world; others say the *law* was as much the church of Christ as the *gospel*; and others that it began at the resurrection of Jesus. To use the apostle's figure we would say, that the first stone of the Christian temple was laid by God —"Behold I lay in Zion a stone" and so forth; and that it was laid on the day when he said, "Behold my beloved Son." Peter alludes to this when he says to the rulers, "This is the stone which you builders rejected, which is now become the head of the corner." Those who believed on Jesus as the promised Messiah, however, had no reason to be ashamed of him; for though the rulers and doctors refused him as the commencement of a new economy—though their religious builders rejected him as the foundation stone, God took him to himself and laid him up in heaven to become the cap-stone, the head of the corner; and when the Christian edifice is about to be finished he shall be brought forth with shoutings, crying, "Grace! grace!" for like Zerubabel of old, God has laid the foundation of this house, and his hand shall finish it. It is wonderful that a stone should be at the same time the first and the last in any building; the foundation stone and the head of the corner! "*This is the doing of the Lord,*" said the Psalmist, "*and it is marvelous in our eyes.*" Thus is Jesus the first and the last, the Alpha and the Omega, the beginning and the ending of Christianity.—God laid Jesus; Jesus laid Peter; and Peter and his fellow apostles laid Jews and Gentiles living stones upon this great foundation. Hallelujah! According to this figure, Christianity commenced when Christ made his first appearance, and will be finished when he makes his second, and comes to be the last stone in this temple; but according to another figure, viz: that of a bride or wife, the church of Christ was not separated from Judaism until the day of Pentecost, when the spirit came, as will be seen immediately.

Some ask whether John the Baptist did not make Christians; others whether Jesus did not disciple men for Moses, and others seem to think it problematical whether Jesus did not make Baptists for John.

Now we think with the Scriptures, that as all these three personages were at different times sent by the Father—their disciples were under God respectively their own. Hence we hear the scriptures speak of MOSES' disciples, JOHN'S disciples, and JESUS' disciples; and when John and Moses' disciples would become Christians, they had to be baptized over again in the name of Jesus Christ. See Acts 19. As therefore, the Jews became ostensibly the disciples of Moses when they were immersed into him in the cloud and in the sea, and as the descendants of these Jews became the disciples of John when they were baptized of him in Jordan, so the disciples of John and of Moses became ostensibly the disciples of Jesus when they were baptized by him; and as the disciples of Moses were the church of Moses, so the disciples of Jesus were the church of Jesus; consequently the church of Christ was formed by himself, when he began to make disciples; and having formed her while alive—having brought his bride into existence,

'HE LOVED HER,' the Scriptures say, 'AND GAVE HIMSELF FOR HER THAT HE MIGHT SANCTIFY HER,' (separate her from Jews and Gentiles,) 'having cleansed her with a bath of water and with the word.' He, therefore, addressed his disciples, after baptism, and before he laid down his life for them, in these memorable words: 'Now ye are clean through the word which I have spoken unto you.' Having washed his bride with water, and bought her with his blood, he arose to separate her from all former, and subsequent institutions, whether religious or political, whether Jews or Gentiles: and this he did effectually by sending down from heaven the Holy Spirit in such marvelous abundance, that 'of the rest,' (whether Jews or Gentiles who looked at the new institution) 'durst no man join himself to them, but the people magnified them.' But every establishment must rest upon some foundation; God, therefore, laid Jesus as the foundation of the Christian building; and he is a rock truly.

The church of Christ, then, was formed by himself before ever he left this world; and previous to the day of Pentecost 'the number of the names together were about one hundred and twenty;' all these, not yet having received the Spirit, continued with one accord in prayer and supplication for ten days, till the day of Pentecost. But as there was a day on which Jesus entered upon his personal ministry among the Jews —as there was a day when the Apostles entered upon their mission to the world—so there was a day when the Spirit came to the church. That day was Pentecost. Accordingly it is written, Acts 2. 'And when the day of pentecost was fully come, they were all with one accord in one place; and suddenly there came a sound from heaven as of a mighty rushing wind, and it filled all the house where they were sitting. And there appeared unto them cloven tongues, like as of fire, and it sat upon each of them; and they were all filled with the Holy Spirit,' &c.

May I entreat the reader to pause, a little over this magnificent event? 'A sound from heaven as of a mighty rushing wind,' shaking the house and filling the disciples with the Holy Spirit![17]

Here, then, we have the descent of the great spiritual missionary into the body of Christ, the church; from which moment he has never

---

[17] If a person would understand the Scriptures on the subject of the Holy Spirit, he must take great heed to his entrance into the Christian body on the day of Pentecost. This is the day when the church assumed her public standing as a divine institution; and a curious and fundamental difference between her and the institution of the law of Moses, is, that persons are filled with this Spirit on becoming members; whereas the Jews might be members of the former institution all their life, and never enjoy the Spirit of God. But in Christianity it is said "If any man have not the spirit of Christ, he is none of his." Christianity is, therefore, called "the ministration of the Spirit."

left it, and never can leave it; for while the personal mission of Jesus to the Jews, and of the Apostles to the world, were only temporary, the mission of the Spirit into the body of Christ is perpetual and will end only at the resurrection, 'For if the Spirit of him who raised Jesus from the dead dwell in you,' says Paul, 'he that raised Jesus from the dead shall also quicken your mortal bodies by his Spirit that dwelleth in you,' 'He shall abide with you forever.' If it be asked why there is no instance of supplication, deprecation, thanksgiving, prayer, or praise being offered to the Holy Spirit in the Scriptures, I answer that the Holy Spirit being in the church, all saints are represented as offering these spiritual sacrifices to God, through Jesus Christ, by the Holy Spirit which dwells in them. Hence the Spirit sheds abroad love in our hearts, groans, helps our infirmities, and makes intercession for the saints. And when the whole church shall be gathered home, there will be seen in heaven this wonderful spectacle—the church glorified by the Holy Spirit, into which she had been baptized: the Son at her head, by whom she had been redeemed; and God on his throne, whom she had worshiped and adored.

The spirit, then, can do nothing in religion, nothing in Christianity, but by the members of the body of Christ. Even the word of God, the Scriptures, have been given by members filled with this Spirit—they spake as the Spirit gave them utterance. But mark, reader, that there is no member of the body of Christ in whom the Holy Spirit dwelleth not; for it will hold as good at the end of the world as it does now, and it holds as good now as it did on the day of Pentecost and afterwards, that *"if any man have not the spirit of Christ he is none of his."* If, therefore, the Spirit convinces the world of sin, or glorifies Jesus, it is all through the agency of the members of the body of Christ, whom he fills—the church. Hence the indispensable duty of all disciples being led by the spirit of God with which they are sealed, and of holding forth in the language of the New Testament the gospel: for where there are no Christians or where Christians do not perform their duties, there are no conversions, as in Tartary, India, some parts of Europe, and so forth. But wherever there are Christians, Christians who hold forth the gospel in the sound words used on Pentecost by the Apostles, there will always be some conversions, more or less.

But now what have we seen in reference to the particular mission of the Holy Spirit? Why, first, that he was to be sent to the church. 2dly, that Christ then formed the church. And, 3dly, that the Holy Spirit was sent accordingly into the institution on the day of Pentecost.

CHAPTER VII

Distribution of Gifts by the Spirit

The church is sixteen times spoken of under the figure of a body, the human body; and this analogy is run out at great length by Paul in the 12th chapter of 1st Corinthians:—"Now, concerning spiritual gifts, brethren, I would not have you ignorant. You know that you were heathens, led away to idols that are dumb, even as you happened to be led. Wherefore I inform you, that no one speaking by the Spirit of God, pronounceth Jesus accursed: and that no one can declare Jesus Lord, except by the Holy Spirit. Now, there are diversities of gifts, but the same spirit. And there are diversities of ministries, but the same Lord. And there are diversities of in-workings, but it is the same God who worketh inwardly all in all. And to each is given this manifestation of the Spirit, for the advantage of all: Now, to one indeed, through the Spirit, is given the word of wisdom; and to another the word of knowledge, according to the same Spirit. And to another, faith by the same Spirit; and to another the gifts of healing by the same Spirit; and to another the in-workings of powers; and to another, prophecy; and to another, discerning of spirits; and to another, divers kinds of foreign tongues; and to another, the interpretation of foreign tongues. Now all these the one and the same Spirit in-worketh, distributing to each his proper gifts as he pleaseth. For as the body is one, although it have many members, and all the members of that one body, being many, are one body, so also is Christ. For, indeed, in one Spirit we all have been immersed into one body, whether Jews or Greeks; whether slaves or freemen; and all have been made to drink of one Spirit. Since, therefore, the body is not one member, but many, if the foot shall say, Because I am not the hand, I am not of the body; is it, for this, not of the body? And if the ear shall say, Because I am not the eye, I am not of the body; is it for this, not of the body? If the whole body were an eye, where were the hearing? If the whole were hearing, where were the smelling? But now God hath placed the members every one of them in the body, as he hath pleased. Besides, if all were one member, where were the body? But now, indeed, there are many members, but one body. Therefore, the eye cannot say to the hand, I have no need of you. Nay, those members of the body which seem to be more feeble, are much more necessary. And those which we think are less honorable members of the body, around them we throw more abundant honor; and so, our uncomely members have more abundant comeliness. But our comely members have no need. However, God hath tempered the body together, having given to the member which wanteth it more abundant honor; that there may be no schism in the body, but that the members may have the very same anxious care for one another. And so whether one member suffer, all the members jointly suffer; or one member be honored, all the members jointly rejoice. Now you are the body of Christ and members in part. Therefore, these indeed God hath placed in the congregation; first, apostles; secondly, prophets; thirdly, teachers; next, powers; then, gifts of healing; helpers, directors, kinds of foreign languages. Are all apostles? Are all teachers? Have all powers? Have all the gift of healing? Do all speak in foreign languages? Do all interpret? Now you earnestly desire the best gifts, but yet I show you a more excellent way." From this analogy we learn that it is in religion as it is in nature. As the human spirit gives to each member of its body all its powers—strength to the arm—skill to the hand—eloquence to the lip, and seeing to the eye; so the Holy Spirit gives to each member of Christ's church or body severally as he wills—pleases.

On this analogy a number of important inquiries may be instituted.[18]

1. Has the Spirit which was sent down from heaven on the day of Pentecost ever left his body? No; never. A human body without the Spirit is dead; and Christ's body (the church,) without the Spirit in her, would be dead also. He shall abide with you forever.

2. Can he be in any person that is not of the body? No, he dwells in the saints; and as well might we hope for a man's spirit to occupy a space beyond his person, as for the Spirit of Christ to be found beyond his body—the church. The spirit of A cannot enter into the body of B; neither can the Spirit of Christ enter the body of a worldly man —'whom the world cannot receive,' says Jesus.

3. How does the Spirit of Christ operate? As our spirits operate in our bodies and by their members, so the Spirit of Christ operates in the body of Christ and by its members. Hence the truth of our former observation, that the Spirit can do nothing in Christianity but by Christians. Therefore, Christians, do your duty, or you will either quench or grieve the Holy Spirit of God, as many, alas! have done, and are now doing at this day by their love of this world and by their prejudices. Alas! if disciples grieve the Advocate, who shall plead for them? Alas! that disciples should quench the Holy Spirit by their lusts and worldly emulations. If the fire is once extinguished, who shall kindle it again? If the salt has lost its savor, wherewithal shall it be salted? It is thenceforth good for nothing, but to be cast out and trodden under foot of men.

---

[18] The use made of the Apostle's analogy is, I hope, strictly proper; and the whole affords a fine argument against the popular error concerning the Spirit that makes him go into a body that is not his; and bids the world hope to receive him before they become members of the church by faith and immersion. This discourse is to inculcate the great truth, that the Spirit is given to every one who becomes a member, but to no one in order to make him a member.

4. Finally, how may a man possess himself of the Spirit of Christ? God has appointed a means for communicating every blessing in nature and in religion. He gives us fruit from the tree; water from the fountain; corn from the soil; and wines from the grape. Join yourself, then, to the body of Christ, and you will receive the Spirit of Christ. How am I to do this? If you believe in Christ, and think that God means what he says, I would venture to quote my text as an infallible direction how you may received the Spirit; "Repent and be baptized, every one of you, in the name of the Lord Jesus Christ, for the remission of sins, and you shall receive the gift of the Holy Spirit." Does this please you? Then obey the Lord.

But now, to approach the mission of the Spirit more closely. The purposes of it are in a summary way comprehended in three words—comfort, glorify, convince. We shall show, then, that first he comforted the disciples by bestowing upon them gifts—gifts of wisdom, power, and goodness. When we were all very young in the knowledge of the Scriptures, much confused about what was right and wrong in Christianity, fifteen years ago, and some time anterior to that most illustrious matter, 'the Restoration of the Ancient Gospel,' an important division of the spiritual gifts suggested itself to me, which very much relieved my mind on the subject of the Holy Spirit; for at that time a number of disciples in New York had ceased to believe that the Spirit, originally from heaven, was any longer in the church.—The division alluded to is this: all the gifts by which the Spirit comforted the church might, I perceived, be classed under the three general heads of power, wisdom, and goodness; so that as a human spirit endows the head with wisdom, the heart with goodness, and the hand with power;—the Spirit filled the body of Christ with these things in order that all the world might be allured or compelled to become Christians. And surely this was a most apt plan for comforting the disciples in the church.

To illustrate this division of the GIFTS, let us arrange a few of them under each head—

1. The gifts of wisdom were, discerning of spirits, teaching, prophecy, tongues, interpretation, knowledge, and all those gifts which enabled the apostles and others to understand the prophecies relative to the Messiah, and to recollect all things which the Saviour had told them on that subject when he showed them in the Law, the Prophets, and the Psalms, the things concerning himself.

2. The gifts of power were those of miracles, healings, signs, wonders, &c. &c.

3. The gifts of goodness were, love, joy, gentleness, meekness, long suffering, fidelity, &c.

The Apostle has divided the world into Jews, Gentiles, and the church: 'giving no offence,' says he, 'to Jew, nor Gentile, nor to the church of God.' Now what relation had the three sets of gifts to these three parties, Jews, Gentiles, and the Church? Why, in order to render the church all amiable herself, the Holy Spirit poured through the souls of all her members the gifts of goodness, filling them with love, joy, gentleness, meekness, &c. &c. And as the Jews had to be coaxed from the rock on which they had split, and the Gentiles to be snatched from the whirlpool into which they had been plunged, the gifts of wisdom were bestowed in order that the church might win the first, and the gifts of power that she might compel the last; and thus the gospel gave an exhibition of the wisdom of God and the power of God to every one who believed, whether Jew or Gentile.—The gifts of wisdom, then, were given to convince the Jews, and the gifts of power to convince the Gentiles; while the gifts of goodness were given an endless and abiding ornament to the church.

The purposes for which the gifts of wisdom and power were given being now accomplished, the Holy Spirit, who dwells in the Christians, will give no further exhibition of his power, until he raises them from the dead. Jews and Gentiles have received the Scriptures, and if the world will not believe them, they would not believe in Christ if a man arose from the dead.

What unbounded comfort must it have yielded to the disciples to have their testimony concerning their beloved Saviour confirmed in the presence of Jews and Gentiles—by both the power of God and the wisdom of God: and to see both parties either won or compelled to bow to the peaceful sway of the Messiah!

The Spirit was to convince the world of sin, of righteousness, and of judgment. At the coming of Christ, sin and righteousness (i. e. good and evil) were wholly confounded in the Jewish nation; so that the tithing of mint, anise, and cummin, was substituted for the weightier matters of the law, justice, mercy, and the love of God. The Sadducees, comprehending the wealthy and the great in the nation, denied the resurrection, and of course were wholly uninfluenced by the higher considerations of a final judgment. And as to the Pharisees, they were so filled with religious pride, that they did not conceive themselves chargeable with sin, even in the presence of the Almighty, as may be seen from the parable of the Publican and the Pharisee.

Now to convince a people of sin, who did not know it from righteousness, who did not know good from evil, who had confounded light and darkness, had put bitter for sweet and sweet for bitter—must have been a very hard task, it must be granted. Where then, reader, was the Spirit to begin? Where was to be the starting point? Where would you have begun? Where would you have started? At Adam—at the Law —at John—or where? Until you have made at least one conjecture on this matter, pray stop; try your skill in the learning of the New Testament. How would you have convinced the Jews of sin at this crisis?

There was one thing on which the whole nation were agreed, both Pharisees and Sadducees. All parties concurred, all sects were unanimous in this—that the ancient Scriptures promised a Messiah. Now, then, if the Holy Spirit in the Apostles proved by the ancient Scriptures, and by gifts of power, &c., that Jesus of Nazareth was the very identical person for whom they looked, then he at the same time convinced them of sin for not having believed on him; and this was just what the Spirit did, and also what he was to do when he came: 'He shall convince the world of sin, because they believe not on me,' said Jesus.

On the day of Pentecost all the apostles were accordingly filled with all the gifts of wisdom, in order that by suitable arguments drawn from the Law, the Prophets, and the Psalms, the Jewish nation, who believed in these oracles as divine, might be convinced that Jesus whom they had crucified was the Messiah.

The proof drawn from the ancient Scriptures relative to the conception, birth place, life, trial, death, burial, resurrection, and ascension of Jesus, is, with great elegance, styled 'the demonstration of the Spirit;' and Paul calls it this because, like a skillful geometrician, who first states his proposition, and afterwards proceeds step by step in the proof of it, from its simplest to its most involved properties, from its immediate to its most remote relations, until all its powers are fully developed; so the Holy Spirit speaking in the apostles, first sets down the great proposition revealed at Jordan to the Jews, (viz. that Jesus was the Christ,) and then proceeds step by step in the proof of it, unfolding its simplest and most complex relations by the most ancient and involved, and the latest and clearest of the Jewish prophecies; by the Law, the Prophets, and the Psalms, he proves that, in regard to his conception, birth, life, ministry, poverty, character, descent, trial, condemnation, death, burial, resurrection, ascension, and reign, Jesus of Nazareth is the very person promised to the nation; and we have only to make a reference to the apostles in the Acts to see how perfectly these remarks harmonize with the word of God. Acts 2. Three thousand on the day of Pentecost were convinced of sin, confessed Christ, and were baptized for the remission of sins that they might receive the gift of the Holy Spirit. To convince a person of a fault we must prove him guilty. The Spirit first shewed that Jesus was Messiah, and then proved them guilty by urging it upon their consciences that they had murdered him. This cut them to the heart, and they cried, "Men and brethren, what shall we do?"

But, reader, is there any thing in all this like the Spirit entering the souls of these sinners in order to produce faith, repentance, or any thing else? Not a semblance of such a thing. The Spirit was in the Apostles, who spoke as he gave them utterance. The Devil was in the people.

In all subsequent addresses Peter and all others proceeded in the same manner, reasoning from the Law, the Prophets, and the Psalms, great additions in this way being made to the church. Stephen cut the members of the Sanhedrim to the heart; and all the Jews and proselytes, such as the Eunuch, Cornelius, Lydia, and so forth, were in this way convinced of the truth; Samaritans and Idolaters were convinced chiefly by miracles, signs, wonders, and gifts of the Holy Spirit, called the powers of the Spirit of God, and conferred on the church for the purpose of converting the nations; concerning which the Apostle speaks thus: "I will not dare to speak of any thing which Christ has not wrought, but of what he has wrought by me in order to the obedience of the Gentiles, in word and deed, by the power of signs and wonders, and by the power of the Spirit of God; so that from Jerusalem, and round about as far as Illyricum, I have fully declared the gospel of Christ." The word of God is the great organ of conversion in the hand of the Spirit, whether he stir up a Prophet, an Apostle, Evangelist, Martyr, or Saint, to declare it now or formerly.

But the Spirit was also to convince the world of righteousness:—How was this to be done? Why, as the Jews had condemned Jesus Christ as wicked, it was only necessary to show the contrary in order to convince them of righteousness. Christ is, therefore, said to be justified by the Sprit; i. e. the Spirit descending upon his disciples, and bestowing upon them the gifts of power, wisdom, and goodness, justified both the pretensions and righteous character and life of Messiah, proving to his murderers in this manner that he had gone to the Father: "Of righteousness because I go to the Father."

The third part, of the Spirit's mission was to glorify Jesus:—We shall show the reader how this was done. The Jews had crucified him because they did not believe him to be the Son of God. When the Spirit came he showed the reverse of their decision; viz: that he was the Son God. By reasoning from the Law, the Prophets, and the Psalms, to the life, descent, doctrine, character, death, burial and resurrection of Messiah, he fairly proved this proposition; and after it was established he so explained and illustrated it as to let the disciples understand perfectly that Jesus was the Son of God in the same strict sense in which we are the sons of our respective parents; and, finally, that he was officially the Prophet, Priest, and King of the human kind.

Previous to the resurrection of Jesus his disciples seem to have entertained no adequate apprehension of the dignity of his nature:

"*Have I been so long with thee, Philip, and thou hast not known me? He that hath seen me hath seen the Father.*"—They did not apprehend him a sacrifice for the world, neither did they understand it to be his destiny to arise from the dead: "*As yet,*" says John, "*his disciples knew not that he must arise from the dead.*" But when the Spirit came he led them into all the truth on this subject. He took of the things which were Christ's, and showed them to them, and acquainted them with all those parts of the ancient Scriptures which related to his origin, destiny, glory, and natural and official characters. "*He shall take of mine and show it unto you.*"

Who would have supposed that the poor fishermen (one of whom betrayed him, another of whom denied him, and all of whom forsook him in his greatest need) would ever have attained to such extended and sublime views of his natural excellency as to have exclaimed, "In the beginning was the Word, and the Word was with God, and the Word was God. All things were made by it, and without it was not any thing made that was made. And the word became flesh and dwelt among us, and we beheld his glory, the glory as of the only begotten of the Father, full of grace and truth." Thus speaking of him as a partaker of all the glorious attributes of his Father, the true and living God: "All that the father hath is mine." Some admire that Jesus should at anytime be called "God;" but it should be remembered that this is his Father's name, and per consequence it is his name also; for every son inherits, of necessity, the name of his father. Hence the Apostle reasons for the superior dignity of the Messiah, from this very consideration: "being made," says he, "so much better than angels, as he hath by inheritance obtained a more excellent name than they; for to which of the angels said he at any time, "Thou art *my* Son?" Being Son he became Heir of the Universe, and sat down on the throne of heaven—the brightness of his Father's glory—an impress of his existence; men and angels, nature and religion being subjected to him: "Let all the angels of God worship him."

In another scripture it is said, "He is the image of the invisible God, the first born of every creature; for by him were all things made that are in heaven and on earth, whether they be thrones, principalities, or powers, whether visible or invisible, all things were made by him and for him; and he is anterior to all things, and by him all things consist—the head of the body—the first born from the dead—that in all things he might have the preeminence; for it pleased the Father that in him should all fullness dwell." He is therefore called "God's dear Son," "God's beloved Son," "God's only begotten Son," "God's holy child;" in short, the New Testament lets us see that the Spirit gave the apostles to understand that Jesus the Messiah was strictly and properly the Son of God. "God, then, hath sent forth his Son, made of a woman;" and we see that, like every other child, he partakes of the nature of his parents

—the infirmities of his mother and the grandeur of his Father; wearied and sitting on Jacob's well, yet himself the well of salvation; fatigued and sleeping on a pillow in the ship, yet allaying the reluctant storm; living with his mother at Nazareth, yet claiming the temple as his Father's house; ("Wist you not that I must needs be at my Father's"); paying tax for repairing the temple, at the same time letting Peter know that, as the King's Son, he had a right to be exempted in this matter, asking whether the kings of the earth taxed their children, and at the same time looking with the omniscience of his Father through universal nature, and bidding Peter go to the lake, and take from the mouth of a fish a small piece of money which it had probably picked up from some person who had dropped it in crossing Genesareth; descended from the fathers, yet God over all; born himself, yet raising the dead; poor yet heir of all; calling Mary uniformly his mother, and God as uniformly his Father; suffering, yet capable of ordering twelve legions of angels to his assistance; wearing a crown of thorns, yet himself the king of glory; judged, yet himself the judge of quick and dead; killed and at the same time redeeming his murderers; ranked among thieves, yet holy, harmless, and undefiled, and separate from sinners; dying, rising, in the sepulcher, on the throne of God, and there swaying a sceptre of righteousness over men and angels, who, in one eternal throng, cry, "Riches, and honor, and power, and dominion, and glory to God who sitteth on the throne, and to the Lamb forever and ever!"

The most famous and distinguished officers among the nations, are Kings, Prophets, and Priests. These dignities are united in the person of the Messiah, who is set forth in Scripture as the greatest of Prophets, the King of Kings, and the High Priest of Mankind.

The great evils which have most of all characterized the nations of the earth, are 1st, Ignorance of the divine character. 2d. Sin, the consequence of ignorance. 3d. War, the effect of the combined evils of ignorance and sin.—The offices of Christ are instituted in reference to these evils, as a Prophet, he enlightens us in the divine character; as a Priest he takes away our sins; and as a King, he rules us in peace; he is therefore called "King of Peace," "Prince of Peace," and so forth.

The time is coming, then, when all Kings, Priests, and Prophets, shall officiate in their respective offices, under and in subjection to the Messiah. We do not, indeed, see this now; but we see Jesus exalted for this very purpose: for he must reign until all his enemies are made his footstool.—The last enemy, Death, shall be destroyed; and when all shall be subdued to him, then the Son himself shall alone be subject to the Father: and all others, whether men or angels, subject to the Son. The whole creation, then, being subject to the Son, and he to the Father, they will spend an endless eternity in the new heavens and the new earth. "The Lamb that is in the midst of the throne shall feed them, and lead them to fountains of living water, and God the Lord shall wipe away all tears from their eyes."

OBJECTIONS REMOVED

1. Is not the word of God, or the Gospel, which is the meaning of the word, *a dead letter?* No; falsehoods alone, when known to be such, are dead letters; but truth is living, quick, and powerful.

2. Was the Holy Spirit, when he came, to make sinners believe? No; he was to convict them of sin because they did not or had not believed.

3. How can he do this if he enter not the mind of sinners? By preaching to them through the members of the church, the Apostles, Prophets, Evangelists and saints.

4. When we reject his teaching by the Scriptures and those who preach them, do we resist the Spirit? Yes; this is the way the people resisted the Spirit of old.—Neh. 9:30.

5. Can we believe of ourselves? This is not required; believe in Christ on the testimony of God and the Scriptures.

6. How does faith come? By hearing the scriptures.

7. Why then have not all faith? Because most men are in love with the world and care not for eternal life.

8. But the word is called the sword of the Spirit? That is because he made it; and, therefore, Paul bids us take it and use it in our own defence.

9. Is not the Spirit given to every man? Yes; to every man in Christ, but to nobody out of Christ.

10. The Lord opened Lydia's heart. Granted, and he will open your's too, if you read his holy book in order to know and do his will.

11. Did not Cornelius receive the Holy Spirit before baptism? Yes; but not, as Protestants teach, before faith.

12. Was not Jesus to grant repentance to Israel? No; God was to do this by exalting their Messiah, and thus grant them repentance by his exaltation to heaven, as he would grant them remission by his death.

13. If you receive the Spirit, why do you not work miracles? Because miracles are now unnecessary. Truth may need miracles to set it

upon a footing with error established by law; as in the Apostolic times, when Judaism and Idolatry prevailed; but truth needs not and will not accept of the aid of miracles to triumph over error.

14. But some say they can work miracles. Do you watch them narrowly; and think it no miracle if you find them guilty of error *and* falsehood.

15. What now, is proof of a professor's having the Spirit? His joyfulness in obeying the Christian religion by a holy walk and conversation.

16. What difference is there between the ordinary and extraordinary influences of the Spirit? It is corrupted and not true Christianity that recognizes such a distinction.

17. Does the Christian religion consist in knowledge or in a right state of the heart, that is, in a moral bias of the soul? It consists in both and more too. The Christian religion lets us first know what is good, second do what is good, thirdly feel what is good. Blessed be God and the Lamb.

A DISCOURSE OF THE TRUE GOSPEL

SECTION EIGHTH–THE RESURRECTION

"Jesus answered and said, Verily, verily, I say to you
unless a man be born of water and spirit, he cannot
enter the Kingdom of God." John 3:5

CHAPTER I

Introductory

There are four matters in the Christian Religion, forming its very foundation and glory, which were not found in the Law of Moses, viz: pardon of sins by the sacrifice of the Messiah, the hope of a resurrection by his resurrection, the Holy Spirit by his elevation to the throne of God, and eternal life by his second advent to this world.

Substitution, or salvation by blood poured from the veins of a person of the house of David, seems never once to have entered the public mind in Judea. It is peculiarly a revelation of the Christian Religion; for though predicted by the prophets, such was the veil upon the heart of that people, that even when the doctrine was preached to them, and prophecy was illuminated by the fact they could not believe and would not receive it; and thus they lost those excellent honors, in hope of which, they and their fathers had served God night and day for fifteen centuries. They imagined their own law to be of perpetual obligation; and mistook the shadow for the substance; the patterns and samples of things in the heavens for the heavenly things themselves.

They knew not that the passing of their High Priest once a year with blood of others through the veil, was a figure of our true High Priest passing through the rent veil of his flesh and entering with his own blood into the presence of God for us; and that the Holy Spirit, by what occurred on the day of annual atonement, signified this, "that the way into the holiest of all was not yet made manifest while the first tabernacle was yet standing; which was a figurative representation for the time being" &c.

Of the resurrection of Messiah, as the event which was to bring life and immortality to light and be the foundation of hope among his people, they were equally ignorant; for although this also was shadowed forth in the law and predicted by the prophets and in the Psalms, yet such were their prejudices of an earthly kingdom that they do not seem even once to have anticipated the Messiah's resurrection or their own as depending on the certainty of that event; for his resurrection being foretold, it is certain that if the Scriptures which relate to that, are not fulfilled, those which relate to the general resurrection never will be fulfilled. If he is not risen, all faith and hope are equally vain, and his people are yet in their sins; for it is in no part of the Old and New Testament more clearly predicted that there shall be a resurrection of the just and the unjust, than it is that the Messiah was to arise from the dead and become the first fruits of them that slept, It is said even of the twelve, after Christ had spoken of his resurrection, that they "wondered what this rising from the dead should mean."

His elevation to heaven was also unknown by them; for although the appearing of their High Priest in the holiest of all as certainly prefigured Christ presenting himself in heaven for us as blood prefigured his death, and the passing through the veil his resurrection, yet every part of the shadows, all these samples and figures were of a nature to hide from their apprehension the facts to which they pointed; so that the death, resurrection, and ascension of the Messiah were equally novel to and unexpected by the nation when they occurred.

Of his second advent also, or his return to this world, the Jews knew nothing; yet this also was prefigured by the return of the High Priest from the sanctum sanctorum and the throne of God in that holy place in which he had been officiating for the sins of the people. The holy and most holy places are acknowledged figures of the earthly and heavenly divisions of the kingdom of God.

Here then are four grand facts in our Religion, which, were kept secret from the foundation of the world, and of which the Jews, like all other nations, were wholly ignorant till the promulgation of them by the Apostles of the Lord our Saviour; and yet they are the facts on which the kingdom of the Messiah rests with all its glory and weight. Deny the first two, his death and resurrection, and you cut up by the roots the first principles of his kingdom on earth, and faith and hope and pardon and the Holy Spirit are scattered to the winds. Disbelieve the last two, his ascension and second coming, and you break upon the pillars of his heavenly kingdom and the glory that rests thereon.

The kingdom of Christ is in many parts of the sacred writings spoken of as divided into two states, the *earthly* and the *heavenly*. For instance, "If I have told you of earthly things, and you have not believed, how shall you believe if I tell you of heavenly things?" This last is, by Peter, called the "everlasting kingdom of our Lord and Saviour Jesus Christ," implying that the present reign on earth is not of an eternal nature, but to come to an end, as the same apostle expresses it, "at the revelation of Jesus Christ." Here then we have in the scriptures two kingdoms of Christ, one temporal in its duration, the other eternal; the former having in it earthly things or things to be enjoyed on earth, the latter, containing heavenly things or things which can be enjoyed only in heaven. These reigns are represented as differing in the following particular also, that the earthly things of the first are to be enjoyed by faith; but that in the second, faith is to give way to knowledge and the heavenly things belonging to it shall be enjoyed by absolute personal communion with them. Here, the blessings are pardon and the Holy Spirit; but in the everlasting kingdom they are eternal life and the personal presence of God and the Lamb. In the present state of the kingdom flesh and blood or men in the flesh are permitted to inherit the blessings, but flesh and blood cannot inherit the kingdom of God which is to come. Even as corruption cannot inherit incorruption, or as our present bodies, which are corruptible and temporal in their duration, cannot inherit a kingdom whose duration is eternal and which is consequently incorruptible. We enter the first with a renovated mind; we shall enter the second with a renovated body also. Now we are raised into his kingdom through the waters of baptism, by faith; then we shall enter his kingdom through the grave by the Spirit. Now we are born of water; then we shall be born of the Spirit also. Here purified by the belief of the truth the Spirit receives us as a temple from Christ; then glorified by his power Christ shall receive us from the Spirit as his redeemed. That which is born of the flesh is flesh and consequently is obvious to sense; that which is born of the Spirit is spirit and like the Spirit shall be invisible to mortal eyes. We must be born again before we can discern the kingdom of God on earth, and again before we enter it in heaven; Christ was born of the water into the first and from the dead by the Spirit into the second kingdom; and we are ordained to be conformed to him in all things that he may be the first born among many brethren; so as we have been immersed in water, and raised up to sit with him in his kingdom on earth, so if we continue in the faith the Spirit will raise us up to sit with him in his kingdom in heaven; for if the Spirit of him, who raised up Christ from the dead, dwell in us, he that raised up Christ will also quicken our mortal bodies by his Spirit which, dwells in us.

With these observations premised, let us here quote the conversation of our Blessed Lord with Nicodemus, and endeavor to ascertain, whether the whole passage may not find a complete interpretation in this view of the kingdom of God and Christ.

"Now there was a Pharisee, called Nicodemus, a ruler of the Jews, who came to Jesus by night, and said to him, Rabbi, we know that you are a teacher come from God; for no man can do these miracles, which you do, unless God be with him. Jesus answering, said to him, Most assuredly, I say to you, unless a man be born again, he cannot discern the Reign of God. Nicodemus replied, How can a grown man be born? Can he enter his mother's womb anew, and be born? Jesus answered, Most assuredly, I say to you, unless a man be born of water and spirit, he cannot enter the kingdom of God. That which is born of the flesh is flesh; that which is born of the Spirit is spirit. Wonder not, then, that I said to you, You must be born again. The Spirit breathes where he pleases, and you hear the report of him, but know not whence he comes, or whither he goes; so is every one who is born of the Spirit. Nicodemus answered, How can these things be? Jesus replied, are you the teacher of Israel, and know not these things? Most assuredly, I say to you, we speak what we know, and testify what we have seen; yet you receive not our testimony. If you understood not, when I told you earthly things, how will you understand, when I tell you heavenly things? For none has ascended into heaven, but he who descended from heaven; the Son of Man, whose abode is heaven. As Moses placed on high the serpent in the wilderness, so must the Son of Man be placed on high, that whosoever believes on him, may not perish, but obtain eternal life; for God has so loved the world, as to give his only begotten Son, that whosoever believes on him may not perish, but obtain eternal life. For God has sent his Son into the world, not to condemn the world, but that the world may be saved by him. He who believes on him, shall not be condemned; he who believes not, is already condemned, because he has not believed on the name of the only begotten Son of God. Now this is the ground of condemnation, that light is come into the world, and men have preferred the darkness to the light, because their deeds were evil. For whosoever does evil, hates the light, and shuns it, lest his deeds should be detected. But he who obeys the truth, comes to the light, that it may be manifest, that his actions are agreeable to God."

It is allowed, that in this passage our Lord Jesus speaks of both his kingdom on earth consisting of his saints, and of his kingdom in heaven consisting of both saints and angels. Well, does being born of water and spirit refer to any thing else but the different means by which we enter these two distinct kingdoms? I think not. Into the present kingdom we are introduced by water, the water of baptism; into the everlasting kingdom we shall be introduced by the Spirit, the Holy Spirit. And in this manner shall we be born of water and spirit; so that the Lord Jesus in this conversation speaks to Nicodemus under the figure of a birth concerning both the great change of condition to which every man must be subjected by the obedience of the gospel viz: his introduction by baptism into his kingdom on earth, and of that mighty change which must pass upon the body also of every man who shall inherit the heavenly things of his everlasting kingdom.

The great objection, which would be brought against this interpretation, by the present professors of our religion, is that it does away from the passage conversion by spiritual operations. Granted; for this is unscriptural; but it militates not at all against the true doctrine of Christianity concerning the Spirit, viz: that he is given to them "who obey the gospel;" for he is sent to the saints not to make them obey, but because they have obeyed. He is the comforter of the obedient, the substitute of our glorious but absent Lord. "What know ye not, says the apostle to the Corinthians, that your body is the temple of the Holy Spirit, who is in you, whom you have from God? Besides you are not your own for you are bought with a price; therefore, with your body glorify God." *You are not your own;*—Whose then are we? Christ's, who has bought us with his blood. To whom has Christ committed us till he comes again? To the Holy Spirit who is in us. I will send you another comforter, who shall dwell with you for ever. He is our Guide, "As many are led by the Spirit &c." At the resurrection day then, the Holy Spirit shall deliver up to Christ the saints, which he has now in charge, and our bodies which are corruptible, dishonored, weak, and natural, shall then be born of the Spirit, and be incorruptible, glorious, strong and spiritual; and then shall we realize this saying of our Lord that "Whatsoever is born of the Spirit is spirit." In that day spirit shall issue from the Spirit as flesh issues from the flesh and we shall be like the angels of God.

Thus, we shall, according to the predestination of the Almighty, be conformed to the image of his Son in all things; for as he himself was baptized into his kingdom on earth, and afterwards received the Holy Spirit; so we also are baptized into his kingdom on earth and afterwards receive the Holy Spirit; and as he has been quickened by the Spirit, and has become the first born from the dead, so we likewise shall be quickened by the same Spirit, if he dwells in us, and be born into heaven; and thus Christ shall be the first-born among many brethren.

But, let us look a little more particularly at the third of John, which we have quoted. We say that the figure must be filled up by facts. Now I know no facts in the Christian Religion, which go to fill up a birth but that of our issuing from the bosom of baptism into Christ's kingdom on earth, after we have been converted by the gospel, and the fact of our issuing from the bosom of the Spirit into his kingdom in heaven, when we are raised from the dead. Is there then any thing in the passage to forbid this interpretation? I know nothing. To an unconfiding person belonging to a nation filled with family pride and the pride of birth, Christ says. "You must be born again before you can discern my reign, that is the nature of my reign." The man is amazed, and asks whether a man can be born of the flesh a second time.

The Lord replies that "Unless a man be born of *water* and *spirit* he cannot enter into the kingdom of God." Now this is a bold figure, but very easily to be understood also, if we allow that a man cannot enter into his kingdom on earth but by baptism, and into his kingdom in heaven but by the Spirit. Nicodemus' second birth by flesh would not have changed the case nor the man, it would have left him still in a state of nature; "That which is born of the flesh is flesh;" but by being born of water, we pass from a state of nature to a state of grace; and by being born of the Spirit, we pass from a state of grace to a state of glory, which is the perfect and everlasting kingdom of God. And so our bodies becoming spirit, the saying of the Saviour is versified, "That which is born of the Spirit is spirit."—The Jewish ruler was confounded. The Saviour adds, "Marvel not that I said unto you, you must be born again. The Spirit breathes where he pleases and you hear the report of him, but you cannot tell whence he comes or whither he goes; so is every one who is born of the Spirit." The person, who believes the gospel, as we said, now receives the Spirit of Christ; and at the resurrection Christ shall receive him from the Spirit, incorruptible, glorious, strong, and spiritual. And so it will finally be with the man "born of the Spirit," as it is with the Spirit himself of which he shall be born, that is, he shall be invisible; for that which is spirit must necessarily be invisible. All this must have been astounding to Nicodemus. Like other Jews he hoped that the kingdom of heaven should appear, be given to the Jews, and be visible to mortal eyes; but here he is told a man cannot discern it but by being born again! and cannot enter it but by becoming spirit and invisible.

Nicodemus was overwhelmed, and ejaculated, "How can these things be!" Well, this faithlessness in him was the very thing to be detected; for the whole passage was introduced to show the character of that faith which some had in Christ when they beheld the miracles which he wrought. "While he was at Jerusalem, at the feast of the passover, many believed on him when they saw the miracles which he performed. But Jesus did not trust himself to them for he knew them all. He needed not to receive from others a character of any man, for he knew what was in man. Now there was a Pharisee, called Nicodemus, &c." Nicodemus confessed his Messiahship, but the Lord Jesus by this strange metaphorical manner of speaking of the way by which men were by water and spirit to enter into the two departments of his reign on earth and in heaven, brings the true state of the case to light; and shows that it was wisdom in him not to commit himself to the professed believers of that time, because their profession was not accompanied with that unreserved confidence without which no man is acceptable to God and Christ.

How can these things be! To this our Lord replies "Are you the teacher of Israel and know not these things?" It was wonderful that a man, holding so eminent a station in those days, had not informed himself most accurately in regard to the preaching of John the Baptist, and the kingdom of heaven; and as a Pharisee he might have understood his own doctrine of a resurrection although veiled under the figure of birth by the Spirit. His ignorance and want of confidence are, therefore, rebuked in the following manner: "Most assuredly, I say unto you, we speak what we do know and testify what we have seen, yet you receive not our testimony. If you understood not when I told you of earthly things, how will you understand when I tell you heavenly things. For none has ascended into heaven, but he who descended from heaven, the Son of Man whose abode is in heaven." Our entrance into Christ's kingdom on earth by water, and into his heavenly kingdom by spirit are two things, which must both take place on the earth, and they are, therefore, called earthly, not that they are of an earthly nature, but that they occur upon this earth.

"Born of God," "born again," then, applies very well to any man that has been baptized on proper principles, viz: love to God and faith in our Lord Jesus Christ; for faith and baptism are of God, and he wills his children thus to be born to him into the kingdom of his Son; but "born of the Spirit," which occurs only in this place, has no fact to respond to it in our religion, but our resurrection from the dead. But it may be objected that Jesus speaks in the present tense, and says, "so is;" not so shall be "every one that is born of the Spirit." This is a trifling objection. The manner of speech is found in many parts of the New Testament. Paul says, "It is raised," not it shall be raised, "a spiritual body." The present is taken for the future, a common enough thing among the Hebrews, and a very sprightly form of speech.

Again: it may be objected that the passage does not speak of two births. This is the very thing disputed by the present exposition. I say it speaks of being born by two distinct things, *water* and *spirit*, importing that we are born of each, of these things separately; and thus amazement in the mind of Nicodemus was doubtlessly doubled; which indeed is the feeling which the Saviour designed to arouse in the Ruler, in order to exhibit how dangerous it would have been in him to trust himself to a person of that time, even when he said, "Rabbi we know that thou art a teacher sent from God." &c.

When the people pretending to believe in the Lord Jesus, followed him and told him how anxiously they had sought him, he said it was for the loaves and fishes they followed him; they were surprised; and declared themselves willing to work the works of God. Jesus replied that then they must believe on him. Immediately they demurred and asked a sign, saying Moses gave our fathers manna in the wilderness. Jesus said his Father had given them in him the true bread from heaven; their surprise becomes astonishment. Then he said he would give them his flesh to eat; their astonishment was heightened to amazement. He adds, his blood also to drink, they are overwhelmed; He closes by saying that, unless they eat his flesh and drink his blood, they have no life in them, they abandoned him in despair, and from that day walked no more with him. Thus he easily revealed the hollowness of their belief, and their total want of confidence in his power and veracity. This was the case with Nicodemus. He said he believed him to be a teacher sent from God. Jesus says you must be born again; the man is astonished. The Lord adds you must be born of water and spirit, he is amazed. Jesus rejoins that the person born would be like the Spirit of which he should be born, invisible, incomprehensible; the Ruler is overwhelmed, and by his exclamation, "How can these things be," shows at once the hollowness of his faith and his total want of confidence in the power and veracity of the Teacher. This was the thing to be exhibited, agreeably to the narrative of the evangelist. "He needed not to receive a character of any man for he knew what was in man;" he knew that Nicodemus had a faith that was wholly unconfiding: and he doubles the darkness of his discourse as the conversation proceeds in order to develop this want of confidence. The man, whose attachment to God or to his Son Jesus Christ is predicated on this irrational idea, that these glorious personages must uniformly or at any time act in conformity with his perceptions of right, will certainly feel himself disappointed. John the Baptist himself was almost stumbled by the course which our Lord pursued; who told that truly excellent man, "Blessed is he that is not stumbled at my course."

In this interpretation, however, as in all others so entirely new, much deference is due to the sentiments of professors in general, and to my brethren of this reformation in particular, who have submitted other interpretations of the passage; for young and old, baptists and pedo-baptists, generally meet on the third of John, and break a lance with each other here, as at the bulwark of their party views, baptism by water on the one hand, and conversion by the Spirit on the other.

According to the interpretation now submitted, no christian is yet born of the Spirit; this event is the resurrection; and consequently, the fact, which fills the figure, is still in the future. But then, professors in general think that the person, who is truly converted to God, is born of the Spirit; and this they call regeneration by the Spirit. Doddridge, Newton, Scott, Henry, Burton, Baxter, Clarke, Pool, Witherspoon, Gill, and ten thousand others, and indeed all, both Catholics and Protestants, espouse this interpretation. Now I differ from them in this, as I have done in the entire arrangement of all the first principles of the gospel of Christ. Well, I grant that all this bares against me in a certain point of view and as a private individual unordained either by Protestants or Papists, and having no particular charge in any congregation. I am even willing to confess to the reader that nothing but my duty as a Christian and a disciple, who would prove his fidelity to his Redeemer by endeavors to correct error and publish the truth, would sustain me in these matters; but what is a man to do, when he believes the world in error on doctrines of such vast importance? For myself I know no other plan of procedure but that of publishing; and by so doing afford to all a fair opportunity of correcting these things if they are wrong, and of being improved by them if they are right.

The public think that in the passage, of which I have offered this as an interpretation, regeneration or conversion by secret and special operations of the Holy Spirit is meant. Now in answer I say that it behooves all such folks to prove that this sort of conversion, namely, by the influence of the Spirit, is a doctrine of the Christian religion. I deny that it is, and if it is not, then "born of the Spirit," cannot of course mean that.

With those who preach the true gospel, however, this is not the objection with which my interpretation has to contend; for like myself they do not believe in conversion but by the word, the word of the truth of the gospel. A solution of the following nature has been submitted by one of the brethren and espoused pretty generally by those who preach the true gospel. Being begotten by the word, (Of his own will begat he us by the word of truth,) and born of the water, the Spirit, it is said, may be regarded as our father; and so having the Spirit for our father and the water for our mother, when born of the last we may be said to be born of the first also.

Perhaps it is George Campbell who says there is such a thing as riding a figure to death. If this is not done in the above criticism, there is at least taken for granted several things which ought to have been proved. First, that the scriptures warrant us in calling or even regarding the Spirit as our father. Second that they warrant us in looking upon the water as our mother.—The ancient fathers called baptism *matrix* but never, I opine, *mater*. And while the Scriptures speak of "being born of the Spirit," they never say or ever hint that we are begotten by the Spirit. It is always the heavenly Father who is said to have begotten us; "he begat us by the word of truth;" "begotten of the Father," "begotten of God." "Him that begat." Hence we are called his children, but in no instance are we styled the children of the Spirit, or the children of the water. It is said that we are born of the water, therefore, only because we proceed from it into the kingdom of God on earth; and born of Spirit only because we shall proceed from it at the resurrection and be ushered into the everlasting kingdom of heaven by its energies in raising us from the dead. Isaac is said to have been born according to the Spirit, because he proceeded from the bosom of her who was dead to childbearing. Christ is said to be born from the dead or the grave, and there to have been quickened by the Spirit; we also shall be quickened by the same power and born from the dead or of the Spirit which raises us from the dead; for without his power we never can be born of a matter so dead and devoid of life as is the grave.

But it may be further objected. If by water here, baptism is meant, and by spirit, the Holy Spirit which is to raise us from the dead, why are the two words put in such close juxtaposition to each other, why are they connected by a conjunction copulative, when in fact the things signified are as far apart as the first and second coming of Christ, as distant as his death and our resurrection?

In answer, I say, that other expressions, of a similar construction, are found in the Holy Scripture; in which two distant things are joined grammatically, thus: "This is he that came by *water* and *blood*, even Jesus the Christ; not by the water only, but by the water and the blood." Here *water* and *blood* are first expressed indefinitely, like *water* and *spirit* in the passage under consideration; but in the latter part of the verse blood is called *the blood*, and water *the water* definitely, referring to certain blood and certain water which John the writer had in his eye. This is also the case in the passage concerning being born again. What is there in the first instance called spirit indefinitely is afterwards by our Lord explained to mean the Holy Spirit. What, then, is meant by the water and the blood? It is thought, that by the water, baptism is meant; and by the blood, family descent; for, agreeably to the prediction of the prophets, he was born of the house of David; and as such recognized by the Spirit at Jordan. Therefore, John adds, "And it is the Spirit that beareth witness; for the Spirit is the truth." Here, then, are two distant things put in the closest possible juxtaposition to each other. But while the water is his baptism, the blood may be his death. Suppose this to be true, still two things distant and distinct from each other, as his baptism and death, are united in the construction; it is probable to me, however, that his death is not meant here, but his descent and baptism; therefore, these are the first points in the narratives of the Evangelists concerning him.

"*Spirit* and *fire*" is also a like construction, and the two connected words signify very different and distant things, the descent of the Spirit on Pentecost, and the destruction of Christ's enemies."

"A resurrection of the *just* and *unjust*." This would seem to imply but one resurrection, yet it is said, "The dead in Christ shall rise first;" and again, "Blessed and holy is he who has part in the first resurrection." Here are two things conjoined which are distinct, and perhaps a thousand years distant from each other; therefore, it is not more improper to say "*born of water*" and "*born of spirit*" than to say *first resurrection* and *second resurrection*. But Jesus absolutely separates *water* and *spirit*, and speaks in the passage of being *born of the Spirit* alone, leaving out water when he refers to our birth into that kingdom in which like the Spirit himself we shall be invisible to mortal eyes. Thus, the while of this long and much vexed passage, in the third of John, is rendered perfectly intelligible, and fearfully significant. And it is proved to refer to the resurrection from the fact that in our religion it can refer to nothing else.

CHAPTER II

The Resurrection of Christ

The great Peter said to his brethren, "Sanctify the Lord God in your hearts, and be ready always to give an answer to every man that asks you for a reason of me hope that is within you, with meekness and reverence. In hope as in faith, three things are to be considered. In faith the first thing is the *fact*, the second is *he that testifies* of it, and the third is *belief* itself, being a state of mind composed of confidence in relation to the *speaker*, and *conviction* in relation to the fact. But the fact may be either before or behind us, in the past or in the future. In hope the first thing is the *thing promised*, the second is the *person* promising, and the third is hope itself or a state of mind composed of confidence in the promiser and desire in relation to the thing promised, which is always in the future. Desire alone and hope differ from each other in this respect. We may desire a thing which there is neither a probability or possibility of obtaining; but we cannot hope for a thing, but upon reasonable grounds that it can be obtained.

That hope, or the object of a Christian's hope, is before and not behind him, that it is in the future and not the past, is very certain from what Paul says of our resurrection by the Spirit in his letter to the Romans, when discoursing of redemption or the resurrection of our body, to wit: "For even we are saved by hope; now hope that is attained is not hope; for who can hope for that which he enjoys? But if we hope for that which we do not enjoy, then, in patience we wait for it." The object, therefore, of the Christian's hope is the resurrection of the dead, and he that promises this is God, and this blessing is in the future and not the past. When, therefore, any one obtains or attains by the Christian religion a hope toward God, he attains to a hope of the resurrection; this is the thing which he desires and God and Christ Jesus are the blessed promisers in whom his confidence reposes for the fulfillment of his desires. The hope of Christians, then, is one, not many. "God," the apostle says, "has called us to one hope of our calling." When, however, modern Christians are interrogated concerning their hope, they too frequently give you a very different account of the matter; the object of desire is very generally laid by them in the past and not the future, behind them and not before them, and is the conversion of their souls to God, and not the redemption of their bodies from death. They hope they have been converted! Now we never read in the scriptures of any professed disciple hoping that he had been converted; for, who could be a disciple without conversion? and if he had attained conversion how could he according to Paul, any longer hope for it, seeing he had already attained it? "for who," says he, "can hope for that which he enjoys?" But professors will still meet to tell over their experience as evidence of their hopeful conversion to God, looking backwards instead of pressing forward, remembering the things that are behind instead of forgetting them, and pressing forward to those things which are before. What would it avail me to know that I was converted ten or twenty years ago, if I am not good now and hastening not forward to the day of God? nothing; it is as useless as to call to remembrance that I was once rich, but am now poor.

But the hope of being raised from the dead, after being resolved into dust, after being the food of worms, and buried for hundreds of years, is a very extraordinary one indeed, and, therefore, Peter bids us be able with reverence to assign a reason for it to every one who requires it of us. Our hope, then, is the resurrection from the dead, and the reason of it is laid in the promise of God, and in the fact that he has already raised our Lord and master from the dead, and consequently, by an instance in kind, he has showed us both the certainty of the thing, and its nature; he has showed us that it is a reorganization of the whole inner and outer man, and the restoration of him to all his intellectual relations to material nature and to social life forever. We shall die no more. The promises of God are these; that the Messiah was to be the first fruits of a resurrection; that his dead men should live, and their bones be made to flourish like a green herb; that he should see a seed, who would publish his praises; that as in Adam all die so in Messiah all should be made alive; that he would raise us up at the last day. But Messiah's own resurrection is the great turning point; this was as clearly predicted in the Old Testament as was the general resurrection, and, therefore, it is only on the fact that God has fulfilled his promise to the Messiah that we his people and disciples can hope to be raised. As the Jews held to remission without understanding the reconciliation accomplished by Messiah, so they held to a resurrection without being aware of the fact on which that resurrection depended, namely, the rising again of Jesus from the dead. It is not so with Christians; to them all this is made plain. We submit the following on the resurrection of our Lord and Saviour. I wrote it some twelve years ago but it is as true now as it was then and will very properly come in at this part of our discourse.

Respecting Jesus of Nazareth, the Jewish nation seems to have been divided into two principal parties—that which favored, and that which rejected his pretensions. That the views of his scheme too, entertained by both, were not almost but altogether political, we have all the reason, I think, in the world to believe. The opposition party regarded the whole as a political cabal, and its abettors as reformers of the state. Radicals, whose ultimate objects were to put down the prevailing party, to abandon allegiance to the Romans; to assert the independence of the Jewish nation; and, under the conduct of Jesus as their general, or, as his own party would have it, their king, to maintain it sword in hand. This is the only view that accords with the warlike spirit of the times, the popular belief respecting Messiah's reign and kingdom, and with what we read in the four evangelists. Now, it was to check the spirit of this enterprise that the leaders of the opposite party voted the destruction of Jesus, who was looked upon by the great men as the life's blood of the conspiracy. From the moment when Caiaphas delivered his sentiments on the grand question, "what is to be done for the safety of the state!" the death of Jesus was eagerly desired by them all. These princes, preferring rank and honor with their present inglorious ease under foreign masters, to the distant and uncertain advantages of a noble and magnanimous declaration of the nation's independence— these lordlings conceived power and pomp to be the chief good and the only thing worthy of ambition. They imagined that to form the object of the Lord's ambition also, and endeavored by mean arts to draw from him the secret. The views of his followers were nothing different in kind from those of his opposers; they were equally worldly and political; and both parties, contemplating the designs of the Lord Jesus under this mistaken and degraded point of view, it is not wonderful that his resurrection from the dead should be an event equally distant from the anticipations of all. Both parties, too, seem to have considered his decease as an unequivocal refutation of his pretensions—as an event which at once reflected the greatest discredit on the party, and gave apparent ponderosity and importance to those who had slain him, and who, during the whole of his public ministry, had steadily persisted in rejecting and disproving his pretensions. Had the Lord then not appeared to some of his followers on that day on which he arose, the dispute of the two parties, would not have been whether he had risen from the dead, but only which of them had stolen the body from the sepulcher. This is evident from the easy assent which the two disciples gave to the hasty suggestions of Mary Magdalene. They believed that the opposite faction had stolen the body; John alleging for it as a reason, that the disciples knew not as yet that he must rise from the dead. The anticipation of such an event was equally foreign from the conceptions of his murderers, who barricaded the tomb, and sealed it with the seal of the state, not to prevent his resurrection, but, as they themselves said, to prevent his followers from taking the body by stealth. I think too, that the rulers really and sincerely believed his followers to have taken away the body, and that, in the first instance, they regarded the wonders told them by the soldiers, of earthquakes and angels, to be nothing more than cunningly devised fables, trumped up by his disciples for the safety of the guards, who, as they believed, had permitted them (the disciples) undisturbedly, perhaps for a sum of money, to bear away the body in the dark. But their bribing the soldiers again, may seem to contradict this opinion. Well then, suppose for argument's sake, that the rulers did believe the report of the guards, viz: that the Lord had risen. If they did, then they must have believed that he would also immediately appear among them again in person, to assert the reality of his claims, and maintain the certainty of the confession, for which he had been put to death; for of his ascent into heaven they had no conceptions. If they believed him to be risen, to have said that his disciples had stolen him, would have been a miserable invention, and nowise suited to the exigency of the case. Such an invention would never have counterbalanced one single well attested appearance of the Lord; and we have seen that they, having no just notions of his reign and kingdom, would have expected to see him again in person, if so be they believed the reports or the soldiers. After all, if the Pharisees expected him to rise, why did they put him to death? The rulers, then, believed the guards to be telling a falsehood, and they bribed them to report what the Pharisees themselves conceived to be the true state of the case. As the opposing faction all along regarded the enterprise as a political one, they foresaw that if once its abettors should get the dead body into their possession, they might make it the instrument of greater mischief to the nation than it had been when alive. They foresaw that one of the reformers might personate their former leader, exhibit himself at a distance, and set up for Messiah on the grounds of having risen from the dead. Such an evidence they foresaw would be altogether irresistible; the Jews would flock to his standard, and the cause would derive accessions from all quarters of the land—such accessions, too, as nothing but the arm of the imperial government would be able to break or dissolve. If once the Romans had engaged in the quarrel, their rulers would have seen a realization of all their former fears. The temple and the city, they forsaw, would ultimately have become the grand bone of contention, and this whole enterprise, or, as they called it, last error, issue in consequences more fatal to their place and nation than the first, under the conduct of Jesus of Nazareth. All these forebodings of the rulers seem to have arisen out of what the Lord said or dropt concerning his resurrection. The Pharisees then suspected his followers of having stolen the body, and his followers, with the exception of those who saw him on the first day, seem to have suspected the Pharisees or rulers; a circumstance which in itself indeed proves that neither party had done it; for if either party had stolen the body it never could have conscientiously blamed the other, as we have seen it did; if the rulers had had it, the disciples would not have dared to say that it was alive; and if the disciples had had it under their control, and said it was alive, they would have embraced the first opportunity of exhibiting him in order to refute the calumny of the rulers, who said the body was in the possession of the party, but it was not alive. These things show us, at all events, that on the third day the body was not where it had been originally laid, and where both parties hoped to find it; they show us that both parties agree in this, viz: that the body was under the control of neither.

There seems, therefore, to be only two ways of accounting for its departure. Seeing it was not removed by any of the parties concerned, it must either have been taken off by some unconcerned party, or have departed itself; which last opinion, indeed, is the more probable of the two; for to suppose that any unconcerned party would endanger themselves, or bribe the guards for a dead person, about whose fate they had been altogether unconcerned whilst alive, would be nonsense. But to suppose that there was any unconcerned party in the capital when Jesus was crucified, would argue great ignorance of the spirit of the times. He was not stolen by any party, either concerned or unconcerned about his fate; and the only conclusion remaining is, that the body departed itself, that "the Lord has arisen indeed;" that "Now has Christ risen from the dead, and become the first fruits of them that slept."

CHAPTER III

The General Resurrection

We now assume it as proved, for the contrary cannot be sustained, that the resurrection is the only fact in our religion, which goes to fill up the measure of that figurative expression, "born of the Spirit."[19] So that this great mystery is that into which all sound hope of eternal life is to

---

[19] To consummate our criticism on the 3d. of John, and to settle the scriptural sense of the word regeneration, I would here observe finally, that the term occurs only twice in the New Testament; and that there, it is used once in relation to baptism, and once in relation to the resurrection, which is the meaning established in our views of the passage. In reference to baptism it is said, "Of his own mercy he saved us by the washing of *regeneration.*" In reference to the resurrection, it is used thus—"at the *regeneration* when the Son of Man shall be seated on his glorious throne, you, my followers, sitting also upon twelve thrones, shall judge the twelve tribes of Israel." See Matthew, 19th Chapter, New Translation. This, I hope, settles the matter.

But although the term regeneration is used with reference to both baptism and the resurrection, it would be as incorrect to call either of these regeneration as it would certainly be unpopular and dangerous. Regeneration, if water is the element, is always baptism; but baptism is not always regeneration; for a person may be raised from the water and not be born to God, because he may not have had the faith which is necessary to make immersion a birth by water. So of the resurrection also; for though regeneration, if spirit is the element, is always a resurrection, yet every resurrection is not a regeneration, because a person may be and thousands will be raised from the dead, who will not be born to God of the Spirit, because they had not in life the righteousness necessary to attain to the resurrection of the just, Regeneration then, into the first kingdom, is the baptism of a true believer. Regeneration into the everlasting Kingdom, is the resurrection of the just.

The New Translation ought to read "water and spirit, not water and Spirit. This capitalizing of the word spirit is demonstrative of the confusion of thought which has heretofore prevailed in regard to the passage.

be resolved at last. This of being born of the Spirit constitutes the final and eternal difference between the righteous of all nations and the wicked. Both of them shall be raised from the dead; but the righteous shall issue forth from the bosom of the Spirit of God, into the everlasting kingdom of our Lord and Saviour Jesus Christ; while the wicked shall be cast forth as dirt, "to shame and everlasting contempt" to share in the eternal punishment of the devil and his angels.

Let us now look at this beautiful creation by the Spirit, when emancipated from the frailty of death, the travail and groans of the present order of things, and ushered into the glorious liberty of the angels, being now children both of God and of the resurrection.

At that great day of God Almighty, "for which all other days were made;" while the unthinking world is busily employed in the affairs of trade and commerce: while Courts and Kingdoms are plotting war and deeds of imaginary renown; while the kings of the earth and the great men, and the rich men, and the chief captains, and the mighty men, and slaves and the masters of slaves, are promising themselves liberty and eternal fame; while fighting armies shake the solid ground, and the din of war carries terror into the hearts of the affrighted nations, and men's souls quail and fail them for fear of the things that are coming upon the earth; while navies ride triumphant o'er the deep, and by their shouts of victory drown "old ocean's roar;" while diplomacy and the affairs of state and all the intrigues of the cabinet flourish; while art pursues her eternal round and mantles the nations with her endless variety; while grave philosophy boasts her triumphs and promises to redeem ten thousand truths to men; while the school, the academy, and university, the alma mater of the land, pour forth the hopes of the State and sow society with the seed of honorable men; while social bliss is still green and mirth and gayety flourish; while men are eating and drinking, and, as now and in the days of Noah and the flood, they were marrying and giving in marriage; while the sun himself turns pale at the thoughtlessness of the world, and the moon becomes like blood with fear for their crimes, and the stars ashamed retire from the heavens, and earthquakes shake the solid land and the very sea and the waves thereof mourn for the iniquities of men; the Lord shall look from the clouds; in a moment—in the twinkling of an eye, and sudden as a glance of lightning, and unexpected as the thief at night and the voice of the bridegroom at the dead of night; the Lord shall look from the clouds of heaven; and the world is at an end.

One blast of the trumpet of the great archangel, for the trumpet shall sound, rends open all the tombs, and the pregnant earth labors; the saints, the dead and the living, issue; from her womb by the power of the Spirit of God into the arms of angels, who reap this great harvest of redeemed men, and bare them like ripened sheaves aloft to eternal life, to meet the Lord in the air.

"Now I would not have you ignorant, brethren, concerning them who sleep; that you may not be grieved, even as others, who have no hope. For if we believe that Jesus died, and rose again; so also, them who sleep, will God through Jesus bring with him.—Besides this we affirm to you, by the word of the Lord, that we the living, who remain at the coming of the Lord, shall not anticipate them who are asleep; for the Lord himself will descend from heaven, with a shout, with the voice of the Archangel, and with the trumpet of God. And the dead in Christ shall rise first; afterwards, we the living who remain, shall at the same time with them be instantly taken up into the clouds to join the Lord, in the air; and so we shall be forever with the Lord. Wherefore, comfort one another with these words."

Let us now collect in order the scriptures which speak of the children of the resurrection. We do not know, and it is perhaps because we cannot precisely know, what we shall be. "Behold," says the apostle John, "what manner of love the Father has bestowed upon that we should be called the sons of God; therefore, the world knoweth us not, even as it knew him not.—Beloved, now are we the sons of God and we know not what we shall be; but we know, that when he shall appear, we shall be like him, that we shall see him as he is; and every one, who has this hope in him, purifies himself even as he is pure." Being here entombed in flesh, it is impossible we should be able to comprehend the nature of that which is but the incorrupted and immediate offspring of the Holy Spirit of God. But neither our own ignorance nor the ignorance of mankind in general, can cut the connection which subsists between Christ and his people by the Spirit; even now, we are the children of God and ripening for the resurrection. In the general, we understand this much, that when he appears, we shall be like him, or as the apostle Paul says, "he will change this humble body and fashion it like unto his own glorious body." "We shall see him." This is the reason for our glorious change; we shall be made like him that we may behold him in his glory. Those who partake not of his likeness in the resurrection, shall never see his face; but will be driven away by his wrath; for he shall be revealed from heaven, with his holy angels, in flames of fire, taking vengeance on those, who know not God, and obey not the gospel. But his saints will glorify and extol his great name and hold him in eternal admiration. He will be admired by all them that believe.

If we know not what we shall be, we at least know what we shall not be. We shall no longer be flesh and blood; for as the apostle says, flesh and blood does not inherit that kingdom. Nor shall we be corruptible; for neither is corruption of a nature to inherit incorruption, even as eternity cannot be measured by time. The result will be that there shall be no more death; nor any pain leading thereto; but, as John says, "the tabernacle of God shall be with men, and he will dwell with them, and they shall be his people, and God himself shall be with them and be their God, and God shall wipe away all tears from their eyes; and there shall be no more death, neither sorrow, nor crying, neither shall there be any more pain; for the former things are past away."

What an admirable state of things! Our rational nature shall be divested of the burden of flesh and blood and of the thousand ills of which they are the heirs! Having attained to heaven through great tribulation and washed their robes and made them white in the blood of the Lamb, men shall "stand before the throne of God and serve him day and night in his temple; and he that sitteth on the throne shall dwell among them; they shall hunger no more, neither thirst any more, neither shall the sun light on them, nor any heat; for the Lamb that is in the midst of the throne shall feed them and shall lead them unto living fountains of water; and God shall wipe away all tears from their eyes."

The Greeks very much contemned the resurrection of the body when preached by the first ministers of our religion; they thought the thing both improbable, and incomprehensible. But this was to their shame, and it proceeded from their utter ignorance of the power and goodness of the Deity. This error creeping into the church, it gave birth to that famous discourse of St. Paul, found in the fifteenth chapter of his first epistle to the church at Corinth. In this discourse the apostle resolves the gospel into remission of sins by the death of Christ, and the hope of eternal life by his resurrection. He founds our faith exclusively upon the testimony of Peter, James, and the other apostles together with himself and five hundred other brethren, who all saw the Saviour after his resurrection. Thirdly he shows that Christ's resurrection is the pivot on which all faith and forgiveness and hope and life rests; and that if this is false all things else in Christianity are vain.

Reader, if no son of man, who is not born of the Spirit, shall ever enter heaven, if no mortal shall ever behold the face of God Almighty in peace who is not born from the dead by the power of the Spirit, and made incorruptible, glorious, powerful and spiritual in his person, to see the Creator of the ends of the earth, how awfully, how fearfully significant are the sayings of Jesus Christ in reference to this matter! "Strait is the gait and narrow is the way that leadeth to eternal life and few there be that find it! Strive ye to enter in at the strait gate, for many shall seek to enter thereat and shall not be able. If once the master has arisen and shut the door, and you begin to knock without, saying Open, open unto us, then shall he say to you Depart from me you accursed, for I never acknowledged you."

"I am the Alpha and the Omega, the Beginning and the End: I will give to him that is athirst, of the fountain of the water of life freely. The conqueror shall inherit all things: and I will be to him a God, and he shall be to me my son. But as for the cowards and unbelieving, and the abominable, and murderers, and prostitutes, and sorcerers, and idolaters, and all liars—their part shall be in the lake which burns with fire and brimstone, which is the second death."

Reader, obey the gospel; enter, by faith and immersion, his kingdom on earth and you shall receive the Holy Spirit; and, when you do so, walk in the Spirit; cherish and reverence his blessed presence in your soul, by a life and behavior becoming the gospel, and all your better hopes and better wishes will be realized, at the appearing of Our Lord Jesus Christ. May the God of peace be with you. May grace, mercy, and peace from God the Father, and from Jesus Christ, with the communion of the Holy Spirit, be with all the Israel of God.

Amen.

TO THE READER

We have now brought our volume to a close; for which we render praises to the gracious providence of God our Father:

In relation to the whole performance, we just say this much; that the distribution of the entire subject into the Fall, the Messiahship, Faith, Repentance, Remission, the Spirit, and the Resurrection, will, we hope, be deemed one of very obvious propriety in a treatise like the present, intended as it is to touch upon all the great landmarks of the True Gospel of Christ.

In regard to the first discourse, the Fall, with the views which I had formed of the subject, it would have been very difficult for me, I presume, to have derived any assistance from others if I had even sought for it. It is a matter which the Protestants, I think, have very much misapprehended. The fact, however, that our First Parents never eat of the Tree of Life, was detected by my brother, Dr. Wright, on reading to him my chapter.

The same holds good of the second discourse also. As a unique topic, Christians have done it but little honor; and have almost universally neglected it for things of an inferior and party nature. We felt ourself alone here also so far as the assistance of others is concerned, and had to pour forth what we have submitted on the topic, from the sources of our own reflections Upon the riches of Christ, contained in the Evangelists.

In regard to Faith, which is the third subject, many excellent things, doubtless, have at several times been published in all the periodicals of the Reformation. But I had neither the time nor the taste so indispensably requisite to search for and collect them together. The three topics just named fill more than three hundred pages, and are turned round and look at from many points for the sake of readers in general.

When I came to Repentance I purposed, if possible, to reach both the head and the heart of the careless and the presumptuous reader. For the accomplishment of the first of these ends I thought it good to rally him upon the many items of internal proof for the truth of Revelation in general and of Christianity in particular. And to attain the second I have transcribed the most striking cases from Mr. Simpson's Plea for Religion. I had felt my own heart touched and awed by them, but thought the argument for which he had introduced them of too general a character. Here they are transcribed and applied to Reformation in particular.

My discourse on Baptism is intended to set in a proper light the authority of the holy apostle, and to throw off from the mind of the reader the useless efforts of erring and uninspired men. That on Remission is formed purposely to bring the offerings of animals and that of our blessed Redeemer, into striking and strong contrast, that the reader may see the greatness and certainty of our redemption.

I could say but little more on the subject of the Holy Spirit than I had formerly done in my discourse on that subject; and, therefore, I have embodied it as an important item of this treatise. Perhaps I have gathered up one additional thought which is expressed in the introduction.

The resurrection suggested itself to me as the only fact in our Religion which could fill up with all fullness the figurative expression, "born of the Spirit," and, therefore, the subject is very briefly discoursed of, under that idea I should observe that I have also occasionally inserted at proper places a piece of my own, written formerly either for the Evangelist or Christian Baptist.

Every book requires to be known by some name. We have called this one, "The Gospel Restored," because it contains the substance of those things, which were brought before the public in 1827, and which, at that time and since, have been recognized as a republication of the true Gospel of Christ.

I repeat here what I tell the reader in the preface, that during the writing of this volume, a period of little more than three months when lost time is deducted, I have enjoyed uninterrupted comfort of mind. But it is, I confess, a very serious task to sit down in a printing office, in the midst of almost a dozen of men and boys, to write so large a volume, with five or six compositors picking up type behind a man, and having the proofs of two presses to correct during a great part of that time, with the cares of other public business.

I now thank God for his tender mercy to me in this business. May he enable us all to become what we ought to be; and to God and the Lamb be present and everlasting honor.

Amen.

ANCIENT LANDMARKS
COLLECTION

This book is part of the *Ancient Landmarks Collection*.

Those in previous generations of what we often call the Restoration Movement produced a wealth of material that is useful for us today – either for instruction or as a matter of historical perspective or both. Many of these materials are rare and difficult to find. In order to make some of these materials accessible to this generation, Gospel Armory is working to republish some of the works by men of the past.

Other titles in the collection include:

> *A Refutation of Hereditary Total Depravity* by Aylett Raines – Originally published in 1859, this book provides a thorough rebuttal to the Calvinistic doctrine of hereditary total depravity.

> *The Reformation For Which We Are Pleading: A Collection of Articles* by Moses E. Lard – This book contains a collection of articles published in *Lard's Quarterly*, a journal Lard published from 1863 to 1868.

For a complete list of titles currently available, visit www.gospelarmory.com/ancient-landmarks-collection

Made in the USA
Columbia, SC
20 January 2019